ANNOTATED TRAVEL GUIDES

Pat and Lester Brooks

Edited and Annotated by
Robert C. Fisher

1985

Fisher Travel Guides / New York

Library of Congress Cataloging in Publication Data

Brooks, Pat.
Spain and Portugal, 1985.

(Fisher annotated travel guides)
Includes index.
1. Spain—Description and travel—1981-
—Guide-books. 2. Portugal—Description and travel—1981-
—Guide-books. I. Brooks, Lester. II. Fisher, Robert C.
III. Title. IV Series.
DP14.B79 1985 914.6'0483 83-1475
ISBN 0-8116-0063-7

Maps and city plans by Pictograph
Text and cover design by Parallelogram/Marsha Cohen
Editorial production services by Cobb/Dunlop Publisher Services

The Fisher travel guides include:

Bahamas
Bermuda
Best of the Caribbean
Britain
California and the West
Canada
Europe
Florida and the Southeast
France
Germany
Greece
Hawaii
Italy
Japan
London
Mexico
New England
Paris
Portugal
Spain and Portugal
Texas and the Southwest

Distributed in the U.S.A. and Canada by
New American Library, 1633 Broadway, New York, N.Y. 10019

Distributed worldwide by
New American Library, Inc., International Department
1633 Broadway, New York, N.Y. 10019

Printed in the United States of America

Contents

Editor's Foreword

Iberia is a word provoking wonder. It makes us pause, whenever we ponder taking a trip to Europe, because this dramatic peninsula is anything but ordinary. Mysterious, haughty, tragic . . . the adjectives roll out easily, begging us to dare a journey to Spain or Portugal. We know before setting off that Spain won't be dull, or Portugal unpleasant. We sense an air of unfamiliarity, of some abience beyond the majesty of cathedrals, the splendor of rugged mountain vistas, or the often unsettling folklore.

From the days of Washington Irving and Edgar Allan Poe, Spain has meant living theater, with characters larger than life, and situations impossible to credit as true. Portugal has been a country even less clearly seen, its history obscured by a language less ubiquitous than Spanish.

Unlike the majority of Europeans, who view Spain as an inexpensive place in the sun, North Americans visit mainly for the culture, the history and the continuing drama of contemporary living in a newly-born democracy. The same visitors to Portugal come looking for evocations of the past, for a country as yet unspoiled by mass tourism, and for a friendly people who still like Americans. (Nobody dislikes Canadians, it seems.) European visitors, including the British, appear to visit Portugal simply to get away from the hurly-burly of modern cities.

I believe you will enjoy a visit to Iberia more than ever today because of the strength of the U.S. dollar and the resulting moderation of expenses when you come to Madrid, Lisbon or your chosen base. If you concentrate on what Spain and Portugal really mean and don't get those identities confused with the artificial life seen on the various playground coasts, you will have enjoyed two of the most entertaining countries on the face of our planet.

About This Book

Over many years of writing and editing guidebooks, I have concluded that what the busy modern North American traveler needs is a concise listing of the best of certain categories . . . the best in hotels, restaurants, museums, and the like. The experienced traveler, in particular, wants sure guidance without having to wade through irrelevant information. The sophisticated traveler already knows how to pack, how to apply for a passport, how to buy an airline ticket, how to use a travel agent, and so forth. What he or she may want to know, for example, is: What are the best and second-best hotels in Madrid; which of the museums in Lisbon are really worth visiting; and what to see in Barcelona if there is only half a day. With the star rating system employed in this book, I think you'll find what you want, and quickly.

Spain and Portugal 1984 and the 15 additional guides published this year launch the new Fisher annotated travel guide series. These will be the first American guidebooks to attempt the classification of hotels, restaurants, museums, and even points of special interest in foreign countries. I do not believe for a moment that everyone is going to agree with all the selections or the ratings that go with them: The authors and editors are, however, as competent as anyone else, in my opinion, to make these selections.

The annotations are intended to provide handy cross-references, some explanation and, I hope, a bit of amusement. The books will be revised each year.

About the Authors

Patricia and Lester Brooks, authors of this guide, live in Connecticut, but spend more than one-third of each year traveling and reporting on various travel destinations for *Bon Appetit, Cuisine, Family Circle, Travel & Leisure, Vogue, Harper's Bazaar, Travel/Holiday, Modern Bride, House Beautiful,* and numerous other publications. Between them, they have written 15 books, six "his", six "hers", three "theirs."

In their travels, the Brookses combine their interest in food and wine. Pat, restaurant reviewer for the Connecticut section of the *New York Times* since 1977, belongs to Les Dames Escoffier; Lester is a member of the Sommelier Society of America. They met, they say, over a jugged hare while fellow students at the University of London. Pat, who grew up in Minneapolis, is a Vassar graduate. Lester, a Des Moines native, earned his M.A. at Columbia University.

Lester credits a Spanish great-grandfather for his long-time love affair with Spain. Pat says it was love at first sight during the Brooks's first visit in 1953. Since then, they have lived in Spain, and elsewhere, and have returned for visits at the drop of a sombrero dozens and dozens of times.

About the Editor

My qualifications are based mostly on my 20 years experience with the Fodor guidebook series, where I was chosen by Eugene Fodor to be his successor as editor-in-chief and president of the company. During my work with that company, I lived for 16 years outside the U.S.A., 8 of them in Europe. In the course of my work, I helped create more than 62 titles in the series of 75 books, including four volumes covering Spain and Portugal. In addition, I supervised all the titles to ensure their proper revision from year to year. This led to constant traveling around the world, as the series eventually covered all or parts of 120 nations.

Prior to the Fodor job, I attended the Graduate School of Tokyo University after graduating from Harvard College, where I studied international relations. I also attended Columbia University Law School, where my subject was international law.

On the professional side, I am a former president of the New York Travel Writers' Association and am now vice-president of the Society of American Travel Writers. I am also a director of a charitable foundation, the International Association for Medical Assistance to Travelers (IAMAT), a group whose services I recommend highly.

If you have read this far, you must be a friend or a relative, possibly a reviewer, or even as I am, a hopeless addict of travel books and guidebooks. Thanks, anyhow. I hope this book fills the bill for you.

List of Maps

IMPORTANT NOTE ON PRICES, ETC.

Prices mentioned in this book were accurate at time of writing, but as all experienced travelers know, nothing in life is forever, particularly costs, hours and days of closing, and the ambience of a hotel or restaurant. Please phone ahead to obtain reservations, confirm price ranges, or check closing times in order to avoid being disappointed. We will be delighted to hear from you, whether it be a recommendation, complaint, or both at: **Fisher Travel Guides, 401 Broadway, Suite 2300, New York, N.Y. 10013.**

IMPORTANT NOTE: The Star Ratings for each country's hotels, restaurants and points of interest are based on each country's merits alone, and are not to be compared with ratings given to places in any other country. Standards and attitudes in each country vary, and so, therefore, must our ratings.

The Hard Facts—Spain

Bay of Biscay
El Ferrol
La Coruña
Santiago
Oviedo
Santander
Bilbao
Leon
Burgos
P O R T U G A L
Braga
Bragança
Porto
Vila Real
Douero R.
Douro R.
Zamora
Valladolid
Medina del Campo
Salamanca
Aveiro
Viseu
Guarda
Avila
Madrid
Coimbra
S P A
Castelo Branco
Leiria
Tomar
Toledo
Tajo R.
Santarem
Tejo R.
Portalegre
Lisboa
Badajos
Ciudad Real
Evora
Guadiana R.
Linares
Cordoba
Guadalquivir R.
Sevilla
Granada
Sagres
Faro
Malaga
Jeres de la Frontera
Cadiz
Marbella
Estepona
Algeciras
Gibraltar
COSTA DEL SOL
SIERRA NEV
0 Miles 100
0 Kilometers 150
ROADS
RAILROADS
Mar
MOROCCO
Spain and Portugal

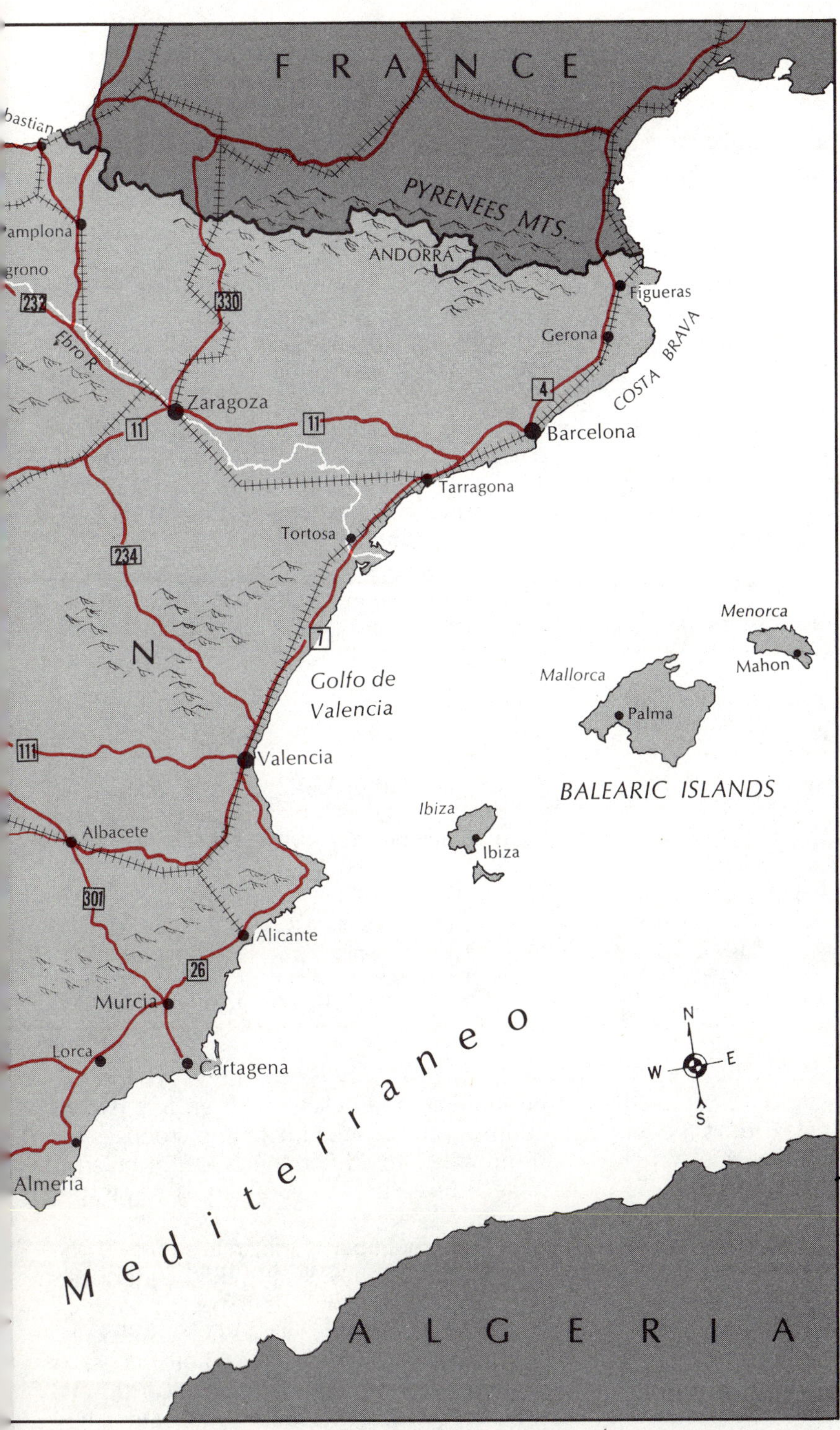
F R A N C E
bastian
amplona
grono
PYRENEES MTS.
ANDORRA
Figueras
Gerona
COSTA BRAVA
Ebro R.
Zaragoza
Barcelona
Tarragona
Tortosa
N
Golfo de
Valencia
Menorca
Mahon
Mallorca
Palma
Valencia
BALEARIC ISLANDS
Ibiza
Ibiza
Albacete
Alicante
Murcia
Lorca
Cartagena
Almeria
Mediterraneo
A L G E R I A
N
W
E
S

PLANNING AHEAD

Costs

Be glad you're going to Spain now. There was a lengthy period when Spain was a backwater. Today, Spain is one of the world's leading industrial nations. It is prosperous and, as you will find, has a high standard of living that you, as a visitor, can enjoy at moderate cost. Translation: You can have a terrific time in Spain without melting your money market fund.

Modern Spain offers you world-class quality in every conceivable category, especially hotels, restaurants and transportation, as well as fascinating, incomparable cultural life and art. You will find that you can live it up in Spain for far less than it would cost in most other popular destination countries.

The U.S. State Department's 1980 cost of living report on cities abroad puts Spain far down the list. Geneva, rated 184, was most expensive; Tokyo, with 183, was second; Paris rated 166; Brussels rated 158 and Madrid rated 120. The dollar at that time had an exchange ratio of about 60 pesetas (pts.)/$1; at this writing the rate is about 150 pts/$1.

And even if living it up is not your purpose, you'll still find that the cost of visiting Spain can be a pleasure rather than a pain in your pocketbook. "I can't afford the things I need, much less those I desire," may be true where you live, but depending on your needs and wishes, it doesn't have to be the case in Spain. Consider the following:

	Madrid/Barcelona	**Provinces**
Moderately priced hotel. Per person, double room, tax and service included	3,500 pesetas	3,000 pesetas
Lunch. Inexpensive restaurant	1,000 pesetas	750 pesetas
Dinner. Moderate restaurant	1,500 pesetas	1,400 pesetas
Total:	6,300 pesetas ($42)	5,150 pesetas ($34)

That local telephone call is about 15¢ or about 11p (U.K.)

We're talking about a country where a phone call (local) is 15 pts., buses are 40 pts. (subways and multiple-ride tickets are even less expensive), taxi rides are less than 200 pts., and air-conditioned microbuses are 45 pts. per ride. When you go shopping, you'll find that a loaf of bread is about 20 pts., milk, 55 pts. per liter, cheese between 380 and 1000 pts. per kilo, navel oranges, 75 pts. per kilo.

A pack of Marlboros costs 100 pts., but Spanish cigarettes cost 30 pts. for *negros* (blacks). Scotch is expensive—Johnny Walker Red Label costs 1,025 pts. per fifth, as does bourbon; Jack Daniel's is 850 pts.; Smirnoff Vodka costs at least 530 pts.; but Spanish vodka may be as little as 205 pts. Spanish Osborne brandy is 220 pts. per bottle and Spanish liqueurs are at bargain prices. A drink made with imported liquor will cost 200–300 pts. per drink, but an aperitif wine or *fino* (light and dry) sherry will come to half that. If wine is one of your interests, you can have a Lafite Rothschild 1970 in one of Spain's top restaurants for 14,000 pts., or a 40 year-old Rioja (Bodegas Riojanos 1942) at the same place for 6,000 pts.; the less-exalted Riojas 190 pts. and up. Beer at such a restaurant will be 150-200 pts. If you buy your Heineken's at a delicatessen, it will be 86 pts. per bottle; the local Aguila costs only 45 pts.

As for entertainment, for a musical such as *Annie* in Spanish, tickets are 600-1,000 pts. At the National Drama Center you can see Ibsen's *Wild Duck* or *The Night of Molly Bloom* for 350 pts. If you prefer a movie, a new first-run feature costs 150-225 pts.

How about music? A chamber music concert at the Teatro Real in Madrid will take you from Telemann to Handel and Bach for 300 pts. If pop rock is your thing, try a double-decker concert featuring Scorpions and Backfoot for 700 pts., or a single concert with 96 Lagrimas at 300 pts. If you prefer a concert by flutist Jose Moreno playing Shubert, you'll be happy to hear that it's free, sponsored by Fundacion Juan March.

For a quintessential Spanish experience, you can enjoy flamenco at Café de Chinitas for 1,350-3,500 pts., depending on your meal choices; it's open from 10 P.M. to sun-up. Bullfights may cost anywhere from 55 to 1,420 pts. at the Madrid ring during March (top-notch fights during the San Isidro Festival will be half again as much).

Entry to Spain's treasure houses is relatively modest in price. The Prado charges 200 pts., and most other museums are less than that.

These prices will give you a few ideas on how to judge expenses in Spain as of this writing. They will undoubtedly change since the exchange rate fluctuates and inflation continues (but even inflation is lower in Spain than in many other countries).

Climate

No, the rain in Spain is *not* "mainly on the plain," regardless of what was said in *My Fair Lady.* The rainiest parts of Spain are in the north, especially Galicia, the northwestern corner, where the climate and the countryside are much like Ireland—lush, green and velvety. On the plain—the Castilian Meseta—and Andalucía and the Mediterranean coastal areas, there are limited amounts of rainfall in February and March.

In general, Spain's climate is similar to California's—dry and warm, except on the coasts where sea breezes moderate or in the mountains where high altitudes keep temperatures down.

It can be quite cold in Madrid during winter

Spring is the most colorful season when the land is green and trees and flowers are in bloom. It's a time for light sweaters or jackets in the evening. Summer can be very hot—especially in Castile and Andalucía—and you'll find short sleeves and light-weight clothing are best. Fall lingers long on the coasts and turns the grape leaves golden in the vineyards. This is the season for sweaters during the day and light jackets at night. In winter, topcoats and light woolens will be comfortable in Madrid and most areas, except in the mountains such as the Guadarrama or along the Mediterranean coast, which is mild and just right for golfing.

To help you plan your trip, here's a temperature chart, giving the average daytime maximums (M) and nighttime minimums (m) for northern, central and southern Spain:

TEMPERATURES IN DEGREES, FAHRENHEIT

Locations		Winter (January)	Spring (April)	Summer (July)	Fall (October)
Northern	M	50	61	75	60
Coast	m	39	43	59	45
Madrid	M	53	67	89	64
	m	26	41	63	42
Málaga	M	60	75	88	77
(Costa del Sol)	m	42	56	64	55

Holidays and Special Events

There are few modern nations where festivals and folkloric events have not only survived but have flourished to the degree they have in Spain. At almost any time of the year you're bound to find a celebration or observance under way somewhere in the country. Of course, there are some holidays that all Spaniards celebrate, whether in the streets, in churches or in bars, depending on the occasion.

Spain observes a dozen national holidays. The religious ones are: Christmas, Epiphany (January 6), Good Friday, Easter Monday, the Assumption, Corpus Christi, All Saints Day (November 1) and Immaculate Conception (December 3), plus the feast days of St. Joseph (March 19), St. Peter and St. Paul (June 29) and Spain's patron saint, St. James (July 25). In addition, Spaniards celebrate New Year's, May Day and the National Day (October 12). Note that in some towns business closes from Maundy Thursday through Easter Monday.

Semana Santa—Easter week—with its costumed penitents and emotional processions is the religious high point of the year. The most famous processions and observances, such as Sevilla's, attract thousands of visitors who reserve hotel and line-of-march seats months in advance. Do likewise.

Some of the interesting and unusual festivals of the year are:

January

2nd, Granada celebrates Ferdinand and Isabella's 1492 final victory over the Moors; 6th, Epiphany is celebrated as Three Kings Day with elaborate parades, especially in Sevilla, Jaen, Murcia; 20th, Tamborrada parades through old sections of San Sebastian.

February

7th, St. Agatha Festival, 12th-century women's lib celebration with two mayors, dancing, at Zamarramala, 3 kilometers (km) from Segovia; 13–15th, Pero Palo Festival, at Villanueva de la Vero, condemned then authorized by Inquisition, it recreates a Moorish trial, execution and banquet; during carnival, International Antique Cars Rallye, 38 kilometers from Sitges to Barcelona.

March

12–19th, Fallas de San Jose fireworks, famous parades, dancing, burning of wood-and-paper buildings and satirical effigies in Valencía; third week of Lent, La Magdalena Festivals in Castellon de la Plana, with cavalcades and bullfights; on Sundays preceding Easter, Passion Plays and tableaux in many towns, such as those at Esparraguera, near Barcelona and at Cervera; *Semana Santa,* holy week ceremonies, processions, festivities all over the country, especially impressive are those in Cuenca, Málaga, Granada, Sevilla, Valladolid, Zamora, Pollensa and Chinchon. Cuenca, for example, has a reenactment of Christ's ascent to Calvary on Good Friday and sacred music festival during *Semana Santa;* 26th, Mercat del Ram, agricultural fair held since the Middle Ages in Vich.

April

3–4th, Bollo Festival of parades and folkloric competitions at Aviles; 9–15th, Burial of the Sardine (remember Goya's picture?), satirical festival in Murcia; 21–24th, Battle of Moors and Christians in Alcoy; end of April–early May, *Feria,* when Sevilla goes all out—hundreds of horses with costumed riders, carriages, floats, parades, pavilions, colored lights, *flamenco* and bullfights.

You'll find Goya's work in the Prado

May

1st–12th, Patios Festival, flowered houses, patios, squares and streets plus flamenco competition brighten Córdoba; last 3 weeks in May–1st week in June San Isidro Festival in Madrid—best bullfights; mid-May, Horse Fair, exhibitions, riding contests, folk dancing in Jerez de la Frontera; 26–29th, El Rocio, annual gathering of hundreds of gypsies in Andalusían dress at the sanctuary near Huelva.

June

5th or 12th, Aplec de la Sardana festival of Catalan dance at Calella; 23–24th. Paso del Fuego in which men walk barefoot on live coals in San Pedro Manrique, Soria; on or about 24th, St. John celebrations in Alicante, Coria, Soria, Barcelona, Segovia; end of June into July, International Festival of Music and Dance in the Alhambra, Granada.

July

6 –14th, Fiestas de San Fermin in Pamplona, as Hemingway described; 25th, St. James Fiesta with processions, fireworks at Santiago de Compostela; 22–27th, International Jazz Festival, San Sebastian; 25th, Shepherds festival at Cangas de Onis.

Hemingway's "Running of the Bulls"

August

Month-long International Festival of Music and Dance, Santander; similar one at Cadaques; 5–7th, festival with folk dancing and *encierros* with women running the bulls in Estella; 11–15th, Mystery of Elche, 13th-century musical at Elche; 15th, Feast of Assumption celebrated with mystery play, ancient costumes, dances at La Alberca; Wine Harvest festivals at Jumilla, Montilla and Requena (among others).

September

(Early), International Cinema Festival, San Sebastián; bullfights or running of the bulls during this month's festivals in Cabra, Albacete, Barcelona, Candeleda, Cardona, Graus, Tordesillas, Carreno-Candas; Wine Harvest festivals during the month in Valdepenas, Jerez de la Frontera, Logroño, La Palma del Condado.

October

International Music Festival, Barcelona; 9th, Shellfish Festival, (a gourmet extravaganza) in El Grove, near Pontevedra; week of the 12th, Fiestas del Pilar with parades, folk dancing, bullfights in Zaragoza; 17–20th, "As San Lucas" livestock and folk dancing fair at Mondonedo; 30th, Saffron Rose Flower Harvest Festival, with bullfights, festivities, wine cellar visits, at Consuegra.

December

6th, Immaculate Conception celebrated with processions and folk dancing at Yecla, Cuenca, Jarandilla; 24th, Christmas Eve ceremonies at all churches and cathedrals, especially at monasteries at Poblet, Montserrat and Guadalupe; Shepherds' Dance medieval procession, singing and ceremony at Midnight Mass at Labastida.

Travel Agents and Tour Operators

A *travel agent* specializes in making transportation and accommodation arrangements tailored to individual travelers' needs. A *tour operator,* by contrast, specializes in taking travelers on "tour packages" that include transportation, lodgings and sightseeing and may include meals, transfers and guides, plus sundry extras such as welcoming drinks.

Some of the leading tour operators who offer Spanish trip packages are:

In the United States

Abreu Tours, Inc. 60 E. 42nd St. New York, NY 10165 (800)233–1580.
American Express, 125 Broad St., New York, NY 10004; (800)241–1700.
Caravan Tours, 401 N. Michigan Ave., Chicago, IL 60611; (312)321–9800.

Five Points Travel, 1 Old State Rd., Media, PA 19063; (800)345–8146.
Iberoamericana Tours, 1440 Canal St., New Orleans, LA 70112; (504)561–8678.
Maupintour, 408 E. 50 St., New York, NY 10022; (800)255–4266.
Mundi Tours, 2390 N.E. 7 St., Miami, FL 33125; (305)649–7066.
Percival Tours, One Tandy Center Plaza, Ft. Worth, TX 76102; (817)870–0300.
Thomson Vacations, 401 N. Michigan Ave., Chicago, IL 60611; (800)621–9543.
Globus-Gateway Travel, 69–15 Austin St., Forest Hills, NY 11375; (800)221–0090.

Airlines

Iberia, 97–77 Queens Blvd., Rego Park, NY 10017; (800)221–9640.
TWA. 605 Third Ave., New York, NY 10016; (800)523–4828.

In Canada

Eaton's Department Store, 677 St. Catherine, W., Montreal, Quebec.
Thos. Cook & Sons, 2020 University St., Montreal, Quebec.

In Britain

Cosmos, Cosmos House, 1 Bromley Common, Bromley, Kent.
Thos. Cook & Sons, c/o Harrod's, Knightsbridge, London; SW1X 7XL.

Tour Packages

Just what do tour operators offer these days? The range begins with bare-bones transportation and lodging and extends to truly unusual, luxury vacations.

Globus-Gateway, for instance, has three economy-style tours that cover Spain, Portugal and Morocco in tandem. One 11-day trip goes from Lisbon to Sevilla, on to Tangier, back to Malaga, then Granada and Madrid. A "Grand Tour" also begins in Lisbon, allows two days in Sevilla, and then to Tangier for two days. The remainder of the 18-day tour concentrates on Malaga, Granada, Madrid and then north to Burgos, León and along the "pilgrimage trail" to Santiago de Compostela. The tour swings back to Portugal—to Oporto, ending in Lisbon.

TWA Getaway Tours offers a 15-day budget-minded tour that includes Portugal, Spain and Tangier with prices inclusive ranging downward from $1,452 for double accommodations. These tours travel by air-conditioned coach from Lisbon via Elvas to Sevilla, Jerez, a side trip to Tangier, the Costa del Sol, Malaga, Granada, Toledo and Madrid. The tour allows time in Lisbon for the Alfama quarter, Jerónimos Monastery and the palaces at Sintra, and in Spain to see the Alhambra in Granada, El Greco's home in Toledo, the Prado and Royal Palace in Madrid, Columbus's tomb and the Giralda Tower in Sevilla.

A deluxe three-week *Maupintour* includes Barcelona's Gothic Quarter, Montserrat, three days in Mallorca, then Andalucía's key cities—Sevilla, Córdoba and Granada—followed by the Costa del Sol at Málaga and Marbella. The tour continues with a visit to Toledo's Alcazar and Madrid's Prado and Plaza Mayor, then a sidetrip to the *Escorial* and Segovia, with its Roman aqueduct. The trip winds up in Lisbon. Tab for the trip, including air connections in Spain: $2,057, double occupancy. Round-trip airfare via TAP or IBERIA, New York–Madrid: $723.

In Spain, you'll want to call at Madrid's Municipal Tourist Information Bureau, 3 Plaza Mayor; 266–5477, for local assistance and counsel. The National Tourist Office of Spain (NTOS) is at 50 María V. Molina; 401–6011. The Plaza Mayor office has literature, lists of hotels and restaurants, current cultural events and handsome posters and can help you locate shops that deal in specific items, from apple presses to *zapatos* (shoes).

Each town and city, of course, has a local *turismo* office usually centrally located and identified with a large sign. Most of them have maps of their localities, restaurant and hotel lists and the basic leaflet distributed by the NTOS about the region.

For current information on the cultural and entertainment scene in and around Madrid, the most complete weekly listings are in *Guía del Ocio* (leisure guide), available at newsstands for 30 pts. It includes movies, theater, music, art, books, sports, television and *tarde y noche* (evening and night) listings of jazz, folk, disco, as well as massage parlors, sex shops, call girls and boys (all in Spanish). For a pale shadow of this in English, there's *Guidepost* for 50 pts. And for the best daily newspaper listing of events, try ABC's *espectaculos* (spectacles) section. A Spanish–English summary of upcoming events and activities called *En Madrid* is distributed free by the offices of the Municipal Turismo. It is prepared by the editors of *Guía del Ocio.*

Packing

Though Spain's climate dictates what clothing to bring, your choices should also reflect your interests.

In every case, you'll want comfortable shoes for walking—perhaps a couple of pairs. (It's true that shoes are excellent values in Spain, but not if you have large, narrow, wide or difficult-to-fit feet.) For the warm months, wash and wear, drip-dry cottons are your best bets. In most areas, except the northern coastal region, the air is so dry that when you wash your clothing, it will dry overnight. Don't forget to take a light sweater to ward off evening chills. For lunch and dinner at the better restaurants in major cities, a jacket and tie or neat sports shirt for men, and a simple dress, separates or pant suit for women should do. Spain tends to be a bit formal, and fine establishments look askance at blue jeans and shorts. Of course, in the casual resort areas, swim suits, sneakers, jeans and shorts are generally acceptable every place but church.

If you'll be traveling in the mountains or in the north, bring a raincoat and at least one cool-weather outfit. And if you'll be visiting in late fall or spring, take some woolen clothing, especially a jacket or heavy sweater and heavy socks. A coat with zip-in lining should help ward off the chilly winds.

You'll find that Spain sells most of your basic needs. If you run out of staples such as aspirin or hand lotion or face cream, there is no need to worry. Also, you can have your drug prescriptions filled at the *farmacias.* There's no need to bring soap—hotels supply fine Spanish soaps—but you may want to carry your favorite shampoo. Spanish hotels rarely supply tissues, but you can buy them at *supermercados.*

For your electric razor, hair drier and iron, the hotels provide outlets that may or may not be 110 volts, alternating current and accept flat prongs. To be safe, bring a plug adapter (with round, European prongs) and a transformer to step down the 220 volt current. Since a hair drier may blow a fuse in some hotels if you plug into the shaver outlet in the bathroom, be prepared to plug it into a baseboard in your bedroom. (You may want to bring a hand mirror.)

Smokers may want to bring their favorite brands of cigarettes or pipe tobacco. Cigar smokers may prefer to buy the good Havana (and other) cigars that are readily available.

You may wish to carry your favorite Scotch or bourbon with you, but gin, vodka, brandies, liqueurs and wines are relatively inexpensive in Spain.

Camera film can be bought in shops in all towns, especially in resort areas. If you carry film with you, you will find the security officials at the airports obliging if you ask them to hand film in transparent bags around the x-ray machine. If you pack your film, be sure to enclose it in lead-shielded bags.

Documentation

A valid U.S., Canadian or British passport is all you need for entry to Spain —no visas are required for a stay of up to six months.

Unless you are traveling directly from some area of the world where contagious diseases are currently a problem, you will not need to show an immunization record. At present, the USA, Canada and Britain are not in that category, so you don't need your shot record.

If you plan to drive in Spain, you will need a valid U.S., Canadian or British driver's license. If you wish, you may secure an international driving license before leaving for Spain; they are available through your automobile club.

Though it's not required, if you have special complications such as pacemakers, allergy to medications, diabetic requirements, you should carry information stating this. Some travelers scotch tape this information inside their passports.

The Handicapped Traveler

Spaniards are solicitous of people who are recognizably handicapped. However, the country is not very easy for handicapped people to negotiate. Hotels, for example, generally have their lobbies up at least one flight of steps, most often without ramps. Nevertheless, there are readily available personnel to help handicapped people at airports, bus and rail depots, hotels and restaurants.

The resort areas along the Costa del Sol are better able to aid handicapped visitors than some of the other parts of Spain. There is, for example, a dialysis center for visitors in Torremolinos (Gambro Dialysis Clinic, Edificio Eurotorre; 385–650), and the Hotel Parasol (Urbanizacion Tres Caballos Vial Benxamina, Torremolinos; 386–022) advertises that it is equipped to handle tourists in wheelchairs.

You may wish to check the advice in Louise Weiss's *Access to the World,* published by Facts on File, Inc. It is designed for the handicapped traveler. Lois Reamy's *Travelability,* published by Macmillan, is also valuable.

Other sources of information for handicapped travelers include Easter Seal Society for Crippled Children and Adults, 2023 West Oregon Avenue, Chicago, IL 60612; Society for the Handicapped, 26 Court Street, Brooklyn, NY 11242; Travel Information Center, Moss Rehabilitation Hospital, 12 Street & Tabor Road, Philadelphia, PA 19141.

GETTING THERE

By Air

Lowest roundtrip fare at press time, New York–Madrid $509 (APEX)

From New York, both Iberia and TWA have daily nonstop flights to Madrid. TWA goes on to Barcelona three or more times a week, and Iberia has daily through service. In summer, Iberia has weekly nonstop flights to Santiago de Compostela.

From Miami, Iberia flies to Madrid three or more times a week and Aeromexico flies nonstop to Madrid four times a week.

From Canada, Iberia flies from Montreal nonstop to Madrid four to five times a week.

From Britain, Iberia flies to Alicante, Almeria, Barcelona, Bilbao, Madrid, Málaga, Santiago, Sevilla, Valencía, Mallorca, Menorca and Ibíza. British Airways also flies to Barcelona, Bilboa, Madrid, and Malaga and Valencia.

In addition to these regularly scheduled air lines, charter flights by the hundreds carry travelers to Spain. Among these are two Spanish carriers, Spantax and Aviaco. Many charter flights are made by major carriers who contract for such business. The travel pages of American Sunday newspapers and some travel magazines generally have ads for Spain-bound charter flights in the form of package tours. In Europe, the *London Times* and *International Herald-Tribune* carry classified ads for charter or group flights to destinations in Spain—at remarkably low rates.

By Car

The Gibralter border is now open, but only for residents of the Rock, and relatives

You can drive into Spain from France or Portugal and, if they ever unlock the border, from Gibraltar.

From France, there are 14 border points from which to enter Spain. Most frequently used are those between Perpignan and Barcelona and between Bayonne and the Basque province. From Portugal there are more than a dozen crossing points. From Gibraltar, the single road leads through La Linea checkpoint.

In general, the border crossing is simple and quick, with easy passport processing and verbal answers to customs officials' questions. Occasionally, a spot check of a vehicle is made.

You can bring your car in by sea via the twice-a-week ferry service from Plymouth, England–to–Santander on Brittany ferries or the weekly Marseilles–to–Palma de Mallorca run on the Algerienne line, to mention two possibilities. For alternatives, check with Sealink Car Ferry Centre, Grosvenor Gardens, London SW1, or French Railways, 179 Picadilly, London W1, England.

By Water

You can come by ferry in ten minutes from Vila Real de Santo Antonio, Portugal to Ayamonte. From Morocco, ferries to Spain leave Tangier, Cevte and Melilla.

By Rail

Many trains serve Spain from both Portugal and France, including fast, reliable express trains.

From Lisbon to Madrid there are two daily expresses—the Lisbon Express or T.E.R., which takes about 11 hours and the Lusitania Express, which makes the journey in 13 hours. There are also trains from Portugal's Algarve to destinations in Spain.

From France, the most popular express trains to Madrid are the Puerta del Sol overnighter, the Iberia Express (which continues beyond Madrid to Algeciras) and the Paris–Madrid Talgo (*Tren Articulado Ligero Goicoechea y Oriol*—the light, swift articulated train of Sr. Oriol), which makes the run weekdays only, from 6:45 A.M. to 9:52 P.M. A Barcelona Talgo operates seven days a week, leaving 9:36 A.M., whistling into Barcelona at 11:27 P.M.

There are sleepers, couchettes, first- and second-class accommodations on some or all of these trains. And there are many other trains that cover these and other routes into Spain. RENFE, the Spanish state railways, has schedules and information about rail routes into and out of Spain. They have offices in all major Spanish towns but not abroad. French National Railroads handles their reservations and sales overseas. In the United States, address them at: French National Railroads, 610 Fifth Avenue, New York, NY 10020; (212)582–2110.

By Bus

Air-conditioned, deluxe motorcoaches with toilet facilities, hostesses, background music, reading lights and airline-type reclining seats have brought a new dimension to bus travel. There are many bus lines using such equipment to bring travelers to Spain.

From Portugal there are regular buses to Sevilla and Madrid. One of the major carriers is Mundial Turismo, Av. Antonio de Aguiar, Lisbon; 563–521.

There are many bus tour operators who have package excursions to Spain from other European countries. One of the most active is Europabus, which cooperates with ATESA, a major Spanish motorcoach tour company. In Britain, Europabus is represented by Sealink Travel, Ltd., Victoria Station, London SW1. Many bus tours are advertised in the *International Herald-Tribune* and *London Times,* especially on the travel pages and in the classified ads.

FORMALITIES ON ARRIVAL

Customs

Customs processing in Spain is generally quick and easy.

At the airport, after you retrieve your luggage, you'll push your cart (in Madrid a limited number of carts are to be found among the baggage carousels) through the doors marked "nothing to declare." Customs officials spot check only rarely. Then you continue through a second set of doors to the lobby where auto rental desks and telephones are located. Go through the next set of doors and you are at the taxi and bus stands.

If you are stopped for a spot check, customs officials will be looking to see that you have no more than 200 cigarettes or 50 cigars (or 100 small ones), 260 grams (9 ounces) of tobacco, 2 liters of wine or 1 liter of spirits (above 22% alcohol), ¼ liter of cologne and perhaps a small amount of perfume.

Spanish customs allow you to bring in the clothing, jewelry and personal effects you need for a visit. These include two still cameras and ten rolls of film per camera; one motion picture camera (16 millimeters or smaller) with ten rolls of film; and field glasses, portable radio, record player, bicycle, typewriter, television set and/or a musical instrument. You may have difficulty bringing in elaborate professional or electronic equipment; you'll probably have to place a deposit on the equipment, which is repayable when you leave the country, and "re-export" the gear by taking it with you.

Pocket calculators, tape recorders, cassette players and new electronic gizmos are generally allowed in so long as they are clearly personal property and noncommercial.

There is no limit on the amount of foreign currency or travelers' checks you may bring in, but the ceiling for Spanish pesetas is 50,000 pts. You cannot take more than 3,000 pts. out of the country.

If you're bringing in sporting equipment, you are welcome to carry a tent and camping gear, bicycle without motor, canoe or kayak shorter than 5.5 m, two pairs of skis, two tennis racquets, fishing tackle and lures. You're allowed two hunting guns—rifles or shotguns—with 100 cartridges for each, but be sure you declare them.

Driving your own bicycle, motorcycle, car or recreation vehicle into Spain for noncommercial purposes should cause no problems at customs. The same is true of boats. If you fly your own plane in, you must land in a customs airport where officials will determine whether you meet regulatory requirements. Contact the closest Spanish consulate before you're airborne for the latest regulations.

The big no-no is drugs. They are illegal, and penalties for possession are stiff.

Money

The peseta (pta.; plural, pts.) is the basic unit of money and is made up of 100 centimos. Peseta banknotes are issued in 100, 500, 1,000 and 5,000 denominations. Coins are 10 and 50 centimos; 1, 2½, 5, 25, 50 and 100 pts. (The 10 and 50 centimos and 2½ pts. coins are rare.) Spanish coins illustrate topical events. Last year's world football championship matches were featured on a popular coin.

All major travelers checks are accepted throughout Spain. U.S., Canadian and British currency is easily exchanged at your hotel, local banks and *cambios* (exchange offices).

Credit cards are widely accepted. The decals on the front windows or doors of restaurants, hotels and shops tell which are welcome. Generally, American Express, Visa, MasterCard, Diners Club and Carte Blanche are honored. Some merchants add on an extra charge for credit card payments. MasterCard is usable where the European Interbank cards are accepted. And some trusting hotels and shops will take your personal check—but don't bank on it. You may as well leave your oil company credit cards at home. They cannot be used in Spain.

Your best exchange rates are offered by the banks, and of these, we have found Banco Exterior is slightly more generous than the others. The *cambios* in the cities are open longer hours than the banks but have lower rates. Your hotel will generally have an exchange rate that is less attractive than the bank's but better than the cambios'. Note that most banks avoid changing small amounts.

Incidentally, while you are at the airport waiting for your luggage you'll notice an office of Banco Exterior. It's kept open to meet the many arriving planes. You'll find that its exchange rate is better than at hotels and cambios, so you may wish to change some money there.

Getting into Town

When you step out of the Madrid airport arrival building, the taxi stand is in front and to your left. Along the sidewalk to your right is the stop for the Madrid bus that goes to Plaza Colon.

If your hotel is located at or near Plaza Colon, simply put your luggage aboard, pay the 100 pts. and arrive there in less than half an hour.

If your hotel is located elsewhere, you have two choices: Take the bus to Colon and taxi the rest of the way, or take a taxi all the way. A taxi will cost from 500 to 1,000 pts., depending on how much luggage you have and other factors. A cab from Colon to your hotel will probably be 200 pts., or less, unless your hotel is beyond the fringe. Rule of thumb estimate: If you are alone or with another person and have minimal luggage, take the bus and cab. If you have heavy luggage and/or are three or more, take the cab. And be sure the driver puts the flag down so the ride is metered.

Taxis take about 20 minutes to cover the 16 kilometers barring a traffic jam. Some flights arrive just in time for the morning rush hour traffic, so you could have a slow trip.

When you take the bus you disembark in the underground parking garage beneath Plaza Colon. Taxis are lined up just a few steps away. Most trips to points in Madrid by taxi from Colon cost 30 –150 pts.

If you arrive by train or bus you'll be in the city, and your best bet, especially with luggage, is to taxi to your hotel.

There is another way to get into town—rent a car. (See the section Getting Around.)

SETTLING DOWN

Choosing a Hotel

A list of all of Spain's hotels and inns is included in a fat volume published annually by the Spanish Tourist Board. It is called *Guía de Hoteles* and can be bought for about 300 pts. at bookshops and tourist offices. However, many municipal tourist offices have printed lists of hotels in their own areas and will gladly give you such a list for free, if you ask. (Don't be surprised if they don't voluntarily load you up with literature—you do *have* to ask.)

The official government publications list alphabetically all the hotels, apartment hotels, and *pensiones.* The Spanish system classifies each establishment on how it measures up to certain criteria. The raters check out the number of lounges, bars, elevators, telephones, hygiene and service facilities and bathing facilities per room. In general, the more a hotel has, the higher its government rating and the higher its prices. The one-star hotel may be 1,500 pts. or less per room and the five-star, *gran luxe,* may be 10,000 pts. or more per room. Every hotel has an official blue plaque at its entrance with the letter "H" and its star rating below. In addition to "H" on official hotel plaques, you may find other letters. "HS," meaning hostal, usually shares its building with another tenant. "HR" meaning hotel-residencia and "HsR," meaning hostal-residencia; they do not have restaurants and serve breakfasts only. "P", meaning pension, is where you must book a room with full board.

But there is great variation in comforts and amenities among hotels in the same category. A four-star, world-class hotel in a fashionable resort area may be far superior to a five-star hotel in a provincial town. In short, the government star system is often not very helpful in comparing hotel accommodations.

Nevertheless, in every hotel star ratings and room prices are posted near the reception desk—in plain sight. And the legal prices of accommodations, accompanying meals and extras must be posted in each room. Taxes and service charges (now 15% and 5% –10%, respectively) also must be shown. Except in Madrid and Barcelona, room rates fluctuate according to the season, and this must be stated. All of this information is helpful.

All hotels are required to give you a card with your room number and room rate when you register. This eliminates confusion at checkout time.

We suggest that you augment the posted information by examining a room before accepting it. This procedure of asking to see a room will be no surprise to management. Does the room have double glazing and air-conditioning (during summer)? If not, the window on the street is going to amplify the night street noises and you should ask for a room on the courtyard instead. Do the lights, radio or television work? Get the idea?

Our ratings (see box) from five stars (best-deluxe) on down to one star (clean, acceptable) are our own evaluations (not the Spanish government's ratings) based on our experiences. These are our personal judgments made on the basis of overall comparisons. We've listed especially worthy hotels, based on their character, amenities, ambience and location, above and beyond their provision of fundamental lodgings.

STAR RATING SYSTEM

Hotels

★★★★★ 5 Stars. Super deluxe establishment, BEST of the best.

★★★★ 4 Stars. Deluxe. As comfortable as your own home, and better service.

★★★ 3 Stars. Superior. Has the facilities that make it stand out.

★★ 2 Stars. Excellent. There is nothing to complain about at all.

★ 1 Star. Good. One or two things may be missing, but an o.k. place.

0 Stars. Recommended.

Restaurants

★★★★★ 5 Stars. Out of this world!

★★★★ 4 Stars. Fantastic!

★★★ 3 Stars. Superb!

★★ 2 Stars. Excellent.

★ 1 Star. Good.

0 Stars. Recommended.

Sightseeing, Museums, Etc.

★★★★★ 5 Stars. You should make a trip to Spain if only to see this.

★★★★ 4 Stars. You should plan your trip to Spain around this.

★★★ 3 Stars. You should plan your day around this.

★★ 2 Stars. You should detour a mile in order to see this.

★ 1 Star. You should detour a couple of blocks to see this.

Spain has a number of very special hotels that you should keep in mind. Over the past 50 years the government has opened more than 80 hostelries across the country. These *paradores* (inns), *albergues de carretera* (motels) and *refugios* (lodges) have been extremely popular since they offer excellent value in reliable, clean and attractive lodgings. The *paradores* often are at exquisitely beautiful sites or at heart-thumping romantic places—old castles, monasteries, palaces and convents. These establishments are located in scenically or historically important areas away from major cities (with some exceptions) and, in the cases of the ancient buildings, have been restored with loving care and minimal changes to bring in modern conveniences.

Tranquility, peace, beauty and scrupulous attention to historic preservation characterize the best of the paradors. They offer you the opportunity of fulfilling, if only briefly (for stays are limited), the fantasy of living in a castle in Spain. Paradors have well-appointed dining rooms and usually offer regional specialties, local as well as national wines and bottled waters. In the USA, paradors are represented exclusively by Marketing Ahead, 515 Madison Ave., New York, NY 10022; (212)759–5170. The *albergues* (roadside lodging or shelter) are fewer in number, simple in style and accoutrements, on main highways, often with swimming pools. The *refugios* (retreats) are like rustic lodges located in mountain spots from which you can easily hunt, fish and hike.

If you visit Spain during the popular months of April through September or during the holiday seasons of Easter and Christmas/New Year's, make sure you reserve rooms in advance. This is especially true for the most desirable hotels and paradors in the most popular destinations.

Granada's *Parador de San Francisco* required booking a year in advance until newly added rooms cut that time in half. Another remarkable chain of hotels is the *Entursa* group. Operated by a Spanish government holding company, these world-class hostelries are deluxe in every respect. Several are installed in national treasures such as the palace/monastery/church/museum of San Marcos in León. Furnished with handsome antiques, outstanding art and superb detail, they cater to customers who wish to experience ancient Spain but with modern comforts. Their service, wines and cuisine are of top quality. It is one of the pleasant discoveries of a trip to Spain that the prices of such luxurious accommodations and coddling are, by contemporary American standards, a bargain. Very few double rooms go for more than $75 a day and most are less than two-thirds that, breakfast included.

Entursa is represented in the USA by Marketing Ahead (see address above). They'll send you information and book your rooms.

Nine Spanish hotels and three restaurants are members of the exclusive *Relais et Chateaux* group. Among these are the well-known Marbella Club Hotel and Los Monteros, both on the Costa del Sol. The Son Vida, on Mallorca, is situated in a 13th-century royal palace and the Landa Palace near Burgos was formerly a royal castle. The *Relais* have a well-deserved reputation for top quality in furnishings, restaurants, service and settings (usually with prices to match). Information and bookings are available from Relais et Chateaus, Hotel de Crillon, 10 place de la Concorde, 75008 Paris, France; 742–00–20.

There are other representatives who specialize in booking rooms directly at Spanish hotels. Among the most active are the following:

Five outstanding Spanish hotels, including Hotel Formentor, are represented by Robert Warner, Inc., 711 Third Ave., N.Y., N.Y. 10017

Loews International, 666 Fifth Ave., New York, NY 10019 (representing *Melia* hotel chain and others); (800)223–0888 or (800)522–5455.
Hotel and Transportation Consultants, 520 North Michigan Ave., Chicago, IL 60611; (800)621–5078
Trusthouse Forte, 810 Seventh Ave., New York, NY 10019; (800)223–5672 (represents the Ritz in Madrid and other hotels)
Jane Condon Corp., 211 East 43 St., New York, NY 10017; (800)223–5608
Utell International, 119 West 57 St., New York, NY 10019; (800)223–9898 (represents 35 hotels in Spain)

Choosing a Restaurant

If your mental picture of a typical Spanish meal is a mound of *paella* or a chunk of lamb swimming in olive oil with a heavy crust of bread and throat-scalding wine to wash it all down, you're in for some pleasant surprises.

There has been a vast improvement in the quality of Spanish cuisine, including a broadening of the menu offerings and a much greater variety on the bill of fare. This has come about mainly because of the increased prosperity and a larger middle class, with the consequent enlarged clientele for better fare.

Spain's tourism ministry ranks all restaurants and awards them from five *tenedores* (forks) for luxury class down to one tenedor for fourth-class. You'll see these tenedor ratings near entrances to eating places. It is important to note that these rankings do *not* relate to the quality of the food but to the number of dishes on the menu in specified categories. A one-tenedor fourth-class restaurant menu is only required to offer appetizers, soups, two entrées and desserts with cheese and fruit. Luxury restaurants, however, must offer at least five choices in each of five course categories, plus a first-rate selection of wines.

Star ratings also explained on back cover of this book

We rated Spanish restaurants specifically on the *quality* of the cuisine and how well the establishments deliver what they promise. We compared restaurants with their counterparts in other countries, in Spain and in their own areas. Our ratings go from five stars for the best restaurant on down. (See box.)

Some of the basics of Spanish dining are as follows: Except for *desayuno* (breakfast), dining hours are quite late. In Madrid, *comida* (midday dinner) is served from 1:30 to 4 P.M. (most Spaniards arrive at about 3); *cena*, (supper) from 8:30 P.M. to midnight (the most popular hour is 10 P.M.) Outside the capital, the hours tend to be earlier.

Servings are more than ample; prices are reasonable. In the entire country there are few restaurants with prices in the Lutece, Dorchester or Tour d'Argent range. The same is true for quality Spanish wines.

Every restaurant posts its menu where it can be read by passersby. Examine it and see if it offers what you want at a price you're willing to pay. You may want to look inside. If the place is empty at 3 P.M. or at 10:30 P.M., *caveat emptor.* Local diners know *the* places—follow their lead to another restaurant.

Restaurateurs are hospitable and will proudly welcome you in to view their dining rooms and maybe even the kitchen. (Exceptions are when the place is very crowded with diners and in deluxe restaurants, where reservations are mandatory.)

If you're assailed by waves of uncontrollable hunger before the restaurants open, take heart. You can survive!

In the afternoons and many evenings, bars, taverns and *cervecerias* (beer pubs) serve tiny saucers of canapes called *tapas* (*pinchos* in Madrid). These tidbits on toothpicks or small portions of "pub food" are eaten at stand-up bars or are taken to nearby tables. Spaniards delight in going on a *pinchos* prowl from one bar or *tasca* (a pocket-sized barroom) to the next. In some quarters, such as Calle Echegaray, Plaza Santa Ana and Plaza Mayor in Madrid, you can sample half a dozen different specialties in as many bars in a single block. Typical tapas include garlic shrimp, mussels, fried mushrooms, bits of spicy sausage and cheese balls.

If you have an insatiable sweet tooth, head for a *patisserie, pastelería, confitería* (pastry or candy shops or both) or cafeteria. (Spanish cafeterias are sit-down, not tray-carrying, places. Brassy and glassy, they specialize in sugary sweets, sandwiches, tea, coffee or aperitifs during the day.)

There are also fast-food shops in each big city. McDonald's, Burger King and Kentucky Fried Chicken have their beachheads in Madrid and they and their look-alikes are expanding.

You'll probably be served promptly, whether you order a gargantuan meal or coffee. But the check may not be delivered until you call for it. After all, you've "rented" your table for the duration. Spanish waiters do not rush their patrons. How do you get your waiter's attention? Call him: *"oiga"* (listen), or *"camarero"* (waiter), or *"por favor"* (please) will do. Not recommended are clapping your hands or calling *"chico"* (boy). Want to be trendy? When requesting the bill ask for *la dolorosa* (bad news).

Tipping

In Spain, restaurants, bars and hotels add service charges to your bill. Spaniards generally leave loose change when paying small bar and café bills. At a restaurant they usually leave change and currency up to 5% of the bill but rarely more than 100 pts.

Think of a peseta as approx. one american cent (or a British ha'penny)

At stand-up eating and drinking counters, you are not charged for service. The custom is to leave the small change on the saucer when you pay your bill.

Hotel bills include service, but porters are tipped 25–50 pts. per bag, maids about 50 pts. per day or 200 pts. per week at the best hotels and room service 50–100 pts. The doorman who calls a cab for you usually receives 10–50 pts.

Porters at airports or stations should be content with 50 pts. per bag, more if your luggage is leaden. If a porter quotes a higher price, ask to see his rate card. There are set rates posted.

Taxi drivers are satisfied with 25 pts. for most rides under 250 pts. Figure 5%–10% beyond that if the driver has been particularly helpful. When your trip is unmetered, the cabbie figures in his tip.

You'll want a supply of 5- and 25-pts. coins for restroom attendants (10 pts.), coat check persons (10 pts.), ushers and keepers of the keys to tourist sights (25 pts. each).

Barbers and hairdressers usually receive tips of 50 pts.

Guides who attach themselves to you at museums or monuments deserve nothing if you don't use their services. If you find them interesting, 25 pts. should suffice. If one of the door openers, whose duty it is to give you access to the building after you've paid an entrance fee, should hold out his hand for a tip, you can shake it, ignore it or simply thank him. Guides who take you on bus tours generally receive a small tip of 50 pts. and up from each person for a brief half-day tour; commensurately more if they are outstanding or the tour is longer.

In general, you won't be hounded by tip-hungry Spaniards.

Perks

Transportation offers some excellent opportunities for you to stretch your dollars if you make the effort to plan ahead. Among the interesting gambits are the following:

Chequetren is a discount ticket booklet that gives you 15% off on rail travel in Spain if you spend a minimum of 15,000 pts. The booklet can be used by as many as six people and there's no time limit on its use. You have to buy it at a RENFE (Spanish rail) ticket office in Spain, and it's good only in Spain.

Tarjeta Dorada (Gold Card) costs 25 pts. if you qualify as a senior citizen, 65 years or over. Present your passport to prove your age. With your Gold Card you then can buy rail tickets at half-price for trips of 100 kilometers or more on all designated "blue days" (more than half the year).

Visit Spain is the Iberia Airlines special fare ticket that gives you 45 days of air travel within Spain for $199. It must be bought in the USA or Canada before you leave for Spain. Just one qualifier: You cannot fly twice to any city but Madrid (it's an exception because so many routes go to it), otherwise you have unlimited travel via Iberia's domestic flights.

The *Eurailpass* is widely known; here are the basics: It is good in 16 member countries on railroads and, in some cases, buses, steamers and ships. You buy tickets that are good for 15 days for $260; for 21 days for $330; for a month for $410, for two months for $560, for three months for $680. The Eurail Youthpass for travelers up to 25 years of age is $290 for one month and $370 for two months. The regular Eurailpass is for first- or second-class unlimited travel; the Youthpass is for second-class travel only. They are good on RENFE's routes, as well as in other countries. Eurailpasses are available and must be bought before departure through U.S. travel agents in the USA and Canada.

Because of Spain's vast size, you may want to combine rail travel with some airplane trips

Want to cut your housing costs to zero? More and more vacationers are doing so by swapping. You exchange with a person/family in another country (Spain, in this case) your home or flat (apartment) for his/hers/theirs for the mutually agreed upon time period. You can do this by yourself, but there are organizations that facilitate it. One such organization is Vacation Exchange Club, 350 Broadway, New York, NY 10013, which distributes an annual *Exchange Book* that is a swappers' marketplace.

Want to rent a home in a Spanish resort area? Interhome is an organization that has such homes on the Costa del Sol and Costa Brava. Its office in Britain is Interhome, 10 Sheen Road, GB-Richmond TW9 1AE; (01)948 41 12.

Business Hours

"Morning" has a different meaning in Spain. Businesses are open in the morning from 9:30 A.M. to 1:30 P.M. Their afternoon hours are generally from 4:30 to 8 P.M., Monday through Friday. Most businesses are open Saturday mornings as well.

Banks have hours much like those in the USA, from 9 A.M. to 3 P.M. weekdays, plus Saturday mornings.

Department stores are the major exception to the midday closing for *siesta.* They are open 9:30 A.M. to 8 P.M. six days a week.

Museums and monuments are usually open from 10 A.M. to 1 P.M. daily, except Mondays. Some do, some do not open Sunday afternoons and holidays.

Theaters and movies generally have performances at 7 and 10:30 P.M. weekdays and about 4:30 P.M. Saturdays, Sundays and holidays. Soccer and other sports events begin at 8 or 9 P.M. in summer, about 4:30 P.M. in winter. Bullfights start at 6:00 P.M. Sunday afternoons during the March-October season.

Restaurant lunch hours are 1:30–4 P.M.; dinner hours are 8:30 P.M–12 A.M.

In August many establishments of all types shut down for vacations. Some of them take off part of July and/or September, as well. There is a six-hour difference between Spain and the east coast of the USA. In summer —April–October—The difference is five hours because of daylight saving time.

Electricity

Much of Spain operates on 220 volt current, but there are places where 110 is in use. Be sure to ask at the hotel desk. In newer hotels it is increasingly common to find 110 volt outlets in bathrooms. However, these almost invariably require a continental round-prong plug rather than the typical U.S. flat-blade plug. Save yourself frustration and buy an adapter, either before you leave for Spain or at the first electric shop after you arrive in Spain. Furthermore, if you plan to take your music with you, take battery-operated radio/-cassette/record players. In some hotels it is impossible to find an electric outlet outside the bathroom. And if you do, the 50-cycle Spanish current will mismatch your 60-cycle USA equipment.

Communications

Mail service is relatively efficient in Spain. Charges are comparable to those in the USA. Rates (at this writing) are: airmail letters (5 grams, about one-third ounce) 55 pts. to Canada and the USA; 33 pts. to England and Europe. Airmail postcards are 40 pts. to Canada and the USA, 23 pts. to England and Europe. Within Spain, letters are 14 pts.; postcards are 9 pts.

You'll recognize mail boxes by their mustard yellow with red trim colors. They are also marked with a post horn and crown.

Rates for mailing packages are high. The hotel porter will mail packages for a fee. If you do it yourself, you may encounter what happened to us. We shipped home a series of identical packages from the same local post office and by the same woman day after day. With a twinkle in her eye, but never a flicker of recognition, she set a different price each day, as the spirit moved her. Good luck.

Spain's telephone system is similar to Britain's. For local calls from a public phone, put three 5 pts. pieces in the sloping slot at the top. Dial your number. When the person answers, the mechanism will gobble up the first coin. If you go beyond the basic time, the machine will gobble up your second, and additional, coins. If there is no answer the coin remains in the slot. If the number rings and then stops ringing, one of the two phones is out of order. Try another. Most hotels do not charge for local calls you make from your room.

For a long-distance call, the hotel operator is your best bet. Give the operator the number you're trying to reach and she will assign you a telephone booth where you can wait until she puts the call through. You pay her after the call is completed. You can place long-distance calls from the local post office in a similar way.

Overseas calls can be shockingly expensive. Some hotels add on a surcharge of 100% or more. To avoid this, call from the post office. The operator will place the call and there will be no surcharge. You can minimize charges by calling collect and asking your respondent to call you back.

Cables can be sent from the post office directly or by your hotel concierge, in which case the charge is added to your bill.

Spanish telephone conversations begin with *oiga* (listen) and *digame* (speak to me).

Language

Just because 230 million people all around the world speak Spanish doesn't mean you have to, but it will make your travel in Spain more enjoyable.

In major cities you will find many people who understand and quite a few who speak English. You'll have little trouble finding English-speaking clerks on the Ramblas or on Calle Serrano. But Spain is not like Scandinavia where English is a second language. In the out-of-the-way shops and small towns you may have to search for someone to translate or fall back on your miming and charade skills. If you're desperate to find an English-speaking person, head for the turismo, leading hotel, bank or department store. Someone in one of these will probably know English. When you're rolling out your

Spanish pronunciations, remember that Spaniards pronounce C before E or I as TH; otherwise as K. Also, Z is pronounced as TH; G and J as H; H nonexistent; LL as in billion; R is rolled as "rrrrrr." Spaniards will love you if you try to speak their language. Do try.

The drives for autonomy by Basque, Catalonian and Galician nationalists have complicated life for foreigners traveling to these areas. There are so many quirks and peculiarities (from the viewpoint of the foreigner) to the spellings of words in these languages that road and street signs present some nightmarish problems. These languages are full of surprising combinations and juxtapositions of consonants. Puzzling them out is difficult enough; pronouncing them is an enormous challenge. Where Spanish-language street and road signs have been replaced with the local language, your only recourse is to find some person who can tell you what the old, that is the Spanish language, names for them were.

Medical Assistance

Most transient afflictions can be cleared up with remedies from the local *farmacia* with the counsel of your hotel concierge.

If you need medical attention, the hotel can call a physician. If you are in a city where U.S., Canadian or English consulates exist, you may call upon them for referral to English-speaking doctors or dentists. (See list of consulates and hospitals under Directory.)

Spain has a well-developed system of practical nurses, called *practicantes,* who can administer medicines and therapy on the prescription of physicians. They will come to your room, if necessary, to give you injections and what else you may need, for reasonable charges.

If you are in southern Spain and have a serious health problem and insurmountable language difficulty, you may wish to head for Gibraltar. There you will find English-speaking physicians and dentists and clinics and hospitals where you can be understood.

Should you need immediate, emergency medical help, ask for a *medico de urgencia.* Call the police, if necessary. If you need a first aid station, ask for a *casa de socorro, pronto.*

Take the precaution of contacting the International Association for Medical Assistance to Travelers (IAMAT) for a free list of approved English-speaking physicians. The roster includes physicians who have had medical training in the USA, Canada or Britain and locates 24 IAMAT member clinics and hospitals. The literature also gives a schedule of fees. Write to IAMAT, 736 Center St., Lewiston, N. Y. 14092; or 123 Edward St., Toronto, Canada; or Gotthardstrasse 17, 6300 Zurich, Switzerland.

Check whether the border is open to non-Gibraltarians, however IAMAT is a charity, so it welcomes voluntary donations when you write for the free list of doctors & clinics

Measurements

Officially, measurements in Spain are metric. Here is a very simple conversion scale:

1 centimeter (cm.) = 4/10 inch. 1 inch. = 2.55 cm.
1 meter (m.) = 3.28 feet or 1.1 yards. 1 ft. = .31 m. and 1 yd. = .93 m.
1 kilometer (km.) = .62 miles. 1 mile = 1.51 km.
1 gram = .035 oz. 1 oz. = 28 grams.
1 kilogram (kg.) = 35.27 oz. or 2.21 lbs. 1 lb. = 450 grams.
1 metric ton (t.) = 1.1 tons U.S.
1 liter (l.) = .26 gallon. 1 gal. U.S. = 3.75 liters.

For a quick estimate, to convert Celsius to Fahrenheit temperature, multiply by 2 and add 32; to convert Fahrenheit to Celsius, subtract 32 and divide by 2. The results will be a bit off, but you'll have a hasty approximation.

To convert miles to kilometers, multiply by 8 and divide by 5; kilometers to miles, multiply by 5 and divide by 8.

A kilogram is just over 2 pounds (2.2 pounds).
A liter is a little more than a quart (1.06 quarts).
A meter is slightly more than 3 feet (3.28 feet).

When it comes to clothing sizes, you'll be happy to know that glove sizes for both men and women are the same as in the USA. But for every other wearable, the sizes are completely different both from the British and the U.S. sizing. Spain follows the continental system; you will find that shops in major hotels and on fashionable shopping streets carry comparitive size charts giving the equivalents from one system to another.

GETTING AROUND

Be sure to get a copy of *Como Viajar Barato en España,* published by the Secretaria de Estado de Turismo, Ministerio de Transportes, Turismo y Comunicaciones, 50 Maria V. Molina, Madrid. (Ask for a copy at RENFE ticket offices.) This 52-page booklet is packed with information about discount and special rate travel on Spain's railways (RENFE), airlines and ships (Compañia Trasmediterranea), as well as unusual vacation possibilities for campers and youths.

By Air

Spain has two domestic airlines—Iberia and Aviaco. They serve more than 36 cities and towns and have offices in major cities throughout the country. The planes are modern, comfortable and speedy. You'll find you can fly from Madrid to most airports in Spain in an hour or so. However, domestic routes radiate from Madrid like the spokes of a wheel, so you often have to return to Madrid and change planes to reach another city.

Many Spanish airports are less than 10 kilometers from the nearest city but some are much further away. Málaga and Murcia, for example, are 50 kilometers from their respective airports (the farthest) and you lose time reaching them. Madrid is 16 kilometers from Barajas.

There is no question that the Visit Spain special ticket offering unlimited air travel on Iberia domestic flights for $199 for 45 days (see Perks) is an excellent time and money saver.

By Car

Spain's highway network covers the country well with all-weather roads. There are limited stretches of *autopista* (superhighways), some of which are toll roads. There are far more *carreteras Radial* (national roads) and *Nacional* and country roads. These are generally two- or three-lane asphalt roads and vary from excellent, new surfaces to poor and heavily weathered ones, especially in remote areas.

Be sure you note and remember that seat belts are mandatory. If you are found "unhitched" driving in the countryside you're in for a ticket and a stiff fine. The Guardia Civil (national police) may stop you and fine you on the spot. You will be given a receipt when you pay. Don't worry, it's not a shakedown, but completely legal.

Roads are well marked with international highway symbols. Mileage distances and turnoffs to towns are usually posted. Other than in the towns, gasoline and service stations are few and far between, so don't tempt fate by allowing your tank to run low. Also, don't spin your wheels "shopping" for gasoline. The prices are identical from one end of the country to the other.

Car rentals are offered by several companies, including Hertz, Avis, Godfrey Davis, Atesa (Budget Rent-a-car) and Europcar (National). You can reserve your car in Spain by calling the company before you leave home. All of the companies carry Seats (Spanish-built Fiats), as well as various other makes, in sizes ranging from subcompact to nine-seat vans.

The usual rentals are either by day or by week, with a charge per kilometer. If you run past your scheduled return time, charges will be added for each extra hour. Included in the rental fee are basic public liability and property damage insurance, oil and maintenance. Full (nondeductible) vehicle damage insurance requires paying an extra charge per day. You pay for all gas, a 4% tax, all traffic fines and tickets. You must deliver the vehicle to a prearranged destination. (Most rental companies will pick up the car at your hotel.)

To drive in Spain you must be 18 years old and hold a valid U.S., Canadian or British driver's license or an international driver's license. Car rental is expedited if you use a well-known credit card. Most companies will deliver the car to you at your hotel during business hours, without charge, in the cities where they have offices. A typical week's rental may come to 17,000 pts. plus tax and gasoline. Seats get 48–69 kilometers (30–40 miles) per gallon, (12.7–16.9 km. per liter), which costs about 331 pts.

Be forewarned that driving in cities is not always easy. Traffic during rush hours is fierce. There is excruciating competition for parking spaces, and Spanish police are tough on traffic and parking violations. They not only fine you, but if you're parked in a no-parking zone, they'll tow the car and you'll have to "ransom" it back. The fine may be 500–2,500 pts., which isn't terrible. The worst part is the Kafkaesque procedure you'll have to follow: Find out where the car is; taxi there; find out where you have to pay the fine; taxi there; pay the fine—do you have enough cash?; taxi back to the lockup with the receipt and hope that you arrive before (a) lunch; (b) closing for the day; (c) the holiday.

Observe with care the parking "allowed" regulations. Look for the big signs marked "P" for parking, and put the car there. Parking on the street in major cities may be chancey. In Madrid, for example, you need to display inside your windshield a *tarjeta de estacionamiento (papel de la hora),* which you purchase at a tobacco shop at 20 pts. per one-half hour; you may stay in any single parking spot up to 1 and one-half hours. In other cities, there are other regulations.

From this you may gather that we are less than enthusiastic about driving in large Spanish cities. Right! We prefer to use the car between towns and for outlying travel and to park it in the hotel garage and walk, taxi or use public transportation within the larger towns and cities. It works, and it saves wear and tear on car and driver.

At present auto theft is not a major concern for car rentals. However, break in and theft are serious problems in some places, most notably in Sevilla. In Sevilla the situation has deteriorated to the point that sometimes youths actually smash car windows to steal goods—even with people in the car. Your only defense is to make sure nothing of any value—not even a sweater—is visible when you leave the car temporarily, and that you empty the car at night if it is not parked in a garage.

By Bus

There is no national bus company. Spanish towns are linked by myriad small bus companies. Generally, they are inexpensive but slow. The only way to determine their schedules and prices is to check with the turismo office in the town from which you will be traveling or to talk on the phone to a travel agent in Madrid, Barcelona or other city before you go there.

By Train

Spain has a well-developed rail network operated by its state railway, RENFE. Nearly all towns of commercial significance are linked by rail, and there are excellent trains to major cities and towns.

The sleek Talgo, air-conditioned diesels, offer express luxury service between Madrid and the largest cities—Barcelona, Bilbao, Zaragoza, Málaga, Cádiz, Sevilla and Valencía. The Electrotren and diesel Ter train also have luxury accommodations but are somewhat slower, make more stops and serve other areas of the country as well. They are also cheaper. Depending on the destination, you may take a sleeper, couchette or coach for either first- or second-class fares. On express trains, a supplemental fare is charged.

RENFE (Red Nacional de los Ferrocarriles Espanoles) offers some attractive price incentives. Its round-trip fares on many routes offer a 25% discount. Children 3–7 years old travel at half-fare. You can purchase a kilometric card (see Perks) that is good for a 20% discount and a Gold Card that is good for a 50% discount (see Perks). Furthermore, RENFE has a calendar of discount days during the year when you can travel at reduced rates. RENFE also offers excursions at substantial savings.

You should not overlook the convenience of rail trips to attractions near Madrid. For example, RENFE runs many trains per day from Atocha station to and from El Escorial, Avila, Segovia, Aranjuez and Toledo, none of them more than 2 hours away.

All in all, rail travel in Spain is clean, comfortable and reliable. It can be cheaper than every other system but bus, depending on your destination and the class of service you choose.

Schedules are complex, as are fares and supplements. If you wish to investigate them before leaving for Spain, ask your travel agent for information or contact RENFE's representative abroad: the French National Railroads, 610 Fifth Ave., New York, NY 10020; (212)582–2100.

GOING HOME

U.S. Customs

The general regulations apply, including the overall allowance of $300 for duty-free retail value allowed citizens and legal residents of the U.S.A. once every 31 days.

The next $600 worth of goods (above the $300 amount) will be assessed at a flat rate of 10% of *retail* value. After this $600 (or a total of $900), goods will be assessed at regular rates of duty on estimated *wholesale* value.

Over and above your quota, gifts (except perfume, tobacco amd liquor) up to the value of $25 may be mailed to anyone you wish, so long as the recipient does not get more than one package per day. These packages are duty free.

Duty-free tobacco and liquor limits are: 1 liter of alcoholic beverages (you must be 21 or over), 100 cigars or 200 cigarettes, or smoking tobacco equivalent. Be sure to buy your liquor at least 24 hours before departure. You'll pay U.S. tax on ¾ gallon for every gallon purchased (couples will pay on half a gallon), and this works out to about $9 or $6, respectively. In addition, you'll pay 10% duty for anything over 1 liter. the duty on wine is quite low, about 12 cents per bottle for table wines (almost $1 on champagne, however).

Canadian Customs

If you have been out of Canada over 48 hours, you can return with $10 worth or goods duty free (not including a alcohol and tobacco). Alternatively, you can claim up to $50 duty free once in each of the four three-month quarters into which the year in divided January to March, April to June, July to September, October to December). This $50 category may include 200 cigarettes and 40 oz. of alcoholic beverage.

If you're absent from Canada more than seven days, you can claim $150 duty free once a year, with same amount of tobacco and alcohol exemptions. You may have this $150 exemption plus all four of your $50 exemptions, but you can't put them together on one trip.

You may also send home gifts up to $15 in value, duty free.

British Customs

From Spain or Portugal, you are allowed on returning to Britain (you must be over 17 for these exemptions): 200 cigarettes or 50 cigars or 250 grams of tobacco, plus 1 liter of spirits and 2 liters of table wine, plus 60 cc. of perfume and 250 cc. of toilet water, plus £28 worth of souvenirs or other articles. If you return to Britain via an EEC country and purchase goods in the other country, different quotas apply, so check beforehand.

Spain is in process of applying for EEC membership, so watch developments

Spain

By major European city standards, Madrid is the new kid on the block. The earliest historical record of Majrít or Majoritum, as the Moors called the town, dates from Moorish chronicles of the early 10th century. Long after the Moors had relinquished their Alcázar overlooking the Manzanares River to Alfonso VI (in 1083), Majrít—or Madrid—was just another dusty little Castilian town, scorching hot in summer, bitter cold in winter, agreeable any time in between.

Old Spanish saying: "The air of Madrid is as keen as a knife, it will spare a candle and blow out your life."

Charles V was the first monarch to pay any attention to the little town. He liked the clear, sharp, dry air and made Madrid his occasional royal residence. Philip II, Charles's son, went a step further. In 1560, while supervising the building of El Escorial nearby, he declared Madrid his *unica corte* (his only court).

IF YOU HAVE ONLY ONE DAY

The *Prado* tops anyone's list of reasons for visiting Madrid. It is one of the very great museums of the world. Its major strengths are the depth and breadth of its Spanish, Flemish and Venetian collections. No where else in the world will you find the number and quality of paintings by Goya (114 works), Velázquez (50), El Greco (34), Rubens (83), Titian (36), Breughel (40), Bosch (8). There is a total of about 5,000 works of art in the Prado.

What is also remarkable about the Prado is that much of the collection represents the tastes and aesthetic judgments of just a handful of people—the Habsburg and Bourbon royal families. More remarkable still, it was just three kings who formed the bulk of the collection—Charles V, his son Philip II and Philip's grandson Philip IV.

Every time we visit this extraordinary museum, we're reminded of two things about the collection: first, how personal it is. These kings bought what they liked. No art adviser suggested diversifying their portfolio as a hedge. That's why there is such depth in works by specific artists. Second, this enormous collection was bought, traded and inherited but always paid for. It wasn't booty seized in war. This also makes it a rarity, given the history of Europe.

As the buses and cars go charging along Paseo del Prado (which turns into Recoletos and then Castellana), it is difficult to remember that the *prado* means meadow in Spanish. When the large neoclassical building was designed, in 1775 by architect Don Juan de Villaneuva, it was intended by King Charles III to house collections of both the arts and the natural sciences. It was to be built in the prado next to his new botanical garden and to be part of the monastery grounds of San Jerónimo—a country setting.

By 1806 the work on the new museum was well advanced. Then came the Napoleonic invasion, and as a poet's lament says, "Its royal salons/in vile uses were profaned." In other words, the French soldiers used the building as stables.

After the Prado's official inauguration in 1819, it functioned as both a science and art museum. There are Madrileños who can recall seeing a stuffed, moth-eaten bird of prey in a glass display case somewhere in the building as late as 1930.

There have been complaints for generations that, rich as its collection is, the Prado makes viewing difficult. The lighting has been dim, and one guidebook recommended visiting the museum only on sunny days. Also the collections were not well-organized, so that you were likely to come upon a Titian here, there and in a hallway.

Note the new lighting in the Flemish rooms

All that, we're happy to observe, has been changing over recent years. Structurally, the building has been shored up to make it fireproof. Inner walls of steel and concrete have been inserted. (Fire has plagued the royal collections. Many treasures were lost in 1734 when the Old Alcazar/Royal Palace burned.)

Inside the Prado

There are two ways to enter the museum: The main entrance in front is on Paseo del Prado (no longer a meadow). Facing the building, there is a second entrance on the left side. Three of Spain's greatest painters seem to be watching over "their" museum. At the left entrance is Francisco Goya, a bronze sculpture by Francisco Bellivre which may have been modeled after Goya's own nonflattering self-portrait. On the right side of the Prado, facing the Jardin Botanico, is the pleasant little Plaza de Murillo. Here stands another bronze, Bartolome Esteban Murillo, looking somewhat pompous today, with one hand on his breast, the other on a lectern or pedestal.

You will probably enter through the main door since this leads you right to the first floor and what many consider the *chef d'oeuvres* of the collection. Just before you enter, you will pass a seated bronze sculpture of an artist with pallette in hand—Diego Velázquez.

At the book and postcard counter inside you can buy printed guides to the Prado with detailed layouts of where each collection is and helpful descriptions of individual works. Guards posted in various rooms will tell you where to find particular works or schools of painters. With the ongoing renovations in the museum, works are moved and sections closed from time to time. This means the guards are more *au courant* about a painting's whereabouts than any guidebook can be.

The Prado's cafeteria and much of the South Wing are closed temporarily

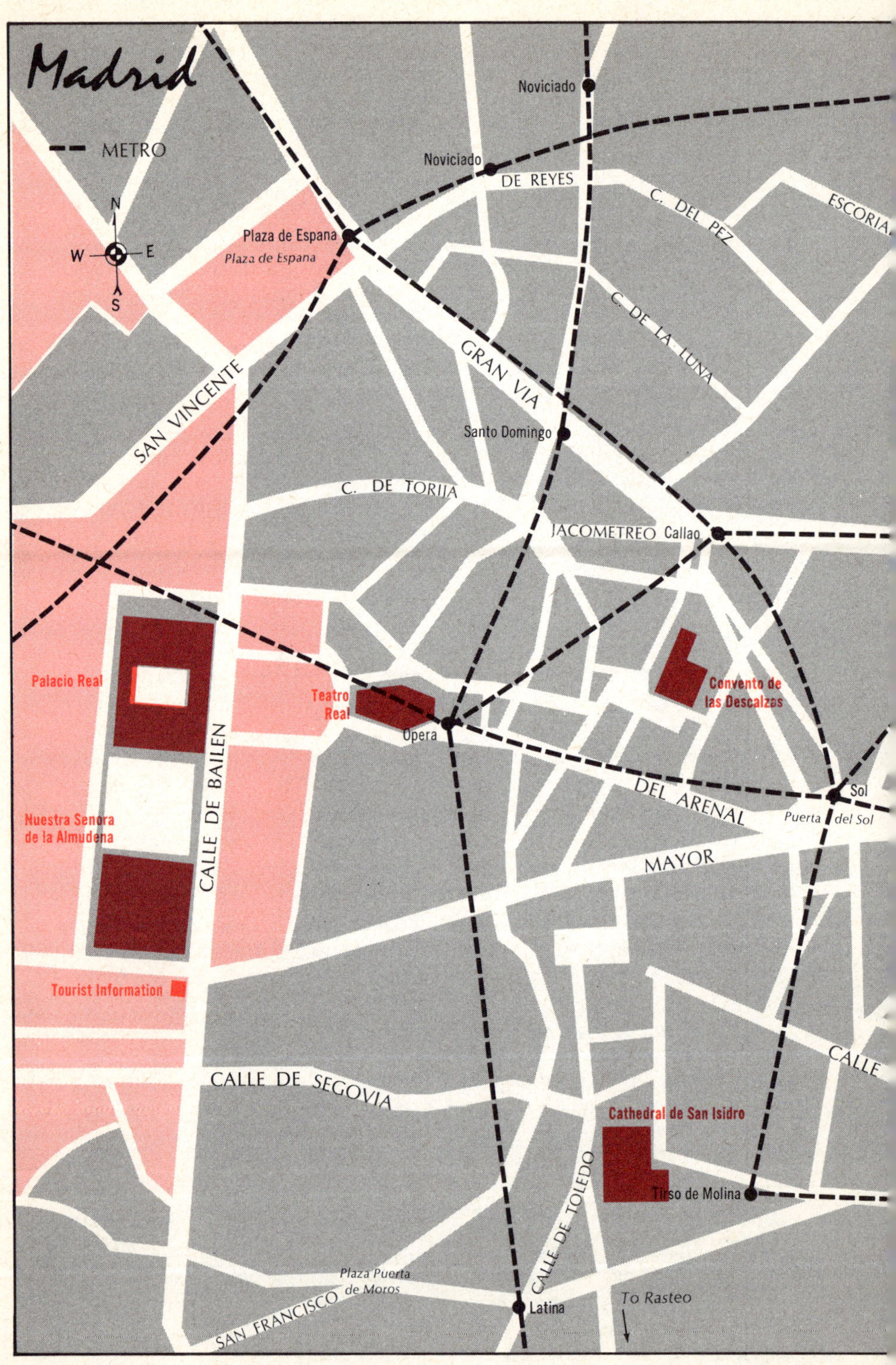
Madrid
METRO
N
W
E
S
Noviciado
Noviciado
DE REYES
C. DEL PEZ
ESCORIAL
Plaza de Espana
Plaza de Espana
C. DE LA LUNA
GRAN VIA
SAN VINCENTE
Santo Domingo
C. DE TORIJA
JACOMETREO
Callao
Convento de las Descalzas
Palacio Real
Teatro Real
Opera
DEL ARENAL
Sol
Puerta del Sol
Nuestra Senora de la Almudena
CALLE DE BAILEN
MAYOR
Tourist Information
CALLE
CALLE DE SEGOVIA
Cathedral de San Isidro
Tirso de Molina
CALLE DE TOLEDO
Plaza Puerta de Moros
SAN FRANCISCO
Latina
To Rasteo

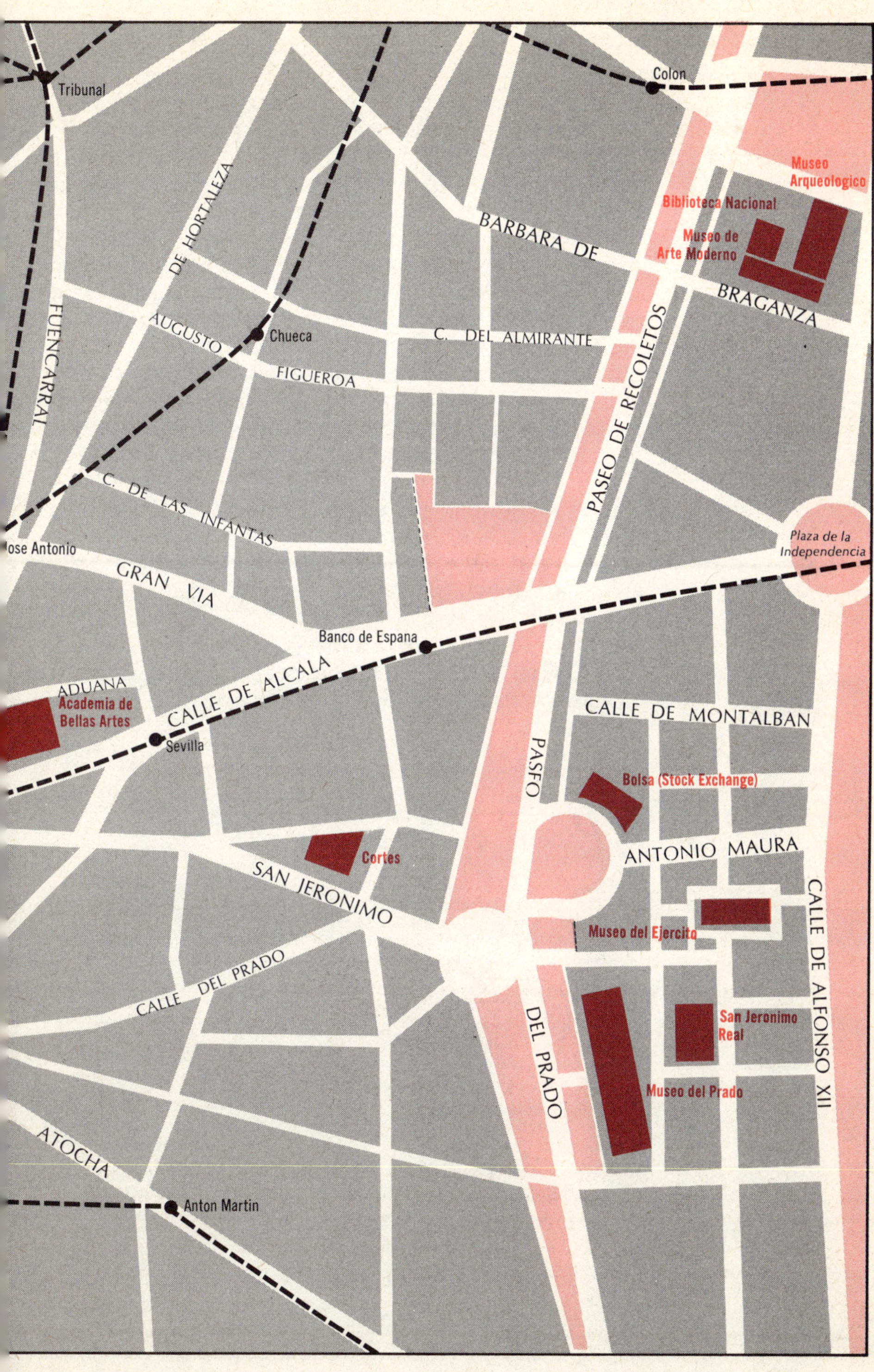
Tribunal
Colon
Museo Arqueologico
Biblioteca Nacional
Museo de Arte Moderno
DE HORTALEZA
BARBARA DE
BRAGANZA
FUENCARRAL
AUGUSTO
Chueca
C. DEL ALMIRANTE
FIGUEROA
PASEO DE RECOLETOS
C. DE LAS INFANTAS
Plaza de la Independencia
ose Antonio
GRAN VIA
Banco de Espana
ADUANA
Academia de Bellas Artes
CALLE DE ALCALA
Sevilla
CALLE DE MONTALBAN
PASEO
Bolsa (Stock Exchange)
Cortes
ANTONIO MAURA
SAN JERONIMO
CALLE DE ALFONSO XII
Museo del Ejercito
CALLE DEL PRADO
DEL PRADO
San Jeronimo Real
Museo del Prado
ATOCHA
Anton Martin

Not all of the works of art the Prado owns are on display all the time, though even with repairs going on the museum tries to keep the most famous works on public view. There are 2,500 or so works regularly exhibited.

★★★★ The Prado

If this is your maiden voyage through this vast art repository, we recommend taking one of two approaches in order to avoid visual indigestion. The best way we've found is to spoon out our visits over several days, spending an hour a day, usually with a single artist or a single school.

This may not be possible if you have limited time in Madrid. In that case, you may concentrate on the Prado's long suits—its Spanish, Flemish and Venetian collections. This will allow you to see some of the greatest works in the world by painters such as Goya, El Greco, Velázquez, Rubens, Pieter Breughel, Bosch, van Dyck, Titian, Veronese, Tintoretto and Tiepolo.

Certainly you'll find your way to Rogier van der Weyden's *The Descent from the Cross* or El Greco's enormous *Baptism of Christ,* both certifiable masterpieces. You'll need time to study the many miniscule details of Breughel's *The Triumph of Death* and Hieronymus Bosch's macabre *Garden of Delights.*

Late development: Las Meninas has been moved—ask the guards where

Then there are the many wondrous works of Velázquez. You will find the famous *Las Meninas (Maids of Honor)* in a room all by itself. Perhaps the best-known room in the entire Prado is Room XII. In it there are 26 Velázquez paintings; it's a museum within a museum. Open 10 A.M. to 5:30 P.M.; Sundays and holidays 10 A.M. to 2 P.M.

The Goya collection in itself is too rich a diet for a single visit. There are the light and classical Goyas; the many court portraits of Charles IV and his wretched family, painted warts and all; the "black paintings," taken literally

Plan of Prado Museum

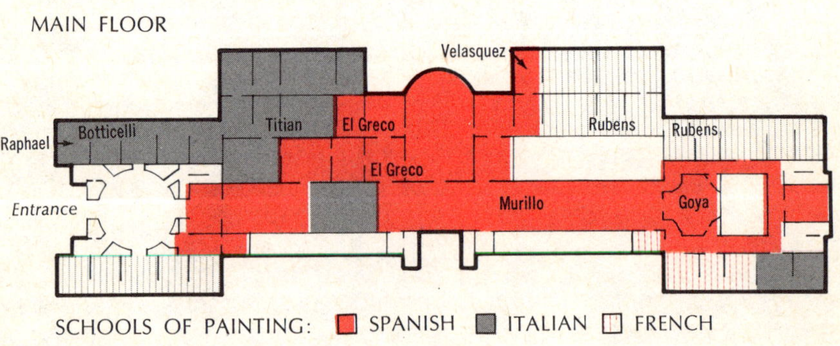

from the walls of Goya's house, Quinta del Sordo; and finally the reams and reams of ethings—the *Caprices, Disasters of War, Bullfights* and *Disparates.* A feast.

Outside the Prado

You may walk behind the Prado for a look at the twin-towered Church of San Jeronimo el Real with its fine Gothic portal. Forget the traffic noises and the encroachments of the modern city. Think back to the time 400 years ago when King Philip II used to hunt here, when the church was just a part of a vast monastery complex whose wooded peacefulness prompted Philip to begin building a summer palace nearby. Earlier, in 1510, Philip's great-grandfather, Ferdinand the Catholic King, held a parliamentary session in the monastery, and off and on ever since Spanish princes and their brides have been married in the church, with the scent of orange blossoms wafting in from the orchards outside.

The streets behind the Prado and across from the Retiro Park are clustered with museums, but save them for another day. After a morning in the Prado, a change of pace is called for. Before heading for Old Madrid, walk north one block on the Paseo del Prado to the small semicircle in front of the Ritz Hotel. This is the Plaza de la Lealtad, and in it you will see an obelisk. Sometimes fresh flowers rest against the base, whose inscription commemorates the heroes of the Second of May, 1808.

This date has fervent emotional connotations for Spaniards. You have just seen Goya's powerful painting with that title in the Prado, and throughout

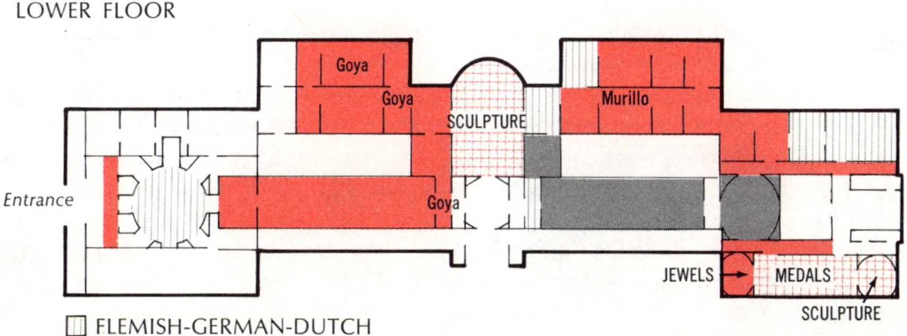

Spain you will discover streets named Second of May. The date refers to the beginning of the Spanish uprising against Napoleon's troops—known in Spain as the War of Independence and known abroad as the Peninsular War.

Carrera de San Jerónimo

By now you may be ready for lunch, and it's easy to pop into the Ritz or the Palace Hotel catty-corner across the Paseo. But you may want a more modest option, so begin your walk along Carrera de San Jerónimo.

Behind the 19th-century parliament building (which was called the Cortes, but is now the *Congreso de los Diputados*—Congress of Deputies), is a touch of Germany in the menu at the Edelweiss restaurant. As you stroll past the *Congreso building,* notice the imposing brass-knobbed doors and two bronze lions "guarding" the doors. The lions are reincarnated from cannons captured from the Moors in an 1860 battle in Morocco, melted down and recast in a more peaceful mold.

The *Congreso* was the scene of the attempted coup in 1981. While the army officers were shooting up the *Congreso,* a government command post was established across the street in the Palace Hotel.

Plaza Mayor

If you have ever felt you were in the middle of a stage set, you know how it feels. Just stepping onto the vast expanse of black and white brick pavement, surrounded on all four sides by arcaded buildings of great architectural harmony is an experience. In the center of the enormous square is a vibrantly alive equestrian statue of King Philip III who made all this possible.

The whole thing was done so quickly. Within two years, 1617–1619, the old square, Plaza del Arrabal, had been demolished and the new Plaza Mayor, consisting of 136 attached houses with arcades on all four sides was built. Sets of twin towers designed by Herrera and placed opposite one another added unity to the square; 437 balconies were another graceful touch. The fact that the town bakery occupied the entire ground floor of the major building from which the king, in elegant upper chambers, presided says something about the hominess of Madrid at that time. The twin-towered building opposite was the town butcher shop. Beneath the arcades members of all the town merchant guilds sold their wares—clothiers, silk salesmen, tool and hardware merchants, haberdashers. The Plaza Mayor was the center of Madrid's mercantile life.

The Prince of Wales (later Charles I) was feted in the Plaza Mayor with a jousting tournament when he came in 1623 to marry the Infanta Doña Maria of Austria. (The fete was spectacular, but the wedding never took place.) In the Plaza there were bullfights, horse races and *cañas* (tournaments on horseback) and ceremonies proclaiming new kingships. There was even a beheading; it was a minister of Philip III's, Rodrigo Calderón.

Then there was the June day in 1680 when the dim young man Charles II (whom Velászuez captured so well on the canvas hanging at the Prado) thought it would make a fantastic spectacle to round up 120 prisoners of the Inquisition and, with spectators jamming the balconies, subject them to a mass trial or *auto-de-fe.* After 14 hours of trial and sermonizing, all except

14 were flogged or sentenced to the galley. The 14 were burned. To be sure his *auto-de-fe* went smoothly, Charles (so they say) had dress rehearsals.)

The magnificent building that the kings and bakers shared has been handsomely restored. You'll recognize it instantly—the *Casa de la Panaderia* (house of the bakery) by the charming paintings all along the pale orange facade; there are rows of nudes, satyrs and distinguished Spaniards such as Cervantes, Calderón, Lope de Vega and Philip III himself.

Old Madrid

From the Plaza Mayor you have several choices, all of which lead into the old section of Madrid and make for fascinating wandering. Let's begin by going down the steps near El Pulpito, through the Arco de Cuchilleros into the narrow calle called Cuchilleros (Knifemakers Street). Here you'll have a glimpse of some vestiges of medieval Madrid. Tiny doorways lead into one-room shops.

Cuchilleros is not only a concentration of knifemakers. One of the street's specialties seems to be *esparto* grass. *Esparterias* dot the narrow street with mats, rugs, chairs and ropes hung from shop walls. Alternating with *esparto* makers are woodworkers, guitar makers and potters.

Cuchilleros is also the street of Botin's, at No. 17, the haunt of Ernest Hemingway and Madrid's oldest and probably most famous restaurant. Cuchilleros also has clusters of *mesónes,* rustic taverns where you can quench your thirst at dusk (or any other time) when the nightlife really begins to hum. Drop by for a *chato* of wine and drink in the ambience along with your *vino de casa.*

Most of the miniscule streets in this area are studded with cosy, rustic restaurants where you can eat heartily at modest cost. Consider Casa Paco (for steaks), 11 Puerto Cerrada (one block from Cuchilleros); La Toja (Galician specialties), 3 Siete de Julio, off the north side of the Plaza Mayor; Aroca (Castilian), 3 Plaza de los Carros; and Esteban, 36 Cava Baja (an extension of Cuchilleros). Casa Lucio, 35 Cava Baja, is known for its seafood, but it is costlier.

As you weave through the warren of little streets, notice the old-fashioned street lamps and the decorated tile street signs on corner buildings. Every time we come upon the Plaza de la Villa, it takes our breath away. This small town hall square is so eclectic and so architecturally rich it is a delight to contemplate. In the center is a bronze statue of Alvaro de Baztán, hero of Lepanto, one of Spain's greatest sea battles (against the Turks in 1541). The sculptor was the same Benlliure who did the Goya bronze outside the Prado.

On the east of the Plaza is the Lujanes Tower, with an Arabic arch, Gothic front and three Lujanes coats of arms. Madrileños enjoy the legend that the tower is where Charles V kept France's Francis I prisoner after the battle of Pavia. Legend it is since no historical evidence has been found to prove it. In this case the reality is fine, too. Inside the building (it is now a branch of the city library with old newspaper archives—Hemeroteca Municipal) are two fine Gothic tombs (one a knight, the other a noted Latin scholar, Beatriz Galinda) and a Gothic staircase.

The *ayuntamiento* (town hall) also has a treasure—a chapel with a fine *mozarabic* (Moorish-influenced) ceiling, believed to be the work of Pedro

Berruguete. From the Patio de Cristales you can enter the house next door, Casa de Cisneros, which dates back to the early 16th century. From the outside all that remains of that vintage is a single window overlooking the Plaza del Cordon. Pay attention to the oldest coffered ceiling in Madrid, which is rich and beautiful. Another legend has it that the Casa de Cisneros was the home of Cardinal Jiménez de Cisneros, Isabella the Catholic's adviser and Inquisition leader. In fact, it *was* the home of the cardinal's nephew, Benito.

Restaurant Area

The Plaza de la Villa is a delightful square; enjoy it before turning right onto Calle Mayor and coming back to the bustle of 20th-century Madrid and its myriad restaurants. Calle Mayor and the streets leading off it are polka-dotted with Galician restaurants (the signs say "Mesón Gallego" or "Casa Gallego"), which offer good respites to the tired or thirsty. Seafood of the Atlantic is a Galician specialty; it includes *merluza,* (hake), bream and, in season, *angulas* (baby eels served sizzling hot in a garlic–chili pepper bath—fantastic!).

"There is no bird so scornful or fish so withdrawn that it does not reach Madrid if it is enjoyed by some region." That was a local booster speaking in the 17th century. True then, even more so today. The tiny *tascas* and *mesónes* that stipple the narrow side streets of Old Madrid are rich sources of regional cooking. Castilian, Galician and Basque dominate here, but if you look hard enough you'll probably find Catalan, Valencian and Andalucian as well.

IF YOU HAVE TWO DAYS

The most crucial must-see on your second day is the Royal Palace and its museums. It doesn't open until 10 A.M.; start out earlier and stop at the Church of San Francisco el Grand on the Plaza de San Francisco, just off Calle de Bailén. From here it's a seven- or eight-block walk along Bailén to the palace.

St. Francis of Assisi wouldn't recognize his old hermitage. The small edifice he supposedly built in the 13th century is long gone. So too is that fine Gothic church where tombs of the Lujanes, Henry IV's queen Doña Juana and numerous other medieval big shots were kept. In their stead, usurping their site, is San Francisco el Grande, a massive overblown structure that was designed in 1764 by Miguel Fernandez but built somewhat later (1784). The rotunda is covered with a monumental dome measuring 33 meters in diameter. Two things you really should look at here are the St. Francis chapel, which Goya was commissioned to paint, and the 50 richly ornamented (in Plateresque style) choir stalls, which were once in the monastery of El Paular near Segovia. You can admire them now in the sacristy of the chapterhouse. When you're ready, move along to the Royal Palace.

Inside the Royal Palace

Inside there are, *mas o menos,* 1,500 rooms. Only 50 or so are shown to the public on guided tours that move at a fast trot from room to room, from tapestries and clocks and crystal chandeliers to libraries. It is exhausting trying to keep pace with the guide, especially if you would like to linger a minute to look longer at the vast collection of clocks that Charles III collected or the Goya portraits of Charles IV and self-indulgent Maria Luisa.

Room by room, from the moment you enter and climb the double marble staircase—three flights of black and white marble, each step made of a single marble slab—the effects are dazzling. The stairs lead you to Charles III's apartments, with a ceiling painted by Anton Rafael Mengs. Mengs came to Spain as Charles's art advisor, but he soon became dictator, official taste maker and arbiter on all matters artistic in the royal circle. His neoclassical painting may be out of fashion, but you must be grateful to him for urging the king to buy Pieter Breughel's *Triumph of Death,* which you have seen earlier at the Prado, and Velázquez's *Portrait of the Count-Duke of Olivares on Horseback.* A dictator yes, but with great taste. A Mengs for all reasons.

The most rococo room in the palace is probably the Gasparini Saloon, containing floor-to-ceiling, wall-to-wall gilded and ornamented paintings and bas reliefs. There isn't an inch of empty space.

In the throne room, illuminated as it might have been when Napoleon Bonaparte saw it for the first time, with walls covered in red velvet and gold, heavy crystal chandeliers and gilded candelabras all around the mirrored room, you don't know where to look first. Should you look at the green malachite table given by the Tsar of Russia, the soft patterned rugs from the Royal Tapestry factory or the gilded lions shielding the ornate throne? No, you may prefer the airy, cloud-filled ceiling that Giambattista Tiepolo was imported to paint for the new palace. Even today it commandeers the attention, with its symbolic figures swirling through the pale blue sky. It was Tiepolo's last great fresco triumph.

Most aesthetically satisfying of the rooms that you are permitted to see are the former apartments of Princess Isabel of Bourbon, who was Alfonso XIII's aunt. Her rooms have been turned into a museum of fine porcelain, embroidery, crystal and paintings. A sampling of the treasures includes Velázquez's *Count Olivares* (the one Mengs persuaded Charles III to buy), Bosch's *Road to Calvary,* four Goyas, several Rubens and Zurbarans, two charming small Watteaus, and a splendid *Duke of Burgundy* believed to have been done by Rogier van der Weyden. If you're a bibliophile, you'll want to see Philip V's library of more than 150,000 volumes, many of which are rare and ancient. There is also the music museum with numerous fine instruments, including several Stradivari violins. Open 10 A.M. to 1:30 P.M. Sundays; 3:30 to 6:30 P.M.; on holidays and state occasions.

The Palace Grounds

Armeria Real

No guide leads you in lockstep through the Armeria Real (Royal Armory) on the palace grounds. You can explore this treasure house at your own pace. This Armeria Real, either the finest in Europe or sharing that title with Vienna's, is an absolute delight. We are not militarists, yet we find this enormous collection of armor fascinating. For one thing, many of the suits of armor are works of art, the highest level of a craftsman's skills. Armor making in medieval Europe was a noble craft.

There is something wonderfully eerie about the display: row upon row of 50 armored horsemen, seemingly riding toward you, in a cavernous hall —almost surreal in the silence. Finally, the sense of history comes into play. There is Charles V, seated on his horse just as Titian painted him. To see the suit of etched and damascened armor that belonged to Charles V will give you pause. Charles V, Emperor of the Holy Roman Empire, conqueror of much of Europe, master of intrigues, most powerful ruler in 16th century Europe was barely 1.5 meters (5 feet) tall! After all those history books, it takes the visual realization, the measuring of the armor, to have an image of the real man.

It was Charles V, that indomitable warrior, who began this collection of armor. His son, Philip II, continued and added to it. Among many rare and valuable items in the royal collection is a suit of armor made for Sebastian I of Portugal, the ill-fated king who sailed to Morocco to battle the Moors and never returned. The armor is engraved with battle scenes in which elephants can be seen, a reference to Portugal's exploits in India.

Museo de Carruajes Reales

The *Museo de Carruajes Reales* (Carriage Museum) is located in a separate pavilion in Campo del Moro behind the Palace. It offers its own insights. Many of the earlier coaches were lost, along with a number of Philip II's rare Bosch paintings, in the 1734 palace fire. This means that the museum contains mostly carriages dating from the late 18th century. That's okay since some of the most spectacularly rococo and baroque carriages are the most fun to look at, great gilded, moveable bonbons with painted tops and panels and heavy, ornate sculptures along the front and rear.

Casa de Campo

In the Casa de Campo are all kinds of recreation and amusement facilities as well as a delightful zoo and the woods and gardens that were once part of the royal hunting grounds. This parkland of 4,000 acres was a royal playground for centuries. In fact, it was in the Casa de Campo that England's Charles I defied Spanish custom by trying to speak unchaperoned with a Spanish princess. It seems that Charles, then the Prince of Wales, was in Madrid to "check out" the possibility of a marriage to the Infanta Doña Maria of Austria. But rather than wait to meet her formally, the impatient prince decided to engineer a more casual meeting. He heard that every morning she walked in the Casa de Campo. So one day, with his friend, George Villiers, Duke of Buckingham, he crossed the river and managed to spring over a wall into the orchard where Doña Maria and her *duenna* were walking. On seeing him, Doña Maria screamed and ran off, and Bonnie Prince Charlie's plan failed, though not for lack of trying. The marriage never did take place, but the reasons were political and religious, not personal.

Plaza de Oriente and Surrounding Area

Across from the Royal Palace on Calle Bailén is a quiet tree-shaded plaza known as Plaza de Oriente. In the center facing the palace is a remarkable horseman, one of the most beautiful of Madrid's many outdoor sculptures. As you approach, if you can take your eyes off the marvelous, lifelike vigor of the prancing horse, you'll recognize a familiar face you have seen in the many Velázquez portraits in the Prado. It's Philip IV in the flesh, or rather in the bronze, with his familiar sharp nose, soft lips and elongated head. It's a splendid piece of work that was planned by Velázquez and cast in bronze by Tacca.

Along the Plaza de Oriente, in rows of ten on each side, are stone statues of ancient and past kings from long before the time Ferdinand and Isabella unified Spain. These sculptures along with 88 others were intended for the roof of the new palace, but you can imagine what 108 larger-than-lifesize stone statues might have done to a roof, even one as long and balanced as the palace's. Hence, they were banished to the square across the way. They seem to provide comfort to the old men in berets who sit sunning themselves on benches beneath them.

The Plaza de Oriente is a peaceful square for snoozing. To Philip IV's left is the Jardines del Cabo Noval. Beyond it, on the corner of Calle de San Quintin, No. 8, is the house where a famous 19th-century composer, D'Hilarian Eslava, lived. His neighbor, Emilio Arrieta, was an artist. It was certainly a good address, opposite the palace, catty-corner from the then newly built Teatro Royal (Royal Theater). The teatro is a handsome mid-19th-century neoclassical creation on three levels, which has recently, after decades of neglect, been repainted grey on grey and now makes an excellent setting for concerts.

Just across the street at No. 2 Arrieta, in a stylish old mansion with window boxes full of ivy, is Clara's, a quiet restaurant with an agreeable bar; it's a good place to stop for a drink at this point in your travels. La Bola, 5 Calle de la Bola, is also handy and attractive, a classic Castilian tasca.

*** Clara's, 2 Arrieta

You may run into Ava Gardner at La Bola

Duck past the statue of Lope de Vega in the minute Plaza Encarnación (at the end of Calle de Saint Quintin) and into the *Convento de la Encarnación* for a peek at the many paintings and chapels in this 17th-century Renaissance convent and church with rococo interiors. The convent was established in 1611 by Philip III's wife, Margaret of Austria. It was the custom, until Philip IV put an end to it, for a widowed queen to retire to a convent after her husband's death. It also seemed to be the custom to bring along fine paintings and endowments that would make life comfortable and enrich the convent.

There's a fine "St. John the Baptist" by Ribera here

Convento de las Descalzas Reales and Surrounding Area

It is a six-block walk from one convent to another, but at the *Convento de las Descalzas Reales* you'll see one of the richest repositories of art in Madrid. The name, incidentally, means Royal Unshods, or, as it is usually called, Barefoot Nuns. The nuns in question are of the Order of Santa Clara, the Poor Clares who are dedicated to the vow of poverty and helping the poor—a fact that some find difficult to reconcile with this palace of treasures.

*** Convent of Barefoot Nuns. a 100 pta. ticket admits you to both convents

The palace, for such it was, was the place where Charles V's daughter, Joanna of Austria, was born. Joanna, not to be confused with that other Joanna, *Juana la Loca* (The Crazy), who was Charles' mother (but that's another story, which we'll come to in the next section on Tordesillas) founded the convent as a home for the nuns and used it as her retreat to which she brought beautiful objects.

Other noble ladies followed Joanna's example, and for several centuries the convent benefited from a vast array of noble visitors bearing gifts. It was only in the 1960s that the convent was opened to the public as a museum.

The collection is fabulous. It would be even more so if you had the luxury of time to enjoy it. Unfortunately, you are led through by a guide who invariably seems to be running a marathon. (We clocked our last visit at 25 minutes.) You are scooted up and down stairs, including a sumptuous grand staircase that leads majestically to the gallery in the upper cloister, in and quickly out again of rooms covered floor-to-ceiling and wall-to-wall with fine paintings. Stop, if you dare risk the guide's reproach to absorb the beauty of Pieter Breughel the Elder's *Adoration of the Magi* or Titian's *Caesar's Pence.* The tiny chapel of Guadaloupe has some enchanting baroque glass paintings. The large chapel on the ground floor is another place you'd like to linger. Open 10:30 A.M. to 1:30 P.M. and from 4 to 6 P.M.

Outside, the Poor Clares's little square has been nibbled away by progress. El Corte Inglés department store is just one block away. Across the street a richly ornamented baroque portal festooned with two voluptuous stone angels—the 1733 work of Ribera, Philip V's architect—now graces the door of a local bank. Across from it is a brick building where Tiepolo lived while working on the Royal Palace ceilings. A plaque identifies it.

Puerta del Sol

If you turn right on Calle Arenal (coming from the convent), you'll soon find yourself in front of the Royal Palace, back at the Plaza de Oriente. Turning left instead and walking two blocks will lead you to the center of Madrid, which is the center of Spain. All roads may lead to Rome, but all Spanish roads lead to the Puerta del Sol.

The Puerta del Sol's mystique is often lost on foreigners, who see it as a smaller version of Picadilly Circus. First of all, there's no *puerta* (gate). The Sun Gate disappeared in the 16th century but the name has lingered on. There's not only no gate, there's no real center. The Puerta consists of a number of intersecting streets pulsating with traffic. The buildings and shops that line the streets are not especially interesting, though there are several bookstores in which you can purchase a map or city guide.

Part of today's fascination with the Puerta del Sol is that it seems to lead to everything. You *can* get there from here, which makes it a handy place for meeting someone and then going to a nearby street for *tapas* and a few glasses of *Manzanilla* (sherry). Just a block away, off Victoria, which is off carrera de San Jerónimo, is one of the best tapas hangouts in town, Vista Alegre, 2 Calle del Pozo. Calle Victoria is no mean shakes for tapas itself. *Its* many tapas tascas are favorites with bullfighters, among others. Casa Vasca, 2 Calle Victoria, has good Basque food at moderate prices.

The Puerta del Sol is also just down the street from the main stores of Madrid's oldest department store chains, Galerías Preciados and El Corte Inglés. The narrow streets surrounding the Puerta del Sol are like arteries flowing from the heart. Part of the excitement is that the crowds are intense, creating a constant feeling of frenzy. Kids hawk newspapers; old ladies sell fresh flowers; somebody's invariably shouting, urging you to buy something.

IF YOU HAVE THREE DAYS

El Buen Retiro

What makes El Buen Retiro different from any big city park? Other parks have small zoos, lakes with boats, walking trails and romantic 19th-century statuary. True, true. But it's the joyous use of El Buen Retiro that makes it special. Only on Sunday mornings in the springtime does the park seem crowded, and yet it is in constant, happy use by every imaginable type of Madrileño. Soldiers ride through on horseback. Old men warm their favorite benches day after day. Sailors walk hand in hand with their girls. Mothers sun their babies in elaborate buggies with hand-embroidered covers. Teen-agers rendezvous on benches by the lake. Working women eat their lunches under willow trees. Rarely is the park deserted.

Museums in the Area

The *Casón del Buen Retiro* has special art exhibits such as the showing of Pablo Picasso's *Guernica.* The *Museo del Ejercito* (Army Museum) is far more than a collection of rusty swords and muskets. El Cid's sword is here along with a piece of the cross that Christopher Columbus took with him on his first voyage. The most dramatic display is the campaign tent of Charles V, a circular affair, 6 meters (20 feet) in diameter, with appliqued designs and Moorish scalloping around the top. Inside, the emperor's four-poster, elaborately carved wooden bed is ready to receive him with its turned-back satin sheets. On each side of the tent door, costumed mannequin halberdiers "stand guard." Open 10 A.M. to 5 P.M.; closed Mondays.

Another fascination of the Army Museum is its "assassination alley." In it is a trio of vehicles in which various past leaders were ambushed and killed: the berliner carriage in which General Jose Prim was assassinated in 1870; the black auto in which Eduardo Dato was shot in 1921 by an anarchist, riddling the rear of the car with machine gun bullets; the original Dodge Dart (now only 3 feet high) in which Admiral Carrero Blanco, Generalissimo Franco's chosen successor, was blown up in 1973. A unique collection, and an unusual building, with painted ceilings and a richly decorated Arabic hall.

If you stroll north on Alfonso XII, you will pass another museum located just in from the street on Calle de Montalban. It's the *Museum of Decorative Arts,* lodged on five floors of a handsome old mansion. The collections are varied and give an illuminating look at Spanish decorative tastes through the centuries. Open 10 A.M. to 5 P.M. Tuesdays through Fridays; 10 A.M. to 2 P.M. Saturdays and Sundays; closed Mondays.

Next, move along to the two major museums further uptown. While strolling, notice No. 4 on Alfonso XII. A stone plaque with a bronze bas relief identifies it as the house where 20th-century philosopher José Ortega y Gasset was born in 1883. Next door is Saskia-Sotheby's, the art auction house. Horcher, No. 6, is a good place for an elegant lunch, but you'll need advance reservations.

You are now at the large traffic circle known as Plaza de la Independéncia, in the center of which is one of Madrid's favorite Bourbon monuments, the Puerta de Alcalá. You may call it the gate that wine built, for to pay for this colossal portal, money was raised by taxing all the wine sold in Madrid *tascas.*

The *Puerta de Alcalá,* built in 1778 by Francisco Sabatini, was a celebration of Charles III, affectionately known as the Mayor of Madrid for all his civic improvements. Pretend for a minute that the traffic doesn't exist. Erase the stop lights and let yourself enjoy the scope of Sabatini's achievement: five triumphal arches in the rounded neoclassical style, beautifully proportioned, with ten Ionic columns attached, all made of Colmenar granite and limestone. Lyrical cupids and angels ornament the cornice in the center and along the sides. The sculptures were the work of Roberto Michel and Francisco Gutierrez, who also created the sculpture of Cibeles in the Cibeles fountain. If you turn away from the Puerta de Alcalá and look westward down Calle Alcalá, you will see Cibeles at the next major intersection. The juxtaposition from one circle to the next, of these two works, Cibeles and the Puerta de Alcalá, is brilliant. Come back after dark to see them lighted and radiant.

Once you round the circle and continue north on Calle Serrano you are in the high rent district. It's also a district with restaurant choices galore, many of which are quite elegant. A sampling includes Club 31, 58 Alcala (2216622), related to Jockey, but slightly less expensive; Alkalde, 10 Jorge Juan (2755168), Basque dishes, also an excellent *tapas* repertoire; La Trainera, 60 Lagasca (phone 2261181), good Galician dishes, especially fine for fish; and El Pescador, 75 Ortega y Gasset (phone 4013026), super for seafood, one of our favorites.

Serrano is one of Madrid's most stylish shopping streets. You'll have plenty of distractions as you stroll. Along the way uptown is the *National Archaeological Museum,* with more than 200,000 *objects* on view, including a reconstruction of the Altamira caves. Madrid's other museums tend to be overshadowed by the Prado, but this museum and one further up Serrano (read on) are sleepers—giants in their own right. One Archeological Museum object alone is worth a special trip—the enigmatic *Dama de Elche,* a polychrome stone head discovered near the town of Elche outside Alicante. The mysterious, beautiful lady is richly coiffed and perhaps narcotized. The finely worked stone shows a high level of sophistication. Another lady who will attract your attention is the *Dama de Baza,* a 4th-century B.C. statue of a goddess that is very realistic for its time. The museum is a harvest of prehistoric Iberian, Roman, and Moorish art and artifacts. Open 9:30 A.M. to 1:30 P.M.; closed holidays.

Your other museum stop today might be the *Museo Lazaro Galdiano,* a showcase for diverse treasures collected by a single man. José Lazaro Galdiano was a writer and scholar who bought what he liked, and his taste was both exemplary and catholic. That's why you'll find Celtic and Iberian bronze figurines, Roman and Visigoth bronze bowls, religious ivories, gold-embroidered church vestments and antique German gold and silverware.

IF YOU HAVE MORE TIME

Even repeat visitors to Madrid find numerous things they haven't seen or done, with rarely enough time to see and do them all. One handicap to scheduling nonstop activities is that Madrid's museum hours are short and broken into two segments, A.M. and P.M., thus limiting the number of visits you can actually squeeze into a single day. Then too, the long midday meal hours —what we would call the three-martini lunch except that in Madrid the time is spent more in eating than in drinking—make for a big block of time (3 hours is average) taken out of a sightseeing day. What this means is that you should do it the Madrid way, at a leisurely pace that ensures full enjoyment.

Gran Vía

For example, an extra day gives you time to promenade up the Gran Vía. This one time grand boulevard has recently undergone another name change. Gran Vía is what it was originally called, and indeed it was a great road. Then, during the Franco regime, the name was changed to Avenida de José Antonio in honor of José Antonio Primo de Rivera, founder of the Spanish Phalanx and a Falangist martyr (he had been assassinated at the time of the Civil War).

Now Franco is gone and Madrid has a Socialist mayor and Gran Vía is Gran Vía once again. It is just one of some 30 streets whose names have been changed, mostly from Franco-endowed names back to the names that existed before the Second Republic of 1931. If you know Madrid from a few years back, you may have a momentary set back trying to figure out what this or that *calle* (street) is now. To add to the confusion, new maps have the new names but sometimes the street signs still bear the old names. Policemen and taxi drivers will help you cope.

The Gran Vía may have its old name back, but it really isn't the same grand old boulevard anymore. There was a time when the best diversion in the late afternoon was to sit at a sidewalk café along the Gran Vía/José Antonio and watch the crowds flow by. This was a major shopping street, full of restaurants, hotels, shops and theaters.

It's still a busy street, frantically so, but you're likely to soak up more diesel fumes than atmosphere in a sidewalk café today. The cafés are there and tourists still find them and you may want a quick *chato* for old times' sake. But you'll soon see how the Gran Vía has declined. It isn't just the density of cars and pollution. The smartest shops, with a few exceptions, have moved over to the Serrano area. It's as though the pollution has settled a dull grey grime over the buildings and spirit of this old thoroughfare.

Having said all this, we still urge you to stroll the Gran Vía and see for yourself. It's still lively, the crowds are as intense as ever and there's always something to see.

More fun than the Gran Via itself, are the dozens of small streets that shoot out from it. It's on the side streets that you find many restaurants, especially the newer ethnic ones, and small shops. Walk upward on Gran Vía from Alcalá. Go off to the left on Tres Cruces, which will lead you to the Plaza del Carmen, always a hive of shops and shoppers. You'll find an old time, still popular landmark restaurant, Valentín, at 3 San Alberto.

If you continue up the Gran Vía, just as it narrows into Calle de Princesa, you'll see the Plaza de España on the left—an oasis of green pine trees, reflecting pool and relative solitude. If it's lunchtime you can get fondues, salads, and so forth, a block north of the Plaza at La Fromagerie Normandie, 9 Ventura Rodriquez (phone 2420146). Below the heroic-style monument celebrating the Spanish Age of Discoveries, you'll see old friends: a stone figure of Cervantes overlooking his charges, Don Quixote and Sancho Panza, their bronze figures glowing with a green patina. In the shadow of two skyscrapers, the Plaza has managed to hold its ground.

Head now for the 4th-century B.C. Temple of Debod, catty-corner from the Plaza de España on its northwest side. The temple, saved from being submerged by the Nile River when the Aswan Dam was being built, was a present to Spain from then-president of Egypt, Gamal Abdel Nasser. The temple was dissassembled and shipped piece by piece; it has been carefully reassembled in a tranquil greenbelt in the *Jardines de la Montaña* at the lower southern end of the *Parque del Oeste.* In bone-dry Madrid, there's no need to worry about this Egyptian monument being submerged by water. "The Manzanares must have been the safest refuge Nasser could think of," a Madrid friend mused.

University Area

You may want to explore the university area of the northwestern part of Madrid, and since you're heading in that direction now, this may be the time to do it.

At the University of Madrid's northwestern campus, there are two attractive museums worth your attention. The Museum of the Americas has a large collection that focuses on Spanish America. The most intriguing objects are from pre-Columbian and Inca days. Open 10 A.M. to 2 P.M.; closed Mondays and holidays. The Museum of Contemporary Spanish Art will give you a perspective on 20th-century art in Spain. The giants—Picasso, Miro—are represented, but there are less well-known painters and sculptors. Discovering them for yourself can be a pleasurable experience. Open 5 to 9 P.M.; 10 A.M. to 1 P.M. on holidays; closed Mondays.

SIDE TRIPS/EXCURSIONS

There are a couple of outings that are so easy to do from Madrid that we're mentioning them now, rather than in the next section on Castile. El Pardo is not to be confused with an anagram for the Prado. El Pardo is a royal palace that dates back to the 16th century. It was built in a deer park used as royal hunting grounds, about 15 kilometers northwest of Madrid.

El Pardo is both a small town and a palace. The palace has been a summer residence and watering hole for Spanish royalty through the centuries. Generalisimo Francisco Franco took it over and lived in it as head of state for 40 years. El Pardo is now open to the public; its 32 rooms are elaborately decorated with antiques, some curiosities and much Franco memorabilia.

A popular half-day outing for Madrileños is to visit Alcalá de Henares, 33 kilometers east of Madrid. Alcalá is more interesting for what it was than for what it now is. It *was* a great university center for three centuries. Isabella the Catholic's confessor, Cardinal Jiménez de Cisneros, founded the university in 1508. It was then called *Colegio Mayor de San Ildefonso.* Much later the university was moved to Madrid and became the University of Madrid. In its heyday, everybody who could make the journey turned up at the *Colegio.* Many of the Golden Age poets, such as Lope de Vega, and philosophers studied at Alcalá.

Alcalá was also home to Cervantes. You can visit the house where he was born. His birth certificate is still on the registry at Santa Maria la Mayor Church, though the church was badly destroyed (as was most of the town) during the Civil War of 1936–1939. Its baptistry has been restored. Catherine of Aragon, first wife of England's Henry VIII, was born here, but there's little left to remind you of the birth.

Inside Information

Hotels

Rates pertain to double rooms: *Very Expensive,* 15,000–21,000 pts.; *Expensive,* 10,000–14,500 pts.; *Moderate,* 6,000–9,500 pts.; *Inexpensive,* 3,500–5,500 pts.; *Bargain,* below 3,500 pts.

In past decades Madrid has suffered severe hotel shortages, especially in the deluxe and first-class categories. All that has changed. Over the past 12 years or so, new hotels have been sprouting as fast as spring grass.

It is worth remembering that hotel prices quoted in Spain usually include continental breakfast and always include service charges and taxes. (At deluxe hotels breakfast isn't generally included.)

★★★★★ FIVE STARS

★★★★★ 1. RITZ

5 Paseo del Prado (phone 2212857). How to do justice with words to this Grande Dame of Madrid hotels? Elegant, graceful, evoking an aristocratic past. Certainly. High-ceilinged public rooms, beautifully furnished with antiques, Royal Tapestry Factory carpets on marble floors. Old but beautifully maintained; formal but not stuffy. Rooms and suites handsomely furnished, spacious, generous closet space, large marble baths. Handy location across from the Prado. 156 rooms and suites. Bought by Trusthouse Forte and newly refurbished. Ravishing! Ask about Crown weekend packages. *Very Expensive.*

★★★ Restaurant. Even if you don't stay here, drop by for afternoon tea, served with great style. Ask for the King's favorite cookie, tejas

★★★★★ 2. PALACE

7 Plaza de la Cortes (phone 4297551). Our favorite home away from home in Madrid. Big sister to the Ritz across the road, with a similar white facade and slate-blue roof, the Palace seems smaller than the sum of its parts. In short, the staff's friendly; the beautiful lounge with regal carpets is large but not cavernous. We revel in tea or drinks under the glorious stained-glass skylight. Large rooms, nicely furnished, equipped with color TV, direct dial phones, large marble baths, vast closet space. In-house hairdressers (men and women), cinema, shops, jogging map in every room. Handy to shopping and Old Madrid. Helpful concierges. 504 rooms and suites. *Expensive.*

Alexander Haig's favorite. The bar is popular with journalists, politicians and celebrities.

★★★★★ 3. VILLAMAGNA

22 Paseo de la Castellana (phone 2614900). Relatively new, slick, popular with foreign visitors, Villamagna has full amenities: radio and TV in all rooms, beauty parlor, men's barber, sauna, drugstore, shops, pleasant garden with hotel set back from busy Castellana. Spacious rooms. Exuberantly decorated. Attractive bars (Mayfair and Villamagna) and restaurant (Rue Royale). 194 rooms furnished in diverse historical styles. *Very Expensive.*

★★★★★ **4. MELIÁ MADRID**

25 Princesa (phone 2485800). An ultracomfortable deluxe hotel, well situated near the Plaza de España, convenient for shopping and sightseeing. Handsomely decorated public areas, rooms and imperial suites with good views and all conveniences (TV, minibar). Services include sauna, gym, beauty parlor, barber shop, shops, two bars, nightclub, two restaurants, convention facilities with simultaneous translation. 250 rooms. *Expensive.*

Nice tapas bar near hotel is El Caseria

★★★★★ **5. MIGUEL ANGEL**

31 Miguel Angel (phone 4420022). A modern skycraper, the Miguel Angel is one of Madrid's newest hostelries. Tastefully decorated public rooms, quiet bedrooms. TV, radio, minibar in each room; heated swimming pool, sauna, hairdressers, drugstore and medical services, shopping center, disco and restaurant (Zacarias) are among bonuses. 307 rooms. *Expensive.*

★★★★ FOUR STARS

★★★★ **1. LUZ PALACIO**

57 Paseo de la Castellana (phone 4425100). Ultraquiet hotel, though in central location. Understated elegance in rooms and public areas. Numerous accoutrements: sauna, beauty parlor and barber shop, conference rooms with translation facilities. 200 rooms and 14 suites. *Expensive.*

Handy for shopping and smart restaurants

★★★★ **2. PRINCESA PLAZA**

40 Princesa (phone 2423500). Newish (1976) hotel, well furnished in modern motifs—abstract prints, modern furniture, subdued and integrated color schemes, comfortable. Artful arrangement of pines and greenery screen the lobby and lounges from street view and traffic. Well planned. 406 rooms. *Expensive.*

Next door to El Corte Inglés, department store

★★★★ **4. WELLINGTON**

8 Velázquez (phone 2754400). Right in the middle of the fashionable shopping district of Velázquez and Serrano. Many amenities in this bustling hotel, though the lobby is unpretentious. The hotel was enlarged and renovated in 1974; swimming pool, saunas, hairdressers and boutiques. Rooms are comfortable, though ask for an inside one—Velázquez is a busy, noisy street. 325 rooms and suites. Newly redecorated. Improved service. *Moderate.*

Hotel owns a bull-breeding ranch near Madrid, and a stuffed bull stands in the lobby

★★★★ **5. ESCULTOR**

3 Miguel Angel (phone 4192729). In a fashionable and handy location, this apartment hotel offers rooms by the day or week; it's perfect for families or long visits. Opened in 1976, decor is modern, attractive, lots of marble, chrome, and glass. Amenities include outdoor swimming pool, kitchens in rooms, balconies, couches that unfold to extra bed, TV, minibars, restaurant, coffee shop, disco. 82 rooms (with sitting rooms). *Moderate.*

★★★ THREE STARS

Suecia, lit. = "Sweden"; and there's a good smorgasbord here twice weekly

★★★ 1. HOTEL SUECIA

4 Marqués de Casa Riera (phone 2316900). Something of a sleeper, this small, stylish hotel is handy to Alcalá and Gran Vía on a relatively quiet side street. (Ask for a room overlooking a small park.) An all-blue contemporary looking lobby sets a cool mood. Some rooms are smallish but comfortable; furnished in Swedish modern with minibars. 64 rooms. *Moderate.*

★★★ 2. EL PRADO

11 Calle del Prado (phone 4293568). Located on one of the best shopping streets in Madrid for antiques; a short stroll from the old part of the city. El Prado takes its name seriously: Walls of the cosy lobby and small bedrooms are decorated with reproductions of masterpieces. (The Prado is also a short walk away.) Opened in 1976 but has the "feel" of another era. Maybe it's all those art works. 45 rooms. *Moderate.*

We've been told bull-fighters stay here. If so, they are discreet.

★★★ 3. VICTORIA

7 Plaza del Angel (phone 2314500). Back in the 1950s when this old-timer was in need of refurbishing, it called itself Gran Hotel Victoria. Now that it's had a facade lift, it's dropped the Gran. But it still offers some of the best value around, a handy-to-everything location (Prado, shopping, Plaza Mayor) and fronts on one of the prettiest tiny squares in town (Plaza de Santa Ana). Small glassed-in balconies, some old rooms with great charm, others modernized. Helpful staff. An old favorite of ours. 125 rooms. *Inexpensive.*

★★★ 4. LIABENY

3 Salud (phone 2325306). Wood-paneled lobby with comfortable couches and chairs extend an inviting welcome to visitors to this newcomer among Madrid hotels. The location is a shopper's dream: near Galerias Preciados and Gran Vía. Also central for sightseeing. 151 rooms. *Inexpensive.*

★★★ 5. AROSA

2 Salud (phone 2321600). Possibly the most delightfully wacky hotel in Madrid. The tiniest elevator takes you from the ground floor to the upstairs reception desk and lobby. Here you'll find a well-appointed, comfortable lounge, TV room, bar and dining room. Bedrooms are small, newly decorated in a bright, somewhat theatrical style, each different from the next. It's an old hotel, recently revitalized. Family run with a caring staff. 121 rooms. Handy location. *Moderate.*

★★ TWO STARS

★★ 1. CALATRAVA

1 Tutor (phone 2419880). Just a block off busy Princesa, near the Plaza de España, this quiet hotel is neat, tidy, well run. Most rooms with pint-size balconies. 100 rooms. *Inexpensive.*

★★ 2. EL GRAN ATLANTA

34 Comandante Zorita (phone 2535900). Opened in 1976, this medium-small hotel strives for the antique look; it has replicas of old Spanish chests and chairs and a tapestry on one lobby wall. Rooms with music panel, minibar. Breakfast only. One drawback (or advantage, depending on your viewpoint): located in an urbanization area, it's a cab or bus ride into the center of the city. Small garden, pool. 180 rooms. *Inexpensive.*

★★ 3. MENFIS

74 Gran Vía (phone 2470900). Large, bright, color-coordinated rooms; some facing rear; large closets. Drawback: right on Gran Vía, one of noisiest central locations. A rear room is imperative. 122 rooms. *Inexpensive.*

★★ 4. BRÉTON

29 Bretón de los Herreros (phone 4428300). Relatively new, in the Paseo de la Castellana area. Cheerful place, with family-style lounge and TV rooms. Quiet street with *supermercado* (supermarket) across the way and Dos Passos Pub next door. Helpful, accommodating staff. 60 rooms and suite. *Inexpensive.*

★★ 5. CARLOS V

5 Maestro Vitoria (phone 2314100). The dining room is gone; it's breakfast only in this old timer. A face lift has modernized the rooms and the comfortable lounge on the second floor. Crackerjack location, down the street from Galerías Preciados on a pedestrian mall. 60 rooms. *Inexpensive.*

★ ONE STAR

★ 1. CONDE DUQUE

5 Plaza Conde Valle Suchil (phone 4477080). Agreeable accommodations compensate for a noncentral location. The setting, on a new square with parklike surroundings, is pretty. *Bargain.*

★ 2. PRINCIPE PIO

16 Paseo de Onesimo Redondo (phone 2478000). A delightful location. Well-run establishment. Noted for its dining room. *Inexpensive.*

★ 3. REGENTE

8 Mesonero Romanos (phone 2212941). Just off the Gran Vía, this "old shoe," family-style hotel is a find. Friendly staff; comfortable lounge and bar; well-kept rooms. *Bargain.*

★ 4. SERRANO

8 Marqués de Villamejor (phone 4355200). Tucked into a small, quiet street between Serrano and Paseo de la Castellana, this miniscule hotel offers good value. Breakfast only; no restaurant. 35 rooms. *Inexpensive.*

★ **5. ZURBANO**
79-81 Calle Zurbano (phone 4414500). Stylish lobby with Chagallesque murals. Recently renovated (1980). Fashionable neighborhood. Rooms adequate, well lighted. 260 rooms. *Inexpensive.*

Restaurants

In Madrid you can sample the cuisines of all regions: Basque, Galician, Catalan, Andalusian, Valencian, and Castilian

Per-person cost for three-course meal, beverages extra: *Very Expensive,* 3,000–6,000 pts.; *Expensive,* 1,900–2,900 pts.; *Moderate,* 1,400–1,850 pts.; *Inexpensive,* 1,000–1,350 pts.; *Bargain,* below 1,000 pts.

The price difference between eating cheaply and dining lavishly in Madrid is very wide indeed. It is still possible to have a hearty meal at an unpretentious eatery for less than $5. At the other end of the scale, luxurious dining in Madrid, in memorable surroundings, costs $20 to $40, much less than in comparable establishments in most other European or U.S. capitals.

Madrileños dine late, as we have already noted in the Hard Facts section of this guide. They also tend to have their *comida* (big meal) in the afternoon, more of a *cena* (supper) at night. You will probably soon discover that servings are large in Spain, both in Madrid and elsewhere. Two large meals a day may be one more than your digestion, metabolism or figure can handle. You may consider shifting your eating patterns, as we do in Iberia, to dinner in the afternoon and a light supper or snack at night. When in Madrid . . . as they say. The restaurant menus and prices are usually the same noon or night.

★★★★★ **FIVE STARS**

★★★★★ **1. ZALACAIN**

For men: jacket at noon, tie and jacket evenings—par for most deluxe restaurants. This is a favorite of King Juan Carlos and Queen Sofía

4 Alvarez de Baena (phone 2614840). Since owner Jesús María Oyarbide opened his doors in 1973, Zalacain has added a new dimension to dining in Madrid and has spawned imitators all over Spain. We'll go out on a culinary limb and say it's *the* best restaurant in the country (with two or three runners-up elsewhere). Dining is flawless here, from the moment maitre d' Barón escorts you to a table in one of four small, elegantly understated dining rooms until you leave (usually 3 hours later). In between you'll have feasted on the *nouvelle cuisine* offerings of chef Benjamin Urdain (who worked 14 years in France) who brings authority and imagination to dishes such as smoked goose salad with truffles, French duck with strawberry sauce (much subtler than it sounds), tartlette of truffles with salsify *en croûte,* fresh salmon in tarragon sauce. Even more familiar dishes are prepared with new flair and subtlety here: *bacalao* (a Spanish standby—salted cod) in a sweet pepper sauce, *gazpacho* with sherry vinegar, sole with fettucini and oregano sauce. Delicate accoutrements complement the superb food: fresh roses on each table, fine silver and china, *demitasse* served in porcelain cups from Luxembourg. A rare dining experience. Closed Saturdays at midday, all day Sundays, holidays and during August. *Very Expensive.*

★★★★★ **2. JOCKEY**
6 Amador de los Rios (phone 4191003). For decades Jockey (pronounced Hokey) was cock of the walk among Madrid's fine restaurants. It's still marvelous, maintaining top performance year in and year out since 1945. In a conservative low-key setting of wood paneling, banquettes and soft light-

ing, you'll lunch or dine on specialties such as Chateaubriand with bearnaise sauce, turbot flambée with pernod, veal kidneys tarragon flambée. For starters, you may try oysters in a blanc de blanc wine sauce or smoked eel mousse. Closed Sundays and August. *Very Expensive.*

Jockey chef, Clemencio Fuentes, is a household name among Madrid gourmets

★★★★ FOUR STARS

★★★★ 1. EL AMPARA

8 Callejón de Puigcerda (corner of Jorge Juan) (phone 2266456). Stunning redecoration of an old loft (keeping the rough-hewn beams, posts and skylight) in pale pink with beige fabric-covered walls. All is *très chic,* including the elegant *nouvelle cuisine* dishes. Super are the duck with vinegar and honey, langosta salad, *bisque de Marisco Armagnac* and *sorbete de mango*—among many boggling choices. *Very Expensive.*

★★★★ 2. HORCHER

6 Alfonso XII (phone 2220731). This is the place to be pampered: A small cushion is placed under each female diner's feet at table. Crisp, cold carrot sticks and celery are there to nibble on as you work your way through the German-accented menu. Decisions, decisions. Cream of lentil soup, watercress soup, sweetbreads in Calvados sauce, escalope of veal in mustard sauce, pork medallion in beer sauce, venison steak in juniper. Horcher is strong on veal and game in season. Sauces are excellent, portions gargantuan and setting lavish and exceedingly comfortable. Helpful and solicitous waiters hover. Closed Sundays. Recently redecorated. *Very Expensive.*

Making advance reservations at all Madrid's top restaurants is essential

★★★★ 3. EL CIRCO

29 José Ortega y Gasset (phone 2760144). Local celebrities love this new, stylish restaurant with a circus theme—and so do we. Live piana, all-white decor (including waiters in "ensign" uniforms) punctuated with greenery, art by the clever Equipo Crónica, all are especially fun for Sunday brunch. Sole in champagne sauce, bass in fennel, hake in green sauce with *angulas,* all are wonderful. *Expensive.*

★★★★ 4. PRINCIPE DE VIANA

5 Manuel de Falla (phone 2591448). A restaurant much favored by chic Madrileños. Stylish accoutrements; seafood a particular specialty—*merluza* (hake), *bacalao* and other fishes are especially well prepared. Awarded one star in Michelín and three suns in the Madrid Gastronómico guide. Closed for Saturday lunch, Sundays and from July 15 to September 1. *Expensive.*

★★★ THREE STARS

★★★ 1. CASA LUCIO

35 Cava Baja (phone 2653252). Casa Lucio is currently very "hot," *the* place Madrileños go to be seen and to see others—notably *politicos,* actors, society people. Located below the Plaza Mayor in Old Madrid, the restaurant doesn't look like anything special outside. Inside, two floors are handsomely whitewashed, with tile floors, wood-beamed ceilings, brick arches, a wel-

It is said King Juan Carlos has been known to come here "incognito"

coming "country" chic. A straightforward menu features excellent seafood: *angulas* (baby eels), shrimp in garlic sauce, smoked salmon, as well as baby lamb chops, Jabugo ham sliced thin (you'll see the hams drying along the beams). Viajo, a restaurant catty-corner from this one with the same ownership, handles Casa Lucio's overflow. Closed Saturday afternoons and August. *Expensive.*

★★★ 2. LA DORADA

64 Orense (phone 2702002). Another "in" spot for seafood *aficionados.* Roomy, located away from the city center in an urbanization area near Paseo de la Castellana. La Dorada has a light Sevilla touch with *fritura de pescados* (fried fish). Simple dishes prepared to perfection. Closed Sundays. *Expensive.*

★★★ 3. IRÍZAR

3 Jovellanos. In spite of its handy location directly across from the *Teatro de la Zarzuela,* this Basque restaurant is a sleeper. White and brass in looks, *nouvelle Basque* in theme, with dishes such as crepes *bacalao* with *salsa pimiento. Expensive.*

★★★ 4. AL MOUNIA

Don't miss the rose-water-scented desserts

5 Recoletos (phone 2750173). Related to the splendid Casablanca restaurant of the same name, Al-Mounia is marvelous to look at—a totally authentic decor. Such dishes as *tajine aux amandes, couscous, poulet aux pruneaux* are beautifully served Moroccan style on brass trays at decorated Arabian couches. From the ewer brought to your table for hand washing to the mint tea served in a glass, you're Morocco bound. Closed Sundays, Mondays at lunch and August. *Moderate.*

★★★ 5. EL BODEGÓN

15 Calle del Pinar (phone 2623137). From the outside, El Bodegón looks like just another handsome house on an attractive residential tree-shaded street off the Paseo de la Castellana near the Museum of Natural Sciences. Inside is another story: one of Madrid's favorite restaurants, with the discreet decor of a private club. Lunch is clublike—a noisy gathering place for business people. Night is more relaxed. The food is robustly Castillian. We're partial to the venison in red wine sauce and capon in wine with mushrooms and truffles. Closed Sundays and August. *Expensive.*

★★★ 6. ANTIGUA CASA SOBRINO DE BOTÍN

Hemingway's favorite. Cuchilleros is one of Madrid's oldest streets. Walk off your lunch by exploring it.

17 Calle de Cuchilleros (phone 2664217). A first-time visit to Madrid wouldn't be complete without lunch or dinner at Botín's. Famous as Botín's has been for generations (it opened in 1725), it's still an authentic purveyor of hearty Castillian cuisine. Roast suckling pig or roast baby lamb are almost compulsory here, and you can watch as the expert chefs haul the little fellows out of the wood-fired *horno* oven onto huge wooden platters. Numerous small dining rooms are cosily decorated with blue and white tiles, beamed ceilings, mullioned glass windows. Sure it's touristy. It's also fun, good value and a fine meal. *Expensive.*

★★ TWO STARS

★★ 1. SAINT JAMES

26 Juan Bravo (phone 2750069). If you crave a good *paella,* this is the place to have it in any of five ways. A Valencian restaurant all the way, all the rice dishes are good here. A good ending to such abundance is a tart, cooling lemon sorbet. Closed Sundays. *Moderate.*

also good seafood; try sole with champignons

★★ 2. LA CHARLOTTE

3 Pasaje Juan Bravo (phone 2750697). This little all-white gem is located in a passageway between two highrise buildings, near the U.S. Embassy. It's made-to-order French cooking, very simple, expert. A good place for a quiche and salad lunch or light supper. *Moderate.*

Convenient to museums (Lázaro Galdiano or Juan March)

★★ 3. KORYNTO

46 Preciados (phone 2212041). Seafood is the specialty here, as can be seen in a window full of succulent samples. There's no special character to Korynto, though it's vaguely *fin de siecle.* Its seafood is everything: *angulas* in season, shrimp, *langostinos,* clams, mussels and fish, fish, fish. (Chicken, partridge and steak as well.) Open 12 A.M. to 12 P.M. daily. Two dining rooms keep devotees satisfied. *Moderate.*

★★ 4. LA FUENCISLA

4 San Mateo (phone 2216186). A relatively new and highly with it *tasca* for seafood of the north. It's possible to spend a lot of money here, for shellfish in Spain can be costly. It's also possible to dine more modestly on bream, *bonito* and other fish, handled with loving and expert care. Closed Sundays and August. *Expensive.*

Cocochas (fish jowls), a Spanish passion, are especially well prepared here

★ ONE STAR

★ 1. AROCA

3 Plaza de los Carros (phone 2651114). Here's a sleeper, a nondescript facade, unpretentious dining rooms, small kitchen. Yet with all this Doña María Izquierdo is something of a Madrid institution, turning out superb fish–incomparable fried sole and *merluza* (hake). It's simple food, consistently well prepared. The *pollo al ajillo* (chicken with garlic) is another specialty. Closed Sundays and August. *Moderate.*

Doña María won the Premio, a gastronomic award in 1976

★ 2. EDELWEISS

7 Jovellanos (phone 2210326). Behind the Cortes, diagonally across from the *Teatro de la Zarzuela,* this homey little place serves a trio of specialties—German, Spanish and Alsatian dishes. It's been a favorite with students and politicians as long as we can remember. Menu of the day is 380 pts. Tops for à la carte entrees is *chuleta de tornero* (veal cutlet with fried potatoes). Closed Sunday evenings and August. *Moderate.*

★ 3. CARUSO

70 Serrano The name's Italian and so is the menu in this tiny restaurant with a flair (formerly Charlot). It's across the street from Sear's. Specialties include

osso buco Milanese (550 pts.), *lasagna verde al queso* (400 pts.), pizza (300–450 pts.). Have a *cassata Siciliana,* a sorbet or share a souffle for dessert. It's a pleasing bistrolike atmosphere. *Moderate.*

★ 4. EMBASSY

12 Castellana (corner of Ayala) (phone 2259480). In the rear of a first-rate food shop is one of the foreign community's favorite hangouts in Madrid. Great for afternoon tea (English owned, so why not?), lunch or a light supper, the Embassy has a restful, old-fashioned air and good food. Chicken breast in champagne sauce; quail *escabeche* (pickled) are especially tangy. You can also buy homemade patés and gourmet items to take out. Open daily. *Moderate.*

★ 5. ARRUMBAMBAYA

23 Calle de la Libertad (phone 2329035). *Caldo Gallego* is the favorite in this old-fashioned, unpretentious Galician restaurant, where Federico García Lorca once hung out. The main dining room seats only 24, but there are several small side rooms where you can dine happily on trout Navarra, *bonito riojano, fabada* Asturiana or *bacalao al pil-pil* and wind up with *tarta al* whiskey or the ubiquitous *flan.* Open daily. *Moderate.*

Shopping

Gone are the days when you could buy everything in sight on a three-day shopping spree and barely feel a twinge in your pocketbook. Inflation has been leapfrogging with the peseta as it has with other currencies.

Still, there *are* values in Spain. You can still get very fine workmanship, specifically in Madrid. And, while things are no longer extremely inexpensive, they cost less than the same high-quality items would most other places.

Examples of good values: anything that is handmade, such as suede and leather jackets, leather handbags and boots. Then there are shoes. Sometimes it seems that Madrid is one giant shoe store. Shoes are usually not handmade, but are of tremendous variety, good-quality leather and moderate prices. The caveat here is sizes: Odd sizes or tricky foot problems make fitting difficult.

The following are some of the best buys you'll encounter in Madrid and some of the best places to shop for them.

Art and Antiques

Top quality contemporary art—mostly paintings and original graphics—can be a very good buy in Madrid. Not inexpensive, but good value. Since the early 1960s Madrid has had a lively and highly professional art scene.

There are dozens of galleries from which to choose; the following are of special interest and reliable. *Galería Theo,* 2 Marqués de la Ensenada, is known for its big name moderns: Picasso, Miro, Juan Gris, Tapies, Sempere, Zóbel and others. *Galeria Celini,* 8 Barbara de Braganza, features graphics, watercolors and drawings by the same group.

You'll find paintings by a younger generation of Madrid artists, along with a large selection of graphics, at *Galería Egam,* 7 Villanueva. More graphics, many produced on the premises, at *Grupo Quince,* 7 Fortuny. There is usually new and interesting work being exhibited at *Kreisler* II, 8 Hermosilla (*not* Kreisler I, which is a somewhat touristy gift shop). Trendy and avant garde art can be seen at *Galería Vijande,* 65 Nuñez de Balboa. Most of these galleries are in the same general area, off Paseo de la Castellana.

Art galleries are generally open from 11 A.M. to 2 P.M., then again from 5 to 8 or 8:30 P.M. Evening is the preferred time in Spain for gallery hopping (after shops and offices have closed). It is a sociable, relaxed time of day when many galleries schedule their openings. You may be lucky and come upon a sherry party for a new exhibition.

The best streets for antiques are Calle del Prado and nearby Carrera de San Jerónimo. Shops of particular interest on del Prado are *Antigüedades J. Pena,* No. 5, *Luis Morueco,* No. 16; *Romero,* No. 23; *El Partenon,* No. 25. On San Jerónimo there is *Deogracias Magdalena,* No. 34. *Antiguedades Abelardo Linares,* across from the Palace Hotel at No. 11 Plaza de las Cortes, is one of Madrid's oldest and largest shops.

The Rastro, which we'll talk more extensively about under Markets, is another important source for antiques. Three shops of special interest in El Rastro are *Luis Carabe* in Nuevas Galerías—with a fine selection of ceramics, antique glass, Renaissance and baroque works; *Los Andes,* Nuevas Galerias —small objects, archeological items, antique glass, prints, drawings and small paintings; and *Lucas,* Galerías Piquer—extremely high-quality (and prices to match) baroque and Renaissance objects.

Prices at art galleries are usually firm, but when shopping for antiques it never hurts to try your hand at negotiating. Bargaining is the name of the game in El Rastro.

Note: A helpful booklet, if you are an art buff, is *Arte y Exposiciones.* It is published three times a year and lists all museums and art galleries with their current shows and has an artist index (invaluable) indicating at which gallery or galleries you will find your favorite artists' works. The booklet can be obtained for 100 pts. from Asociación Professional de Galerías de Arte,

7 Rollo, Madrid 12. It can also be found at most of the city's art galleries or at the Fundación Juan March, 77 Castelló for free.

Shopping Custom-Made

Madrid is a center of custom-made articles, whether it is couturier clothing, riding boots and saddles, book bindings or embroidered pillow cases. Such handwork does not come cheap, but it does exist and is a better buy than in most of Europe.

For example, boot wearers insist that the best boots in the world are made at a small hole-in-the-wall shop in Madrid. Ernest Hemingway and Anthony Quinn, to say nothing of every horseman from Argentina to Zambia, have been customers of Hijos de García Tenorio, 9 Calle de la Bolsa (phone 2213194). In a tiny workshop the García brothers and a friend are carrying on a 150-year old tradition, making every boot painstakingly by hand from a pattern drawn to the foot of the purchaser. (The García foot pattern collection—which they save for reorders—looks like a paper version of Grauman's Chinese Theater footprints in cement.) Each pair of boots takes a minumun of 3 months to make. They may last forever.

Balenciaga was no fluke. Spanish couturiers have long had a reputation for superior workmanship and stylish designs. There are at least three dozen working in Madrid now. Among the best are Elio Berhanyer, 25 G. Mena (boutique), 124 Calle Ayala (atelier); Manuel Pertegaz, 8 Matias Montero; Antonio Nieto, 22 Calle de Prado; and Herrera y Ollero, 9 Almirante. *The* best men's custom tailor is Angel Collado, 21 Almirante (phone 4194676).

If you covet a real Spanish cape, one of the places you can have one made to order is Seseña Capas, 23 Calle de la Cruz, which has been making capes for the rich and beautiful since 1901.

Suede jackets and coats can be found in shops all over Madrid, but rarely will you see the quality of Loewe, which has turned the craft of leatherworking into a fine art. Prices are high, but even if you decide not to buy, just browse and admire. Two main shops, at No. 8 and No. 26 Serrano, are supplemented by (at last count) 15 branches throughout Spain. Loewe is for men and women and all seasons—the most beautiful suede and leather jackets, skirts, suits, vests, coats and accessories.

Madrid is full of boutiques in which you will find a wide range of smart, trendy clothing for men and women. The formal styles of times past have given way to more casual, sporty wear. Just browsing along Calle Serrano could keep a dedicated shopper busy for days. Doncarlos has attractive men's wear. Yves St. Laurent has a branch at No. 100, Ted Lapidus at No. 53; you'll find familiar international fashion names all along the way, as well as on Goya and Ortega y Gasset. One of our favorite boutiques is Rango, just below street level at No. 19 San Jerónimo, which always seems to be on the crest of a new wave of fashion. It also carries some of the Miss Dior and Yves St. Laurent lines.

Handicrafts

Authentic Spanish handicrafts are harder and harder to come by. (The fact that Spain is now the fifth most industrialized country in Europe probably has a lot to do with it.) What passes for handicrafts in Madrid, especially in the myriad tourist shops along the Gran Vía, could more accurately be labeled souvenirs.

Ceramics have always been a strong Spanish craft. If you can't get to the source, that is Talavera outside of Madrid, or Manises outside of Valencía, you can find a good selection of pottery at any of the major department stores (see listing below). In addition, Alfaijar Ceramica, 72 Ortega y Gasset, has ceramics from all over the country in a variety of styles. La Ceramica de Talavera, 44 Lagasca, features plates, bowls and other works in the classic Talavera patterns and colors. At Cantaro, 8 Calle de la Flor Baja, off Gran Vía, you'll find offbeat ceramics, terra cotta masks and pots and amusing things. Gavilla, 7 Ortega y Gasset, is upscale, a select gallery of handicrafts with an emphasis on contemporary, not folk, pottery.

Shoes

Shoe stores, like banks, seem to have taken over Madrid's downtown shopping areas. Charles Jourdan, 1 Gran Vía, has a stylish boutique at prices to match, though lower than in the USA, devotees tell us. Petits Suisses, 41 Claudio Coello, with another store at 68 Serrano, has an excellent selection, also at the upper end of the price scale. Don't worry about finding shoes. Window after window will distract you a dozen times a day.

Books

If you are looking for books in English, Herman Miessner, 14 Ortega y Gasset (phone 2250978), has a good selection of foreign and Spanish books, as does Libreria Turner, 3 Genova (phone 4191784). A source for old Spanish and foreign books is Mirto on Espalter. There are used bookstalls near the Atocha railroad station where it is fun to browse. There are also secondhand bookstalls set up each Sunday at the Rastro. (Details under Markets.)

Food and Cookware Shops

There are numerous marvelous food shops—*ultramarinos*—throughout Madrid. They are good sources for supplies if you plan an excursion out of town and want to take a picnic lunch or if you want to take home some culinary reminder of Spain. (Cheese, candy and canned foods are permitted by the U.S. Department of Agriculture, but sausages or meat products and fresh produce are not.)

Some of the most interesting and unusual food shops, with a variety of offerings, include the following: Mantequeria Leonesas, 15 Castellana (phone 4351701, 7394200 or 2764658), with many other branches in various parts of the city; Embassy, 12 Castellana (phone 2259480 or 2760080) for cheese, homemade patés, cookies. Mantequeria Alemana, 88 Padilla (phone 4019821), has a fine selection of German sausages, hams and smoked salmon. Pastelería Riosal Mantequeria, 112 Serrano, specializes in ultrafancy foods, many imports.

One of the best is Ferpal, 7 Arenal (phone 2215108) with an unusual assortment of cheeses from all over Spain, regional hams (piled high in the window), sausages and other goodies. It's also a good place to stop for a quick, inexpensive sandwich and a glass of beer taken stand-up style.

If you have a sweet tooth, head for Casa Hijos Sucesores de Luis Mira, 30 Carrera San Jerónimo. In this splendid old wood-paneled shop that dates back to 1855, you'll find a world of *turrone,* a Spanish nougat that could hook you for life. To addicts like us, it is difficult to find a turrone that isn't good, but here is the best of the best, in dizzying variety, with or without almonds and with citron, plain, light, dark, darker, soft, firm or hard. Make your choice; it is cut off huge, crumbly blocks on a marble counter.

If you enjoy large public food markets with their attendant noise, clutter and aromas, a good one is on Calle Alonso Cano at the corner of Viriato. Another, considered the best for fresh fish, is on Calle del Potosi near General Mola.

Markets

A market to end markets is the Rastro (flea market) or El Rastro to be Spanish about it. Every Sunday morning you get the feeling that the entire city of Madrid tilts to the southwest below the Plaza Mayor. Rain, snow or shine, Madrileños and tourists descend on this area in search of bargains, hidden treasures and mostly, we suspect, entertainment.

The Rastro *is* entertainment; it's a five- or six-block long happening. Actually, there is no street named Rastro. It is an area that extends down Ribera de Curtidores from the Plaza de Cascorro to wide Ronda de Toledo, spilling over into narrow side streets all along the route. The Rastro seems bigger than it really is because movement through it is so snail-paced slow. By noon Sunday the area is wall-to-wall people. Then, miraculously, by 2 P.M. or so, the crowd disperses to go home with their new treasures or off to lunch.

What are these treasures that lure people in? Nowhere is the saying "One man's trash is another's treasure" more applicable. You'll find anything from live birds to baggage, silver to samovars, firearms to fire stokers. The gamut. Anything, everything is fair game for sale or resale at this fantastic open-air weekly event. You'll find brand new fleece-lined cowhide mittens and slippers for 200 pts. or 19th-century bona fide queen's guards uniforms for 20 times that. Not too many years ago someone uncovered Michaelangelo drawings for a pittance. It happens.

But mostly the fun is just being there, enjoying the mix of buyers and sellers, the haggling, the shouting, the singing that goes on. As we said, it's a happening. If you can organize your trip so that you are in Madrid on a Sunday morning, the Rastro is the place to be. Note: Pickpockets also find it the place to be so be prudent about your cash on hand.

Prices, should you find the perfect trinket, are almost always negotiable. In fact, for regular Rastroites, bargaining is where the fun begins. The only time you really can't expect a vendor to budge on his prices is when an item is ticketed P.V.P. This stands for *precio venta publico*—or fixed price—and it is most likely to be found in the shops that line the streets rather than in the moveable vendors' stalls.

The 40% or so permanent shops in the Rastro, located around pleasant courtyards just off the main shopping street, are mostly high-quality antique shops. They are not portable. In fact some of them are among the most elegant, and expensive, antique galleries in the city. Almost all of these galleries or shops are open during the week. If you are contemplating a purchase, it is advisable to do so on a weekday. On Sunday mornings the dealers seem far too busy socializing with friends who drop in or watching out for shoplifters to do any serious haggling. We listed several of the more reliable shops for antiques in the section Art and Antiques.

There is another Sunday market that is fun and colorful, even if buying isn't the primary object. It's the stamp market held from 10 A.M. to 2 P.M. all along the shaded arcades of the Plaza Mayor. You'll find coins old, new, foreign and rare as well. But the majority of vendors sell stamps. It is a great place for people watching. Fun to poke among the treasures too. Filatelia Castellana, No. 28 Plaza Mayor, is a permanent stamp-and-coin shop, considered reliable.

Department Stores

If you are in a hurry, Madrid's many department stores offer the convenience of one-stop shopping, along with a wide range of reliable, quality goods. Department stores are something more as well; they are a mirror of local life. They give you an instant picture of what's new, current and of interest to local residents.

Prices are fixed. Unlike most of the city shops and boutiques that close for the midday meal, department stores keep regular hours and are open all day. Most of the major stores have interpreters on hand to help visitors.

Most exclusive, expensive and with the highest level of taste, is Celso García. "It's our Bloomies," a Spanish friend said. But it is smaller, and is also smaller than the two Madrid giants. Celso's main store is on Calle Serrano; a larger branch is at 15 Avenida del Generalisimo. Both are good sources for women's, men's and children's clothing.

Madrid's oldest department store, with branches all over Spain, is Galerías Preciados, which many Madrileños consider the lowest common denominator of the three large stores. Maybe so, but it has wonderful selections of gift items, books, pottery and porcelain, handcrafts and household wares. It's also a good place to replenish toilet goods, with large hand soap, make-up and toiletries selections. Pure glycerin soap is an especially good buy. Galerías, as it is called, has three Madrid locations. The main one, Plaza Callao, is just off Gran Vía with a large annex nearby; another is at Calle Goya and Conde de Penalver and the third is at the Arapiles shopping center.

El Corte Inglés, like Galerias, has stores in major cities throughout Spain. In Madrid you'll find its main store right near its competitor, Galerías, on Calle Preciados just off the Puerta del Sol. The other three branches are on the Avenida del Generalisimo, Goya and Alcalá, and Calle Princesa and Alberto Aguilera.

Other, smaller department stores include Galeprix, a Galerias Preciados budget spin-off, and Simago, a Spanish version of the French chain Uniprix. Woolworth is in Madrid, on Calle Juan Hurtado de Mendoza, with a much upgraded image and lots of imports. Another familiar face is Sear's, located on the corner of Serrano and Ortega y Gasset. It too has an up-graded image here, with somewhat higher prices than the old Madrid standbys.

Museums and Galleries (in addition to those mentioned in text)

★★★★ Prado; and for other museums, see pp. 30-43

★ MUSEO CERRALBO

17 Ventura Rodriquez. A 19th-century mansion that belonged to the Marqués de Cerralbo is the stage set for an imposing collection of furniture, tapestries, fine porcelains, armor and paintings. These include works by El Greco, Zurbaran, van Dyck, Tintoretto, Titian, Ribera and others. Open 9 A.M. to 2 P.M., closed Tuesday and August. Admission 100 pts.

★ FUNDACIÓN JUAN MARCH

77 Castelló. Outside a stunning, severely modern building are two authoritative stone sculptures by Eduardo Chillida, contemporary Spanish sculptor. In a small garden area are other abstract sculptures. These sculptures set the tone for the high level of professionalism maintained inside this interesting art gallery. Changing exhibits—usually every month—are shown, sometimes of Spanish work, often of internationally known modern artists. Matisse, Klee, Braque, Motherwell, Mondrian have all been shown here. There are also lectures and free concerts held in this stimulating place. Open 10 A.M. to 2 P.M., 5:30 to 9 P.M.; holidays 10 A.M. to 2 P.M. Admission free.

MUSEO NACIONAL DE ETNOLOGIA (ETHNOLOGICAL MUSEUM)

68 Alfonso XII. Primarily a collection of artifacts from the Philippines—Ifugao and other Luzon tribal groups, there are some items from Africa, the Canary Islands and prehispanic Incas as well. Open 10 A.M. to 1:30 P.M.; closed Monday and August. Admission 300 pts.

Cool off with a glass of alcoholic Asturian cider at casual Casa Mingo, next door

★★★ PANTEON DE GOYA—SAN ANTONIO DE LA FLORIDA

Paseo de la Florida. In the cupola of a late 18th-century church, Francisco Goya's frescos are as fresh as spring time. The frescos, which Goya was commissioned to paint for the then new church, depict one of St. Anthony's miracles. But it is the individual faces of the people in the crowd who are watching the saint that command our attention. Goya has captured various types of Madrileños of his day in rich and sure portraits. The studies are brilliant, the colors airy and light. This is Goya at his most ebullient. His tomb is here as well. Open in winter, 11 A.M. to 1:30 P.M., 3 to 6 P.M.; in summer 10 A.M. to 1 P.M., 4 to 7 P.M.; closed Wednesday, Sunday and holiday afternoons. Admission 25 pts.

MONASTERIO DE LA ENCARNACIÓN (CONVENT OF THE INCARNATION)

1 Plaza de la Encarnación. In a quiet little square stands a convent founded in 1611 by Queen Margaret of Austria, Philip III's wife. Inside, in a rococo setting, are dozens of paintings, sculptures and reliquaries. Open 10:30 A.M. to 1:30 P.M., 4 to 6 P.M.; closed national holidays and Sunday afternoon. Admission 100 pts. (same ticket admits you to Descalzas Reales).

CASA MUSEO DE LOPE DE VEGA (LOPE DE VEGA'S HOUSE)

11 Calle Cervantes. An impeccably restored 17th-century house projects a strong sense of how a middle-class Madrileño lived at the time. Don't think of it as the playwright's house per se, nobody knows for sure just how his house was organized, that is, where the kitchen and other rooms were. Think

of it instead as an example of a comfortable house of his period. Open 11 A.M. to 2 P.M.; closed Monday and from July 15th to September 15th and major holidays. Admission 50 pts.

Historic Buildings and Sites (in addition to those mentioned in text)

TEATRO REAL (ROYAL THEATER)

Facing the Royal Palace across the Plaza de Oriente this 1850, three-story neoclassical confection in grey stone with a darker grey trim is beautifully restored and maintained. It is now a concert hall.

★ OPEN-AIR MUSEUM

Just below the overpass where Paseo de Eduardo Dato (which changes names to Calle de Juan Bravo) crosses Paseo de la Castellana, are a number of gigantic abstract sculptures, the work of the 1960s school of Spanish artists. Two huge bronze egglike forms by Madrid sculptor Pablo Serrano are especially notable. The city was awash with controversy over whether the heavy stone piece by internationally known Eduardo Chillida was or was not too heavy to be hung by cables from the bridge overpass. It was not, and there it is. Wags irreverently call it "the earring."

★★ PALACIO DE LIRIA

This splendid neoclassical palace, the 1773 work of Ventura Rodriguez, belongs to the Duchess of Alba. With luck and special permission the fine art collection inside can be visited (see **Perks**). It has greenery and breathing space at the edge of Calle de Princesa.

★ PLAZA DE COLÓN AND THE PLAZA OF THE DISCOVERY OF AMERICA

If you have been away from Madrid for awhile, you'll be surprised to find the 17-meter high monument to Christopher Columbus gone from the busy circle on Paseo de la Castellana. Worry not. It isn't far away; it's just across the street in a new park, building and garden complex called Plaza of the Discovery of America. The Plaza is dominated on the Calle Serrano side by a monumental stone memorial to Spain's explorers (which vaguely resembles an elongated oversize page of a book), designed by Madrid artist Joaquin Vaquero Turcios. Also in the plaza is a new cultural complex, Centro Cultural Villa de Madrid, installed below and behind a wall of water, a modern fountain. The only problem inside is the roar of the water.

Entertainment

"When a man is tired of London," said Samuel Johnson, "he is tired of life." If he had been a Madrileño, Johnson's statement would more likely have been "if a man is tired of Madrid, he is dull-witted and a blockhead to boot."

The problem is to learn about and locate Madrid's many and varied presentations. Best sources are: *ABC* (the national daily newspaper), under the heading "Espectaculos"; *Guia del Ocio* (leisure guide), a weekly that carries comprehensive listings, addresses, times and usually admission charges; and *En Madrid,* a monthly English–Spanish-language leaflet distributed by the Madrid municipal tourism offices.

Here is an admittedly incomplete catalog of some of the glitter and glow from Madrid's jewel case.

Theater

Ten-thirty P.M. is the theater hour in Madrid (matinees are generally at 7 or 7:30 P.M., and frequently all 23 major theaters are in action simultaneously.

Variety is the spice of Madrid theater. Three theaters are supported by the government: The Teatro Español and the Maria Guerrero stage Spanish classics by authors such as Lope de Vega or plays by internationally known playwrights. Teatro Zarzuela hosts opera, ballet and the season of *zarzuelas,* those 19th-century operetta sugar plums. If your Spanish is weak you may especially enjoy the performances at Teatro Zarzuela. There grand opera and ballet speak in international languages and the *zarzuelas'* simple plots are self-evident. You are there for the music, dancing and costumes of these delicious period valentines.

Satirical reviews and experimental or avant garde presentations use the Teatro Alcazar or La Latina, and musicals are often at the Maravillas and Calderon theaters. The rest of the theaters present a variety of shows such as Ibsen's *The Wild Duck, Amadeus,* Arthur Miller's *The Price,* Pirandello's *Six Characters in Search of an Author,* current Broadway musicals, and Spanish plays with the tempting titles *Cantata for F. Garcia Lorca, Nothing is Late if the Night is Good, Crazy for Democracy, Teresa de Avila* (in the 4th century since her death), and the award-winning *Bicycles are for Summer* about the 1936 siege of Madrid.

Theater prices are modest: They start at 200 pts. and top out (for example, for the smash hit *Evita*) at 1,200 pts.

Perhaps the city's most beautiful theater is the Teatro Real. This 19th-century galleried opera house is used for concerts.

Opera

Madrid's opera season runs from April through June, often featuring Spain's own sons and daughters such as Placido Domingo and Montserrat Caballé in world-famous works with international casts. Operas are presented at the Teatro de la Zarzuela.

Cinema

Movies are popular and plentiful in Madrid. You'll find the latest Spanish and top foreign releases in Gran Vía's movie houses. Imports of less than blockbuster dimensions, classics and revival may play at smaller specialty theaters. Seats are 250 pts. or less. Tip ushers 5 pts.

Look for showings of older films of interest sponsored by Filmoteca Nacional de España. They usually are shown at the Circulo de Bellas Artes, 2 Marques de Casa Riera or the Museo Español de Arte Contemporaneo, 2 Juan de Hererra. Admission 100 pts.

Concerts

The range of serious music covers the entire classical literature and avant garde experiments. Concerts run the gamut from symphonies to soloists performing in the grand Teatro Real (for 150–600 pts. per seat) or the Madrid Cultural Center auditorium under Plaza Colon (200 pts.) or in the auditorium at Fundación Juan March (whose many concerts are free), or the French, German or American cultural centers (usually free) or on Sundays in the Plaza del Maestro Villa in Retiro Park.

Pop, jazz and rock concerts are found all over the city at almost any time of year. Some are held in movie theaters (taken over for the concert), discotheques, college auditoriums and, on occasion, open-air bandstands in the parks.

In addition to splashy concerts, pop, jazz and rock groups appear at pubs, bars and *discotecas.* For jazz, two highly recommended spots are Whisky Jazz Club, 7 Diego de Leon (phone 261-1165); and Balboa Jazz, 37 Nuñez de Balboa.

Ballet

Ballet, whether classical or exotic, generally is seen in the Madrid Cultural Center, Plaza Colón; Teatro Real or Sala Olimpia, Plaza de Lavapies.

Gambling

There is now a Casino Gran Madrid in the small town of Torrelodones, some 20 kilometers northwest of the city. Casino gambling was only legalized in 1978. You have to be 21, show your passport and pay about $5 admission before you can play blackjack, roulette or baccarat, or feed the slot machines.

Far more popular is an old familiar gambling game: bingo. You'll find more than a dozen bingo parlors in Madrid, some of them in surprising places such as the hotels Melia, Plaza and Palace. The stakes are not like home, though; they get higher as it gets later. Most games start about 5 P.M. and continue to 3 A.M. Locations are listed in the *Redi Guide Madrid* distributed by Redi, S. A., 55 Gran Vía, or, as always, ask your concierge.

Nightlife

Nightlife entertainment depends on what interests you, of course, but there are now *post-Franco* nightclubs that run the gamut from decorous to gamey in any or all of three sexes. Among those places presenting shows with pretensions beyond flashing flesh are Pasapoga, 37 Gran Vía, with shows at midnight and 1:15 A.M.; and the Lido Music Hall, 20 Alcalá, with a show at 1 A.M.

The roster of *discotecas* is lengthy and fluctuates as some die and others are born. Among those that have been operating successfully and are doing so at this writing are Vanity, 3 Miguel Angel; Bocaccio, 16 Marqués de la Enseñada; Mau-Mau, Edificio Eurobuilding; and Golden Village, 3 Agustin de Foxá. Most discos open about 7 P.M. and close around 3 A.M.

If you have a taste for satirical revues, a café–theater setting, El Biombo Chino, at 6 Isabel la Catolica may satisfy you.

Folklore

Flamenco, the fiery gypsy art form that at its best fuses castanets, guitar music, singing and dancing with the intensity of a rocket can be seen mostly in the *tablao flamenco* places in side streets off Gran Via. Most are small restaurants with raised stages or bars. Meal and drink charges include the show. Generally such spots open about 10 P.M. and you'll finish dinner before the show starts around midnight. It isn't necessary to go for dinner. In fact, the best performances come on after the dinner crowd has gone home. You may not go the distance, as the show could end as late as 3 A.M. That's when government regulations decree that clubs must close. But if you have the stamina, stay for the 2nd show. The first is a warm-up only and is often poor.

Recommended for the torrid barefoot dancing of "la Chunga" and the *bailadores* (dancers) who accompany her and "Serranito," the guitar virtuoso, is Café de Chinitas, 17 Torija (phone 248-5135). The restaurant is a re-creation of a 19th-century Andalucían concert café. Don't let the unprofessional warm-up team scare you off. The longer you stay, the better the flamenco gets. (Sr. Llorente, director of Chinitas, was for years a mainstay of the famed *Spanish Pavilion* in New York.)

Other flamenco places are Las Brujas, 15 Norte; Corral de la Moreria, 17 Moreria.

Pubs

Many bars and cocktail lounges use the name "pub" and they are of several types.

Some *cervecerias* specialize in German beer imported by the barrel. It is served along with *tapas* of a supposedly Teutonic character. The Henninger-1, 85 Puerto de la Castellana and L'Alsace, 3–5 Domenico Scarlatti are among them.

Madrid pubs also may turn out to be piano bars—one such is El Avion, 99 Hermosilla. And a more recognizable Irish-style pub is the Dublin, 29 Princesa. For a more mature crowd, we recommend the Balmoral, also on Calle Hermosilla just off Serrano.

A variation on the pub theme is the classical music coffee house. Some feature live performers. La Fidula, 57 Huertas, has live music accompanied by cheese, tea and patés or vice versa. El Juglar, 37 Lavapíes, styles itself as a café burlesque and features Renaissance and baroque music with its crepes, canapes and patés.

If Latin American music moves you, Pena Tres, 79 Alcalá and La Carcelera, 10 Monteleon will rattle your maracas.

Tours

Some rugged individualists insist that the only way to see a "new" place is by your very own self with your very own local guide. We've always wanted to make the rounds in a sedan chair with our guide trotting alongside pointing out the highlights. Alas, the sedan chair seems to have gone the way of the ricksha, and most people now have to settle for guided tours in groups. Fortunately, modern motorcoaches and guides with high-quality intercoms make seeing a "new" place pleasant.

Madrid has dozens of tour operators but only a limited array of city tours. The standards are these:

"Artistic" Madrid. A half-day tour that includes a visit to the Prado and the 18th-century Royal Palace. (When either of these is closed, the tour substitutes the Pardo Palace near Madrid, where Francisco Franco lived for 40 years.) Departs about 9:30 A.M.; fee 1,350 pts.

"Panoramic" Madrid. A half-day tour through the university area, Casa de Campo, the old Moorish quarter, Puerta del Sol, Retiro Park, the Alcalá gate and Madrid's fountains. Departs about 3:30 P.M.; fee 975 pts.

"Madrid by Night." Drive through Old Madrid and past the illuminated fountains to a flamenco show followed by a nightclub for an "international show." Departs at 10 P.M. Fee 3,100 pts.

There are variations on this tour—one skips the flamenco show and goes to a nightclub for dinner. Fee 4,800 pts. Another goes to a restaurant for dinner, then to a *tablao flamenco.* Fee 4,100 pts.

The night tours will return you to your hotel safe and sound about 1 A.M.

Among companies offering these or similar tours (plus tours to other attractions outside the city) are:

American Express, 2 Plaza de las Cortes (phone 222–1180).
Atesa, 59 Gran Via (phone 247–0202).
El Corte Inglés, 3 Preciados (phone 221–3858); and its many branches.
Melia, 3 Plaza Callao (phone 231–3809).
Wagons-lits Cook, 23 Alcala (phone 433–5600).

Perks

Just as hotel reservations need to be made ahead of time during the height of season or as a Eurailpass must be purchased before your trip begins, so there are certain other advance preparations that may help heighten your trip's enjoyment.

Special House or Exhibition Visits

It is possible to see the art collection at the *Palacio de Liria,* which we have mentioned under Historic Buildings and Sites. To do so requires advance planning. Write ahead and make a request to Director, Fundación Casa de Alba, Princesa, 20, Palacio de Liria, Madrid.

The Banco de España also has a collection of art, including paintings by Goya, tapestry and fine antique furniture. To view the collection, it is recommended that you write to Señor José Manuel Ferrer, Conservador, Colección del Banco de España, Alcala, 50, Madrid.

It is possible to use the National Library by showing your passport and paying a modest fee. There are special exhibitions in the salons.

Cooking School

Gourmets who would like to blend a little food experience into their travels might consider taking cooking classes at Madrid's Alambique, a combination cookware shop–cooking school. Madrid's top restaurant chefs often give demonstration lessons. You can write ahead to inquire to Alambique, 2 Plaza de la Encarnación, Madrid. The fee is 7,000 pts. for four or five 2 one-half-hour lessons. Regional Spanish cooking is a specialty, along with French and Italian. Alambique also offers special cooking tours of Madrid and Castile that can be arranged through Marketing Ahead, 515 Madison Ave. New York, NY 10022.

Club Memberships

A woman who is a U.S. citizen or the wife of a U.S. citizen may get temporary membership in the American Women's Club for 1,500 pts. that is good up to 6 months. What's the point? Well, some of the group's activities and options may be of interest. For example, there is an English library, helpful tips, special luncheons, and nominally priced excursions (such as a 3-day trip to Córdoba—hotels, transportation, lunches, admissions—for 8,300 pts.). For information, write Señora Erme Huidobro, American Women's Club, Plaza Republica del Ecuador, 6, Madrid 16.

Business Aid

While any deluxe hotel is equipped to help line up secretarial services (the Palace Hotel, for example, has such services available in English, French and German and three telexes for business use), advance planning is sometimes useful. If you are considering Madrid as a site for a conference or convention, there are a number of organizations that can help make the arrangements for you. One is Central de Congresos, Avenida General Perón, 26 piso 2°, (2nd floor) Madrid 20, c/o Sr. D. Julio Abreu, Director General. There is a list of 12 others that may be obtained by writing: CISET (Circulares Informativos de la Secretaria de Estado de Turismo), Sección de Información Turistica, Alcalá, 44, Madrid 14.

Sports

Football (Soccer)

Futbol is the most popular spectator sport in Madrid, in fact in all of Spain. The season runs from September to June. There is usually a game played every Sunday in Madrid, as the city has two teams. The *Real Madrid* team plays in the Santiago Bernabeu station on Avenida del Generalisimo. The *Atletico de Madrid* team plays in the Vicente Calderón Stadium, Paseo de los Melancolicos. Matches usually begin at 5 P.M. Tickets can be bought at the stadium or through your hotel concierge. The cost is 500–2,500 pts., depending on the location and seating.

Bullfights

The season runs from March to October, the day is Sunday, the time is 5 or 7 P.M. The best *corridas*—with the top matadors and bulls—are held during the San Isidro Festival from May 15th to 31st. It is very difficult to get tickets during this time except at scalpers' prices. Normally, tickets run from 55 to 855 pts. for seats in the sun, 85 to 1,025 pts. for *sol y sombra* seats (half-sun, half-shade) and 110–1,420 pts. for seats totally in the shade. Tickets can be bought at the *plaza de torro* itself, through your concierge or from the official box office at 3 Calle de la Victoria. If you are planning to attend your first bullfight, inquire if it is a *Novillada.* If so, we'd recommend skipping it. These are *corridas* with inexperienced matadors and over- or underaged bulls. The end result is often disastrous and will turn you instantly against what can be a sport of skill and beauty. There are two *plaza de torro* in Madrid: Plaza de Toros Monumental de las Ventas (largest and handiest) and Plaza de Toros de Vista Alegre (Carabanchel) located across the river.

Jai-alai

This Basque-originated sport is played at its fastest and most exciting in Spain. A super spectator sport, it's fun to bet on too. The time of play is 5:30 P.M. daily at the Fronton de Madrid, 10 Calle Doctor Cortezo.

Horse Racing

The modern track, El Hippódromo de la Zarzuela, in La Carretera de la Coruña, in season is usually crowded with enthusiasts whether it's for betting or just enjoying the excitement. There's no racing in summer.

Greyhound and Auto Racing

Greyhound racing, a traditional Madrid pastime, can be seen at the dog-racing tracks at 57 Via Carpetana. International auto racing—and there are some big competitions here—is held at the Jarama racecourse on Carretera de Burgos, 28 kilometers north of Madrid.

Participation Sports

There are good municipal facilities for many participation sports in Madrid. For example, you can play tennis on one of 15 all-weather courts at the Casa de Campo. You can jog on two well-marked circuits at Casa de Campo and El Retiro. You can swim in a number of public or hotel pools. If you want to bicycle, in addition to the parks, there's a closed-off section of the city streets, Calle Principe de Vergara between Alcalá and Maria de Molina, reserved for cyclists every Sunday between 9 A.M. and 3 P.M.

There is a very handy, all-purpose phone number—4623161—for sports information. This can provide you with a listing of the private clubs, prices, temporary memberships that are possible, where you can golf, ride horseback, hunt, fly, even ice skate. It's a useful number to carry along. Hunting and fishing can often be arranged through your concierge, especially at the four- and five-star hotels where such requests are not uncommon. A booklet called *Sports in Madrid* lists 35 sports federations in the city, such as wrestling, canoeing, archery, sailing, with addresses and phone numbers. It is available free from the Municipal Office of Tourist Information, 3 Plaza Mayor.

GETTING AROUND

By Car

Cars, the most obvious index of Spain's increasing prosperity, clog the streets of Madrid. Parking is a serious problem; signs marked with a big "P" (for parking) seem elusive just when you need them. The city government asserts that there are 43,757 parking places in designated facilities and garages. Good luck in finding them.

If you decide to park on the street in the central city (south of the east–west line from Calle de Cea through Maria de Molina), follow the rules or you'll be ticketed and fined.

If you park on these streets between 9 A.M. and 8 P.M. Mondays through Fridays or 9 A.M. and 2 P.M. Saturdays you will need to display inside your windshield a *tarjeta de estacionamiento.* These tickets are yellow for 30 minutes, green for 60 minutes and red for 1-1/2 hours (the maximum time possible) of parking in one spot. The tickets cost 20, 40 or 60 pts., respectively, and are bought at tobacco shops. They are popularly called *papeles de la hora*—papers of the hour.

You can drive around Madrid's wide boulevards and avenues easily. You'll find that many Madrid streets are one way. And you'll soon learn that Madrileños drive fast. You can also thrill to cutting in and out of the city's roundabouts, but you'll have a devil of a time driving in the old sections of the city, with their twisting, narrow streets.

There are many car rental agencies in Madrid. Atesa, Avis, Europcar, Hertz, Godfrey Davis, Inter-rent and others are all eager to serve you.

By Train

Madrid's public transportation system is modern, efficient and inexpensive.

The subway system consists of nine lines with interchange points. You can go the distance for 25 pts. in clean, safe, graffiti-less comfort. Look for *Metro* entrances. You can buy 10 tickets for 215 pts.

By Bus

There are two basic types of buses in Madrid—large blue or red buses and yellow microbuses. They cover many of the same routes, but you pay a premium (35 versus 30 pts.) for riding on the air-conditioned micros. At each bus stop is a pole with stylized route drawn to show the number of the bus and where it will stop; each bus carries a sign with its destination clearly printed.

When it is a driver-only bus, you enter through the front door; when there's a conductor as well, you enter through the rear door. You don't need exact change. Be sure to signal, wave and shout if necessary when you want to get off. Buses do not necessarily stop at designated stops unless signaled.

Though many routes run from about 6A.M. to midnight, some through routes continue all day and night. Plaza Cibeles is the key junction point for bus arrivals, departures and all-night service. There's an unobtrusive kiosk on the sidewalk in the middle of Paseo del Prado, almost in front of the Palace Hotel, where you can get a free bus map—*Plano de la Red*—and buy ten rides for 210 pts. There are no free transfers.

By Taxi

Madrid's white taxis with red stripes and the all-black ones are all licensed and metered. Drivers are usually honest. However, if the cabbie forgets to start the meter when you begin to move, ask him to turn it on. Often the driver will ask you for a supplemental amount beyond the meter figure. Is it legitimate? Yes. There are allowable surcharges for night, holiday, airport, train station and bullring trips, as well as for baggage. The driver will show you the printed surcharge chart if you insist. Cabs are still inexpensive.

There is one uncomfortable taxicab encounter that you can expect. It happens when you are going to the airport and ask the cabbie to take you to the bus terminal underneath the Plaza Colón so you can catch the airport bus and save some money. He may counter with an offer to take you to the airport for a flat rate (it should be 800–900 pts.). Or he may pretend ignorance of where Colón is. If he pulls this one, point it out on your map. If he still plays dumb, don't enter the cab, get another.

Rule of thumb for the airport ride: If there are two or more of you with luggage and the driver offers to take you for less than 900 pts.—*completo (no extras)* that's probably your best bet in terms of convenience and comfort. The airport bus tab is 100 pts. per passenger plus cab fare to Colón. The difference may not be worth the hassle.

Directory

The following are addresses and telephone numbers that may be of assistance during your Madrid stay, whether you need help or just a haircut.

U.S. Embassy, 75 Serrano (phone 2763600, 2763400)
British Embassy, 92 Avenida Pio XII (phone 7664329)
Canadian Embassy, 35 Núñez de Balboa (phone 2259119)

Madrid's Municipal Office of Tourist Information, 3 Plaza Mayor (phone 2664874). Hours: 10 A.M.–1:30 P.M.; closed Saturday afternoons and Sundays. For information in English, phone 2666609 or 2665477.

British–American Hospital, 1 Paseo de Juan XXIII (phone 2346700). An English-speaking doctor or nurse on duty 24 hours a day.
American Express, 2 Plaza de las Cortes (phone 222-1180).
Thomas Cook, 45 Banco Serrano (phone 2768837).
Ambulance service, call 2524394.
Police, call 091.

Places of Worship

Information about specific services in English (and other non-Spanish languages) may be obtained by calling 2419927. One of the most fashionable Catholic churches is San Jerónimo El Real, 4 Moreto (behind the Prado) (phone 2391537), but the Mass is celebrated in Spanish. For Catholic services in English, consider Las Calatravas, 25 Alcalá (phone 2218035); St. Francis Borja, 104 Serrano (phone 2750973); Our Lady of Consolation, Plaza Madre Molas (phone 2590217); and Convent Chapel, 165 Alfonso XIII (phone 2332032).

There is an Episcopal Anglican Church at 43 Nuñez de Balboa. (phone 2765109). Other denominations include British Bible Society, 133 Joaquín García Morato (phone 2545298); Immanuel Baptist Church, 4 Hernandez de Tejada (phone 4074347); German Lutheran Church, 6 Paseo de la Castellana (phone 2258045); Christian Science Society, 61 Alonso Cano, 1° (1st floor) (phone 2592135); Church of the Latter Day Saints, 135 Guzmán el Bueno (phone 2539120); Greek Orthodox Church, 12 Nicaragua (phone 4574085); and the Community Church of Madrid, 34 Padre Damián (phone 4422427). The Jewish synagogue is at 3 Balmes (phone 4459843 or 4459835).

Hairdressers

You can have satisfactory work done by the hairdressers in deluxe hotels such as the Palace or Ritz. Elizabeth Arden, 4 Plaza Independencia, is a familiar, reliable name. Chic Madrileños go to Duran, 11 Calle Velázquez (phone 2768817).

For men's barbers, again the choice may be a major hotel or the mainstay of Madrid fashion and reliability, Benitez, Calle Serrano (in front of Sears), a tradition with elite Madrileños.

Cleaners

Tintorería Olimpia, 106 Lagasca (phone 2752458).

Central Spain–Castile

To Spaniards, Madrid is the hub of the Castilian wheel. Good roads radiate like spokes from Madrid to a number of fascinating cities and towns nearby.

Near enough from Madrid for easy day trips—but it's sacrilegious to think of trying to compress so many treasures into so little time—are Toledo, Avila, Segovia and Cuenca, which form a circle, or wheel, around Madrid. Smaller spokes lead to El Escorial, Aranjuez and Chinchon, each one even more easily managed in a single day. Further afield are Salamanca, Valladolid and Burgos, with the possibility of side trips to Zamora, Tordesillas and Palencia.

See for yourself. Were we to recommend a route for the first-time traveler to Castile, we would suggest going south from Madrid to Toledo and following the rim of the wheel northwest to Avila, west to Salamanca, north to Zamora, Valladolid and Burgos, and then back down to Madrid. Cuenca to the southeast is a long day or overnight outing from Madrid. To avoid backtracking we would recommend a separate side trip to El Escorial and Segovia, both part of the "wheel" and both close to Madrid.

This "wheel" route would take a week of good sight-seeing

That's presuming you have the time—lack of which is the bane of tourists—to spend a night or two in each town.

An alternative plan would be to pick and choose a cluster of towns near one another and "do" them together—Avila, Segovia, El Escorial are obvious choices for such clustering if you are pinched for time.

A third plan would be to do certain towns on the way to other regions. If you plan to visit Santander and Santillana del Mar, Burgos is on a direct line north; if you are driving northwest to Santiago de Compostela, Salamanca, Valladolid and Zamora are easy possibilities; Toledo makes a natural overnight stop on the road south to Andalucia. Cuenca is an easy detour if you are driving to Valencía.

TOLEDO

When Domenicos Theotocopoulos arrived in Toledo, he expected it to be a short stop on the way to fame and glory at El Escorial. Things didn't work out that way.

"El Greco," as he quickly became known, did receive one commission from Philip II—for an altar piece in the king's church at El Escorial. But when Philip saw the work, he neither liked nor understood the strange new treatment, the strong colors, the elongated figures and dramatic compositions. He paid for the painting, but did not make it his altar piece and promptly ignored the artist. That was that.

Well, not exactly. El Greco remained in Toledo, and for the last 35 years of his life painted up a storm (sometimes literally, as in *Toledo in a Storm*). The Crete-born painter, who had studied with Titian, learned from Tintoretto and Michaelangelo in Rome and wandered the Mediterranean, brought it all together, so to speak, on an arid hilltop overlooking the Tagus River in Castile.

Cervantes called Toledo "that rocky gravity, glory of Spain, and light of her cities"

Inch by inch, street by street, Toledo probably has more treasures than any other city in Spain. If you can make just one trip from Madrid, let it be to Toledo. But let it be for more than the day-trip excursion of the tour buses. You need to spend at least one night to absorb the still-medieval feeling of the town. And you need to rise early and begin your round of sightseeing—at least to the most obvious places, El Greco's house, the cathedral, El Transito—before the crowds of tour-bus passengers make seeing anything very difficult.

Besides, it's impossible to cram almost 2,000 years of history into a single day. The impossible takes a little longer—two days at the absolute minimum.

*** Parador Nacional Conde de Orgaz. Sample the sopa de ajo (garlic soup) and roast lamb, regional specialties

What first will astonish you about Toledo is how harmonious it looks. No neon leaps out at you from the hilltop. No chrome-and-glass modern condominiums intrude on the skyline (you'll find them at the edge of town, outside the perimeter of the old city). Then you'll remember that the entire city is a National Monument that must be preserved, in amber as it were. New building—and there's plenty, as you'll discover winding your way around scaffolding and brick piles on labyrinthine streets—must conform on the outside to the look of the old, to the traditional terra-cotta tile roofs and brick or limestone exteriors.

If you drive around the edge of the town, cross the Tagus and follow the Parador signs, you will have your second astonishment. From the terrace of the Parador Nacional Conde de Orgaz (phone 221850 or 221858)—a good place for lunch or a drink—look across at the city. There it is, El Greco's own "View of Toledo," the same rugged promontory of rock into which houses have been lodged, the same magnificent profile against the sky. If you are there at the right time of day, mid-afternoon, even the colors are right, the same shadows and golden light bathing the stone.

**** View of Toledo from the Parador

El Greco Trail

** Hospital de la Caridad. Don't miss "San Ildefonso" above the altar

El Greco cut a wide swath through Toledo. Just following in his footsteps will keep you busy. Before you even reach town, you'll want to stop in *Illescas* to see the five Grecos in the small, unprepossessing convent church—Hospital de la Caridad. Several of the knock-outs are in the sacristy to the left of the altar (a magnificent *Coronation of the Virgin* and a *Nativity* in which you will see the infant from the novel perspective of a cow's horns in the manger).

Once in Toledo, your El Greco trail will transport you to the Church of Santo Tomé and one of the painter's masterpieces, *El Enterrio* (*The Burial of Count Orgaz*). It depicts a miracle in which the saintly knight, Count Orgaz, is being buried by St. Stephen and St. Augustine who have descended from Heaven for the occasion. A row of mourners in black with white ruffs at their necks watch. Their heads form a frieze across the picture. Above them we see the count being received in Heaven. The skill in which the artist joins the real and supernatural worlds is fascinating to behold. It is hard to pull yourself away. Hours: 10 A.M. to 1:30 P.M., 3:30 to 7 P.M.; closes at 4 in winter. Closed Holy Week and Corpus Christi.

But think of all that's left to be seen. There are more Grecos in the sacristy of the cathedral, including the *El Expolio* (*Stripping of Christ before the Crucifixion*), which was one of his first Toledo paintings and his most controversial. First, there was the matter of payment, to which the church fathers finally agreed. Then, there were "certain improprieties" that they wanted painted out—namely, the "Gentle Marys" in the lower part of the picture. It was deemed unseemly that women were present at such a scene. El Greco refused. Finally, under threat of imprisonment he agreed. By then the fire had gone out of the argument; somehow the Marys remain.

Then there are the 22 Grecos in the Museum of Santa Cruz (more about this remarkable museum in a minute); those in the 16th-century Hospital de Tavera (where you will also see a bizarre painting by José de Ribera of a bearded woman nursing a baby, based on a true episode); and, of course, the El Greco House and Museum with its 20 paintings (including the magnetic *View and Plan of Toledo*) and private chapel with a Mudejar ceiling encrusted with stars and other heavenly designs.

The Greco house shows what a prosperous 16th-century house was like. It is attractive from that point of view, with small, dark wood-paneled rooms, uneven floorboards that squeak, period furniture, a small rose garden and river vistas. Greco lived nearby—with the same view of the river—in 24 rooms of the Marqués de Villena's palace. The artist reportedly had a fine book collection of Greek and Latin first editions, of no small value at the time. The books, like the palace, are long gone. Hours: 10 A.M. to 2 P.M., 3:30 to 7 P.M.; closes at 6 P.M. in winter; closed Sunday and Monday afternoons.

History's Impact on Toledo Today

With El Greco, you have barely touched the surface of Toledo. What gives this ancient town such multi-layered texture is the interweaving of the cultures and civilizations that have dominated it. The Romans left Toledo its name—*Toletum.* The Visigoths left a lot, if one is to believe the Moorish chroniclers who waxed ecstatic over the treasures left behind in 712 when the Moorish army routed them. But most of what the Visigoths left was incorporated by the Moors in their own buildings (note the Visigothic capitals in the 10th-century mosque that later became the church of El Cristo de la Luz). What else the Visigoths left can be seen in columns, fragments and incised stones in the Visigoth Museum. This is installed in the San Román church, which in turn was a mosque—note the fine Arabic tower and arches.

The Moors were in Toledo four centuries (half the length of time they spent in the south). You'll see traces of their presence everywhere—in the use of brick, in the Arabic underpinnings of several churches, bridges and town gates (notably Puerta Vieja de Bisagra), even in the addiction to (and production of) *mazapán,* a Toledo trademark. Similar to marzipan, mazapán has a natural color with a slight browning of the top and is usually sold in the shape of a crescent with pine nuts or an almond on top. Try it at Santo Tomé, a tempting pastry shop in the Plaza Zocodover, Toledo's main square.

Most of Toledo's Moorish traces date from the period after the Moors left as rulers but remained as artisans, scholars and builders. Their architectural and decorative work during this period is called "Mudejar," signifying traditional Moorish work done by Moors under Christian rule. (To add to the confusion, "Mozarabic"—a term you'll encounter frequently in Spain—refers to Moorish *style,* but actually Christian-executed work.)

The Mudejar influence in Toledo is enormous; it was most productive between the 12th and 15th centuries when Moors, Jews and Christians worked side by side. You'll see examples of Mudejar work in the Christian churches of Santiago del Arrabal, San Vicente, Santo Tomé, El Cristo de la Vega, San Miguel and San Román (now the Visigoth Museum). Part of the pleasure of your Toledo wandering will be to find examples on your own—an arch here, a bit of brickwork there.

What you're most likely to see is an overlay of cultures, such as El Cristo de la Luz, which we've mentioned, a tiny gem with Visigothic, Moorish and Romanesque elements. Hours: open all times. El Tránsito, a 14th-century synagogue, is elaborately decorated in Mudejar designs with Hebrew wall inscriptions praising King Peter I (Pedro the Cruel) and Samuel Ha-Leví, who was the king's treasurer and the synagogue's founder. Levi was later tortured & killed by his boss, and there are those who think the red-bearded Levi haunts the area where he once lived. (The El Greco house is on land that was once part of Levi's estate.) The synagogue became a church when the Jews were expelled from Spain in 1492. Attached to it is the Sephardic Museum with tombs, maps and memorabilia of the Jews in medieval Spain. Hours: 10 A.M. to 2 P.M., 3:30 to 7 P.M.; closes at 6 P.M. in winter.

Another synagogue-to-church-back-to-synagogue is Santa Maria la Blanca Synagogue, which had still other transitions—to an asylum for women, a barracks and again a church. Now it is a museum, whose splendidly restored interior is a forest of beautiful Mudejar arches. Hours: 10 A.M. to 2 P.M.; 3:30 to 7 P.M.; closes at 6 P.M. in winter. You will find both synagogues, the only two remaining of more than a dozen, near each other: El Tránsito on the Calle de Samuel Leví, Santa Maria la Blanca on Calle de los Reyes Católicos in what was the old Jewish quarter or Juderia. If it's thirst-quenching time, you'll find Bar Sinai nearby on Reyes Católicos.

Also nearby is one of our favorite Toledo sights, the monastery of San Juan de los Reyes (St. John of the Kings). Ferdinand and Isabella had it built (or rather started, for construction took two centuries) as their burial place. You'll see their escutcheons and monograms all over the interior. (Royalty spent a lot of time planning their own deaths—the big production of their lives.) That was before the Catholic Monarchs conquered Granada and chose *it* for their tombs. We're partial to the Flamboyant Gothic bays in the cloister and the Mudejar vaulting on the upper floor. The chains attached to the facade of the church were taken off Christian prisoners of the Muslims when they were freed by Ferdinand and Isabella's reconquest. You'll see similar chains on church and cathedral walls elsewhere in Spain. Hours: 10 A.M. to 2 P.M., 3:30 to 7 P.M.; closes at 6 P.M. in winter.

No question, Toledo vibrates with history. In the restored 14th-century Fuensalida Palace, Charles V's queen, Isabel of Portugal, died while giving birth to her fourth child. In the Mudejar church of Santiago del Arrabal, St. Vincent Ferrer reportedly preached and so inflamed Christians to convert Jews, they flung those who refused conversion off nearby cliffs.

The center of Toledo life, scene of the daily *paseo,* is the Zocodover, which Cervantes (who was married and lived awhile in Esquivias, near Illescas) knew well (he supposedly stayed at the Pousada de la Sangre) and described in his book *Novelas Ejemplares.* Playwright Tirso de Molina called Toledo "the heart of Spain," in which case the Zocodover is the heart of the heart.

Bars, coffee houses and pastry shops surround the Zocodover

Just one block off the Zocodover is the Museum of Santa Cruz, so near, yet so often overlooked by visitors. The building itself (formerly a hospital) is a delight in the heavily ornamented Plateresque style, the work of Enrique de Egas (who did the Royal Chapel in Granada) and Alonso de Covarrubias (whose greatest triumph is the Toledo cathedral's Chapel of the New Kings).

*** Museum of Santa Cruz

Inside, in enormous halls (with coffered wood ceilings) formed in the shape of a cross, there is a remarkable collection of art and artifacts: paintings by Goya, Veronese, El Greco, Ribera; a splendid altar piece by Pedro Berruguete; primitive sculptures and paintings; 16th-century Flemish tapestries; a room full of Emperor Charles V memorabilia. There is a cloister attached. It is a marvelous caprice of Plateresque "embroidered" arches, which houses a small archaeological museum and a museum of tiles and ceramics. Hours 10 A.M. to 7 P.M.; closes at 6 P.M. in winter.

You'll see Don Juan of Austria's banner from the Battle of Lepanto here

We've saved the cathedral for almost last, though it will surely be one of your first stops. Long before *Juana la Loca* (the Mad) and Philip (The Fair) were proclaimed successors to the Spanish throne in great pomp in this splendid Gothic building, there had been a Visigothic church on the same site.

The cathedral began as a *French* Gothic building in 1227, but two and a half centuries later, when it was finished, it had become *Spanish,* with numerous Flamboyant and Plateresque touches. You will want time to examine the elaborately carved 15th- and 16th-century choir stalls; the Mozarabic chapel (beneath the dome) where a special Mozarabic liturgy is still performed; Covarrubias's Plateresque New Kings Chapel with tombs of Henry III and his wife, Catherine of Lancaster (daughter of John of Gaunt); the sacristy with paintings by El Greco, Titian, Van Dyck, Rubens and others. Hours for museum, Sacristy: 11 A.M. to 1:30 P.M., 3:30 to 6:30 P.M.; closes 5:30 P.M. in winter.

**** Toledo Cathedral. Behind the sanctuary, look for Tomé's Transparente sculptures

AVILA

Another spoke in the Castilian wheel is Avila, 112 kilometers (70 miles) northwest of Madrid and, at 1,200 meters (4,000 feet) above sea level, both the highest and the coolest city in Spain. Needless to say, it's a better place to visit in May than in December.

*** In warm weather, the walls are illuminated at night.

Avila's single most memorable sight is its city walls, unique in all Europe for their completeness. They are the oldest and best preserved in Spain; coming upon them from any direction, they are an incredibly dramatic sight.

Depending on the time of day, they look golden, grey, pink, or deep purple (in the late afternoon shadows).

Best view of the walls is from Cuatro Postes, a look-out on the road to Salamanca. Have a drink and enjoy the vista at the Hotel Cuatro Postes right at that spot.

When Count Raymond of Burgundy—who was in charge—ordered the walls built in 1090, the feat took only 9 years, rather brief a time, one would think, to encircle the city with walls one and a half miles long and ten feet thick and an average height of 40 feet.

Taken as a whole, the walls are a remarkable architectural achievement: 88 bastions and towers, nine gateways into town, incorporating (later in the 12th century) the apse of the cathedral, itself a major example of military architecture.

Enter the city through the Puerta de San Vicente, one of the oldest gates. But stop briefly just outside the walls to pay respects to San Vicente whose Basilica is on the right just before the gate. The church is ravishing, stretching transitionally from the Romanesque style of the 12th century when it was begun to the Gothic of the 14th century when it was completed.

The golden-hued sandstone church boasts two fine portals. The south one is called "Sin and Virtue" with the inevitable struggle between the two depicted in marvelous detailed sculptures on the cornice. On the west door is a portal reminiscent of the famous *Portico de la Gloria* in Santiago de Compostela. A 13th-century Romanesque work, it consists of a series of well-carved figures of apostles and saints, many of whom, alas, have had their noses knocked off and their faces marred.

Inside is the sarcophagus of San Vicente, Archbishop of Zaragoza, with concise, exquisite 13th century carvings on all four sides. The panels depict the martyrdom of San Vicente and his sisters, Sabina and Cristera, with graphic renderings of them stretched on the rack having their heads smashed with boulders. The church was built on the very spot where the saint is presumed to have died. Hours: 11 A.M. to 1 P.M., 4 to 6 P.M.

Once through the Puerta de San Vicente, a right turn will lead you to the cathedral, another transitional structure but more Gothic than Romanesque. Built right into the town wall, the cathedral seems squatly defiant. Its fortress-like quality is relieved somewhat by the graceful carvings on the portal. Note especially the stylized heads carved into the capitals of the columns.

Appearances are often deceiving in Spain. Inside the cathedral you will find much more delicacy than the outside would lead you to expect. Pedro Berruguete and Juan de Borgoña have painted a magnificent retable depicting events from Christ's life. Berruguete will be crossing your path frequently in Castile. He was a great Castilian painter of the late 15th century, heavily influenced by the Italian Renaissance style.

Behind the main chapel in Avila's cathedral is the fine, monumental Renaissance tomb by Vasco de la Zarza of one of Avila's leading lights, Bishop Alonso de Madrigal. The bishop, known as *"El Tostado"* because of his complexion, was a noted author and theologian and is shown writing. Sacristy and treasure hours: 10 A.M. to 1:30 P.M.; 3 to 7 P.M.; closes earlier in winter.

The real stamp put on Avila de los Caballeros, to give the town its full, rarely used name, was not by El Tostado but by a remarkable woman of the

16th century—Saint Teresa. Writer, reformer, founder of religious institutions throughout Spain, St. Teresa is best remembered as a mystic; she influenced the Catholic church for generations.

In Avila, you can follow St. Teresa's footsteps through a series of shrines: the site of her house, now the Convent of Santa Teresa; the Convent of *Nuestra Señora de Gracia,* where she was educated; the Convent of San Jóse (known also as the Convento de Las Madres), the first convent she founded, now a museum of her artifacts.

Avila had a second saint, a poet named *San Juan de la Cruz* (John of the Cross) who helped Saint Teresa in her work and became the first prior of the Barefoot Carmelites. In his attempts to reform his own Order, he was imprisoned by his superiors (who liked things as they were) and persecuted much of his life. His poetry reads fresh even now across the span of four centuries.

The mood changes somewhat outside the town walls at the Royal Convent of Santo Tomás, which was founded by Ferdinand and Isabella. Inside this Gothic monument there is much to see: a retable of the life of Santo Tomás (St. Thomas Aquinas) by Berruguete; three ornate, embroidered stone cloisters; an imposing alabaster tomb of Prince Juan, only son of *Los Reyes Católicos* (the Catholic Monarchs, as Ferdinand and Isabella were known), who died at age 19. The cloisters are richly decorated with the royal symbols, the yoke and arrows and the Spanish letters for them, "Y" and "F." The Y is for *yugo* (yoke), just as Isabella in medieval times was spelled Ysabella; the F is for *flechas* (arrows), the F of Ferdinand. The other symbol used extensively by the Catholic Monarchs was the pomegranate, which signified Granada. At the time Santo Tomás was being built, the Catholic Monarchs were preparing for their assault on Granada. There were royal quarters here, where Ferdinand and Isabella stayed (less frequently after the death of their son). Hours: 10 A.M. to 1 P.M., 4 to 8 P.M.; closed Sunday mornings.

SALAMANCA

Most of the Castilian towns, built as they originally were for protection, look like stage sets from the road.

Salamanca is no exception; in fact, it is more dramatic than most. Set alongside the Tormes River, it casts a silhouette of spires, domes and city walls against the sky.

The city may seem off the track today, unless you are on the way to Portugal or Santiago de Compostela in the northwest corner of Spain, but Hannibal didn't think so. He captured it from the Vettones. The Romans also found it useful as one of their stops on the Roman road from Merida to Zaragoza. The bridge they built is still in use. Visigoths and Moors passed through as well. The latter were driven out in 1055.

What really put Salamanca on the map, though, was when Alfonso IX of León founded a university here in 1230—the first on the Iberian Peninsula and the oldest of Salamanca's three universities. Under the scholarly Alfonso X (the Wise) the university prospered, and its schools of canon and civil law drew students from as far away as Paris and Bologna. Columbus lectured here on his discoveries. The Copernican system was taught here long before it had been accepted elsewhere. In 15th–18th-century Spain if you were serious about scholarship, Salamanca was the place to prove it.

Three names were heavily associated with the Salamanca of this Golden Age. You'll soon encounter all three as you make your rounds of the sights —of which there are enough to keep you busy for several days.

We are fondest of Fray Luis de León, a 16th-century theologian and poet, who was known throughout Spain for his brilliance. Somehow he got into trouble with the Inquisition and was imprisoned for almost 5 years without ever being told for what. When he was released, he returned to his classroom, stepped up to the lecturn and began his first lecture with: "As we were saying yesterday. . . ."

You'll see a bronze statue of Fray Luis in his Augustinian monk's robes in the tiny plaza—*Patio de las Escuelas*—that faces the ornate Plateresque facade of the university. Inside the university building is the chapel where Fray Luis's remains are kept and the austere classroom with the old wooden lecturn (*cátedra*) where he taught.

Pause a minute at the Renaissance facade to admire the rich ornamentation. Sacheverell Sitwell describes this facade as "a tapestry or needlework" —one of the finest specimens of Plateresque in Spain. The name "Plateresque" evolved from the extremely detailed chiseling of stone done by Spanish artisans on Italian Renaissance forms. The chiseling looked more like silver work—*platero*—than stone, hence the name. You'll find the style in many places in Spain, but it is at its richest in Salamanca.

Inside, the building itself *has* to be anticlimactic, but of interest are the Paraninfo Hall, a magnificent room of wood beamed ceilings and stone arches hung with eight Brussels tapestries and a Goya portrait of Charles IV and a grand staircase with delightful stone carvings all the way up, some with bullfight scenes, some with mildly bawdy village carryings-on. A plaque inside lists many of the University's famous students. They include Fray Bernardino de Sahagún, a Franciscan, born in 1499. He was a "missionary to New Spain til 1529"- died in Mexico City 1590. "He studied the language and culture of ancient Mexicans, and was father of Anthropology in the New World."

Fray Luis's Patio de las Escuelas (School Patio) is small and choice. As you face it, having just left the university building, you'll see a more modest Plateresque portal on the left, the rectory, where poet-philosopher Miguel de Unamuno lived until 1936 as rector. The *Escuelas Menores* (School of Minorites) at the far left has another excellent Plateresque portal. See the library inside and the Fernando Gallego painted *Sky of Salamanca* ceiling. Library hours: 9:30 A.M. to 1:30 P.M.; 10 A.M. to 1 P.M. on Sundays and holidays; in summer also 4 to 7 P.M., rest of year also 4 to 6 P.M. Next is the Alvarez Abarca House, the 15th-century home of the doctor of Isabella the Catholic. It is now the Belles Artes Museum with paintings from the 15th to 18th centuries and some interesting rooms—one with a colorful Mudejar ceiling.

Right around the corner from the university is one of Salamanca's other major monuments. Or perhaps we should say *are,* for we're speaking of the New and Old Cathedrals, one of which (the old—12th century) is enveloped by the other (the new—16th-going-on-18th century).

The other two names threaded through Salamanca's Golden Age (besides Fray Luis) are those of Churriguera and Quiñones—not single architects but entire families of architects. Among them they seem to have been responsible for most of the lavish ornamentation—during the 18th century—of Salamanca's many churches.

*** New Cathedral. El Cid's crucifix—"de las Batallas"—is hidden in the curlicues of angels in a Baroque retable

José Churriguera introduced the style that now bears his name in Spain—Churrigueresque—with twisted columns entwined with fruit, vines and other decorative elements. His brothers, Alberto and Joaquín, followed suit, along with sons and nephews. Andrés Garcia de Quiñones carried the excess even further, as did several other architects of the time.

Whether you like Churrigueresque or not is a matter of taste, but you'll see it to a fare-thee-well in Salamanca (along with almost every other type of Spanish architecture we might add). As local boys, the Churrigueras and Quiñones were especially productive here.

The New Cathedral, for example, spanned two and one-half centuries before it was completed. While many beautiful late Gothic elements are in play, you'll see the Churriguera hand in the ornate organ loft and baroque choir stalls, among the other decorative touches.

**** Old Cathedral

But wait until you step from the New into the Old Cathedral. The contrasts are astonishing. Now you are thrust back into another age, a Romanesque time of powerful primitive frescoes and sculptures. Look especially for the San Martin chapel (to the right of the entrance) with its brightly colored Romanesque frescoes; the Gothic chapel of Santa Barbara and the beautifully carved alabaster sepulchre of Bishop Diego de Anaya, surrounded by a fine grill in the Anaya chapel. There you'll also see one of the oldest organs in Europe (16th century) with Renaissance side panels and a gilded inlaid Mudejar front.

There's a great view of the cathedrals lighted at night, from the Parador across the river

In the Old Cathedral you will be riveted to the main altar with a wall-to-wall reredos consisting of 53 separate painted panels by 15th-century artist Nicolas Florentino. Each painting depicts a scene in the lives of Mary and Christ; each is separately framed by a gilded Gothic or rounded arch. Above the painted panels on the vault is a Last Judgment scene with the penitents in white on the lower left pleading to be admitted to Heaven and the naked damned on the lower right being banished by a stern Christ for eternity. Altogether, the dazzling panels and vault painting combine to make an extraordinarily powerful viewing experience. Hours: 9:30 A.M. to 1:30 P.M., 3 to 6 P.M.

After exhausting both yourself and the treasures of the Old Cathedral (don't forget the cloisters and Diocesan Museum with paintings by Fernando Gallego), head down the Rua Mayor, past the unique *Casa de las Conchas* (House of Shells) with 400 stone "scallop shells" carved on its 15th-century facade, to the Plaza Mayor. The shells may seem a caprice, but were the original owner's tribute to Santiago (St. James), whose symbol was the shell. The owner, Doctor Talavera Maldonado, was a knight of the Order of Santiago. Hours: temporarily closed, consult local tourism office.

*** Plaza Mayor

In the Plaza Mayor, a monumental open square, largely the triumph of the Churriguera brothers, you can sit at one of the many sidewalk cafés, sip a glass of *vino* and contemplate their achievements. There are no cars allowed, so your sight lines are unimpeded. Four-story buildings completely surround the square, as in Madrid's Plaza Mayor, with arcades and balconies and 90 arches on Corinthian columns. A bust of Philip V who financed the building of the Plaza overlooks the proceedings from the facade of the Royal

Pavilion, just as the king himself must have in the days when horse races and bullfights were held here while 20,000 spectators cheered. Diagonally across from the graceful Royal Pavilion is its match, the *ayuntamiento,* or town hall, which Quiñones designed—an equally ornamented 18th-century masterpiece.

As you contemplate the elaborately decorated facades of houses, palaces and churches on street after street, think what the city must have been like before the French demolished the entire southwest section to fortify their position against the Duke of Wellington's attack in 1811. Napoleon's General Marmont, Wellington noted later, "destroyed 13 out of 25 convents and 20 out of 25 colleges." Impartial sources have confirmed that.

Among remaining buildings that you may want to look in on are the *Convento de San Esteban* (St. Stephen's) with an imposing Plateresque facade (hours: 9:30 A.M. to 1 P.M., 4 to 7 P.M.; closes at 6 P.M. in winter); *Colegio Fonseca,* also known as *Irlandeses* because for some years it was a training college for Irish priests (Spanish Renaissance patio, fine altar piece by Alonso Berruguete); *La Clérica,* Philip III's enormous baroque church (two lovely towers, dome and courtyard); Palace of Monterrey (16th-century Renaissance style, now owned by the Duke of Alba); and *House of the Dead* (Plateresque facade, mysterious title—no one quite knows why the nickname persists).

Sidetrips from Salamanca

Salamanca, its golden stone countenance gleaming in the sunlight, is not only dense with worthy things to see, but it makes a good focal point for several side excursions to nearby attractions.

Alba de Tormes

Take C-510 south about 17 kilometers (10 miles) and as you cross the Tormes River you'll be in *Alba de Tormes,* the little town where Saint Teresa of Avila died in 1582. You may wish to visit the Carmelite Convent to see (behind a grill) the cell and narrow deathbed where she spent her last days and her tomb in the main altar. If you fancy Romanesque art, you will be surprised and delighted by San Juan de Evangelista y de Baptiste, a small 12th-century church with a redone 18th-century interior. It possesses fine early polychromed Romanesque sculptures of saints. Iglesia Santiago, another 12th-century church, has a retable of note. There is also the castle keep, the last memory of the Duke of Alba's once large castle.

Buen Amor Castle

Just 21 kilometers (13½ miles) north of Salamanca, following the signs to a private road, you will find *Buen Amor Castle,* which was the base camp for the Catholic Monarchs when they were fighting for control of Castile. The castle was later given palatial amenities, including a Renaissance patio, when the Archbishop of Toledo, Alonso II, was prettying it up for his mistress.

ZAMORA

This westerly town of 52,000 people on the same Duero River that flows through northern Portugal isn't exactly on a direct road to Nowhere (it *is* on a direct line between León and Salamanca and just 50 kilometers from the Portuguese border), but it is somewhat off the route taken by most tourists. And that's a pity, especially if you lust after Romanesque architecture and are keen about antique tapestries. Zamora is rich in both.

If you find yourself in Zamora, a good stopping place is the *Parador Nacional Condes de Alba y Aliste,* a medieval palace converted into an excellent hotel. It is a handy starting point for walking all over town, and Zamora is just the place for walking.

Strolling through Zamora is like being in an open-air Romanesque museum. There are at least seven 11th–12th century churches in recognizably Romanesque condition and several others with Romanesque elements intact.

Prime destination, however, should be the cathedral, completed in 1175. It's small as cathedrals go, but choice, with a south portal well-organized in its elaborate decoration (it's called the Bishop's Door). Above is what has been identified as a Serbo–Byzantine cupola with four baby cupolas, all finished in overlapping, rounded stone shingles that resemble fish scales.

Note, amid the many fine early sculptures, a filagreed stone tomb; a *reredos* by Fernando Gallego; the carved wood choir stalls—a blend of the sacred and profane that characterized the work of the free-lance craftsman who did them, Rodrigo Alemán. Rodrigo, believed to be a southern German, left his imprint on choir stall bottoms (and backs) all over Spain. You'll find his most impudent work in Plasencia, but here he is now in Zamora, up to his old tricks.

All this is a prelude to the main attraction, the tapestries, which are exhibited in the upstairs of the cloister. There are two series. The oldest series, believed to be 15th-century Flemish, depicts scenes from the Trojan War. Originally there were 11, now there are four, not in sequence. The accumulation of detail and the clarity are stunning to behold: Battle scenes, dense with knights, horses, banners and shields are virtuoso performances, both in the concept and in the skill of the handwork. One tapestry is 8 meters (9 yards) long, a festival of flowing movement, color and design. Adding to the lyricism of each work is a woven inscription along the top in Chivalric Age French, with a second flow of writing in doggerel Latin woven along the bottom edge.

The second series of tapestries depicts the history of Tarquinius, king of ancient Rome. Hannibal and his elephants in the Alps are also alive & well in these tapestries. The figures and weaving are of a finer quality, suggesting a later, more developed period. Here black is a dominant color. The delicacy and precision of workmanship linger in the memory long after leaving the cloister. Hours: 10 A.M. to 1:30 P.M.

TORO AND TORDESILLAS

To go from Zamora to Valladolid, drive east on N-122, then veer northeast on N-620 and you'll roar right into town. But wait, there are two stops en route worth considering.

Toro

Toro comes first, a serene little hilltown with a renowned collegiate church —*Santa Maria la Mayor.* It is proud of its richly carved Gothic west portal, its delightful polychrome wood, Romanesque sculptures of saints inside and a painting by Fernando Gallego called *The Virgin of the Fly.* The picture is said to include the best portrait of Isabella the Catholic. Hours: ask at town hall.

Tordesillas

Further along the same road, is Tordesillas. This is the town where the Spanish and Portuguese divided up the "New World" between them (giving Spain all Latin America except Brazil) in the 1494 Treaty of Tordesillas. The Treaty division was known as the "Line of Demarcation." The palace is gone, but do visit the *Convent of Santa Clara* where Juana la Loca lay buried for 22 years before joining Philip and the Catholic Monarchs in the Royal Chapel in Granada. In a small Mudejar-style room (the *Capella Dorada*) Juana's compact, decorated wooden organ is kept, along with several 15th- and 16th-century clavichords and Romanesque statues. One clavichord has a lid with flute players painted on it—a charming work. The famous treaty between Spain and Portugal (see above) was signed here, and the church is well worth seeing for its gilded Mudejar ceiling frescoes (in the former throne room) 12th-century Romanesque cloister screen, Gothic arches and four finely sculpted alabaster tombs (note the intricately-carved stone clothing) of the Saldañas family who founded the chapel in which they lie. Hours: 9 A.M. to 1 P.M., 4 to 8 P.M.; winter, 3 to 7 P.M. A few miles south of Tordesillas at Medina del Campo is La Mota Castle, where Queen Isabella died and where Cesare Borgia was once imprisoned.

VALLADOLID

Just 96 kilometers (60 miles) from Zamora, 121 kilometers (75 miles) from Burgos and 191 kilometers (119 miles) from Madrid, Valladolid is convenient as a stopover no matter which way you're heading.

A word about sightseeing in Valladolid. If you drive into town, you'll be in turn startled, annoyed and confused by the maze of one-way streets and stream of traffic. Your best bet is to park your car as fast as possible and rely on your feet or, if need be, a taxi. The areas you'll want to visit are close together, and the town is much smaller than it appears at first (true of many provincial towns in Spain). But parking is a real problem, so relax and hoof it.

You will find many things of interest, but at the head of the list is the *National Museum of Polychrome Sculpture,* located in a remarkable 15th-century building, the San Gregorio College. The college was founded by Isabella the Catholic's confessor, Fray Alonso of Burgos (Bishop of Palencia), and its architectural style is the definitive Isabeline. In the patio is a flowery working of stone with arches filled in with fanciful and symbolic figures—angels, demons, flowers, thorns—all intricately carved. Along the top, above the arches of the patio, the regal yoke and arrows are carved. Above them gargoyles are perched ready to spring. The sculptor was probably a Dutchman, Gil de Siloé, who lived in Burgos and was a master of the Isabeline style.

As unusual as the building itself is, it's only the beginning. The collection of painted wooden sculpture is unique in Europe. Basically, it consists of more than 30 rooms (which are architectural gems in their own right) filled with religious sculptures (and a few paintings, one of which is a rare *Veronica's Veil* by Zurbarán that looks like a modern abstract work). Most of the sculptures are masterpieces created for specific churches. Over the years as churches were torn down or damaged in war or whatever, these pieces were collected.

The National Museum of Polychrome Sculpture is no clutter of jumbled-together sculptures, as you may expect in provincial museums. First, this is a *national* museum, and considerable attention and money have been lavished upon it. The result is a dramatic display, with much space used to highlight particular pieces and modern museum effects used to make these art works look as the artists created them but as they are rarely seen in dimly lit, dust-collecting niches in churches.

Naturally you'll see the main rooms (Nos. 1, 2 and 3) with remarkable retables by Alonso Berruguete (son of Pedro, and a leading 16th-century sculptor). But pay attention also to the carving on the two rows of dark wood choir stalls by Diego de Siloé (room No. 11); Juan de Juni's *Entombment of Christ,* with six anguished people burying Christ, whose bruised and ravaged face is so hauntingly real it almost hurts to look at (room No. 15); an 18th-century tableau of St. Michael the Archangel going after a fish-tailed devil with such vigor you can almost hear the devil shrieking "Ouch!". Pedro de Mena's *Mary Magdalen* is a stark, dolorous, moving work; and the ceilings—some Mudejar, one from an ancient Royal Palace in Valladolid, one 18th-century Portuguese baroque—are all uplifting (no pun intended) constructions (room Nos. 10, 12, 14, 18, 19, 20). Step out onto the balcony and drink in the loveliness of the Isabeline–Plateresque cloister. It is ornate and enjoyable on this second-floor level. Hours: 9 A.M. to 2 P.M. summer; rest of year 10 A.M. to 1:30 P.M., 4:30 to 6:30 P.M.; closed Sunday afternoons, holidays.

Outside, there are more visual delights in store. As you leave the museum, turn right. The very next building is the church of San Pablo, which began life as a 15th century monastery. Its facade, around the corner, takes our collective breath away no matter how many times we have seen it. Between twin, plain cream-colored stone towers is a facade so ornamented it looks like a larger-than-life retable. It was the work of Simon of Cologne in 1492, and will keep you riveted to the spot studying it for half an hour. Gothic Plateresque or Isabeline Gothic is what it's called, and you'll want to study each figure and tableau separately (binoculars help with the fourth and fifth tiers). Fortunately, it's a big square in front of the church with no one to crowd you, so on a clear day you can take forever. There are lions holding royal coats of arms, saints holding coats of arms at another level, crowns, saints, bishops and San Pablo (St. Paul) just above the door—the richness and variety both exhaust and thrill. While you are in the Plaza de San Pablo, notice the huge bronze statue of Philip II in breast plate and bare legs. He seems to be staring across at the very house where he was born. It is *Pimenteles Palace,* and functions as local army headquarters. It bears a plaque telling the date of Philip's birth (May 21, 1527) therein. If you can peek inside you'll see wood beamed ceilings, crystal chandeliers, and Moorish-style glass-and-metal lanterns over the staircase. Across the street and around the corner from it is the church of Las Angustias with one of Juan de Juni's finest carvings, the statue of *Virgen de los Cuchillos* (Our Lady of the Knives). Nearby is the cathedral, which began as the work of Juan de Herrera (who built El Escorial), but construction stretched into the 18th century and Alberto Churriguera put a baroque hand to it. It is still unfinished, but Herrera's interior is starkly impressive, as is the splendid altar piece by Juan de Juni (which was intended for Santa Maria Antigua but ended up in the cathedral). Hours: 9 A.M. to 2 P.M. summers; rest of year 10 A.M. to 1:30 P.M., 4:30 to 6:30 P.M.; closed Sundays, holiday afternoons.

That leaves, among numerous palaces and other churches, Christopher Columbus's last house. There's not much of a personal nature here—a few etchings of him, a map of his four voyages, a huge totem from Colombia and other Latin American artifacts. Hours: 11 A.M. to 2 P.M., 4 to 7 P.M.; holidays 11 A.M. to 1 P.M. Across the street from Columbus's house is the Church of Magdalena, with possibly the world's largest escutcheon—three-stories-high—of the Bishop who founded the church—a lesson in hubris for all to see.

Cervantes's house, a two-story 17th-century brick building with a garden that should be prettily restored by the time you get there, is a nicely furnished example of a modest house of the period. Dark wood paneling, terra cotta tile floors, and a rounded, concave *bovadilla* ceiling highlight furniture of the time—a canopied bed, desk, Moorish brazier on the floor, and a traveling chest. It may not be totally Cervantes (he was both peripatetic and poor), but it looks as though it *should* be. Hours: 10 A.M. to 6 P.M.; Sundays and holidays 10 A.M. to 3 P.M.; closed Mondays.

Within a short walk of the Plaza Mayor there are numerous sights worth your attention; one is the Gothic Church of Santa Maria la Antigua with a rather fine high Romanesque tower. For an after-lunch constitutional, a walk along Paseo de España through the park will lead you to the door of the Convento de los Filipinos (Convent of the Order of the Philippines). Here you'll find a Museum of Oriental Art, with 13 rooms full of Chinese bronzes, sculpture, coins and jade, as well as ethnic Philippine *objets*—musical instruments, armor, baskets and sculpture from tribal areas.

BURGOS

The road N-620 from Valladolid to Burgos is a pretty one, especially in springtime when it is lined with bursts of golden broom and wild poppies carpet the fields beyond. At 44 kilometers (27 miles) from Valladolid, there's a turnoff to Palencia. We recommend this 10-kilometer detour for one major reason: a late Gothic cathedral that is virtually a museum of 16th-century Spanish art.

Palencia

Palencia is essentially just a long ribbon of a town. One of the endless surprises of Spain is that a town like Palencia, with a population of 63,500, that has lived and thrived on the coal mining industry of the Cantabrian

Mountains to the north and the grain fields to the south, should be a repository of so many artistic treasures.

Palencia's Cathedral of San Antolin, recently scrubbed back to its original all-white stone, has a long history. Back in the 7th century a chapel was built on the site to honor San Antolin, whom the Visigoths first killed and then, in a paroxysm of remorse, turned into a martyr and hero. The chapel went to weeds during the Moorish occupation. It was Sancho the Great of Navarra, they say, who stumbled upon it while chasing a boar. In 1034 Sancho built a Romanesque chapel over the ruins. You'll see this in the crypt today. In front of the Visigothic section of the crypt is a pool of water. In it you can see reflected the star-decorated Visigothic capitals (which aren't visible-they're too high—when you're looking at the columns head-on). Eerie, fascinating.

Everywhere you look inside this amazing cathedral there are visual feasts: an ornamented screen separating the choir stalls from the main altar; an organ decorated with a fantasy of turbaned musicians and cherubs; a heavily "embroidered" stone Plateresque screen on the other side of the choir stalls. The main altar retable is an extraordinary work consisting of 12 paintings interlaced with 26 gilded and polychromed sculptures, dominated by a dolorous crucified Christ (the work of Juan de Valmaseda) at the top.

That's for starters. A sacristan lights each chapel so you can see the intricate detail in the myriad paintings and sculptures. He then leads you to the museum and cloister where there's another banquet: Romanesque and Gothic paintings; 15th century Flemish tapestries; and a triptych by Pedro Berruguete. A tableau by Felipe Bigarny of Christ's removal from the cross has a distraught Mary that is unusually touching. This is just a partial inventory of the riches here. The guide saves the most unusual for last: a tiny, elongated portrait of Emperor Charles V by Lucas Cranach that is an optical trick. Viewed straight on, you can't make head or tail of the painting on a thin sliver of a wood panel. It's like a fun house mirror—distorted. But if you view it from the side, it's a real portrait, beard and all. Hours: 10 A.M. to 1 P.M., 4 to 6:30 P.M.

Burgos: El Cid's Hometown

In Burgos, as in most Castilian towns, the faster you lock up and leave your car, the faster you come to grips with the town. A heavy flow of traffic, a maze of one-way streets, a sense of confusion—all this can be quickly forgotten with map in hand and comfortable shoes on feet.

Burgos: Three Main Sights

The Cathedral

Burgos has three main sights, two of which are located just outside town. In town, the cathedral dominates all else. And why not? It's the third largest in Spain (behind the ones in Toledo and Sevilla) and one of the definitive statements of Spanish Gothic. Begun in the 14th century, it took over a century to build and very cleverly utilizes a sloping terrain with a series of small closes or enclosures.

We call your attention to El Cid's grave in the floor of the main aisle. A trunk of his is suspended on the left-hand wall in the sacristy. In the chapter-house, the room beyond, is an arresting two-sided diptych by van Eyck with a graphic rendition of Christ being nailed to the cross and having the crown of thorns hammered into his head.

The most grandiose work is probably the resplendant Constable's Chapel, designed by Simon of Cologne in the Isabeline style. Sculptures of the Constable of Castile, Hernández de Velasco, and his wife can be found atop their carved Carrara marble tombs, sleeping peacefully, their double chins preserved for all posterity.

As a change of pace, be sure to check out the backs of the inlaid wood choir stalls near the main altar. The mischievous wooden satyrs and naughty cupids peeing into fountains strike an amusingly incongruous note in the midst of such solemnity. Hours: 9 A.M. to 1 P.M., 3 to 7 P.M. in summer; shorter hours rest of year.

One usually enters the cathedral from the Plaza de Santa Maria, facing the finely fret-worked spires of John of Cologne. When you leave through the Sarmental Portal on the right, you'll find yourself in the Plaza del Rey San Fernando. Turn back to admire the well-preserved carvings above the portal, with Christ seated and giving his blessing while an angel hovers to his right and a bird to his left.

You may want to take note of Casa de los Condestables de Castilla, also known as Casa del Cordón, on Calle de la Puebla, for the huge stone cords on the facade resembling a monk's knotted cord. As a 15th century constables' palace, it is notable for its flamboyant Gothic facade alone, but is of special interest as the palace where the Catholic Monarchs received Columbus on April 23, 1497, on his return from his second voyage. In the same *casa* Juana la Loca's husband, Philip The Fair died suddenly after playing a game of pelota.

Before heading for Burgos' two other major sights, pause to admire the Santa Maria Arch, a free-standing gateway that once had city walls attached. The arch, just opposite a bridge, dates from the 14th century, though the statues of Emperor Charles V, El Cid and others took up their vigilant postures two centuries later.

Las Huelgas Reales

Las Huelgas Reales (Royal Leisure Hours) Convent is a short 1.5 kilometers (1 mile) west from Burgos. It began life as a summer palace for Castilian kings. In 1180 Alfonso VIII's wife, Eleanor (whose father was Henry II of England), turned the place into a convent for high-born Cistercians, nuns of the nobility. The abbess was so regal and powerful that it was once said: "If the Pope were to marry, he would need look no lower than the Abbess of Las Huelgas." Obviously her credentials were in order.

The plain, simple-lined grey stone facade is a Cistercian landmark. But it certainly bears no hint of the variety of riches kept within. To see them, you pay a small fee, then wait for a guide to lead the way. A tour theoretically takes an hour—and indeed it easily could, depending on the temperament of the guide. Our last visit may have set a record—35 minutes, click, click, room after room, through the Gothic cloister with its fragments of Mudejar stucco vaulting (the peacock panel is most delicate and complete), in and out of the lovely Romanesque cloister with the fountain in the center and the inlaid pavement. *"Vamos, vamos,"* insisted our guide, and so we went, meek as lambs.

Linger, if you are allowed, in the Materials Museum, a long room with 12th- and 13th-century memories. There is a fragment of a gown of foundress Eleanor's—with a castle shield on it. There is also her coffin cover—delicate white brocade with gold dots and beige crosses woven into it. You will see all kinds of 800-year-old fabrics. It boggles the mind.

In the oldest part of the building, off the Romanesque cloister, are rooms of Alfonso VIII's, decorated Moorish style. Beyond the chapel, with its brick Arabic arches and wall designs, is another room with a Mudejar ceiling in red, gold and brown and, in the corner, a curious statue of Santiago (St. James) with a sword in his articulated arms. Legend has it that he dubbed as knights those whose pedigree passed muster. Only those of royal blood need apply. Hours: 11 A.M. to 2 P.M., 4 to 6 P.M.

Cartuja de Miraflores

On the other side of Burgos, 4 kilometers (2½ miles) east of town, is another royal legacy. The *Cartuja de Miraflores* (Miraflores Carthusian Monastery) is a somber, austerely simple building that shelters a rich collection of art.

The centerpieces of the *Cartuja* are two exuberantly carved stone tombs, the works of the late 15th-century Flemish sculptor, Gil de Siloé. The subjects of the tombs are King John II (Isabella the Catholic's father) and Isabel of Portugal (his second wife). It was King John who made the gift of the monastery to the Carthusians, with the idea of a pantheon for himself and his wife probably lurking somewhere in the back of his mind. Presto, 12 years later he needed it, but by the time his daughter got around to commissioning a sculptor to make a tomb, it was 44 years after his death. The result is full-fledged Isabeline Gothic by a master. John looks at peace, as does his unsmiling wife. Notice the vitality of the other figures carved on their bower-like tombs, and the lions at the king's feet. Hours: 10:15 A.M. to 3 P.M., 4 to 7 P.M.; Sundays 11:15 A.M. to 12:30 P.M.; holidays 1 to 3, 4 to 7 P.M.

CUENCA

At the end of the southeasternmost spoke of the Madrid wheel is Cuenca. Approximately 167 kilometers (104 miles) from Madrid (on N-111, then at Tarancon left, or east, on N-400), Cuenca is approached through a lunar landscape. It is on the edge of La Mancha, and you can almost picture Don Quixote riding his horse Rocinante over the buff, rough-textured plains and sun-baked hills.

Casas Colgadas

What has put Cuenca on the map in recent years is the Museum of Spanish Abstract Art. The art in this collection, assembled and donated by Fernando Zóbel, one of the generation of "new wave," 1960s modern artists, is displayed in Cuenca's most historic buildings, the *Casas Colgadas* (or hanging houses). These three houses are joined together and perched on a rock. Their balconies are cantilevered and seem to float high (600 feet) above the Huécar, as they have since the 15th century. Their construction is considered unique in Europe for their time.

Inside the first two buildings are paintings and sculptures by internationally known Spanish artists such as Antonio Tápies, Antonio Saura, Luis Feito, Eduardo Chillida and Eusebio Sempere. The Casas Colgadas were in decay before the museum was developed in the mid-1960s (though they were once used as the town hall). In the renovating, plaster was peeled away to reveal an early Gothic stairway and arches and a primitive Gothic fresco. These finds have been kept and make interesting counterpoints to the stark white walls and bright and somber abstract art. Hours: 11 A.M. to 2 P.M., 4 to 6 P.M.; Saturdays 4 to 10 P.M.; closed Mondays and Saturday mornings.

The Cathedral

The Cathedral, in *Plaza Mayor,* the main square, is a Norman–Gothic–Romanesque building, eclectic outside but with several things worth popping in for—two El Greco paintings, a beautiful, bejeweled 14th-century Byzantine diptych and a series of delicate, ornate, even playful ironwork screens by 16th-century local artisan, Hernando de Areñas. The *Virgin del Sagrario* (Virgin of the Sanctuary) statue is the one hooked to Alfonso VIII's saddle when he liberated the town. Julian The Tranquil—Cuenca's patron saint—wasn't always so tranquil: during the 1936–39 Civil War his casket was dumped in the river. The remains were later retrieved and are now back in the cathedral. Treasury hours: 10 A.M. to 1:30 P.M., 4:30 to 7:30 P.M.; closes at 6:30 P.M. in fall and winter.

Around Town

The upper town is where a number of the Madrid artists (whose work can be seen in the museum) have summer homes in 17th-century houses. This section is full of winding streets and old buildings, many with grillwork done by Areñas four centuries ago. The colorful, mysterious stripes of blue paint around many of the white-washed houses are there because of an old belief: that they keep flies away. The old town's official lamp lighter was kept busy with the gas street lamps until just recently.

The lower town has moved more into the 20th century. But it has its moments too. As you walk down the hill through the old 18th-century gate, which is the town hall, you will eventually pass the mysterious Casa de las Rejas (House of the Grills), known more commonly as the House of Crime. No one is 100 percent sure what the crime was—it was all so long ago—but the most widely-circulated story is of the nobleman who killed his beautiful wife for infidelity. Whatever the offense, it was severe enough to have the coat of arms on the facade effaced. Some sculpture and a Renaissance cornerstone remain. There's a small Museo Arqueológico (Provincial Archeological Museum) at the bottom of the hill (on the Húecar's right bank) with coins, mosaics and ceramics.

For a pleasing side trip, follow the Júcar 35 kilometers (22 miles) to *Ciudad Encantada* (Enchanted City)—with amazing and eerie rock formations. En route is *Ventano del Diablo* (the devil's window)—a fantastic 1,500 foot drop through a cliff to the river bed. It is an astonishing sight.

ARANJUEZ

Go right onto superhighway A-4, south from Madrid and 64 kilometers (40 miles) away, and in just over an hour you will be in Aranjuez. If you are Spanish, it will probably be in late spring, just in time for the fresh white asparagus or the tiny wild strawberries.

Aranjuez is so conveniently located, with good train and bus connections, it is a very easy and enjoyable day or half-day excursion from Madrid. As such, it is a quick two-step back into the 18th century. The *Palacio Real* (Royal Palace) has had more than its share of royal fires—at least two serious ones (in 1660 and 1665)—but each time it was rebuilt as elegant as ever.

Spanish royalty have long enjoyed Aranjuez's location along the Tagus River. Ferdinand and Isabella contented themselves with a simpler summer residence, as did Charles V. Philip II ordered his Escorial architects to build a new palace at Aranjuez. It was the French Bourbons who enlarged, embellished and enjoyed it to the fullest, dreaming as they may have of far-away Versailles.

Historically, Aranjuez looms most vividly in Spanish history as the scene in March 1808 of an abdication. The unregal royal family of Charles IV and Maria Luisa (of the pursed lips in Goya paintings) was in Aranjuez packing to flee to America on the advice of their inept Prime Minister Manuel Godoy, when the mob struck. Angered at the Godoy-style "neutrality" that gave the French army free reign in Spain, Spaniards attacked Godoy's palace. Charles IV was forced to abdicate in favor of his son, Ferdinand VII. (It didn't do much good. Napoleon just made his brother Joseph king instead.)

The Royal Palace is a showcase, as you might expect, for fine period furniture, Louis XIV-style appointments, Brussels tapestries and rococo embellishments. Surprises include the *chinois* tiling of the Porcelain Saloon; the Arabian Saloon, a replay of the Hall of the Two Sisters in the Alhambra.

If ennui sets in at the mere thought of another royal residence, enjoy the many walks, the French type formal garden (Parterre), the delightful informal garden *Jardin de la Isla* on a manmade island in the river; and the parklike *Jardín del Príncipe* (Prince's Garden). The latter offers you the chance to see how royal "farmers" lived in the *Casa del Labrador* (Farmer's Cottage). It's just your usual humble "cottage" with such bibelots as green malachite chairs and table (from Czar Alexander III), billiard room, Pompeiian ceilings, embroidered silk hangings and solid mahogany doors. Hours: 10 A.M. to 1 P.M., 3 to 6:30 P.M. in summers; earlier closing rest of year.

Don't forget the strawberries. They're the world's best.

SEGOVIA, EL ESCORIAL

We've come full circle, or wheel, on our Castilian escapade, omitting several important sights that could be included on a Toledo–Avila–Madrid run or could be separate, individual day trips from Madrid.

We include them now, with the suggestion that taken all together they make an agreeable 2- or 3-day self-conducted "package tour."

Leave Madrid on N-V1, a superfast autopista that takes you most of the way to Segovia (just 88 kilometers or 55 miles from Madrid). You may wish to stop en route for a halfday visit to El Escorial and a peek at General Francisco Franco's *Valle de los Caidos* (Valley of the Fallen) memorial. Using Segovia as your base, you can visit La Granja and Rascafria and wander through the quaintly medieval village of Pedraza de la Sierra.

El Escorial

Spanish rulers paid great attention to how they died. And no one did so more than Philip II, who lavished 20 years on the building of El Escorial—the monastery, palace and his final resting place, the *Panteón de los Reyes* (Royal Pantheon) in the *Capilla Mayor.* The first architect, Juan Bautista de Toledo, died before the building was completed, and his assistant, Juan de Herrera, finished the job. But all the while Philip worried it into existence, too, poring over plans, altering this or that (much of the design should properly be credited to him), climbing over scaffolding to see what progress had been made since his last visit.

Philip's decision to build Escorial was based on a vow he made to San Lorenzo (Saint Lawrence) just before the Spanish troops launched an attack on the French at St. Quentin in Flanders. The attack was scheduled for the feast day of Saint Lawrence, August 10, 1557, so it was only natural that Philip prayed to Saint Lawrence: "Help us, and a monastery will be yours," or words to that effect. San Lorenzo had special meaning to Philip and to Spaniards in general. He was a martyr of the early Roman occupation of Spain, roasted on a grill.

Spaniard to Spaniard, San Lorenzo answered Philip's call. The Spanish forces beat the French, and Philip soon began building El Escorial (which means, literally, grill or gridiron which is how the complex looks from above). For a deeper understanding of Philip II, one of Spain's most complex and interesting monarchs, we recommend the late Garrett Mattingly's marvelously readable book, *The Armada.* To know Philip may not be to know Spain, but it helps. And it also gives you insight into the austere, forbidding El Escorial.

A single ticket admits you to seven sections of the vast complex. In the early 1950s when we saw it for the first time, a guide took us in hand and, like an old retainer poking into closets while the master was away, told anecdotes and showed us this and that. Times change. Nowadays you wait in a postcard and souvenir sales room until there is a sizeable enough group to march through in rapid lockstep behind an army sergeant-type guide.

There is much to see, and the inside is much more human scale than you would guess from the exterior. One would like to linger longer in the monk cell-size 2½ by 3 meter (8 by 10 feet) bedroom that Philip built for himself (and in which he died in 1598). Beyond his red canopied bed be sure you glimpse the Hieronymous Bosch triptych *Seven Deadly Sins.*

The Escorial offers a harvest of fine art. Fortunately, the guide leaves you in the gallery to wander through at your own speed, and you can savor Gerard David's *Descent from the Cross,* Velázquez's luminous *La Tunica de Jose,* various Titians, Tintorettos, Rubenses, Rembrandts, Veroneses, the wickedly satiric *Los Improprerios* by Bosch and dozens of other splendid pictures. Philip had an eye.

One painter he didn't have an eye for, though, was El Greco, and here you'll see the famous painting that was commissioned by the king but never hung. It's hung now, in all its haunting sobriety and acid yellow and blue tones —*The Martyrdom of St. Maurice and the Theban Legionary.* It tells the story of St. Maurice who offers to be executed in the place of another man who refused to offer sacrifices to the pagan gods. You'll find the painting in a position of honor on the ground floor. Hours: 10:30 A.M. to 1 P.M., 3:30 to 6:30 P.M. in summer; rest of year afternoon hours are 3 to 6 P.M. closed major holidays.

Segovia

From Escorial it's a beautiful drive north to Segovia through the Guadarramas. This is hunting and fishing country, and weekending Madrileños make the most of it in season. There are sweeping vistas on both sides of the highway and clumps of vibrant yellow gorse dotted through the pines.

Roman Aqueduct

Segovia has sights to make larger towns weep with envy. First, and it alone is enough to make the trip for, is the Roman aqueduct. This monumental grey stone structure, made of huge dressed boulders, carefully fit together without cement, dates back to the 1st and 2nd centuries and was in constant use until a few decades ago. Its 148 arches are over 9 meters (30 feet) high and stretch half a mile across the valley linking two distant hills. In the Plaza del Azoguejo at the center of town, the aqueduct rises to a height of 29 meters (96 feet). Statistics don't begin to convey the drama of it. Considered the finest Roman structure left in Spain, it casts a shadow literally and figuratively over the entire town. A timeless sculpture on the horizon.

Alcázar

Segovia's location in the stirring Guadarramas must have inspired past builders. High on a hilltop overlooking the town stands another substantial building —the Alcázar, a golden stone fortress with slate roofs, turrets and towers straight out of the *Arabian Nights.* "Disneyland," sniffs our resident Spanish skeptic, critical of restorations undertaken in the 19th century.

We disagree. If the Alcázar is not Arabic, it is what later Christians thought a Moorish castle *should* be. The Moors ruled Segovia for 200 years, *más o menos,* from the 8th to the 10th century. There wasn't much left of their fortress except its name and foundation. The 13th-century Christians co-opted both and combined Moorish and Gothic elements using the wall structure of the original building. After a fire gutted the building in 1862, it was rebuilt with its current romantic profile and turrets.

For one of the best views of the Alcázar we suggest crossing the Eresma River and looking up at its fairytale towers from the Knights Templar 12th-century Romanesque church of Vera Cruz (a 12-sided gem itself).

Once inside the Alcázar the views outward are spectacular, especially if you climb all the way to the top of the crenellated Mudejar tower. In 1474 Isabella was named Queen of Castile here, and the furnishings of the throne room and various halls and chambers are decorated as sparsely and handsomely as they might have been then. There is a royal chapel with a splendid wood Mudejar ceiling inlaid with "stars" and a Hall of Armor with a considerable display of firepower—guns, cannons, spears, armor and the like. Hours: 10 A.M. to 7 P.M.; closes at 6 P.M. in winter.

Cathedral

Segovia's third major sight is the graceful cathedral, the last Gothic cathedral built in Spain (16th century). You'll discover a lifesize *Burial of Christ* by Juan de Juni and a quintessentially baroque chapel of the Sagrario by José Churriguera. Hours: 9 A.M. to 7 P.M. summers; holidays, and October to April 9 A.M. to 6 P.M.; winters 9 A.M. to 1 P.M., 3 to 6 P.M.

Stroll through Segovia

With three such sights as the aqueduct, Alcázar and cathedral, it's not surprising that Segovia's many other charms are overshadowed. Yet a walk through the twisted, curving medieval streets of town is richly rewarding. There are some superb Romanesque churches to be enjoyed (San Millan, San Esteban, San Lorenzo, San Justo). There is a synagogue-turned-church (Corpus Christi) and an old Jewish quarter. There are palaces and manor houses such as the prickly, bumpy-walled Casa de los Picos, as well as numerous delightful little plazas—discoveries to be made around many a corner. As you stroll, notice the pastel pink, avocado and baby blue buildings with decorative squares or designs incised into their facades—a Moorish legacy that gives Segovia a unique look.

It's a short 11 kilometer (7 miles) spin out to *La Granja* (farm) *de San Ildefonso,* a *petit palais* built by Philip V to remind him of his French roots. The palace is supremely Frenchified. Many visitors driving up the chestnut tree-bordered carriageway simply park and tour the gardens. The big treats here are the fountains, dozens and dozens of them (as many as 42) at many tiered levels of the hedge-lined, blossoming tree-lined walkways. Three times a year all stops are pulled, and anyone lucky enough to be around enjoys a display of hydrotechnics that is unforgettable: spurts, spirals, cascades, sprays, multileveled waterfalls. Water, water everywhere. Hours: 10 A.M. to 1:30 P.M., 3 to 6:30 P.M.; closes at 6 P.M. fall and winter.

Inside Information

Hotels

For prices, see Madrid, page 50.

★★★★★ **FIVE STARS**

★★★★★ **1. PARADOR NACIONAL DE SEGOVIA**
Carretera to Valladolid; phone 415090. A new departure for a government-run parador, this dramatic newcomer (1978) is built in tiers on a hillside, more like a super luxury hotel but at giveaway prices. Imagine: Stunning public rooms (lobby, bar, lounges) on different levels; handsome modern furniture and paintings; plantings—trees and hanging plants; swooping overhead beams; fireplaces, skylights, floor-to-ceiling picture windows with wide-angle views of Segovia across the valley. Add both indoor and outdoor heated swimming pools, exercise room, sauna, gardens, snack bar, elegant restaurant plus color-coordinated guest rooms with comfortable modern wood furniture, sliding glass doors to private balconies with the same fantastic view of the city. Every room with a view. Even without Segovia across the way, this would be a great vacation choice. Only drawback: Car or taxi is needed to reach the city (has large parking lot). 80 rooms. *Inexpensive.*

*** Restaurant here

★★★★★ **2. LANDA PALACE**
Carretera to Madrid, km 236, Burgos; phone 206343. The cavernous lobby of this air-conditioned, all-comforts luxury hotel is part of the squat, stone dungeon tower of a medieval palace. Jesus Landa incorporated it into a hotel that has every room and service feature you'd expect of one of the deluxe Relais et Chateaux members. Also attractive garden, nearby swimming pool, ample parking, and adjoining a theatrically decorated restaurant. Located on a highway outside the city. 39 rooms. *Moderate.*

★★★★ **FOUR STARS**

★★★★ **1. HOSTAL DEL CARDENAL**
Plazoleta de Alfonso VI, Toledo; phone 220862. You can't get a more romantic ambience than this, our favorite Toledo hideaway built into the city walls next to the 9th-century gate through which El Cid and Alfonso VI triumphantly entered after defeating the Moors. An 18th-century archbishop's palace built around a garden courtyard reminiscent of Granada with 27 simple rooms with whitewashed walls, tile floors, antique carved wood furniture, handwoven bedspreads and drapes, but also baths, lights, telephones. Some rooms have anterooms or balconies with views over the city walls; others look out on tiny fountains, patios or the garden. Attached is a restaurant in the same style, built and managed by Botín's of Madrid. A delightful, unique oasis with a large parking area. Only drawback: many stairs, no elevator. *Inexpensive.*

*** Restaurant here

★★★★ 2. SANTA MARIA DEL PAULAR

Roscofría (95 kilometers from Madrid); phone 8693200. In the foothills of Navacerrada Mountains, this modern hotel has been installed in a monastery that dates back to the 1300s. Air-conditioned from top to bottom, the hotel has a Castilian-style lounge and bar. Rooms are elegantly simple—linen sheets, Spanish provincial furniture, wrought-iron light fixtures—also with direct-dial phones, radio, color TV. There are views of the ancient patio or pine woods and mountains. New amenities: heated pool, tennis, winter sports and parklike grounds. 62 rooms. *Moderate.*

★★★★ 3. PARADOR NACIONAL DE CHINCHÓN

1 Avenida Generalisímo, Chinchón; phone 8940836. It took ten years to restore this old convent, which opened its doors as a parador in 1982, but the results are dazzling: red-brick walls hung with modern tapestries; alcoves with naive religious paintings; a lovely dining room (***) overlooking a terrace, with views of a hilltop castle; swimming pool; many gardens. All 38 rooms handsomely tile-edged, well furnished. *Inexpensive.*

★★★★ 4. PARADOR NACIONAL DE ALMAGRO

Ronda de San Francisco, Almagro; phone 860100. One of our favorites, this enormous former monastery is built around various delightful patios and gardens. Amenities include swimming pools, cloisters, fountains; excellent three-star restaurant; cosy lounge with fireplace; *bodega*-bar; charming paintings and tapestries throughout. 55 rooms, simply but handsomely furnished. *Inexpensive.*

★★★★ 5. PARADOR NACIONAL CONDES DE ALBA Y ALISTE

Plaza de Cánovas, Zamora; phone 988/514497. This Renaissance palace has carved stone arches and portals, timbered ceilings, graceful double-deck arcaded patio, 16th-century tapestry and armor-suited "knight" on the staircase. It also has a garage, swimming pool, bar-lounge and restaurant. 19 comfortable rooms. *Inexpensive.*

★★★★ 6. PARADOR NACIONAL DE SALAMANCA

2 Teso de la Feria (Carretera de Cáceres), Salamanca; phone 228700. One of Spain's newer paradors (1981) is a dramatic, starkly modern structure across the river from the city. Guest rooms are attractive with coordinated rattan furnishings, natural pine floors, "Hollywood" baths, sliding glass doors to large individual terraces with splendid views of Salamanca (romantic at night when the city is illuminated). Air-conditioned throughout; elevator; pleasant restaurant. 67 rooms. *Inexpensive–Moderate.*

★★★★ 7. PALACIO VALDERRÁBANOS

9 Plaza de la Catedral, Avila; phone 211023. Once a bishop's palace, this 15th-century granite building has been a four-star hotel since 1971. It has all the 20th-century travelers' requisites—air conditioning, central heating, elevators, modern baths. Most rooms are furnished in Spanish provincial style with carved wood chests, beds and chairs, and handwoven rugs and bedspreads. Across from the cathedral, the hotel is ideally located for sightseeing. 73 rooms. *Inexpensive.*

★★★ THREE STARS

★★★ 1. OLID MELIÁ

10 Plaza San Miguel, Valladolid; phone 254200. This ten-story modern hotel near the Plaza Mayor is a handy (and popular) gathering place for local residents. Guest rooms are adequate in size and well designed with coordinated furnishings that include minibar, radio and direct-dial phone. There are writing and games rooms, a roomy lounge, a bar, garage, hairdresser and boutiques, air conditioning throughout. 250 rooms. *Inexpensive.*

★★★ 2. TORREMANGANA

9 San Ignacio de Loyola, Cuenca; phone 211906. This modern all-conveniences hotel at the edge of Cuenca makes a handy overnight stop. Good dining room (**), simple but comfortable rooms, pleasant lounges. 116 rooms. Attractive views. Parking. *Inexpensive.*

★★★ 3. PARADOR NACIONAL CONDE DE ORGAZ

Paseo de los Cigarrales, on the Circunvalación Carretera, Toledo; phone 221–850. Perched on "the Emperor's Hill" above the Tagus River, this modern brick building has an incomparable view of El Greco's city. The large lounge, bar, patio and restaurant (regional specialties) look out across the valley, as do some of the neat, comfortably furnished rooms. All are air-conditioned. There is a garage and ample parking. *Drawback:* Because of the distance from town, a car is a must. 58 rooms. *Moderate.*

★★★ 4. PARADOR NACIONAL RAIMUNDO DE BORGOÑA

16 Marqués de Canales and Chozas, Avila; phone 211340. This building was reconstructed early in this century, carefully preserving elements from the 15th-century palaces once on this site. Built into the city walls, with a lovely garden and steps leading up the parapet surrounding the city—great for nighttime viewing of the city or countryside. Beamed ceilings, Spanish provincial carved wood furnishings, modern baths and fixtures. Limited parking. 27 rooms. *Inexpensive.*

★★★ 5. PARADOR NACIONAL DE TORDESILLAS

Carretera N-620, 1 kilometer from Tordesillas; phone 770051. In the midst of a pine grove next to the highway is this motel-type parador. With its own swimming pool and garden, air conditioning throughout, a welcoming bar and lounge, attractive dining room decorated with handcrafts and tiles. Rooms are equipped with modern bathrooms and furnishings. Plenty of parking. 73 rooms. *Inexpensive.*

★★★ 6. GRAN HOTEL

Plaza del Poeta Iglesias, Salamanca; phone 213500. Located at the edge of the famous Plaza Mayor, this hotel is convenient to shopping and sightseeing areas. Air-conditioned, its comfortable rooms are furnished with desk, chairs, reading lights, minibar and direct-dial phones. The lounge and bar areas are roomy, light, nicely furnished. Its restaurant, Feudal, is well known locally and popular with visitors. Garden; garage for parking. Get a room away from busy, noisy plaza. 98 rooms. *Inexpensive.*

★★ TWO STARS

★★ 1. LAS SIRENAS

30 Juan Bravo, Segovia; phone 411897. An unpretentious, old-fashioned hostal–residencia on a quiet square handy to everything: shops, bars, restaurants, cathedral. Rooms are adequate, with quality furnishings, standard baths. Completely furnished and well-lighted lounges and bar areas. Air-conditioned. Parking is difficult. 39 rooms. *Bargain.*

★★ 2. ALFONSO VI

2 General Moscardó, Toledo; phone 222600. This well-located, reliable hotel has all the necessaries and amenities (except air conditioning) to keep you comfortable. 65 rooms. *Inexpensive.*

Restaurants

For prices, see Madrid, page 540.

★★★ THREE STARS

★★★ 1. HOSTAL DEL CARDENAL

Plazoleta de Alfonso VI (next to Bisagra Gate), Toledo; phone 220-862. Enter through the brick gate and Moorish garden, past the willow-shaded pool and fountains into the cool, tiled interior. Appetizers, desserts, fruit and cheese are arranged around a giant copper kettle overflowing with seasonal flowers on a central "well." The elaborate wood ceiling carries out the Moorish motif.

The restaurant is run by Botín's, the Madrid restaurant that has specialized in roast lamb and suckling pig for over 250 years. Those specialties, as well as veal, chicken and beef, are offered along with game in season. Especially memorable: partridge, either stewed or pickled; venison ragout, rich with chunks of deer, ham and mushrooms in a winey brown sauce; and wild boar in a dark, mildly sweet sauce with pureed turnips, artichokes and chestnuts on the side. Desserts include Toledo specialties *marquesitas*—tiny, paper-wrapped eggy cakes that melt in your *boca.* The wine list is extensive (perhaps a Paternina Gran Reserva 1920), including a house wine at 150 pts. *Moderate.*

★★★ 2. PARADOR NACIONAL VIRREY DE TOLEDO

1 Plaza del Palacio, Oropesa; phone 430000. At this beautiful old castle-parador, you'll find some of the very best regional food: game in season, chicken with walnuts, wild rabbit in wine, pigeon in pink peppercorn sauce, trout in tarragon sauce, wild mushrooms with salmon, almond mousse, *tarta del Beato.* Superb food enhanced by dining room vistas of *Sierra de Gredos* mountains. *Inexpensive.*

★★★ 3. SANTA MARIA DEL PAULAR—RESTAURANTE MESÓN TRASTA MARA

Rascafría; phone 8963200. The elegant modern dining room of this Entursa hotel in an ancient monastery is as pleasing to the eye as the palate. Windows look out on a cobblestoned patio.

Castilian regional dishes are well prepared: roast or grilled meats and poultry, *cocidos* (stews), soups (such as garlic) and *tortillas* (omelets). But try trout, fresh from the monastery pond; puff potatoes; baked sea bream; tomatoes stuffed with liver paté and, for dessert, almond ring filled with creamy egg custard.

There's a solid wine list, strongest in Riojas; as Entursa has suppliers who bottle especially for them, house brands are bargained priced for their quality. *Moderate.*

★★★ 4. MESÓN PANERO

1 Marina Escobar, Vallodolid; phone 221467. Closed Sunday nights. It is only a few steps downstairs to dining rooms with beamed ceilings from which hang colorful pitchers and garlands of garlic, peppers and chilis. Rooms are brightened by blue and white *azulejos* (tiles) on the walls, ladder back chairs and red tablecloths.

Here even simple beverages are served with a flourish, such as frosted globe glasses and an ice bucket for chilling beer bottles or cider. Chef Angel Cuadrado has an imaginative flair: Olives served as *tapas* are enhanced by wild thyme and onion; rabbit stew combines tomatoes, ham, mushrooms and olive oil; shrimp and mushrooms have a zingy garlic and hot pepper treatment; an appetizer of spinach is sauteed with pine nuts and raisins, and there are infinitely more.

Panero's features a special dish each day—Sunday it's *paella;* Monday *cocido Castellano* (Castilian stew); and so on. Service is fast, good natured and efficient. The wine list is lengthy and reasonable. (Try the red Rueda or Toro wines or the local Cigales.) *Moderate.*

★★★ 5. PARADOR NACIONAL DE SEGOVIA

Carretera to Valladolid; phone 415090. Choices, choices. In the stunning restaurant of this dramatic new hotel you can sit with a view of (a) a contemporary painting and trees; (b) the gleaming modern kitchen and grill; (c) a contemporary painting and guests cavorting in the swimming pool; (d) all of Segovia spread before you. Fortunately, the food measures up.

The menu offers classical Castilian dishes. *Cochinillo asado* and *perdiz* (roast suckling pig and partridge) are done with authority under the gaze of assembled diners in the open, airy hall. The parador offers several wines bottled especially for them; good quality at attractive prices. *Inexpensive.*

★★★ 6. MESÓN DE CANDIDO

5 Azoguejo, Segovia; phone 428102. "To visit Segovia without dining at Candido is not to visit Segovia at all," goes a saying about this historic, folkloric restaurant, now a certified national artistic monument.

Though the building has been next to the aqueduct since the 15th century, it's been a restaurant in this family's care "only" since 1860. Visitors—famous or anonymous (and everyone ends up at Candido's)—appreciate the hanging hams, fireplaces, decorative flowers and plates in the many small, whitewashed rooms with beamed ceilings. *Best bets:* Roast pig, lamb, veal, beef or chicken, game in season, garlic soup, trout (from Candido's own trout farm), fresh beans and strawberries in season. For dessert, the Segovian specialty *ponche* (punch), which is a marzipan–rum–egg yolk–

biscuit concoction. The house wine is a sturdy one from La Mancha, but Riojas and others are also available. *Expensive.*

★★ TWO STARS

★★ 1. MESÓN CASAS COLGAL

Canónigos; Cuenca; phone 211822. Closed Mondays. In these 500-year-old hanging houses, whitewashed walls and high, timbered ceilings plus sweeping views of the Castilian countryside make a rustic setting for well-prepared regional specialties.

Palate pleasers include fresh-caught Júcar River trout, partridge, quail, rabbit, lamb, beef and pork dishes. The rabbit paté is a winner. Regional wines, as well as Riojas are on the list. Try the Valdepeñas. *Moderate.*

★★ 2. PARADOR NACIONAL CONDE DE ORGAZ

Paseo de los Cigarrales, Carretera de Circunvalación, Toledo; phone 221850. Eating here is only half the fun. The awe-inspiring sight of El Greco's city across the Tagus may distract you from the cuisine. That would be a pity, for the Castilian specialties are well prepared and tasty. The *cochinillo* or *ternera asados* (roast suckling pig or lamb) and *cocidos* for instance. The parador wine list is also dependable, as is the *vino del casa. Inexpensive.*

★★ 3. PARADOR NACIONAL DE ALBA Y ALISTE

Plaza de Cánovas, Zamora: phone 514497. Zamorans like their food hearty and strongly seasoned. The kitchen here responds to the challenge, and you will find solid Castilian regional specialties with some Extremadura additions such as *caldereta de cordero* (spicy lamb stew), *jamon y embutidos* (ham and sausages), pheasant or partridge in red wine. Desserts include tasty fritters and *perunillas* (Extremaduran cookies) in addition to flan, goat cheese and fruit. Usual parador wine list. Usual parador bargain price for four-course menu. *Inexpensive.*

★★ 4. PALACIO DE VALDERRÁBANOS

Plaza de la Catedral, Avila phone 211023. Though the hotel is actually a 15th-century archibishop's palace, the kitchen and the dining room have been updated. The kitchen turns out toothsome fare, whether of regional specialties or continental dishes. The wine list is a good one (try a Cebreros), and pastries are appealing. *Expensive.*

★★ 5. MESÓN LA FRAGUA

10 Paseo Zorrilla Valladolid; phone 232008. Closed Sunday nights. Though the smithy is long gone, his forge is now an oven where roasting is done. As you enter, you'll see it beyond the busy bar. The menu features Castilian dishes, but includes international as well as other Spanish fare. Baked artichokes *gratineé,* lamb liver in whisky, sole *en brochette* are a few of the imaginative products of the kitchen. In addition, a wide selection of French and Spanish cheeses and dessert specialties such as flambéed strawberries or nuts with whipped cream. Among the wines of the region the white from Medina del Campo or the red from Toro is recommended. *Moderate.*

★ ONE STAR

★ 1. RESTAURANTE RIO DE LA PLATA

1 Plaza del Peso, Salamanca; phone 219005. Closed Mondays and July. Down half a dozen steps from street level is a lively bar (with good tapas) and tiny dining room. Both are packed with local patrons. The whitewashed walls are decorated with blue and white Manises plates. Portions are generous: Mushrooms sauteed with ham, garlic and parsley, an appetizer for one, can easily serve two. Try the rib of roast goat—tender, with crisp garlicky skin—and French fries; roast suckling pig; or quail spiced with rosemary and ham in casserole. Desserts are the usual flan and rice pudding. The wine list is adequate; try the red Cigalas. *Inexpensive.*

★ 2. MESÓN DEL CID

8 Plaza de Santa María, Burgos; phone 205–971. Closed Sunday nights and February. In these 15th-century walls were published, among other classics, *La Celestina* (the big hit of 1499) and *El Lazarillo de Tormes* (book of the year in 1554). Today this thriving restaurant draws patrons looking for new, daily first editions. Castilian roast and grilled meats and fowl are served here, augmented by Basque favorites such as trout and *bacalao* (dried cod), fried milk and local specialties such as Burgos cheese with honey and nuts. The wine list includes those of Navarra, Aragon and Rioja. A Ribera del Duero is suggested. *Inexpensive.*

★ 3. CASA DEL DUQUE

12 Cervantes, Segovia; phone 411–707. This may be the Mama Leone's of Segovia, if not Spain. Dionisio Duque's popular eatery is the "roast of the town." Since the 1890s the Duque family has specialized in roasting everything it could lay hands on, and it has proudly touted the *maestro asador* (master roaster) title awarded in 1895.

Today, in this *casa* that roasting built, you'll find walls cluttered with framed bank notes, awards, plates, pitchers and photos of patrons and family. When in Duque's, as the saying goes, order the *asados*—pork, lamb, chicken or veal. If it's the veal chop, you'll receive it garnished with pimento on a wood platter bearing a dagger to help you do battle. *Ponche Alcazar,* the local dessert, is a delight.

The grand finale, however, is best: Into a huge (25-centimeter or 10-inch diameter) brandy snifter with the house escutcheon on it your waiter pours hot water to heat the glass. He empties it, then from a porcelain flask pours enough brandy for double the number at your table. This is passed from diner to diner to finish the meal. *Moderate.*

★ 4. CASA DAMIÁN

9 Martinez de Azcoitia, Palencia phone 744-628. Closed Mondays and from July 25th to August 25th. This family establishment, founded in 1910, serves classic Castilian cuisine with interesting variations. Try the excellent planked fish, a different bean casserole each day, fresh fried hake and an old specialty, 12 vegetables with ham and veal, for which the restaurant is famous. Good cheese selection and Rioja and Castilian wines. *Inexpensive.*

Entertainment

There are many opportunities for attending theater, movies, concerts and dance in the region. However, these cities are too small to sustain regular "seasons" of opera or ballet such as you find in Barcelona or Madrid. Several special international festivals are held in various cities including:

Almagro. Classical theater Festival in Corral de Comedias; September.

Avila. International Festival of Polyphonic and Organ Music; July.

Burgos. International Music Week; August.

Cuenca. Festival of Religious Music; Holy Week.

Escorial. International Festival of Ancient Music in 18th century Royal theater; mid-summer.

Segovia. Festival of Chamber Music; July.

Valladolid. International Week of Films on Religious and Human Values; April.

The dates of these events often fluctuate from year to year. If you are interested in one or more, contact the nearest office of the National Tourist Office of Spain or the local tourist office in the town where the event will be held. (See Directory listings for addresses.)

Folkloric

Folkloric events are plentiful in Castile. Many center on religious observances, especially Christmas and Easter. Cuenca, Toledo and Valladolid are celebrated for the fervor and beauty of their *Semana Santa* (Holy Week) processions. Here are some other noteworthy events in the region.

Almagro. St. Bartholomew's Fair, August 24. District-wide festival and *feria.*

Avila. St. Teresa Week, October 8th–15th. *Verbenas* (evening and night carnivals), fun fairs, parades of club-headed giants through the streets, dancing, singing, merry making.

Fiestas de verano. (Summer festivals) July 17th–25th. Folk dancing, fireworks, poetry contest, bullfights, "Festivals of Spain" (typically theater, concerts, ballet and handicraft or art exhibitions).

Burgos. International Folk Festival around Feast day of St. Peter and St. Paul, June 29. Several days of festivities, bullfights, sports competitions, regional dancing, folkloric performances.

Cuenca. May or June. "Mayos," competition by round singers, folk dancers of *jotas, torras* and *seguidillas.*

Salamanca. At La Alberca (77 kilometers from Salamanca) August 15th–16th. Celebration of Assumption. People assemble in the Plaza Mayor wearing traditional costumes. Then mystery play, *Loa* is performed in front of the church.

Valladolid. "Festivals of Spain" with concerts, ballet, drama, opera, recitals. October–November.

Medina de Rioseco. (41 kilometers from Valladolid) has beautiful Maundy Thursday procession with floats and 16th- and 17th-century images carried along its Calle de la Rúa. The entire street has been declared a National Monument.

Segovia. Festival of St. John and St. Peter, June 24th–29th. Parades and dancing with giants and big-headed monsters, *verbenas,* fairs, bulls, cattle market, races, sports competitions.

Zamarramala. Fiestas de Santa Agueda (festivals of Sta. Agatha). Women take over the town for a day in traditional dress; a parade, "wheel dance" and running of the bulls are part of this ancient "women's lib" celebration. Takes place on Sunday closest to February 5th.

Shopping

Much of the shopping you may be tempted to do in Castile you can do quite as well in Madrid. Exceptions are handcrafts you may find serendipitously at a local fair or antiques which pop up surprisingly in odd places. The following are a few places to look should you feel the urge. They are listed alphabetically by town.

Cuenca

In *Cuenca* the best buys are in art, and the place to buy is at the *Museum of Spanish Abstract Art.* There is a small shop in the museum with original posters, graphics and art books. None of them are really cheap, but they *are* collectibles and represent good value. There are also a few antique shops in the upper town, at the edge of the Plaza Mayor, where you can buy old and not very old ceramic plates, as well as the popular ceramic Cuenca bull.

Segovia

An attractive art, handcraft and gift shop in Segovia is *Galería La Casa del Siglo XV,* 32 Calle Juan Bravo; it's a second-floor shop with one room full of modern art and a second room with contemporary gifts; a good selection.

Talavera

When it comes to ceramics, go to the source. The source, if you are attracted to the tawny, lemony, blue, green and white pottery plates and bowls of *Talavera* can be bought in, yes of course, Talavera de la Reina at any of 15 different ceramic workshops. This ancient pottery-producing town (going strong for 800 years) is an easy detour if you are on the Toledo–Avila road (just take N-IV west where it crosses at Maqueda). You'll find shops along the highway and all over town. The largest is Artesanía Talaverana, 32 Avenida de Portugal.

Toledo

Talavera antique and new plates can also be found in *Toledo,* along with almost any other souvenir item. Toledo has been known for its blades—not Dapper Dans, but sword and knife—for over 1,000 years. Nowadays, the skills used in forging swords for warriors past have been turned to making letter openers. The big Toledo commodity is damascene ware—black steel objects inlaid with gold, silver or copper thread. Judging by Toledo's many gift shops, every object conceivable seems to have been damascened—bracelets, rings, pendants, cigarette boxes, knives, plates, ashtrays, yes, and letter openers, too. So popular is the ware that it was probably inevitable that some sham has entered the damascene scene. Tin can masquerade as steel. To be sure you're getting real damascene ware, buy at reliable stores. One such is *Artespaña,* 2 Calle de Samuel Levi, a branch of the government-sponsored handcraft shops (there are 24 scattered all over Spain emphasizing regional crafts). Artespaña offers such crafts in Toledo—ceramics, embroideries, weavings—but the emphasis is on damascene.

Toledo is more tourist-conditioned than most towns in Castile. Nowhere is this more apparent than in the many souvenir shops near the star attractions and along the *calles* leading into the Zocodover. You will find some bona fide antiques shops even so, tucked among the more blatantly commercial tourist shops. Look for some along Calle de Samuel Levi.

Valladolid

Shopping in *Valladolid* is most interesting in the shops along the arcades of the Plaza Mayor and on Calle Pasion leading from the Plaza Mayor. To catch a glimpse of the local and all-Spanish contemporary art scene, drop by Galería Carmen Durango, 2 Calle Fray Luis de Leon. Paintings and prints are for sale.

Museums and Galleries (in addition to those described in text)

Avila

★ **CASA DE LOS DEANES**

Calle de Eduardo Marquina. The deans of the cathedral once lived in this 16th-century mansion that now houses the fine arts museum. On view are ceramics from Talavera and Manises and carpets, furniture and art—pay special attention to a 15th-century triptych by Memling. Hours: 10 A.M. to 2 P.M.; Sundays and holidays 11 A.M. to 1:30 P.M. Closed Mondays.

Burgos

★ **CASA DE MIRANDA**

Calle de la Calera. This 1545 noble's mansion is now the Archaeological Museum with artifacts from Roman to modern times. Worth the visit: 12th- and 16th-centuries altar pieces; 11th-century ivory casket; de Siloé's tomb of Isabella's page. (Closed for restoration at this writing.)

Segovia

★★ **MUSEO PROVINCIAL DE BELLAS ARTES**

Calle San Agustin. Called "the squire's house," it houses art from defunct churches and convents, includes Durer and Rembrandt engravings and 15th- and 16th-century Spanish and Flemish works. Fine 16th-century room with tiles, covered bed, furnishings. Hours: 10 A.M. to 1 P.M., 3 to 7 P.M. summer; closed Mondays; closes an hour earlier rest of year.

Toledo

★★ **IGLESIA SAN ROMÁN**

On street of same name. This 13th-century Mudejar church is the *Museo de los Concilios y de la Cultura Visigoda* (Museum of the Councils and the Visigothic Culture). The horseshoe arches, red and white decoration are reminiscent of the mosque at Cordoba; frescoes of Biblical scenes; jewelry and fragments of Visigothic work give rare look into this lost culture. Hours: 10 A.M. to 2 P.M., 3:30 to 6:30 P.M. Admission 150 pts., including entry to Santa Cruz Museum.

Valladolid

★ **MUSEO ARQUEOLÓGICO PROVINCIAL**

Plaza Fabionelli. In 20 rooms of this 1582 banker's palace are objects from prehistoric to 17th century times. Worth the trip: Roman mosaics, sculpture; frescoes from 13th and 15th centuries; tapestries. Hours: 9 A.M. to 2 P.M., summer; 10 A.M. to 1:30 P.M., 4:30 to 6:30 P.M. rest of year; Sundays and holidays 11 A.M. to 1 P.M.; closed Mondays.

Zamora

MUSEO DE LA SEMANA SANTA (HOLY WEEK MUSEUM)
Across from church of Santa Maria la Nueva. Here, where you can see them at rest, are the remarkable figures carried in the Easter week processions. Open 10 A.M. to 2 P.M., 4 to 7 P.M. For admission, ask for key at Santa Maria la Nueva.

Historic Buildings and Sites (in addition to those described in text)

Burgos

★ IGLESIA SAN NICOLÁS
Opposite the cathedral. This 1408 church features sculpture of Simon of Cologne. The high altar (1505) has more than 460 of his carvings in alabaster of St. Nicholas's life, Virgin crowned, Last Supper. Tombs are worthy of note.

PLAZA MAYOR
In Burgos it's the circular, porticoed Plaza José Antonio, with the 14th-century Iglesia San Gil (notable Pietá) and 1791 *ayuntamiento* (town hall) on perimeter.

Chinchon

Picture a medieval town *plaza mayor* used as a bullring during fiestas. That was—and is—Chinchon.

Coca

★★ COCA
This castle, 50 kilometers from Segovia, is the epitome of the castle in Spain. On what had been first a Roman then a Moorish fortress site, the 15th-century archbishop of Sevilla built Coca using Moorish workmen. The result is massive, big as a town, yet delicate in design details. Powerfully impressive. Church and central keep are open. Hours 10 A.M. to 1 P.M., 4 to 6 P.M.

Medina del Campo

★ LA MOTA
One of Spain's great castles, this was a favorite of Isabella La Catolica. The original fortress was built in the 13th century and enlarged in the 15th century. After it was turned into a state prison, it held Hernando Pizarro and Cesare Borgia among others.

Pedraza de la Sierra

35 kilometers (22 miles) northeast of Segovia. This wall-girdled, medieval

maze of streets under the brooding oversight of a powerful castle is a fortified town that has changed little in centuries.

Segovia

CASA DE LOS PICOS

House of the "points" is a much-photographed 15th-century facade covered with square pyramids of stone, like giant nail file.

★ MONASTERIO DEL PARRAL

This monastery, founded in 1459, is across the Eresma River. A Renaissance complex, impressive doors, niches, altar piece, 16th-century retable, alabaster tombs. Hours 10 A.M. to 1 P.M., 3 to 7 P.M., summer; closes an hour earlier the rest of year.

★★ IGLESIA DE VERA CRUZ

On Calle Marqués de Villena near El Parral, this church built by Knights Templar, 1208–1217, is decorated with frescoes of the period. Building modeled after Jerusalem's church of Holy Sepulchre.

PLAZA DEL CONDE DE CHESTE

At the center of this plaza with its palaces of nobles is the 13th-century fortress-palace of the Marquéses de Moya who served Ferdinand and Isabella.

★ PLAZA SAN MARTIN

In this monumental open space are stairs on which the two marble sphinxlike sirens crouch; other features are *Torreon de los Lozoyas* (tower of the Lozoyas family) and the 12th-century San Martin Romanesque church (with museum, pictures, baroque altars) with galleries and a fountain at top of stairs.

Toledo

ALCANTARA BRIDGE

For ages this was the most important bridge across the Tagus River to Toledo. There is a 13th-century Mudejar tower at its west end.

ALCÁZAR

Reincarnated once more after its destruction during the 1936–1939 Civil War, the Alcázar towers above the city and the Tagus, its slate-topped turrets gleaming in the sun. Charles V converted the 13th-century fortress on this site into a royal palace and castle. It looks today much as it did then. Hours 9:30 A.M. to 7:30 P.M.; closes 6 P.M. in winter.

★★★ GATES

Gates are some of Toledo's most impressive monuments. The *old Bisagra Gate* on the north, Madrid road, side was the Moorish portal entered by conquering Cid and Alfonso VI in 1085. The *new Bisagra Gate,* built in 1550 by Philip II, has immense Habsburg eagles in stone. Behind it are two square towers topped by black and white checkerboard tiles. The *Puerta del Sol* is classical Moorish portal along, rather than through city walls; it incorporates earlier Mudejar arches, arcades and brickwork and adjoins *Visigothic Valmardán Gate.*

★★★ HOSPITAL DE TAVERA

Madrid highway, just outside Bisagra Gate. This 16th-century palace of the dukes of Lerma is a neoclassical building. Its church has Berruguete marble tomb of Cardinal Tavera, El Greco retable. Paintings by Titian, Coello, Tintoretto, Greco, Zurburán and Ribera's extraordinary portrait of bearded mother breast-feeding her baby. Hours 10 A.M. to 1 P.M., 4 to 7 P.M.; in winter, 10 A.M. to 1 P.M., 3 to 6 P.M.

Valle De Los Caidos

13 kilometers (8 miles) north of Escorial. In this "valley of the fallen," the monastery and basilica hewn out of granite hillside memorialize the dead of the Spanish Civil War, 1936–1939. They contain tombs of Francisco Franco, other Falangist leaders and 40,000 soldiers. A lift runs to the base of the 125–meter (410-foot) high cross on the hillside above the basilica. Hours 10 A.M. to 7 P.M., summer; 9:30 A.M. to 6:30 P.M., winter. Admission 150 pts. for car with two passengers; 300 pts. for car with more than two passengers.

Valladolid

★ CONVENTO DE SANTA ANA

Plaza Santa Ana. Built by order of Philip II and rebuilt in the 18th century by Charles III from designs by Sabatini. The church contains three Goya canvases and statues by Gregorio Fernandez and Pedro de Mena.

CONVENTO DE LAS HUELGAS

On street of same name. Founded in 1282 by Queen Maria de Molina. Mudejar doorway leads to works by Juan de Juni and Gregorio Fernandez.

★ IGLESIA DE LAS ANGUSTIAS

Calle Angustias. Mixes Romanesque and Gothic styles and is famous for Juan de Juni's masterpiece *Virgen de los Cuchillos* (our Lady of the knives). Also has high altar designed by Cristobal Velázquez and sculptures by Francisco del Rincon.

IGLESIA DE SAN MIGUEL

Plaza San Miguel. Noted for the sculptures it contains: St. Francis Borgia and St. Ignatius by Fernandez; tombs of the Perez de Vivero family (who built the church) by de Praves; and a reredos by Adrian Alvarez in the rectangular chancel.

UNIVERSITY OF VALLADOLID

The university's main facade is a baroque wonder by the Tomé brothers: San Gregorio, Cadenas de San Gregorio, a 15th-century college, is a masterpiece of Isabeline style (built by Queen Isabella's confessor) with lavish carved stone decoration covering it (see National Museum of Polychrome Sculpture).

Rascafria

★★★ SANTA MARIA DE EL PAULAR
An active monastery from the 14th through 18th centuries. Now San Bruno, its baroque church, and cloister, Gothic retable and sanctuary are incorporated in or adjoin the luxury hotel recently established there by the government-run Entursa chain. Hours 10 A.M. to 2 P.M., 4 to 7:30 P.M., summer; 12:45 to 2 P.M., 4 to 7 P.M., Sundays, holidays and winter; tours at 12 A.M. and 4 P.M. 92 kilometers (58 miles) from Madrid.

Tours

In every large city, regular organized tours are offered. Often these are conducted by local tour operators—whose names and addresses you can secure from the municipal tourism office. Among the national tour operators with long experience are Atesa, Melia, Pullmantur, Juliatours, Trapsatur, American Express and Wagons-lit Cook. From provincial cities, comfortable motorcoach tours to interesting towns nearby go almost daily. For example, one tour from Toledo includes the following: Torrijos, where the Palace of the Count of Altamira and Convent of the Franciscan Nuns are visited; Talavera de la Reina, the famous ceramics center, to see its factories in operation and its museum of pottery; Oropesa, for the medieval castle that now is a Parador; and Puente del Arzobispo to visit the handsome *capilla mayor* in the local church—a total of 137 kilometers (85 miles). You can get information about such tours from the local municipal tourism office.

Perks

If hunting or fishing are your passions, Spain is the right place for you. In the rugged areas of Old Castile, exceptional big game hunting is possible. Among the unusual quarry are stag, ibex, roebuck, several types of mountain goat, boar, wolf and bear. Small game abounds, particularly birds such as partridge, quail, bustard, pheasant and waterfowl.

Spanish hunters favor several types of hunts, including "driven" game, high mountain, woodland and field hunts. You need a license and personal-risk hunting insurance for taking the field in the national reserves and game preserves. The government agency to contact is *Instituto Nacional para la Conservación de la Naturaleza* (ICONA). Hunting season schedules, license fees and regulations can be secured from ICONA's provincial headquarters.

The seasons are set each year by government officials. If you wish to participate in a hunt, you will find that there are many companies that specialize in organizing them. Many are located in Madrid, and the Spanish National Tourist Office (SNTO) can supply names and addresses.

If you wish to hunt big game with a camera in these reserves, you will need a permit (which is free) from the authorities. Again, SNTO can supply necessary addresses.

Salmon, pike, black bass, perch are all on Spain's menu for ardent anglers. The country's 73,600 kilometers (46,000 miles) of rivers and streams are also home to barbel, carp, bogue and trout. SNTO can supply information on how to secure a fishing license, seasons, regulations, as well as other information.

Sports

Winter Sports

In the Guadarrama Range and Navacerrada, Valcotos and Valdesqui areas of Castile winter sports are expanding. You will find Spanish ski resorts have all the familiar facilities and amenities, generally at modest prices. From Madrid and cities close to the resorts, buses and trains operate frequently during the snow season. Segovia is a central point for slaloming to the ski resorts. In Segovia, *La Sociedad Deportiva Excursionista* (Society of Sports Excursions) works out ski competitions and sponsors bus tours and train service to Navacerrada. In spring and summer it offers tours, hikes and competitions in the mountains. If these interest you, write the Sociedad at 15 Calle Muerte y Vida, Segovia.

GETTING AROUND

By Car

Roads in Castile vary from *autopistas* (excellent, divided superhighways) and good three-lane, well-surfaced roads to pothole-pocked, cracked roads that look as though Hannibal's elephant convoy was the last to use them. N-403 south of Avila has some of these antique axle-breaker sections.

By Bus

Frequent bus service connects cities and towns in Spain nowadays. But since the companies are local, you'll have to check with the municipal turismo office for schedules and tariffs.

By Train

Train service to popular destinations such as Toledo, Avila, Segovia, Escorial, Valladolid, Burgos, Cuenca and Salamanca is good. You have a choice of trains; on the close-in destinations served by electric trains, there may be a dozen or more trains a day. Fares are reasonable, and the express trains are excellent. RENFE's overseas agent, the French National Railways, can give you specific information about schedules and prices (see Directory for address and telephone number). Once you are in Spain, check in at RENFE's offices or the local railway station for timetables and information about special offers, tours and excursions to popular destinations and/or events.

The South–Andalucía

MÁLAGA

Madrid-Málaga by air takes 40 min.

Málaga, in our pressed-for-time era, is the way most visitors approach Andalucía. There is direct air service from the USA with a customs stop in Madrid, from London and most European capitals. Málaga is the springboard both to the *Costa del Sol* and inland to the "triangle cities" of Granada, Sevilla and Córdoba.

A handy and pleasing restaurant for seafood is La Alegria, 18 Martin García (224143). Try Málaga's famous gazpacho, made with white garlic and grapes

Málaga itself is too often given short shrift. It deserves better. A ride in a horse-drawn carriage (with a little parasol over the horse's head to stave off the sun) takes one along the palm-fringed Paseo del Parque, next to the harbor, past cascades of fountains that glow orange at night and old-fashioned street lamps with an amber cast.

In spite of its proximity to the foreign enclaves that rim the Sun Coast, Málaga has retained its Spanishness. A visitor quickly discovers this in the little side streets of the town center, the bustling shopping section along Calle Marqués de Larios, and the many cobbled plazas and outdoor cafes.

Málaga's Spanishness, like much in Andalucía, is laden with Moorish undercurrents. You'll see this when you pass the *Santiago el Mayor* church's Mudejar tower and Arabic arch on your way to inspect the plaque on the house where Pablo Picasso was born, at 15 Plaza de la Merced. In the Museum of Fine Arts, 6 Calle San Agustin, after you've looked at schoolboy Picasso's early efforts and those of his tradition-minded teacher, Antonio Muñoz Degrain, your eyes will surely turn to the graceful courtyard and tiled patio of the 14th-century Moorish palace of the Condes de Buenavista in which the museum is housed.

Two Moorish monuments dominate Málaga's eastern edge.

** Alcazaba

Walk through the tranquil gardens of the hillside fortress, the Alcazaba, which the Moors built in the 11th century on a site the Romans had usurped when they set up housekeeping there before Christ was born. The gardens' perfume of honeysuckle, lavender and jasmine will linger as you look at the Roman theater nearby and the Archeological Museum with its many Roman and Arabic fragments. Puerta del Cristo (Christ's Door) is the last entrance gate to the Alcazaba. It is the place where Mass was celebrated in 1487 to give thanks for Ferdinand's and Isabella's reconquest of the city. Hours: 10 A.M. to 1 P.M., 5 to 8 P.M.; closes at 7 P.M. in winter: closed on Sunday and holiday afternoons.

Up the hill, crowning the top, with magnificent views of the sea, is the other major Moorish memory in Málaga—the 13th-century fortress, with Phoenician foundations, called Gibralfaro. For centuries the Moors stalked these ramparts, using their many watchtowers to guard the luscious paradise they had created below. Now Gibralfaro is only a garden, but a beautiful one festooned with purple bougainvillea, geraniums, pines and cypress. Hours: same as Alcazaba, above.

COSTA DEL SOL

From Málaga, one has many choices. A sun-lover often heads south to the *Costa del Sol.* Those who remember Torremolinos when it was just a yawning stretch of sun-warmed beach and a gleam in a developer's eye are continuously surprised at the high-rise buildings that seem both endless and seamless. Every comfort and convenience known to modern beach and nightlife is yours for the asking (and paying) at Torremolinos—and in any language. Gregarious, sun- and fun-loving, sometimes frenetic, this hyperactive resort is not everybody's glass of sherry. If it's yours, enjoy!

South along A-7 you'll come to Benalmadena whose whitewashed villas overlook the coastal highway and the sea beyond. Next is the sparkling all-white village of Mijas in the Sierra Mijas Mountains with an overview of the Mediterranean. Beyond is Fuengirola, whose Moorish castle ruins above town contemplate the long expanse of tiled walkway, *Paseo Maritimo,* along the waterfront.

Just 30 kilometers farther along the shore (and 59 km total from Málaga) is the fashionable resort of Marbella, playground of the chic from all over Europe and the USA. There are super-deluxe hotels (see Inside Information), elegant restaurants and shopping, high-powered yachts parked offshore at Puerto Banus. Low-keyed lotus-eating diversions—that's Marbella.

Oddly enough, the beaches are the least of the *Costa del Sol's* attraction. Many are pebbly and grainy and grey. There are better beaches elsewhere. But the weather and the all-purpose resort facilities make this a recreation paradise. With more than 326 days of almost-guaranteed sunshine per year, it's easy to understand the pull southward. There are enough championship golf courses for you to play at a different one for two weeks straight. Big name tennis and golf professionals do stints here as pro-in-residence at some of the better resorts (in Marbella especially). Well, you get the idea.

Below Marbella, in the fast-developing little village of San Pedro de Alcántara, you may have a moment of decision. You can continue circling the coast all the way around the bend to Cádiz, then inland to Jerez de la Frontera. Or you can turn inland now to Ronda.

RONDA

Ronda epitomizes Andalucía. Its whiteness is so blinding you need sunglasses to face it. The road to Ronda from San Pedro is a twister. So is the road from Málaga, whose switchback turns are redeemed somewhat by the sparkling whiter-than-white towns of Alhaurin de la Torre, Coin and El Burgo that you will pass en route.

Still, it's better than the bad old days when only one road threaded its mountainous way into Ronda. This made the town ideal for the Moors to defend—which they did to the bitter end. The town also suited brigands in centuries past. They were safe here at the "end of the line."

There are plenty of picturesque white towns in Andalucía. What makes Ronda special is, first of all, its location on the edge of a 500-foot ravine, called *El Tajo.* The old town (*Ciudad*) is separated from the new (*Mercadillo*) by a splendid, high 18th-century bridge (*Puente Nuevo*) from which you have a swallow's eye view of the craggy gorge, the Guadalevin River and the town's two lower bridges; one of which, *Puente Viejo,* dates back to Roman times. In spite of Ronda's inaccessibility, conquerors seem to have had no trouble finding it. The old town is built on the site of a town the Romans called *Arunda,* and many Moorish elements such as the mosque foundation and minaret tower of the church of Santa Maria la Mayor remain.

Hemingway liked Ronda . . . so did Goya . . . so did poet Rainer Maria Rilke, who visited in 1912–13 and stayed at the Hotel Reina Victoria. You can see his statue in the garden and memorabilia in Room 208. Tauromachophiles gravitate to Ronda to see the oldest extant bullring in Spain with its wrought-iron balconies decorated with bullfight scenes. The bullfight equivalent of the Marquis of Queensberry rules were first drawn up in Ronda by Francisco Romero in the early 18th century. Until he introduced the cape, the "fights" were pretty much a case of daunting, daring and running. His grandson Pedro, one of the great 18th- 19th-century bullfighters, sired a Ronda school, noted for its adherence to his grandfather's rules. There are *aficionados* who see a resemblance between the *torero*'s costume and that worn by the old Ronda smuggler-brigands. (Goya has also been credited with designing the costume or a variation thereof.)

We could tick off all the sights one should look at—the Casa del Rey Moro (near the Roman bridge), the Marqués de Salvatierra's palace (with enchanting views and a triple terrace). But Ronda's principal charm is itself. Discovering it involves walking the narrow streets, savoring the views that differ from street to street, enjoying the immaculate plazas and patios, such as Patio de Cabaleria with its profusion of flowers, and maybe sipping a *fino* on the terrace of the Hotel Reina Victoria, the oldtime local gathering place.

From a single entry point in the past, Ronda now bristles with choices. You could take C-344 to Málaga, but it's a tricky road. Instead, climb the spectacular mountain road C-341 to Campillos and then N-342 to Antequera, which leads past mountainsides that are checkerboards of green and gold fields with long green cypress fingers prodding the clearest of blue skies. Around the curve of one mountaintop—Romeral—you can peer into three provinces - Sevilla, Granada and Málaga.

At Antequera where the ruins of a Moorish castle offer commanding countrywide views, you can opt to go south to Málaga along the pleasant Málaga-Sevilla road or continue east past Loja (another Moorish castle and views) to Granada. Choices, choices.

If you choose the Málaga route and then from Málaga circle along the coast and north to Granada, this gives you a look at the low-key resort of Nerja, 52 kilometers east of Málaga. Nerja is known for its cobbled and painted promenade, called the Balcony of Europe, which overlooks two scenic inlets edged by mammoth boulders. Paleolithic caves with ancient paintings inside have been discovered recently and are now open to view. The caves are just seven kilometers east of town, on the road to Almuñecar, which the Romans knew as Sexi (and the locals are tired of *those* jokes). Here you'll find the remains of a Roman aqueduct and a Moorish castle, captured during the *Reconquista* (Reconquest) by Ferdinand and Isabella. All in all, a peaceful little town, Almuñecar.

GRANADA

A turn north on N-323 at Motril, with time out to look back down on the sea from a hillside vantage point, and then it's 70 kilometers to Granada. Shortly beyond Padul, look for the *Puerto del Suspiro del Moro*—the gate of the Last Sigh of the Moor. When Boabdil, the last Moorish king of Granada, relinquished his beloved city to Ferdinand and Isabella, he left on this Motril road.

He is said to have paused and turned back sadly for one last look. His mother, Aisha, noted bitterly, "You do well, my son, to weep as a woman for the loss of what you could not defend as a man."

The Alhambra

Boabdil's feeling of loss can be understood the moment you see the Alhambra. The hill which it caps is the westernmost foothill of the Sierra Nevada Mountains. In its prime it was unassailable. Where now there are cypress and pine trees, there was then a sparsely covered hillside, the better to see and repulse any possible sneak attack. What you see from afar or from the noisy quarter called *Albaicin* (Falconers' Quarter) across the Darro River is a magnificent terra cotta brick fortress with 13 towers crowning the hilltop. This may well be the most romantic group of buildings in the world, excepting perhaps the Taj Mahal.

One moves into the Hall of Secrets, designed so that you can hear distinctly what is being whispered at the opposite end of the room. The Hall of the Two Sisters refers to two similar marble slabs in the room's floor. On the walls stucco is carved into lacy, embroidered calligraphy of famous poems in Arabic.

This hall leads into what is probably the most photographed and famous part of the palace, the Court of the Lions. In the center of an open courtyard is a round alabaster fountain surrounded by 12 stone lions facing outward. The courtyard is covered with sandy earth in which stone paths lead from four sides of the fountain to the arcaded pavilions surrounding it. The pavilion roofs are supported by more than 100 pencil-thin white marble columns seemingly irregularly spaced, to provide a rich and varied optical effect. The simplicity of the lions and their fountain contrasted with the delicate tracery and embroidered stone of the arcades is sheer poetry.

Facing the Court of the Lions on the south (the Hall of the Kings is on the east side) is the Hall of the Abencerrajes, named after a prominent Muslim family whose members were lured to this room and slaughtered on Boabdil's orders. Their heads were then dumped into the center fountain. A guide often points to an ineradicable stain in the marble and speaks of blood and Lady Macbeth's similar cleaning problem.

The architects planned for every pleasure. In the Queen's Dressing Room a perforated marble slab permitted perfumes to be wafted in, scenting the room as the queen dressed. Below the lovely cypress-and-orange-tree-accented Garden of Daraxa are the three large Royal Bathrooms. Here too every comfort was guaranteed. Starlike openings in the roof let daylight filter in. In the largest room, where bathers rested after their steam baths on raised, tiled platforms, there is a gallery where musicians played or girls sang to divert the bathers. Throughout the marble-tiled bath rooms the walls are faced, to a level of six feet, with the green, black, red, blue and mustard-colored *azulejos* the Moors admired so much.

Throughout the palace the brilliance of Moorish craftsmen is impressive —in the "Star of Solomon" *azulejo* designs; the cedar ceilings and doors so painstakingly carved; the honeycombed and stalactite decoration in wood and stucco; the tapestries of stone in the walls, arches and screens. One salutes Yusef I for commissioning it in the first place. Hours: 10 A.M. to 6 P.M.

The Alhambra itself was the palace of the sultan and his harem. But the enormous hill, which is half a mile long and 550 feet across at its widest, sheltered an entire city of half a million people by one estimate. There were shops, baths, houses, a college and a mosque.

Your ticket to the Alhambra also admits you to the enormous *Palacio de Carlos V* (Palace of Charles V), which is considered by many to be the finest example of Renaissance civil architecture in Spain. It was begun in 1526, on the ashes of a harem that went up in flames two years before. The palace, cooly perfect in its two-story, completely circular Palladian-style courtyard, was the work of a Michelangelo student, Pedro Machuca. Outside, the square stone building is decorated in its cornices, windows and portals with stone medallions, garlands and sculpture. In another setting, the palace would be a triumph; unfortunately it suffers in esteem because of its proximity to the Alhambra. It is out of sync with the style and philosophy of the Moorish monuments that preceded it.

Palacio del Generalife

Another part of your Alhambra ticket is for the *Palacio del Generalife,* but before making the 15-minute hike down one hill and up the Cerro del Sol slopes nearby, you might want to stop for something cool to drink-or maybe even for lunch—at one of the three hotels in the area: the Parador Nacional de San Francisco (delicious lemon and coffee ice cream, and a three-course menu of the day for 950 pesetas); the Hotel Alhambra Palace (where you can snack on sandwiches in the bar if you don't want a full meal); the Hostal America (very handy, tiny, and with a pleasing dining room). See Inside Information—Hotels for addresses and phone numbers.

The word Generalife translates into "Garden of the Architect." It is believed that this serene palace may have been designed by the Alhambra's first architect as his own home. But a far-sighted sultan saw its advantages, felt its cool breezes and snapped it up in 1320 as a summer palace, a retreat when the Alhambra became too warm.

Experts in such matters call the Generalife one of the oldest and finest examples of a Moorish garden. And it is certainly the gardens and fountains that rivet our attention. The palace itself is modest, though the views from the enclosed balcony just off the Hall of Kings are marvelous. You can see the Alhambra in glorious profile, as well as the river valley below.

As you enter the grounds, you parade past columns of cypress and under an oleander arcade. From this walk you can admire the Alhambra and parador across the way. The Moorish love of water comes into full play in the Generalife. Some fountains murmur softly, subtly. Other fountains cascade and splash in noisy exuberance. Water burbles in the handrails of the staircase in the upper garden. And throughout the grounds are walls banked with wisteria, gardens of peonies, roses, magnolia, and pines. The perfume of oranges and jasmine fills the air. For a desert-parched people, the conspicuous use of water and greenery was the equivalent of today's "if you've got it, flaunt it." Hours: 10 A.M. to 6 P.M.

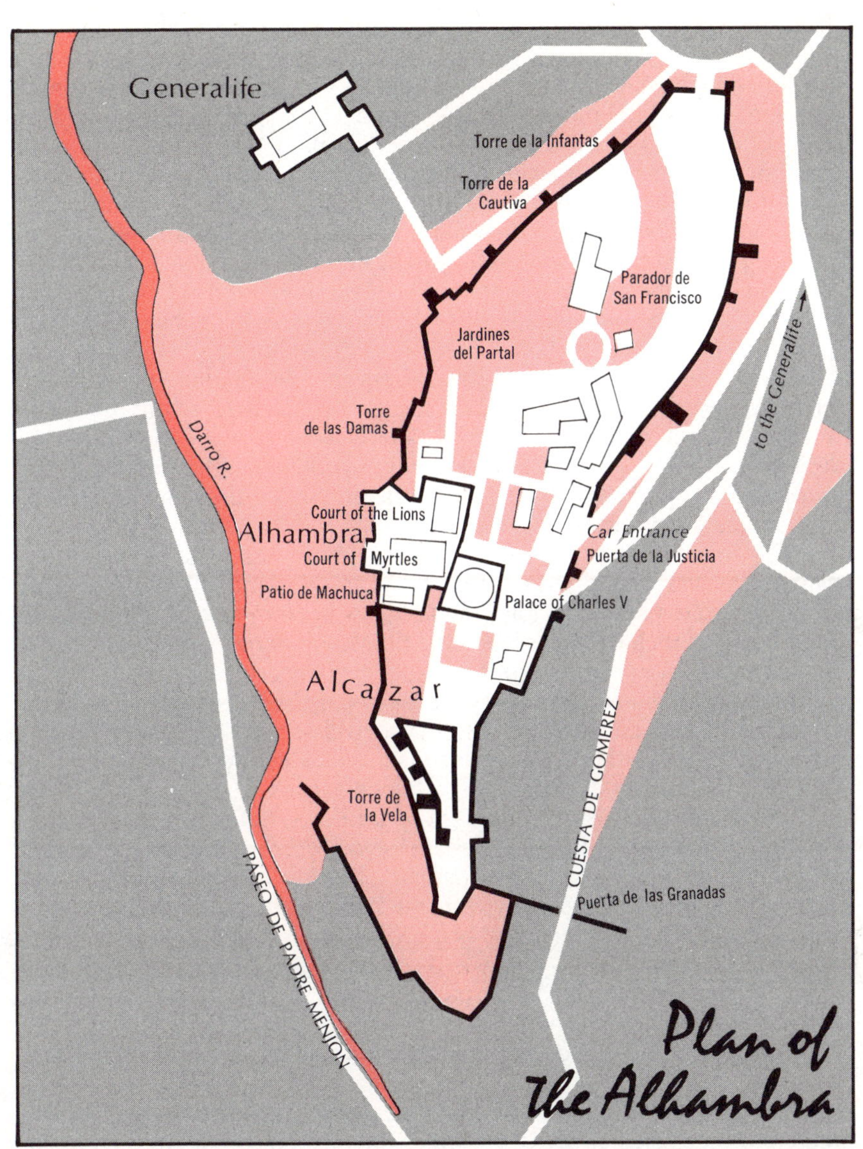

Generalife
Torre de la Infantas
Torre de la Cautiva
Parador de San Francisco
Jardines del Partal
to the Generalife
Torre de las Damas
Darro R.
Court of the Lions
Alhambra
Car Entrance
Court of Myrtles
Puerta de la Justicia
Patio de Machuca
Palace of Charles V
Alcazar
CUESTA DE GOMEREZ
Torre de la Vela
Puerta de las Granadas
PASEO DE PADRE MENJON
Plan of the Alhambra

The Insider's Granada

It would be halcyonic to limit one's Granada visit to the Alhambra hillsides. But there is one important "must-see" attraction in the center of the lower city and many other extras if one's schedule permits. The cathedral is the downtown magnet, along with its attached Royal Chapel or *Capilla Real.*

After the Reconquest, the *Reyes Católicos* (Catholic Monarchs) Ferdinand and Isabella, changed their plans and decided to make Granada, not Toledo, their life-after-death masterpiece. In a rare example of cart-before-horse building, the chapel was started in 1506, finished in 1521. The cathedral wasn't begun until 1528. Isabella didn't even live to see her tomb chapel started. She died in 1504, but there it sits, a tribute to her perspicacity, intelligence and achievements. The Carrara marble sculpture of Isabella on top of her sarcophogus doesn't really suggest the character of this remarkable woman. Plain and somewhat pudgy, she was nevertheless resolute in her desire to see Spain united as a single Christian country and farsighted enough to gamble on the dreams of a Genoese sailor. *NOW* (the feminist organization) should be proud of her.

The Royal Chapel is a museum full of riches. Its focal points are two gigantic Renaissance tombs—elaborately carved islands of gleaming white Carrara marble. One is the joint sarcophagus of Ferdinand and Isabella, the other is that of their daughter Juana the Mad and her husband Philip the Fair. Their sculpted stone figures repose serenely, if uncharacteristically, considering the turmoil of their lives. They are surrounded by bevies of cherubs and caryatids. (If you go down the steps you will see in the lighted chamber beneath the tombs the five severely plain, black lead coffins that hold the remains of the four plus Juana's son, Prince Miguel.)

The major treasures are in the royal art collection that was pledged by the monarchs as part of the chapel. Here you will see Dirk Bouts' powerful tryptych of the *Passion* plus outstanding paintings by Hans Memling, Botticelli, Perugino, Van der Weyden and Pedro Berruguete, among others. Notice especially the gilded and black wrought iron grill that separates the chapel from the cathedral—a masterpiece rich in scenes from Christ's life by Master Bartolomé. You'll find the painted wood sculptures of Ferdinand and Isabella warmly lifelike. These were carved by Felipe Bigarny (who also did the main altar piece) and are idealized portraits of the monarchs in their youth.

The cathedral itself, built on the site of the city's main mosque, deserves attention too. Its chapels are dense with paintings and retables by Spain's 16th and 17th century finest: Pedro de Mena, Alonso Cano, Jose de Mora and others. In the chapel of *Nuestra Señora de la Antigua,* there is a 15th-century German painting of the Madonna and Child in which the child holds a pomegranate in his hand. *Granada* means pomegranate, and the fruit was a symbol of the reconquest of this prized city long before the event took place. This particular painting was carried by the Christian army when it entered the city. Hours for Royal Chapel and Cathedral: 11 A.M. to 1 P.M., 4 to 7 P.M.; winter afternoons 3:30 to 6 P.M.

An unhurried visitor will wander through the area around the cathedral. This was the old Moorish section and silk market. All that suggests it now are the covered, *souk*-like arcades along the Alcaiceria, with numerous touristy

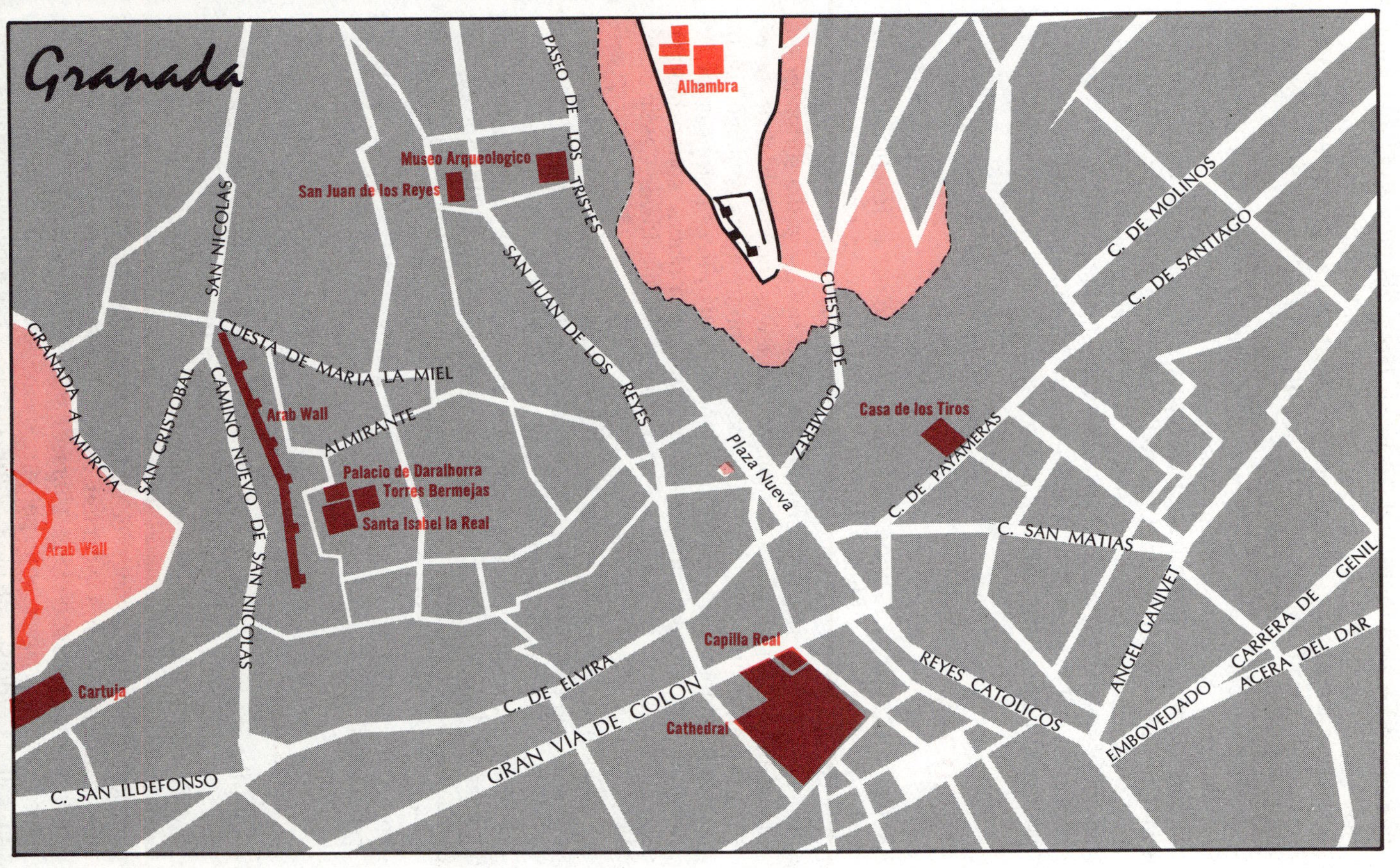

Granada
Alhambra
Museo Arqueologico
San Juan de los Reyes
PASEO DE LOS TRISTES
SAN JUAN DE LOS REYES
CUESTA DE GOMEREZ
Casa de los Tiros
C. DE MOLINOS
C. DE SANTIAGO
C. DE PAYAMERAS
Plaza Nueva
C. SAN MATIAS
ANGEL GANIVET
CARRERA DE GENIL
ACERA DEL DAR
EMBOVEDADO
REYES CATOLICOS
Capilla Real
Cathedral
GRAN VIA DE COLON
C. DE ELVIRA
C. SAN ILDEFONSO
Cartuja
Arab Wall
GRANADA A MURCIA
SAN CRISTOBAL
SAN NICOLAS
CAMINO NUEVO DE SAN NICOLAS
CUESTA DE MARIA LA MIEL
Arab Wall
ALMIRANTE
Palacio de Daralhorra
Torres Bermejas
Santa Isabel la Real

(but fun to browse) shops and the many *tascas* on the side streets. Lunch might be timely at the *Bar Sevilla* (see Inside Information) or the Alcaiceria, 8 Oficios, across from the Cathedral. A really cheap (but tasty) lunch can be had at Zeluan, 49 San Juan de Dios (try the *gambas pilpil* or *chanquetes*).

Local poet García Lorca and composer Manuel de Fallas popularized flamenco in the 1920's

To most of us, Granada is synonymous with flamenco. Alas, it is difficult to find good flamenco singing or dancing in the entire city. In desperation, visitors often snap at the bait of the gypsy cave flamenco of Sacromonte, which bears as much resemblance to the real thing as homemade wine does to *Chateau Lafite.* An assortment of children and tone-deaf elders perform an out-of-step, jaded shuffle that is a travesty of what flamenco can be. Save your money. Or invest it in a polka-dotted Sevillana costume and work up your own flamenco. It can't be any worse.

CÓRDOBA

Santafe is just 12 km outside Granada

Route N-432 spins and turns 172 kilometers or so before reaching Córdoba, another jewel in the Muslim tapestry of Andalucía. En route you will pass through Santafe, the village where Ferdinand and Isabella set up camp, Roman-style, for the siege of Granada. It's also the place the surrender was signed and the contract for Columbus's voyage was confirmed. What you will see today is a small town of 10,000 persons, pretty much contained within an area four blocks wide, nine blocks long, served by three historic gates. The twin-towered church in the center of town has a plaque commemorating Santafe's place in history, along with profiles of the Reyes Católicos and Columbus. A moment in the sun.

Wear comfortable walking shoes; Cordoba's cobblestones play havoc with high heels

Our procedure in Córdoba is to park our car, usually for the duration of our visit, and proceed to the old town on foot. In spite of its size, (240,000) Córdoba, like most Spanish cities, has a walkable central core.

First, walk down to the Puerta del Puente to look at the solidly built Roman bridge over the Guadalquivir River. Visualize all those Roman legionaires crossing during the era, from 151 B.C. when Córdoba was the center of Roman Andalucía and the heart of its intellectual life. Two Senecas were born here, as were Lucan, Martial the satirist, and Pomponius Mela the geographer.

The Mezquita

**** The Mezquita

From the river, we walk quickly into Moorish Córdoba in the astonishing mosque-cathedral called the Mezquita. The grace of the *Patio de los Naranjos* (Courtyard of Orange Trees) is almost pleasure enough. We like to sit here and contemplate the Moorish city of Córdoba as it was, which the Mezquita's interior arches and ceilings recall. For ten generations Córdoba was one of the great Muslim learning centers, as well as the epitome of the good life. In the 9th century Europe's largest library had 36 books; Córdoba's had 50,000. One Arab writer, overcome, perhaps, by the scent of orange blossoms in the air, called Córdoba "the Bride of Andalucía . . . Her long line of sultans forms her crown of glory; her necklace is strung with the pearls which her poets have gathered from the ocean of language."

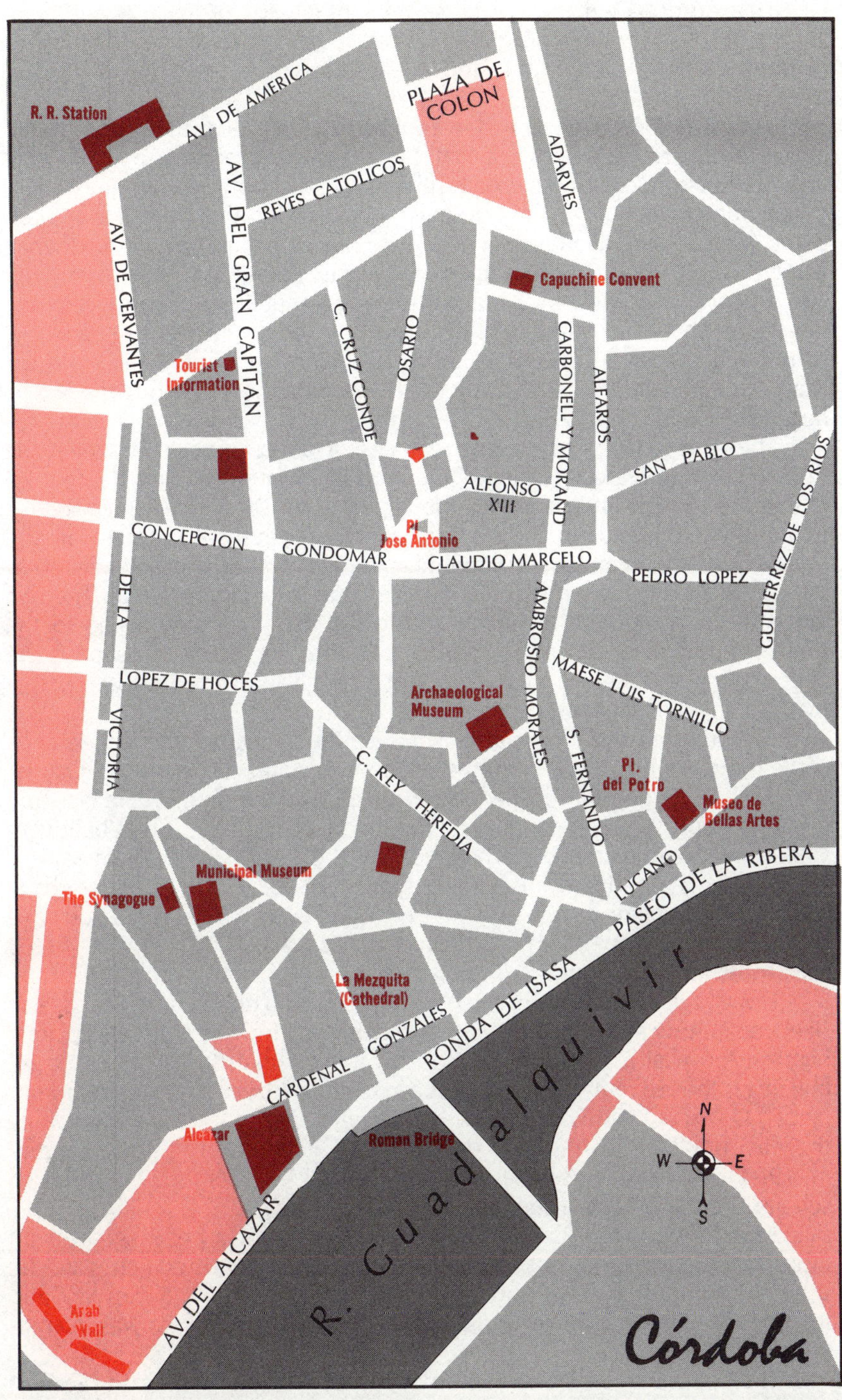
R. R. Station
AV. DE AMERICA
PLAZA DE COLON
ADARVES
REYES CATOLICOS
AV. DEL GRAN CAPITAN
AV. DE CERVANTES
Capuchine Convent
C. CRUZ CONDE
OSARIO
CARBONELL Y MORAND
ALFAROS
Tourist Information
SAN PABLO
ALFONSO XIII
GUITIERREZ DE LOS RIOS
Pl Jose Antonio
CONCEPCION
GONDOMAR
CLAUDIO MARCELO
PEDRO LOPEZ
DE LA
AMBROSIO MORALES
LOPEZ DE HOCES
MAESE LUIS TORNILLO
Archaeological Museum
VICTORIA
C. REY HEREDIA
S. FERNANDO
Pl. del Potro
Museo de Bellas Artes
LUCANO
PASEO DE LA RIBERA
Municipal Museum
The Synagogue
RONDA DE ISASA
La Mezquita (Cathedral)
GONZALES
CARDENAL
R. Guadalquivir
Alcazar
Roman Bridge
N
W
E
S
AV. DEL ALCAZAR
Arab Wall
Córdoba

That Córdoba tended to excess. Think of it—50,000 palaces and mansions of the nobility, 700 mosques, 900 public baths, profusions of fountains, gardens and sybaritic delights, and the largest mosque this side of Mecca, covering six acres.

That was the Córdoba that *was.* We can only fantasize about it. But inside the Mezquita a sense of that city's bygone splendor survives in the forest of horseshoe arches painted with red and white stripes, hundreds (850) of columns made of jasper, porphyry and marble, and lavishly "embroidered" stucco and painted ceilings. Visualize it as it must have looked when lighted by its 800 silver lamps filled with perfumed oil. The Moors were not above borrowing. Some of the lamps were upturned bells pillaged from one of Christendom's most sacred shrines at Santiago de Compostela, just as some of the capitals in the arcade of arches are Ionic and Corinthian from the Roman temple and Visigothic church that stood on this site before the Moors began their building in 785.

The Mezquita's size alone captivates. It almost equals St. Peter's in Rome. The Courtyard of Orange Trees and its cloisters fill almost one-third of that area. Inside, after enjoying the impact—which is never diminished—of the splendid parade of arches, turn to the jewel in the southeast wall: the *mihrab* or prayer niche. Its entrance facade is intricately, byzantinely ornamented in a rising crescendo of scroll work and calligraphic design. Then, in the pattern of Moorish architecture, the surprise. You step inside to the simplicity of a small, scantily ornamented room. Its major attraction is the huge scallop shell ceiling—carved in great simplicity from a single piece of marble. The audacity leaves us gasping.

As you turn from the *mihrab,* you face the inevitable: the Renaissance cathedral ensconced in the middle of the Mezquita. As Théophile Gautier wrote, "It is not destitute of merit and would be admired anywhere else, but it is ever to be regretted that it occupies the place it does." It was built with Charles V's permission, but when he saw the results in 1526 he said to Córdoba's mayor, "Had I known what you were doing, you would not have done it. What you have built here may be found everywhere. What you have destroyed exists nowhere." Mezquita hours: 8:30 A.M. to 1:30 P.M., 4 to 8 P.M.; in winter, afternoons 3:30 to 6 P.M.

Down Calle Almanzor (named for the vizier who doubled the Mezquita's size) you quickly find yourself in the old Jewish quarter, the *Juderia.* A plaque high on the wall at 20 Calle de los Judios notes that the small 22' X 24' building is the last remaining synagogue in Córdoba. (Ask caretaker for admittance.) Down the narrow street, with geraniums spilling from windows along the way, is a little square, Plaza de Tiberiades, with a bronze statue erected in 1964 of a seated, serene Moses Maimonides, Córdoba-born Jewish scholar, doctor and philosopher who died in 1204.

Around the corner is *El Zoco,* once a *souk,* now a petite square with a handcraft center and a bar where you might sip a *fino,* contemplate the birds singing in their cages and watch silversmiths at work. Silverwork and tooled leather are tangible Moorish legacies for which Córdoba was internationally famous.

The Mezquita is obviously Córdoba's number one attraction. Second place goes to the city itself, and one should try to save hours - even a day or two - for wandering its old section. Plazas, patios and palaces are Córdoban *specialités.* A sense of discovery and delight comes around every corner. It might be that you've stumbled upon the statue of an illustrious Córdoban of the past in his own tiny plaza. One such is the Plaza de Santa Marina, with its bronze statue of native son Manuel Rodriquez—better known as Manolete, considered the best bullfighter of the 20th century. He stands, cape in hand, facing the Romanesque church of Santa Marina.

Sometimes the discovery comes in a square itself, such as the Plaza de los Dolores, with its eight old-fashioned wrought iron street lamps and stone crucifix, which people in the neighborhood call "Christ of the Lanterns."

Most famous of the city's squares is Plaza del Potro, Square of the Colt, named for the "bucking bronco" sculpture on top of the fountain in the square's center. On one side of the square is the Museum of Julio Romero de Torres, a local artist who specialized in nudes. But the focal point is the old Posada El Oitro, opposite. It is a whitewashed coaching inn with cobbled courtyard ornamented with flowers. It looks much as it might have when Cervantes wrote about it in *Don Quixote.* Both inn and square were once the gathering place for merchants, gamblers and travelers. Currently it functions as a cultural center of sorts. You might find a Miró exhibit mounted here, as we did recently. It is also a good source of information about current cultural happenings—concerts, exhibitions, et al. There's not a gambler's den in sight. Times change.

The fastest route from Córdoba to Sevilla is N-IV, a distance of 138 kilometers. Break the ride and stretch your legs at Ecija. Besides being an ancient Roman town on the Genil River, it has a perfectly grand rectangle of a main square, *Plaza de España,* lined with palm and orange trees, with an ochre stone fountain in the center celebrating Spain's Golden Age of exploration, and a promenade that encourages walking.

Aside from being the hometown of 15th-century writer Luis Velez de Guevara and a town rich in attractive churches (San Juan has a brick and tiled tower that reminds one of Sevilla's Giralda), Ecija has one other claim to fame. It has the reputation of being the hottest town in Spain. "The Stove of Andalucía" they call it. But if your're there in April or October you'd never believe it, it's so lovely.

Next stop on the road—and it's an ideal coffee or lunch stop—is Carmona and the Parador Alcázar del Rey Don Pedro, nestled into the remains of a Moorish *alcázar* with a windswept ridge view that sweeps over the Rio Corbones and a Grant Wood landscape of creamy wheat fields to the Sierra Morena Mountains beyond. Carmona is a glistening white-on-white town with two fine old gates. One, the Puerta de Sevilla, has a Roman center and a section of wall that could date back to 300 B.C., making it one of the most elderly pieces of masonry in Spain. A church, San Pedro, has a tower modeled on the Giralda in Sevilla. There are also remains of a Roman amphitheater.

A traveler with time to spare could inspect the *Necropolis Romana,* just one kilometer outside of town on the Sevilla road. Some 900 tombs in a network of underground chambers date from the second century B.C. to A.D. 400. Small niches in the walls were for offerings.

SEVILLA

Just 33 kilometers away is Sevilla, capital of southern Spain and the essence of all things Andalucían. At the thought of Sevilla a tourist's images turn instantly to *Carmen, Don Juan* and *The Barber of Seville.* There's little evidence of any of the three in modern day, industrial Sevilla, but even so, there is much more to this ancient city than first meets the eye. "Sevilla is an acquired taste," a Sevillano confided, "it takes longer than a two-day visit." Still, in two or three days of intensive enjoyable sightseeing, one can get caught up in the Sevillano spirit. Fortunately for the time-short visitor, many of the city's major sights are close together, and walking is the name of the game here. Even the bullring is an easy walk from most places in or near the center of town.

Sevilla's three most treasured monuments are just steps from each other —the Alcázar (*Reales Alcazares*), cathedral and Giralda Tower. Yet each of the first two is so rich, so full of choice details that one could spend a day in each and still not be satisfied.

The minute you enter the gate of the *Reales Alcazares* you step into an Arabic world, or at least one simulated by Christian kings using the skills of Muslim artisans. Nightingales sing in the ivy-covered walls, and one patio leads to another revealing new vistas. The palace itself is extraordinary, with all the artifice and mystery of a Moorish interior: horseshoe arches, gilded honeycombed ceilings, walls lined with *azulejos* in classical designs, and "needlepoint" tracery on the walls and arches.

Then there are the collections and furnishings. The first elongated hall is lined with Goya tapestries—25 in all—that depict light, airy country scenes of frolicking, picnics and a wild boar and hare hunt. There are also the tapestries delineating Charles V's Tunisian war campaigns. One has an enormous topographical map of the Mediterranean illustrating villages, hillsides and land contours in such fine detail that one stares with awe at the precision. Hours: 9 A.M. to 12:45 P.M., 4:30 to 7 P.M., May to September; afternoon hours rest of year 3 to 5:30 P.M. on Sundays and holidays, closed afternoons.

Sevilla's cathedral is laden with art masterpieces commissioned and paid for with New World monies. So, to a lesser degree, are its many churches and convents. Relating the art one finds in the many cathedral chapels (almost two dozen) and throughout this monumental structure would be like reciting from the telephone directory. Every prominent artist who ever set foot in Sevilla (over a 300-to-500 year time span) is probably represented.

You'll want to pay special attention to the *Patio de los Naranjos* (Courtyard of Orange Trees) which is entered by the main gate, the *Puerta del Perdon.* In the center of this formally-laid-out courtyard is an octagonal fountain, originally Visigothic, but used by the Moors as their purification or handwashing fountain. The patio itself was once the courtyard of the mosque. Horseshoe arches in the southeast corner are further echoes of its Muslim past. Hours: 10:30 A.M. to 1:30 P.M., 4:30 to 6:30 P.M., in summers; afternoon hours are 3:30 to 5:30 P.M. rest of the year.

The Hospital de la Caridad is a repository of considerable treasures. The chapel itself is an ornate Churrigueresque work of art with ceiling bas reliefs in plaster, gilded serpentine columns and walls full of paintings, several by Murillo. Most commented-on are two somewhat ghoulish works by Valdes

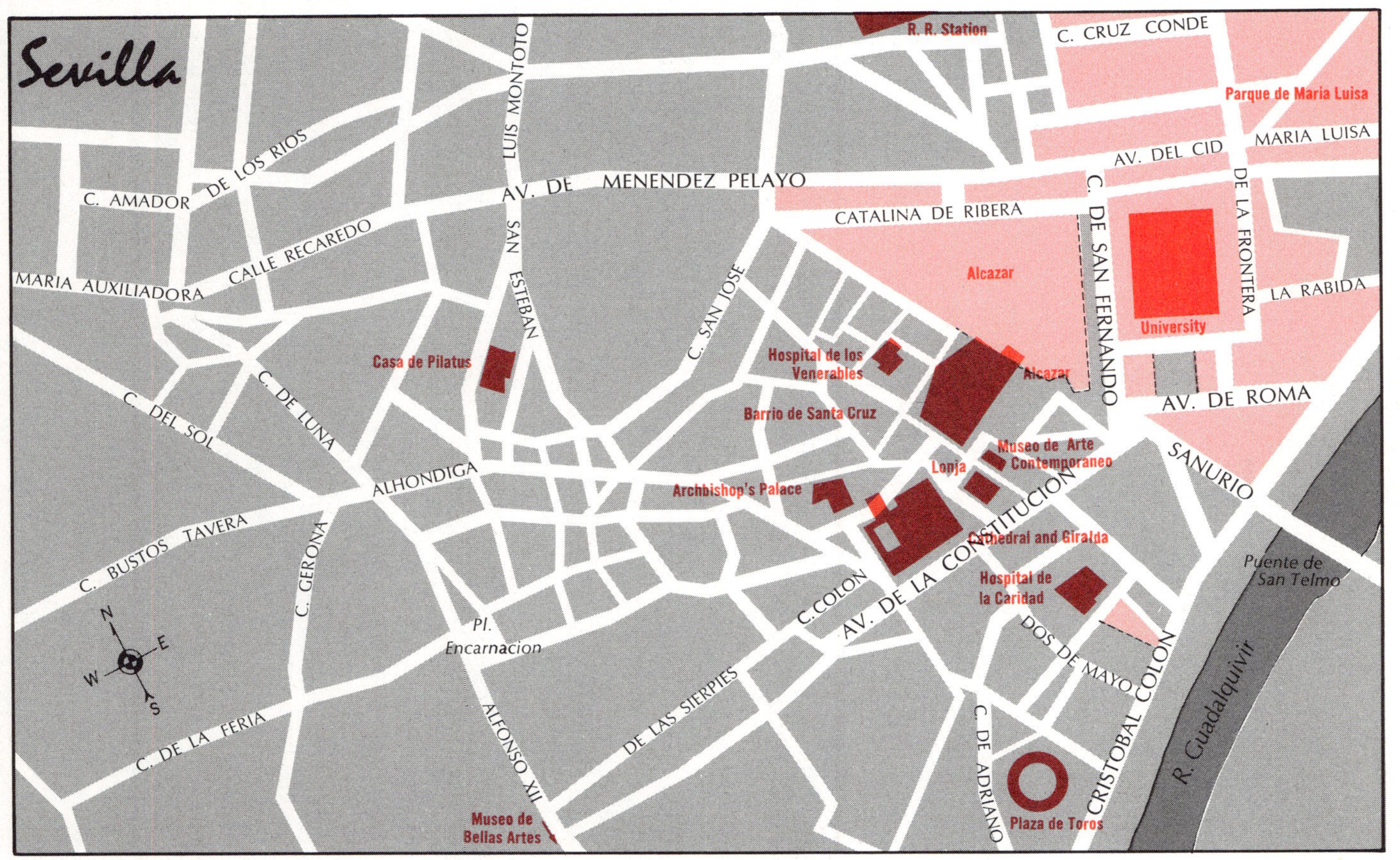
Sevilla
R. R. Station
C. CRUZ CONDE
Parque de Maria Luisa
MARIA LUISA
AV. DEL CID
DE LA FRONTERA
LA RABIDA
University
C. DE SAN FERNANDO
AV. DE ROMA
SANURIO
Puente de San Telmo
R. Guadalquivir
CRISTOBAL COLON
DOS DE MAYO
C. DE ADRIANO
Plaza de Toros
Hospital de la Caridad
Cathedral and Giralda
AV. DE LA CONSTITUCION
C. COLON
Museo de Arte Contemporaneo
Lonja
Alcazar
Alcazar
CATALINA DE RIBERA
AV. DE MENENDEZ PELAYO
Hospital de los Venerables
Barrio de Santa Cruz
Archbishop's Palace
C. SAN JOSE
DE LAS SIERPIES
LUIS MONTOTO
SAN ESTEBAN
Casa de Pilatus
ALHONDIGA
Pl. Encarnacion
ALFONSO XII
Museo de Bellas Artes
C. AMADOR DE LOS RIOS
CALLE RECAREDO
MARIA AUXILIADORA
C. DE LUNA
C. DEL SOL
C. BUSTOS TAVERA
C. GERONA
C. DE LA FERIA
N
E
W
S

Leal. "*Finis Gloria Mundi*" (*End of Worldly Glory*) shows in super-realistic detail a deceased bishop rotting in his casket, another near him in a similar state of decay, and in the rear a skeleton. The second work, equally grim, is *In-Ictu-Oculi,* (*In the Stroke of an Eye*) in which a skeleton, with Time's scythe in one hand, holds a scale in the other. On the scale are a bishop's hat, a crown, and more worldly goods. The implication: it's all gone at the moment of death. Very instructive for their time no doubt.

The old Royal Tobacco Factory is now part of the University of Sevilla, but you are free to wander the courtyards and to admire the overblown portal, with its tobacco allegories and stone tributes to Columbus and Cortes for making the industry possible. Entering the old cigarette factory is in no way hazardous to your health. You'll find the factory just beyond the Alfonso XIII Hotel on Calle de San Fernando. (The hotel, by the way, has an attractive Old World bar and lounge area around an inner courtyard—conducive to late afternoon or pre-lunch refreshments.)

From here, have a look at the splendid facade of *Palacio de San Telmo.* It looks like a palace and is called a palace but was built—it took 114 years —as a school of navigation. It was underwritten by Sevilla's businessmen, proof of the importance of the Guadalquivir River, which brought the New World trade right to the city's door. You'll spot the neoclassical building instantly, either through the courtyard of the Royal Tobacco Factory or just behind the Alfonso XIII, on Calle de Palos de Moguer, by the ripe, russet-colored facade with mustard vertical panels and bachelor-button-blue striped trim. In front of the building are *fin de siecle*-style amber and gilt street lamps. On the roof of the building are stone figures representing Sevilla's glory days: Velázquez, Murillo, sculptor Martinez Montañes (with a sculpted head in his hands), dramatist-actor Lope de Rueda, Ponce de Leon, benefactor Manuel Mañara and others.

The time to visit the *barrio Santa Cruz,* Sevilla's old Jewish quarter, is when it bustles with activity—late morning or late afternoon. The crooked mews are alive with people shopping, browsing the art workshops and galleries, sitting in *tascas,* or just enjoying the "quaint" look of the white-washed houses with grilled windows, spilling ribbons of flowers from their sills. In the past, the grills "protected" young girls, but permitted them to whisper discreetly—and safely—to their lovers or fiances late into the night. Today's new, more permissive Spain needs no grills.

From almost anywhere in barrio Santa Cruz you can see Sevilla's symbol, the Giralda tower, looming in the near distance, its *giraldilla* (little weather vane) turning in the breeze. If you'd like to see the weather vane—a bronze female figure signifying the "Triumph of Faith"—close up, pop into the courtyard of the *Ministerio de Cultura,* located diagonally across from the cathedral (and from the entrance to the Giralda itself on Plaza de Virgen de los Reyes). Beyond the courtyard is the old weather vane, removed in 1981, replaced by an identical one flying from the Giralda today. Hours: 10:30 A.M. to 1:30 P.M., 4:30 to 6:30 P.M. in summer; afternoon hours 3:30 to 5:30 rest of year.

Inside the Giralda looking out, the views vary from side to side. To the west, the tower overlooks the *Plaza de Toros,* the Guadalquivir, and Triana (once the old gypsy quarter, now mostly industrial). It used to be said that "table olives can be seen from the Giralda." Today, the way the city has expanded, you can barely see the silver of the olive trees. Yet the Giralda remains for most Sevillanos the symbol of Andalucía—built on a foundation of Roman and Visigothic stones, a Moorish structure, with a Christian topping.

The *Giraldilla* currently in place on top doesn't move much during Sevilla's hot, hot summers when the heat can reach 118°F. Fair warning that the best seasons to visit this city of grace and flowers are spring and fall. In the spring Sevilla puts its best fête forward. It all begins with *Semana Santa* (Holy Week) when 100 incredibly decorated *pasos* or floats (some dating back to the 16th century) are moved in beautiful emotion-charged processions to the cathedral from churches all over the city during the days (and nights) of the week before Easter. If you plan to be in Sevilla at this time, check the daily newspapers for each day's procession route. The highlights are the exit of "El Gran Poder" and the return "home" of "La Macarena" (Our Lady of Hope of La Macarena), Sevilla's patron Madonna, to her own church.

Then comes *Feria* with its parades, horses, festooned carriages, Andalucían costumes, fireworks, bullfights, and *flamenco* singing and dancing. In 1847 Doña Isabel II gave Sevilla the right and privilege to hold a livestock fair. With typical Sevillano exuberance, Feria is what this simple beginning evolved into—a celebration *par excellence.* The season ends with the pomp and panoplies of Corpus Christi. Sevilla in spring is spelled s-e-n-s-a-t-i-o-n-a-l. It's also spelled "stage set," according to a cynical Spanish friend. It's true. If you want to see the city more relaxed, less " on show," then September or October might be a better time to visit. But springtime *is* spectacular!

Jerez de la Frontera

Wine fanciers may want to take N-VI, or A4 the *autopista,* south 123 kilometers to Jerez de la Frontera for a bit of the grape. This is sherry country, and on 55,000 acres between Jerez (as it's usually called) and Cádiz 4,000 owners produce the strong white wine known as sherry. By international agreement (such as those that limit the use of the name Champagne) no other wine, however similar, can be legally called sherry. The Sherry Triangle's geographical parameters are Jerez to Puerto de Santa Maria to Sanlúcar de Barrameda.

What's in a name that isn't better in a glass, and what better way to enjoy a Jerez visit than sipping one's way from bodega to bodega? Time out, for the non-thirsty, to admire Jerez's many pretty plazas (Plaza de la Arenal, Plaza de la Asunción, Plaza del Arroyo), its *alcázar,* the rich facade of the Archeological Museum, and great flying buttresses of the fine Collegiate Cathedral. There is much to see in this sybaritic little town that good wine built.

Sanlúcar de Barrameda

Just 21 kilometers northwest of Jerez on C-440 is the historic port of Sanlúcar de Barrameda. Magellan shipped out from here in 1519 on his round-the-world voyage, as did Columbus, on his third trip (1498) to the New World.

Sanlúcar's claim to fame today is its Manzanilla (a sherry matured in the town's special salty sea air), produced by 23 bodegas. You may enjoy as much as we do the somewhat lazy air of the village at the mouth of the Guadalquivir River. We like the tiny Bar Bisotes right on the main street opposite the sandy beach, where fishermen bring their catch "wriggling

Seville's ladies loan their jewelry, to be pinned on the Madonna's cape during Holy Week

If you like antiquities, you can ruinate at Italica, 6 kms from Sevilla. Whole Roman theater mosaics and columns

The sherry harvest is in September

Notice the Spanish Georgian architecture in Jerez; an English touch, unique in Spain

Bodegas Barcena, on shore here, good for sardines, clams and sole

fresh" to sell and to barter in exchange for coffee and brandy. (It's open 24 hours a day for the fishermen, but not on holidays.) Next door is *Nuestra Señora del Carmen,* the fishermen's chapel, a tiny stucco building with a mural inside, done by local native artists, with portraits of town residents depicted as the saints surrounding the Virgin. (A white haired man in the left front is Manolo Sanlúcar, a famous flamenco guitarist from the town.) For 100 pesetas round trip you can take a boat across the river to Coto de Doñana, a bird sanctuary that protects endangered species.

Cádiz

Cádiz is just 31 kilometers south of Jerez on N-VI or A-4. Considered the oldest town in Spain, Cádiz was founded by Phoenicians in 1100 B.C. After the discovery of the Americas, when trade flowed like the tides in and out, Cádiz was the richest port in Europe. Consequently it attracted Barbary pirates like flies, as well as England, Spain's main enemy at the time. In 1587 (the year before the Armada sailed) Sir Francis Drake whisked in and out, destroying by fire 10,000 tons of shipping and boasting that he had "singed the king of Spain's beard." The port was used by Napoleon's fleet as a launching pad that ended in a rout by the British at Trafalgar.

Things are a lot more peaceful today. Visitors enjoy the seafront promenade and the knit-together streets and sunny palm-lined squares of the old town. One can visit the old Hospital del Carmen de Mujeres to see the El Greco painting in the chapel or the Chapel of San Felipe Neri to view Murillo's *Immaculate Conception.* But mostly, it's fun just to wander, sit in a sidewalk cafe, sip a *fino* and ruminate on the old port's checkered history. Or something.

In its B.C. Greek phase, Cádiz was widely known for its cuisine. We wouldn't know about that, but do suggest you try El Faro, 15 Calle San Felix (211068,) for sole and other fish expertly prepared.

A CAUTIONARY NOTE

Sevilla, for all its orange blossom charm, has some big city problems tourists should keep in mind. With 24.7% unemployment in Sevilla province—one of the highest rates in the Western World—there is bound to be some unrest. In Sevilla this takes the form of gangs of two or three youths, often on motor bikes, who cruise the streets looking for careless or unwary tourists carrying handbags, shoulder strap bags or cameras. To prevent being "ripped off," the following are recommendations of the U. S. Consulate in Sevilla as of this writing:

1. If you drive through Sevilla, keep all belongings out of sight in the trunk. One gang tactic is to smash a car's window at a traffic light and grab or hook whatever they can—camera, handbag, radio and then ride off.
2. Never leave your car unlocked nor with anything visible inside, except perhaps a road map.
3. When walking, do not enter isolated, empty streets with a camera over your shoulder, especially during the long hot siesta hours of 1–4 P.M.
4. Both men and women should carry their wallets in inside pockets, not in a bag that can be pulled away. Keep your passport locked in a suitcase in your hotel room. (You'll only need it when you have to show identification at a bank.)
5. Best precaution is to be alert to motorcycles and teenage boys in groups of two or more. They won't attack; they avoid confrontation. They want to snatch and run.
6. Sevilla's nightlife is lively and people dine late. Taxi, do not walk, to and from any isolated restaurants.

Inside Information

Hotels

For prices, see Madrid, page 50.

The south of Spain as we have organized it may seem slightly schizophrenic: the *Costa del Sol* revved up and ready for sun-and-sports lovers, a perfect choice for R & R. The interior, with its many historic and cultural connections is more the target of the sightseer and the traveler with touring in mind.

The hotels in both areas reflect these separate proclivities. In a resort area, you obviously want a hotel with more than the comforts and facilities of home. In a city, being near the action makes sightseeing easier. Selections have been made with these thoughts in mind. Thus each star category reflects the area's dichotomy and geographic spread.

★★★★★ FIVE STARS

★★★★★ 1. PUENTE ROMANO

Chances are you may run into the likes of Faye Dunaway, Charlotte Ford, or Diana Vreeland in the pool or lobby

Carretera Cádiz–Málaga, kilometer 184 Marbella; phone 770100. New money talks, old money whispers. At the smart, newish, younger (but bigger) sister of the chi-chi Marbella Club Hotel, money both talks and whispers. New money and old titles mix in the pampered, hedonistic experience provided by this all-for-comfort resort hotel. Puente Romano was originally an apartment annex to the Prince Hohenlohe Langenberg–run Marbella Club, but in 1979 it became a hotel.

Now, beyond the luscious oleander and purple bougainvillea-hedged entrance drive of the Marbella Club you'll find the gleaming white pueblo-style private villas of Puente Romano. Seemingly no convenience has been overlooked: space, glorious space to move around in, double closets, double brass sinks, direct-dial phones, bookcase-hidden minibars, four-channel color TV, rooms decorated in color-coordinated restful motifs, balconies recessed and sheltered by lemon trees for privacy. In a pair of suites you'll even find saunas.

Sports are just a stroll away on the lushly foliaged, flamingo-inhabited grounds: seven tennis courts (and instruction by the likes of Bjorn Borg, pro-in-residence), two pools with a bar at each for handy libations, the use of Marbella Club's golf course, shops, lounges, and three dining rooms-*cum*-terraces. And in the evening, one can drop into Regine's disco on the grounds for a nightcap or a "hustle" around the floor. Pampering is only slightly less complete at sister *Marbella Club* down the road. At Puente Romano: 180 rooms. *Very Expensive.*

★★★★★ 2. LOS MONTEROS

Urbanizacion Los Monteros, Marbella; phone 771100. For the totally sports-minded this would surely be *Numero Uno* on the Sun Coast, for the range of activities available boggles. Part of a handsomely designed development of condos and villas, the hotel is understated elegance all the way. Spacious rooms, abstract art by Madrid artists on the walls, pleasing color schemes, doors that close softly and never slam, all the expected comforts of direct dial phones, color TV, minibar. There's a superb golf course, tennis, horseback riding, five squash courts, and a beach club with every facility you can think of and a few extra besides. Add to that the Incosol Health Spa for the get-or-stay-in-shape types. As you might expect from a member of the *Relais et Chateaux* group, the French cuisine is so good people check in just for that. 171 rooms. *Very Expensive.*

★★★★★ 3. CASTILLO DE SANTA CLARA
1 Suecia, Torremolinos; phone 383155. You can hear the surf at night in this luxury beachside hotel, right on the water in Torremolinos. By day it's play, play, play—water sports galore, good tennis, golf course, and a pool if you prefer it to the sea. By night you have all the resources handy in this lively (to say the least) resort town. If one chooses to be in Torremolinos, the Castillo is a class act. Great views. 212 rooms. *Expensive.*

★★★★★ 4. HOTEL JEREZ
41 Avenida Alvaro Domecq, Jerez de la Frontera; phone 330600. We admit a special fondness, a personal preference, for this oasis of greenery in the heat of Jerez. Just 15 minutes from the airport and on the edge of town, this *Entursa* hotel is a sanctuary of quiet, with each room overlooking a well-groomed garden or the L-shaped swimming pool. The hotel dates from 1969, but all the trimmings look spanking new: brown leather couches and banquettes in the lounge, subtle tile work along the smooth pine bar (where 40 different brands of sherry are stocked—a tip of the hat to the many visiting experts), flower boxes filled with pink geraniums, white stucco walls and cork-ceilinged lounge area. Bedrooms are spacious and airy, with portable TV, double closets, marble-floored baths. You can dine in the large, gracious El Cartujano dining room or on a terrace surrounded by palms, banana plants and pines. For tennis, there's the El Bosque Country Club directly across the road. There's even *merienda* (tea) with *churros* in the late afternoon. 120 rooms. *Moderate.*

Orson Welles and Plácido Domingo have stayed here often. A nice cocktail time custom: delicious hot canapes passed throughout the bar & lounge areas

★★★★★ 5. ALFONSO XIII
2 Calle de San Fernando, Sevilla; phone 222850. Four years, hiatus in the late 1970s for $8 million worth of renovations, and *olé!* Sevilla's landmark luxury hotel is back in business, better and more charming than ever. Renovations have been discreet, and the pseudo-Arabic character of the hotel remains intact. The hotel took 12 years to complete and was finished just in time for the Ibero-American Exposition of 1929. You'll see the bust of the hotel's namesake, King Alfonso XIII, who inaugurated it.

What makes this hotel, now part of the government's *Entursa* chain, so special, aside from the superb low-key, unostentatious service, is its fine attention to detail; hallmarks of times when things were built to last forever. With beige brick three-story exterior, decorated with ornate wrought iron balconies, multicolored *azulejos,* horseshoe-arched windows and cupolas, the Alfonso XIII is even more of a treat inside. Lobby walls 22 feet high, an abundance of soft carpeting, tiled walls (10,000 tiles in the main staircase

King Saud once kept goats (and gold-scimitared bodyguards) in his suite, Hemingway used to "hold court" here, and Eva Peron once made this her diplomatic headquarters

alone), brick-edged Arabic arches, parquet wood floors, brocade-and-damask-covered antique furniture—these are elements of the public areas. The Andalusian Patio with its rounded arches and tranquil fountain delights you as you sip drinks in the lounge surrounding it. In the basement, the modern looking *Italica* restaurant offers regional and international specialties with flawless service. (You can even be served on gold plates if you request.)

Bedrooms are large, roomy as older hotels tend to be, with a phone extension in the bath and balconies big enough for small cocktail parties. You will enjoy the nighttime balcony views of the nearby Giralda Tower and the little park across Avenida de Roma, also the handiness to Sevilla's major sights just two or three blocks away. If a normal king-size bedroom isn't big enough, there's always the royal suite that comes complete with formal salons, king-size beds, totally marble baths (tub, walls, ceiling, floor and fixtures), and a royal dining salon that serves 16 with ease. Other amenities: gardens, garage and parking, hairdresser, shops (Loewe branch), swimming pool, banquet halls. 150 rooms. *Moderate–Expensive.*

★★★★ FOUR STARS

★★★★ 1. ALHAMBRA PALACE

2 Peña Partida, Granada; phone 221468. A handy location, just down the road a piece from the real Alhambra, this pinkish-red pleasure palace of a hotel is a pseudo-Arabic, slightly campish delight. *Azulejos,* Arabic arches and even a "honeycomb" decorative effect bordering the walls conspire to make you feel you're really in Granada. Only the neon sign outside jars (inexcusable in the surroundings). A plaque over the fireplace in the lounge states that King Juan Carlos and Queen Sofía stayed at the hotel in 1980. Bedrooms are large and modern, with thrilling views of the city and mountains, yet quiet at night. If you sip an aperitif at one of the hotel's two lively bars, you'll see much of Granada society float in and out, en route to lunch, dinner or sundry celebrations. Manuel de Falla's tiny house (*) is just a step or two away (open 10–2. Free). 124 rooms. *Moderate.*

★★★★ 2. PARADOR NACIONAL SAN FRANCISCO

Alhambra, Granada; phone 221493. With the best address in town, this parador has a history most hostelries would envy. Queen Isabella was once interred in what is now the interior patio. This is almost everybody's favorite parador and first choice for a Granada visit. We shared that feeling in years past, but a modern addition (to deal with the flood of reservation requests) has done public areas in vivid purples and diminished our enthusiasm.

Most of the guest rooms however are still lovely, simple, and in the original character of Old Granada with handwoven rugs, old carved furniture, lantern lights. And nothing can reduce one's thrill in the views of gardens and the cypress paths of the Generalife Palace across the ravine. The public areas in the old part of this mosque-turned-convent are still their charming selves, with antique wood *santos,* old pitchers and burnished copper casually displayed on antique tables. You may even like the handsome modernity of the purple bar, abstract paintings and spacious but plain restaurant (the food is good!). We're just a little spoiled by memories of times past. Even with additional space, demand continues to outrun availability. This means you should reserve as far ahead as possible, i.e., months and months, especially for the prime spring season. 50 rooms. *Moderate.*

★★★★ 3. DOÑA MARÍA

19 Don Remondo, Sevilla; phone 224990. A tiny gem in full sight of, and a hop-skip-jump *to,* the cathedral, *Alcázar* and the *barrio* Santa Cruz. Not only is there a profusion of antiques used throughout—in attractive groupings in the lounge, painted headboards and furniture in the bedrooms—but there are 1980s comforts as well; namely, air conditioning, a rooftop swimming pool and a small garden in the rear of the lobby. Public areas, including elevator, are small, but guest rooms are ample enough and boast double sinks in bathrooms. Corner room 110 is a special delight, with a head-on view of Giralda Tower. This hotel is a sleeper, just off Plaza Virgen de los Reyes. Parking is a problem. 61 rooms. *Inexpensive–Moderate.*

★★★★ 4. PARADOR NACIONAL ALCÁZAR DEL REY DON PEDRO

Carmona; phone 141010. Let your imagination soar like the hawks circling this hilltop parador, where the views seem to go on forever. Your view is the same as that of Pedro the Cruel, who built a little love nest palace for his *paramour,* just below the rim where the parador now rests. (A parador for a paramour? It'll never make the Top Ten.)

One of the newest of the paradors, Carmona is one of our favorites. Blue-and-white tiles border the entrance, the terrace with its extravagant vistas, and the guest rooms (with views of their own). A melding of marble floors, wood ceilings. Mudéjar brick arches and wood screens plus generous use of tiles give this handsome small hotel the feeling of a traditional Andalusian villa. Patio, fountain, a profusion of palms and flowers add to the effect. The rooms are furnished in handsome local fabrics. A large swimming pool adds to one's comfort on hot summer days. 55 rooms. *Inexpensive.*

★★★★ 5. PORTA COELI

49 Eduardo Dato, Sevilla; phone 251800. Note the one drawback: a location on the rim, not in the center, of Sevilla. Thus noted, the pluses are considerable: large and comfortable guest rooms, with good luggage space and TV; welcoming lobby and lounges with fresh flowers; tapestries, wood paneling and carpeting, soft music as background. A member of the *Husa* chain, new in the late 1970s. 250 rooms. *Inexpensive–Moderate.*

★★★ THREE STARS

★★★ 1. INGLATERRA

10 Plaza Nueva, Sevilla; phone 224970. What a face lift will do! Not that this old-timer is any less comfortable than it was when we first encountered it in the mid-1950s, but a refurbishing inside has brought new furnishings and an altogether modern air. Guest rooms are simply outfitted, with color

TV, radio, good space. Wide, carpeted halls, discreetly attractive public areas. Excellent service and a fine central location make this a reliable, Sevilla-ized choice. 120 rooms. *Moderate.*

★★★ 2. PASARELA

11 Avenida de la Borbolla, Sevilla; phone 231980. A smallish hostelry but a lively one, the Pasarela is on the edge of Maria Luisa Park. Its decor is the most modern in town, which will please or provoke, depending on your taste. Nothing avant-garde, but modish for tradition-minded Sevilla. Small lobby, cute bar, pleasing combinations of browns, beiges and orange. Finnish sauna, garage, large bedrooms overlooking the park, with minibars. 82 rooms. *Inexpensive–Moderate.*

★★★ 3. MELIÁ CÓRDOBA

Jardines de la Victoria, Córdoba; phone 298066. Within walking distance of the Mezquita and Córdoba's old quarter, the hotel is located on a busy boulevard, with the noise screened somewhat by a setback and skillful use of protective greenery. Comfortable rooms (with minibars) play second fiddle to a lively lounge and lobby, with such features as a swimming pool, nice antiques shop on premises, garden and restaurant. Popular with *Thompson Tours* and other groups. Location is *the* big plus. 99 rooms. *Moderate.*

★★★ 4. REINA VICTORIA

25 Jerez, Ronda; phone 871240. Picture yourself sitting calmly, sipping a *fino,* gazing over at an abyss and there you are at the Reina Victoria! Well, that may be a slight overstatement, but Ronda's precipitous location and the hotel's advantageous position with its gorgeous views of the ravine and mountains add to the fillip of staying in this old-fashioned Victorian hostelry. The lounge furniture could do with a touch-up, but the rooms are generous, there's a swimming pool, and a view to knock your socks off from many of the guest room windows. 73 rooms. *Inexpensive.*

★★★ 5. MÁLAGA PALACIO

1 Cortina del Muelle, Málaga; phone 215185. Málaga's major hotel is very handily located for sights and shopping, and if you luck into a corner room you'll have a balcony with full view of the lopsided cathedral with its single tower. Some of the plain, simple rooms have seafront promenade views that are really special. Public rooms are nicely appointed, and the dining room's big rounded windows offer views in three directions. There's also a swimming pool, handy in the heat of summer. 228 rooms. *Inexpensive–Moderate.*

★★ TWO STARS

★★ 1. MAIMÓNIDES

4 Torrijos, Córdoba; phone 223856. This small hotel's big asset is its proximity to the old-quarter sights. (It's within touching distance of the Mezquita, across the street.) Quiet and cozy. Nothing fancy, but comfortable rooms with wall-to-wall carpeting; a small cafeteria, marble-floored lounge, all make this *hotel residencia* a handy spot to be. 61 rooms. *Inexpensive.*

★★ 2. WASHINGTON IRVING

2 Paseo Generalife, Granada; phone 227550. What better name for a hotel within a shout of the *Palacio del Generalife?* Devottes are charmed by the Mudéjar look of this hotel. Adequate rooms, quiet setting, a stairway lined with Granada tiles with pomegranate motifs, and a dining room that would satisfy a vizier with its Moorish tiles and ceiling. 60 rooms. *Inexpensive.*

★★ 3. CAPELE

58 General Franco, Jerez de la Frontera; phone 346400. Handy, if slightly noisy, location in the center of Jerez's action on a pleasant street. The Capele has comfy rooms, some with small balconies. An acceptable choice. 30 rooms. *Inexpensive.*

★★ 4. FRANCIA Y PARIS

2 Plaza de Calvo Sotelo, Cádiz; phone 212318. Modest, but pleasing, and located on an attractive plaza, this is an agreeable overnight choice in a compact city where all sights are within easy walking distance. *Bargain.*

★ ONE STAR

★ 1. HOSTAL AMÉRICA

53 Calle Real de la Alhambra, Granada; phone 227471. The location's perfect, a hop-scotch from the Alhambra. This 19th-century house is immaculate, with two tiny lounges full of antiques and a Spanish equivalent of *gemütlichkiet.* Windows open to a postage-stamp-size patio. The setting is restful, the value is excellent, a super budget-minded choice. 14 rooms; (Tariff includes two meals a day). *Bargain.*

★ 2. MARISA

6 Cordenal Herrero Córdoba; phone 226317. Compact, modest *residencia* conveniently located directly across from *Mezquita. Bargain.*

★ 3. KENIA

65 Molinos, Granada; phone 227506. Here's one we like even better, outside small garden, with orange trees and fountain, lovely villa facade. Inside are suggestions of faded grandeur. There's a small dining room, bedrooms that are adequate, reminiscent of English Bed & Breakfast places. 19 rooms. *Bargain.*

Restaurants

For prices, see Madrid, page 54.

It is easy to underestimate Andalusían cuisine. We were good at it once, but have now come to appreciate its variety and subtlety. There are 30 versions of gazpacho, for instance, including the kind so popular in Málaga, made with white garlic and grapes.

Andalucía's specialty, though, is seafood, especially the tiny fish, miniature anchovies called *chanquetes,* which are so delicious when lightly dusted with flour and deep-fried in steaming hot, fresh olive oil. The region that made sherry famous also uses it in cooking with kidneys, chicken and veal.

Sevillanos claim that *tapas,* which they sometimes serve on a huge platter, originated in their city. They will show you a wide variety to prove it: *chocos fritos* (fried octopus tentacles); *riñones al Jerez* (kidneys in sherry); *cazón* (shark) *frito, tomate* or *marinara;* and *boquerones* (similar to tinier sardines). And more. Starters only.

Andalusíans also have a tradition of sweet desserts, many made with egg yolks. The belief is that since vast numbers of egg whites are used to clarify wine, the yolks had to made into *something.* Thus an entire dessert line evolved, of which *yema* is the most famous.

★★★★ FOUR STARS

★★★★ 1. LA FONDA

9 Plaza Santo Cristo, Marbella; phone 772512. Add the culinary guidance of Horcher's Madrid kitchen to a charming 18th-century house and you have good omens for a memorable dining experience. The signs augur accurately: *las crepes de sardinas, riñones al jerez, crema de mejillones, el ragout de langosta*—are just a few of the excellent dishes in the German-accented international menu. Service is, as you would expect if you know Horcher's in Madrid, professional and pampering. Closed Sundays, except July to October. *Very Expensive.*

★★★★ 2. LA HACIENDA

Carretera Cádiz-Málaga, km 200 (Las Chapas), Marbella; phone 831267. Under the guidance of the Belgian Paul Schiff, this attractive restaurant has become a magnet for gourmets all along the coast. Schiff's imaginative offerings include a paté of shrimp served hot, mushroom salad, *gambas* in puff pastry with a Montilla wine sauce, chicken with olives, seafood terrine and various mousse specialties. The almond crepes for dessert are superb. Closed Sunday night and Mondays from October 1st to May 31st; Mondays from June 1st to September 30 only open for dinner. *Very Expensive.*

★★★ THREE STARS

★★★ 1. EL CABALLO ROJO

28 Cardenal Herrero, Córdoba; phone 223804. Pepe García Martin manages a neat juggling trick: a restaurant that serves flocks of tourists visiting the Mezquita across the street which still maintains quality food. You begin, the minute you are seated in one of the four cheerful, white-walled dining rooms, with a complimentary glass of sherry (*fino* for men, a sweeter *oloroso* for women) and spicy slices of *chorizo* and other *tapas.* The menu is classically Andalusían—almond gazpacho with apples, red sweet pepper salad, rabbit ragout in an almond sauce, lamb stew Mudéjar, sea bream with garlic and parsley—these are a few of the excellent choices. Expect to feast in a very *simpatico* setting. *Moderate.*

★★★ 2. GAITAN

3 Gaitan, Jerez de la Frontera; phone 345859. The *ambiente* is secluded, *intimo* and appealing, the seafood specialties even more so. Consider gazpacho (it's different no matter where you try it), duck with olives Sevilla

style, *merluza* (hake) with anchovy sauce, stuffed squid, fish casserole, or any of the daily fish specials. *Moderate.*

★★★ 3. SAN MARCO
6 Calle Cuna, Sevilla; phone 212440. Currently very "in" with local *politicos* and fashionable Sevillanos. With reason. Lovely, airy, spacious decor—white walls, high beamed ceilings, marble floors—a back drop for delicious fish and pasta dishes. *Nouvelle cuisine.* Try the sole souffle or *papillote de pez Espada. Expensive.*

★★★ 4. LA DORADA
6 Virgen de Agua Santa, Sevilla; phone 455100. The *pièce de resistance* in this popular house (with branches in Madrid and Barcelona) is fried fish, accompanied by a red pepper salad. Or try the shellfish with garlic. Dessert should be the Andalusían sweet, *tocino del cielo,* a very eggy *creme caramel.* Closed Sundays and from July 5th to September. *Moderate.*

★★★ 5. FIGÓN DEL CABILDO
Plaza del Cabildo, Sevilla; phone 220117. You will love the light airiness of this new establishment in a new complex (see Shopping). A bar and informal dining room are on the ground floor, with a large open hearth complete with hanging kettle. Upstairs, the rustic, somewhat folkloric dining room, with tiny balcony, is festooned with palms and potted plants. Try the calves liver and spinach with a pine nut-studded brown sauce, *frito variado* or clams with artichokes. The wine list is unusually strong here, priced from 150 pts. for the house wine to 4,500 pts. for *Reserve Excelso. Moderate.*

★★ TWO STARS

★★ 1. SEVILLA
12 Oficios, Granada; phone 221223. We like the family hominess of this old-time favorite in downtown Granada. Right across from the Cathedral, it attracts Granadans coming from Mass and tourists coming from sightseeing. All the same, the *"típica"* folkloric look is real, and the robust food in generous portions is just fine. Try the wispy-crisp fried *calamari,* grilled fish and shrimp, and the specialty—burnt walnuts in whipped cream for dessert. More than you can eat costs less than you can believe. *Moderate.*

Also 2-stars for El Rincón de Pepe, 1 Sancho Murcia (212249)

★★ 2. ANTONIO
Muelle Ribera, Marbella; phone 812190. Fried fish is the *raison d'etre* here, and this popular Puerto Banus eatery does it to a turn. *Inexpensive.*

★★ 3. VENTA LOS NARANJOS
Carretera de Jerez-Sanlúcar, kilometer 6, Jerez de la Frontera; phone 330535. The decor is roadhouse plain, the food simple. What you get is an abundance of the freshest shrimp, sole and other fish imaginable. No fancy touches, just marvelous marine fare. Try a *Privilegio del Rey Sancho* if you want an inexpensive local dry white wine, or a *Domecq Rioja blanco seco. Moderate.*

★★ 4. OR-IZA

6 Betis, Sevilla; phone 279585. Across the river you'll find this new classical Basque restaurant, popular with locals wanting a change from their Andalusian diet. *Moderate.*

★★ 5. EL BENI

Muelle Benabola, Marbella; phone 811625. Even jet-setters like the simplicity of Beni's fried fish, and this Puerto Banus marine restaurant is as "in" as ever. Yet considering the mountains-to-sea stage-set locale, prices aren't all that devastating. Try the cream of mussels soup, among other lovely dishes. Closed Sundays and from November 1st till December 15th. *Moderate.*

★★ 6. CUNINI

14 Capuchinas, Granada; phone 223727. Stylish, cool-looking place near the cathedral, here's *the* seafood eatery in Granada. Grilled or fried, the fish, oysters and other shellfish are wonderful. *Moderate.*

★★ 7. LA BARRACA

34 Pedro Antonio de Alacón, Granada; phone 265061. "The" place for local fashionables. A somewhat old-fashioned decor unfolds to offer good Andalusian and Continental standards. Try gazpacho Andaluz, *sopa Sevilla* or grilled swordfish. *Moderate.*

★ ONE STAR

★ 1. MESON DE DON RAIMUNDO

36 Argote del Molino, Sevilla; phone 223355. A Sevillano version of a Neapolitan fiesta. The wall and ceiling decorations are a cacophony of garlic buds strung on the wall, a deer head, antique glass chandelier, copper pots, old plates and glass sconces. You'll find certain Andalusian specialties that have Arabic origins. Try the clam and *piñones* soup; pigeon or wild rabbit in sherry; suckling pig. For dessert, Moorish-accented figs and dates in cream. Closed from November to *Semana Santa. Moderate.*

★ 2. SECUNDINO

Bajo de Guía, Sanlúcar de Barrameda; phone 362088. Some of the best food in Andalucía is in the simplest, least atmospheric places. Secundino is a case in point. An informal glass-sided eatery with tin ceiling, facing the beach, it packs in locals and knowledgeable beachophiles. They sit at plain tables too close together, wolfing down tiny clams in garlic sauce, fried squid, baby hake and sole, diluted with a dry *vino blanco de mesa.* The din is deafening—a sign that Spaniards are enjoying themselves. *Bargain.*

If you like muscatel, you'll like Málaga wine; it's best served as a liqueur. Try Carlos Primero, one of the best

★ 3. ANTONIO MARTÍN

4 Paseo Maritímo, Málaga; phone 211018. Sit on the terrace in the harbor, watch the nautical world go by, and munch on chilled gazpacho and *fritura Malagueña,* the in-house way of frying a mix of seafood to perfection. Closed Mondays. *Inexpensive.*

★ **4. DON MIGUEL**
4 Villanueva, Ronda; phone 871090. Fish is the specialty here, next to the view, which looks up to the bridge above. Try the wines of Carineña as a companion to the fried fish, mountain trout, hare, or partridge. Closed Wednesdays and from January 16th to February 18th. *Bargain.*

★ **5. MESÓN DEL CONDE**
10 Medina y Corella, Córdoba; phone 223083. Tucked into a side street of the old *Judería,* this unpretentious place serves hearty fare—oxtail stew, vegetable soup, rabbit—competently prepared, pleasantly served, at modest prices. *Bargain.*

Entertainment

Theater is popular in Andalucía and is generally part of the Festivals de España and other broad-guage celebrations. Films, especially in air-conditioned theaters in the dog days of summer, are popular too. Almería has hosted a film festival in years past during the month of January (check with the National Tourist Office of Spain on this and other such festivals).

Film

TORREMOLINOS
International Film Festival in March.

Concerts and Ballet

GRANADA
International Festival of Music and Dance has been an annual feature for more than thirty years in late June, early July. Held in the Generalife and Alhambra, it presents internationally famous performers. (For festival information write Palacio de la Madraza, 1 Oficios, Granada, or call 225231.)

MÁLAGA
Festivales de España, August to September, includes music by well-known performers. (For information, write tourist office.)

NERJA
Its Festivales de España includes music and dance performances in its famous caves—a cool way of dealing with the August heat. (Write tourism office for information.)

SEVILLA
Sevilla organizes a "Musical May" month of concerts each year. (Check with its tourist office for details.)

Gambling

There are currently four casinos operating along the coast between Murcia and Algeciras. Casino Nueva Andalucía de Marbella in Marbella; Casino de Juego Torrequebrada in Benalmadena; Azarmenor in San Javier just outside Murcia; and Casino Bahia de Cádiz at Puerta de Santa Maria. Each of these has a fancy restaurant, bar and show in addition to the standard exercise fields with slot machines, roulette, chemin de fer, *punto y banco,* blackjack and baccarat. Admission is about 500 pts. and you will need your passport—in addition to money.

Folklore

CÓRDOBA

Fiesta de los Patios Córdobeses in May, when the city opens up like a flower, with patios on display, pilgrimage in honor of Virgen Conquistadora; elaborately decorated carriages, horses, riders, augmented by celebration, singing, dancing, bullfights and flamenco competition.

ESTEPONA

Fiesta de la Virgen del Carmen in July; solemn procession, bringing image of Virgin to the sea, then carried by fishing fleet. Races, regattas, dancing, fireworks.

JEREZ

Feria del Caballo, first part of May. All-out horsey fête, with races, dressage, carriages with 2–6 horse teams. Everyone in Andalucían costumes; top-notch bullfights.

Vendimia (wine harvest festival), early September. After fiesta queen presents new grapes on silver platter to be blessed for good wine, all kinds of celebration break loose—especially bullfights and flamenco festival.

MURCIA

International Mediterranean Folk Festival, mid-September.

RONDA

International Folk Gala, early September.

SEVILLA

Semana Santa (Holy Week). From Palm Sunday on, daily processions through Saturday, of images, penitents and clerics in a palpable outpouring of faith. Fascinating, beautiful, haunting.

Feria, a fortnight after Easter, Sevillanos take to an exuberant, improvised tent city. Horses, carriages, Andalucían garb and open house with singing, dancing, sipping. Superb bullfights. Bellringer of a gala.

Corpus Christi is a solemn and elaborate procession at 8 A.M., then a celebration that includes dancing, singing, flamenco, and the best of bullfights.

Baile de los "Seises" (Dance of the "Sixes") is a dance of six (or as many as nine) boys between 6 and 16 years of age in the cathedral on Corpus Christi, Immaculate Conception, Sunday, Monday, and Tuesday of Carnival and August 15th. By special dispensation they are allowed to dance, with castanets, as long as their original medieval costumes last (the costumes have been patched and triple patched for hundreds of years).

Semana Santa is celebrated all over Spain, but the observances are especially outstanding in Sevilla, Málaga, Murcia, Carmona and Ecija.

VENDIMIA

The wine harvest festival—is the year's major event in many communities. Among the most renowned are Jerez's and Málaga's and the Montilla-Moriles celebration in late August or early September.

SANLÚCAR DE BARRAMEDA

Fiesta of the Guadalquivir River, August, decorated boats, cars; dancing, flamenco, bullfights.

Nightlife

For traditional flamenco, stay out of those gypsy caves in Granada and try some more reliable flamenco places in Sevilla.

Sevilla

El Arenal, 7 Calle Rodo; phone 216492; Los Gallos, 10 Plaza. de Santa Cruz; phone 213198; La Trocha, 23 Ronda de Capuchinos; phone 355028. Remember to go for the second show, after the *hors d'oeuvres* have been run past the tourists and the real artists settle down to serious work. For something more modest, pop into the bar at the *Porta Coelli* Hotel where you'll find a practitioner of the art warmly filling the room with flamenco guitar music.

In Jerez, you may wish to contact *Cátedra de Flamencologia,* which fosters *flamenco* studies, conferences and recitals, to find out who's playing where and when. Check with *turismo* office for current address and phone number.

For more familiar types of after dark music and gaiety the Mediterranean shore is your best bet. Near major tourist magnets such as Torremolinos, Benalmadena, Fuengirola and Marbella, to name but a few, you will find many a dimly-lit, well-attended parlor pulsating with high decibel, familiar music. Whatever your particular favorite type of fare, you'll find it in many places along the major highways near the key tourist towns and in the lounges and discos of the top resort hotels.

If you're seeking the nightclub show experience—showgirls, comics, dance and song—head for the nearest casino in the region. (See listing of casinos under Gambling.) Otherwise, look for shows in what the Spaniards call "Salas de Fiestas."

Shopping

Specialties of Andalucía are all the things one thinks of as "Spanish"—fans, mantillas, shawls, combs, leather and dolls. You will find shops throughout the region with such items. The best source for regional handcrafts is usually the local Artespaña outlet. There is one in Córdoba at Posada del Potro, in Granada at Corral del Carbon, and in Sevilla at 4 Rodriguez Jurado.

If you are in the market for contemporary art, there is Galería Laguada, 44 Puentezuelas, Granada. Galeria Juana de Aizpuru, 10 Canalejas, Sevilla, sells Picasso graphics and exhibits work by many Madrid abstract artists.

In Córdoba the specialty is hand-worked leather—shoes, boots, bags, luggage, and clothes. The prime place for briefcases, handbags, and other top quality leather goods, and embossed leather purses and jewel boxes is Meryan, 2 Calleja de las Flores in the old quarter. You might look in at El Zoco, a complex of leather and silver shops at Averroes—but be wary of cheap, machine-stamped Moroccan leather imports.

Granada's long-time special craft has been weaving. You will see the typical Granada multi-colored stripes in wool shoulder bags, bedspreads and skirts. A central shopping place is the arcade called Corral del Carbon, near the Cathedral along the Alcaiceria in the downtown area. Many of the Corral shops have a touristy look, but it is possible to find buys in woven goods and in Granada pottery—plates, bowls, pitchers. This local earthenware comes in blue/green and white, often with pomegranate designs symbolizing Granada.

In Jerez de la Frontera the big buy is sherry, whether at the *bodega* of your choice or a supermarket in town. (Actually, even if you don't go to Jerez, sherry is available at good prices throughout Andalucía.)

Sevilla's bustling Calle de las Sierpes is a favorite shopping street for Sevillanos. Loewe, the Madrid leather store, has a branch in the Alfonso XIII Hotel. A bookstore with many English language titles is Vertice, 24 Mateos Gago, on the edge of the *barrio* Santa Cruz.

An elegant new shopping complex, Plaza del Cabildo, can be reached via 22 Queipo de Llano, across from the cathedral. It is a beautiful semi-circular four-story building reminiscent of a "crescent" in England, with graceful arcades and painted arches. Among the record, book and other shops is a particularly attractive antiques shop, Antigüedades Lola Ortega.

For an inexpensive lunch or snack, the Galerias's second floor cafeteria is a good buy

There are branches of El Corte Inglés, 10 Plaza Duque Victoria, and Galerías Preciados, 1 Plaza General Franco in Sevilla.

Sevilla's many convents make ends meet by selling homemade specialties, often cookies or cakes of some sort. Anyone with a yen for something *dulce* might take note that the Convent of Santa Ines is known for its *tortas* and *bollitos* (tarts and little cakes); the Convent of San Leandro for its egg-yolk-and-sugar *yemas* (ultra-sweet); and the Convent of Santa Paula for marmalade. The Convent of Madre de Dios breaks the trend and sells paper flowers. To make a purchase, simply ring the bell at the convent, ask for the specialty, which is usually packaged and neatly tied, and pay whatever the modest amount is. The sweets are freshly made. All in all it is a pleasant and different travel experience.

Museums and Galleries (in addition to those described in text)

Cádiz

★ MUSEO DE BELLAS ARTES

Plaza del Generalisimo. The painting collection includes excellent Murillos, Canos and Zurburáns, plus others. On the ground floor are archaeological exhibits. Hours: 9:30 A.M. to 1:30 P.M.; closed Sundays and Mondays.

Córdoba

★ MUSEO ARQUEOLÓGICO
Plaza de Jerónimo Páez. The museum is actually located on a part of an old Roman plaza. You walk on its huge paving blocks and stairs, enjoy its marble fountain and tiny pool with mosaic floor, where they were in the ancient Roman capital of Baetica. Roman mosaics, amphorae, sculpture, Visigothic gold crosses, plus fragments from Medina Azahara. (Rooms may be closed for restoration.) Hours: 10 A.M. to 1:30 P.M.; afternoons 4 to 6, January through April and September through December; 5 to 7 P.M., May and June; closed July and August, and on Sundays and holiday afternoons.

★★ MUSEO PROVINCIAL DE BELLAS ARTES
Plaza del Potro. This palace built around a patio shows the works of Córdoban painters. Notable for the 16th-century works and for the paintings of Ribera, Zurburán, Murillo, and others. Hours: 10 A.M. to 1:30 P.M. except July, August, Sundays and holidays; 10 A.M. to 2 P.M.; afternoons 4 to 7, April through September; 3:30 P.M. to 6 P.M., rest of year; closed July and August.

MUSEO TAURINO Y DE ARTESANIA CÓRDOBESA
Plaza de Bulas. Bullfighters' hall of fame, Córdoban-style. Costumes, photos, wax figures, posters of all-time greats such as Manolete and "El Córdobes." Other two sections show prize examples of Córdoban silver and leather artistry. Hours: 9:30 A.M. to 1:30 P.M.; afternoons from May to October, 5 to 8 P.M.; rest of the year, 4 to 7 P.M.

Granada

★ CASA CASTRIL
Carrera de Darro. In a Renaissance palace, with plateresque gateway by Siloé, are displayed sculpture, ceramics, textiles, jewelry and coins from Granada's Muslim, Visigothic, Greek, Roman and prehistoric heritage. It's the city's archaeological museum. Hours: 10 A.M. to 2 P.M., 6 to 8 P.M. in summer, 4 to 6 thereafter; closed Sundays, holidays and Monday afternoons.

Jerez

★ MUSEO ARQUEOLÓGICO MUNICIPAL Y BIBLIOTECA
City Archeological Museum and Library, Plaza de la Asunción. The Renaissance facade (1575) is as intriguing as the exhibits of Greek, Roman, and Moorish sculpture, ceramics, and calligraphy. Greek 7th century B.C. helmet links the Greeks with ancient Tartessos nearby. Also, library is installed in handsome barrel-vaulted marble room. Hours: 10 A.M. to 1 P.M., closed Sundays, holidays and August.

CLOCK MUSEUM
Atalaya Palace, 3 Cervantes. Installed in a 19th-century palace, the clocks are only part of the interest in this handsome headquarters of Ruiz Mateos, S. A.,

(Rumasa), the large sherry company. Hours and admission (free) by arrangement: Call 332–100 (Rumasa), ask for public relations department.

Sevilla

★★★ MUSEO ARCHEOLÓGICO

Renaissance Pavilion, Plaza de America. Installed in a building of the Ibero-American Exhibition, the 27 halls display pieces ranging from crude prehistoric tools through the priceless, 8th century B.C. "El Carambolo" gold jewelry cache plus Phoenician, Greek, Punic and Roman finds. Roman portraits in stone of gods, demi-gods and emperors from nearby Italica and Carmona. Hours: 10 A.M. to 2 P.M. Closed Mondays.

★★ MUSEO DE ARTE CONTEMPORANEO

Modern art museum, Calle Santo Tomas. In the former offices of the Cabildo Cathedral (begun 1770). Three floors of works by dozens of contemporary Spanish abstract artists (including witty Equipo Crónica satires on famous Spanish classical paintings). Hours: 5 to 9 P.M.; holidays 10 A.M. to 1 P.M. Closed Mondays. Admission free.

★★ MUSEO DE ARTES Y COSTUMBRES POPULARES

(Folk Arts and Customs Museum), Plaza de America. In an Ibero-American Exhibition building this museum displays entire rooms of 19th-century Spanish life in the city and provinces—kitchens, bedrooms, workrooms and parlors. Also gaily decorated *Feria* booth and exhibits of pottery, leather, wine and metal crafts from a century ago. Hours: 10 A.M. to 2 P.M. Closed Mondays. Admission 75 pts.

★★★★ MUSEO PROVINCIAL DE BELLAS ARTES

a gem of a museum, with first-rate works. Murillo's statue is in the pretty plaza outside.

Plaza del Museo. A museum such as this, that displays superbly many of the best works of Zurburán, Murillo, Ribera and Jan Breughel and includes also paintings by El Greco, David, Teniers and Pacheco demands the attention of art lovers. All these and more are in the splendid collection in the former Merced Convent. The 16th to 18th-century halls, refectory and chapel are rich and beautiful settings for the art.

Be sure to see the *sala* with the powerful 12th-century Catalan crucifix and Romanesque statues. The Gothic 14th and 15th century paintings in Sala II are compelling. There is a strong El Greco portrait of an artist (himself?) in Sala IV. The former chapel, Sala VI, has an ornately painted Renaissance ceiling, white marble floor and vast expanses of white walls as settings for huge Murillo (and other) canvases. The Zurburán room shows him at his most dramatic.

The cloister, with its *azulejo*-lined walls, and a tiny patio near exit, give refreshing respite from sun and heat. Convent buildings are a treat for the eye, with cool white stucco facades trimmed in saffron around windows, doors, and arches. Hours: 10 A.M. to 2 P.M. Closed Mondays and holidays. Admission 150 pts.

Historic Buildings and Sites

Arcos de la Frontera

Like roosting doves, Arcos's white cube houses with their red tile roofs cluster on a steep hill. This is one of Spain's famous "white villages." Navigate its tortuous alleys to the main square at the top where you'll find *Santa Maria de la Asunción* Church, with its Plateresque facade. Walk across the square to the parador built into the edge of the cliff. Its patio gives a 180° view of hawks and swallows swooping over the countryside and the Guadalete River far below.

Córdoba

★ ALCÁZAR DE LOS REYES CRISTIANOS

Calle Torrijos (opposite the Mezquita). It looks like a Moorish fortress because it was begun in 1328 by Alfonso XI and built with Moorish architects and workmen. Renovations and enlargements were made in the same style. Views from the parapets and towers of the Guadalquivir River, Moorish mills, Roman bridge, and the Mezquita. In the main hall now used for occasional concerts, Ferdinand and Isabella received Columbus before he sailed for the Indies. The Inquisition was established here in 1490 and continued until 1821. Handsome fortress, stunning gardens. Hours: 9:30 A.M. to 1:30 P.M., 5 to 8 P.M.; afternoons: 4 to 7; October through April. In summer, gardens are floodlit 10 P.M. to 1 A.M.

★ MEDINA AZAHARA

9 kilometers west of Córdoba on C-431 is the site where Abdu'r Rahman III built his pleasure dome about A.D. 957 and named it for his favorite wife—"The Fairest." The luxury of the original can be deduced from the lavishly carved bits now being painstakingly pieced together like a giant jigsaw puzzle, to show the three levels of palace buildings destroyed by Muslim fundamentalists. Vizier's Hall and Mosque are partially restored. Xanadu undone. Hours: Closed Mondays; 9:30 A.M. to 1:30 P.M.; afternoons mid-March to mid-September, 4 to 7:30 P.M.; rest of year, 3 to 5:30 P.M.

★★★★ PALACIO DE LOS MARQUÉSES DE VIANA

Calle Morales. This palace has 14 different patios, each a flowering delight. One has a Roman pavement mosaic, others have fountains. You tour 24 rooms of treasures—remarkable 15th to 19th-century furniture, Mudejar ceilings above halls carpeted with Moorish rugs, a wall of tiles, an 18th-century *sala* all in red brocade; porcelains from China, India and Europe in one room. Paintings by the score, including six Jan Breughels, four pictures of the Hundred Years War, a moving Jordans of *Adoration of the Magi*—and more. Goya tapestries; collections of textiles; rare books and 13th to 19th-century *azulejos;* and then there's the red-sashed Francisco Franco's official portrait, formerly in Córdoba's town hall. Hours: 10 to 12 noon, 4 to 6 P.M. Closed Wednesdays. Admission is 100 pts.

Granada

★★ MONASTERIO DE CARTUJA

Camino de Alfacar. This extraordinary monastery was begun in the 16th century, but its 18th-century baroque sacristy and *sagrario* generate the raves. Hours: 11 A.M. to 1 P.M., 4 to 7 P.M.; in winter, 3:30 to 6 P.M.

★ IGLESIA DE SAN JERÓNIMO

Calle Gran Capitan. This church is a showcase of Granada's exuberant Renaissance architecture, sculpture and painting. Contains tomb of Cordoban hero "El Gran Capitan" Fernando Gonzalez. Hours: 10 A.M. to 1:30 P.M., 3:30 to 6 P.M.

★★ ITALICA

6 km north of Sevilla on the road to Merida. The Roman city founded in 205 B.C. by Scipio Africanus was the birthplace of emperors Trajan and Hadrian. To be seen: baths, mosaic pavements, museum, amphitheater (where open air performances of classics are given). Hours: 9 A.M. to 7 P.M.; in winter closes at 5:30 P.M. (Buses from Sevilla every half hour; 30 pts.)

The amphi-theater once seated 25,000 spectators

Jerez de la Frontera

ALCÁZAR

Pérez Galdós. Brick and stone walls and towers of this Moorish fortress still stand, surrounded now by public gardens. Inside you can visit the small mosque with its horseshoe arches and *mihrab.*

IGLESIA SAN DIONISIO

Calle Pinar. Built in 1430, redone in baroque 1728–1731. Has a notable retable. The adjoining *Torre de la Atalaya,* a starkly simple square tower with Moorish windows on four sides, was built in 1449 originally to signal approaching danger.

★ LA CARTUJA DE SANTA MARIA DE LA DEFENSIÓN

4 kilometers southeast of Jerez. A major artistic monument established 1477. On the highway is an impressive Renaissance stone gate (1571). The Gothic church has a 17th-century retable, gilded choir screen, marble and marquetry doorway, and other gems.

For generations the monks operated a stud farm, and developed a breed called *Cartuja* or *Carthusian.*

Nerja

★ LAS CUEVAS

The caves are 4 kilometers from town near village of Maro. Walks through some lighted, accessible portions with prehistoric paintings are possible. Hours: 10 A.M. to 2 P.M., 4 to 7 P.M., May to mid-September; 10 A.M. to 2 P.M., 4 to 7 P.M. rest of year.

Sevilla

★ ARCHIVO GENERAL DE INDIOS

Archive of the Indies. Plaza del Triunfo. In Escorial architect Herrera's stately building (begun 1582) are the records of Spain in the Americas. You'll find current scholars at work (names listed on bulletin board), maps, diagrams, and reports on all the places where Spain had interests overseas. Hours: 10 A.M. to 12:30 P.M. Closed Sundays and holidays. Admission free.

★★ CASA DE PILATOS

Plaza de Pilatos. The palace of the fabulously wealthy dukes of Medinaceli bears this name only because the Marqués of Tarifa, who built it in 1540, was inspired by Pilate's house in the Holy Land. Splendid Gothic and Plateresque elements; its Moorish decorations include tilework some consider Spain's finest. Hours: 9 A.M. to 1 P.M., 3 to 7 P.M. Closes an hour earlier in winter.

★★★ CONVENTO DE SANTA CLARA

Calle Santa Clara. There are 17th- and 18th-century baroque retables and architectural elements in the church; the lower choir has heavily carved wood ceiling, confessional and furnishings of the 16th century. The *azulejos* on stairs, walls and ceilings in the buildings are outstanding. Hours: 5 P.M. to 9 P.M.; 10 A.M. to 1 P.M. holidays; closed Mondays.

★ IGLESIA DE SANTA MARIA LA BLANCA

Calle Santa Maria la Blanca. Originally a synagogue, this became a church after the Jews were expelled in 1492. In the 17th century the interior was redone in baroque style with lavish carvings. Murillo's painting of *The Last Supper* is here. Hours: check with tourist office.

★★ MONASTERIO DE SANTA PAULA

Calle Santa Paula. In addition to a handsome 17th-century cloister and Renaissance retables, this convent has astonishing 17th-century *azulejos* by Hernando de Valladares and a small museum of choice artworks and furniture. Hours: 9 A.M. to 1 P.M.; 4 to 7 P.M.; holidays 9 A.M. to 1 P.M.

The Sisters' marmelade is delicious, and for sale

★★ REAL MONASTERIO DE SAN CLEMENTE

Calle del Reposo. This is a huge convent built on what had been a Moorish palace. It is a Renaissance work decorated with paintings and sculpture by leading artists of the 16th, 17th and 18th centuries in Sevilla. The chapel frescoes and *azulejos* are remarkably rich. Hours: check with tourist office.

TORRE DEL ORO

Gold tower, Paseo Cristobal Colón. This twelve-sided, 13th-century Moorish tower once was the linchpin in the city's defense network. It anchored a chain across the river, among other duties. Today it contains a maritime museum. Hours: 10 A.M. to 2 P.M. weekdays; 10 A.M. to 1 P.M. Sundays. Closed on Mondays.

Escamillo, where are you?

★ REAL PLAZA DE LA MAESTRANZA DE CABALLERIA

(*La Maestranza* for short—the bullring) Plaza de Toros. This most famous of bullrings may be the most beautiful as well. Begun in 1760, it is a stunning composition in white with saffron and deep paprika-trimmed arcades and windows, and a red tiled roof. It seats 14,000.

Spectacles and Displays

Almonte

Romeria del Rocio. Any time 700,000 people or more turn out for an event, they, as well as the event, are a spectacle. Every Whitsunday and Monday hundreds of thousands make this pilgrimage to the shrine of *El Rocio,* in decorated carts, wagons, and on horses. All participate in the blessing Whitsunday morning of the image of the Virgin (dubbed affectionately *la blanca paloma*—the white dove).

Ronda

If you ever have seen Goya's series of bullfight engravings *La Tauromaquia* you'll have an idea what to expect at Ronda's annual *Corrida Goyesca* in September. Dressed in the bullfighters' costumes of Goya's day, daredevil *toreros* also attempt the caprices he captured with his pen—pole vaulting over the bull and leaping through the bull's horns. (For information, write the nearest Spanish National Tourist Office or *Oficina de Turismo,* Ronda.)

Perks

Jerez

Horse lovers will be in their element in Jerez. Some of the world's best educated horses in training as well as in exhibitions featuring their Spanish riding school education. These "dancing horses of Andalucía" are famous for good reasons, as you will find. Performances can be seen by groups of ten or more by prearrangement. Write or call ahead: *Oficina de Turismo,* Alameda Cristina, Jerez; or Pedro Domecq, S.A., 3 San Ildefonso, Jerez; Telephone week days 10 A.M. to 1 P.M., 221800.

The Spanish army stud farm, Deposito Caballes de Sementales, is on the outskirts of Jerez. Periodically there are training exercises and exhibitions. Call the *Oficina de Turismo* for possibilities.

Polo games are played weekly at certain times of year. Inquire of *turismo* for place and time.

SHERRY SAMPLING

No visit to Jerez would be complete without a visit to one of the major sherry operations. The vintners age their wines in warehouses called *bodegas.* Most of them welcome visitors—with advance notice. Write or telephone at least two weeks ahead. And plan your Jerez trip remembering that the *bodegas* are closed Sundays and shut down for a period each summer, usually in August (varies from company to company). Among the companies that welcome visitors, offer samples and have English-speaking guides are:

Gonzalez, Byass & Co., Ltd., 12 Calle Manuel Gonzalez,

Jerez de la Frontera, phone 340000; 10 A.M. to 1 P.M. The company has many unusual *bodegas* with spectacular grounds, including an 1862 building designed by A. G. Eiffel (no, it isn't a tower).

Pedro Domecq, S.A., 3 San Ildefonso, Jerez de la Frontera; phone 221800; 10 A.M. to 1 P.M. Domecq's *bodegas* range from very old to quite new. Sherry tastings are in flowery patios and reception halls.

Williams & Humbert, 1 Calle Nuno de Canas, Jerez de la Frontera; phone 331300; 9 A.M. to 1 P.M. A *venenciador* (wine tester) takes groups on tours of the premises. A 20-minute film follows that explains and shows the wine-making process and the colorful way of life in Jerez. Guests may taste three sherries and receive a token souvenir.

Garvey, S.A., 14 Calle Guadalete, Jerez de la Frontera; phone 330500; 10 to 2 P.M. The Garvey tour includes a chance to see Spanish coopers making wine casks of white oak from America; view old wine presses and equipment; and taste a 400-year-old wine.

Antonio Barbadillo, S.A., Sanlúcar de Barrameda. This family-run sherry company was founded in 1821 and is Sanlúcar's largest. Its offices are in an ancient Bishop's residence (with beautiful tiled floors, frescoed ceiling, carved wood tables and chairs, Moorish *azulejo*-lined *sala* with beamed ceilings and flower-flooded patios and balconies).

For information about the sherry companies, the industry or related matters, the wine shippers maintain an office. Write or call Promotion and Communications Manager, ESESA, 2 Avda. A. A. Domecq, Jerez de la Frontera.

In the United States, there is the Sherry Institute of Spain, 220 East 42 Street, New York, NY 10017; phone (212) 907–9381.

Málaga

For a tour of a typical winemaking operation in this area contact *Bodegas Scholtz Hermanos,* the largest and best-known winery in the region.

Sevilla

Want tickets good for discounts at such attractions as the Roman town at Italica, the Bellas Artes museum, boat trip on the Guadalquivir River and flamenco performances as well as purchases at shops in Calle Sierpes and meals at 13 restaurants? You can secure the coupon book without charge from *Patronato Provincial de Turismo,* 24–3º Avda. de la Constitución (Pasaje de los Seises); phone 211091.

Sevilla

Tapas, anyone? A *Guía de la Tapa,* a pocket-size directory of *tapa*-types and where to find them in Sevilla has been issued by San Miguel beer. This Spanish-language booklet tells you the ingredients that are in a variety of *tapas* and the bars that specialize in specific ones. The booklet is free from the local tourism office. (*Tapas,* you'll recall, are those canapes served with drinks in taverns. They originated in Sevilla—so Sevillanos claim.)

Sports

Andalucía is an area in which sports are very much in fashion. However, fashions in sports, as in dress, change. So you will find some sports that were popular here in yesteryear or yestercentury (such as bear-baiting and gladatorial combat) have dwindled in popularity and availability. Others are perennially popular—fishing, hunting, swimming and bullfighting are widely available. Still other sports are relatively new—golf, tennis, wind-surfing, water and snow skiing, hang-gliding—but have become popular. Here are some tips on how and where to keep up with fashions in your favorite sport:

Bullfights are on Sundays and holidays in major cities such as Córdoba, Granada, Sevilla, and on festival days in the smaller towns. Corpus Christi is the occasion for the best fights of the year. The season starts as early as mid-March and continues into October in major cities. For dates and ticket information contact local *turismo* offices.

Car rallye is held every December on the Costa del Sol, racing through the provinces of Granada, Almería and Málaga.

Fishing of several types can be done in the area. Trout and other fresh water fishing is popular in the streams of the Sierra Nevadas. Underwater fishing near the shore is very big along the coast between Málaga and Almería. And deep-sea fishing can be pursued by chartered or rented boat in the same area, with swordfish a preferred quarry. *Turismo* offices have license and equipment information.

Golf has become a major sport along the coast with many luxury resort hotels operating their own links. Among the centers for golf are Torremolinos, Marbella, San Pedro de Alcántara, Estepona and Sotogrande—all of which have courses in the championship/tournament category.

Hang-gliding your thing? You can pursue it at Borreguiles or Veleta in the Sol y Nieve ski resort area of the Sierra Nevadas.

Hunting of small game, birds and field animals is permitted throughout Andalucía. Big game, especially deer and wild boar, are in special preserves. For hunting big game you need the appropriate license which you secure through Provincial Headquarters, ICONA, 2 Laiva Aguilar, Córdoba; telephone 223552. (Some of the best big game preserves are near Córdoba.) For general assistance, contact the area's hunters' association: Federacion Regional de Caza, 3 Alta de Santa Ana, Córdoba.

Skiing and winter sports are available November through May at the Sol y Nieve winter sports center, 31 kilometers from Granada in the Sierra Nevadas. If you want to go above 8000 feet, you may ski there year-around. And if you want to swim the same afternoon, the Costa del Sol beaches are only 60 miles away.

Tennis is ubiquitous. There is scarcely a first class hotel on the Costa del Sol beachfront that does not have tennis courts. Some of them are hosts to international tournaments and many offer special tennis package vacations. Local *turismo* offices have the particulars.

Water sports of all types are widely available along the coasts from Torrevieja to Sanlúcar de Barrameda. The most popular beaches are found near Torre de Mar, Torremolinos, Fuengirola, Marbella, Estepona, San Roque and Los Barrios. The superb marina at San Pedro de Alcántara rents boats, as do resorts in these other areas, for fishing, sailing, water-skiing or what have you.

Getting Around

In Andalucía adverse weather is a rarity (except in the mountains) and so the roads, rails and airways offer reliable ways to get about.

Bus transportation along the Costa del Sol is carried on by two companies that cover it from Jerez de la Frontera to Almería and inland to Sevilla and Granada. RENFE's rail lines link the major cities and leave the coast pretty much to frequent bus and auto traffic. Buses depart Málaga every half hour for destinations on the coast, for instance. And there are modern electric trains running from Málaga to Fuengirola (30 km in 25 minutes) and Torre del Mar. Both buses and trains are cheap and the equipment is clean and comfortable.

In the cities you will find the bus systems are adequate and inexpensive. For a romantic change of pace you can hire a carriage in Sevilla, Córdoba or Granada. They have set fare structures, by the half hour. Check with the local office of tourism or ask the hackman to see his printed rate chart before you get aboard.

Taxi rates are reasonable in the region, but be sure you are on the meter, or dicker first for a flat rate charge to your destination.

Though there are narrow, twisting streets in Sevilla, Córdoba and Granada that you cannot navigate in a car, a taxi can bring you fairly close to your destination. And after dark, especially in Sevilla, a taxi should be your preferred way to return to your hotel.

If you wish to rent a car, you'll find offices for one or more rental agencies (Avis, Atesa, Hertz, Europcar, Ital and others) in these cities and towns: Algeciras, Almería, Benalmadena, Cádiz, Córdoba, Fuengirola, Granada, Huelva, Jerez, Málaga, Marbella, Murcia, Sevilla and Torremolinos.

The major ports in the area are Algeciras and Málaga, from which there are ships to and from Barcelona and Mediterranean ports. Transatlantic ships stop at Algeciras.

Air connections in the region use airports in Málaga, Almería, Jerez, Granada and Sevilla, linking these cities with Madrid and Barcelona via Iberia Airlines. There are direct international flights to and from both Málaga and Almería by Iberia and several foreign airlines.

The roads in Andalucía, especially along the coasts, are quite good. However, only from Málaga to Estepona and Sevilla to Cádiz do you have *autopistas* completed and operational at this writing.

Barcelona and the Balearics

BARCELONA

Barcelona—"a fountain of courtesy, refuge for foreigners, an asylum for the poor, a home for the courageous, a revenge for the offended . . . in a unique and beautiful location."

This paean of praise for the capital of Catalonia sounds as though it might be a blurb written by the local chamber of commerce. But no, the words are Miguel Cervantes' back in the 16th century. And, 400 years later, they aren't the exaggeration they may seem to be.

To see almost everything in this fascinating city would take a minimum of three days running at full speed. We have divided the city into threes—though of course you can pick and choose which aspects of the three sections interest you most if you don't have the three days. The sections are the *Gothic,* neatly compressed into the center of the old town, near the harbor, *más o menos*; *Parque de Montjuich* and its diverse attractions; and the *Gaudí* monuments, following a citywide trail to the creations of visionary architect, Antonio Gaudí.

Gothic Barcelona

Gothic Barcelona is pretty much confined to a specific area known as the *barrio gotico*. The so-called Gothic quarter runs more or less from Avenida Catedral, in front of the cathedral, along via Layetana on the east, a little south of Calle Jaime I, and west alongside Calle Banos Nuevos. Keep in mind, though, that not every building in this 20-to-30 block (tiny blocks) area is a medieval treasure. But walls, stones and foundations of the city's earlier days do exist. You will pass excavated Roman columns, and the massive stone wall behind the bronze horseman (Ramon Berenguer, a medieval hero) is pure Roman. Nor is Barcelona's early history confined to the *barrio gotico.* It spills over right and left to adjacent areas.

The centerpiece of the old Gothic quarter is the late 13th–14th century cathedral, an exhilarating example of Catalan Gothic. It was built to replace a Romanesque church, which in turn was on the site of a 4th-century Visigoth structure.

From the outside, the fretted spires and lacy valentine windows look their best at night when they glow in amber light. Inside, the enormous grey stone vaulted ceilings soar up, higher and higher. It is an inspiring elevation —and how miniscule it makes us feel gazing upward (the intention, no doubt, of the master builders).

We have counted and recounted 28 chapels along the cathedral sides, though other sources list 30 and 32. No matter, there is much to see providing you have light enough to see it; dimness and dustiness are problems here. Even many of the gilded baroque retables fade into the gloom.

Be sure to go below the stairs to see the beautiful alabaster sarcophagus of St. Eulalia for whom the cathedral was named. And pause en route to look at the baptistry. According to tradition, it was used to baptise the American Indians brought back to Spain by Columbus after his first voyage.

When you leave the cathedral, you'll be facing the Royal Palace, but a backward glance will show you a door in the cathedral wall that was the Spanish kings' private entrance. The palace was once home to the counts of Barcelona, and now shelters the *Museum of Federico Marés,* with its extraordinary sculpture collection. On the ground floor several rooms display wall-to-wall crucifixes from different countries, different periods, in varying styles, some almost Grand Guignol-like in their blood-and-guts depiction of Christ's suffering. Open 9 A.M. to 2 P.M., 4 to 7 P.M.; closed Monday and Sunday and holiday afternoons.

The barrio gotico has a surprise around every corner: a medieval fountain, a gargoyle jutting from a roof edge, a door opening to a Gothic patio with graceful stone arches. In the *Museum of the History of the City,* on the Plaza del Rey, look in on the Roman excavations and on the grand Gothic hall or throne room called El Tinell. In this great hall, with its elongated arches that are almost half-circles, Ferdinand and Isabella received Columbus on his return from the New World. Open 9 A.M. to 2 P.M., 3:30 to 8:30 P.M.;holidays 11 A.M. to 2 P.M.; closed Mondays.

At the edge of the Gothic quarter is the Plaza de San Jaime I with the *ayuntamiento* (town hall) across the splendid black brick square from the Disputación Provincial or *Palacio de la Generalitat.* Both are marvelous buildings erected on land where the Romans once haggled over the price of olives, wine and grain. Pop into the town hall to see the magnificent *Salon de Ciento* (Council of the Hundred) where the 100 members of the medieval municipal parliament met. The hall has huge rounded arches, a high ornate coffered wood ceiling and myriad wrought-iron and glass chandeliers hanging from it. Open 9 A.M. to 2 P.M.

If you turn right as you leave town hall and continue along Calle Jaime I, with its "inverted" 19th-century street lamps, past busy Vía Layetana, you will find yourself in another old section of town. Calle Jaime I turns into Calle de la Princesa. Four blocks on the right beyond Layetana make a right turn onto Calle Moncada.

This is the street where the Picasso Museum is located, appropriately in the same part of town where Picasso's family once lived. The museum is installed in the old Palace of Berenguer de Aguilar, No. 15, which dates back to the 13th century. In fact, murals of that period depicting King Jaime I's camp as his troops were leaving to conquer Mallorca were uncovered during the renovations. The Gothic palace is a beauty and makes a graceful counter-

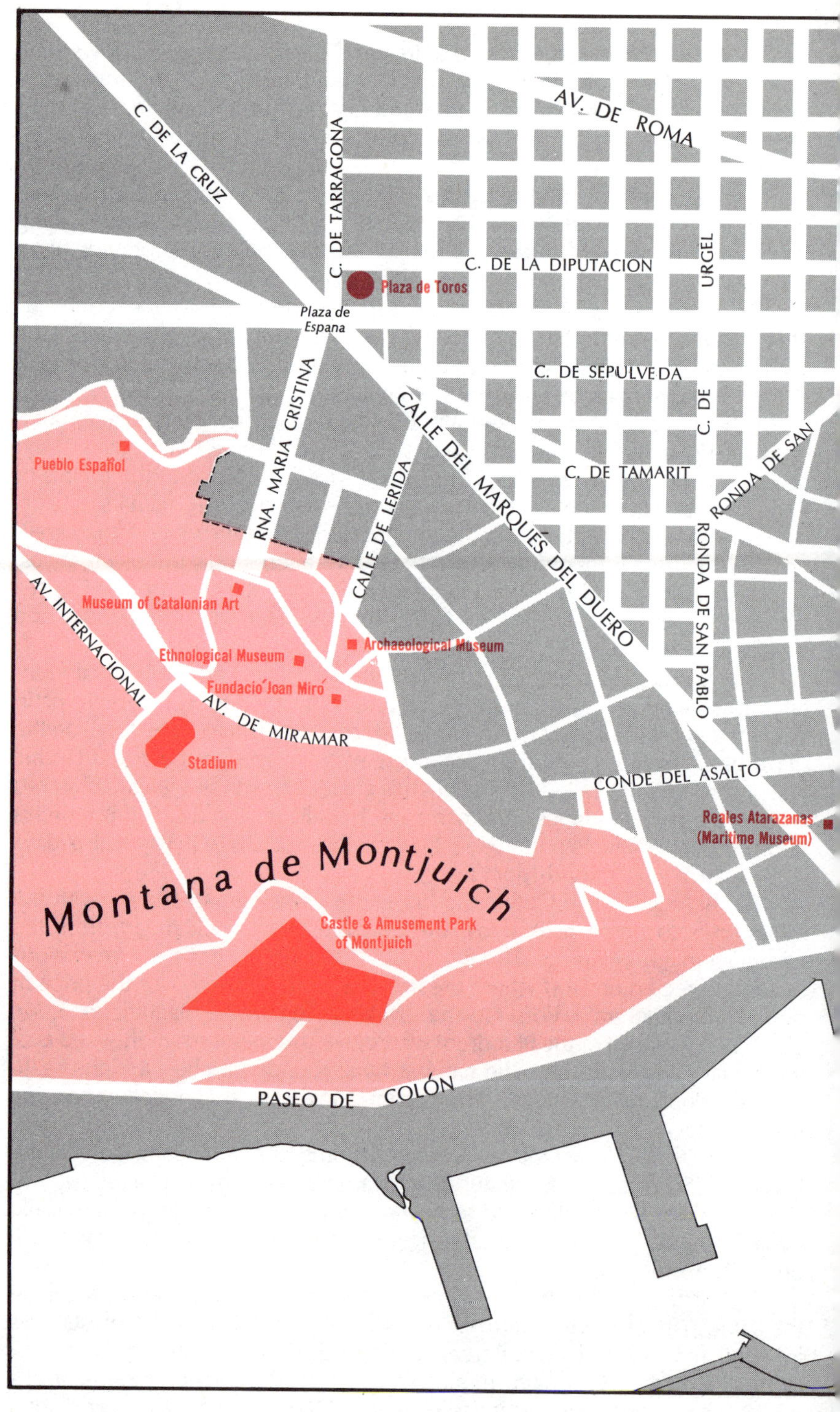
C DE LA CRUZ
C. DE TARRAGONA
AV. DE ROMA
C. DE LA DIPUTACION
URGEL
Plaza de Toros
Plaza de Espana
RNA. MARIA CRISTINA
C. DE SEPULVEDA
CALLE DEL MARQUÉS DEL DUERO
C. DE
C. DE TAMARIT
RONDA DE SAN
Pueblo Español
CALLE DE LERIDA
RONDA DE SAN PABLO
AV. INTERNACIONAL
Museum of Catalonian Art
Archaeological Museum
Ethnological Museum
Fundació Joan Miró
AV. DE MIRAMAR
Stadium
CONDE DEL ASALTO
Reales Atarazanas (Maritime Museum)
Montana de Montjuich
Castle & Amusement Park of Montjuich
PASEO DE COLÓN

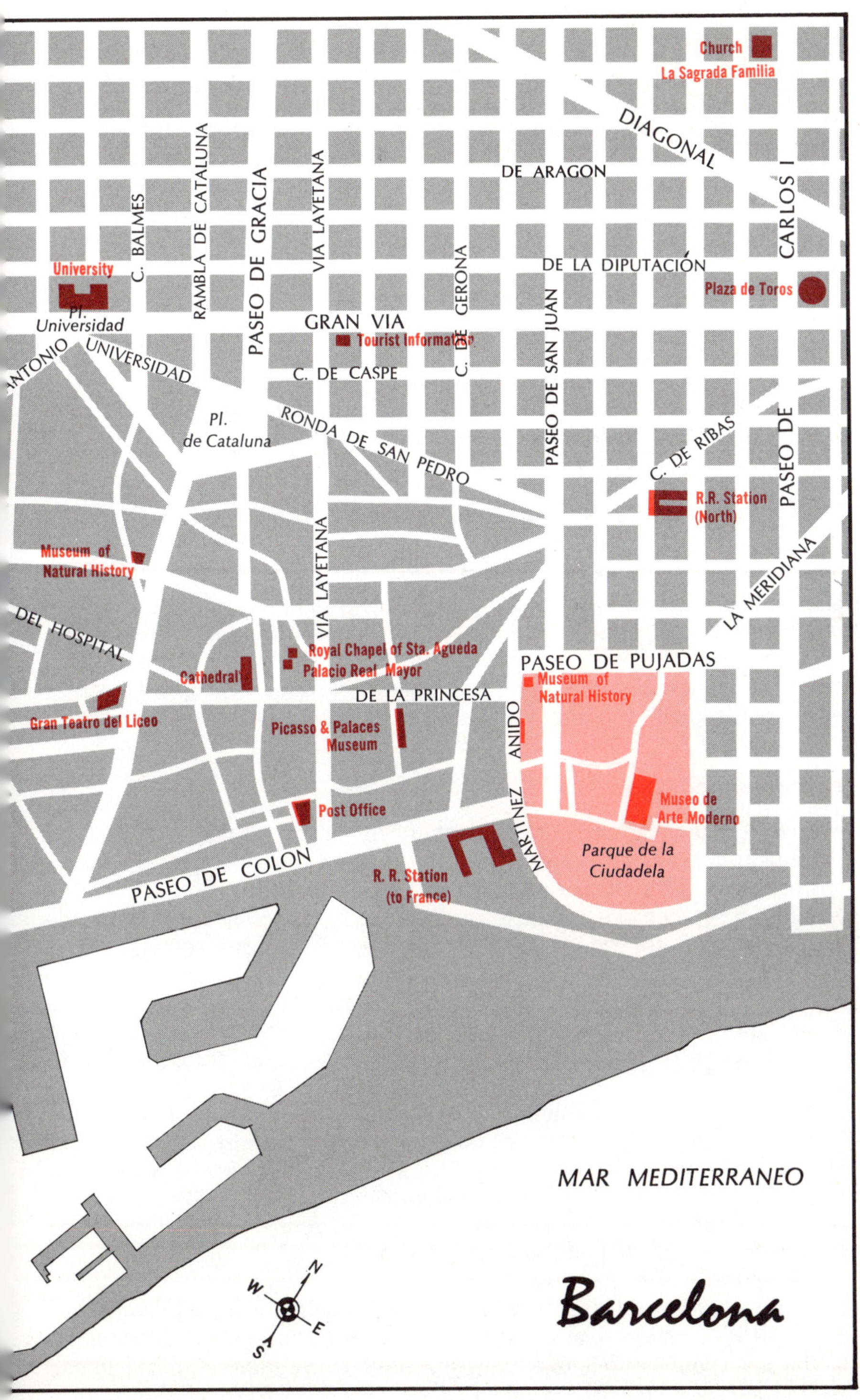
Church
La Sagrada Familia
DIAGONAL
DE ARAGON
CARLOS I
C. BALMES
RAMBLA DE CATALUNA
PASEO DE GRACIA
VIA LAYETANA
C. DE GERONA
DE LA DIPUTACIÓN
University
Plaza de Toros
Pl. Universidad
GRAN VIA
Tourist Information
PASEO DE SAN JUAN
ANTONIO
UNIVERSIDAD
C. DE CASPE
Pl. de Cataluna
RONDA DE SAN PEDRO
C. DE RIBAS
PASEO DE
R.R. Station (North)
Museum of Natural History
VIA LAYETANA
LA MERIDIANA
DEL HOSPITAL
Royal Chapel of Sta. Agueda
Palacio Real Mayor
PASEO DE PUJADAS
Cathedral
Museum of Natural History
DE LA PRINCESA
Gran Teatro del Liceo
Picasso & Palaces Museum
MARTINEZ ANIDO
Post Office
Museo de Arte Moderno
PASEO DE COLON
R. R. Station (to France)
Parque de la Ciudadela
MAR MEDITERRANEO
N
W
E
S
Barcelona

point to the enormous collection of Picasso graphics, drawings, paintings and ceramics on exhibit. There are some 1,000 works in all. Open 9:30 A.M. to 1:30 P.M., 4:30 to 8 P.M.; holidays 10 A.M. to 2 P.M.; closed Monday mornings.

It is easy to linger on Moncada, for this is a street where the nobility once lived, and house after house is a former palace. The *Galería Maeght* is installed in one, *Galería Dalí* in another, and the *Sala d'Exposicions de L'Obra Cultural de la Caixa de Pensions* (No. 14), where art and photography exhibits and musical concerts are held, in still another. You can wander down the street just peeking into patios.

At the far end of the short street is a tiny plaza—*Plazuela de Marcus*—with the Marcus chapel on the corner, named after the merchant who founded it.

It is a Romanesque church built in 1116 and restored in the 19th century. It is dedicated to *Nuestra Señora de la Guía* (Our Lady of the Guide), patroness of mailmen. Many of the streets in this old section are named after medieval guilds: *Calle Carders* (combers), *Plaza de la Lana* (wool), *Calle de la Platería* (silversmiths), among others.

Reverse your steps, and on the south end of Moncada you will come to Plaza Borne and the *Church of Santa María del Mar* (Saint Mary of the Sea), also known as *Santa María de las Arenas* (Saint Mary of the Sands). At the time the church was built (14th century) it was right on the beach; money raised by port stevedores made the construction possible. The church, a favorite for weddings, is the second most important Gothic church in Barcelona (after the cathedral). Pure and simple, with slender, elongated columns that provide great elevation, it is an unadulterated delight.

Parque de Montjuich

A second day could be spent almost entirely on the hillside of Parque de Montjuich. It is a short taxi ride from the center of town; or you can take a bus or Metro to the Plaza de España and climb up from there. Still another way (the most scenic) is via cable car from the harbor. During the short ride you will have a stupendous aerial view of the city and sea beyond.

If you choose the harbor route, take a little time to see the harbor attractions as well. First, there's the enormous column with Columbus's statue at the top. His name in Spanish is *Cristobal Colon*, in Catalan *Colom*, and there are Catalans who will insist he was really a Catalan not a Genoese at all.

Across from the Columbus monument is the Customs House, and beyond it is the harbor. You can board a wooden caravel, a *Santa Maria* replica (built long ago for a movie), which gives a graphic picture of what that sea voyage must have been like in a ship so tiny and cramped. The harbor is full of small, more modern craft—geared for tourist excursions—called *golondrinas* (swallows) and *gaviotas* (sea gulls).

Diagonally from the customs house across the wide *paseo* is the *Maritime Museum*—worth the price of admission for the building alone. It is a 14th-to-15th-century royal shipyard, an imposing grey stone building in the Gothic style with vast beams and arches—unique in Europe. A motto on one wall says it all: *"Navegar es necessario, vivir no es necessario"* (to sail is necessary, to live isn't). There is an extensive collection of ship models and equipment, the oldest map in Spain of the New World (with Amerigo Vespucci's name on it) and the prize—a lifesize red and gilded replica of Don Juan of Austria's galley, *Real,* in which he sailed to win the Battle of Lepanto against the Turks in 1571. The painted panels, gilded lions and nude and clothed figures at the bow are impressive even now. Open 10 A.M. to 1 P.M., 5 to 7 P.M.; holidays 10 A.M. to 2 P.M. Closed Sunday afternoons and Mondays.

You could easily spend a day romping through the hillside of Parque de Montjuich. A cluster of museums make this 210-meter (699-feet) high hill a magnet for tourists. In addition, there is the *Pueblo Español* (Spanish Village), a collection of re-created buildings from towns all over Spain. While it's far better to see the real thing on site, the replicas are authentic and well done if you have limited time in Spain and want an overview. Within the various houses in the village are practicing craftsmen who demonstrate and sell their work *à la* Colonial Williamsburg. Open 9 A.M. to 8 P.M. (7 P.M. in winter); closed Mondays and Sunday and holiday afternoons.

Your real target at Montjuich should be the *Museum of Catalonian Art,* lodged in what was the Spanish pavilion for the International Exhibition of 1929 (the *Pueblo Español* was part of the same fair). It is an incredible museum, the finest collection of its kind in the world.

What you'll see are rare 11th-and 12th-century frescoes transported apse and all from tiny Romanesque churches and chapels in the Catalonian Pyrenees. The colors are fresh and bright; the paintings have an almost Byzantine quality. Many are full of mysterious, evocative symbols whose meanings have been lost in time. These are apses that make the heart grow fonder and ever fonder of Romanesque art.

But that's not all. The museum's 33 rooms are full of other treasures too: Gothic paintings and sculptures, altar pieces by Jaume Huguet and one room with 16th- and 17th-century work by El Greco, Velázquez, Ribera, Tintoretto, Claudio Coelli, Zurbarán and others. On the second floor is a Ceramics Museum with beautifully displayed 15th–18th-century tiles, plates and other objects mounted throughout nine rooms. The numerous scenes depicted on the tiles, such as the 1710 rendition of a *corrida de toros* in Barcelona that shows all the local gentry watching a bullfight from their balconies, are especially charming.

A word or two more about the Romanesque sections of the museum. Some very helpful explanatory material tells you from which churches the frescoes were brought and there are photographs (interior and exterior) of the little village chapels and churches. In addition, one of the guards, veteran Ricardo Benllach, speaks crystalline English and is extremely informative (and witty) on the interpretation of the frescoes. (He's fluent in French and German as well.) Open 9 A.M. to 2 P.M.; closed Mondays.

The *Museum of Catalonian Art* is located at the top of the hill. If you climb the steps to it, you'll pass two "heroic" statues by Federico Marés that are just above the double staircase. As you leave the museum, turn right and wind your way slowly down the hill, stopping at other museums as the spirit moves you.

The *Ethnological Museum* will be in your path; it's a modern building with a handsomely-displayed assortment of artifacts, crafts and textiles from India, Latin America and Africa. (A Spanish section of the museum is inside the Pueblo Español.) Open 10 A.M. to 2 P.M., 4 to 7 P.M.; closed holiday afternoons.

Farther along is the Archaeological Museum, where you will see sculptures and finely preserved floor mosaics from Roman Ampurias, along with tiny Mallorcan bronze figures and other Iberian relics. Open 10 A.M. to 1 P.M., 5 to 7 P.M.; closed Mondays and holiday afternoons.

Also in the park is the Joan Miró Foundation. The Catalan painter's works —dozens of prints and paintings—are displayed in a dramatic, raked concrete building of rounded, square and oblong forms with skylights, terraces and airy patios. Designed by fellow Catalan, architect Josep-Lluís Sert, the building is definitely worth seeing. It is a center for concerts, lectures, film festivals and special exhibits. Open 9:30 A.M. to 1:30 P.M., 6 to 9 P.M.; closed Mondays.

Gaudí Trail

Another Catalan whose handwork is visible all over Barcelona is Antonio Gaudí. Following the trail of his work can keep you busy for a full day or more. Gaudí burst on the scene just as Barcelona's new-found energy, harnessed by the 19th-century industrial revolution, was finding an outlet in new buildings. Art Nouveau was the rage, and architect Gaudí was part of it; he turned the style into a unique personal statement. You may not like his work —people love it or loathe it—but you won't forget it. Gaudí's work and other more traditional Art Nouveau edifices dot Barcelona, giving the city a flavor totally its own.

You may as well begin your Gaudí pilgrimage—or voyage of discovery —on the Ramblas. The *Ramblas* themselves have little to do with Gaudí, but they lead to some of his work and besides it would be unthinkable to leave Barcelona without a stroll up this one-of-a-kind boulevard. The name Ramblas derives from river bed, and what is now a lovely tree-shaded promenade was once a sandy bed down which the southern fork of the Collcerola River streamed. When the river was diverted in the 18th century, the sandy bed became an avenue, which came into full flower in the late 19th century.

The Ramblas begin near the harbor, at *Puerta de la Paz,* by Columbus's statue and amble, changing names from *Rambla de Santa Monica* to *Rambla de los Capuchinos* (or *Centro*) to *Rambla de las Flores* to *Rambla de los Estudios* up to Plaza Cataluña. They are *all* part of the *Ramblas,* and the plural, *Las Ramblas,* is how most people refer to the area.

The Ramblas are a wide swath of boulevard bordered by streets with frenetic traffic, which in turn are bordered right and left by narrower sidewalks. The central ribbon of boulevard is where the action is: flower sellers with vibrant festoons of color; bird, fish, dog, even monkey vendors; perambulating shoeshine men; newspaper hawkers; lottery and gadget vendors; sidewalk kiosks and cafés. All of this is under the feathery greenery of rows of sycamore trees. It is a panorama of Barcelona life—low-level at the lower end of the street (with *el-cheapo* hotels and strip clubs), more fashionable as Las Ramblas wind into the better shopping area. Above all, Las Ramblas mean people—sometimes wall to wall.

Your first Gaudí building is just off the lower Ramblas, on the left (as you walk upward). It is the *Palacio Güell,* at 3 Calle Conde del Asalto, a dark, grey stone and somber metal facade that now houses the Museum of Theater Art. Almost directly across Las Ramblas is the *Plaza Real,* once one of the city's loveliest squares, now a bit seedy. But look closely at the street lights. The old-fashioned metal lamp posts seem to be wearing winged helmets — pure Gaudí, one of his early efforts.

Your stroll will take you up Las Ramblas to *Paseo de Gracía.* It's a lovely street with distinctive ceramic tile pavement in slate-blue to grey-black bas relief designs. Attractive as it is now, one wishes one had been here 100 years ago when the sides were bordered with gardens and fountains and band concerts were given in small kiosks at various junctions.

Between the cross streets of Consejo de Ciento and Aragón, Paseo de Gracía is known as the "Discord block" because of three vintage buildings on the left hand side, built by three leading Barcelona architects: the Lleó building by Doménech Montaner, the Amatller by Puig and Cadafalch, and Casa Batlló by Gaudí. The entire block bursts with creativity. Even so, Casa Batlló (no. 43) stands out with its ground floor columns that look rooted in the sidewalk and its undulating roof of ceramic tiles. Cast iron balconies curve in and out, and no two windows are the same size or shape.

Casa Milá, (no. 92) three blocks north (opposite side) on the corner of the Paseo de Gracia and Calle de Provenza, is an apartment building that is considered one of Gaudí's major works. Known as *La Pedrera,* it is monumental, wrapping its concrete self around an entire corner in a cascade of flowing, moving, wavy forms.

Ten blocks east (right) on Provenza will lead you to Gaudí's unfinished masterpiece, Templo de la Sagrada Familia (Temple of the Holy Family). "It's melting," someone once said about the eclectic facade of this multi-spired church, whose towers seem to be sprouting flowers from their tips. "Awesome," say admirers; "Awful," say others. See for yourself. It was begun in 1884 and was still a work-in-progress when Gaudí was hit by a streetcar and died in 1926.

There's little controversy over his *Parque Güell,* located near Monte Carmelo, a short taxi ride north. Kids old and young love the wacky ceramic tile dragon fountains, the bizarre forms and motley color combinations, the columns that lean but don't fall, the roofs that bend but don't break, the textures that clash but coalesce. It's a place to walk, to dance the *sardana* (a Catalan dance that breaks forth like an epidemic in the spring and lasts throughout the year), to sit and sip *vino* in the sunshine, just as Gaudí would have wished.

His own pink "Hansel and Gretel" house is in the park. Inside you'll see the curved and rounded furniture he designed and his decorated ceilings. The house is more conventional than one might have expected.

And so it goes in Barcelona. Other Gaudí buildings are *Casa Vicens,* 24 Calle de Carolinas; *Bell Esguard,* 46 Calle Ganduxer; *Casa Calvet, 48 Caspe; and the Colegio Teresiano,* 85 Calle Ganduxer.

So much for Gaudí. But in strolling up Las Ramblas, you will pass—and should drop in—the *Palacio de la Virreina,* at 99 Rambla de las Floras, the 18th-century home of the Viceroy of Peru. The high-ceilinged graceful rooms harbor three separate museums: the Postal Museum on the ground floor; Museum of Decorative Arts, on the first floor—with elegant furniture, a few paintings; the Cambó Collection, on the second floor—a small but choice display of paintings by famous artists such as Botticelli, Raphael, Titian, Tintoretto, Tiepolo, Rubens, Van Dyck, Fragonard, Goya, El Greco and Zurbarán. Decorative Arts Museum hours: 9:30 A.M. to 1:30 P.M., 6 to 9 P.M.; closed Mondays.

And we haven't even mentioned *Tibidabo,* Barcelona's other mountain (524 meters or 1,745 feet high), reached by road or funicular. Once there, you will want to see the *Pedralbes Monastery,* a 14th-century Gothic complex, with galleried cloisters, a church with 15th-century stained glass windows and assorted gems. Open Sundays only 1–2:30 P.M. There's also a splendid view of the city.

Three days are not enough.

MONTSERRAT, COSTA BRAVA AND GERONA

Montserrat, 60 kilometers (36 miles) from Barcelona, represents a good half-day trip for most visitors. Gerona, 100-kilometers (60 Miles) from Barcelona, is an easy day trip, but may be better combined with a trip along the Costa Brava.

Montserrat

Montserrat—"jagged mountain"—is one of nature's wonders. Sacheverell Sitwell compares it to Greece's Meteora in its austere, textural grandeur. Richard Wagner was supposedly inspired by Montserrat's eerie, foreboding ambience to make it his setting for *Parsifal.*

A trio of attractions draws tourists to Montserrat: the physical beauty and spectacular views of and from the mountain (on a clear day you can see Mallorca); the singing of the *Escolania,* the boys' choir at the monastery; and the Monastery of Montserrat with its Black Madonna, one of the most revered shrines of Spanish and European Catholics.

There are several ways to go to Montserrat from Barcelona, each dramatic in its own right. By car, twisting around breathtaking mountain roads, take the N-11 from Barcelona or the *autopista* to Martorell. You will pass through olive groves and vineyards, little hamlets such as Colonia Gomis and Monistrol, and up, up, up steep roads and hairpin curves. A second way is to take the train from Barcelona and then go by cable car (an 8-minute ride) up to the monastery. It is also possible, of course, to drive and then take the cable car for the final distance.

We would recommend that you plan to be at the Monastery during one of the occasions when the Escolania sings: 7 A.M. Mass weekdays (hard to manage unless you stay overnight); 7 and 11 A.M. Mass Sundays and feast days; 1 P.M. *salve* daily; 7 P.M. vespers daily. Otherwise your visit can include enjoyment of the views, hiking or going by funicular to several hermitages, and a peek at the museum to see El Grecos, Corregios and other prides and joys. The monastery itself is off limits, but you can visit the church with its sacred Black Madonna, a polychromed wooden statue black with age not pigmentation.

It is easy to understand why the Benedictine monks who founded the monastery back in the 9th century chose such an isolated place. The enormous, gnarled, eroded, protective boulders that shelter the site bespeak timelessness and spirituality. Less understandable is why Napoleon's troops would have sacked and devastated the place so ruthlessly in 1812. What you will see now is not the original Romanesque monastery but a somewhat boring 19th-century complex of buildings.

The Montserrat setting, 1,117 meters (3,725 feet) high above the river valley, produces its own mystique, the stuff of which legends are made. It was once credited as the site where the Holy Grail was kept, a claim made elsewhere as you'll see. The *Moreneta* (Black Madonna) revered by pilgrims and still patroness of Catalonia, is believed to have been carved by St. Luke; it was found many centuries later by shepherds in a cave—now known as the *Santa Cueva*—in the mountainside. Art experts believe the statue to be a 12th-century work. Believe what you will.

Costa Brava

The Costa Brava begins at Blanes, about 64 kilometers (38 miles) northeast of Barcelona, just beyond the estuary of the Tordera River, and stretches some 100 kilometers (63 miles) to Port Bou at the French frontier. Visually, it is a stimulating coast of hidden coves, rocky ledges, expanses of sheltered beaches. The best view of this romantic coast is the one the ancient Greeks had—from the sea.

Unlike the southern, warmer Mediterranean coast, the Costa del Sol, the Costa Brava has managed to maintain quite a lot of its character (in spite of the masses of summer visitors). There are still small fishing villages, and even the urbanizations—the tourist communities—are generally smaller and more human than some of the large highrise complexes to the south. For the nonbeachophiles, there are other things to do and see; there is no need to feel stranded on the sand.

Blanes is a sizeable town of 16,000 persons, once a major fishing port with a life of its own. Hill-backed, with a colorful harbor, the town has an attraction for botanists: Marimurtra Botanical Gardens with some 3,000 examples of coastal (and more far-reaching) plant life and scenic views of the harbor. There's a little Romanesque church, *Santa Maria la Antigua,* as well as the ruins of an old convent, *Santa Ana,* on a promontory.

At *Lloret de Mar,* a very lively resort with an attractive promenade, there's a pleasant hotel, Roger Flor, Turo del Estelet (phone 364800), where you can awaken to the scent of orange blossoms wafting through the air and have terrace views of the Mediterranean. Next along the way is *Tossa de Mar,* which combines a good horseshoe-shaped beach, sea-bordered promenade and active resort area with Roman ruins, 12th-century walls and a lighthouse on the promontory. What has saved Tossa from excessive tourism is its Old Town—*Vila Vella*—with interesting walks and sea views.

The road dips, loops and bends from here to San Felíu de Guixols, leading to such delightfully secluded sandy coves as *Cala Bona* and *Cala Salions.* San Felíu has only a modest beach (a superb one is just a short bus ride to S'Agaro), but it does have lots of nice little bars and restaurants, the most popular bullring on the coast and a 14th-century church with a Romanesque facade and an unusual Mozarabic–Romanesque arcade leading to it.

S'Agaro means "Little Dry Stream," which is no more apt for the fashionable resort with its lovely little half-moon beach than the name "Inn of the

Seagull'' is for the *Hostal de la Gavina,* the superb deluxe hotel that dominates the village.

Playa de Aro has an inviting mile-long beach and an ever-increasing highrise population to enjoy it. Nearby is *Palamos,* where you may drop by to see the 14th-century church of Santa Maria with its Flemish *reredos* (altar screens). From here to Rosas the road moves inland, with spurs down to specific, off-the-track resort areas such as Llafranch and Tamariu. At *Aiguablava,* a government-run Parador Nacional de la Costa Brava (phone 622162) is a dramatic, modern hostelry on a cliff overlooking the sea and one of the area's prettiest beaches. It's just 3 kilometers from Bagur, whose 17th-century castle has a sweeping seaview.

For an inveterate sightseer, rather than sun seeker, *the* destination along the Costa Brava is *Ampurias,* with ruins of Greek and Roman settlements that date back more than 2,000 years. Actually, there was an even earlier Phocean Greek settlement here called Emporion, whence derived the name Ampurias. Many of the prize finds have been hauled to museums in Barcelona and Gerona, but there's still plenty to see and still more to be excavated. Museum hours: 9 A.M. to 2 P.M., 4 to 8 P.M. You can wander through *Neapolis,* a Greek town, and then climb a hill to the Roman town Caesar built overlooking both the Greek settlement and the Bay of Rosas.

The *Bay of Rosas* spans a lovely 16-kilometer beach, crowned at the northern end by Rosas, a fishing village-cum-resort, known for the glory of its sunsets and its daily fish auctions. The last coastal village of great touristic interest is *Cadaqués,* which seems to be everybody's favorite. In the 1950s a number of artists and writers settled in and have been largely responsible for keeping the lazy tempo and white-washed small village look. One kilometer away is the even tinier *Port Lligat,* which Salvador Dali put on the map by building a house there. Swimming in the area is at its best around *Cabo Créus,* reachable only by boat or foot. Open 11 A.M. to 12:30 P.M., 4:30 to 7:30 P.M.; holidays 11 A.M. to 1:30 P.M.; Sundays 5:30 to 7:30 P.M.

We recommend taking C-26, the road from Rosas, to Figueras, where a Dali fan may head for the *Teatro Museo Dali* to see works by hometown boy Salvador installed, appropriately, in an old theater.

Gerona

There's much to see in *Gerona;* it's 37 kilometers via *autopista* south from Figueras. The same autopista will take you 100 kilometers further to Barcelona.

A strategic location in almost every conqueror's path has given Gerona (*Gerunda* to the Romans) the nickname *La Ciudad de los Sitios* (City of a Thousand Sieges) and close encounters of an unpleasant kind with Romans, Moors, Charlemagne's forces (in 785) and Napoleon's troops three separate times (1809). And still there are treasures left: a Gothic cathedral, 90 steps up a fine old 17th-century stairway, with a 14th-century retable, an unusually daring wide nave, cloister, and 11th-century embroidered tapestry; a Provincial Archaeological Museum with Roman relics (from Ampurias) and medieval art, located in the desanctified cloister of the Romanesque San Pedro de Galligans church. Of major interest are the 12th-century *Baños árabes* (Arab baths) with intriguing Mudejar screens with star and orb perforations and unusual Moorish designed capitals on the columns.

TARRAGONA AND THE COSTA DORADA

Dorada means gilt, and the coast that runs from Barcelona south to Tarragona is indeed a golden sandy coast, with beaches stretching much of its 80 kilometers (50 miles). Actually, this least exploited of Spain's Mediterranean coasts extends north of Barcelona too, 64 kilometers (40 miles) or so, until it melts into the Costa Brava.

Sitges

Still, if you are driving south to Tarragona, you may make a stop at the scenic little town of *Sitges,* possessor of a splendid silken beach, a scenic *Paseo Maritimo* (seaside promenade) and several museums. The *Museo Romántico Provincial* in Casa Llopis, an 18th-century manor house, shows off decorative arts of the past two centuries and an enchanting doll museum with toys and dolls spanning three centuries. Another museum, *Museo Cau Ferrat,* pays homage to a painter–writer, Santiago Rusiñol, and has two El Greco paintings and drawings by Picasso, Miguel Utrillo and others as well.

Wine area of Panades

From Sitges, you can go north to visit the Wine Museum, located in the 14th-century palace of the Kings of Aragon in the little town of Villafranca del Panadés. Open 10 A.M. to 2 P.M., 4 to 8 P.M.; closed Mondays. This is the area of Panades, an excellent red wine locked in palate-to-palate combat with Riojas. About 12 kilometers northeast is San Sadurni de Noya, where *espumoso,* a champagne-like white wine, is produced.

Tarragona has changed a lot since the days when Roman emperors Hadrian and Augustus found it, at different times, a restful retreat. There's still much they and local boy, Pontius Pilate, would recognize, for Tarragona's Roman memories are tangible, more so than in any other town in Spain.

Roman Memories in Tarragona

There are the splendid Roman mosaic pavements including a ferocious Medusa's head, and remnants from the Temple of Jupiter, which you'll find with many other excavated items in the Archaeological Museum. Open in summer 10 A.M. to 1 P.M.; 4:30 to 8 P.M.; rest of year 10 A.M. to 1:30 P.M., 4 to 7 P.M.; closed on Mondays. The *Paseo Arqueologico* will lead you on a walk past the mammoth walls which the prominent Scipio family supposedly built, past others built by Augustus, and still earlier Iberian ones. Shaded by cypress, you'll pass six ancient gates and numerous statues, grottoes and artifacts.

Four kilometers north of town, on the road to Lerida, is the way to the Las Ferreras Aqueduct, a two-tiered Roman monument with 25 arches, dubbed *Puente del Diablo* (the Devil's Bridge). If you take the Constanti road northwest from Tarragona, after 9½ kilometers (6 miles) you'll come upon the Centcelles Mausoleum, its two pink-tiled buildings straddling a vineyard. One theory has it that the Emperor Constantine ordered the Mausoleum built for his son, Constans. Another belief is that it is the work of a patrician 4th-century Roman. No one knows for sure, but the buildings are fascinating.

One, with a gigantic cupola, painstakingly restored by German archaeologists, has mosaic decorations—mostly with Christian themes such as Daniel in the Lion's den. This compounds the Centcelles mystery.

Fascinating as Roman Tarragona—or *Tarraconensis,* as the Romans said—is, it isn't the entire Tarragona story. There's a medieval city as well. The cathedral, on the site of a Roman Temple of Jupiter (and later a mosque) is a blend of Romanesque, Mudejar, Gothic, Plateresque and Baroque (with a sprinkling of Churrigueresque). The cloister is splendid, and in the Diocesan Museum you'll find a harvest of 15th–17th-century tapestries—52 in all. The prize Gothic one is in the chapterhouse. Tours from 10 A.M. to 12:30 P.M.; 3:30 to 7 P.M.

Along the southern edge of the city's medieval quarter is a square atop a cliff called the *Balcon del Mediterraneo,* from which you can have wide-angle views of the harbor and sea. From here you can go down a few steps to the Roman amphitheatre, near the sea, where three early Christians were burned alive in A.D. 259 Retrace your steps to the *Balcon,* then walk along the tree-shaded Ramblas or have a refreshment at one of the numerous sidewalk cafés along the way. Sol Ric, 227 Via Augusta (phone 201026), is a good place to sample the local seafood.

Poblet, one of Catalonia's most important and beautiful monasteries, is a side trip from Tarragona, 46 kilometers (28 miles), via N-240, with a turnoff at *Esplurga de Francoli,* a small spa.

Santa Maria, to give the Poblet Monastery its full name, was Ramon Berenguer IV's gift to Catalonia. After driving the Moors from the region, he expressed his thanks to God by building the monastery for the Cistercians in 1150. Royal patronage through the centuries enriched the place, and every visiting monarch paused in passing for a royal retreat. Eventually Poblet became the royal pantheon. You'll see the tomb of King Jaime I of Aragon among others. In 1835 an anticlerical outburst devastated the monastery, but in 1940 the Cistercians returned and have been carefully restoring the fine buildings ever since. You'll now find the Romanesque church, Gothic cloister and Palace of King Martin the Humane much as they may have been in their prime. Tour hours: 10 A.M. to 12:30 P.M., 3 to 6 P.M.; closed at 5:30 P.M. in winter.

VALENCIA AND ALICANTE

Via the Autopista A-7 you can cover the 259 kilometers (155 miles) from Tarragona to Valencia in record time, though you may prefer to fly. If you drive, you'll be passing through *La Huerta*—fields and farms of highly productive gardens, the most fertile land in Spain. First the Romans, then the Arabs developed the irrigation systems that made this so. If you regard an artichoke as a special treat, it is a curious experience to drive past fields and more fields of them and to have them served as commonly as peas. From artichokes to tomatoes, melons and orchards of almond, figs, oranges and apricot trees (thousands and thousands of trees), the terrain is a wonderland of productivity. It's called *Costa del Azahar,* the orange-blossom coast.

Valencia

Valencia itself is possibly Spain's most underrated major city. Its beauty is more than skin-deep, but it takes time to become acquainted. The time to do so is not in the humid sultry summer but in spring or fall. In spring during the March *Fallas* (see Inside Information, Folklore), Valencia is its gayest and most extroverted.

What astonishes one about Valencia is that it is so walkable. As Spain's third largest city, it has a very human scale core. If you are staying at a midcity hotel, you can walk to any of the major sights with little effort.

Palacio del Marqués and Surrounding area

Begin at the *Palacio del Marqués de Dos Aguas* (Palace of the Two Waters) on Rinconada de Garcia Sanchiz, just three blocks off the city's major promenade, Plaza del Caudillo. The palace is important for two reasons. In itself, it is a ripe and luscious rococo building of the 18th century that amazingly presages the Art Nouveau style of more than 100 years later. Its richly ornamented alabaster portal was the Churrigueresque work of Ignacio Vergara. He based the stone sculptures on cartoons of the painter, Hipólio Rovera, who later went mad. (We don't think there's a connection.) Originally, the entire building was covered with Rovera's paintings, but they were later destroyed. A scant sense of them is apparent in the faint gold and green glimmers of color on the facade. Vergara's portal depicts two pumping-iron-type Titans pouring water from amphorae, representing the *Dos Aguas* (Two Waters) in the Marqués's name.

The second reason you should head immediately for the Palace of Two Waters is what's inside—the *National Ceramics Museum,* with a collection of about 5,000 ceramics from Iberia's earliest beginnings right up to Picasso's works. In point of fact, the four huge Picasso plates and pitcher—which can be found in a glass case on the third floor—are insignificant compared to some of the treasures here. A prize is the delightful kitchen, covered tip to toe with scenes in tile and arranged as it may have been in real life with gleaming copper pots hanging above the tile. Open 10 A.M. to 2 P.M., 4 to 6 P.M.; closed Mondays and Sunday and holiday afternoons.

Turn around the block and you'll soon find yourself back on Plaza del Caudillo. But before making that turn, have a look at two other important sights in the Dos Aguas vicinity. The *Church of San Juan de la Cruz* (also called San Andres), built on the site of a mosque, at Calle Poeta Querol, is notable for its *azulejos* from Manises that surround each of the side altars to a height of 1–½ meters.

A street away, on Calle de la Nave, is *Colegio del Patriarca* (Museum of the Patriarch), a Renaissance complex of a museum, the Church of Corpus Christi (with a *Last Supper* by Francisco Ribalta) and the Chapel of the Conception (hung with six Flemish 15th-century tapestries). In the graceful patio is a sculpture of Blessed Juan de Ribera who founded the college. It is the museum, though, that will draw you to this complex, with its cache of works by El Greco, Ribalta, van der Weyden and others. Open 11 A.M. to 1 P.M.

Plazas

As you stroll along Plaza del Caudillo, you'll see a bronze statue of El Caudillo, the late Generalisimo Franco himself (a bit paunchy), with red paint scrawled across the base denouncing him and an adulatory wreath laid beneath him. These two opposing gestures pretty much sum up the ambivalent political feeling of the moment throughout Spain.

The plaza comes to a "V." If you turn left onto Calle Maria Cristina you'll wander into the *Plaza del Mercado.* Here, where tournaments were once held, is the noisy, lively, rambunctious *Mercado* (Central Market), which is at its best midmorning. Pop inside; among some 1,300 stalls selling fruits, vegetables, meat, fresh fish, and flowers, and admire the tiles covering the huge domes, one of oranges (over the produce side of the market), the other a blue scallop shell design (naturally over the fish market). Outside, look up at the bronze cockatoo weather vane over one cupola, a fish over the other. Popular art at its most charming.

Next to the mercado is *Iglesia de los Santos Juanes* (Church of the San Juans) named for both Johns, the Baptist and Evangelist, with a richly ornamented Churrigueresque facade and a vaulted ceiling fresco by Antonio Palomino. This church once had the richest interior in Spain, we are told, but it was burned and pretty much demolished during the Civil War.

Across the street is the *Lonja,* a late 15th-century flamboyant Gothic stone building, built as a silk exchange for the prosperous silk merchants of town. Notice its airy facade, gargoyles, and, inside, the gently twisted columns and graceful Orange Tree Courtyard. As everywhere in Valencia, the scent of oranges perfumes the air.

Within a few twisting and turning blocks are many sights of interest. *San Nicolas Church,* one of the oldest in town, with a Churrigueresque face lift and an altar piece by Juan de Juanes (a 16th-century painter) can be reached by following the Plaza del Mercado northward.

Cathedral Square

Eventually you will find your way to the vast cathedral square. To simplify or expedite matters, you can return to the "V" at the end of Calle Maria Cristina and make a sharp left up Calle de San Vicente. This leads you past the *Church of San Martin* on the right, where you may want to stop a minute to admire the façade with the bronze sculpture of St. Martin in plumed cap on horseback, cutting his cloak to give half to a beggar. The rest of the story is that later that night, Christ appeared in St. Martin's dream and thanked him for the gift of the wrap.

Coming up on the left is the *Church of Santa Catalina,* all modern inside, with a splendid hexagonal tower of weathered golden stone, dating from 1688. The Plaza Santa Catalina is the place to stop if you're feeling listless or in need of a quick sugar "fix." We call it "Sweet Street" because every other shop on it seems to be a candy vendor or *horchatería.* Valencia is the place to try a *horchata* if you haven't yet sampled this cooling, almond-scented drink made of crushed ice and *chufas* (ground earth almonds).

Now you are at the end of the lively, spacious Plaza de la Reina and *voila,* here is the cathedral or *La Séo,* as Valencíans call it. As you walk around its four richly ornamented sides, you will understand why it took from 1262 to 1482 to complete it and why it is a mix of Romanesque (south door or *Puerta del Palau*) and Gothic (north or Apostle door), with a later baroque facade. The baroque elements are being peeled off, and before long the cathedral will be mostly Gothic again. Note the high, Gothic octagonal tower at the southwest corner. It is called *Torre del Miguelete* or *Micalet* after the bell inside, which dinged its first dong on Michaelmas Day in 1418.

There is much to see inside as well as outside the cathedral. The museum has fine polychrome sculptures and paintings by Zurbarán and Ribera and two large Goyas. One Goya shows St. Francis Borja exorcising satanically smiling monsters (as only Goya could paint them) from behind a dying man's bed. The other painting, in lighter colors and mood, shows St. Francis Borja bidding farewell to the deceased man's family at the church. The Borjas, you may be as surprised as we were to learn, were an old Spanish family who changed the family name to Borgia when they moved to Italy. Francis was a different kind of Borja than his notorious Italian relatives. The story goes that he was converted from living a traditional court life (he was fourth Duke of Gandia, a town near Valencia) by the sight of the corpse of Queen Isabella of Portugal. Francis, or Francisco, was requested to accompany her funeral cortege from Toledo, where she had died in childbirth, to Granada, for burial. It fell to Francis to open the casket to identify the Queen's body for the civil authorities. So foul was the sight he vowed never again to serve a temporal sovereign who could suffer so degrading a change. Later he became a Jesuit.

Also in the cathedral is the *Holy Grail Chapel.* Behind feathery Gothic stone tracery, in back of the altar, protected by glass, is a small, deep violet agate cup about 15 centimeters tall. This is reputedly the legendary Holy Grail or chalice used by Jesus at the Last Supper. The story persists in this part of the country that the Grail was brought to Spain in the 4th century and was kept at the monastery of San Juan de la Peña until presented by the King of Aragón to the Valencia Cathedral in the 15th century. Museum hours: in summer, 9:30 A.M. to 1 P.M., 4 to 7 P.M.; rest of year closes 1 hour earlier; closed Sundays and holidays. Tower hours: 10 A.M. to 1 P.M., 4 to 7 P.M.; closed Monday afternoons.

Plaza de la Virgin and Palacio de la Generalidad

If you leave the cathedral at the north door you will come out into the *Plaza de la Virgen,* one of the most delightful of all Spanish plazas. Its pink and gray marble pavement teems with life. Three sidewalk cafés as well as a horchatería are located on the left (a good refreshment stop). Old-fashioned gas lights line the plaza, and in the early evening it is a joy to sit in the lavender light and watch the world of Valencia promenade past. At the far end of the square is an enormous male nude statue in bronze, reclining nonchalantly in a huge fountain with white pigeons roosting randomly all over him. Disproportionately small nymphets pour water from their marble urns and water spouts in exuberant abandon all around the vast fountain.

At the left (north) end of the plaza is a pocket park full of orange trees. Beyond, on Calle de Caballeros, is a handsome 15th-century Gothic structure, the *Palacio de la Generalidad.* It was the meeting place of the Valencia

Cortes, until Philip V took their power away. Their job was to collect the general tax, which is how the building got its name.

There are numerous reasons for peeking inside the palace. To cite just a few: the coffered ceiling and *azulejo* (glazed, color tile) frieze around the Grand Council Chamber; the retable by 16th-century painter Juan Sariñena; the gilded *artesonado* ceilings (marquetry with star designs) ceilings in the 17th-century tower connected to the building; an impressive bronze tableau of *Dante's Inferno* with souls writhing in Hell—the work of local sculptor, Benlliure. Open 11 A.M. to 1 P.M. on Saturdays and Sundays only, and by permission; telephone 331–3790.

Provincial Museum of Fine Arts

We have saved the best for last because it is furthest from the city core—though still within walking distance—the *Provincial Museum of Fine Arts* on the other side of the Turia River. Cross via the Puente de Mar or Puente del Real, both 16th-century bridges with two small shrines and statues nested in their centers. Near the Puente del Real is the Chapel of San Vicente Ferrer, another local person who became a famous and then sainted churchman.

The museum faces the river and is next to the Royal Gardens with their mini-zoo and maxi-restaurant, Viveros Anfitrión (see Inside Information). Four floors—50 rooms or more—in an old palace are packed with interesting pieces. The ground floor has a large Roman floor mosaic and other Roman items, as well as 16th- and 17th-century polychrome sculptures and Iberian and Moorish archaeological items. Upstairs you will find paintings and altar pieces by Valencían primitives during the city's Golden Age of the 15th century—artists such as Jacomart and Reixach. Valencia's three greatest names—Jose de Ribera, Bartolomé Esteban Murillo and Francisco Ribalta—are well represented with some of their finest work. In room 49 there are 11 Goyas, several very nice Goya drawings and a letter signed by him. In an alcove next door is a Velazquez self-portrait, a singular work, hung dramatically against soft orange velvet. In room 30 is a prize—Hieronymus Bosch's *Los Improperios* triptych. Open 10 A.M. to 2 P.M.

Admirers of the current abstract school of Spanish art (we are among them) will find many familiar names—Valencían Manolo Mompó, Eusebio Sempere, Juan Genoves, Equipo Cronica. Much of the second floor is devoted to contemporary works. The museum is, all in all, a rich feast indeed.

South of Valencía—Costa Blanca Road

South of Valencía is *La Albufera,* the rice fields that make all that delicious paella Valencíana possible. If you drive the 185 kilometers (111 miles) south to Alicante, you will find a good motorway, A-7 autopista, for the journey. Along the way, you may want to look in on *Gandia* where all the Borjas (Borgias) originally came from, including St. Francis's grandfather, the decadent Pope Alexander VI. The old Borja Palacio del Santo Duque still stands as a Jesuit college, but in summer if you take the hour-long tour you can peek into some of the elaborately decorated rooms.

After Gandia comes *Denia,* a small resort, which has so far avoided the sleek Miami Beach look. If you want to replenish a traveling flask, there's an amazing wine and liquor store, Bodega Llobell, 51 Calle Marquis de Campo (the main street in town) where you can buy wine, port, gin, Campari, and other liquors *from casks* at low, low prices.

At nearby Javea there's the modern Parador Nacional Costa Blanca, Playa del Arenal (phone 790200) where you can have a good lunch, tea, cocktail, dinner or bedding-down on your coastal drive.

The most spectacular natural sight along this Costa Blanca (White Coast) road is coming up now—*El Penon de Ifach.* Rising from the sea like the proverbial rock of Gibraltar to a height of 323 meters (1,076 feet), this magnificent rough-hewn rock formation provides a stunning landmark as you drive either north or south along the coast (we like to look at it from Punta de Moraira). If you are ambitious you may want to climb to the top of Ifach; supposedly it takes about 2 hours following a decent path. Nearest to Ifach is *Calpe,* a tiny town with several fine beaches close by.

The largest resort on the Costa Blanca and the area's answer to Miami is *Benidorm.* You know you're close when you start seeing the discos and nightclubs and signs with English-sounding names along the highway. Benidorm is popular with English tour groups, and row upon row of hotels cater to charter tours. All kinds of restaurants, nightlife, shopping and amenities are available in this highrise heaven.

The beach *is* heavenly, which of course is why all the building started in the first place. We remember it when.

From Benidorm to Alicante, resorts begin to melt into one another, and if it's sun, sand and beach you're after, this could well be the spot for you.

Alicante

Alicante, capital and focal point of the Costa Blanca, has kept its own identity amazingly well through the years of change along this coast. We love its essentially cheerful look and its 700-meter (2100-foot) long *Explanada de España,* a palm-sheltered seaside promenade whose sidewalk tiles in red, black and white wave-like designs have an eerie optical effect on you as you stroll.

There isn't a lot to see in Alicante. You can take an elevator to the top of *Santa Barbara Castle,* whose underpinnings are Carthaginian. Views of the surrounding countryside and sea are far ranging. Open 9 A.M. to 9 P.M. July to September; 9 A.M. to 8 P.M. May and June; 9 A.M. to 7 P.M. October to April. If modern art interests you, we recommend a visit to the newly installed Museum of 20th Century Art, on Calle de Villavieja near Plaza de Santa Maria, catty-corner from the church of the same name.

Eusebio Sempere, a local son, is a Madrid painter and sculptor who remembers his roots. Thus, his large collection of paintings and sculptures—by the likes of Miró, Picasso, Dalí, Clavé, Chillida, Saura, Nuñez, Tapies, Manrique, Guerrero, Zóbel, Mompó—are the Museum of 20th Century Art's collection, on display in three floors of an old town building. Foreign artists—Alexander Calder, Vasarely, Tamayo, Arp, Braque, Kandinsky, Francis Bacon and Cocteau—are also represented in the collection. Sempere has several works of his own included too. Open 10 A.M. to 1 P.M., 5 to 8 P.M. October to April; 10:30 A.M. to 1:30 P.M., 6 to 9 P.M. May to September; closed Mondays and Sunday and holiday afternoons.

Just south of Alicante on N-340 is Elche, notable for its annual 13th-century mystery play. Its *Palmeral de Europa,* east of town, is a unique palm forest, planted by the Phoenicians, where the only date-producing palms in Europe flourish. You'll be inundated with dates if you hang around town long, for dates are the major crop, the prime negotiable commodity. If you don't succumb to the dates, you may end up with a basket made from the fronds.

THE BALEARIC ISLANDS

The word *balearic* derives from "slingers," and in eons past, the islanders of this Mediterranean group were known for their pitching arms. The Carthaginians conscripted them by the score to help in their battles with Rome. The location of the four islands made them easy prey for any conqueror who came along. And many did: Vandals, Visigoths, Franks, Moors and other Spaniards; even the British and French dropped by later on.

The largest and most developed Balearic Island is *Mallorca.* In 1981 almost 3 million people flew into Mallorca. (That doesn't count the ones who came by boat.) Only visitors to Madrid exceeded this number. If you want to combine sun bathing and swimming with sightseeing, Mallorca is *the* island to visit. The other three have a different, lazier kind of charm.

Mallorca

There is a surprising lot to see in Mallorca, but you really need a car to do it. If you stay in Palma, plan one day to sightsee the west coast, a second day for the east and inland.

Palma

First, there's the capital, *Palma de Mallorca,* a dynamic, interesting and ancient city with considerable history. In spite of all the modern highrise buildings that clog the town, the cathedral, *Séo*, and the *Palacio de la Almudaina,* two long pinkish golden sandstone expanses in the sunlight, are stirring sights as you drive in from the airport along the seafront paseo, for the very first time.

La Almudaina, once the ancient Moorish citadel of the Walis' caliphate and later a palace of the Christian kings, is worth a look. So is the cathedral, which Jaime I of Aragon built to celebrate his defeat of the Moors. We should say Jaime began it and conceived its monumentality. Building it spanned four centuries. It has often been likened to a great golden galleon washed ashore. To Sacheverell Sitwell it is "the most beautiful of Catalan buildings." We may quibble about his superlatives, but *La Séo is* remarkable, notably for its enormous height, the width of the nave and the dramatic double row of flying buttresses. Gaudí fanciers will want a peek inside at the wrought iron high altar canopy he designed. The mausoleums of Mallorcan kings Jaime II and Jaime III are the works of 20th-century sculptor Federico Marés (donor of the fabulous Marés Museum in Barcelona). Cathedral museum hours: 10 A.M. to 12:30 P.M., 3:30 to 6 P.M.; closed Sundays and holidays.

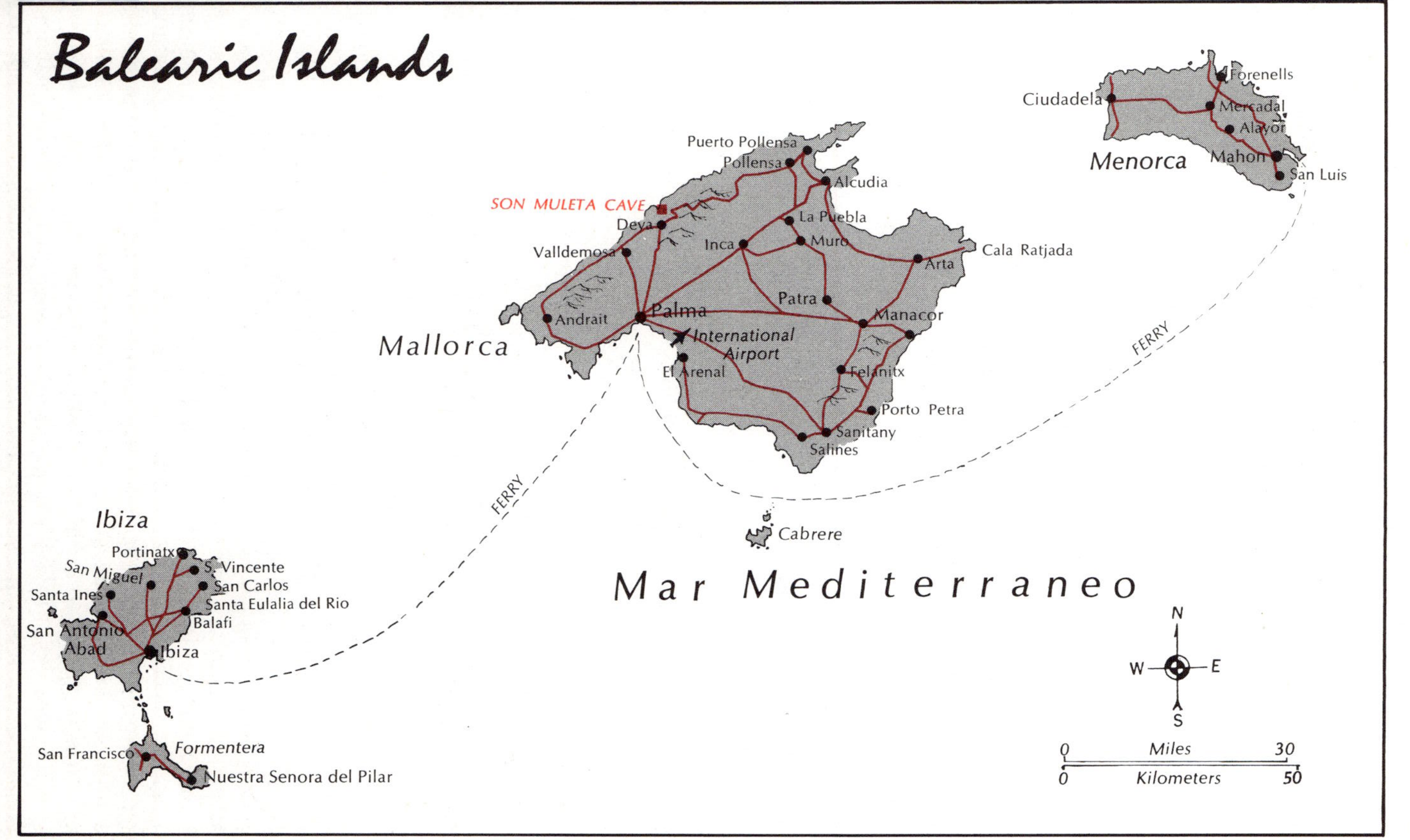
Balearic Islands
Menorca
Ciudadela
Forenells
Mercadal
Alayor
Mahon
San Luis
Mallorca
Puerto Pollensa
Pollensa
Alcudia
SON MULETA CAVE
Deva
La Puebla
Valldemosa
Inca
Muro
Cala Ratjada
Arta
Patra
Andrait
Palma
Manacor
International Airport
El Arenal
Felanitx
Porto Petra
Sanitany
Salines
FERRY
FERRY
Cabrere
Mar Mediterraneo
Ibiza
Portinatx
S. Vincente
San Miguel
San Carlos
Santa Ines
Santa Eulalia del Rio
Balafi
San Antonio Abad
Ibiza
Formentera
San Francisco
Nuestra Senora del Pilar
N
W
E
S
0
Miles
30
0
Kilometers
50

Old Part of Palma

Most of your sightseeing in the old part of Palma can be done on foot. In fact, that's the ideal way. Many of the old palaces and churches were built of the same glowing Santañy limestone. A special jewel is the Gothic *Church of San Francisco;* its cherub-decorated baroque facade is punctuated by a lavish splash of color from red hibiscus and pink oleanders. Inside, the cloister is the gem, a haven of cypress, lemon trees, roses, hibiscus and oleanders framing slender Gothic arches. Franciscan Father Junipero Serra, missionary in Mexico and California (when *it* was part of Mexico), studied here. In the church notice the tomb of Ramón Llull, Mallorca's other famous native son. Llull, a 13th–14th century philosopher, mystic and missionary, was stoned to death during his third mission to Africa.

You can wander on foot to *La Lonja,* the beautifully proportioned building (by local architect, Guillermo Sagrera) used in the 15th century as a commercial center or exchange; to the *ayuntamiento,* which has a painting by Van Dyck; to the Arab baths; and all along El Borne (the major shopping, café and restaurant street), but you'll need a cab for the best view in town —at Bellver Castle.

Bellver Castle commands a superb site, with views of the bay that extend for miles. Built as a summer residence by Mallorca's 14th-century kings, the castle has played host to prisoners for most of its long life. Only in 1915 did it cease being a prison. Open 9 A.M. to sunset.

While Palma is where the Mallorca action is and is the major magnet for restaurants and nightlife, it is not really typical of the island as a whole. For the serious away-from-it-all vacationer, a better choice would be the northern tip, the Formentor peninsula, an area still relatively wild and secluded.

West Coast

Mallorca is known for the company it keeps or has kept. Most famous visitors were George Sand and Frédéric Chopin, who holed up on the island during the winter of 1838–1839. A main place to visit is the monastery in Valldemosa on the west coast where they lived.

The Carthusian monastery in which they lived dated from 1399, though it had been rebuilt in the 18th century. The monks were driven out in 1835, and the 12 cells that existed were leased to tenants who sublet them in turn. Today eight families own different parts of the monastery, except for the church and museum, which explains why when you visit you buy a ticket admitting you to separate sections. It also explains why the ticket price is higher than most in Spain and why there is a kind of frenetic commercialism about the place (with a repetition of postcard and souvenir stands in each section). An ironic note that Sand would have enjoyed is that the place she loathed would 150 years later be so exploited for its charm. Open 9:30 A.M. to 1:30 P.M., 3 to 7 P.M.; closes one hour earlier in winter.

The west coast is lovely, and explains why so many people, including poet Robert Graves, have become enchanted by it. From Puerto de Andraitx, inland to Valldemosa, to Deya (where many artists, including Graves, have settled) on to Soller, with its pretty little port, it is a drive of winding, often squiggly turning roads, past olive groves, rocky cliffs that drop precipitously to the clear blue sea, and orchards full of orange, lemon and almond trees.

Inland

A second day's tour can take you inland, past *Inca,* a small town noted chiefly for its factory outlets of local crafts. The much revered *Monastery of Our Lady of Lluch,* with its aged Gothic statue of Our Lady, the Virgin, has an adjoining ethnological museum with bronze artifacts dating back to B.C. times.

Moving with dispatch, you can loop around to see the sheltered bay at *Puerto de Pollensa,* with mountains looming behind like a stage set, then over more twisting roads to *Colomer,* the windswept tip of *Cape Formentor* with its bleak lighthouse, then back to see the partially excavated Roman theater near Alcudia.

Inland, you may also stop at the tiny village of *Petra,* to see the modest whitewashed home in which Junipero Serra was born. After seeing it and its red-tile-roofed neighbors, you can understand the source of all the mission architecture along the California coast.

Distances aren't great in Mallorca. It's just 75 kilometers (45 miles) from north to south, 100 kilometers (60 miles) from east to west. But because of the mountains that rise and drop with unexpected suddenness, it takes more time than you may expect to cover ground.

That's why a third day might be spent exploring the east coast. Beyond Petra to the east is *Porto Cristo.* Just outside town are the Drach caves, one of several groups (and perhaps the most rewarding) of underground caves on this part of the island. There are group tours throughout the day that will guide you down into a stalagmite wonderland of limestone caves and pools that cover 2 kilometers. The formations are, progressively (in our interpretation), a Chinese mountain landscape sculpted in ivory, a Gothic cathedral, a sculpture by Louise Nevelson, Giacometti multiples, Indian totems, a harvest of Gaudí constructions, a fakir's bed of nails, the world's largest candle factory, a mammoth organ, an Aztec temple, stacks of dental casts, the Snow Queen's palace, a Louisiana swampy bayou and a scene from *The Princess and the Goblin.* They may look like something completely different to you. The eye of the beholder and all that.

Ibiza

What makes the Balearics so compelling is that each is completely different. Ibiza, 45 nautical miles west and south of Mallorca, is another terrain entirely. In looks it is more like a displaced Greek island—its totally white, rounded North African-style houses are dazzling in the sunshine, its foliage often sparse and scruffy.

The drawing cards are the many lovely beaches scattered throughout the island. Sun lovers hop local buses to change venue from day to day, returning, if they are gregarious types, to Ibiza for its lively night scene or to San Antonio Abad, which is giving it a good run. The local bus system is reliable (hourly from Ibiza), inexpensive (50 pts. one-way to San Antonio), and fast (half an hour for a 15-kilometer ride). The bus to and from the airport is equally inexpensive. Many visitors are even tempted to take a boat outing to the

Balearics' fourth and smallest island, *Formentera,* just 3½ nautical miles south of Ibiza. For 800 pts. round trip, you can leave San Antonio, say, at 10 A.M. and return at 5 P.M., with half a day to explore this least developed island.

Ibiza's major sight is its old town *Dalt Vila,* rising like a somber fortress of tan stone above the cheery all-white lower port city. A 16th-century wall protects and encloses Dalt Vila, and you must spiral up its cobbled streets to reach the cathedral. There you'll have enviable views of the harbor and sea below for miles and miles.

Inside the cathedral is a mix of Renaissance and baroque (the nave was rebuilt in the 17th century). Next to the cathedral is a classily-displayed Archaeological Museum whose main attractions are jewelry, terra cotta statues, fragments from the Phoenician–Carthaginian Necropolis on Windmill Mound. The museum gives a quick lesson in the many cultures that overran this small island's coasts in the past—Phoenicians, Carthaginians and Romans are most prominent.

Behind the town hall is a splendid mirador with fine views of the town and sea below. As you stroll down to the old town, you'll pass the Museum of Contemporary Art and may want to drop in to see one of its frequently-changed exhibits—mostly of local artists' work.

Menorca

Roughly rectangular with 200 kilometers of coastline, Menorca is Spain's easternmost land. Though it is young in terms of touristic development, it is ancient in terms of visitors, settlers, conquerors and occupiers. In the past it was not beaches but booty that lured visitors here.

Today *Mahon* has roughly half the island's population (25,000) and a distinctly European look, with boutiques and fashionable shops (on pedestrian streets such as Gen. Goded and Calvo Sotelo). Second city *Ciudadela* is more overtly Spanish, with tiny, twisting streets, palaces and walled courtyards.

In Ciudadela's city hall amid portraits of assorted saints, kings, and Isabella la Catolica, you'll suddenly come upon David Farragut, first U.S. admiral. Farragut's father was born here and when the admiral visited in 1867 he was made an honorary citizen.

From Ciudadela's Plaza del Generalisimo you can see the tiny port below with its many small boats. The square is bordered by golden-hued Renaissance buildings with tall, third-floor loggias beyond which peeks the tower of the Gothic church. For shopping, the boutiques around Plaza Pio XII are contemporary and attractive. Entertained by canaries' songs, you can stroll along Calle del Rosario to check out the Episcopal Palace facade or along Calle Los Dolores to see a magnificent old palace with an unusual open stairwell.

Inside Information

Hotels

For prices, see Madrid, page 50.

The area we have covered in this section—Barcelona and the East Coast—is one known for its recreational facilities (Costa Brava, Costa Blanca, Costa Dorada and the Balearic Islands). This means that you have a wide choice of accommodations in all price ranges. The following are our personal choices of hotels over the entire breadth of the area.

★★★★★ FIVE STARS

★★★★★ 1. HOTEL FORMENTOR

Puerto de Pollensa, Mallorca (phone 531300). The seclusion of world's end, but all the comforts a deluxe hotel can dream up—that's the Formentor. Its peninsula location, with bedroom views of either the Mediterranean or the mountains, and a beach at the door, makes this elegant, understated hotel a genuine hideaway. Yet Palma's busy, glittering nightlife and shopping areas are just an hour's drive away. Gardens full of roses and bougainvillaeas, terraces, two swimming pools (one heated), a gorgeous long stretch of secluded sandy beach, lighted tennis courts, minigolf, water sports, horses for riding—all the elements are here for a super vacation. 131 rooms plus suites. *Expensive.*

★★★★★ 2. HOSTAL DE LA GAVINA

Plaza de la Rosaleda, S'Agáro (phone 321100). Looking like a stage-set-version of a Mediterranean villa with red tile roof, cypresses and riotous flowers everywhere, this delightful *gran luxe* hotel owes its success to the caring attention of a single remarkable man, the late Don José Ensesa, who began the enterprise in 1934 and treated each guest like a welcome friend. Each luxurious guest room is furnished differently and exuberantly with antiques. There's tennis (where professional matches are held), a swimming pool, gardens and a first-class dining room. 73 rooms. *Expensive.*

Has *** restaurant. Ava Gardner & Salvador Dalí have stayed here

★★★★★ 3. HOTEL SON VIDA

Castillo de Son Vida, Palma de Mallorca (phone 232340). Just 13 kilometers (8 miles) outside Palma in a mountain setting, this superb resort hotel was once part of an old castle (renovated and added on). Decor is restrained elegance, part antiques, part classical modern, with handsome color schemes throughout. Large public and private rooms, terrace (and guest room) views of Palma Bay, combine with a heated swimming pool, 18-hole golf course, tennis courts, shops, horseback riding, to make this an all-purpose vacation spot. 171 rooms, plus sumptuous suites. *Expensive.*

★★★★★ 4. HACIENDA "NA XAMENA"

San Miguel, Ibiza (phone 333046). The setting couldn't be more glamorous: high on a clifftop overlooking a tranquil bay with great rocks looming in the Mediterranean below. Fortunately the all-white interior of the all-white, North African-looking hacienda is as beautiful as the setting. Each guest

a Relais de Campagne hotel

Has *** restaurant

room is decorated differently (some with antiques, some with an African look, some Spanish). Accoutrements are first rate, as is the attentive, helpful service. There's an indoor pool (with exercise room) as well as two outdoor pools in a starkly handsome setting. A dream place—our personal preference—but isolated. 65 rooms (including six suites, 11 singles). *Moderate.*

★★★★★ 5. RITZ

668 Gran Vía, Barcelona (phone 3185200). Since 1919 the Ritz's generous flower-bedecked central oval lounge with mirrored walls and beautiful rugs has been the place to meet for tea or talk in old world splendor. Rooms are conservatively modern, sound-proofed, air-conditioned—and equipped with handsome furnishings that include TV. The summer garden, patio bar, grill and restaurant are notable delights. (A long-range refurbishing is under way: Ask for newly decorated rooms.) Shops, hairdressers, services on premises. 200 rooms. All-weather pool. *Expensive.*

★★★★ FOUR STARS

★★★★ 1. EL MONTÍBOLI

8 Apartado de Correos, Villajoyosa (phone 890250). 30 kilometers (18 miles) north of Alicante, 14 kilometers (8½ miles) south of Benidorm. Visualize a flower and palm- ringed Moorish "palace" gleaming on a crag overlooking the sea—and there you are, in one of two swimming pools, or on the tennis court, or in the air-conditioned lounge or restaurant. This modern Moorish fantasy of tile and white stucco offers all the luxuries typical of hotels of the *Relais et Chateaux* association. It's a haven for lotus eaters, complete with sauna, hairdresser, access to golf, horses, beach and water sports. 33 rooms. *Moderate–Expensive.*

★★★★ 2. COLÓN

7 Avda. de la Catedral, Barcelona (phone 3011404). With a lacy, lighted Gothic cathedral in your front yard to distract you, you may never notice the roomy, well-appointed lounges and bar or comfortable, air-conditioned guest rooms. A convenient location for shopping and sightseeing in Barcelona, with a congenial, accommodating staff. Try for a front room with balcony overlooking the cathedral (and *Sardanas* dancing on its forecourt on weekends). *Note:* It's a busy street—you'll have traffic noise as well as cathedral bells to contend with—but it's worth it. Hotel garage nearby. 200 rooms. Continental breakfast included. *Moderate.*

★★★★ 3. DERBY

21–25 Loreto, Barcelona (phone 2392003). On a quiet, tree-lined semi-residential street just off the Diagonal, the Derby is up to the minute (new 1980) with its amenities and furnishings. Modern, well-designed rooms are air conditioned and equipped with refrigerator, TV, direct-dial phones. Contemporary without being *outré.* Live piano music in Epsom lounge; the Dickens English-style pub has brick-and-timber authenticity. Large garage. 116 rooms. *Moderate.*

★★★★ 4. DIPLOMATIC

122 Vía Layetana, Barcelona (phone 3173100). The glass and marble lobby and ultramodern room interiors are outward signs of the "mod" orientation of this hotel. Two-bath and TV-equipped, soundproof rooms, smoke detectors, air conditioning and parking garage. Relax in the vest pocket tenth floor pool with a view. 225 rooms. *Moderate.*

★★★★ 4. PALMYRA

San Antonio Abad, Ibiza (phone 340354). Palm trees surround the pool; grass umbrellas and beach chairs dot the sandy shore. All guest rooms with private balconies. Air-conditioned public rooms and restaurant, bridge room, terrace-solarium and snack bar plus dancing nightly in Ses Voltes club. 160 rooms. *Moderate.*

★★★★ 5. GRAN HOTEL SARRÍA

50 Avenida de Sarriá, Barcelona (phone 2391109). Twenty-one stories of spacious accommodations (314 rooms), this deluxe Entursa hotel is *known* for super service—air conditioning, TV in all handsomely furnished rooms. Good restaurant *San Jorge. Moderate–Expensive.*

★★★ THREE STARS

★★★ 1. HUERTO DEL CURA (THE PRIEST'S ORCHARD)

14 F García Sanchiz, Elche (phone 458040). This resort hotel 10 kilometers (6 miles) from Alicante is right in the middle of Elche's famed palm grove, unique in Europe. Towering palms and lush, beautifully tended flowering gardens line reflecting pools among one-story bungalows for guests. An oasis without camels. There is a free-form pool, light and airy lodge with lounge, grill, restaurant, all of them in a "ski-lodge modern" style. Air-conditioned throughout; plenty of garage and parking space. 51 rooms. *Inexpensive–Moderate.*

** Els Capellans here has excellent regional dishes

★★★ 2. DON PANCHO

Avda. del Mediterraneo, Benidorm (phone 852950). A typical highrise resort hotel near a magnificent beach. Don Pancho's lobby seems to have been decorated by the last of the Aztecs, but guest rooms are chipper, have individual balconies, sliding glass doors, air conditioning. The pool is directly in front, the beach a block further. Lighted tennis court; nurse, wading pool and meals for children; resident band. 251 rooms. Continental breakfast included. *Inexpensive.*

Pleasant garden

★★★ 3. GRAN SOL

3 Avda. Mendez Núñez, Alicante (phone 203000). Upper rooms are quiet; tastefully done with antique-style chairs and couches in inviting, separate TV-equipped sitting room. Breakfast (or twilight drink) in the 26th-floor snack bar where you get stunning views of countryside and sea—only slightly more sweeping than from your room. Tear yourself away from the china leopards, Japanese vases and turquoise Fu dogs in the lobby, and you'll find the guest rooms much more appealing in this high rise that juts above Alicante's skyline. It's just one short block from the palm-lined *Explanada.*

Note: No parking on busy one-way streets around the hotel (closest public garage is eight blocks away); difficult to stop at entrance in heavy traffic. 150 rooms. *Inexpensive–Moderate.*

★★★ 4. ASTORIA PALACE

5 Plaza Rodrigo Botet, Valencia (phone 3229590). On a tiny tree-shaded plaza, complete with Victorian fountain, just two blocks from the main city square, this quiet hotel has a solarium-like lobby, is air conditioned throughout and has parking for guests' cars. Rooms are comfortably outfitted with couch, tiny writing table, TV and small modern bath that features double sinks. Attractive wood and brass finishing in public areas, hallways. 207 rooms. Continental breakfast included (that means croissant and rolls, tea, coffee or chocolate and soft-ball-sized navel oranges; for a bargain 100 pts. extra you have a selection of breakfast buffet of cold cuts and cheeses as well). *Moderate.*

★★★ 5. REGENTE

76 Rambla de Cataluña, Barcelona (phone 2152570). At first you'll think you've entered an Art Nouveau showroom (sinuous door pulls, stained glass door panels, frosted light globes and more stained glass in lobby) but the rest is eclectic, ranging up through 1950s moderne. Rooms are air-conditioned, have handsome, simple furnishings; baths are two rooms (separate tub and lavatory). Small balcony looks out on one of city's main boulevards. Small swimming pool and solarium on roof. Garage. 78 rooms. Price includes continental breakfast. *Moderate.*

★★ TWO STARS

★★ 1. REGENCIA COLÓN

13–17 Calle Sagristans, Barcelona (phone 3189858). This is Barcelona's first post-World War II hotel and is *not* showing its age. Well-planned solidly built and furnished with quality materials, it has spacious guest and public rooms, pleasingly passé wood furniture, conservative lighting and drapes. Air-conditioned and quiet; excellent housekeeping and a friendly staff. One block from cathedral square, Gothic quarter and shopping area; garage across the street. 50 rooms. Continental breakfast included. *Inexpensive.*

★★ 2. PALAS

Plaza del Mar, Alicante (phone 209309). This handsome old-fashioned building, three stories tall, has an awning-shaded balcony on each guest room window. Located at the end of Alicante's famous *explanada* and across from the pier. Renovated in 1973, its guest rooms are now furnished with rustic chairs and Granada handwoven bedspreads; no TV or radio. Inviting sidewalk café, adequate restaurant. Location is the thing. Busy streets and noise are inescapable here. Parking nearby. 48 rooms. Continental breakfast included. *Inexpensive.*

★★ 3. GRAN VÍA

642 Avda. Gran Vía, Barcelona (phone 3181900). Step into another era in this once sumptuous establishment as you view its palatial staircase made

for Gloria Swanson entrances, its 19th-century salon with gilded furniture and crystal chandelier. Guest rooms are high ceilinged, equipped with sturdy furniture, adequate baths. Because of heavy street traffic, opt for room away from Gran Vía. Parking garage behind hotel. 48 rooms. *Inexpensive.*

★★ 4. LAS GARZAS

Avda. de la Marina Española, Benidorm (phone 854850). A highrise glass and concrete hotel several blocks from the beach is one of a chain of places built to accommodate tour groups. Impersonal, clean, designed for efficiency with compact rooms, adequate baths, tiny balconies. Lounges for games, TV and reading. Also swimming pool and patio buffet. 306 rooms. *Bargain–Inexpensive.*

★ 1. CLUB NAUJICO

20 Contramuelle, Palma, Mallorca (phone 221405). Thirty-five simply furnished rooms with great marina views. (King Ivan Carlos sails from there.) Swimming pool, good seafood restaurant are among the assets—along with modest prices. *Bargain.*

★ ONE STAR

★ 1. HOTEL DEL ALMIRANTE

Carretera, Villa Carlos Fonduco Puerto Mahón (5 kilometers from Mahon), Menorca. They still talk about Menorca's most famous visitor, Lord Horatio Nelson. His vice admiral, Lord Collingwood, owned this comfortable manor in 1798. The present owner, Paco Montanari, has decorated with homey British evocations. History abounds: the house was once a convent; once (until 1941) the German consul's home. The stair well sports Collingwood's portrait, military weapons, Spy's *Vanity Fair* drawings of British officers. The British-style sitting room with fireplace and gas grate has Victorian chairs and romantic etchings of Greek myths. In addition to six rooms in the mellow old house, modern rooms are arranged about pool and patio, lovely views of bay and bucolic countryside. So popular with British that the manor is booked months in advance. 39 rooms. One-Half board. *Bargain.*

★ 2. SUIZO

12 Plaza del Angel, Barcelona (phone 3154111). The Suizo, at the edge of the Gothic quarter, across from the Metro entrance, is three blocks from the harbor, one from the cathedral. Serviceable, clean, small, on a busy thoroughfare (noisy but secure), it offers good value in convenience and accommodations (and there's a good *pastelería* on the ground floor). 44 rooms. Continental breakfast. *Inexpensive.*

★ 3. MAR SOL

Playa dela PINS (phone 330108). Santa Eulalia, Ibiza. This Hostal Residencia was brand new in 1982. Facing the sea, it has guest rooms with balconies overlooking the water, date palms at the entrance and a folkloric restaurant. Easy walk to nearby village. 12 rooms. *Bargain.*

Restaurants

For prices, see Madrid, page 54.

★★★★ FOUR STARS

★★★★ 1. JAUME DE PROVENÇA

88 Calle de Provenza, Barcelona (phone 2300029). In a series of small attractive dining rooms and alcoves Barcelona's elite—politicos, socialites, theater people—dine on Catalan dishes with a *nouvelle cuisine* accent. Asparagus mousse (made with tender, baby stalks of fresh asparagus) in a mousseline sauce, canoli of spinach in a creamy champagne sauce, sole in a subtle dry vermouth sauce, are just a few of the imaginative offerings beautifully prepared and served here. Ice cream flan with a thin veneer of caramel crusting and a crushed almond sauce lingers lovingly in the mind as an end to dinner. Closed Mondays, holiday evenings, *Semana Santa* (Holy Week), August and Christmas Day. *Expensive.*

★★★★ 2. AGUT D' AVIGNON

3 Trinidad (corner of Aviñon), Barcelona (phone 3026034). You may have trouble finding this small restaurant at the end of a cul-de-sac, but once found, you may not want to leave. The ambience is sophisticated rustic: whitewashed walls, exposed overhead beams, big sprays of fresh flowers, rush seats on ladder-back chairs, fresh flowers on each table, dining areas artfully arranged at five different levels. The menu isn't large, but is unusual—mussels in a wine, onion and garlic sauce; fresh tuna fish with baked red peppers and eggplant; Navarra-style trout filled with ham, duck with figs, rabbit simmered with red peppers and tomatoes, goose with pears. For dessert try *lionesas*—three tiny, cloudlike cream puffs with chocolate sauce or, in season, *fresas del Bosco*—minuscule wild strawberries with fresh whipped cream. Expect to make reservations—as at all Barcelona's best restaurants. Closed Sundays, *Semana Santa* (Holy Week) and August. *Expensive.*

★★★★ 3. AMPURDÁN

Carretera N-II, kilometer 763 Figueras (phone 500562). *Aficionados* call this unassuming restaurant (part of a hotel by the same name) one of the best in Spain. We can't argue with that assessment. If you're driving into Spain from France, it's on the main highway. If you're not, but are in Gerona (37 kilometers south), it's worth the trip. Many devotees make the trip all the way from Barcelona—137 kilometers away. And what awaits you? Expertly prepared Catalan style food with a nouvelle cuisine accent, using the freshest ingredients in unusual combinations. Among the notable dishes: *dorada al horno a la pescadora* (a delicious baked fish dish), stuffed leg of lamb, veal steak in a delicate cream sauce, and *ensalada de habas a la menta* (cold bean salad). *Expensive.*

★★★★ 4. HACIENDA EL BULLI

Cala Montjoy, apartado 30, Rosas (phone 257651). Located just south of a delightful Costa Brava resort fishing village and not far from Figueras, this attractive restaurant offers a harvest of Mediterranean dishes laced with aspects of Paul Bocuse's nouvelle cuisine and hints of Alsace. The goose liver terrine is a winner as are turbot in a morel-accented cream sauce or slices of duck with lemon and green peppercorns. Homemade ice creams and fruit sherbets round out the picture. A fine wine list specializes in Riojas (reds), Catalan and Alsatian whites. Closed Mondays and Tuesdays for lunch, and from January 15th to March 15th. *Expensive–Very Expensive.*

★★★★ 5. AMA-LUR

275 Calle Mallorca, Barcelona (phone 2153024). Finding this discreet Basque restaurant isn't easy. Only a small brass sign identifies the restaurant's presence. A bell ring admits you. Once inside the building, you climb a few steps, ring another bell (speakeasy style) and enter a beautiful establishment—light, airy, decorated to look like a comfortable living room, with fireplace, couches and an air of understated good taste. The dining rooms with well-spaced tables for privacy, lots of fresh flowers everywhere and pleasing accoutrements continue the sense of fine living. Service is outright pampering by waitresses in black and white uniforms. Fortunately, the kitchen measures up, for the most part, to the overall high standards. Hot rolls and miniature black "skillets" with slices of hot broiled, spicy *chorizo* (sausage) are served just after you sit down. Memorable entrees include a robust *merluza* (hake) in garlic, veal steak in wine sauce and kid and kidneys in a brown sauce. Marvelous desserts include a four-layer orange cake, lemon and honey crepes, plum ice cream with Armagnac. Exquisite tiny cookies are complimentary with coffee. Closed Sundays, holidays, Semana Santa (Holy Week), August and Christmas Day. *Very Expensive.*

★★★ THREE STARS

★★★ 1. EL DORADO PETIT

11 Rambla Vidal, San Feliu de Guixols (phone 321019). Catalan food, with the flair of nouvelle cuisine, makes for numerous imaginative offerings in this charming Costa Brava restaurant. Try the *rodaballo con salsa de erizos* (turbot in sea urchin sauce) or *filetes de pechuga de pato al vinagre de escalomas* (breast of duck in a vinegar–scallion sauce). Rioja reds and Catalan whites are prevalent in a well-stocked wine cellar. Closed Tuesdays during winter. *Expensive.*

★★★ 2. VIVEROS-ANFITRIÓN

Jardines del Real, Valencia (phone 3692350). Sometimes known as El Anfitrión, this delightful restaurant is smack in the middle of the Royal Gardens. From the wall-to-wall, all-glass, floor-to-ceiling windows you have a fine view of the park. Service is attentive, and the menu features many Valencian specialties. *Paella Valenciana* (with chicken, snails and seafood) is a specialty here as is *arroz con marescos* (rice with prawns and fish). An orange souffle—orange sherbet, with meringue on top and flaming Cointreau over all—is superb; so is the lemon champagne sorbet served gratis with a plate of macaroons at the meal's end. Closed Sundays and August. *Expensive.*

★★★ 3. DELFÍN

14 Explanada de España, Alicante (phone 214911). An upstairs dining room (with bar on the ground floor) gives diners a wide-angle view of the harbor—that's why we prefer lunch here rather than dinner. A creative menu features stuffed sea bass with crab sauce, smoked eels calvados style, filet of sole in puff pastry with pistachio sauce (the pastry is cleverly shaped into a fish tail), partridge pie with mushroom sauce and sea bass with lobster mousse baked in pastry. For starters, try the quail paté, leek pie or a salad of endives, walnuts and Roquefort cheese. *Expensive.*

★★★ 4. HOSTAL DE LA GAVINA

Plaza de la Rosaleda, S'Agaró (phone 321100). This delightful dining room in an equally attractive deluxe hotel sets the stage for an excellent dining experience. Seafood is a *specialité.* Try the *sopa de pescado* Costa Brava, a luscious soup with a medley of sea treats; *gambas de Palomós al ajillo* (shrimps in garlic); and, for dessert, a house trademark—*crema Catalana con buñuelos* (a richer Catalan version of *flan*). Superb cellar. *Expensive–Very Expensive.*

★★★ 5. HACIENDA "NA XAMENA"

In Ibiza it is believed that the herbal liqueurs are aphrodisiacs

San Miguel, Ibiza (phone 333046). The setting is a knock out. Whether you eat in the dining room or in front of it on the terrace by the swimming pool, you have a wide, sweeping view of the Mediterranean, mountains and boulders in the sea. The Hacienda is also a superb hotel, isolated on its own clifftop, all white on this dazzling white island. Seafood such as *merluza* in garlic and parsley or red snapper *en papillote* is a specialty. Afterwards, sip an *hierbes*—a local liqueur made of anise, rum and wild herbs. Closed November 1–March 31. *Expensive.*

★★ TWO STARS

★★ 1. SIETE PUERTAS

14 Paseo de Isabel, Barcelona (phone 3193033). Year in, year out, this old-time waterfront establishment keeps going strong, a favorite with tourists and locals alike. Dark wood banquettes, mirrors and blue and white tile paneling combine to make this a very comfortable place in which to enjoy fine seafood dishes such as *soupe aux Baudroie* (sailor's soup), *bullabesa* (Bouillabaisse), *zarzuela* (filet of sole in white wine), paella three different styles and grilled fish. The *crema Catalana* and *turrón* ice cream (almond) are especially good here. *Moderate.*

★★ 2. HOSTAL DE LA GRANOTA

Carretera Barcelona, La Junquera, Sils (phone 853044). Lodged in a former postoffice, this long-time favorite, just 24 kilometers south of Gerona on the highway, is strong on traditional Catalan fare such as lamb chops in garlic, but you'll also find piquant snails, frogs legs, *balcalao* salad on the menu. Closed Wednesdays and November. *Moderate.*

★★ 3. MESÓN QUO VADIS

3 Plaza Santísima Faz, Alicante (phone 216660). Wooden walls and wood-beamed ceilings with blue and white Manises pottery plates along the walls

give this small restaurant a warm, rustic look. The robust cuisine matches. A varied hors d'oeuvres tray with marinated sardines, anchovies, tuna and other seafood makes a good beginning. Baked bass in fennel, bream in salt brine and chicken in a wine-laced vegetable casserole are all good entree choices. *Moderate.*

★★ 4. ANCORA

Ensenada Can Barbara, Palma de Mallorca, Mallorca (phone 401101). In a well-furnished and agreeable setting, imaginative food is the password: puff pastry filled with lobster and green asparagus; sweetbreads with pears; beef with a mustard and oregano sauce. Closed Sundays and Mondays at midday. *Moderate.*

★★ 5. EL TÚNEL

33 Ancha, Barcelona (phone 3152759). A standby in the old section of Barcelona, El Túnel does familiar dishes extremely well: *pescados al horno* (baked fish), *cabrito asado* (roast kid), sauteed octopus, plus many other choices. Closed Sunday evenings, Mondays and from July 15th to August 20th. *Moderate.*

★ ONE STAR

★ 1. AMAYA

24 Rambla de Santa Mónica, Barcelona (phone 3021037). Handy to the lower, harbor end of the Ramblas, Amaya is an old-time favorite of those in search of good, reliable Basque cooking. The menu is extensive, with emphasis on seafaring dishes. Be sure to look at the large wine list. *Inexpensive.*

★ 2. CASA COSTA

Calle Juicio, Barceloneta, Barcelona (phone 3195028). A plain pipe-rack-type place directly on the water. You can watch the swimmers and sailboats skimming the sea on summer days. Grilled shrimp with *Romescu* sauce (a Tarragona dish, hot and peppery, made of tomato, chili pepper, garlic, hazelnuts and oil) is a specialty, but all the seafood is fresh and wonderful. And the price is cheap. Ask to sit in the older section. It's more fun. *Bargain–Inexpensive.*

★ 3. LOS CARACOLES

14 Escudellers, Barcelona (phone 3023185). Long popular with tourists, as well as locals in search of old favorites. Done with expertise at modest prices. We like the house paella Valenciana–beautiful looking, generous, and inexpensive. Enter through a busy bar, then go up the stairs, past the hams hanging from the ceiling and the corn and red pepper strung decoratively along the walls. You can eat bountifully here. *Bargain.*

★ 4. SA PUNTA

Isidoro Malabrich, Santa Eulalia del Rio, Ibiza (phone 330033). On the ground floor of an all-white apartment building, directly facing the Mediterranean, this delightful looking restaurant serves marvelous food at astonishingly low prices. Try hake in red pepper sauce, roast leg of lamb, hake in champagne sauce or crisply roasted pork. Closed Mondays and from January 15th to March 1st. *Inexpensive.*

★ 5. GRAN TABERNA RIO-SIL

10 Mosén Femades, Valencia. In a rustic setting, with nautical decor (ship models, ships' figureheads), you can sample the famous paella Valenciana in natural habitat. Garlic bread and a wide selection of tapas are other house specialties. *Bargain–Inexpensive.*

★ 6. CELLER C'AN AMER

39 Calle Miguel Durán, Inca, Mallorca. This 19th-century wine cellar is one of the most popular spots on the island for *frito Mallorquín* (mixed fried fish) and other seafood. *Inexpensive.*

★ 7. CELLER CAVOSTRA

Puerto de Pollensa (corner of the Pollensa and Alcudia roads), Pollensa, Mallorca (phone 531546). The beach is just across the highway. Feast on hearty bean soup or *zarzuela de pescado,* roast kid or pork, rough-hewn local bread, *flan* and a pitcher of wine. Closed Wednesdays (except in summer). *Inexpensive.*

Barcelona

Barcelona, as a manufacturing city in a manufacturing region, has all kinds of interesting buys and shops in which to buy them. The most fashionable shopping areas are Plaza de Cataluña (where a branch of *El Corte Inglés* is located, with *Galerías Preciados* on Avenida Puerta del Angel nearby); Paseo de Gracia; and the Diagonal (formerly called Avenida del Generalísimo Franco). *Loewe,* at 570 Diagonal, is a branch of the famous Madrid leather shop. On the corner of Diagonal and Vía Augusta is *Gonzalo Comella,* a fashionable women's and men's clothing shop. Off the Diagonal is a small street, Calle Tuset, where Barcelona's young crowd hangs out. There you can find, in addition to with-it discos, a number of small boutiques with "mod" and offbeat fashions.

If your shopping thoughts turn automatically to food, or if you want to shop for picnic items, *Montequerías Leonesas,* 5 Rambla de Cataluña, has an unusually large and varied selection of grocery and delicatessen items and a wide liquor and wine selection. (There's also a cozy bar in the rear.) Another attractive shop for food and wine is *Colmado Quilez* on the corner of Calle del Consejo de Ciento and Rambla de Cataluña.

The art fancier will want to amble along Rambla de Cataluña. *Galería Joan Prats,* at No. 54 is an interesting contemporary gallery. Paseo de Gracía and a street that crosses it, Calle del Consejo de Ciento, are both fertile art shopping turf. Note especially Vinçon, 96 Paseo de Gracia, a super emporium of *objets* (home accessories, toys, stationery, fabrics) as well as well-designed modern furniture. Another fruitful street for both art and handcraft shopping is Calle Moncada near the *barrio gótico,* in the oldest part of town. *Galería Maeght,* No. 25, has a large selection of graphics by big international names (it's a branch of the Paris gallery). Further down the street is *Galería Dalí,* with Salvador Dali's graphics for sale.

Handicraft shops on Moncada include *1748,* at No. 2, with imaginative handmade pottery, ceramic chess sets, casseroles, papier mache sculptures, and 18th-century plates; and *Populart,* No. 33, with ceramics, hand-blown glassware and folk art objects. A tiny street near the cathedral in the *barrio gotico,* Carrier de la Freneria, has two shops side by side: *La Caixa de Frang*—for folk pottery, casseroles and kitchen objects—and *Grafiques El Tinell*—for handcolored woodcuts made from antique blocks (there's one of a family tree that's especially charming), maps and old etchings. The entire Gothic quarter is good for antiques browsing. Note *Antiguedades Maria Esclasans,* 8 Calle de la Piedad (a tiny street behind the cathedral) for a wide selection of antiques. *Papirum,* 2 Calle de la Libreteria, is a shop that specializes in antique, hand-colored papers made up into desk sets—beautiful work; costly.

There are two government-run handcraft outlets in Barcelona, known as *Artespaña*. One is at 121 Rambla de Cataluña; the other is at 419 Diagonal.

Mallorca

On Mallorca, shopping is a favorite pastime (though it will never replace the beach). Leather is a major island product, and in the town of Inca you will find a number of factory outlets, such as *Segui,* at 314 Calle General Luque, with good buys in shoes, luggage and handbags. Many of the shops claim to offer discount prices. Whether yea or nay, the prices are generally good.

Another Mallorca specialty is artificial pearls. At Manacor, 48 kilometers from Palma de Mallorca, is the *Majorica Pearl Factory.* Visitors watch the pearl-making process through a huge window and then, if the spirit moves you, you can browse and buy in the attached store outlet. Prices range from a few dollars to a few hundred for the better necklaces and other pieces. Mallorca pearls are also available in many shops in Palma.

Other locally produced crafts in Mallorca are ceramics, embroideries, wood products and glassware. *Artespaña,* 27 Avenida Jaime III, Palma, has a good selection of local crafts, as well as crafts from elsewhere in Spain. (It's a branch of the government-run handcraft shops.)

If you drive through the Mallorcan countryside, you will find *Madera de Olivo Oliv-Art* on the road to Cuevas del Drach. It has both hand- and machine-made olive wood products—everything from back scratchers to salad bowls. There are many shops for ceramics, glassware and gifts along the roadside. Many are tourist traps, where picking and choosing carefully is essential—if you stop at all.

Menorca

In Menorca the major local products are cheese, British-style gin (of the type and bottle popular when Lord Nelson was stationed here in the late 18th century) and leather goods, especially shoes (made for Bally and Clark's, among others). If you have a sweet tooth, you might try a local cake specialty, *ensaimada,* made in a horizontal spiral shape 1-1/2 inches thick, dusted with powdered sugar and sold in flat, pizza-type boxes.

The principal shopping streets in Mahon are Rosario, Hannover and Goded and in Ciudadela the area around Plaza Pio XII. Discount stores on the highway near Mahon and Ciudadela sell leather goods; some feature gin and locally made liqueurs as well. *Novus Boutique*, near Ciudadela, has a vast array of shoes, gloves, slippers, belts, handbags, boots and sandals displayed in a factory-type building—no frills. Leather boutiques of note in Mahon include *Nelson*, 2 General Goded—for shoes; and *Musupta,* 26 Calvo Sotelo—for jackets and leather clothing.

It is possible to visit gin distilleries. One such, *Xoriguer,* 91 Anden Poniente, Mahon, invites visitors and offers tastings. A stand at the airport sells Menorcan cheeses and sausages at fair prices, but it isn't always open at arrival or departure times.

Valencia

In Valencia, there is another branch of *Artespaña* at Paseo de las Damas. You will find smart boutiques, such as Sirah, located around Plaza de Rodrigo Botet, and others on a little street, Calle de la Nave—notably *Ibiza Boutique* for sporty cotton clothes for women and *Bamboo,* with Dior and Charles Jourdan fashions. Nave leads into the Plaza de Alfonso El Magnanimo where there is a branch of *El Corte Inglés* department store. Just outside Valencia is a pottery village, *Manises,* known throughout Spain for its production of distinctive blue and white ware. You can buy Manises plates, platters and bowls at various Valencia shops. For a larger selection, it's a short drive to Manises to visit some of the pottery show and sales rooms there.

Entertainment

Opera

Barcelona. The Grand Opera season is exceedingly grand (white tie and formal dress for the opening) from November through March. Most seats are by subscription, and you'll be lucky to find any available at any price for openings of the 20 or more different operas each season. Featured are top stars and musicians from the world's opera stages in rarely heard operas, as well as familiar war horses. The breadth and excellence of the performances prompted James Michener to comment "a season's attendance at the Liceo would give one a wider purview of what was happening in [the opera world] than a season in New York or London." Works are staged at the regal *Gran Teatro del Liceo*—aptly named—one of Europe's most beautiful opera halls.

Concerts

Barcelona. This is a music-happy town. It has a municipal orchestra and several chamber orchestras, with a year-round diet of concerts. Outstanding are two concert series: the series during Lent and the International Festival of Music each October. The latter has large group performances in the *Palau de la Musica* (the madly eclectic, uniquely decorated concert hall whose acoustics are so admirable) and small group and soloist performances at halls around the city. If you wish to attend, write the Festival c/o 3 Calle Amadeus Vives, Barcelona 3 or phone 3179928.

Cadaques. An International Music Festival is mounted in this Costa Brava resort center at the height of its busy season—the end of July through August.

Cambrils. (Near Gerona) This tiny seaside village sponsors a well-regarded chamber music festival during the month of July.

Mahón, Menorca. An annual International Music Festival held each September features organ, piano and chamber music concerts, with performers from all over Europe. Many free concerts.

Ballet

Barcelona. The ballet season is each spring.

Gambling

Casinos in Catalonia, the Balearics and Levante are ready and waiting for you. In their gambling salons you can exercise on the roulette, blackjack, chemin de fer, or baccarat tables. A few have slot machines. You're welcome from 3 P.M. to 3 A.M. at most of them. Many augment their gaming parlors with luxurious bar–lounges, five-tenedor (fork) restaurants (a government rating, on a scale of one [low] to five [highest]) and attractions that range from shops, buffets, nightclubs with floor shows and dancing to beach and yacht clubs, tennis and discos.

Casino requirements are similar if not identical for all: Admission—about 500 pts.; age—21 or over; valid passport. Among those keeping a light in the window for you are

Gran Casino de Barcelona, San Pedro de Ribas
Casino Costa Blanca, Villajoyosa (near Alicante)
Casino Castillo de Perelada, Perelada (near Gerona)
Casino de Ibiza
Casino de Lloret de Mar (near Gerona)
Casino Monte Picayo, Puzol (near Valencia)
Sporting Club Sol de Mallorca, Calvia (near Palma de Mallorca)

You can arrange to visit the nearest of these casinos through your concierge, travel agent or tour operator.

Theater and Films

Alicante. Two theaters that show movies in the original languages are *Astoria I* and *Astoria II.*

Barcelona. They call them *cine arte y ensayo* but you'll call them movie houses that show foreign films in their original undubbed language. Showings generally begin as early as 4 P.M. (Don't forget to tip the usher 15 pts.) Make note of *Filmoteca*, 63 Travessera de Gracia. It presents continuing series of foreign films, at 100 pts. per admission. The *Institute of North American Studies,* 123 Vía Augusta shows U.S. films once a week, free. What's on? Call 2090945 for current schedule. The *Spring Theater* shows undubbed foreign films at all times and seems to screen a U.S. film every Friday. *Fundación Miró* frequently has film showings and discussions–lectures about films. Miró Museum, Montjuich Park.

Nightlife

Alicante. Just outside the city on the way to Villajoyosa to the north is a *Playboy Club* at San Juan Beach.

Barcelona. Flamenco in Barcelona? Yes—try the *tablao Flamenco* at *Los Tarantos,* 17 Plaza Real, phone 3178098. For up-to-date word on what's going on, check the Espectaculos section in the daily newspapers *Vanguardia* and *El Periodico* or *Gula del Ocios,* the weekly entertainment guide. The local Municipal Tourism Office should have advice (as well as current entertainment schedules) for diverse diversions in the area and an update on the current "in" discos and flamenco spots. They change with some frequency.

Benidorm. You'll find disco row along the highway to Valencia—night clubs, taverns and pubs as well.

Folklore

Alicante. The city goes all out for St. John's birthday, June 23rd. Merry makers carry on with fireworks, parades and street dancing, winding up with spectacular bonfires as they burn satirical wood and paper figures in a *nit de Foc* (night of fire).

Barcelona. Making a big thing of San Jordi's Day (St. George's), April 23rd, which is also Cervantes' birthday, Barcelona has an old book market and bargain book fair. Roses, associated with San Jordi, and books traditionally are given by lovers this day. You may find just the book you want at the book fair. (Carry a rose—maybe you'll find a lover—too.)

During the week of September 24th, Barcelonans celebrate the Feast of Nuestra Señora de la Merced, the city's patron saint. There are parades of extravagant floats, cavalry, bands and almost everything movable and celebratory. Theater, film and music festivals also play a role.

About mid-September *Cardona,* near Barcelona, has its annual festival, which includes running of the bulls.

Corpus Christi is widely celebrated all over Catalonia, but is especially notably in *Sitges.*

Elche. The town's acclaimed medieval mystery play is performed from August 12th to 15th at the *Basilica.* It tells the life of the Virgin in verse.

Holy Week. Among the most beautiful, fervent and spectacular of Spain's Holy Week observances are those in *Higar* (Teruel), *Moncada* (Valencia), *Pollensa* on Mallorca, *Valencia* and *Verges* (Gerona).

Note that local patron saint's day festivals (as well as more elaborate celebrations mentioned above) usually include bullfights and band concerts.

Lloret de Mar. (Near Gerona) has its Santa Cristina celebration July 24th–25th. "S'Amorra" is a water-borne procession of gaily decorated boats in which fishermen pay respects to their patron saint.

Onteniente. (Near Valencia). Moors and Christians Festival (the final week of August) is staged with a lively re-enactment of battles past. *Villena,* near Alicante, holds its own "Moors and Christians" battle September 4–9; *Alcoy's* (most famous) is in April; *Alicante's* in May.

Sitges holds its 21-kilometer antique car rally in late February or early March each year. It attracts dozens of veteran auto entries, many of them from abroad.

Sueca. (Near Valencia.) Its Rive Festival is held about mid-September, with a challenging paella contest and parades.

Wine Festivals. Wine festivals are held in the coastal area during harvest time, which in this region may be as early as August. Valencia's celebration (64 kilometers west at *Requena*) is notable for consumption and gaiety, not necessarily in that order.

Valencia. *Fallas de Valencia* also known as *Fiesta de San José* is held annually March 15th-19th. St. Joseph (San José)–carpenter, is patron saint of artisans, hence papier mache, rag and wood *ninots* (caricatures) in mocking, satirical tableaus or floats are displayed at every street corner or plaza. Then it's parades, flowers, up to 4,000 musicians marching and tootling and nightly displays of fireworks. At midnight the final night the larger-than-life *ninots* are draped with firecrackers and the whole works go up in spectacular flames—all over the city. Not with a whimper, but a bang! There are also bullfights, dances, fairs—and incessant nocturnal gunfire and popping firecrackers! Heads of some of the more inspired, prize winning fallas, however, are saved from cremation and put on permanent display in the *Fallas Museum,* 4 Plaza de Monteolivete. Hours 10 A.M.–2 P.M., 4–7 P.M.; closed Mondays and afternoons in August and September.

Museums and Galleries (in addition to those described in text)

Mallorca

★ **ARCHAEOLOGICAL MUSEUM**

Plaza de Catedral, Palma de Mallorca. This small museum is of interest because of its Carthaginian collection. Dating from the 7th to 3rd centuries B.C., exhibits are from digs and 2,000 tombs in the necropolis on *Puig des Molins* (windmill mound) nearby. Other Greek and Roman finds—jewelry, glass, coins—also on show. Hours 10 A.M. to 1 P.M., 4 to 7 P.M., closed Sundays, holidays. Admission of 100 pts. also includes entrance to necropolis.

Sitges

★ **MUSEO MARICEL DE MAR**
Calle Fonollar 25 (phone 8940364). Opened in 1970, this museum in a 14th-century Gothic hospital is a sleeper. Strong in Romanesque and Gothic paintings and sculpture, it includes altar pieces from Catalonian medieval churches and Hispano-Flemish works of the 16th century. Especially moving is a tiny (c. 1300) chapel decorated with Aragonese paintings of the life of Saint Bartholomew. Also rooms of period furniture. Hours 10 A.M. to 2 P.M., 4 to 8 P.M.; closed Mondays in summer and an hour earlier in winter.

Historic Buildings and Sites (in addition to those described in text)

Tarragona

★★★ **MONASTERIO DEL POBLET**
46 kilometers from Tarragona, this is not your usual little roadside monastery. The walled complex of stone buildings dates from the 12th century when the Cistercians began to build at the invitation of Raymond Berenguer IV. The monastery prospered as the pantheon for the kings of Aragon and became rich and powerful. This is reflected in the Romanesque church, cloister and alabaster tombs of the royal families. The kitchen, refectory, library, dormitory and chapter house are well worth a look. Sacked by the French in 1809 and damaged after 1835 by anticlerics, the monastery has been carefully restored. Tour hours 10 A.M. to 12:30 P.M., 3 to 6 P.M.; half hour earlier closing in winter.

★★ **MONASTERIO SANTES CREUS**
32 kilometers from Tarragona. Established in 1157. Its abbot was chaplain to the kings of Aragón and this monastery, linked to Poblet, became wealthy. The 12th–13th-century church looks like a fortress (and was) but has a fine rose window and royal tombs of Peter, son Jaime II and his queen. The great adjoining cloister has tombs of nobles. Stairs lead to the monks' dormitory, and nearby is the entry to Old Cloister with its austere simplicity. Beyond it are the refectory, kitchens and 14th-century royal palace. Tour hours 9 A.M. to 1 P.M., 4 P.M. to sunset.

Tours

Barcelona

Boat tours of the harbor circle the open area, skirt the breakwater and lighthouse. In a small, covered launch the ½ hour trip will cost you 300 pts: in the large, open *Las Golindrinas* the same journey is 95 pts. Tours leave from Muelle Atarazanas.

Half-day tours of Barcelona are useful for covering more of the city than you might otherwise see. In an air-conditioned motorcoach you'll be taken to visit the cathedral and its cloister, Gothic quarter and the palace of the town hall. You then go to the seafront to see the *Santa Maria* in the harbor. Next is a panoramic view of the city from Montjuich and a visit to the Spanish Village, then back to the Plaza de España and Gran Vía. Tours last about 3 hours and are priced at 950 pts.

A second half-day tour goes via Gran Vía past the bull ring to Gaudí's Templo de la Sagrada Familia, then up to the top of Tibidabo mountain for a panoramic view of the city and a look at the amusement park, and then to the Pedralbes Palace built for King Alfonso XIII. Then it's down to the old Gothic quarter and a visit to the Picasso Museum (or Parque Güell if the Picasso Museum is closed.) The 3-hour junket costs 950 pts.

"Barcelona by Night" tours depart at 10 P.M., take you along the streets to see the illuminated cathedral and fountains, then to a tablao flamenco tavern for singing and dancing. This is followed by a music hall nightclub review and then back to your hotel by about 1 A.M. For the two shows and a drink in each place the tab is 2,800 pts.

A variation on this is the "Noche de Gala," which adds a visit to a well-known night club for an international show and dances and one more drink. This tour costs 3,250 pts. And if you want dinner at a renowned and elegant restaurant plus your tablao flamenco, consider the "Noche Flamenca con cena" for 3,500 pts.

These tours are available from a number of tour companies such as Juliatours and Pullmantour. (Autocares Juliá, 5 Ronda Universidad, phone 3176454; Autocares Pullmantour, 635 Avda. José Antonio, phone 318519.)

A popular and useful way to see the bullfights is the "Corrida de Toros" tour. It leaves at 1½ hours before the bullfight, cruises the city, stops for a peek at Gaudí's Sagrada Familia Church, arriving at the ring in time for the preliminaries. After the six fights, the guide analyzes and explains what it all meant. These tours are priced at 2,600 pts. for seats in the shade, 2,150 pts. for those in the sun.

Mallorca

The tour visits *Valldemosa's Carthusian Monastery* where Chopin and Georges Sand stayed and where there are folk dance presentations, then to Son Marroig miramar and the Gardens of Alfabia. Tour begins and ends at Palma de Mallorca.

Among dozens of agencies in Palma offering these and other tours are Corte Inglés, España Mundial, Melia and Wagons-Lits Cook.

Perks

Trips through the *Codorniu winery* in San Sadurni de Noya, 40 kilometers southwest of Barcelona, to see its *espumosa* (champagne-type wine) made can be arranged through the company's Barcelona office, 644 Gran Vía (phone 3014600) or by writing ahead.

Jijona, 24 kilometers from Alicante, is Spain's "turrone capital." In its factories local products—especially almonds and honey—are transformed into the famous candy. Visit a factory (such as Teclo Hijos—sons—de Manuel Sirvent Miralles) in Jijona and receive a free sample.

Sail the Balearics? You can rent a boat and do it yourself or hire a local skipper. *Best bet:* Contact one of the boating–yachting clubs in the islands or on the coast from which you'd like to sail. You can secure the appropriate address(es) from your nearest Spanish National Tourist Office and arrange it all in advance. If you decide to do it after you arrive, the local Municipal Tourism Information Office will have the addresses.

Sports

Pelota

They call it hand ball, but it should be named cannon ball because of its speed. It's the Basque sport of Jai alai or *Pelota,* played by bouncing a *Pelota* (small hard ball) off a large hard wall with a scoopshaped, basketweave "glove" until your opponent misses. The ball moves at speeds in excess of 100 miles per hour, slightly faster than the money that changes hands in spirited betting on each game's outcome.

Barcelona has two *frontons* (the courts where the game is played): Colón, at 15 and 18 Rambla de Santa Monica; phone 3173197 and 3173080, respectively, for game times and prices.

Dog Racing

Another popular sport in the area is dog racing. There are three dog tracks in Barcelona: Pabellon, 2 Llansá (phone 2430993); Avenida, next to Club de Polo, Avda. Generalisimo (phone 2033092); Meridiana, 165 Concepción Arenal (phone 3173080).

Bullfights

In addition to special bullfights held during Feria and fiestas, there are regularly scheduled *corridas* in Barcelona and Valencia and less frequently held corridas in other towns along the coast and in the Balearics. Season schedule information can be obtained from the tourism office in the specific city or town.

Futbol (soccer)

Futbol (soccer) is Spain's major spectator sport. Games are usually played September to June on Sundays at 5 P.M. Don't be surprised if you're only able to get standing room. Check with your concierge or tourism office.

Horse Racing

Some places in this region (Menorca, for example) are very big on horse racing. Trotting and straight racing are featured at the hippodromes near Mahon and Ciudadela. More information from tourism offices in the specific locale.

Participation Sports

Whatever your participation sport interest, you'll find an organization for it. There are golf, tennis, sailing, cycling, skiing, hockey and underwater sports, as well as hunting and fishing. You can even link up with clubs for billiards, bob sleighing, bridge and polo. Get addresses from the Spanish National Tourist Office.

Golf courses are found at many resort areas on the coast. Usually foreigners are welcome by paying visitor's and greens fees; you can rent clubs and caddy services. Carts are found at only a few courses.

Skiing is an increasingly important activity in the Pyrenees, with some of the finest runs in Europe found there. Though their names may be unfamiliar, Nuria, La Molina, Masella and Vallter 2000 are outstanding ski resorts with all the latest equipment and facilities.

In a radius of 160 kilometers or less, Barcelonans can reach at least seven skiing centers with altitudes of up to 3000 meters (10,000 feet) and seasons of five to seven months. Some are reached by train; package ski tours are available through travel agencies in the major cities. Information: SNTO or local tourism offices (see Directory).

Water sports are, as you'd expect, major interests along the coast and the islands. Boats may be rented (and skippers hired, if necessary) for day sailing, touring or fishing. Local tourism offices have specifics.

Go-carting and horseback riding are other popular pastimes. In Menorca you can rent either type of steed. Contact the local tourism office for information.

GETTING AROUND

In this eastern coastal area of Spain getting around is relatively easy and you have a choice of modes. For the long hauls by car there is the *Autopista*—622 kilometers of superhighway between Gerona and Alicante, which you can zoom through in 6 hours. Or you have the luxurious TER train from Port-Bou along the coastline as far as Murcia. There are also long-distance motorcoach lines along the coast, running modern buses. And there are regular links between coastal cities via ships of the Trasmediterranea and other lines. If you're really in a hurry, you can fly from Barcelona to Valencia or Alicante or vice versa daily on Iberia Airlines. You can reach the Balearics from Valencia and Barcelona in about an hour on flights via Aviaco or Iberia. And there are regularly scheduled overnight trips to these islands via Aucona's Trasmediterranea ships.

Along the Costa Brava there is a sea-link system called Cruceros that gives regular service to most of the coastal towns. And, if you're driving yourself, you'll find that the local roads, as well as the Autopistas, are generally well maintained.

Local Travel: By Subway or Bus

In Barcelona there's a tidy subway that will whisk you to city destinations in safety and clean comfort (but you can tell when you're at the university stop by the spray-painted graffiti). However, Barcelona's bus system is far more extensive and service is frequent, with capable equipment and drivers. The same is true of Valencia and other communities along the coast. Most people use buses to get around in the local towns as well as between them, and to go to and from popular beaches and resorts. Unless you are staying in a remote location or need to reach off-the-beaten-track destinations constantly, the bus should do for you as well. Trips to tourist destinations—major sites, museums, monuments and events—can be arranged through travel agencies by motorcoach, most of the time.

By Car

There are exceptions, of course. You may want to rent a car on Menorca or Mallorca or perhaps even Ibiza. By the week, about 14,000 pts., minimum, with unlimited mileage on one of the Balearic islands.

Mallorca has many scattered places to see and is fairly large, so depending on the bus could be frustrating. Menorca's bus system is limited and if you want to reach the various villages or tucked-away beaches, you'll need a car. Ibiza, however, is quite small and it is a simple matter to walk from town to beach and to use the bus for cross-island and beach-hopping excursions.

A car, of course, gives you freedom to zoom off to the beach or Roman ruins or a museum, to a concert or *al fresco* picnic of broiled sardines and wine by the sea—or all of the above. However, if you can plan ahead, you may find that on the mainland reliable, cheap transportation by bus, train, funicular or boat is available to reach almost any destination you can think of, especially along the Costa Dorada and Costa Brava and inland to such places as Montserrat, Poblet and Vich.

Atesa, Avis, Hertz, Europcar, Ital and others have car rental agencies in towns up and down the coast and on each of the Balearics.

By Taxi

In the cities and major resort areas such as Benidorm, you'll usually find an adequate supply of taxis for most of your needs. In general, taxis are bargain-priced compared with places such as New York and London.

One factor of supreme importance in the transportation picture is timing. Be aware that when the jumbo jets disgorge their charter loads of sun-starved Nordics from Scandinavia, England and Germany, you may find considerable competition for public transportation, not to mention other facilities.

Spain's Northern Tier

There are several ways to plan a trip in the north, depending on how you want to slice it. If it's the pilgrimage route alone, you could drive straight north from Madrid to Burgos and head west from there. You could also hop-scotch by air from San Sebastián to León and Santiago de Compostela. Or you could, and this is the way we will route you now, fly into San Sebastián, drive from there to Pamplona (to see what Hemingway was so excited about), and then follow the pilgrims' route to León and Santiago, with a detour to the seashore at Santander and to visit the Altamira Caves next door at Santillana del Mar.

Two facts you should know in advance in planning a trip north: it rains a lot. That's why all those hillsides are so apple-green. If rain deters, depresses or makes you suicidal, maybe you should consider Andalucía. Generally, the northern rain is light and misty and quite often the sun shines through (making for some Oz-like rainbows). But it can rain for several days at a time, and if a tourist is on a time-conscious schedule, this can be inhibiting. The second caveat is this: if you plan to drive the *Camino de Santiago*, bear in mind that it is a twister of a mountain road for much of the way. Some of the mountain peaks in the area reach 8,000 feet. The vistas are breathtaking, maybe too much so for a timid trekker. If this is you, you might prefer to aero-hop or take the train (though trains go to all the cities mentioned, none follows the old pilgrims' trail).

SAN SEBASTIÁN AND PAMPLONA

When you fly into San Sebastián, you are, to be exact, actually flying into Fuenterrabia, which faces France across the Bidasoa River. You can pick up a rental car at the airport and drive the 23 kilometers into San Sebastián, or (our recommendation) bed down in Fuenterrabia, a small and peaceful little resort in its own right.

You are now in Basque country, distinguished by many things—language (which to a non-Basque sounds like *X* and *Z* almost entirely), customs different from the rest of Spain, independent spirit, and, above all (at least as far as visitors are concerned) its cuisine (which is in a dead heat with Catalan for culinary honors). To gourmets, a trip to San Sebastián is a pilgrimage in itself.

But stop a minute in Fuenterrabia. For centuries it was a prime target of French attack. Sancho Abarca, king of Navarra in the 10th century, had the smarts to build a hilltop castle fortress to keep an eye on the French across the river. Charles V *re*built it six centuries later. The French kept the town under siege for two months in 1638, until Our Lady of Guadalupe came to Fuenterrabia's rescue. There's a festival honoring this event every September 8th.

The views from the castle are serene today; no massing of troops across the border. Just brightly colored fishing boats in the harbor. The castle is everything a castle is supposed to be, with turrets and Great Hall and inner courtyard. Even if you don't spend the night—it's now a government-run *parador*—have a drink in the bar which is tucked into a gallery upstairs, overlooking the Great Hall.

The petite square in front of the castle is made for color photos. The houses facing it range the color palette: violet stucco with white trim, white with pink shutters and purple trim, white with green or red shutters. The entire town, for that matter, is highly photogenic. It can't be the altitude (it's sea level after all). Many houses look as though they had been parachuted in from Switzerland or Austria—neat little chalets with wooden balconies, sometimes painted bright green or red, and an alpine tidiness.

The history-minded might drop by the Gothic church of Santa Maria to see, in addition to the baroque tower, the altar where France's Louis XIV was married by proxy to Spain's Infanta Maria Teresa in June 1660, six days before the real event. However, when in Fuenterrabia do as the Fuenterrabians do —especially at *paseo* time in the early evening—gather along Calle San Pedro and promenade. It's a charming street with cute shops, many restaurants in chalet-like houses and even more *tapa* bars.

The N-1 is the fast road to San Sebastián, but Americans might want to detour briefly to Pasaje de San Juan, a pleasant little fishing village facing the Bay of Biscay. The Marquis de Lafayette set sail for America from here in 1776. Today it's a village of narrow streets and of houses higgledy-piggledy hugging each other. Victor Hugo spent time here; and there's a little restaurant where he dined—and you might also—*Casa Camera* (see Inside Information at end of this section). Here you can watch the ferries, freighters and fishing boats as you dine.

Suddenly signs tell you that you are approaching Donostiarras in the province of Guipuzcoa, but the high rise buildings and international air are reminders that this is San Sebastián, Basque nationalism notwithstanding. One of the problems for tourists is that the Basques insist on using their language, not Spanish, in road and street signs. This is more than just quaintly confusing for foreigners, it is downright mind-boggling.

San Sebastián (or Donostiarras if you prefer) was Spain's answer to Biarritz. Twenty years after Empress Eugenie made the latter famous as a chic watering hole for the French, Queen Maria Cristina built the Miramar Palace here in 1889 so her young son, Alfonso XIII, could escape the Madrid heat and enjoy the seashore. Where the Queen led, the Court following, loving every minute of the breezy air.

As a beach resort San Sebastián is a natural. Strung like a jewel around a gorgeous half circle of beach, *Bahia de la Concha*, with a small island, Santa Clara (now a water sports complex), San Sebastián is sheltered from the ocean waves. As if this weren't beauty enough, Mount Igueldo to the west and Mount Urgull on the east present their dramatic silhouettes.

The city does its best to live up to such spectacular natural resources. The wide *Avenida de la Libertad,* a two-lane boulevard lined with trees and fashionable shops, and with splendid old white metal street lamps along the center divider, must have seen some grand carriages in its heyday. The grandly ornate Maria Cristina Bridge, with its grey stone horses rearing eternally from their huge white pedestals, and the *Paseo de la Concha,* the beachfront promenade, with its celebrated cast-iron railing painted white (a landmark on most of the city's tourist literature), are part of San Sebastián's legacy.

There are even a few non-water-oriented sights in town. There were lots more, of course, before a fire razed much of the old city in 1813—at the time Wellington's English and Portuguese troops had the French at bay on top of Mount Urgull. Climbers might march up the hillside—more than 600 feet—to see old *Castillo de la Mota,* where the French were holed up during that engagement of the Peninsular War (Spanish War of Independence). There is a military museum there now. Museum open 10 A.M. to 1 P.M., 3:30 to 7 P.M.; closes 5 P.M. in winter; closed Sunday and holiday afternoons, Monday mornings.

A curvaceous sea road will transport you to the city's other mountain top, Igueldo, where you can sip a glass of *vino* and enjoy a panoramic view of the city, Santa Clara Island and the *other* mountain from the bar of the *Monte Igueldo* hotel, which crowns the top. It's a good spot for watching regattas.

Still, San Sebastián's main tourist attractions, other than that seductive conch shell beach, are its major places of worship: the 16th-century Monastery of San Telmo and the 20th-century restaurants. The monastery has Renaissance cloisters with carved stone funeral crosses in the Basque style and a chapel-turned-conference hall with modern paintings depicting Basque history by the late José Maria Sert. The art lover will be pleased to find in the rooms off the cloister paintings by Zuloaga, Ribera, El Greco and others. Open 10 A.M. to 1:30 P.M., 3:30-7 P.M.; closed Monday mornings, Sunday and holiday afternoons; closes 5 P.M. in winter.

The mere thought of San Sebastián's restaurants, dozens of them, can bring a Pavlovian response to even the most disciplined Madrid gourmet. You will find favorites among the restaurants cited in the Inside Information section, and a complete list is available from the San Sebastián tourist office.

There is no joy in another Basque event. In fact, it is downright unnerving to the visitor to see soldiers with machine guns in hand standing along the palmy boulevards and stylish shopping streets of San Sebastián. But in recent years small bands of Basque terrorists have robbed banks and shown their contempt for authority by spray painting graffiti messages all over walls, fences and buildings in this and other Basque cities.

It is a pity that so few could intimidate so many, but they have succeeded in scaring many tourists away from San Sebastián. Yet for the tourist who visits, there is the discovery that the majority of Basques are warm, friendly people, hard-working, religious, and it is more than a little rewarding to learn something of their ways. As an ethnic group, Basques are not Spanish (which explains part of their need for a separate identity) and their roots go back so far, no one quite knows when or where they began. Some believe the Basques were the earliest inhabitants of Europe; their language seems unrelated to any other.

There are three Basque provinces in Spain (there are also French Basques over the border in the Pyrenees)—Guipuzcoa, Vizcaya, and Alava. When you head southeast to Pamplona, if indeed you do, you will be in Navarra where many Basques also live. Before doing so, a beach addict might scoot along the coast west of San Sebastián for a look at the Cantabrian corniche which begins at the delightful little resort of Zarauz (reached by an overshoot from A-9 *autopista* west toward Bilbao).

The naughty (some say nymphomaniacal) Queen Isabella II put this small resort on the map when she made it her summer residence in the mid-19th century. Isabella's carryings-on, both amorous and political, led to an army ultimatum, and in September 1868 (she was in San Sebastián at the time) she abdicated, with the sad words, "I thought I had struck deeper roots in this land." Exit Isabella to France.

Zarauz survived. Its beach is a grand swath of powdery sand. Two palaces and many handsome houses add to its interest. A few minutes west, punctuated by a huge boulder called *El Ratón* (The Mouse), is Guetaria, another pleasing, minuscule resort. Many Guetaria fishermen, like others along the Basque coast, sailed with the early explorers. But only one has a monument celebrating the fact. Juan Sebastian Elcano brought fame to Guetaria as the first navigator to circumnavigate the globe. When Magellan was killed in the Philippines, Elcano brought the ship safely home in 1522. In the Town Hall are frescoes illustrating Elcano's trip, painted by Basque artist Ignacio Zuloaga.

At the next town, Zumaya, is still another tiny resort. Here Zuloaga installed a museum of his works, El Greco's, Goya's and others in a 12th-century convent, now known as Villa Zuloaga. Zumaya is the point where religious pilgrims—and anyone else curious about the man who was a prime founder of the Jesuits—will turn down C–6317 to Azpeitia, a brooding stone village in a pine-darkened valley. This is where St. Ignacio (Ignatius) of Loyola was baptized.

The church is San Sebastián, a large grey granite building in the Gothic style, with a statue of St. Sebastian punctured with arrows on the top as a signpost of the church's identity. "Handball players using this wall will be fined one peseta" a faded sign on the wall next to the church cautions. It is a fair warning, though probably ignored, for every male in Basque country seems to be an amateur *pelota* player. Even priests can be observed practicing against church walls, but not, perhaps, in Azpeitia.

Just three kilometers from town is Loyola, and the Monastery of St. Ignatius, a monumental complex which envelops a Jesuit college, a neoclassical basilica and a *Santa Casa,* the birthplace and home of the saint himself.

Poverty is not what strikes you first (if at all) in visiting the Jesuits' home base at Loyola. The church—with a huge 165-foot-high dome, somber use of stone columns and pilasters, a black-and-tan marble checkerboard floor and light coming only from the cupola and upper windows—is mysterious and overpowering.

The attached *Santa Casa* is something else. It was built by the saint's grandfather in 1461, and Ignatius was born here. There has been much overlay since, with wall mosaics, "rusticated" ceilings, elaborate use of marble, gilt, stone, and baroque curliques and ornamentation. It is really hard to find the saint for the house.

It's heresy to say so, but San Fermin's Day is *not* the time to visit Pamplona. Yes, yes, we know, Hemingway had a different story. But the fact is, Hemingway bears a large responsibility for popularizing both the town and the event. If you insist on visiting on July 7th, you'll find the old Roman city ("City of Pompey") wall-to-wall tipplers, most of them fellow tourists. Poor old San Fermin, or St. Firminus, bishop, native Pamplonan, martyr, probably deserves better. Still, if you're under 30 and in the neighborhood, the days and nights between the 6th or 7th and the 16th of July are filled with processions of *Gigantes* (giants) and *Cabezudos* (big heads), ear-splitting fireworks, dancing (in the streets and cafés all over town), and a general air of gaiety and combustible excitement. Highpoint, as every reader of *The Sun Also Rises* knows, is the running of the bulls through the town streets to their bullring stalls (the *encierro*), which occurs early in the A.M. (7 o'clock). Half the young men of the town try to run fast enough ahead to keep from meeting the padded ends of a bull's horns.

At calmer times, that is the rest of the year, Pamplona behaves with rather staid decorum. Among its wide avenues, arcaded squares and fountains, there are certain things a tourist might look for. Notice the monument to Hemingway outside the Plaza de Toros on Calle Amaya and the marker in the pavement on Calle San Ignacio where St. Ignatius fell wounded in the battle of 1521.

There isn't a lot to see in this pleasant, prosperous city, but do look in on Charles III of Navarra and his queen Leonora of Castile in the cathedral Charles commissioned. They share an alabaster tomb. The carving of the mourners around the base, with each highly personalized, is remarkable. It's the work of a Flemish sculptor of the 15th century, Janin Lomme of Tournais. While you're in the cathedral, continue to the cloister, noteworthy for the delicate Gothic arches and sculptured doors. Opening off the cloister is the *Sala Preciosa*, where the Cortes met, and the tiny *Capilla de la Santa Cruz,* whose grill was made from Moorish tent chains "liberated" in battle in the 13th century. Gourmets will observe the enormous open hearth and chimney in the kitchen of the Refectory of the Canons, suggesting there was more than food for thought among the clergy in medieval times. Pamplona is a Basque city after all. Cathedral museum open 9:30 A.M. to 12:30 P.M., 4 to 7 P.M., mid-May to mid-October only.

THE PILGRIMS' WAY - WITH A DETOUR TO SANTANDER *and* SANTILLANA DEL MAR

It should be said at the outset that this route through spiraling mountain passes is not for the tourist in a hurry. One can pull all the stops in praising the scenery—"breathtaking", "Olympian"—but nearer-my-God-to-Thee isn't what you want to be if you've budgeted just a week for all the highlights of Spain. True, you could probably *traverse* the distance from the French border to Santiago in two days of hard, long driving, but you'll have missed all the charm of the route. Consider, it can take much of a day just to "do" the 139 kilometers from Pamplona to Santo Domingo de la Calzada.

That's assuming you stop, not far from Pamplona, to photograph the *Puerto del Perdon* (Gate of Pardon), through which all pilgrims passed. And surely you'll want to admire the rare six-arched bridge over the river Arga, that Queen Doña Mayor built for pilgrims in the 11th century and which gave the tiny town of Puente la Reina its name. (This was the town where the pilgrim routes from northern and central Europe converged.) There are spontaneous sheep stoplights along the road where you have to wait patiently while a flock precedes you through a narrow village gate.

A real purist will even backtrack 47 kilometers from Pamplona to Roncesvalles, the pass in the Pyrenees through which foreign pilgrims entered Spain. This was also the gateway invaders used, not always successfully, as Charlemagne learned to his discomfort when Basque and Navarrese guerrillas ambushed and routed his troops in 778. (In the epic poem, *Chanson de Roland,* written by a Frenchman, the emphasis is understandably different.)

Roncesvalles is rich in pilgrim reminders. A 13th-century collegiate church is a French Gothic masterpiece. A Romanesque chapel inside contains a silver-covered wooden statue of the Virgin and Child venerated by pious travelers.

A joy of the *Camino de Santiago,* which was also known as *Camino de Francés* because so many Frenchmen traveled it, is the almost constant discoveries it brings. At its peak, the route was studded with churches, hospices, inns and places the tourist—for that's what these pilgrims were, really the first *mass* travelers of all—could stop to pray, rest, eat and be diverted.

Estella is an example. Today a town of 10,000, it has clusters of choice Romanesque buildings. The kings of Navarra lived here during medieval times, and the town was a major stop for Santiago-bound pilgrims. In fact it was so rich in monuments it was once called the "Toledo of the North."

In Estella a skeptic can quickly become a convert to Romanesque art and architecture—which had its flowering in the late 10th through 12th centuries. At the Church of San Miguel note especially the superbly carved high reliefs of St. Michael slaying a dragon and weighing souls. The Church of San Pedro de la Rua has a richly carved portal.

There are also palaces, such as the Royal Palace and the Palace of the Dukes of Granada, the latter reputedly the very first civic building in the Romanesque style. Just outside of town (three kilometers) is a Benedictine monastery, *Santa Maria de Irache,* with roots in the 10th century (a Romanesque apse) and branches in the 16th (a Renaissance dome and Plateresque cloister). A few kilometers further are the ruins of a still earlier monastery, Iranzu. Hours: 9:30 A.M. to 1:30 P.M., 2 to 7 P.M.

Sampling the diverse and fine reds of the Rioja vineyards is a time-consuming hobby in itself (and we don't recommend driving very far after you have spent time tippling). A side trip for oenophiles might be to Haro, via N–232. Haro is Rioja's second largest wine center, after Logroño, and a town of pleasantly narrow, cobbled streets, handsome houses that wine built, fountains and a generally fine demeanor. Oh yes, and two agreeable restaurants where food and wine meet convivially: *Beethoven II,* 3 Santo Tomas (tel. 311181), and *Terete,* 27 Lucrecia Arana (tel. 310023).

In the Rioja region the terrain levels off somewhat, and the road—if you continue along the *Camino de Santiago*—becomes N–120 westward to Burgos. You'll pass green fields, orchards and vineyards. Go through Navarrete where you will see the statue of Santiago on horseback in a niche in an old manor house. Just 11 kilometers from Logroño is Nájera, where the kings of Navarra first minted coins, and where in the 11th century King García and Queen Estefaña built the Church of Santa Maria la Real, whose cloisters you can still admire today.

A good place for bedding down is Santo Domingo de la Calzada (St. Dominick of the Causeway), with its *parador* of the same name, that once functioned as a hospice for pilgrims. (See Inside Information—Hotels) Before dining, walk across the road to the Cathedral to see the tomb of the hermit-saint for whom the town is named. Domingo de Viloria built this section of the Pilgrims' Road, as well as the 24-arched stone bridge, and a hospice to aid travelers on their journey to Santiago.

On the wall opposite Santo Domingo's tomb is a curious sight: a chicken coop with a gilded and painted Gothic roof. Inside the brightly-lit coop are a live hen and rooster, hopping around happily as a reminder of a miracle that occurred in medieval times. Each year there is a changing of the guard, or chickens, as new ones replace the old. Pilgrims still treasure "capturing" a white feather as it floats down through the cathedral's air as a memento of their trip.

Burgos is the next major stop, and an important one in the Middle Ages, on the pilgrimage trail. (See the section on Castile for its many treasures.)

This is the junction for choices. If you continue westward, it is between Burgos and León that you will find some of the most remote and fascinating Romanesque villages, beginning with Olmillos de Sasamon, with a 15th-century castle and Romanesque tower. Then one goes from N–120 to BU-4010 to see the ruins of the hilltop castle, a camp that Caesar built, and the 12th-century Church of San Juan at Castrojeriz. Another spur off N–120 (near Osorno) leads south a few kilometers to Frómista, a favorite pilgrimage village, with its near-perfect Romanesque Church of San Martín (built in 1066), considered by experts to be one of the finest examples left of Spanish Romanesque. Back on N–120 at Sahagún (at an altitude of 2500 feet) one passes the ruins of a famous Cluniacensian abbey, four 12th- to 13th-century Romanesque churches (note especially San Tirso), and the 12th-century convent of San Benito. León is just a pilgrim's hike away.

But for a change of pace, let's detour for a moment north 155 kilometers from Burgos to Santander, Madrid's favorite Atlantic watering hole, and its near neighbor, the exquisite village of Santillana del Mar. The road north, N–623, is a good one, and some of the scenery is dramatic. You'll pass right through, with an eye-blink, Vivar del Cid, where El Cid lived as a child. You'll also pass the pretty village of Tutilla del Agua with its golden stone houses with red tile roofs and roadsides lined with yellow broom. Just beyond, before you reach Covanera, high, ridged grey stone cliffs loom, contrasting eerily with the yellow earth. Gnarled plane trees make formal columns through this canyon. Between the Ebro Reservoir and Entrambasmestas the terrain swings dramatically again—symptomatic of Spain—to one of brilliant green hillsides crisscrossed with stone fences and with spectacular mountain views that seem suspended in mistiness. Then once again the road straightens, is lined with heliotrope and more broom and *voila!* you are in the seaside surroundings of Santander.

As befits a popular seaside resort, Santander has a prize location, on the U-shaped Bay of Santander, sheltered from the Atlantic, with a wide swath of sand that almost matches San Sebastián's *La Concha* and a lively ambience that excels it, at least nowadays. What distinguishes Santander from many resorts, especially northern ones whose season is short, is its bustling year-round life. Art galleries, chic shops, and good restaurants make it a convenient stop-over almost any time of year. Its many glass-fronted balconies were built to catch even the winter sun's rays.

Santander is almost a completely modern city—but not by design. In the winter of 1941 a tornado dropped in, driving a wall of water from the sea and spreading flames throughout the central district. The result: hundreds of buildings destroyed and 20,000 homeless people.

The rebuilt city is notable for its wide boulevards, plazas and flower-stippled parks. Walking along *Paseo de Pereda* is pleasant enough anytime, but when ships are tied up broadside, their super-structures and painted forms look like modern sculptures bordering the boulevard. And when a cruise or training ship docks, outlined at night with strings of lights along deck and masts, the seafront becomes a gala.

Santander's beach, *El Sardinero,* is the major attraction. It is anchored at one end by a large park, where Alfonso XIII and his English wife once discreetly cavorted in the surf—after the city had built the Magdalena Palace for their royal use in 1912. The palace now is used for summer courses in Hispanic culture. *Sic transit.* At its other end, the beach climbs to high ground and the Cabo Mayor lighthouse.

Santander is one of the few places in northern Spain where the compulsive sightseer needn't feel guilty if he pauses to linger longer over lunch or a drink. All that's really essential to see will take little time. The 13th-century Gothic cathedral was restored after the 1941 disaster. Its crypt (circa 1200) contains the remains of two martyred saints, Celedonius and Emeterius. The literary-minded might look in on the tomb of Marcelino Menéndez y Pelayo, who died in 1912. Scholars consider him Spain's greatest 19th-century prose writer and critic.

You might then pass by the Museum of Fine Arts, which has Menéndez y Pelayo's library, in addition to some interesting art, old and new. Hours: 11 A.M. to 1 P.M., 5 to 8 P.M. A garden separates the museum from Menéndez y Pelayo's house.

It's only 30 kilometers and seven centuries from Santander to Santillana del Mar, curving along the narrow, heavily trafficked N–611 most of the way. Industry has come to this once bucolic area, and it isn't until you turn off N–611 that the landscape turns green and cows can be seen in fields again.

Santillana itself is all medieval serenity—except in the height of summer, when its half dozen cobbled lanes are dense with tourists, mostly French, en route to the Altamira Caves, less than three kilometers from town. (See Inside Information Historic Sights—for information about the caves.)

To find this tiny gem of a village at its most natural, we'd strongly recommend a spring or fall visit. The population is only 4,000, but in summer you'd swear it was four times that.

Santillana is just a one-cattle-track village, and its two remarkable sights stand at opposite ends of that single track or street: the exquisite *Colegiata,* a 12th-century Romanesque church, and four blocks away the Diocesan

Museum, installed in a 16th-century convent, Regina Coeli. Hours: 10 A.M. to 1 P.M., 3-6 P.M.; closes 2 hours earlier in winter; closed Wednesdays.

We aren't kidding about the cattle track. At the top of the few steps leading to the Colegiata's main portal is a wide metal grill with rollers—designed to keep cows from wandering into the church. "The mooing at Mass got to be a real pain," a friend said matter-of-factly. A washing shed, where local women used to do their laundry, has been turned over to the cows—proof of a new prosperity in the village.

There is much to admire in this fine old church. The sacristan may show you, if you ask, the rare Romanesque stone panel in front of the altar, with vividly carved portraits of Matthew, Mark, Luke and John. Normally an embossed silver panel (made in Mexico in the 17th century) covers the original.

The prize is the cloister with its precisely carved stone capitals showing all the vigor and imagination of medieval artisans. Some details are as graphic as a modern horror film: a knight disemboweling a dragon, whose intestines spill forth; a horse being rent by wolves and gobbled by vultures; Samson breaking a lion's jaws. Oh the times we live in! An angel counting souls seems almost peacefully out of place. Hours: 10 A.M. to 1 P.M., 3 to 8 P.M.

It isn't just the designated "sights" that make Santillana fascinating. The whole village has the flavor of the Middle Ages. Many of the large stone houses are actually small palaces, called *casas solares.* You can tell them by the coats of arms on their facades. In the late 19th century it became fashionable for Madrid nobility to summer in Santillana (they rushed here when their favorite San Sebastián was suffering a cholera epidemic, and then stayed on). But most of the village's palaces date back to the 16th and 17th centuries when many local families acquired fortunes (and titles to go with them) in the New World.

In looking at the coats of arms, each grander and more ostentatious than the last, one senses a game of keeping-up-with-the-Santillanas played in stone. Actually one of the smallest coats of arms is on the house that may be the oldest in town. It is on the corner of Cantón and Racial and belonged to Leonor de la Vega, mother of the Marqués de Santillana, a very good 15th-century poet.

Facing the Colegiata, the palace closest to the church on the left belongs to the Archduchess Margaret of Austria. Across from it, diagonally, are the attached palaces of the Cossíos and Quevedos. The Quevedos have deep roots in Santillana. One of them, Francisco de Quevedo y Villegas, wrote a classic novel, *Los Sueños,* in the 17th century.

The coat of arms that is the standout—and no wonder, it almost covers the full front of the building and the *bas* is really *haute* relief—is on the Villa palace. The stone palace is nicknamed *Casa de los Hombrones*—House of the Big Men—for the gigantic knights who seem to be holding up the coat of arms. In the center of the escutcheon is the family eagle wearing a plumed helmet beneath which is the motto "A noble death gives honor to an entire life."

On Santillana's only parallel street, facing the petite *Plaza de Ramon Pelayo,* is the village's oldest civil monument, the *Torre del Merino*—or Tower of the Magistrate—built in the 9th or 10th century with some later 13th-century additions. It is a rare example of a medieval defense tower in the Santander area. The *merino* was a sort of governor of the *"Merindad"* or area, representing the King. On the ground floor of the tower, guards would have lived, with the *merino's* living quarters above that, servants still higher up, and the top used for defense—a neat, compact, all-in-one building. Inside, a "central tree" of perpendicular posts branches into a support system for the upper floors. A few years ago, the tower functioned as a modern art gallery, but it is currently closed.

One palace and attached tower that can be visited are diagonal to the Torre del Merino. The 16th-century tower once belonged to a branch of the Spanish Borgias, and its 18th-century neighbor was owned by the daughter of Queen Isabella II. Together the two buildings form the Santillana Foundation, where art exhibitions, lectures and current happenings take place. The buildings, impeccably renovated recently, have *bovadilla* ceilings and a 16th-century patio; they are a pleasure to inspect.

Another palace on the same plaza has been turned into the *Parador Nacional Gil Blas,* named after the hero of an 18th-century French picaresque novel by Alain-Rene Lesage, set in Santillana. It is a delightful building, to dine in, to sleep in, just to admire.

From Santillana you can explore the Cantabrian coast. Following C–6316 brings one first to Comillas, with a hilltop location and beautiful beach, and then to San Vicente de la Barquera, a little port, with excellent beach, a photogenic ruin of a castle, and a church *(Santa Maria de los Angeles)* with two fine Romanesque portals.

LEÓN TO PONFERRADA AND LUGO

León may be one of Spain's most under-appreciated cities by tourists. "That's because it can't decide whether it's Castile or France," a Madrid friend said, without any noticeable sympathy.

Mostly, we think, it's because the busy, traffic-clogged modern city of 120,000 (which seems bigger) tends to swallow up the old city, whose lineage goes back to Roman times. For two centuries—the 10th to 12th—when the Lion of León roared, much of Spain listened. The kingdom of León *was* Spain, Christian Spain, during a considerable part of the Moorish domination of the south. But when León and Castile were joined in 1230, the León's roar became more of a purr.

There are three major monuments in the city that should be on any "must-see" list. León boasts one of the finest early Gothic cathedrals in Spain. What commands the attention are its 125 magnificent major stained glass windows, which date from the 13th to the 20th century. Two of the three rose windows—on the north and west—are among the oldest glass in the building. The largest chapel, Santiago, is a reminder of León's importance as a station on the *Camino de Santiago,* and in it you will find some of the finest of the windows.

The effect of all the glass and light and color is mesmerizing. On a sunny day, the best kind, of course, for a visit to this glass palace, the light dazzles, and the colors seem to glow, dance, melt, and vibrate almost magically.

There is much else to delight the eye in this remarkable place, but it is the glass that one remembers, and the delicate stone tracery that supports it.

Hours for museum and cloister: 9 A.M. to 1:30 P.M., 4 to 6 P.M.; in winter 10:30 A.M. to 1:30 P.M., 4 to 5:30 P.M.; closed Sunday afternoons.

León's second major sight is just a few streets away from the cathedral. The Basilica of San Isidro was begun in 1063 and dedicated to San Isidro (Isidore), not the patron saint of Madrid, but the Isidro who was Archbishop of Sevilla when he died in 636. He had been in turn a scholar, hermit, teacher and reformer. His remains were brought to León after the Moorish occupation of Sevilla, to be entombed in the church named for him.

The pantheon of the Basilica houses the tombs of all the early kings of León, Castile and Aragón, but they were badly ravaged by Napoleon's troops, who opened them all in search of buried kingly treasure. Now no one knows who is where. What captures the attention, though, more than the tombs, are the exceptional Romanesque wall and ceiling frescoes that completely cover the crypt. The restored colors are crisp and fresh—copper, slate blue, russet, grey and white. But it is the animation of the figures and scenes depicted that enchants: Gospel scenes, with figures that must have been drawn from contemporary medieval life—grape pickers, farmers, boxers, brawlers. Dominating the center ceiling panel is *The Last Supper.* Another ceiling panel shows Christ in the middle of His four gospel writing disciples, each with the animal head that was used to depict him in medieval symbolism—St. Mark as a lion, Luke as a bull, and so on—painted ingenuously and with sly humor. Hours: 9 A.M. to 2 P.M., 3:30 to 8 P.M.; closed Sunday and holiday afternoons except in July and August, when schedule is 10 A.M. to 1:30 P.M., 4 to 6:30.

Now it is surely time for a restorative sip, and the place to enjoy it is the bar of León's third important monument—the Hotel San Marcos, which in various metamorphoses has been a hospice for pilgrims, a monastery, a prison, and a barracks. It has now come full circle—providing accommodations for travelers.

It *really* is a hotel *plus* museum *plus* Gothic church. The monastery-hotel is in itself a museum of sorts, for it has kept its many fine old ceilings, portals, cloister, and arches. It has added handworked tapestries, rugs and paintings and prints by Spain's modern artists. The dark painted wood ceiling panel in one of the main lounges (called, curiously, a tearoom) is the work of Madrid abstract artist Lucio Muñoz. As a hotel, it is probably the most beautiful in Spain; as a museum, it is choice and worth a visit, whether you bed down there or not. Museum hours: 10 A.M. to 1 P.M., 3 to 6 P.M.; closed Sunday and holiday afternoons, and from January 15 to February 15.

N–120 will take you from León westward. As it does so, fertile fields, orchards and groves of trees give way to a more austere mountainous landscape. As you cross the river Obrigo, 17 kilometers this side of Astorga, think briefly of Don Suero de Quiñones. In 1434, a year and century when *camino* traffic was at an all-time peak, he decided in a fit of pique (brought on by being jilted by his true love) to force any knight who tried to cross the bridge over the Obrigo to joust with him first. The loser got tossed into the river. Don Suero was a strong fellow; in a month he doused 727 would-be challengers before he decided enough was enough.

In Astorga if you are a cathedral collector you will head for the three Plateresque portals (with finely detailed scenes from Christ's life) of the 15th-to-16th century edifice. Once inside, you will want to study the fine 16th-century retable behind the main altar.

Fanciers of Antonio Gaudí will go to the Episcopal Palace, but they might be disappointed by the master fantasist's restraint. That is, it would look restrained in Barcelona. In staid Astorga it is rather daring—a grey stone pseudo-Gothic pastiche. Inside is a Museum devoted to art and memorabilia relating to the pilgrimage trail.

Pliny called Astorga a "splendid city." That was in Roman times. Since then poor Astorga has been razed and trampled all too often—by Almanzor and the Moors, by the kings of León and Castile, and finally by Napoleon's forces under Marshal Junot. If you decide to lunch before moving along to Ponferrada, consider the homey *Quiñones* restaurant on Carretera de Madrid-La Coruna (N-VI) (tel. 615599), just outside town.

Once again the terrain changes, the road becomes steeper, more hazardous. Here the old *camino* became impassable by car. The modern highway follows what is believed to have been the original Roman road through these steep mountain passes, leveling off just a bit before it reaches Ponferrada.

One can imagine how the Knights Templar castle looked in silhouette to the pilgrims, as they struggled over treacherous, snow-capped mountains. The castle is in ruins now, but it offers some superlative views. Another stop might be made at the tiny 10th-century Mozarabic Church of *Santo Tomas de la Ollas.*

Beyond Ponferrada, luscious green fields, apple orchards, and more fertile hillsides begin to appear. Asturias is nearing—land of strong cider. Yet the mountain curves are tight and precipitous. Speed is *not* the password as you continue to climb.

Finally you reach the Piedrafita Pass, 3,638 feet above sea level, with a stone cross marking it. From here you'll see peaks twice the height. It's a thrilling sight—better when sheltered by car we must admit than in even the strongest sandals and pilgrim's cape. This is the pass the British troops straggled over in 1809, retreating from French cavalry. It was January, and more than a few British soldiers died of the cold right here. This is the spot (and that was the time) where General John Moore pitched 150,000 gold guineas into the ravine—to keep them from the French.

The road to Lugo slants slowly downward. The worst of the mountain driving is behind you. Lugo's main claims to fame are its high (30-to-40 foot) slate walls that date back to the third century when the town was known as Lucas Augusti. The walls are 20 feet thick with four gates and 85 towers. Through the centuries they have been incorporated into everyday life—houses are built right into the sides, forming a sort of collage.

Reasons for tarrying in Lugo might be its cathedral, which is rather eclectic with many fine individual parts; a church (Santo Domingo) with a nicely carved Romanesque portal; and an astonishingly pretty little square, Santa Maria. Here you'll find an 18th-century episcopal palace with coat of arms and wrought iron balconies; and behind the palace, through a network of old streets, is still another little square, Plaza del Campo, faced with interesting old houses and a center fountain.

You are now in Galicia, and the temperature becomes balmier (and possibly mistier). N-640 gives way to C-547 through Mellid, where you will see two Romanesque churches, Santa Maria and Sancti Spiritus. Then finally, as millions of pilgrims in centuries past have done, you climb the hill called *Mountjoy.* From here, as the name of the hill suggests, you can see in the distance the three towers of Santiago de Compostela's cathedral. Some say the hill derived its name from the exclamation French pilgrims made on seeing the cathedral—*"Mon Joie! Mon Joie!"*

The arduous passage is over. Santiago and its cathedral, churches and other gems await.

SANTIAGO DE COMPOSTELA *and* A GLIMPSE OF GALICIA

Santiago de Compostela can gobble up weeks of your time if you let it. But even if pinched for time, plan *at least* two days here, for there is much to see.

Fortunately, the old city is so concentrated that most of the sights, pubs, restaurants, and shops are within a relatively small, walkable area. If you arrive by car the sensible thing is to ditch your vehicle on arrival, never to see it again until you leave town. Although a motorway and modern housing rim the distant edge of the city, the old medieval center is still marvelously intact. Its rabbit warren of labyrinthine passages and arcaded streets make foot travel mandatory.

Your initial impression of this still medieval city will be much the same whether you drive or come by plane, though a plane ride (it's just 55 minutes from Madrid by air) makes the transition from the present to the past that much more abrupt. The airport is a ten-minute taxi ride from town. As your car—whether taxi or self-driven—wriggles through the narrow cobbled lanes, then suddenly turns into Santiago's main plaza, the century-shock is dramatic.

This grand square—sometimes called *Plaza del Obradoiro,* ("Golden Work") sometimes Plaza de España, sometimes just Plaza Mayor—is large enough to have swallowed many bands of pilgrims. To see it as it was during peak travel times you'd have to be here on the birthday of Santiago, July 25th, during Holy Year. St. James's birthday is always special—he is after all the patron saint for all Spain—but Holy Year is something else again—more fireworks, more nighttime illuminations, more displays of the *Botafumeiro* (and more about *it* in a few minutes).

But we digress. The square in front of Santiago's cathedral is surrounded by buildings representing the four major architectural styles used throughout the city. The cathedral's facade is baroque. Facing it, and turning clockwise, you come in turn to the Romanesque College of San Jeronimo; the neoclassical *Palacio de Rajoy* (City Hall); and the Plateresque *Hostal de los Reyes Catolicos,* a former hospice for pilgrims, now a deluxe *Entursa* hotel.

It is the cathedral that will rivet your attention. First, its monumentality. There is a glint of gold to the granite (which is nothing more than the accumulation of lichen over the centuries). One will want to walk around to each of the richly carved doorways in turn—the *Puerta de la Azabacheria* (named for the jet or obsidian carvings made in the nearby plaza even today—as souvenirs for tourists) on the north side; the *Puerta Santa* or Holy Door in the east in the *Plaza de los Literarios* (this is the one only opened during Holy or Jubilee years); and the *Puerta de la Platerias* (silversmiths), the oldest portal, on the south. Any *one* of these portals would be a lesser city's "claim to fame."

It is the west entrance you will approach, the *Obradoiro.* Its baroque ornamentation—the work of Fernando Casas y Novoa—is so richly interwoven, one could spend endless time gazing at it alone. But wait, the best is yet to come. As you pass through this portal there is another one, a facade within a facade. The outer one was completed in 1750. But until then, from 1188 it was the inner one that put its many faces forward to greet arriving pilgrims.

This is the *Pórtico de la Gloria,* one of the most important statements of Romanesque sculpture in the world. We should be grateful that it has been sheltered from Galicia's rains for at least 200 years. In the space of 51 feet (lengthwise) X 13 feet (depth) X 60 feet (height) is a sculptural masterpiece, an achievement by a single man known only as Maestro Mateo. What *is* known is that this great work—three large archways peopled with wonderful, real, human figures and faces that you know from life—was begun in 1168 and took Mateo more than 20 years to complete.

Amidst the array of wonders that emanate from the central column of the *Tree of David* with Christ's genealogy stretching from the heart of Jesse, through David and Solomon to the Virgin, one notices two very earthly things. The first is the space worn into the marble on the *Tree of David*—worn by hands touching a specific place where five fingers fit among the carved leaves and vines. Were St. Ignatius and St. Francis of Assisi among those who put their fingers in these spaces and said a prayer, as was and still is the custom for new arrivals to the cathedral? Might they also have genuflected before the kneeling stone statue just inside one column, facing the altar, and rubbed heads with him? If so, they did as many before and since have done, causing the flat-faced, large-eared figure, which Mateo intended as a self-portrait paying respects to Santiago, to be nicknamed *Santo dos Croques*—Saint of Bumps.

There is another custom pilgrims and other believers follow inside the cathedral. Santiago, looking faintly like an Oriental potentate in gilded splendor, sits in the center of the main altar, baroquely resplendent with silver and framed with winged silver cherubs. It is the custom to climb a few steps to a small passageway behind the altar, embrace the saint from the rear, and then descend to the crypt where he is entombed. Museum hours: 10 A.M. to 1:30 P.M., 3:30 to 7:30 P.M.

The churches and convents and monasteries could keep you busy for days. But Santiago is no dead, pinned butterfly under glass, and you could be kept just as busy wandering the streets without going indoors—admiring sculpted facades and fountains (such as the eerie faces on *Plaza de Fonseca*), discovering tucked-away squares, exploring the marvelous, noisy, exuberant open-sided market. Galicia is known for its seafood, and you will find fish and shellfish you may never have seen before—percebes (goose barnacles), cockles, winkles, eels, spider crabs, centolla (giant crabs), and of course *vieiras,* the symbol of Santiago—scallops.

Santiago at night is surprising. One would expect this city of 70,000 to close early. It is a virtual museum city after all, chockful of saintly monuments. Ah, but it is also a university city, and after 10 P.M. the narrow side streets reverberate with disco sounds and groups of young people clustered on every corner. Insomniacs will have company. Other tourists will be grateful that there are no hotels in this central core.

The hotel in town—as it was for some pilgrims in the past—is a former royal hospital, which Ferdinand and Isabella ordered built to care for the ill among the visiting hordes. They even chose a favorite architect, Enrique de Egas, who built the Hospital of Santa Cruz (now a museum) in Toledo, and to support it they alloted one-third of the taxes collected from newly liberated Granada. The building was of such interest to the Catholic Monarchs that they made decisions about details, such as where to put the fireplaces, what wood to use for floors, how to paint and gild the chapel ceiling.

If you tour the hospital, which is now (since 1954) the deluxe hotel called *Hostal de los Reyes Católicos,* you may be shown the *Observatorio de Agonizados* that looked out over the chapel. It was used as a room where dying or contagious patients could hear mass in isolation. When Andres Segovia began visiting Santiago some years ago, he stayed at the hotel and blocked the look-out window with a mattress and turned the room into a practice chamber.

Those of us addicted to the "golden stone and red tile roof look" of this medieval town can never get enough of it. But there is much else to be seen in Galicia, an independent-minded region whose language and habits sometimes seem more akin to Portugal than to the rest of Spain.

A car and a little patience, for the roads are sometimes clotted with traffic and slowed by rain, will take one from Santiago on N–550 south to Pontevedra, a cheerful town of 60,000 with many spritely squares and lively air. Mostly in Galicia, aside from the artistic richness of Santiago that requires one's total attention, one is content to breathe in the sea air, enjoy the vistas and the *rias* (a less dramatic version of a fjord or firth) that "pink" the shoreline, giving it a scalloped edge, and cut one's internal motor back to cruising speed.

There are things to be seen and savored. In Pontevedra the three-house Provincial Museum has treasures and surprises unexpected in a town of this size. Hours: 11 A.M. to 1:30 P.M., 5 to 8 P.M.; closed Sunday and holiday afternoons. And the *Plaza de la Lena,* where the museum sits, is just one of the little town squares where it is pleasant to be. An aura of unhurried antiquity seems airborne—visible in the many arcaded buildings, the old granite houses (a Galician touchstone) with *escutcheons,* and especially in the delightful *Parador Nacional Casa del Baron,* which has made itself at home in a 16th-century palace. With little ado, one can lunch very happily here on fresh squid, scallops or fish, washed down with a bottle of *Ribeiro,* a young dry white wine of the region.

A dedicated sightseer with a compulsive edifice complex will of course move briskly along to see Cornelis de Holanda's splendidly carved facade on the 16th-century church of Santa Maria Mayor, as well as the all-wood interior of San Francisco.

In Vigo, down the road apiece on the water, a bustling fishing port (Spain's major one) co-exists with an extremely pretty and liveable city of gardens, pine woods, and three soft sand beaches. Vigo's history goes back to Roman days. Its most trying times were during the 15th to 18th centuries, when the port was fair game for raiders and pirates—especially English versions of the same—in search of galleons returning heavy with riches from the Americas.

From Vigo it is a short drive along the coast southward to Bayona on C-550. Here a landscape laced with grapevines and round and pointed haystacks features inlets and fishing boats, handsome and properous-looking farms, and unusual little stone or brick granaries on stilts, which look oddly like miniature Japanese Shinto shrines, except for a cross at each end.

At Bayona one might reward oneself with lunch, a drink or both at the relatively recent *Parador Nacional Conde de Gondomar* built on an ancient site. (See Inside Information—Hotels.) One can even climb around the old fortress walls into which the *parador* has been set for some of the most super views along the coast. The exercise doesn't hurt either. This is the spot where the Pinta landed in 1493 with word that Columbus and crew had reached the Indies (as they still believed). As proof, an "Indian" was shown off to any doubting Tomáses among the crowd greeting their arrival.

From Bayona to Túy it is a hilly but lovely ride through vine-covered fields, where the vine leaves are reddish (and so is the local wine they produce) and strung like roofing over small square wooden frames. Túy is another delight, low key, charming, with an 11th-to-13th century cathedral that will keep you busy briefly. But mostly, Túy is a pleasant, easy place for sitting and sipping the local *Ribeiro* on the terrace of the *Parador Nacional San Telmo* at the edge of the River Miño and gazing across at Portugal. On the hilltop, on the other side of the river, which the Portuguese call Minho, other tourists are very likely sitting in the Portuguese equivalent of a *parador, the Pousada de Sao Teotonio,* in the hillside town of Valença do Minho, sipping a local *vinho verde,* staring across at *you.*

Inside Information

Hotels

For prices, see Madrid, page 50.

As you might expect in an area of proud ethnic groups striving to preserve their traditions and cultural treasures, the hotels are neither flashy nor splashy. The past has a strong claim on the best ones and where tradition combines with enlightened management to produce a superior hostelry, we have included it in our selection.

You will note more than the usual proportion of *paradors* in our list. We consider them superior choices because they are often steeped in history and are so conducive to a guest's enjoyment of that history that no other accommodation comes close. Such *paradors* add dimension to a trip for the wayfarer with enough romance in the soul to appreciate the handcarved door, wrought iron lighting fixtures, handwoven rugs and antique furnishings. And yet all these *paradors* are equipped with the luxuries we take for granted today, including first-rate bathrooms, central heating and good lighting.

★★★★★ **FIVE STARS**

★★★★★ **1. HOTEL DE SAN MARCOS**

7 Plaza de San Marcos, León; (phone 237300). Without question, this is one of the world's finest hotels. It is not every day you can stay in a palace, museum, convent and grand-luxe hotel simultaneously and sumptuously for such a modest amount. Your taste for the regal life can be fully indulged. Rooms are furnished with original art and antiques. Some bedsteads have elaborately carved headboards, others have four posters with ornate canopies of gilded wood or brocaded valances. Handwoven rugs (from the Royal Tapestry Factory), bedcovers and embroidered linens are standard equipment. The convent walls, three feet thick in many places, are decorated with 1027 original works of art—many by Spain's leading contemporary artists.

*** Rey Sancho restaurant

You can be coddled in the bridal or tower suites with their 20-foot ceilings, brocade-upholstered chairs, traditional candelabras, canopied beds, antique writing desks, tapestried walls and thick carpets. Each room has an all-marble bath with heated towel racks and direct-dial phone. The Royal Suite, No. 364, has a foyer as big as many hotel rooms, opening into the living room, laden with sculpture, art and antiques (including an ivory-inlaid writing desk). In the bedroom you'll find two full-size canopied beds whose wood headboards have handpainted decoration, carved wood walk-in closets. A marble bathroom is roomy enough for a basketball team. There's a Mudéjar wood ceiling in the hotel's TV lounge, a Moorish canopy in the bar. The cloister, museums and church are added, inimitable attractions, so are the vistas of formal gardens, sculpture, river and city. Parking. Cathedral is 12 blocks away. 258 rooms. *Moderate.*

Plaza del Obradoiro, Santiago de Compostela; (phone 582200). At this historic hotel, one of Europe's finest, you can enjoy luxurious accommodations, immersion in the past and the closest location to the fabulous cathedral.

Started by Ferdinand and Isabella, this golden stone building covers a city block and was completely modernized for the 1954 Jubilee Year. The most modest of its 159 rooms is merely elegant—furnished with carved wood or canopied beds, polished wood floors, parchment-shaded lamps and the most modern of bathrooms. If you prefer something grander, there is the ego-enlarging Cardinal's Suite, with huge granite fireplace, oversized red velvet-canopied bed and, on a dais, an antique writing desk and high-backed red chair. There's an iron-railed balcony facing the plaza, if you wish to address the multitudes.

On walls of the galleries surrounding the four Renaissance courtyards (named after apostles Matthew, Mark, Luke and John) are copies of El Greco portraits, gilded mirrors and wall sconces. Furnishings include handcarved tables, antique wooden sideboards, ancient statues of saints and fat Talavera porcelain jars surmounting old chests and writing desks.

Note the beautiful wrought iron grille at the entrance to the Gothic chapel and the white marble carvings inside. The chapel is now used for concerts and art exhibits. The hotel's *Relais* restaurant is in what were ancient stone stables; its *Peregrinos* restaurant overlooks the great plaza. Shops, hairdresser, parking and garage. 159 rooms. *Moderate–Expensive.*

★★★★ FOUR STARS

★★★★ 1. LOS TRES REYES

Jardines de la Taconera, Pamplona; (phone 226600). You couldn't be closer to what's happening in Pamplona than here. The deluxe *Three Kings* is near the Plaza Mayor on the pleasant Gardens of Taconera. It has its own swimming pool and parking facilities. All rooms are air-conditioned. Its *Enrique IV* restaurant is noted for local specialties and wines. 168 rooms. *Moderate–Expensive.*

★★★★ 2. LONDRES Y DE INGLATERRA

Zubieta 2, San Sebastián; (phone 426989). In spite of the name, neither staff nor guests are exclusively English. Location is all in this resort town and the century-old Londres has a super site right on the beach promenade. "Old world charm" aptly applies here, though renovation has made rooms and public areas stylishly conservative–modern with cheerful color schemes and quality furnishings. Rooms have all the basics plus TV, radio, direct-dial phone, minibar, reading lights and balcony. Helpful, friendly staff. The casino is in the hotel, FYI. Parking. Attractive restaurant and delightfully fresh and cool green-and-white "American bar." 130 rooms. *Moderate.*

★★★★ 3. BAHÍA

Alfonso XIII, Santander; (phone 221700). A modern hotel right on the seafront where you can watch ship and port traffic, it is close to shopping and the cathedral. Classy, contemporary (not daring, but pleasant) lobby and lounge. Rooms are fresh and attractive, well-coordinated (beige walls, cocoa drapes and bedcovers) with excellent lighting. Outstanding hall and room maintenance. Handsome dining room; generous continental breakfasts; parking garage nearby. 181 rooms. *Inexpensive–Moderate.*

★★★★ 4. PARADOR NACIONAL CONDE DE GONDOMAR

Carretera de Bayona, 1.6 kilometers (55 kilometers from Pontevedra). On the Monte Real peninsula, this *parador* is built on the site of pre-Roman fortifications overlooking the Vigo *ria* or fjord.

Ensconced in an 18-hectare pine and eucalyptus park, surrounded by 3 kilometers of battlements on top of Roman walls, its views are of crashing waves and craggy headlands as far as the eye can see. Air-conditioned rooms are completely modern; there is a beach, also pool, tennis, sauna, marina, parking plus garage, shops. Good kitchen, serving Galician specialties. Drawback: Slightly isolated from town. 108 rooms. *Inexpensive–Moderate.*

★★★★ 5. REAL

28 Perez Galdós, Santander; (phone 272550). This roomy and rambling 19th-century model of a Victorian resort hotel tops spacious hilly grounds. It is noted for its gardens, splendid service and old-fashioned charm. Convenient to one small beach (walking distance) but miles from city or Sardinero beach; quiet; parking. Too bad it is open only July to mid-September. 124 rooms. *Moderate.*

★★★ THREE STARS

★★★ 1. PARADOR NACIONAL GIL BLAS

8 Plaza de Ramón Pelayo, Santillana del Mar (phone 818000). We're partial to this 16th-century palace converted to *parador* because it fits so well into the village, giving that "you were there" feeling. It's authentically simple from its pebble-paved lobby, beamed ceilings, smoky wood paneled bar and cozy lounges to upstairs guest rooms that are light, spacious, with modern baths, minibars and balconies overlooking either gardens, cobbled streets or village. Black beams and white *bovadilla* (concrete plaster) ceilings throughout. Armor on stairway, tapestry banner, stone fireplace in "TV room." Though it's in middle of everything, you'll find quiet you can eat with a spoon and the scents of meadows, cattle and blossoming plants. 22 rooms. *Inexpensive.*

★★★ 2. PARADOR NACIONAL SANTO DOMINGO DE LA CALZADA

3 Plaza del Santo, Santo Domingo de la Calzada (47 kilometers from Logroño) (phone 340300). On this historic spot Santo Domingo established his original hospice in his 11th-century hermitage. The *parador* has modernized the later building on the site with its massive rounded arches and thick stone walls, and offers pleasant, well-furnished accommodations in the very heart of this ancient town. 27 rooms. *Inexpensive.*

★★★ 3. LOS INFANTES

1 Avda. Le Dorat, Santillana del Mar; (phone 818100). In a 300-year-old building, Los Infantes is a small, very bourgeois, 19th-century Spanish hotel. Its charm is its approximation of a middle-class home of a century ago (though with modern plumbing and lighting). Victorian brass beds and old-fashioned furniture; parlorlike lounges on each floor, with petit-point chairs in groupings; attractive lobby and downstairs lounge. Quiet; good views from small balconies. 31 rooms. *Bargain–Inexpensive.*

To add authenticity, the inner courtyard wall has been left unrestored.

★★★ **4. PARADOR NACIONAL EL EMPERADOR**
Plaza de Armas del Castillo, Fuenterrabía (23 kilometers from San Sebastián); (phone 642140). Sancho Abarca, king of Navarra, built the original castle on this site in the 10th century. It was updated by Charles V in the 16th century and much more recently outfitted as a comfortable *parador.* The Great Hall, with banners, suit of armor, carved wooden furniture, is a knockout. At night, you're back in the 16th century (almost) because of dramatic lighting and rough stone walls. Rooms are cozy and modern with views of harbor as well as jacaranda trees below. Drawbacks: several blocks from town down a steep hill; the climb to one's room up many flights of tower stairs, along irregular corridors and stiles are not for the lame, the halt or those short of wind—there is no elevator. 16 rooms. *Inexpensive.*

★★★ **5. PARADOR NACIONAL CASA DEL BARÓN**
Calle Maceda, Pontevedra; (phone 855800). The 16th-century palace of the Maceda family has been redone as a *parador* in this lively town on the Lérez River. Convenient to the museum and shopping areas of the city, the *parador* is comfortable and rooms are spacious, well-maintained; handsome garden and a library; parking. 47 rooms, doubles: 3000–3900 pesetas.

★★ **TWO STARS**

★★ **1. EL SARDINERO**
1 Plaza de Italia, Santander; (phone 271100). Views of the beach are only part of the story at this venerable hotel. Rooms range from small to spacious, have wall-to-wall carpets, brightly lit tile baths. Lounge is comfortably furnished. No restaurant, but easy access to eating places nearby. Drawback: minimal lights in rooms. Noisy on side street—ask for seaside, where the views and breezes are. 113 rooms. *Bargain–Inexpensive.*

★★ **2. HOTEL RESIDENCIA MONTE IGUELDO**
Monte Igueldo (at the summit), San Sebastián; (phone 210211). The view's the thing here—of San Sebastián's harbor, beaches and boats—compensating for rather uninspired rooms that seem to have had much traffic. The breezes never stop here, 600 feet above sea level. The barnlike lounge is light and airy and the self-service restaurant has a panoramic terrace. Garden, pool and parking help to make this attractive. *Inexpensive–Moderate.*

★ **ONE STAR**

★ **1. ALTAMIRA**
Calle Cantón, Santillana del Mar. The Valdivieso family mansion, built three centuries ago, has been the Altamira Hotel since 1955. Wood floors, heavy stone walls, high, beamed ceilings and authentic, and the central heating, telephone and modern but basic baths, adequate furniture make this a rustic, agreeable place to stay. 27 rooms. *Bargain.*

Restaurants

For prices, see Madrid, page 54.

In the north, as throughout Spain, but even more so, the operative food word is *pescado*—fish of all kinds, wriggling-off-the-hook fresh, prepared any number of ways. The seafood capital of Spain is Galicia. Its bounty includes scallops, mussels, giant crabs called *centollo* (small ones weigh over five pounds) goose barnacles known as *percebes* (ugly as elephant feet, with only a modicum of meat that is surprisingly delicious), lamprey and baby eels *(angulas)* that should be tried once. From then on they're an addiction.

In Asturias, the more industrial part of the north, the favorite standby is *fabada,* a hearty white bean stew made with smoke-cured *chorizos* and *lacón* (air dried beef). You'll find it on menus in other regions as well. Washed down with the potent local cider, it's a meal in itself.

It is the Basque cooking whose reputation has spread, as have its cooks, all over Spain. Note in a Basque restaurant how many of the dishes are described as *pil-pil,* which means "simmered." That is a key to the Basque cuisine—fresh ingredients living together long enough for the flavors to become comfortably familiar, blended into succulent creations. Take time to make this acquaintance.

★★★★★ FIVE STARS

★★★★★ 1. ARZAK

21 Alto de Miracruz, San Sebastián (phone 285593.) An orange brick facade is the most ostentatious thing about this extraordinary restaurant. Inside, all is quiet, subtle, elegant, deceptively simple. Juan Mari Arzak is the third generation of Basque restauranteurs, but he has turned traditional Basque cooking on its ear by folding into it certain aspects of French *nouvelle cuisine.* An observer of Paul Bocuse and other French chefs, Arzak has developed the appropriate *nouvelle* elements into a fresh approach to his native Basque cooking. The result for diners is an array of imaginative, original dishes that combine typical Basque ingredients with the careful visual presentation, *al dente* preparation and unusual juxtaposition of foods.

The menu changes frequently, but among the dishes we have liked especially in the recent past are *hojaldre de sesos y gambas con Juliana de calabacin* (brains and baby shrimp *vol-au-vent* with snippets of chives on top, in a lovely cream sauce with very thin slices of zucchini); *pimientos rojos rellenos de cigalitas* (red peppers stuffed with bits of shrimp, crayfish, fish and beans in an elusive tomato-based sauce); *escalopes de pechuga de pato a la naranja* (slices of rare duck breast decorated with orange slices and cepes mushrooms on a green noodle bed); and a specialty—walnut souffle. Brains with carrots (a salad) is a dish that is magic with the Arzak touch. Reservations are essential here, as space is limited. Closed Sunday night and all day Monday. *Very Expensive.*

★★★★ FOUR STARS

★★★★ 1. AKELARRE

Barrio Igueldo, San Sebastián (phone 212052). Another of San Sebastián's chefs who has fallen under the spell of *nouvelle cuisine* Basque style, Pedro Subijana, like Arzak, uses it to enhance his native Basque cooking. The Monte Igueldo setting is a lovely one, and such dishes as *filete de lenguado al chacolí* (sole in the famous Basque white wine *Chacolí, lubina a la pimienta verde* (fish with green pepper) and endive, nut and apple salad serve to enhance it. Here, as at Arzak, the choices are boggling. Closed Sunday night, Monday, October and *Semana Santa. Very Expensive.*

★★★★ 2. NICOLASA

Try the guinea hen in Armagnac

4 Aldamar, San Sebastián (phone 420755). An 80-year-old landmark restaurant in San Sebastián must be doing something right, for Basques don't put up with average cooking when they dine out (they can do better than average at home). Among many notable specialties: chicken stuffed with truffles, crayfish with spinach, and for dessert, perhaps *tocino de cielo* or an apple pudding. The wine list is a fine one here. Closed Sundays. *Expensive.*

★★★ THREE STARS

★★★ 1. REY SANCHO

Hotel de San Marcos, 7 Plaza de San Marcos, León (phone 237300). A table display of inviting dishes and dazzling kitchen with burnished copper pots visible behind a picture window do much to whet the appetite in this handsome dining room. The food doesn't disappoint. Memorable dishes include grilled trout with the essence of rosemary, veal with toasted pine nuts in a brown sauce, ham cooked with citron and grapes (sweet and tender). *Moderate–Expensive.*

★★★ 2. EL MOLINO

Carretera N–611, Puente Arce (12 kilometers west of Santander) (phone 574000). No newcomer to the Santander restaurant scene, Victor Merino has turned this, his prime establishment, into a temple of *nouvelle cuisine,* with such *spécialités* as spinach mousse, salmon or *lubina* with clams, and mushrooms or partridge in pastry. But traditionalists need not worry. Such hearty Cantabrigian dishes as squid in their own ink, fish *en papillote,* stuffed peppers, and *tortilla* with leeks are as well prepared as ever. Closed Sundays. *Moderate–Expensive.*

★★ TWO STARS

★★ 1. VILAS

88 Rosalía de Castro, Santiago de Compostela (phone 591010). Seafood lovers, take heart. Galicia is the land of marine life, and *Vilas* is a marvelous source for some of the best there is. There's nothing fancy here, just a variety of sea dishes expertly prepared. The restaurant is simple, pleasantly rustic, but handsomely done (it's on the outer rim of the old town), and the emphasis is on the table and such dishes as *gambas, centollo, prawns,* and little prawns called *santiaguinas* (because they have what looks like the shape of the St. James cross on their shells). Hake and turbot with onions, pimiento and tomato Galician-style is a hearty, delicious dish. And if you're trying eel or lamprey for the first time, this might be the place to do it—in a red wine sauce. A dessert specialty is *membrillo* (quince jelly) with a soft cheese—an agreeable combination. Closed Sundays. *Expensive.*

★★ 2. CASA CAMERO

79 San Juan, Pasajes de San Juan (phone 356602). Just 12 kilometers east of San Sebastián, this waterfront restaurant offers seafood so fresh you can watch it being hauled up via pulleys from the water from a "well" inside the dining room. Ships' lanterns as overhead lights accentuate the nautical menu. You might try the *cocóchas* (fish jowls), a Basque specialty done to perfection. A place for leisurely dining as you watch the boats glide past outside (even as Victor Hugo once did). Closed Sunday evenings, except in summer. *Moderate.*

★★ 3. LA SARDINA DE PLATA

3 Doctor Fleming, Santander (phone 271035). A creation of Victor Merino, *La Sardina* is so nautically decorated you'd almost swear you were aboard a ship, with rope chairs, ship models mounted on the walls, ship lights, and the dining room decorated to resemble a ship's saloon. *San Martín a la pimienta verde* is a delicious, fine-textured fish, but there are many other finny choices. Good wines too. Closed Sunday evenings and Mondays. *Moderate.*

★★ 4. JOSETXO

73 Estafeta, Pamplona (phone 222097). Here, in pleasant surroundings, you'll experience a number of Basque classics, such as *bacalao al pil-pil.* You might try the partridge with grapes, rabbit with land snails or lamb with chili peppers—all triumphs. Closed Sundays and August. *Expensive.*

★★ 5. HOSTAL DEL REY NOBLE

6 Paseo Sarasate, Pamplona (phone 211729). Pamplona is lucky to have two equally special restaurants, and fans rate them a toss-up. Vegetables here are done with special care, but so is the lamb. The ambience is fancier here. Closed Sundays and from July 15th to August 15th. *Expensive.*

★ ONE STAR

★ 1. DON GAIFEROS

23 Rúa Nova, Santiago de Compostela (phone 583894). If looks alone were the determining factor in rating restaurants, this would zoom to the five-star category. It is stunning—all-white *chic,* with stone walls and old arches and capitals, bentwood chairs. This is the setting—Santiago—for *vieiras* (scallops.) You might splurge and have a *zarzuela* too—a seafood medley that's native to Catalonia. Closed Sundays and Christmas. *Moderate–Expensive.*

A surprisingly sophisticated ambiente for old-fashioned Santiago

★ 2. LOS BLASONES

Plaza de Gandara, Santillana del Mar (phone 818070). Nothing fancy here, but a tidy, sparkling setting and competently prepared dishes. There's always a daily fish special, in addition to regular entrees such as hake Roman-style, trout with ham, *bacalao* with tomato, and sea bass. Good value is the menu of the *casa:* three courses—soup or salad, a choice of three as an entree, and flan or fruit or ice cream. Ice-cream tart with whiskey and cheese with honey are dessert specialties. Closed from September until *Semana Santa. Inexpensive.*

★ **3. IRIS**
5 Castelar, Santander (phone 215225). The setting—soft lights, grey and lavender color scheme, rattan chairs, vintage popular music (often jazz)—will remind you of many smart restaurants at home, if home is a sizeable American, English or Canadian city. The menu, though, blends a dash of *nouvelle cuisine* with classical Cantabrian seafood specialties. Try the San Martín fish with *salsa verde. Inexpensive–Moderate.*

The Basques tend to be better than other Spaniards with beef dishes

★ **4. NOVELTY**
4 Independencia, León (phone 250612). A solid, dependable choice for hearty Castilian fare, popular with local clientele. Here's the place for such dishes as oxtail stew, veal shank and all kinds of river and stream fish. *Moderate.*

★ **5. CASA SALLA**
Carretera a La Toja, San Salvador de Poyo, near Pontevedra (phone 852678). The old palatial background is good company for a menu rich in Galician seafood specials: crayfish, sole, crayfish omelet, all kinds of fish. Closed Sunday evenings and Thursdays. *Moderate.*

Entertainment

Concerts

Estella. Week of Medieval Music, Plaza de Toros; July.

León. "Music in the Kingdom of León," in major monuments; first half of July.

Santander. International Festival of Music and Dance, open-air performances at Plaza Porticada; July–August.

San Sebastián. International Jazz Festival, Palacio de Deportes; late July.

Loyola. International Festival of Religious Music, Monasterio de St. Ignatius de Loyola; August.

Gambling

Of course there's gambling in such sophisticated watering holes as San Sebastián and Santander—but it is a post-Franco phenomenon. The casinos are:

Nuevo Gran Casino de Kursaal de San Sebastián. In the venerable Londres y de Inglaterra Hotel.

Gran Casino del Sardinero. Right at the shore in Santander, a birthday cake of an Edwardian building. It's where four roads intersect. (All roads lead to roulette?)

You'll find the usual exercise mats: roulette, *chemin de fer,* baccarat, and blackjack. They may have slot machines by the time you arrive. In any case, they do have bars, restaurant and nightclub facilities and live entertainment. You have to be 21, carrying identification (your passport will do) and have the necessary scratch (about 500 pts.) for admission.

Folklore

Alfaro. Fiesta with folk dancing, music, *encierros*—(running of the bulls) makes this a scaled-down "San Fermin;" August 15th–18th.

Estella. Fiesta with folk dancing, parades of "Gigantes" and "Bigheads," bullbaiting, bullfights; first weekend in August.

Logroño. *Vendimia*-A wine harvest festival (one of the largest), second half of September.

San Sebastián. Basque festival with traditional folk dances, flute and tambourine music, competitions (tree chopping, tug-o-war, and so forth); first two Sundays in September.

Santiago de Compostela. St. James's Day fiesta. On the day before this patron saint's day celebration a monumental fireworks eruption ("Apostles' Fire"); on July 25th, parades of Gigantes, Bigheads, more fireworks, folk dancing.

Santiago de Compostela Tuna Serenades. These are sung some evenings in the Plaza by groups of university students wearing academic robes, rainbow-beribboned, accompanied by guitars and tambourine. Ask your hotel for news of when, where; time is *usually* 10:30 P.M.

Shopping

Shopping runs the gamut in the north, from the sophisticated boutiques of San Sebastián and Santander to the more folkloric shops of smaller and less urbane towns inland. Much of what you find in the resort boutiques you could possibly find in Madrid, though there is probably greater emphasis on sporty resort clothes. As always, shopping buys are where you find them, but the following might help in the finding.

In Pontevedra, there's an attractive antiques shop on the same square as the museum, Plaza de la Lena. *Platería Antigüedades* is the name, featuring, last time we looked, old wooden religious figures (*santos*) and baroque angels, among other things. Just strolling the streets in the old section of town you will find other antiques shops as well.

San Sebastián's main shopping streets are Avenida de la Libertad and Alameda Calvo Sotelo. If you're collecting goodies for a picnic, Casa Arrieta y Garagorri, 3 Alameda Calvo Sotelo (not far from the delightful *Belle Epoch* bandstand), is a wonderful liquor and pastry shop with a big selection. For regional handcrafts, there is a branch of the national Artespaña at 3 Penaflorida.

The best buy in Santander could well be art; there is a busy and productive contemporary art scene in town. The best galleries for prints or paintings that might appeal to you are: Galería Sur, 20 Calle San José (phone 226813;) Galeria Dintel, 8 Calle Santa Clara (phone 227876); Galería Rua, 9 Calle Medio (phone 226397); Galeria Trazos Dos, 5 Francisco de Quevedo (phone 312821); and Galería Union Arte, 13 Arrabal. An Artespaña branch is at 80 Cádiz. Two streets in Santander for general boutique and gift shopping are Calvo Sotelo and, parallel to it, Hernan Cortes.

Chief buy in the little village of Santillana del Mar is the earthenware pottery being produced in the area. There are just a handful of gift shops in town. Most have the bowls, plates and pitchers. Otherwise, the gift items are much the same tourist objects found all over Spain.

As the focal point of the *Camino de Santiago* it is probably natural that Santiago, though 36 kilometers from the sea, is awash with scallop shells—silver ones. You'll find them in the form of ashtrays, jewelry pins, bowls, bracelets, charms, geegaws, but find them you will—in shops all along *Rúa* Nova and *Rúa* del Villar, two arcaded shopping streets that run parallel from the *Praza das Platerias* (that's Galician for Plaza). A shop near the horse fountain with nice terracotta and golden-striped pottery (a Santiago specialty) is Tenda-Galería de Arte, 1 *Rúa* del Villar. Sargadelos, 16 *Rúa* Nova, is an art gallery; it also sells Portuguese and local ceramics.

The scallop shell is the symbol of St. James (Sant'Iago)

In Santiago we enjoy making a sweets pilgrimage. As in Sevilla and other towns where there are many convents, Santiago's nuns keep the Gothic roofs over their heads by selling homemade baked goods. Certain convents have specific specialties. Many of the Santiago convents are cloistered, so to buy the cakes or cookies, you must ring a bell at a window near the entrance. When the window is opened, state what you want—one dozen, one cake, or whatever—and wait a minute or two. Then presto a neatly tied cardboard bakery box is handed out and you put your pesetas on the counter or window sill. At the Convento de Belvis, for instance, a list of sweets (and prices) is posted next to the window grill. It also lists the hours when one might buy the sweets (9:30 A.M.–12 noon, 4–5 P.M.) The list is longer than at many bakeries (some 20 items, though not all are available at a given time) and includes *brazo de Gitano* ("arm of a gypsy"—a cream filled cake), tarts (apple, chocolate, egg yolk [*yema,*] almond), Magdalenas, Glorias (delicious glazed French donutlike) and a number of Galician specialties. At San Pelayo, just behind the cathedral, we buy *almendrados,* paper-thin, almond-flavored cookies, boxed by the dozen, to be nibbled while sipping strong coffee at a nearby café.

We also like to amble over to the *mercado* or public market to buy a huge wheel of *borona,* a crusty, grainy bread with a *soupçon* of cornmeal in it. It goes well with *chorizo* and the sharp, robust Galician cheeses which we also buy to take along on picnics through the Galician countryside. Note especially the orange San Simon cheese and *tetilla,* a big creamy breast-shaped cheese (whose name means, ironically, *male* teat). Local lore has it that farm women created the cheese in this shape in sympathy with a revered martyr, Saint Esther, whose breasts had been cut off. If you don't want the fun of haggling over prices in the market, you'll find a wide selection of cheese and sausage at *La Casa de los Quesos* on *Rúa* Bautizados, just off Plazuela del Toural. An interesting antiques shop, *Casa Hortensia,* is next door. This is a fine street for food shopping, with bakeries, pastry shops and *ultramarinos* all along the way.

If the aroma of all the good food gets to you, there're always the red-hot chestnuts, fresh from the black-red-and-green "locomotive" of the vendor on the corner to provide a "quick fix," or a café or bar you can duck into at a number of given spots on the route from the *mercado* to Bautizados. A glass of local white wine, purchased *al fresco* in the market costs about 15 pesetas, prompting a wicked friend to call the pick-me-up stop "the 11th Pressings Cafe."

The public market is the place to sample the Galician one-stop meal: an empañada, a huge pizza-shaped flat "pie" filled with onion, fish or meat, potato—a variety of tasty things

Museums (in addition to those listed in text)

Pamplona

★ **MUSEO DE NAVARRA**
Plaza de Santa Ana. Twenty-four galleries with Roman mosaics, Romanesque capitals, Gothic and Renaissance paintings; unusual panels of Charles V's campaigns and of Adam and Eve, in reconstruction of 16th-century Palace of Oriz interiors; murals from provincial churches. Hours: 10 A.M. to 2 P.M. and 11 A.M.–2 P.M. Sundays, holidays.

MUSEO PROVINCIAL DE PREHISTORIA Y ARQUEOLOGÍA
Paseo de Canalejas. Finds from prehistoric caves in the province include bones engraved with animal pictures, batons from antlers, stone tools, Roman coins, pottery figures and more. Hours: 10 A.M. to 1:30 P.M., 5 to 7P.M.; Closed Monday mornings, Saturday afternoons, Sundays and holidays.

Santiago

★ **MUSEO MUNICIPAL Y MUSEO DE POBO GALEGO**
Town museum and Gallegan museum in Convento Santo Domingo de Bonaval, Plaza de Santo Domingo. In these 14th to 17th-century monastery buildings is a unique triple spiral staircase, each of which leads you to a different floor where there are displays of Galician costumes, handcrafts, and life; *sala* of antique furniture, mementos of Alfonso VII. Observatory at top gives sweeping views of city. Hours: check with tourism office.

Rosalía Castro, Galicia's most famous poet, is buried here.

Historic Buildings and Sites (in addition to those mentioned in text)

León

CASA DE BOTINES
Plaza de San Marcelo. A fortress-like stone building designed by Gaudí, it

included textile merchants' store, residence and tenants apartments. Built 1891–1894.

Najera

★ **MONASTERIO DE SANTA MARIA LA REAL**
Church has royal tombs; see that of Doña Blanca de Navarra; highly praised choir stalls, ogival cloister. Remarkable 11th-century church with carved color guards, figure of founder King Don García III of Navarra in full armor. Hours: 9:30 A.M. to 12:30 P.M., 4 to 7:30 P.M.

Santiago de Compostela

COLEGIO DE SAN JERÓNIMO
South side Plaza del Obradoiro, has fine 1490 doorway, charming tiny patio inside; is part of Colegio Fonseca (1544).

★ **GELMIREZ PALACE**
Palacio Arzobispo, Plaza del Obradoiro. Named after the first archbishop who was the driving force in building the cathedral, the palace's 12th-century Romanesque rooms include synod hall nearly 100 feet long with corbels carved with scenes from the wedding of Alfonso IX of León. Hours: 10 A.M. to 1:30 P.M., 3:30 to 7:30 P.M., April to mid-October.

★ **MONASTERIO DE SAN MARTIN PINARIO**
Plaza de la Immaculada. This grandiose 16th–18th-century monastery has a stately neoclassical facade topped by a statue of St. Martin. Its interior includes a wildly Churrigueresque main altar and three serene patios. See especially the fountain by Casas y Novoa and the monks' choir stalls. Hours: Open all day.

★★ **SANTA MARIA LA REAL DE SAR**
Calle Castron D'Ouro, on the banks of the river Sar. Architecturally pure 12th-century Romanesque church (with 18th-century flying buttresses to keep its leaning pillars and walls from toppling). Tombs (13th–16th centuries) along walls and a cool, quiet Romanesque cloister. Hours: 10 A.M. to 1 P.M., 4 to 6 P.M.; closed Sundays and holiday afternoons.

Santillana del Mar

★★★★★ **CUEVAS DE ALTAMIRA**
2 kilometers north, were discovered in 1879 and the paintings have remained remarkably fresh and delicate. More than 150 animals pictured. The cave paintings were done more than 10,000 years ago by Magdalenian/Cro-Magnon men. Nearby caves (without paintings) and small exhibition building are open 10 A.M. to 1 P.M., 3 to 6 P.M. (closes an hour earlier, November through February). Fear that paintings may deteriorate from traffic has caused virtual shutdown of chambers with paintings; for admission see *Perks*.

★ **FUNDACIÓN SANTILLANA**

Combining a venerable palace and tower, this foundation has installed the finest modern facilities for exhibitions and audio-visual presentations. It presents fresh exhibitions of contemporary artists, scientists, literary leaders, with programs, discussions, conferences. Be sure to look in. Hours: 11:30 A.M. to 1:30 P.M., 4:30 to 8 P.M.; closed Monday and Tuesday and month of June. Admission: 50 pesetas.

Santo Domingo de la Calzada

★ **CATHEDRAL**

This is a rebuilt edifice of 1158, enlarged again in the 16th-century. See the Saint's alabaster tomb—a 12th-century Romanesque figure on a 16th-century sarcophagus. Fine *reredos* carved by Forment in 16th century; and chapels. Hours: 8 A.M. to 8 P.M.

Túy

★ **CATHEDRAL**

Built 1170, on summit of highest hill; with crenellated towers, it's a regular fortress. Fine Gothic door and portico; Romanesque cloisters finished in 15th century with guard walk above, from which you can look at Portugal across Miño River.

Spectacles and Displays

Najera

Son et Lumiere in Knights' cloister of Monasteria de Santa Maria la Real during second half of July tells town's history.

Pamplona

"San Fermines"—the fiesta to end all fiestas, with more than 100,000 visitors packed into the nonstop music, wine, dance, firecracker fest that not so incidentally includes *encierros* (running the bulls) and bullfights. July 6th to 16th.

Every few years, one who runs with the bulls gets killed

San Sebastián

Son et Lumiere in Monasterio de San Telmo during special events such as International Film Festival and Basque Week.

Santiago de Compostela

★★ **EL BOTAFUMEIRO**

The giant incense burner. On solemn occasions (such as Easter, Corpus Christi, St. James's Day) this extraordinary, ornate, perforated silver urn three feet tall is so heavy two men in red carry it suspended from a pole into the cathedral. Hot charcoal and incense are poured in as six more men in red tie El Botafumeiro to a rope suspended by a pulley more than 100 feet above them. The Botafumeiro then swings like a pendulum; by rhythmical tugs the eight men on the other end of the hawser increase the swing. At its zenith the censer nearly touches the transept ceiling, only to swoop downward again, sending out a trail of perfumed smoke and sparks over heads of the multitudes as it roars toward the ceiling of the other transept. Clouds of smoke fill the great church as the gigantic silver pot zooms to and fro manipulated by the skill of the eight–man team. Sight, sound and scent combine for an awesome experience. (The Botafumeiro is displayed in the cathedral treasury when not swinging.)

Perks for the Experienced Traveler

Rioja

Rioja aged in oaken casks has a specially fine flavor

If fine wines interest you, maybe you'd like to visit the *bodegas*—wineries—where Spain's finest wines are produced. To do so, make arrangements ahead. Logroño is the center of the Rioja wine trade. (There are 41 bodegas in and around this Ebro River wine district.) Write Consejo Regulador de Denominacion de Origen, 9 Calle 11 de Junio, Logroño, stating your interest and when you expect to visit. A more direct approach can be made by contacting Rumasa, the Spanish conglomerate that owns several bodegas in Rioja (and Jerez). Write or call Rumasa, 370 Lexington Ave., New York, NY 10017; (212)683-3850.

In Rioja villages there are other customs and perks of interest: In the tiny village of Laguardia, *Bodega de Abuelo* (Grandfather's Bodega) is literally a cave carved out of solid rock, whitewashed, large enough for just two picnic tables. Its red wine is kept in a vat, also carved in stone. Here, on Sunday afternoons, the Paternina Wine company representative traditionally has hosted *tapas* and wine for visitors who manage to squeeze in. If you're in the area, stop by and see if he still does.

Santiago de Compostela

Want to dine at one of Europe's finest hotels, free? You may, if you qualify. When the government renovated the Hostal de los Reyes Católicos as a luxury hotel, it agreed to provide three meals a day for three days to genuine, certified pilgrims. The qualifying certificate is obtained at the cathedral upon completion of the pilgrimage.

Genuine pilgrims to the shrine of Santiago are few and far between these days (except during Holy or Jubilee Years), but those who qualify are entitled to have their free meals at this marvelous hotel. How to prove you really *are* a pilgrim? Requirements: Documentary evidence from your parish that you are going on a pilgrimage; written evidence from religious or secular authorities at two (generally the last two) stops on the pilgrimage route before Santiago itself that you have stopped there as a pilgrim. For more specific information write Manager, Hostal de los Reyes Católicos, Santiago de Compostela. And if you think you can talk your way into a free meal or so, forget it—they've heard it all before for 400 years . . . in 40 different languages.

Santillana del Mar

Cuevas de Altamira: Fears that tourist traffic, changes in temperature and humidity were endangering the irreplaceable cave paintings at Altamira forced a shutdown. Only limited numbers of visitors are permitted to view the paintings, and only by prearrangement. If you wish to do so, write *at least* a month ahead to: Director del Centro de Investigación y Museo de Altamira, Santillana del Mar, Cantabria, requesting a date. You may also be interested in the cave where a 14,000 year-old shrine—the oldest known—was discovered. This was in El Juyo cave, an archaeological site. Dr. J. Gonzalez Echegaray, director of the Altamira Museum, was one of the team that found the unparalleled sacrifice site and can tell you if it may be visited yet.

San Sebastián

If you're serious about food and a card-carrying member of a national gourmet organization, you may be able to visit one of the two dozen men's cooking societies in this city. These gourmet clubs have their own kitchen and dining facilities. In rotation, each member prepares a sumptuous repast for fellow members. Though neither the meals nor the dining halls themselves are generally open to tourists, you might have a try (good luck!) at securing an invitation to visit one. Stress your gourmet credentials and serious purpose and write Cofradia Vasca de Gastronomica, Subida al Castillo; and to *Officina de Turismo,* 13 Calle Andia, San Sebastián, Guipuzcoa.

Tours

There are tours of the individual cities in this northern region, and there are tours making circuits of the smaller towns and destinations. However, the offerings are so diverse that the wisest course here seems to be to suggest agencies known to be reputable and recommend that you discuss with them your interests and their offerings.

León. Viajes Meliá, 8 Generalisimo; (phone 211563) Wagons-Lits/Cook, 28 Avda. Republica Argentina (phone 216518)

Pamplona. Wagons-Lits/Cook (agency), Hotel Los Tres Reyes, Jardines de la Taconera (phone 226603)

Pontevedra. Wagons-Lits/Cook, 39 Benito Corbel (phone 850946)

San Sebastián. ATESA, 1 Hernani; (phone 418119) Viajes Meliá, 39 Avda. de España (phone 417946)

Santiago de Compostela. Viajes Melia, 26 Gen. Franco; (phone 582081) Wagons/Lits Cook, Edificio Viacambre, Gen. Franco; (phone 583003)

For other tour information, call on the local tourism information office (see Directory listing).

Sports

As one Basque chauvinist puts it, "autochthonous *Basque sports* require notorious muscular strength and great skill to save effort and to overcome the resistance of the other competitors." He's talking about rowboat races, *soka-tira*—tug-o-war; *aizkolariak*—tree-trunk chopping; and *arrijasotzaileak*—stone lifting. All of these "autochthonous Basque sports" can be enjoyed by spectators at the annual *Fiestas Euskaras*—Basque Festival—the first two Sundays in September, in San Sebastián.

Bullfights are scheduled during Ferias in all the larger towns in the region during the summer season (April through September). The key ones—Santander and Pamplona in July, Logroño in September—are so popular that you must book ahead through your travel agency.

Horse races lure to San Sebastián an international group of spectators as well as breeders and trainers during the months of July, August and September. The Hipódromo race course at Lasarte is the place. (It's the only one open in summer in Spain.)

Horseback riding is popular in the north country. If you're interested, make arrangements through the Real Sociedad Hipica de San Sebastián, Bº de Loyola, San Sebastian; tel. 459142. There are riding stables southwest of the city in the foothills of the mountains.

Hunting—the entire northern region has a reputation for excellent hunting for birds, small and large animals. In the San Sebastián area, you can secure a license through ICONA, 2 Aguirre Miramon, San Sebastián.

Pelota or Jai Alai is the Basque national sport. Nowhere are you likely to see it played better—or with more variations or panache—than in the Basque provinces. There are 100 pelota courts in the San Sebastián area, so from 4 P.M. onward, almost every single day, there is a game under way somewhere near the city. Just 5 kilometers from town on the Hernani road is Galarreta Pelota Court where daily games feature variations using bats, and two kinds of wicker baskets. Tickets can be obtained through your hotel concierge.

If you want to play pelota or conventional handball write or call Trinquete Club, Calle Anoeta, San Sebastián; phone 452703.

Skiing—from the Pyrenees in the east through the length of the Cantabrian range there are now modern ski facilities. What's more, there are roads or rails to make them accessible. And there is an array of modest resorts and refuges for ardent skiers. Among the leading ski resorts with slopes above 2000 meters are these, with the city listed from which they are most accessible:

Pamplona—Burguete is close by, near Roncesvalles.
Logroño—Valdezcaray and Valle del Sol are less than 130 kilometers distant.
Santander—Alto Campoo and Picos de Europa (where there is a *parador*).

León—Valgrande-Pajares, San Isidro, Riaño-Maraña, each 90 kilometers or less from León.

For information about skiing at any of these, write or call the tourism information office of the four cities listed. For general information about skiing in Spain, write Federación Española Deportes de Invierno, 4 Modesto Lafuente, Madrid; phone 4469118.

Summer is sea time on the north coast and those who choose to be are water borne as often as possible. Power boating, sailing, rowing and kayaking are among the usual activities and you as a tourist are invited to participate. Various craft can be rented in key places such as San Sebastián, Santander, Pontevedra, and Túy (especially for kayaks). The local tourism information office is your essential contact for arrangements.

Getting Around

Unquestionably, a car gives you the greatest flexibility and makes it possible to see many fascinating out-of-the-way places, which this northern region has in abundance.

If it hadn't occurred to you before, you will certainly realize quickly here in the north that Spain is one of the most mountainous countries in the world. You will find yourself driving through, between, over and around mountains much of the time. If heights bother you, let someone else take the wheel.

True, it is possible to take the north coast route which avoids much yo-yo-ing through the mountains, but if you do so, you will miss many appealing areas and unusual historic sites. In any case, keep in mind that the distance from the French border at Irún to La Coruña in the northwest corner of Galicia is 350 miles as the seagull wings it. It is much farther on the ground. And when reckoning ground speed, remember that *Autopistas* are few and limited: From La Coruña to Santiago; San Sebastián to Bilbao; around Pamplona and south to Tudela. The National Road, which is 3–4 lanes in many places, runs from La Coruña southeast toward Segovia, and from Villafranca Beasaín southwest to Burgos. On these, a 100 *kph* speed limit is easily possible. Other roads are mostly 2–lane, asphalt surfaced and their twisting nature in mountainous terrain makes it unlikely that you can average even 50 *kph*. If, as often happens, you're behind heavy freight haulers, you'll be lucky to average 30 *kph* for any long distance.

Another caution: This is the region of Spain where there is precipitation at all times of year. In the mountains especially, condensation and frost are almost predictable in early morning. All of which is prelude to the warning: Be sure you have plenty of tire tread, proper inflation and be wary of slick road surfaces.

Still another red flag: Spanish police officers use radar traps and unmarked cars to nab speeders and traffic violators, as you've been warned. Local police, however, in some of these northern, independence-minded provinces, have another twist: They target out-of-province cars, especially for illegal parking. (We found it out the hard way once when we parked behind a local car in one northern city, came back in two hours and found our car gone—towed away. The local car was still there. Two hours and $20 later we had retrieved our car with the aid of a local samaritan who was incensed about the inequity of targeting for ransom a "foreign" [Madrid] vehicle while ignoring the local one. You can't hide your license plates, but you can either rent a car locally or make sure you find a legal parking spot. Whatever the fee, it will be cheaper).

You can rent a car in Bilbao, La Coruña, León, Pamplona, San Sebastián, Santander and Santiago from one or more of the following: Atesa, Avis, Europcar, Hertz and Ital.

Plane travel in this region is limited to direct flights between Santiago—Bilbao, Santiago—Oviedo on Iberia; and Oviedo—Bilbao via Aviaco. You can fly between other cities but you have to go to Madrid and change planes to do so, i.e., Santiago to San Sebastián via Madrid; Santander to Pamplona via Madrid, and so forth. The flight time is not great (Santiago—Madrid, 55 minutes, for example), but the delay between planes can sometimes be annoying.

Rail lines link the towns on the seacoast from the French border all the way to La Coruña, Santiago, Pontevedra and Túy on the Portuguese border. There is, however, no such thing as an express train to whisk you from one end of this corridor to the other. Instead, you will find links between major cities and suburban service around such cities as Santander, Bilbao and San Sebastián. This suggests that unless you are traveling just a short distance along the total north coast you may find that the numerous train changes and lay-overs eat up too much time and require too much baggage wrestling. Note that in the Picos de Europa area many of these are picturesque narrow gauge railroads in beautiful terrain.

Buses between towns and around major cities are generally modern, comfortable, frequent and inexpensive. Consult local bus companies and tourism offices on schedules and prices.

If you lack information or time to learn local bus systems, taxis are still your best bet for city transportation. They're available, comfortable and relatively inexpensive.

One slightly different transportation factor in this coastal area is travel by ship. From Santurce, the port for Bilbao, for instance, there are regular runs by ship to Santander, La Coruña and Cadiz. (There are also ships that make regular circuits from Santander to Plymouth, England.)

A Bit of Background

Inside Today's Spain

"Why is it," an aristocratic Spanish friend of ours once asked rhetorically, "that we Spaniards so often export our worst image?"

He was living in England at the time, commenting on the opposite situation—the success of the British in "exporting" positive images of their country. He cited the youthful beauty of Princess Diana, the handsome urbanity of the late Duke of Windsor and the rugged sensibility of Sir Edmund Hillary—as opposed to such Dickensian types as Mr. Micawber or Bill Sykes.

Our friend José may have been right. The "export" Spaniard is a pastiche of a bullfighter, Figaro, Don Juan and a *flamenco* dancer all rolled into one. He is a stage character who may have elements of truth, but to say he, and only he, is the prototypical Spaniard is like calling Sylvester Stallone's Rocky or Alfred E. Newman the definitive American.

Some visitors to Spain are disappointed to find that the Spaniards they encounter on the streets don't look nor act like Latin lovers, ready to break out the castanets, strum a guitar or burst into an impromptu fandango. "I thought they'd be more Italian," said one acquaintance, explaining that she meant mercurial, emotional, warm and extroverted.

There may be such Spaniards, but we haven't met them offstage. If Spaniards are not all saturnine gypsies or smiling Neapolitans, what then are they?

Spaniards—as you might expect of a polyglot population of 37.5 million descended from waves of invaders and occupiers—notably Arabs, Berbers, Romans, Visigoths, Celts and Iberians—are many things. But first of all they are proud.

If a single word had to be used to describe a Spaniard it would surely be pride. You see it in the way they dress for the evening *paseo.* Even in this day of new casualness, a Spanish girl in tight blue jeans will wear them neatly pressed, with stiletto-heeled pumps to accent her figure. Over the jeans will be a sweater—clean, shaped, and probably cashmere. In cities, the well-groomed middle-aged or elderly gentleman, smelling faintly of lavender toilet water, his nails trimly manicured, his suit custom tailored, may still be seen.

Pride in Spain is shown in how one looks. We can recall when the first hippies appeared in Madrid cafés in the early 1960s. A Spanish acquaintance commented, only partly in jest, "A Spaniard would have to be very rich to dress like that."

But pride isn't just appearance. There is the famous Spanish story of the old man who is starving. Rather than accept charity, he dresses up as usual for the day's promenade or *paseo* and carefully places a crumb or two on his vest so that his acquaintances will notice and assume he has eaten.

To say in Spanish that someone *es un hombre* has much more significance than the mere English words "he is a man." Such a phrase isn't just a statement of the obvious. To be a man has nothing to do with women's lib or its antithesis. It means that the person knows his own worth, is in command of himself, can cope with life, has dignity as a human being—in short, he is a survivor; he lives.

In the past that's been no small accomplishment in Spain. Until very recent times life hasn't been easy. Wars, conquests, occupations, coping with the land—the mere art of survival—has demanded a stoicism and a life force that commands respect. An old Aragonese expression: "We are as noble as the king but not as rich." Every Spaniard believes this. And if you watch how lovingly Spanish children—especially boys—are treated, you'll understand why.

Once long ago we rounded a sharp curve on a country road in La Mancha and ran straight into a dog. Family members had been calling him from each side of the road. Confused by the conflicting signals, he didn't know which way to run. The road was narrow and without shoulders. To avoid him, we would have hit members of the family on either the left or right. We stopped, of course, agitated, contrite, wanting to compensate for the accident. The people were obviously poor, weather-lined farmers, and the dog was not just a pet but a herder of the family sheep. We reached for our wallets. "No, no," said the man of the family. *"Es nada."* We pressed a handful of pesetas on him. He shook his head resolutely. "No, no, no. It is nothing. It doesn't matter. It is life."

That is Spanish pride, dignity, sense of self. Somewhere else in the world that poor little mongrel dog might have been called by its owner a pedigreed prize, the family treasure, winner of awards—to be sold, bargained for, transformed into a bounteous ransom. But not in Spain.

An aspect of the pride you encounter over and over in Spain is an honesty that may not be unique but is increasingly rare elsewhere. Even in the past ten tumultuous years, with the 20th century sweeping them on its crest into the 1980s, Spaniards retain their honesty. Oh yes, you say, you were shortchanged on the Costa del Sol. Well, perhaps. Areas that have become international playgrounds may have become tempting targets for a new avarice. But in most places there is still the kind of pared-clean honesty we have always remarked in Spain.

"How many postcards do you have, sir?" the clerk asks. "Ten," you say. *"Muy bien."* No double checking, suggesting that you might have sneaked in an extra one or two. A man's word is honored. A sense of honor, like independence, is an aspect of Spanish pride.

Another Spanish characteristic born of the pain of survival is humor. Wry, sometimes cynical, self-deprecating, often mocking, humor exists in casual encounters and in big ones. And, of course, it is always used in speaking of the government, never mind which government—any government. Take the official license plate that reads PMM. It is a widely repeated joke that the initials really mean *Para mi mujer* (For my wife), a jab at the fact that an official's wife may often be using the government car on a shopping expedition.

It is a truism to say that Spaniards enjoy life. Can you see more than two of them together during the *paseo* and doubt that? The sidewalks almost vibrate with noisy chatter, laughter, gesticulating. People walk arm in arm, three and four abreast, and you may almost be run down by their togetherness. But it is animated and spirited; there is a sense of enjoying the moment, whether it's a walk, a meal, a conversation.

A first-time visitor to Spain is usually amazed at the variety of facial types. Just as a Spaniard is an individualist in spirit, often his looks defy any easy categorizing. In addition to the invaders of centuries past, there have been more recent ones. Just since 1800, armies on Spanish soil have included British, French, Portuguese, German and Italian. No wonder Spanish "types" range from dark to fair, blue-eyed to black, short to tall.

In politics, that prideful sense of self, or *yo* (I), has often had anarchical strains. It has been said that with two Spaniards in a room, you'll find three differing points of view expressed. Twentieth-century Spanish history does much to confirm that.

Racked by economic and social problems, Spain managed to stay neutral during World War I. But in 1923 a military dictatorship was formed by Miguel Primo de Rivera, with the approval of King Alfonso XIII. Financial, tax and land reforms were inadequate and led to protests, strikes and political assassinations. In 1930 Primo de Rivera resigned. The following year the Republicans won the election, and Alfonso XIII followed Primo de Rivera into exile, as a Spanish Republic was formed.

Monarchist and Falangist victories in the 1933 elections were followed by a victory in 1936 by the Popular Front, made up of Republicans, Socialists, Syndicalists and Communists. Factories were occupied, estates divided and turmoil reigned. Then the assassination of Monarchist Calvo Sotelo triggered a revolt led by Francisco Franco y Bahamonde and other generals who set up a rebel "nationalist" government in Burgos. Franco was appointed *caudillo* (leader), supported by the military, Fascist Falange, Monarchists and most of the clergy.

Germany and Italy sent troops, weapons and bombers to aid the Franco forces; Portugal helped in every way short of outright participation. Russia and Mexico supported the Republicans. The Democracies remained aloof from what many at the time called the dress rehearsal for World War II.

Three years of bitter and intense fighting finally led in early 1939 to the capitulation of Valencía and Madrid to Franco's Nationalist forces—in large part because of the powerful, decisive intervention of the Axis powers. The Civil War devastated Spain's cities, towns, road and rail systems, drove out many of the country's most talented people, killed at least 1 million and impoverished an already poor country.

Though beholden to both Germany and Italy for his victory, Franco proved himself a consummate political juggler by managing to stay out of World War II. With one exception. Volunteers in a Spanish "Blue Division" battled against the Communists in the Nazi drive into the Ukraine.

Ostracized and condemned by the United Nations after the war's end, Spain in 1953 signed a treaty with the United States for air and naval bases to be used in the Cold War against the Iron Curtain bloc. The U.S. needed the bases; Franco needed the capital (1 billion dollars in economic and military aid) and the international acceptance the treaty provided.

By 1955, Spain was a member of the United Nations. Its downward spiral was turning upward.

Throughout the 1950s and 1960s as Western Europe prospered, Spain shared in the economic boom. Tourists began to visit the little-known, long-isolated bargain-priced country. Industry and trade flourished, and thousands of Spaniards worked abroad and sent remittances home.

In 1969, after years of hints, whispers and rumors, General Franco designated his successor at last: Juan Carlos de Bourbon, grandson of Alfonso XIII. Spain would become a monarchy again.

TODAY'S SPAIN

Juan Carlos assumed power November 22, 1975, at Franco's death. And in 1978 a democratic constitution was approved and the present constitutional monarchy was born. The country is now actually governed by an elected parliament—the *Congreso de Diputados,* still commonly called "the Cortes" —and a prime minister. Free trade unions are now allowed, as well as political parties that cover the entire spectrum, including the Franco-outlawed Communist party. Freedom of religion and opinion are now guaranteed—no small change.

As concessions to nationalist independence groups, Basque, Catalan and Galician have been recognized as official national languages. Basques and Catalans now are allowed to elect their own parliaments and run their own "show." Similar freedoms to be extended to Aragon and Galicia have stimulated the same demands from other regions. The Spanish state may be headed for a federal form of government similar to Canada's or West Germany's.

This great rush of extreme political change seems to have mollified regional factions everywhere but the Basque areas. There the extremist ETA organization continues to impose a "revolutionary tax" on businesses and to terrorize the army and Guardia Civil.

Still, most Spaniards are bemused and delighted with their new monarchy, a phenomenon they haven't experienced in half a century. Handsome Juan Carlos and his pretty Queen Sofia are a class act and make it easy to be Monarchists. The king's prestige is high because of his decisive action in staving off a coup attempt in 1981.

Monarchy isn't the only news in Spain today. A sizable middle class, expanding widely over the past 20 years, is reasonably prosperous. Cities have mushroomed too, some almost doubling in size in two decades. Their inhabitants are now leading lives closer to those of their counterparts in London, Chicago or Toronto than to their parents back in the *barrio* or fishing village. Their jobs, needs, desires, clothing and leisure-time pursuits are those of a cosmopolitan rather than a provincial type.

The Cultural Scene

Spain is not a chameleon, though when you travel around the country you may find its many faces nearly as changeable and as bewildering. Its monuments and art speak from its past; its towns and people are of today; past and present are contradictory, impressing you variously as ornately grandiose or starkly austere, exuberant or inhibited, intensely devout and primitively pagan.

What else could you expect from a land where so many conquerors have fought and built palaces, shrines, fortresses—and where there have been so many of them? It is fortunate that traces of so many of the cultures that left an imprint on Spain have survived and, doubly so, that their quality is often so high. Mile for mile, Spain probably has more monuments of artistic merit than any other country you can name.

The best of Spanish art in every age has had a high quotient of mystery, magic or emotion beyond its technical competence.

This is apparent in the haunting prehistoric art of 10,000 to 20,000 years B.C., found in the Altamira caves at Santillana del Mar. It is apparent also in the stone constructions on Menorca in the Balearic Islands. You cannot help wondering who the people were, from 2000 B.C. onward who piled stones into burial mounds, built towers (for lookouts?) and the heavy, dressed stone, T-shaped structures reminiscent of Stonehenge.

The most remarkable example of this from the Celtiberians who lived in the peninsula just before the historical dawn is *La Dama de Elche* (the Lady of Elche)—a life-size stone portrait found at Elche on Spain's southeast coast. This Nefertiti of the Celtiberians (a treasure of Madrid's Archaeological Museum) comes from the 3rd to 4th centuries B.C.

While handsome and enigmatic fragments—and better—were left behind by the Phoenicians, Carthaginians and Greeks, Spain is especially rich in Roman art. No wonder, since Iberia was a vital part of the Roman empire from 200 B.C. through the 5th century A.D. Some of Rome's relics or "calling cards" are still viable as well as visible: the aquaduct at Segovia, Tarragona's triumphal arch, theaters at Italica and Merida and walls of fortresses and towns. But there are also dazzling mosaics and sculptures in museums or on sites from Ampurias to Córdoba (which was the Roman capital of Iberia) and

Jerez to Zaragoza (whose very name is a corruption of Caesar Augustus).

The Visigoths, who seized control in about A.D. 484, were only 200,000 nobles and military in a population of some 6 million. Their artistic legacy was relatively small, even though they ruled the roost until the Moorish conquest 200 years later. The best Visigothic work, in greatest variety, is seen in their capital, Toledo, in the Iglesia San Román. There you'll see their horseshoe arches, mural art and heavy gold jewelry thick with precious stones.

When the Muslims of North Africa crossed into Spain and vanquished the divided and bickering Visigoths in 711, they opened the door to a Moorish garden, flowering with a far superior Arab culture. The Moors brought a higher standard of living, advanced knowledge and technology into Spain. These percolated into Christian areas through the former Christians who had adopted Islam and the former Moors living in Christian areas. Interchange came through the western scholars who attended the great Moorish universities and studied with outstanding Moorish and Jewish teachers in centers such as Córdoba, Toledo and Granada.

The Moorish impact was profound. Many of today's most highly treasured monuments are from the hands of Moorish architects or craftsmen. No less treasured are the marvelous buildings, ceilings, tiles and decorations constructed by those who learned their craft under the Moors. When you look at the Alhambra in Granada, Alcázar in Segovia, Giralda in Sevilla or Mezquita in Córdoba, their alien beauty may obscure the fact that Moorish art was not seamless, all part of a static period with a single artistic ethic. Far from it. Moorish architecture and art evolved and changed, just as did architecture and art in the Christian areas of Spain and Europe.

As church and secular building and art in the Christian kingdoms metamorphosed from Romanesque through Gothic to Renaissance during the 700 years of Moorish occupation, so, too, did Moorish art and architecture change. The forms seen in the earliest section of Córdoba's Mezquita use alternate red brick and white stone horseshoe arches, progress through multilobed to intersecting multilobed and pointed arches. The walls also progress from severely plain decoration to the elaborately rich ceiling, dome and walls of the prayer niche and emir's area that have exquisite mosaic work in geometric, floral and calligraphic designs. The evolution took place from 785, when the mosque was begun, to 987, when it was completed. In other buildings, calligraphy, pierced marble screens and delicately carved floral designs, as well as ornamental brickwork, were typical features during the 8th through 11th centuries (El Tránsito Synagogue, Toledo).

An abrupt change came with the puritanical Almohades, Muslims who swept through Moorish Spain with reforming zeal. They considered decadent the delicate, infinitely interwoven decorations and subtly colored mosaics and carved stone of the Cordoban Caliphate and imposed their own artistic ethic during the 12th and 13th centuries. It concentrated on geometric designs in brick construction, elaborately carved and inlaid star pattern wood ceilings and decorative ceramic tiles (called *azulejos*) that sported bright colors. Calligraphy had more variety, and floral elements were allowed in the same panels.

During the final 250 years of the Moorish era, the cultural center was the sophisticated city of Granada under a self-proclaimed, breakaway caliphate of the Nasrid dynasty. The focal center of that reign was concentrated in the fortress-city of the Alhambra.

Decoration was raised to a new level, with carved stucco, stalagtite ceilings, "collars" around doors and windows and panels of carving as intricate as an Oriental rug pattern on the walls. The sum of the parts—the many buildings, pavilions, patios—of the Alhambra is greater than the whole in this case because the complex was not a unified architectural plan or result, but a cluster of individual masterpieces. The Alhambra's design and decoration, so light, airy, lacy and intricately delicate, using water, space and sunlight as factors, have been tremendously influential.

The hallmarks of Moorish architecture—infinite elaboration of geometric designs (such as stars) in wooden inlaid ceilings (called *artesonado*), glazed *azulejo* tiles, brickwork in geometric patterns and carved plaster ceiling, wall or column decorations—were used wherever they could be afforded. These elements that so enrich an interior were prized by Christian kings, churchmen and nobles through the succeeding centuries, long after the Moors were expelled.

Meanwhile, back across the frontier on the Christian side, the church was the major factor in continuing the arts. It was the patron for new buildings—chapels, churches, monasteries. It contracted for paintings and sculpture for the interiors of buildings, sponsored illumination of manuscripts and production of furnishings for churches and convents.

North of the Cantabrian Mountains, where the Moorish invasion had driven the resisting Christian forces, Asturias became an important haven. There, as streams of pilgrims poured across the northern tier from France to Santiago de Compostela's shrine, French and Lombard influences were fused in the Romanesque architecture used in the many chapels, hospices and churches along the route. By the 11th century small Romanesque churches with separate bell towers were appearing in many small towns in the Pyrenees in what is now Catalonia. And here the brightly painted wood sculpture and vivid, almost Byzantine murals were extraordinary (to be seen in Vich, Santa Maria de Ripoll and Barcelona's Catalan Museum). Early in the Pilgrimage era, Sancho the Great of Navarra welcomed Cistercian monks who built abbeys, monasteries, churches and hospices to care for the flood of pilgrims. Typically Romanesque in form, these buildings were adorned with carved and painted figures in portals, porches and interiors, representing saints, Savior and/or Biblical events, such as the Nativity, Annunciation and happenings from the lives of the Virgin or Christ. These sculptures were emotionally charged when done by gifted artists (as seen in the great cathedral at Santiago de Compostela, for example).

The Romanesque ideal was stubbornly retained in Spain even when Gothic architecture was spreading throughout Europe. Many buildings in Spain show compromises that incorporate both styles. Major Gothic achievements in Spain were the cathedrals in Burgos, León and Toledo and finally the incredibly large, late Gothic masterpiece in Sevilla.

The Renaissance was foreshadowed in Spain by a style called Isabeline because it was commissioned by or during the reign of Isabella the Catholic (1474–1504). Notable for its lacy carved stone decoration of entire facades, it became the Plateresque style, so-called because its minutely carved exteriors were reminiscent of silversmiths' filagree work. It was busy and intriguing and was subordinated to overriding architectural purposes and designs.

Parallel with this, disengaged, cerebral architectural elements superseded Gothic in buildings and interiors in Renaissance works built by Pedro Machuca, Bartolome Bustamante and Philip II's chosen architect, Juan de Herrera (who did the Escorial). Rhythmical round arches, arcades, columns and pediments are seen in works such as the palace of Charles V at the Alhambra and Valladolid Cathedral and were used throughout the 16th century. There was a tremendous surge of building at this time, thanks to the torrents of gold and silver flowing in from the Americas. Architects Alonso de Covarrubias, Andres de Vandelvira, Rodrigo de Hontañón and Diego de Siloé set their marks upon the landscape in stone monuments admired yet today.

In the 17th and 18th centuries the fantastic, exuberant ornamentation of baroque and rococo flowered and reached an apex in the Churrigueresque style (named after the three Churriguera brothers who initiated it). It used twisted, serpentine columns, vine adornments and every conceivable decorative element from cornucopias of flowers, fruit and leaves to platoons of cherubs, gilded, painted or toned as the purpose might dictate. (Salamanca's San Esteban Monastery and Valencía's *Palacio de Dos Aguas* are among hundreds of examples.)

Neoclassical styles were a reaction to the overadornment; they continued until modern architecture in the 19th century, using new tools, concrete, steel, elevators and electricity, changed the ground rules for building. Spain's most original architect of the late 19th-early 20th centuries was Antonio Gaudí, the Catalan genius whose individual vision produced striking, unforgettable buildings. His best work, which seems Gothic and organic simultaneously, is seen in Barcelona's Sagrada Familia church, Parque Güell and the Milá and Battló apartment buildings.

PAINTING AND SCULPTURE

Though visitors to Spain are deeply impressed and often fully prepared for the rich diversity of the Prado's fabulous art, many do not understand the fundamental reasons for the international character and high standard of the works. And they may not be aware that similar diversity—and quality (but not quantity)—are to be found in many towns and cities around the country.

There are several reasons. First, the royal and noble patrons and the Catholic church commissioned and/or bought works by the best artists of their times. Second, the art market was in Spain—the richest European country of the 15th-17th centuries. Third, it was a stimulating place for artists to be. Fourth, royal patrons such as Isabella the Catholic, Charles V and Philip II personally chose both the art they bought and their court painters; they didn't delegate their authority to an arts committee. Fifth, Spain included (for centuries in some cases) parts of Italy and the Netherlands and was linked through Charles V's Habsburg family with German-Austrian areas of Europe and through the Bourbons with France and Italy.

For decades, many leading architects, painters, craftsmen and sculptors working in Spain were from Flanders, Italy and Germany. Some stayed and settled. The roster of Spain's leading artists of the 15th and 16th centuries is liberally sprinkled with foreign names. It is this international aspect of Spain's history that accounts for superb art by "foreigners" being found in what might be considered out-of-the-way churches, chapels or convents. An active "network" insured that a small church in Zamora, for instance, might have panels, reredos or portals by leading artisans of the time.

In the Christian kingdoms during the Moorish period artists specialized in religious motifs. They worked in wood or stone (and a few, later, in precious metals) and painted on wood, walls and, later, cloth.

The influences of Byzantine mosaics and icons are evident in the early murals and sculpture (especially in Catalonia), which is not surprising, considering the Crusader contacts with the Middle East and the fact that the Byzantines had conquered and occupied Spain's eastern coast from 551 to 624. The primitive painters of the Gothic era were greatly influenced by Flemish and Italian schools. Jaime Huguet, Bartolome Bermejo, Fernando Gallego, Ferrer Bassa and the Serra brothers were among the leaders.

Sculpture in the Gothic period moved from the primitive stiffness of the Romanesque (Master Mateo's *Portico de Gloria,* Santiago de Compostela) to portrait altar pieces, tomb effigies and choir stall figures that have warmth, human emotions and expressions. Some of those whose works are both signed (many were still anonymous) and exceptional were by "immigrants" such as Gil de Siloé of Antwerp, Nicolas of Florence (Salamanca's Old Cathedral), Egas Cueman of Brussels and Rodrigo Alemán. Siloé was Burgos's most prolific purveyor of Plateresque sculpture; Alemán did lively, bawdy choir stalls in the Toledo cathedral, among other things.

It was in the 16th century that Spain fielded a number of competent painters and two exceptional ones—Pedro Berruguete, who synthesized all the styles he observed, and the Crete-born El Greco, who put on canvas his singular visions of men and angels. Sculpture of the era emerged as astonishingly powerful in the works of the gifted Alonso Berruguete (in Valladolid), Diego de Siloé and Felipe Bigarny (in Burgos Cathedral), and the master of drama, Juan de Juni (Segovia Cathedral).

There was a flowering of painting talent in the 17th century, with Spanish painters turning out huge canvases, made to fill vast spaces. The outstanding talents of the time were Ribalta, Ribera, Murillo, Zurburán, Coello and the genius Velázquez. Much sculpture of the period was destined for *pasos,* those floats carried during *Semana Santa* (Holy Week) parades in every village and town, as well as for monasteries and churches. Alonso Cano, who was also an architect and painter, and Pedro de Mena were two leading lights in this period (Toledo cathedral).

The 18th century was Goya's (though he lived until 1828) and his virtuosity in etchings and lithographs pioneered these forms in Spain. The country's sculpture burned itself out in overkill; overembellishing altars, retables and chapels in baroque and Churrigueresque decoration, for the most part, and in "heroic" memorial monuments. It did not revive until mid-20th century with the work of contemporaries Eduardo Chillida, José de Ribera, Pablo Serrano and Amadeo Gabino, among others.

In paintings, however, the picture was quite different. During the 19th century and into the 20th Joaquin Sorolla painted placid landscapes, Ignacio Zuloaga and José Solana dramatized ordinary *barrio* people and José Maria Sert made an international reputation painting murals of historic and legendary subjects (as in Rockefeller Center and San Sebastián's San Telmo chapel).

The radical changes in art in this century, breaking completely with the past, have been led by Spaniards working outside Spain: Pablo Picasso, Juan Gris, Salvador Dalí and Joan Miró. They have been enormously influential. Looked at now as "old masters" of modern art, they have been superseded by a younger generation of Spanish artists who emerged on the world scene in the late 1950s. They worked within Spain and used abstract expressionism as a vehicle. Among these, perhaps the most widely known are M. Cuixart, Antonio Tápies, Manolo Millares, Antonio Saura, Luis Feito, Eusebio Sempere, Manuel Rivera, Gustavo Torner and Fernando Zóbel. These artists have been joined by an increasing number of younger painters in what is now an extremely active Spanish art scene.

LITERATURE AND THEATER

The literary tradition in Spain stretches back two millenia to the Roman era when satirists and moralists dominated the scene. Among Iberian Romans were the two Senecas, father and son (54 B.C.–A.D. 39; 4 B.C.–A.D.65) and Martial, the epigramist (A.D. 42–104). During the Visigothic period the outstanding literary achievement was the compilation of an encyclopedia by Isidore, the Archbishop of Sevilla (A.D. 570–636).

In Moorish Spain there was a tremendous amount of academic and literary activity. It was stimulated by the free exchange of ideas and easy accessibility of books and teachers who had knowledge of Greek, Latin, Arabic, the Middle East and the far reaches of the Muslim world—India, central Europe, Africa. This world view produced thinkers, scientists, physicians, historians, mathematicians, geographers and astronomers of high achievement. Among those whose work filtered through from Arabic to Latin were Averroes, who reintroduced Aristotle's works; Avicebron, a neo-Platonist; Maimonides, the Jewish philosopher; botanist Ibn Baitar; historian and physician Ibn al-Khatib; mathematician and geographer al-Khwarizmi (with his maps of the heavens); and Ibn Khaldun who wrote a profound 7-volume history of the rise and fall of civilizations.

Meanwhile, in the Christian north, one early type of literature consisted of ballads of the troubadors. Brought by the French *jongleurs* and pilgrims to Santiago de Compostela, this lyric form was the epic, which inevitably was about struggles with the Moors and competing Christian kingdoms. In the 12th century, one such epic was fashioned from the legend of El Cid.

In the following century Alfonso X, *El Sabio* (the Wise) put scholars to work to translate Arabic books and to compile a *General Chronicle of the Spanish People.* This included fact, fable and myth in a work that proved an inexhaustible source for writers who came after. Written in Castilian, it gave that language an early and fundamental advantage toward becoming the accepted common tongue. Alfonso is also credited with 417 "Songs of the Virgin Mary" in Galician, setting a pattern of using that language for lyrics and poetry.

Religious dramas and mystery plays (such as the one still performed at Elche) and recreations of battles of the *Reconquista* were the dramatic staff of life until Italian influences (from Spanish campaigns in Italy) stimulated secular theater.

Generally cited as the first of "modern" plays is Fernando de Rojas's *La Celestina* (1500), named after its leading character, an earthy bawd. By the middle of the century, theater and literature were flowering with the plays of Garcilaso de la Vega and Juan Boscán, the books of John of the Cross and Fray León and Santa Teresa's *Autobiography.* The first of the picaresque novels appeared in 1554: *Lazarillo de Tormes.* Author unknown, it told the adventures of a *picaro* (social outcast) as he moved from master to master. It punctured romantic notions of chivalry. But it was Miguel de Cervantes Saavedra who demolished the age of chivalry in his universally appealing *Don Quixote* in 1615. Many scholars call this the first modern novel, precursor of *Tom Jones* and *Moll Flanders* and others.

In the theater, Lope de Vega's output numbered an astonishing 700 authenticated plays and an unbelievable 1,100 more attributed ones. They incorporated gaeity in comedies of manners and cloak and sword intrigues. Guillen de Castro wrote about the Cid (and Corneille used it for *Le Cid*) and Tirso de Molina wrote *The Sevilla Deceiver,* prototype of Don Juan. Calderón de la Barca (1600–1681) is best known outside of Spain for his *Life is a Dream.* He specialized in religious-moral drama but wrote light comedy and cloak-and-sword plays as well.

The 17th century saw the Benedictine monk Feijoo shaping opinion with his essays. Ramon de la Cruz wrote witty, brief playlets of manners that, set to music, became *Zarzuelas*—Spanish light operas.

Decadence and resistance to the Bourbons characterized the 19th century in letters. Pérez Galdós (1843–1920) wrote some 80 novels recreating Spanish life of the times (especially life of the common folk of Madrid). He won international stature for these. His contemporary, the Basque Pío Baroja, wrote anarchistic adventure novels. But it was José Echegaray (1832–1916), author of violent melodramas, who earned Spain's first Nobel prize for literature.

The impact of the Spanish-American war on writers of the time was such that they were known as the "generation of '98." They dealt more with ideas than plot or action, trying to blast the Spanish public out of its apathy. Miguel de Unamuno (1864–1936) and Baroja were two such writers. Ortega y Gasset (1883–1955) is internationally known for his philosophical writings such as *The Revolt of the Masses.* Salvador de Madariaga (born 1886) was one of the writers who went into exile when the Civil War broke out.

Meanwhile, Catalan writing revived in the 1830s after centuries of being moribund. Its poets and novelists of stature included Rubio' i Ors, Jacint Verdaguer, Joan Maragall and dramatist Angel Guimerá.

In poetry, the towering figures were the 14th-century archpriest of Hita —Juan Ruiz—the Chaucer of Spain, remembered for his *Libro de Buen Amor* (*Book of True Love*); Garcilaso de la Vega (1501–1536); Luis de Góngora (1561–1627), noted especially for his *Soledades.* All of these people wrote lyric poetry of the first rank. The Marqués de Santillana (1398–1458), one of the most powerful men of his time, wrote courtly poetry. San Juan de la Cruz (1542–1591) proved to be capable of beautiful lyric flights. His contemporary, Francisco de Quevedo, used scalding satire directed during much of his lifetime (1580–1643) to denunciations of institutions via Hieronymus Bosch-like scenes. Some critics give the *villancicos* (country songs) of the 16th century high marks for vitality and lyric qualities. Critic Gerald Brenan cites the Galician *cantigas de amigo* (love songs sung by women) of the 13th century as "the most beautiful song poetry of the middle ages." The tradition and strength of poetry in Galicia strongly influenced all of Spain.

At the turn of the 20th century Nicaraguan Rubén Dario, working in Europe, wrote French Symbolist-influenced works. Antonio Machado, poet of the Castilian countryside, has been compared to Yeats in his later years. The poetry of Juan Ramon Jiménez (1891–1958) was extremely influential, and he won a Nobel prize with his deceptively simple book about a boy and his donkey, *Platero y Yo.* One of the casualties of the Civil War was Andalucían poet Federico García Lorca, executed at age 38 by Franco's Falangist followers in 1936. Lorca's poetry and plays are alive and still produced today. José Maria Gironella's acclaimed trilogy described life just before and during the Civil War. Ana Maria Matute, Antonio Ferres, Juan Goytisolo, Rafael Sanchez Perlosio, Carmen Laforet and Ramón Sender are among active writers of the postwar period.

MUSIC

Spanish music traces its written origins back to Alfonso X's *Songs of the Virgin.* Beautifully illuminated on parchment manuscript pages, they appeal to the eye as well as the ear.

Ballads were sung and songs were important elements in Spanish dramas. The *vihuela,* (a primitive pre-guitar) and the organ were the two leading instruments for Spanish composers. But it was folk music and dance of the people that accentuated the vitality of Spanish music. French composers of the 19th century seized upon this wonderful storehouse and, transmuted, Spanish themes emerged in Bizet's *Carmen,* Chabrier's *España,* Lalo's *Symphonie Espagnole* among others. Catalan Felipe Pedrell's life researches into Spanish folk music served as a seed bed for composers.

In this century Spanish composers who have captured an international audience include Isaac Albeniz (1860–1909) with *Iberia;* Enrique Granados (1867–1916) for his *Goyescas* and Manuel de Falla (1876–1946) with *El Amor Brujo* and *The Three Cornered Hat.*

Leading contemporary composers are Joaquin Rodrigo (*Concerto de Aranjuez,*) Federico Mompou, Joaquin Homs and Xavier Montsalvatge.

Spain's musicians have earned international reputations as scholars, interpreters and popular performers. Sarasate, the dexterous Basque violinist, was such a one in the 19th century, as was cellist-conductor Pablo Casals in the 20th century.

Andres Segovia is credited with reviving the classical guitar, an instrument with which Narciso Yepes has distinguished himself. Pianist Alicia de Larrocha is well-known on the concert stage. Spanish singers have become opera stars too. Among those presently celebrated are Montserrat Caballé, Victoria de los Angeles and Placido Domingo.

You should be aware that Spain's folk music and dance are truly living arts. At *ferias* (fairs) and on special local or regional occasions, the *jota, muñeira, sardana* or other local folk dances are performed often by people in traditional costumes. There are also frequent folk dance and music festivals that feature regional groups. These are staged by Spaniards, for Spaniards; visitors are welcome.

Spain has one type of traditional music that is popular enough to be a genuine expression of one segment of the people and commercially successful at the same time. This is *flamenco,* played by guitarists, sung by male vocalists and danced by either or both males and females. The word is a mystery, for *flamenco* in Spain usually refers to anything Flemish. But the Arabic and gypsy origin of *flamenco* is apparent in its stylized form and emotional content. Tremendous tension is created by its dancers, the tight vocal control of its singers (especially in *cante "jondo"* or deep song) and the intense haunting quality of its music. The best works of *flamenco* singers, musicians and dancers are to be found on tape, record or radio in Andalucía and in live performances in Jerez, Sevilla and Málaga during Feria.

The performers at many tourist-oriented *tablao Flamenco* are all too often tired, unskilled and untalented. This is particularly true in Granada's gypsy caves. They give visitors a poor and false impression of *flamenco.* But one inspired, taut and fiery performer can redeem a dozen lackluster experiences and reveal why *flamenco* continues to have devotees.

Some observers contend that *flamenco* is cyclical, with good periods alternating with poor. It was down in the early 20th century until Manuel de Falla and García Lorca revived interest in it with a *flamenco* congress in 1922. There followed a long period in which greats such as Escudero, Antonio and Rosario and Rosa Durán danced. *Flamenco* enthusiasts, who see the current period as a trough in the "flamenco cycle," contend that the art form is in the early stages of an upswing. *Hasta pronto!*

Food and Drink

The Spanish may not have a special shrine to the kitchen god as the Chinese do, but they are just as concerned with food and drink. "He eats well," or "They eat well in that town," are sentiments frequently expressed. Food is a preoccupation, a fixation, a dedication, and, if you observe the conviviality of a gathering of Spaniards, a fiesta.

In the past, to "eat well" meant quantity; today, with the increased prosperity of the past ten years, "to eat well" is a more selective undertaking.

There has been a tendency in gourmet circles abroad to criticize Spanish food. That's because in the poor dark days of the 1950s the country's impoverished economy was reflected in its diet. In those days, outside the major cities, bread was coarse, restaurant menus were severely constricted and portions were miserly. The price was low, but often so were the quality and quantity. You were reminded of Alexandre Dumas's passage through Spain some hundred years before when he resorted to carrying his own food and preparing his own meals because the country inns were so ill-equipped they often didn't have so much as an egg. Life was never that Dumas-bad in our experience.

In recent years, a spartan cuisine has flowered into a new richness of choices. There are dozens and dozens of attractive restaurants in Madrid and Barcelona, and the smaller cities reflect prosperity in a similar fashion. Local and regional specialities have been embellished, repertoires have been enlarged.

We noted in the various chapters how the outside world, in the form of France's *nouvelle cuisine,* has made itself felt and has been interpreted in regional ways by inventive local cooks. What this means for you is that you now have an opportunity on your visit to Spain to sample regional Spanish cooking in much greater depth and breadth than at almost any time in the past (unless you were the guest of an aristocratic gourmet with the interest and means to lay it all before you in style).

Though nouvelle cuisine in France may be on the wane, its influence is paramount elsewhere

We mentioned earlier (Hard Facts) the obsession of Spanish chefs with freshness and the delight of being able to dine in season on fresh-killed game, fresh fruits and vegetables whose ripening time has come naturally and the freshest of seafood. When it comes to certain foods, Spaniards take pleasure in thinking small: tiny strawberries, so delicious and flavorful; skinny stalks of baby asparagus.

Spaniards eat varieties of sea life unknown to most foreigners. Feel brave, and you will be rewarded when you try *angulas* (white baby eels). "I didn't have my glasses on when I first tried them," a devotee admitted, "and I thought it was spaghetti." It's that first time that poses a problem for many. Sauteed in garlic and olive oil, with spicy red pepper pods, *angulas* are customarily served in the individual earthenware casseroles they are cooked in and eaten with special wooden *angulas* forks. Dressed angulas salads have become popular of late. Though a Basque dish, *angulas* are enjoyed all over Spain.

Spanish food speaks of its origins—fish from the Mediterranean and Atlantic and rivers and mountain streams; veal, lamb and goat from the farms, fields and hillsides. It is robust and earthy as befits a country of hard-working farmers and fishermen.

You will find echoes, too, of past conquests, both *of* Spain and *by* Spain. When the Phoenicians arrived they planted olive trees, and the rich oil has been basic to Spanish cooking ever since. The Romans brought garlic. The Moors introduced the joys of black pepper, saffron, cinnamon and cumin and did their own planting—of lemon, orange and almond trees. We can thank them for Spanish marzipan and perhaps *turrone.* Their cross fertilization with the East may have brought Persian *pilau* to the Levante, which has evolved through time to the succulent *paella.*

Conquistadors returned from the New World and in their luggage were tomatoes, paprika, pimientos, potatoes, chocolate and vanilla beans. Spanish cooks learned to combine ingredients and make rich olive oil-and-tomato sauces, which became a basic element in many stews.

There are certain constants in Spanish cooking that are used in various dishes throughout the country: garlic, onions, olive oil, almonds, pine nuts, walnuts, hazelnuts, tomatoes, thyme, sweet and hot red and green peppers, pepper, cloves, bay leaf, various types of pork sausage (*chorizo, salchichon, butifarra*) and ham (used in tiny diced bits as seasoning in meats, sauces, vegetables). And, of course, we can't overlook what may be the national dish, *tortilla española* (a potato omelet) eaten for breakfast, lunch, dinner, *merienda* (late afternoon snack or tea), supper and always on picnics (cold).

The menu you encounter in Jerez de la Frontera will differ from that in San Sebastián, but you may be sure that the noontime meal, the *comida,* is ample. It will begin with soup or appetizer, called *entremeses,* to be followed by a fish course, then a meat course, possibly a dessert and coffee. Noontime meal is a misstatement. The meal usually begins after 2 P.M., sometimes as late as 3 P.M. After so much food, you can understand the *siesta* custom.

Preceding this major meal of the day one may have stopped first at a bar or at the bar of the restaurant for a glass or two of wine or sherry, accompanied by a selection of *tapas,* tidbits to nibble before the serious business of dining. The word *tapa* means, literally, cover or lid, and the custom originated, they say, when the first bartender, whoever he may have been, served a beer or glass of wine with a small lid on it. On the lid were a few toasted almonds or ripe olives. Little by little, the lids became small dishes and multiplied along the counter. Nowadays a good bar is often evaluated by the quality and quantity of its *tapas.* It is possible to skip dinner completely, just by moving from tapa bar to tapa bar, sampling each one's specialities.

Because of the tapa and wine custom, most Spaniards are ready to eat when they finally reach their table in a restaurant. The bar is for drinking; the restaurant is for eating (with table wine accompaniment of course). Rarely will a waiter approach you, after you are seated, to take a drink order. He assumes your drinking hour is over. (An exception is a restaurant in an international-type hotel.)

Drinking, eating, socializing—that's the way it goes in Spain, whether you're sampling the hearty *cocido* (the Castilian stew) or the garlic soup or enjoying as *entremeses* thin slices of air-dried mountain ham (either *Jamon Serrano* or *Jamon Jabugo*).

Just as all roads meet in Madrid, so do all the regional cuisines of Spain. Yet there are dishes that are at their best when sampled in the specific air and ambience of their place of origin. Could any *paella* excel that eaten in the sultry air of Valencia? And despite the marvelous Basque restaurants all over Spain, on home turf the *bacalao pil-pil* seems more succulent. *Fabada Asturiana,* that thick, long-simmered stew of broad white beans, pork and sausage, seems at its peak in Oviedo when consumed with glasses of feisty Asturian cider. "That's because of the water," says one Asturian. "No," says another, "it's the *lacón,* the pork hock used here." "Wrong," says still another. "It's the special *chorizo,* cured in wood smoke."

In Pamplona you will eat lamb prepared as *cordero a la chilindron,* a spicy mix of red peppers, tomatoes, onion, garlic, and pimientos with a mere hint of ham added.

When you see an entree on the menu listed as *à la viscaya* or *vasco,* you'll know it's Basque, so leap. It will have a sauce, perhaps red with tomatoes and peppers or green with parsley and, perhaps, in season, asparagus tips. Most Basque dishes are baked in *cashuelitas* (little earthenware dishes). Basque fish specialties include *cocochas merluza* (hake "cheeks") in a peppery sauce; *changurro* (king crab) baked with cheese; *merluza* in green sauce; and cod cooked perhaps in a hundred different ways.

If the Spanish north is the land of the bean (Asturias) and the cod (Viscaya), it is also—in the northwest (Galicia)—the land of the *empañada* (a meat- or fish-filled sealed pie), *Caldo Gallego* (a vigorous meat and vegetable soup), lamprey pie and *Lacón con Grelos* (pork leg and turnip greens).

In León they will show you 30 ways to prepare the freshly-hooked trout from their mountain streams. Here and throughout Castile the hare and the wild deer play, but when they are caught, Castilians pickle them in a wondrously tart and tangy *escabeche* sauce. Originally devised as a means of preserving game, *escabeche* now endows partridge, pheasant, and even chicken with a special piquancy.

Castilian and Manchego dishes still lean heavily toward one-pot simmered stews, called *olla podrida,* familiar to Don Quixote and to today's wanderer as well. In Segovia, Salamanca and Toledo you will find with ease succulent suckling pig and lamb, crisp of skin, tender of meat. Toledo's *chanfana* (a one-pot shepherd's stew with lamb) vies with its *perdiz estofada* (stuffed partridge) for your attention.

Spaniards like variety meats—sweetbreads, kidneys, brains, liver. A popular Madrid *tapa* is tripe. As you leave the bull ring in Sevilla, look for a restaurant near the *Plaza de Toros* for a specialty—*rabo de toro* (bull's tail) simmered in wine with tomatoes, potatoes, saffron and garlic.

Sevilla is also home of the gossamer-fried and grilled fish. *Gazpacho,* which began life as a farmer's stew, now has dozens of identities according to each cook's whim or family hand-me-down recipe. Córdobans like theirs made with tomato, broad beans or almonds. In Granada, you must sample *sopa de ajo blanco*—soup made with white garlic and ground almonds. Málaga's white garlic and grape *gazpacho* is famous.

Granadans savor the snow-cured Trevélez ham, the famous Sacromonte omelet and chicken stewed with tomatoes.

Barcelona's seafood medleys—*Zarzuela, opera* and *paella a la Parellada*—deserve your indulgence. Its special mushroom, *moixarnon,* unknown in the rest of Spain, is an aromatic addition to many meat dishes. Rabbit *a la alioli, secas judias amb butifarra* (beans Catalan style) and artichokes stuffed, grilled and sauteed with ham bits or in omelets are all Catalan specialties.

La dulce vida—and the Spanish do like sweets—comes not only at breakfast with pound cake served with a continental breakfast or with *churros* and thick hot chocolate served as an *almuerzo,* (light lunch) snack or mid-morning pick-me-up. Have something sweet at *merienda* (afternoon tea), and then, of course, there's dessert at supper. *Flan,* Spain's all-purpose ubiquitous dessert, a richer, carmelized version of *creme caramel,* is as much a menu regular as is ice cream. In Catalonia *crema Catalana* is a still richer variation on the flan theme with a higher density of egg yolks.

Other sweets have their regions, but they share one basic characteristic—they *are* sweet, sometimes too much so for anglicized tastes. They often emphasize the yolk, not the white of the egg, providing a density and egginess that is unique to Spain.

The Basques like fried custard squares they call *tostadas de crema,* a sponge cake made with ground almonds (*colineta*), and an egg-yolk sponge cake called *capuchina.* In Santiago de Compostela you will be urged to try the local tart with a powdered sugar cross on top in honor of St. James.

Toledo is proud of its marzipan, made from an ancient Moorish recipe, and its *melindres* (honey fritters) from Yepes.

Andalucía is a heavenly place, no argument there, and sweets lovers find it especially so because of the candied egg yolks of San Leandro (in Sevilla), Córdoban quince jam and almond and honey pastries.

Sweets such as *yemas, bizcocho con crema* (a sponge cake with cream filling), *arroz con leche* (rice pudding, often served with whipped cream on top), and *almendrados* (almond cookies) can be found in variations all over Spain. So can the popular and simple dessert, *zumo de naranja* (fresh orange juice served in a tall glass).

Cheeses in Spain often stay close to home. You can seek out the blue ewes' cheeses from the north, called *cabrales.* The Burgos type is especially creamy and soft. In Santiago de Compostela there are the *tetilla* and *San Simon* cheeses. Navarra takes pride in its strong, sharp *roncal,* and throughout La Mancha you will find version after version of *manchego,* everyone's favorite in Spain.

Not all Spanish food has a peasant derivation, a Spanish friend reminded us. She's right of course, but few people know that some of Spain's most elegant dishes are erroneously attributed to France. Sauce *Espagnole, riz a l'Imperatrice,* and *mahonesa* (mayonnaise, created in Mahon) are examples. Even puff pastry can be traced back to a Spanish cookbook of 1495. *Pot au feu* derives from *olla podrida.*

Most of these dishes traveled to France with the Spanish women who married French kings. Some recipes were carried by Dumas. But one Spanish cookbook, the property of the friars of the Monastery of Alcántara, was rescued when Napoleon's troops looted the friars' library. The book landed in the lap of General Junot's wife, and her chef, the famous Carême, introduced many of the recipes to France. One such, *pheasant a la Mode d'Alcántara,* was described by the great Escoffier as the only booty of value in the Peninsula War.

WINES AND OTHER POTABLES

Man does not live by bread alone—certainly not in Spain. It's a country that prides itself on its potables . . . with good reason.

You will find that thirsty is not a Spanish word. That is, no Spaniard would carry a thirst long enough to be "thirsty" and neither need you. The country is so well supplied with libations—in variety as well as quantity—that you face the happy problem of many choices.

Everywhere in Spain, it seems, water is bottled and sold. It is a country where water is a treat and, in many cases, a treatment as well. Certain Spanish springs are famous for the healthful qualities of their waters. So many bottled waters are marketed that some Spaniards keep collections of their favorites, just like wines, in "water cellars." Some Spaniards pride themselves on being able to identify the waters of specific springs by taste alone. You don't need such finely tuned taste buds to appreciate the freshness and, in some cases, the tang of Spanish waters. Just order the *agua minerale* in full or half-liter bottles (*litro* or *medio-litro*) with or without carbonation (*con* or *sin gaz*).

Many beer *aficionados* believe that the best beers are produced with pure, superior water and so they are doubly delighted with the Spanish products. Spaniards make an excellent German-type brew. Certain delicious beers can be ordered from one end of the country to another (such as San Miguel and Aguila brands); some are local (Málaga's *Vitoria,* Sevilla's *Cruz Campo,* Granada's *Alhambra*).

Typically, beer in Spain is served ice cold (but never with ice in it). You'll usually find three types—regular, light and dark (*negra*). Beer is riding the crest of a popularity wave and you will see it widely advertised and served by restaurants that a few years ago would not have deigned to have it on their premises. *Cervecerias* are taverns that specialize in serving beers (though they serve wines, too).

Sidra (cider), in the verdant north of Spain, is "the wine of the country." In the Normandy-like areas of *La Montaña,* orchards cover the hillsides with pink blossoms in spring, and in fall yield apples that are prized for cider. You can find two types: still and sparkling.

The still cider is full bodied, with just enough sweetness to take the edge off. It is amber, and though some compare it to British "scrumpy," the raucous, country drink of Somerset, we have found the Spanish cider not nearly so astringent, thin nor harsh. You'll find still *sidra* in and around the northern tier of provinces or in Asturian restaurants, wherever they may be.

Spain's other cider is produced in Asturias but found almost everywhere in Spain—at restaurants, bars and shops where bottled beer, wine and spirits are sold. This extraordinary champagne-like cider—*sidra champaña*—is one of the outstanding palate pleasures of Spain. Asturias's *El Gaitero* (the piper) brand *sidra* is as famous as its soccer team—though it doesn't have as much kick.

Spain's wines are as varied as the topography, climate and moods of its people. They range from the sparkling wines of Catalonia to the astringent Valdepeñas of La Mancha, the crackling Chacoli of Vizcaya or Ribeiro of Galicia to the silky *claretes reservas* of the Rioja, the syrupy nectar of Málaga's muscatels to the incomparable span of superb sherries from Andalucía.

No one can say for sure who brought grapes to Spain first. Some say the Phoenicians, 1,100 years B.C. Others say the Greeks, or the Carthaginians or the Romans. Certainly the Romans, during their 600 years on the Iberian Peninsula, made wine a major industry. Spain was a primary wine source for the Roman world. Some of the Spanish wine regions were famous in Roman times—with good reason. You can try their products—some are of more than local interest and are bottled and sold throughout a region or the entire country. And some are so unusual or superior that they are shipped abroad and have become world famous, such as sherry, Málaga and the champagne-like *espumosos.*

One of the joys of Spanish travel is sampling the many different wines. There are so many that you're not likely to do more than skim the barrel.

Perhaps Catalonia's most widely known wine is its *espumoso*—the sparkling white wine that by any other reckoning would be called champagne. The leading company in the business is Codorniu, a little family wine maker since 1551. It has used Dom Perignon's method of hand turning and double fermentation to pour out 3 million cases of sparkling wines per year. Codorniu estates at San Sadurni de Noya, 64 kilometers (40 miles) west of Barcelona, are surrounded by landscaped gardens and have the world's largest underground wine cellar—26 kilometers (16 miles) of caves, five deep, with 125 million bottles maturing—unusual enough to be declared a national monument.

Around Barcelona, the Panadés region produces outstanding red table wines. The *priorato* of Tarragona has been famous for centuries. Its red reminds many people of Lambrusco; its white wine has its devotees also. *Ampurdán* from Gerona and *alella* from the Barcelona area are other refreshing choices.

From the banks of the Duero River as it flows toward Portugal comes a complex red wine called *Vega Sicilia.* It is Spain's most expensive wine and is often chosen for state banquets given by Spanish embassies abroad.

Around Santiago de Compostela in Galicia you will find a "green wine" similar to the Portuguese *vinho verde.* Spaniards call it *ribeiro,* and it is an aromatic and refreshing cooler, low in alcohol, with enough natural carbonation to be a *petillant,* or crackling, wine. It comes in either red or white, but white, with its fruity bouquet and flavor, is far and away more popular and is the drink of choice with Galicia's famous seafood.

Málaga's celebrated wines are from grapes grown in land shot through with slate. This unusual soil gives a special flavor and aroma to the muscatels of the region.

Spain's premier table wine comes from the Rioja region along the Ebro River in Old Castile and Navarra. Here, superb Bordeaux and Burgundy style wines have been produced with great success, especially in the last century. French wine makers migrated here after the phylloxera blighted vineyards on their side of the Pyrenees in the 1860s. Though most Rioja vintners now use modern techniques for crushing grapes and controling temperatures, wines are made as fine Bordeaux were a century ago. The wines are aged in wood for at least 2 years and often much longer, yielding a mellow, superior wine with great aroma, body and flavor.

For their *Reservas,* Rioja vintners select wine from extraordinary, choice harvests and age them 10 years or more in oak. The results are frequently wines of remarkable complexity, character and finish. It is not unusual to find 50-year-old wines offered by better restaurants—sometimes at prices in the 2,000–40,000 pts. range. Wine lovers should aim to try at least one of these. Among the leading Rioja vintners at present are Paternina, CUNE, Bodegas Bilbainas, Bodegas Franco-Españolas, AGE, Lopez de Heredia and the wine companies of the three Marquéses—de Cáceres, de Murrieta and de Riscal.

The white and rosé wines of Rioja are generally not up to the quality and sophistication of the reds. However, the whites from Ollauri have a pleasant, clean, Riesling character.

The *corriente* or *de mesa* (house wine) you find in Madrid generally comes from New Castile—especially Don Quixote's La Mancha—and is likely to be a Valdepeñas. These are dry, astringent whites and light but flavorful reds.

Well worth trying among the reds are the sweet *carineña* from around Zaragoza, the *cebreros* from Avila, strong *cacabelos* of Leon, heavy *toro* of Zamora (which may reach 18% alcohol) and the *alavesas* of Vitoria. One of the most delightful whites is the *petillant,* golden *chacoli* of the Basque area—though it is sometimes difficult to find because of limited production.

The most famous of Spain's white wines is its sherry. The entire production comes from a 50,000 acre triangle of Andalucían earth demarcated by the towns of Jerez de la Frontera, Puerto de Santa Maria, and Sanlúcar de Barrameda, where the Guadalquivir empties into the Atlantic. The chalky soil gives a singular flavor to the grapes and the wines.

Sherry as we know it today has only been made since the 17th century when the *solera* method was developed. In it, the newly pressed juice goes only into new casks made of American white oak. In December or January the wine is racked off and fortified with grape brandy, bringing its strength to nearly 16%. Then begins the *añadas* stage, during which the wine "decides" whether it is to be dry or sweet according to the development of *flor* (yeast) on top of the liquid. The young wine is put in barrels at the top row of casks that are stacked from four to 12 rows deep. The mellow, aged wine drawn off for bottling always comes from the bottom, or *solera,* casks. The amount taken is replaced from the row just above, and the amount taken from *it* is replaced from the next highest row of casks, and so on to the topmost, most recent row.

The resulting wine is one of five types: *fino*—driest and palest of all, but heavier and stronger than table wines: *manzanilla*—very dry, only from Sanlúcar where the salty sea air enriches the flavor; *amontillado*—more body, color and slightly sweeter, nutty flavor; *oloroso* (fragrant)—still larger body, amber color, sweeter; *cream*—rich, golden brown, heavy, sweet and fragrant. The *fino* and *manzanilla* are generally aperitif wines; the rest are for after dinner or to accompany desserts.

Brandies, liqueurs and spirits are produced in huge quantities in Spain. Perhaps the best brandies are made in Catalonia and Andalucía. Many leading French, Italian and other internationally known aperitif wines, liqueurs and spirits are made in Spain under license from the home distillery. The prices are surprisingly reasonable. And you may find a liquor store where brandies, spirits and liqueurs are sold from the cask at unbelievably low rates. (Among the popular types you will find are *Cointreau, Chartreuse, Grand Marnier, kirsch, amaretto, creme de menthe, aquavit, pernod, triple sec, gin, vodka, vermouths* and *fortified wines.*)

Label Language

Bodega—wine cellar or vintner.
Cosecha—year in which the grapes were harvested.
Embotellado en la bodega—bottled at the winery.
brut or *seco*—dry.
medio seco and *demi-sec*—medium dry.
dulce—sweet.
reserva—from an exceptional harvest, aged at least 6 years in oak.
gran reserva—aged at least 10 years in oak.
tinto—red, full-bodied, usually in slope-shouldered Burgundy-type bottles.
clarete—red, but lighter and softer, usually in high-shouldered Bordeaux-type bottles.
rosado (rosé)—may be in long-necked Riesling bottles or conventional Bordeaux bottles.
blanco—white, in long-necked Riesling bottles or conventional Bordeaux-type bottles.

The Hard Facts–Portugal

PLANNING AHEAD

Costs

The good news is that Portugal is a bargain. Some observers contend that it's the least expensive country in Europe, next to Turkey. Whatever the comparisons, it is, without doubt, a delightful place where your money—in modest outlay—commands both quality and quantity. (Be aware, however, that the inflation rate since 1982 has been 20%.)

The major elements of holiday life—food, lodging and transportation—are relatively less expensive in Portugal than most other places. Furthermore, hotel and restaurant bills include taxes and service. And lodgings *always* include Contintental breakfast. Here are some figures to give you an idea of prevailing rates at this time:

	Lisbon, Porto and Faro	
	Escudos	**$U.S.**
Moderately priced hotel. Per person in double room (½ of double room average) with taxes, service and continental breakfast included:	1400	11.50
Lunch. Inexpensive restaurant, per person, tax and service included	600	4.90
Dinner. Moderate restaurant, per person, tax and service included	750	6.15
Total (escudos)	2750	
Total (dollars)		22.55

More good news is that this garden spot is so fertile, the people are so industrious and the quality of workmanship so high that the standard of living your money buys is remarkably high also. Consider that in Lisbon and prime resort areas the super-luxury hotels charge about 6,000 *escudos* (Portugal currency) per person for a double room, taxes, service and Continental breakfast included. The tab in the finest restaurants may average 1750 escudos—tax, service and regional wine included. Transportation, too, is remarkably inexpensive: Taxi rides anywhere in Lisbon seldom exceed 100 escudos for short rides, 200 for long rides. The modern, clean and efficient buses and trolley buses take you quickly and safely about the city for 16½ to 50 escudos. On the old-fashioned trams you can have an open-air, hang-out-the-window joyride for 16½ to 32½ escudos. Three-minute local telephone calls are 7½ escudos at some public booths and 2½ escudos in the countryside. And you can satisfy your thirst with Luso or Calda da Rainha spa-bottled water for a mere 35 escudos per half-liter, a small bottle of Sagres beer for 25 escudos or a full bottle of the wine of the region for 80 to 150 escudos.

Portuguese prices for luxuries are also reasonable—except heavily taxed imported items such as Scotch (Chivas Regal, 12 year-old, at 2,844 escudos) or American cigarettes (Marlboros, 97 escudos; Winstons, 94 escudos per pack).

For a man's haircut you'll pay between 150 and 250 escudos (and leave a tip of 20). For a woman's wash and set at one of the finest hairdressers the price will be from 300 to 400 escudos and a permanent will run from 900 to 1,600 escudos. A shoeshine will cost 50 escudos or less.

Entertainment is reasonably priced. Opera tickets are about 250–800 escudos; ballet 120–350 escudos; concerts, 80–400 escudos; movies 80–200 escudos. Tickets to bullfights can be as little as 300 escudos and as much as 2,200 escudos. First-division soccer games cost between 150 and 800 escudos. A ticket to the zoo is 120 escudos, the aquarium, a mere 30 escudos. And you'll find *piscina* (swimming pool) tickets are about 30 escudos.

Climate

Portugal is a country for all seasons—depending on where and when you decide to enjoy it. The climate is mild *somewhere* in Portugal even in the depths of winter and is cool and comfortable *somewhere* even on the most sizzling summer days. Whether it's the Algarve's Costa do Sol, with its almond trees in blossom in mid-January or the Costa Verde (Green Coast) in the north with its apple, orange and olive orchards and silky sand beaches, the weather smiles in Portugal.

For example, in mid-July in the Douro River valley, where port wine grapes are grown, temperatures frequently hit 104°F, while just 128 kilometers (80 miles) west, where the Douro meets the Atlantic, the beaches are full and in the Minho hills people are wearing sweaters.

Portugal, for all its Atlantic border, enjoys a Mediterranean climate. From north to south, the coast is washed by gentle (usually) Atlantic breezes. Winter's worst is generally two weeks of frost plus crisp nights and sunny days. Rain and sun alternate in spring and autumn, but summer features almost flawlessly clear skies and brilliant sunshine.

AVERAGE MEAN TEMPERATURES (° F)

	Winter (January)	Spring (April)	Summer (July)	Autumn (October)
North (Porto):	49	60	74	58
Lisbon:	53	62	78	62
Algarve:	61	68	81	64

Holidays and Special Events

Here is a listing of some of the outstanding and enjoyable festivals of the year:

January

11th, Vila Nova de Gaia pays its respects to St. Gonçalo and St. Christopher with 18th-century costumes in a madcap shouting–drumming procession.

February

Mourão—Évora observes Our Lady of the Candelas with religious procession, fun fair, bullfight, fireworks; last week—Loulé in the Algarve celebrates carnival and Almond Blossom Festival: battle of flowers, parades, folk dancing.

March

Ovar holds the first of Lenten processions, called Tertiaries with 14 famous floats, hundreds of marchers in robes of St. Francis; 15th, Lisbon's Graça section has Procession of Senhor dos Passos.

April

The bullfighting season begins on Easter Sunday

Holy Week is an important event observed throughout the country. Notable celebrations are those in Braga, where penitents carry lighted torches and lamps in a procession of floats that takes hours; in Ovar, penitents swing rattles by the light of torches and bonfires.

May

Barcelos—Festival of the Crosses, bands, stilted men, big heads, folklore festival and costumed procession with 50,000 fires along banks of Cavádo River. 12–13th, Fátima—first of annual religious pilgrimage dates.

June

12–29th, Festival of Saints, Lisbon, starting St. Anthony's eve in Alfama, lights, decorations, street dancing, singing, bonfires. 23–24, Porto—Festival of St. John, with all-night folk festival, swatting with garlic and balm-mint switches, dancing, singing.

July

Festival of Colete Encarnado, 2–3rd, Vila França de Xira, with competition of fandango dancing, amateur bullfighting in streets. Faro, 15–31st, Festival of Senhora do Carmo, annual fair with folk dancing, singing. 18th, Guimarães, São Torcato International Folklore Festival.

August

5–8th, Guimarães, Festas Gualterianas, three days of parades, musical bands, folk singing, dancing. 8–10th, Portuzelo—Festival of Sta. Marta, traditional costumes, dance, music competitions, International Folklore Festival. 5–8th, Setúbal, Festival of Barrete Verde—running of the bulls, folk music and dance, bullfights, grilled sardines. Late August, Viana do Castelo—Festival of Senhora da Agonia, with a vast handcrafts market, folk music and dance, men on stilts, and big heads, women in traditional costumes.

September

6–8th, Viseu, Pilgrimage of Senhora dos Remédios, hundreds of thousands of pilgrims, procession, battle of flowers, folk music and dancing. First week, Palmela, Grape Harvest Festival with song and dance, running of bulls, bullfights. Third week, Ponte do Lima, Feiras Novas—folk music and dance, pony race, bullfight, folklore festival.

October

Faro, 12–13th, Santa Iria Fair, including folk music and dancing. Third week, October Fair, Castro Verde, where a great handcraft exhibition and sale and cattle show take place.

November

8–12th, Golega, Santarém, St. Martin's Fair, the national horse show, with races, competitions, parades accompanied by chestnuts and *água-pé.*

In addition to these events, there are recurring market days in many places, which are colorful and fun: Albufeira—third Sunday each month; Azeltão—first Sunday; Barcelos—each Thursday; Lagos—first Sunday; Portimão—first Monday; Silves—second and third Mondays; Sintra—second and fourth Sundays; Tavira—third Monday.

Travel Agents and Tour Operators

No matter where you live, your town is likely to have at least one travel retailer—a travel agent. And today, most travel agents can custom tailor a trip to your needs with little difficulty. In larger cities, travel agencies put together itineraries, or packages, and market them at considerable savings over the custom-tailored trips.

Tour operators are travel wholesalers, specialists in putting together all the ingredients of a trip, from departure to return and all the major elements in between. Because Portugal is such a popular destination, you will find many package tours arranged by tour operators are offered through travel agents and directly to the public via advertisements in magazines and newspapers. Here are some of the tour operators and retailers who specialize in package trips to Portugal.

In the United States

Abreu Tours, 60 E. 42nd St. New York, NY 10165; (212)611–0555.

American Express, American Express Plaza, New York, NY 10004; (800)241–1700.

Atesa Marsans, 500 Fifth Avenue, New York, NY 10036; (212)730–0417.

Catholic World Travel Service, 1019 19th St. NW, Washington, D. C. 20036; (202)293–2277.

Thomas Cook, 380 Madison Avenue, New York, NY 10017; (212)-949–0400.

Cosmos of London, 69–15 Austin Street, Forest Hills, NY 11375; (800)-221–0742

Globus/Gateway, 727 West 7 Street, Los Angeles, CA 90017; (213)-485–8733.

Maupintour, 900 Mass. Street, Lawrence, KS 66044; (800)255–4266.

Olson Travel Organization, 5855 Green Valley Circle, Culver City, CA 90230; (800)421–2255.

Percival Tours, Inc., 1 Tandy Center Plaza, Ft. Worth, TX 76102; (817)-870–0300.

RN Tours, 666 Old Country Road, Garden City, NY 11530; (516)-222–9090.

Travcoa-Travel Corp. of America, 875 North Michigan Avenue, Chicago IL 60611; (312)951–2900.

In Canada

Aviz Holidays, 4136 Bathurst Street, Toronto; (416)630–5024.

CP Holidays, 69 Yonge Street, Toronto; (416)675–4344.

Thos. Cook & Sons, 2020 University St., Montreal, Que.

In Britain

Cosmos, Cosmos House, 1 Bromley Common, Bromley, Kent.

Thos. Cook & Sons, c/o Harrod's, Knightsbridge, London SWIX 7XL.

There's a remarkable range of vacation packages available through operators—from "stay-put" holidays to escorted bus groups and do-it-yourself, fly–drive arrangements. Among the many, here is a sampling to give you an idea of the range.

RN Tours, with TAP-Air Portugal offers a package called "Portuguese Quest," which takes you on an 11-day tour to some of the country's outstanding sites: Obidos, the 12th-century walled city, the monastery at

Batalha, the shrine at Fatima. You also visit Coimbra and its ancient university, the fairy-tale castle of Buçaco, and Aveiro, with its swan-necked boats. There are stops in Porto and in medieval Guimarães, where Portugal was "born." Visits to fishing villages and the old city of Évora, the castle of Saint Philip at Setúbal and the resort city, Sesimbra, are also included. For the nine nights, all breakfasts, eight lunches, seven dinners the package price, double occupancy, high season, is $508 for land arrangements.

Abreu Tours, with TAP Air Portugal, offers "Free and Easy" fly–drive vacations featuring six nights in luxury hotels chosen by you. In one, Abreu's "Freedom Algarve" package, you drive to Portugal's southern coast, where you have reservations for the first night plus vouchers valid in leading resort hotels so you can move on—or stay put and enjoy the sun, sea and golf in one place, such as Vilamoura's Hotel Dom Pedro (per-person double occupancy rate is $26 per night plus $84 for car rental).

TWA's 15-day luxury motorcoach tour "The Flamenco" visits choice sights and sites in Portugal: white-walled Elvas; Lisbon's ancient Moorish Alfama quarter and Jeronimos monastery; Sintra's shining palaces; Nazare's plaid-clad fishermen; Fatima shrine; storied Coimbra and Guarda, with its 16th-century cathedral. The Spanish portion includes Salamanca, Avila, El Greco's Toledo, Madrid's Prado and Royal Palace, Cordoba, Granada, Sevilla, the Costa del Sol and an excursion to Tangier. The tour tariff tops out at $598 per person double occupancy, plus air fare.

"Captivating Kingdoms," offered by TAP with many tour operators, is a deluxe way to go. Chauffeured by an experienced English-speaking guide, you'll visit Lisbon and its Moorish Alfama quarter; medieval Obidos; Nazare's boats and beaches; Fatima shrine; Tomar's haunted Knights Templar headquarters. Overnights include Bucaco's royal hunting lodge palace; Estremoz's 13th-century palace Pousada da Rainha Santa Isabel; posh luxury in a Moorish fortress at Pousada de Palmela; Sintra's elegant Palacio dos Seteais. The tour price ranges from $799 per person downward, plus air fare.

From Britain's Gatwick airport you can fly directly to Faro (Algarve) from £132 (approx. $185) round trip, midweek (YLXAP fares).

Sources of Information

The Portuguese National Tourist Offices (PNTO) are excellent resources for useful, up-to-date information. They supply literature about regions, cities, specialties—cuisine, handcrafts, festivals—where the action is and where the historic as well as religious features are. They also have the money-saving "Portugal on a Silver Platter" booklets (see Perks for details). The PNTO address in the United States is: 548 Fifth Avenue, New York, NY 10036; (212)354–4403.

In Canada, PNTO is at 1801 McGill College Avenue, Suite 1150, Montreal, P.Q. H3A 2N4; (514)282–1264.

In Britain, PNTO is at New Bond Street House, 1–5 New Bond Street, London W1Y 0DB, U.K.; 4933873.

Another source to tap is TAP-Air Portugal; check the yellow pages of your telephone directory for nearest office. TAP's WATS line telephone number in the USA is 1(800)221–2061.

In Portugal you will find well-marked local *Turismo* offices, staffed by people fluent in English, in every city and virtually every hamlet, village and town. A bonus for travelers: These offices are open beyond the call of duty hours—often until 9 P.M., as well as Sundays and holidays.

The major ones are Lisbon: Avenida Antonio Augusto de Aguiar, 86 (phone 575086); Praça dos Restauradores (Palacio Foz) (phone 367031); Lisbon Airport (phone 885974); Santa Apolonia Railway Station (phone 867848). Porto: Praça Dom João I, 25 (phone 317514). Faro: Faro Airport (phone 22582).

In Lisbon, for information by telephone in English, call 369450 or 575086.

The Portuguese radio network broadcasts a daily program in English, "Holidays in Portugal." It carries useful information for visitors and is heard from 8:15 to 8:30 A.M. on standard band 765 kHz and via FM at 94.3 MHz.

Packing

Because Portugal's climate is moderate, you'll want to pack lots of drip-dry and cotton clothing. Evenings are cool, so include a light sweater or light-weight wool suit. In case you're heading into the mountains or plan to visit in a cooler season, carry a raincoat that can double as windbreaker. At the coldest, Portugal requires only the normal topcoat and fall woolens worn in the northeast. And in the balmy summery areas, shorts and sports shirt will suffice during the day. (You can pick up an inexpensive straw hat at the beach.)

Two advisable carry-alongs are sun lotion or screen for your skin type and insect repellents (to give you peaceful sleep in places that do not have screens).

Kodak and other brands of film are widely available. Kleenex is in short supply, though boxes can be bought. You're not likely to find it in your hotel. If you're planning to picnic, either bring along a corkscrew and Swiss army knife or purchase one of the excellent corkscrews and knives available in Portuguese hardware stores.

The security people at the airports are very accommodating and will hand your camera and film past the X-ray machine. However, if you want to make sure your film is protected, put it in a lead-shielded bag.

Portugal's quaint cobbled streets and uneven, tesselated marble side-walks play havoc with flimsy shoes. Bring sturdy ones (or plan to buy replacements—leather goods are well made and bargain priced).

Don't forget your pocket calculator. You'll find it handy for currency, mileage and temperature conversions.

Documentation

Your passport is the only document needed to enter and enjoy Portugal for up to two months. (If you plan to stay longer than 60 days, you will need to secure a visa from a Portuguese consulate.) No health certificate is required. If you're going to rent a car and drive it yourself, bring along a valid driver's license.

No visas required for American, British or Canadian visitors for stays of 60 days

Handicapped Traveler

Portugal isn't ready for people who can't walk and climb easily. First, it's a hilly terrain in towns and cities, as well as in the countryside. This is especially true of Lisbon and Porto. Second, hotels and restaurants make few concessions to people's handicaps. Not that you have to be a goat to scramble up and down steps, over curbs and through uneven cobblestoned alleys. However, hotels have several steps up or down to their lobbies and some of the most interesting hostelries, such as the *pousadas,* are built into old castles on hills, rocky promontories and isolated spots purposely chosen for their inaccessibility, which means that today's visitors have to climb. Restaurants are often on upper floors or sites that capitalize on views—without the benefit of elevators. Wheelchair access from street to sidewalk and from street to hotel or restaurant is relatively rare in cities, even in Lisbon, and almost nonexistent elsewhere.

GETTING THERE

By Air

Major ports of entry to modern Portugal are its international airports in Porto, Lisbon and Faro. TAP serves these three cities from major European and U.S. cities, especially London, New York and Chicago, with daily flights and from other cities such as Boston, weekly. Flying time from the USA is about seven hours; from Britain, only two hours. Other airlines serving Portugal are British Airways, CPAir, TWA.

Lowest round trip APEX midweek airfare at press time, New York-Lisbon, was $582 in mid-summer

By Car

If you drive, you'll enter Portugal through one of the Spanish border points. The roads are decent and you'll have no difficulties or special delays at border check points. Your only complication may come from the droves of Spanish tourists who flock across the border to buy handcrafts and port and Madeira wines, which are such bargains in Portugal. We've seen bumper-to-bumper traffic on the Valença-Túy bridge inching along for hours on a holiday weekend. Try to time your border crossing for non-rush-hour periods. Border posts are usually closed at night.

Be sure to have insurance that covers you in Portugal as well as the country you're leaving. Driving is on the right side of the road, and international signs and symbols are used. Most roads are two lanes, so your patience is likely to be tested thoroughly and often as you find yourself behind slow-moving trucks, buses or flocks of sheep, cattle or pony carts.

By Train

There are express trains from Paris and Madrid (the daily Sud Express makes the Paris–Lisbon run in 25 hours; the Lusitania Express/TER from Madrid does it in 11 hours). Within the country the well-developed electric rail system has good equipment and a well-deserved reputation for efficiency. Both Eurailpass and Youth Passes are good on Portuguese trains.

By Bus

Portugal's state-owned and-operated bus system uses modern buses that are quick, clean, comfortable, air-conditioned and have tinted glass, picture windows. You can travel nearly everywhere in the country via bus, if you have the time.

FORMALITIES ON ARRIVAL

Customs

You may bring in 200 cigarettes or half a pound of tobacco; a quart of alcohol; a bottle of wine; a reasonable amount of perfume for personal use. In general, you are allowed items for noncommercial use, such as still and movie and video cameras, recorders, radios, typewriters and sporting equipment. (If you are a hunter and bring more than one rifle and 50 cartridges you'll have to make special arrangements with the Portuguese consulate ahead of time.) If you plan to take your pet with you, Rollo will need a veterinarian's certification that he has had his distemper and rabies shots. As for cash or travelers' checks, you may bring in reasonable amounts.

In our experience, Portuguese customs authorities are relaxed. When you arrive at the Lisbon airport, for instance, after you retrieve your bags you simply head for the "nothing to declare" exit and go out to the taxi ramp. If you arrive by car or train at a border point, the officials will ask what goods you have to declare. If there is nothing, chances are that you will be waved through without even a spot check.

Money

Portuguese money is based on the *escudo,* which consists of 100 centavos. In general use are ½, 1, 2½, 5, 10 and 25 escudo coins and paper notes for 20, 50, 100, 500, 1,000 and 5,000 escudos. Since most transactions are in the 5 to 500 escudo range, you'll use these lower denominations most, especially the 20 and 50 escudo notes. Prices are quoted in escudos, with the sign ($) where we would expect the decimal: thus 1024.5 escudos is quoted 1,024$50. This *can* be confusing at first.

Travelers' checks and major international credit cards are welcome in hotels and most shops and restaurants in cities, towns and resort areas. In smaller shops and bistros in remote villages, of course, escudos are necessary. In some instances an establishment will accept a personal check. Sometimes you will find clerks reluctant to accept credit cards for small value purchases. You will also find that bank credit cards are preferred because they cost merchants less and they can secure payment from their local bank faster.

Banks are open 8:30 A.M.–12 noon and 1–2:30 P.M., Monday through Friday.

Getting into Town

From Lisbon's airport the green bus runs to the city center every 15 minutes. The trip takes 20 to 30 minutes, depending on traffic, and stops at designated *paragems* (stops), some of which are close to major hotels (ask the driver). The fare is a modest 100 escudos. The alternative is the taxi, one of Lisbon's great bargains. The metered ride from the airport to a Lisbon destination should cost approx. 250 escudos ($1.96 as of this writing), with a possible 100 escudos supplement if bags are placed in the trunk.

In Porto and Faro, taxis may be your best bet to go from the airport to your destination. They are reasonable, quick and available.

SETTLING DOWN

Choosing a Hotel

The several types of accommodations in Portugal are categorized by the national tourism organization, which also inspects and rates them. The categories are hotels; residential-hotels (which do not have restaurants and serve only breakfasts); apartment-hotels; *estalagens* (which are supposed to be of historic or touristic interest and are "inns" rather than hotels; there is great latitude in this category); *pousadas* (government-owned and-run inns); *albergarias;* boardinghouses; motels; and *pensões.*

Realistically, you are likely to be most interested in the *pousadas,* hotels and estalagens. They are the most appealing and widely available accommodations. The *pousadas* are similar to the Spanish *paradors.* There are 27 of these "resting places" or inns dotted around the country. Many are in castles, palaces, monasteries or historic buildings. Loving attention has been given to the use of handicrafts, art, regional cuisine and wines, and each pousada is completely modern in plumbing, wiring and heating. Their only handicap is their few rooms, which means that advance reservations are a *must* and can be made through Marketing Ahead (see Tour Operators).

Excellent hotels exist in Lisbon and resort areas. They carry government ratings of from one to five (top) stars, which help you determine the quality of accommodations. In a three- or four-star hotel you can expect a clean, well-kept room with one or more chairs, desk and telephone, private bath that includes tub and shower, as well as WC, lavatory and bidet. Five-star and grand luxe hotels have all these features plus numerous luxury touches—more space, air conditioning, balconies, swimming pool, sauna, shops and more. All hotel quotations include Continental breakfast, service and taxes.

Estalagens and *albergarias* are hybrids. They are supposed to resemble pousadas—in locations or buildings of unusual interest—but are owned and run by private entrepreneurs. Though they are star rated, on a lower scale, they vary tremendously and have no verifiable claim to quality or esthetic interest in their furnishings or kitchens. Thus, a four-star estalagen or albergaria must be viewed in a different light from a four-star hotel.

Pensãos are to be found in most towns and cities and run the gamut from dreary to dramatic, some with cascades of flowers spilling from sunny balconies and cosy rooms. You are expected to take full or demiboard.

Your best strategy in deciding upon accommodations is to ask to see a room. This is a perfectly acceptable procedure in Portugal and, indeed, is often expected. Clerks at the reception desks are almost without exception extremely helpful and friendly and understand and speak English.

If you do not have the opportunity to see the room before booking, our hotel ratings will help you select the best for your money in various categories. Our categories, however, do not always coincide with the official ratings.

There are only a few hotel chains in Portugal. The Sheraton, Intercontinental and Penta are members of international chains. And there is one local chain, Dom Pedro, which has a half dozen hotels in Portuguese cities. They are all four- or five-star establishments.

For advance information on hotels in Portugal ask the Portuguese National Tourist Office for copies of the latest pocket hotel guides. Each booklet includes listings of hotels in two regions. The most popular one contains Lisbon and Costa de Lisboa and gives the name, address, telephone number, number of rooms, star category and features (such as pool, tennis, bar, shops, garage) the hotels offer and information on pricing regulations. The booklets are free. The listings do not give prices.

When you arrive in a Portuguese town, ask the local Turismo office for an up-to-date list of hotels and accommodations in the area.

There is a premium on parking in the cities. Be sure to check whether the hotel where you're thinking of staying has parking space or a garage.

Choosing a Restaurant

You can eat well at nearly any price level in Portugal. The challenge and the delight are in choosing from the many dining places available. Some terms to help you focus on the kind of place you may be seeking are as follows:

Cervejarias—specialize in beer and hearty, simple fare.
Churrascurias—charcoal grilled seafood and meat entrees.
Tascas (means pocket)—tiny bistros where wine and simple dishes are served.
Casas do Fado—late-night taverns–restaurants featuring singers and instrumentalists presenting *fado* music. Expect a minimum charge per person.
Pastelerias and coffeehouses (sometimes called Brasilerias)—traditional espresso and pastries are served; they range from handsome, 19th-century settings to dayglow plastic and neon.
Snackbars and cafeterías—new on the scene and include burgeoning burger restaurants.

Eating places post their menus outside or in their windows. This gives you an excellent indication of what's being served and the prices. A "menu of the day" includes choice of soups, entrees and desserts with wine for a set price.

…ually bargain priced and feature the fresh fare of the day. If the m… …osted, by all means step inside and ask to see it—and look about to … the decor and hygiene appeal to you. Decent lighting, clean walls, ceiling, spotless tablecloths and shining glass and tableware are standard and you should have no difficulty finding them. (In *tascas* and *cervejarias,* fresh, clean paper often substitutes for a cloth table covering.) The maitre d' will help explain alien terms on the menu; if his English isn't that good, you'll still enjoy the sign language.

Good restaurants? The government awards from one to four crossed spoon-and-fork symbols to eating places (four is tops), but we discovered wide discrepancies in the quality of food and appearance of the places rated.

One index of quality and value is the number of Portuguese dining at a restaurant. (Which ones are the Portuguese? The men often wear their jackets cape style over their shoulders.)

A useful listing of all restaurants, hotels and pensions in Portugal with their official ratings, addresses, phone numbers and useful information about wines and regional specialties is the annual *Roteiro Gastronomico Hoteis, Pensoes and Restaurantes de Portugal,* published annually and available, free, from the central Turismo office in Lisbon at Palacio Foz.

Learning to Cope

Tipping

Hotel and restaurant bills include tax and service, but it is customary to round off the bill and leave perhaps 50 escudos in an inexpensive restaurant, 100 escudos in a more expensive place—but no more than 5% of the bill's total in any event. For a metered ride in a taxi, tip 5 or 10 escudos on a small fare or up to 20 for a considerable ride (but not more than 10%.) For the bellman at a deluxe hotel, 50 escudos per bag is plenty; at a small establishment, 20 escudos will do. And after your stay, leave the maid 50 escudos if you're alone; 100 escudos for two or a family. If the concierge renders a valuable special service of some sort, 100 escudos should suffice. On a bar bill, leave a few escudos on the plate.

If you use a credit card to pay a restaurant bill, you may prefer to leave your tip in escudos, on the plate, rather than include it on the credit card slip. *Reason:* The credit card process is still imperfectly understood in many areas and though you may write in a tip in the proper space, it may not find its way to the waiter.

Business Hours

In general, the business offices are open from 9 or 9:30 A.M. to noon or 12:30 P.M. and from 2:30 to 6 or 6:30 P.M. daily except weekends and holidays. Banks are usually open 8:30 A.M. to noon and 1 to 2:30 P.M. Monday through Friday.

Shops are usually open from 9 A.M. to 1 P.M. and 3 to 7 P.M. Mondays through Fridays and 9 A.M. to 1 P.M. Saturdays. However, there are now modern shopping complexes—called drugstores, curiously enough—which are open from 10 A.M. to midnight, day in, day out. They make shopping possible on rainy days or after downtown shops have called it a day. One such complex is *Centro Commercial Imaviz* at Avenida Fontes Pereira de Melo, 35 in Lisbon. It has 54 boutiques, shops, stores, and restaurants under one roof (more or less).

Most restaurants now serve lunch from 12 noon and dinner from about 7 P.M.

For theater, you'll make the opening if you arrive before 9:30 P.M.

Church hours vary, but figure 7 A.M. to 1 P.M. and 4 to around 7 P.M.

Museums and monuments are closed on Mondays and open from 10 A.M. to 5 P.M. other days, but often are closed from 1 to 2:30 for lunch.

Electricity

Don't be shocked to learn that the current is 220 volts, 50 cycles, AC. The sockets take round plugs—except in some luxury hotel installations where special ambidextrous sockets accommodate both the round European and flat U.S. plugs. Best take an adapter and a transformer with you.

Water and Drink

The United States Embassy says the water in Lisbon and Porto is safe to drink, though high mineral content may upset some stomachs. In the suburbs during the dry season and in other parts of the country all year around you're advised to stick to bottled water. There are many excellent types available at modest cost, *sem gás* (still) or *com gás* (carbonated).

Pasteurized milk is safe, but untreated milk may transmit tuberculosis.

Turista, or the "Portuguese complaint," though rare, may afflict travelers here, as elsewhere, because of unfamiliar food and drink and an overtaxed digestive system. The amount of olive oil Portuguese use in cooking may upset some stomachs, but experienced travelers cope by ordering dishes that avoid or minimize it, such as broiled, boiled or baked entrees. And though the temptation of gorgeous shellfish may be overwhelming, be warned that some visitors have reported severe indigestion and diarrhea from raw clams and oysters consumed in inland areas of Portugal. Raw vegetables should be washed carefully, and fresh fruits should be washed or peeled.

Communications

Letters can be mailed by leaving them with the hotel concierge, who also sells stamps. Other stamp sellers are found in shops designated *correios* and at the local post and telegraph center in each town. You'll find red, cylindrical post boxes on the streets; each has a small dial that tells when the next pickup will be.

You can place a telephone call from pay phones (red, British-type call boxes), post offices and nearly any hotel. The easiest way is to present the telephone number to the desk clerk who will have the switchboard operator make the call while you use the hotel phone booth. You'll pay the deskman after the call. In large cities the post office telephone desk is open all day for long distance and overseas calls. The operator will place your call and charge you for the time units used.

Portugal's pay phones are reliable and easy to work. At the top of the box is an inclined slot in which you place one or more coins. You lift the receiver and dial your number; if the call goes through, the first coin drops automatically. The second one rolls down the inclined slot into position and will be gobbled up by the machine only if needed. To send a cable, take your message—preferably printed or typed—to your concierge. He will phone it in and add the charges to your bill. In Lisbon, you can go directly to the Marconi office, 131 Rua de S. Julião and place the call yourself. All Portuguese hotel staffers recommend long distance telephone over cable because of the speed, certainty of delivery and economy.

Avoid hotel surcharges on your international calls by calling collect or using your telephone company "calling card"

Language

It may look like a dialect of Spanish, but when you hear Portuguese spoken you'll find it doesn't *sound* at all like Spanish. Nevertheless, if you can read Spanish you can often puzzle out the meaning of many Portuguese phrases. Don't expect all Portuguese to understand or respond to your spoken Spanish, however. Many don't or won't. Far more useful are spoken English or French. The ancient "English connection" going back to 1308 has resulted in relatively widespread study and understanding of the language. You'll find that almost all hotel clerks understand and speak some English, as do many restaurant personnel. Though many guides in museums do not speak English, a fair number do. In the country at large, English comprehension dwindles in direct proportion to the distance from Lisbon or Porto. In the Algarve and the Estoril-Cascais resort areas where so many British people have sunned for so many years, English is virtually a second language.

The peaceful cooperation between England and Portugal is the world's oldest alliance

Portuguese has certain peculiar characteristics, the most baffling being that a number of its sounds are not pronounced as written. The *ao* (as in *São*) has a *sa-on* sound. The *s* (as in Cascais) has a *sh* sound. A *c* with a tail (ç) has an *s* sound: Praça is pronounced "prasa."

Medical Assistance

First stop is the concierge, who can call the necessary medical practitioner, dentist or required facility.

For all-out emergency (or ambulance,) telephone 115 or call the appropriate American, Canadian or British embassy or consulate.

If you need first aid or quick action of some type in Lisbon, ask for the closest *Centro de Enfermagem.*

There is no American hospital, but there is a small British one in Portugal. It is at 49 Rua Saraiva Calvalho, Lisbon, phone 602020. All the staff members speak English and there is a daily outpatient clinic between 10:30 A.M. and 1 P.M. and 6 to 8 P.M. The night emergency phone number is 603785.

You may prepare yourself by securing the free listing of physicians supplied by the International Association for Medical Assistance to Travelers IAMAT. see section of Spain - The Hard Facts

Measurements

Portugal uses the metric system of weights and measures. This chart for converting one to the other can be useful.

1 centimeter (cm.) =.39 inch	1 inch = 2.54 cm.
1 meter (m.) = 3.28 feet or 1.1 yds.	1 foot = 0.31 m.
	1 yd. = 0.91m.
1 kilometer (km.) = 0.62 miles	1 mile = 1.61 km.
1 liter (1.) = 0.26 gal.	1 gal. U.S. = 3.79 l.
1 gram (g.) = 0.035 oz.	1 oz. = 28 g.
1 kilogram (kg.) = 35.27 oz. or 2.21 lbs.	1 lb. = 454 g.
1 metric ton (t.) = 1.1 tons U.S.	

In short, a liter is very close to a quart, a meter to a yard, and a centimeter to a half-inch.

Perks

Don't buy a Eurailpass if your European trip is confined solely to Portugal — buy a kilometric or tourist ticket, instead

Perhaps the most frequent money-saving perk used by travelers to Portugal is Eurailpass or Eurail Youth Pass. Information and the tickets are available through your travel agent or the Eurailpass offices. For the USA and Canada, the office is at Eurailpass, Box Q, Staten Island, NY, 10305.

Eurailpasses are sold for periods of 7, 14, 21 days, 1, 2, or 3 months and entitle you to unlimited first-class train travel during that period.

The Eurail Youth Pass is sold to people under 26 years of age in the USA and Canada and gives you 1 or 2 months of second-class transportation through any or all of 15 countries of Europe. You have to pay extra for seat reservations.

An Interrail Pass is sold for use in more than 20 countries of Europe. It gives you the right to travel at half-fare, second class. These tickets can be bought in Europe.

If you're over 65, you can travel all year for half-fare on the Portuguese railways.

A kilometric ticket is offered by Portuguese railways. It is in the form of a passbook that is good for 3 months or 3,000 kilometers (1,800 miles). You can buy these for either first- or second-class travel. That's not all: You can specify "express" or regional trains and either first or second class and pay the appropriate amount—a considerable saving, however you figure it.

Tourist Tickets are offered to families of three or more people (children up to age 18). They are good for a minimum of 150 kilometers (90 miles) and cost full fare for one adult, half-fare for others who are 12 or more and one-fourth for those between 4 and 11 (children under 4 ride free on Portuguese trains).

The group ticket may be of interest. It's available to groups of 10 or more who are traveling 100 kilometers (60 miles) or more. They have a 20% discount. (If your group is 15 or more, you qualify for one free ticket.)

When you're in Lisbon, remember that you can buy discount tickets that are good on buses and streetcars at the ticket office, Rua da Aurea, Santa Justa elevator. A tourist ticket that is valid for 7 days entitles you to ride on any public transportation in the city during that time—bus, streetcar, subway, funicular and elevator its price is 620$00. You can buy 20 bus or streetcar tickets for 11$25.

Portugal's museums are free on certain days, generally Saturdays and Sundays. Though the fees are seldom as much as 40 escudos per person, every little freebee helps pay for something else.

Which brings us to the "Portugal on a Silver Platter" promotion. The Portuguese National Tourist Office has a 24-page booklet listing hotels, restaurants, shops, auto rental agencies, beauty salons and a wide range of commercial establishments that offer discounts or gifts (such as a half-bottle of wine with a meal). The discounts range up to 20%, with presentation of the booklet, which is free from PNTO.

For tourist information by telephone, in English, the Lisbon Tourist Council will respond if you call 706341.

Oenophiles can pursue their interest in depth. By writing ahead, a group of people with a serious desire to learn more about Portugal's wines may be welcomed by both the port wine and Dão wine associations. Experts will talk to you, describe the magic of wine production from vine to bottle and provide literature and opportunities to observe the process. The port wine organization is Instituto do Vinho do Porto, Rua Ferreira Borges, 4000 Porto, Portugal. The Dão wine producers are at Federacão dos Vinicultores do Dão, Rua D. Duarte, 102, 3500 Viseu, Portugal.

If you have a car and wish to visit some *quintas* where the wine is produced, check with the tourism office in cities in the wine districts, such as Porto and Viseu. They will be able to tell you which nearby quintas welcome visitors. One such quinta is Quinta de Aveleda in the town of Penafiel. It's open weekdays; closed noon to 2 P.M.

The "American Women's Club of Lisbon" is an organization that maintains a library and thrift shop and plans cultural and social activities and trips in which you may be able to participate. Address American Women's Club of Lisbon, Avenida de Sintra, 3, Cascais (phone 280252.)

If you're in the country on business, you may wish to look in on the American Chamber of Commerce in Portugal, 155–5 Esq., Rua D. Estefania, 1000 Lisboa (phone 572561.)

The American Club of Lisbon sponsors a monthly businessmen's lunch. Prominent figures speak on topics of current interest. Visiting businessmen may inquire about attending: American Club of Lisbon, 38–1° D, Rua Castilho, Lisbon (phone 539650.)

GETTING AROUND

By Air

Portugal has a well-developed, modern air transportation system. On its Lisbon–Porto and Lisbon–Faro runs TAP uses Boeing 727 jetliners. For charter and regularly scheduled flights to 29 destinations in smaller cities, TAP Regional Service uses 12-passenger planes. The distances are, after all, not great. Portugal measures only 560 kilometers (350 miles) north–south and 218 kilometers (137 miles) east–west.

Nevertheless, flying saves valuable time. Regular jet service from Lisbon to the Algarve takes only 40 minutes (and costs 3,500$00). Trains make the trip in four hours, but to drive may take you five or six hours. From Lisbon to Porto, flight time is 45 minutes (also 3,500$00), the express trains take three hours; you'll be lucky to drive it in six hours. The 90-minute flight to Madeira costs 8540$00.

By Train

The rail network reaches 38 of Portugal's 40 towns with well-maintained equipment. The key runs of interest to most visitors are the several daily express trains from Lisbon to Porto and the special *Rapido Sotaventos* to Algarve points. There are also night sleeper trains; on some you can ship your car. Another heavily used line links Lagos, Faro and other Algarve spots.

The fare structure has a number of clauses in it that may be to your benefit: Children under four years travel free; children from age 4 to 12 travel for half-fare. Seniors (over 65) travel for half-fare if the trip is more than 50 kilometers. There are also three types of reduced rate tickets: (1) tourist ticket—for unlimited travel for 7, 14 or 21 days; (2) family tickets—used by married couples, or by unmarried brothers and sisters under 21 or by a husband or wife with children under 21 for distances over 150 kilometers; (3) kilometer booklets—sold for 3,000 kilometers to be covered within three months. Another possibility is group tickets—ten or more persons going more than 100 kilometers receive a 20% discount.

There is excellent service on the heavily traveled Lisbon–Estoril–Cascais run via electric trains. The trip to Cascais takes 25 minutes and costs 65$00; there are 100 trains per day, both ways.

International rail service goes to both Porto and Lisbon. Major trains connect with Madrid and Paris—the famous Sud-Express, Lusitania-Express, Lisbon-Express and International.

By Car

There are at least a dozen auto rental agencies in Portugal, including Avis, Auto Europe and Inter Rent, Hertz and Atesa.

The road system varies from multilane, divided superhighways (called motorways) to "goat tracks" in remote interior regions. Sections of some motorways are toll roads.

Driving is on the right side of the road and the operating speeds, according to Portuguese traffic and highway regulations, are 60 kilometers per hour in towns, 90 kilometers per hour out of town on "regular roads," and 120 kilometers per hour on Auto Estradas (where the minimum speed is 40 kilometers per hour). Portuguese drivers observe these limits about as rigorously as they adhere to the one that requires them to decrease speed when being passed by another vehicle. Many Portuguese drivers zoom along as though blissfully unaware of speed limits.

International motoring signs are used; cars entering an intersection from the right have the right of way unless contrary information is posted.

Because so much of the countryside is stitched together by two-lane roads, driving can be frustrating when traffic is heavy and you are behind a slow truck spewing acrid diesel smoke that engulfs cars following it. Reckon on averaging 50 kilometers per hour in the areas beyond superhighways. Road hazards (pony carts, sheep, and so on), heavy traffic, construction work and the possibility of single-lane or gravel-surface travel, hairpin turns and snaking mountain roads plus wet or slick surfaces will slow you down.

If you have a breakdown, the distance to a roadside SOS telephone, service station or village is likely to be short. Be aware, however, that service stations are open from 8:30 A.M. to 7 P.M. Monday to Friday. Most gasoline stations are open from 7 A.M. to midnight daily and some around the clock (but don't plan on it). The Automovel Club de Portugal has reciprocal arrangements with counterparts overseas such as American Automobile Association and Royal Automobile Club. It operates a towing service and you can telephone for assistance: north of Coimbra—292712; south of Coimbra—775402, 775475, 775491.

Incidentally, gasoline prices are identical from station to station, so don't waste time shopping around.

By Bus

Several motorcoach companies run regular daily service to popular destinations such as the Algarve towns, Porto, Espinho, Braga, Aveiro and Covilha. Among these are RN, Capritur, Mundial Turismo and Concorde. You can check schedules and book tickets through concierges or travel agencies.

By Boat

There are ferry services that cross the Tagus to and from Lisbon. It was the only way to go until they built Europe's longest suspension bridge. The ride gives you a pleasant, cooling "sea" voyage for 30$00 one way.

GOING HOME

Be ready to pay 1000$00 airport tax before you fly home.

American Customs

If you haven't taken advantage of the exemptions within 30 days previously, Americans returning to the USA from abroad may claim as exempt any purchases made up to the value of $400 retail (keep your receipts), provided you have been out of the country for at least 48 hours. Above your exemption, the next $1,000 worth of goods will be assessed at 10% of the retail value, and after that, things get more complicated. Every family member is allowed the same exemptions, and they can be pooled, but exemptions for alcohol and perfume can't be claimed by children under 18.

Don't try to bring in fruit, plants, soil, meats, etc. If you plan to acquire foods abroad, you might be wise to write for the following pamphlet: "No. 1083, Travelers' Tips on Bringing Food, Plant and Animal Products into the U.S.," available from the U.S. Dept. of Agriculture, Federal Center Bldg.,

Hyattsville, Maryland, 20782. You may mail home small packages valued up to $25 without paying duty (no booze, perfume or tobacco, however.)

British Customs

If you return to Britain directly from Portugal, you are allowed, duty free, the following: 200 cigarettes (or 100 cigarillos, or 50 cigars, or 25 gr. of tobacco); 1 liter of strong spirits (or 2 liters of other spirits or fortified wines, such as sherry); plus 2 liters of still wine; 50 gr. of perfume and .25 liter of toilet water, plus other gifts up to the value of £10.

If you return to Britain via a Common market (EEC) country and buy goods there, you get EEC allowances, which are 50% higher for tobacco and spirits, or 75 gr. of perfume, .375 liter of toilet water and gifts up to the value of £50.

Canadian Customs

You may bring in duty free a maximum of 50 cigars, 2 lbs. of tobacco, 200 cigarettes, and 40 oz. of liquor, with a total exemption of $150. You may mail home unsolicited gifts up to $15 each.

Portugal

Lisbon

Lisbon is a born-again city—literally.

Much of modern Lisbon is less than 200 years old. People still talk about the earthquake and tidal wave that instantly followed it, as though they happened yesterday. Small wonder. You don't recover easily from a trauma in which 600 years of architectural treasures are wiped out in 15 minutes.

"Lisbon town—saw the earth open and gulp her down'" Oliver Wendell Holmes wrote later. That's practically what happened that All Saints Day, November 1, 1755. Two-thirds of the city was destroyed, some 39,000 people killed, 9,000 buildings collapsed. Among the buildings were 42 palaces and mansions, 30 monasteries, untold numbers of churches and public buildings—the accumulation of the wealth of centuries that had accrued to Lisbon from the Age of Discoveries when Portuguese ships ruled the seas.

"Bury the dead, feed the living, close the port." That was the advice of a sage at the time. And the Marquês de Pombal took it. Prime Minister to King José I (who wasn't much interested in the job of governing), Pombal cleaned up the debris, then sent an architect and engineer to London to study the reconstruction that had taken place there after the Great Fire of 1666.

What you see in downtown Lisbon today, the Baixa area, is Pombal's doing. The straight, gridlike, intersecting streets that lead from the Rossio down to the Praça (Plaza) do Comércio were built according to his plan.

The Praça do Comércio is a special triumph. It had seen its share of history since medieval times when King Manuel I built his palace there. (It would see more in 1908 when King Carlos I and his heir were assassinated there while riding through in an open carriage. But that's another story.) It is an unusually beautiful square—open, graceful, with integrated architecture on three sides and the Tagus River facing it on the fourth.

In the center of the Praça, atop a grandiose white marble pedestal, is a bronze sculpture of a plumed José I, looking more authoritative in the management of his horse than he ever looked at the head of his government. The sculpture was the work, in 1775, of Machado de Castro. (You'll see a fine baroque crib by him in the cathedral.) For reasons obscured by time, the Praça is more widely known as Black Horse Square, though the patina on the horse is still visibly green.

Pombal had been Ambassador to the Court of St. James

British sailors nicknamed the Praça "Black Horse Square" because from their ships in the harbor the statue's silhouette looked black.

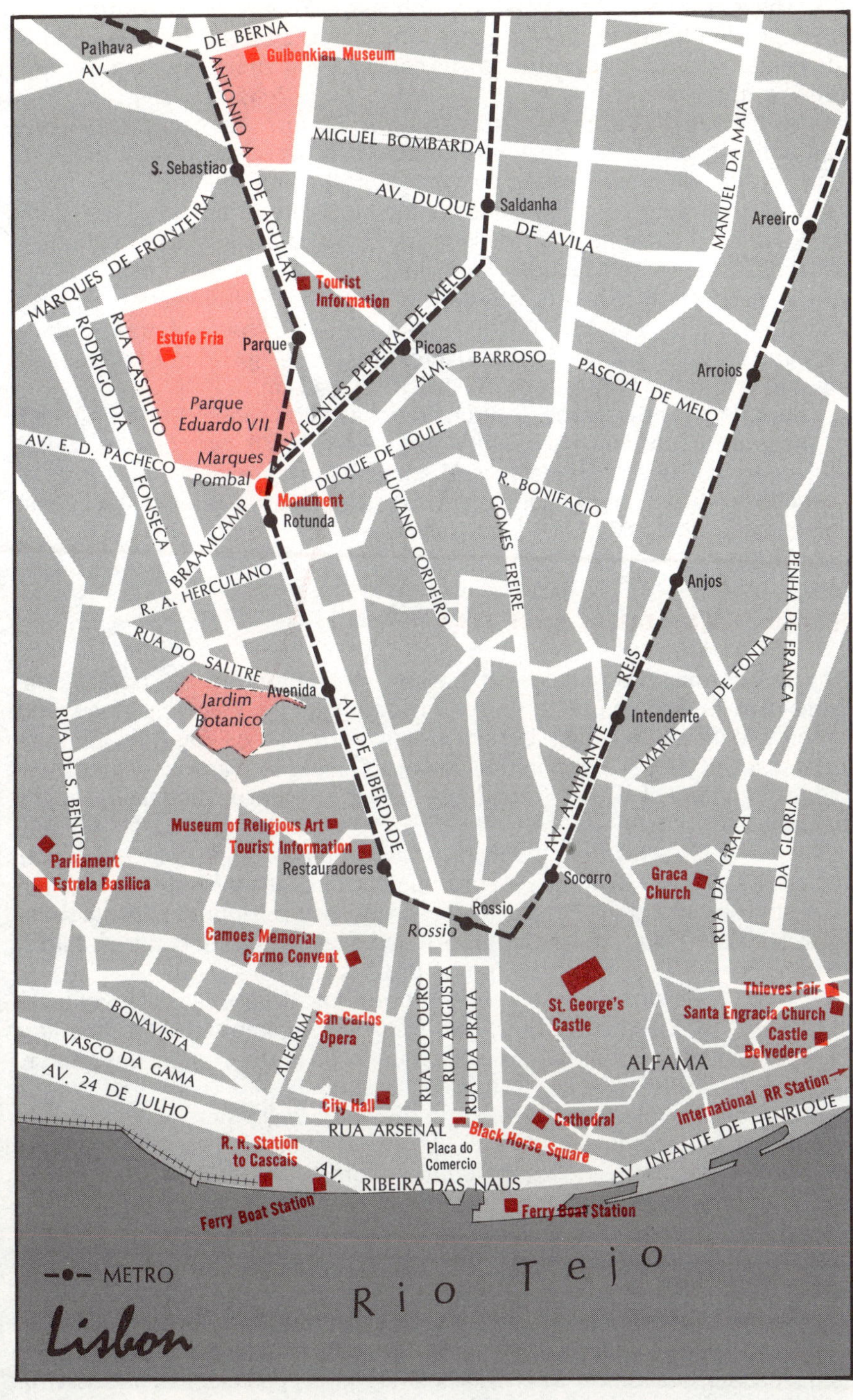

Palhava
AV.
DE BERNA
Gulbenkian Museum
ANTONIO A. DE AGUILAR
MIGUEL BOMBARDA
S. Sebastiao
AV. DUQUE DE AVILA
Saldanha
MANUEL DA MAIA
Areeiro
MARQUES DE FRONTEIRA
Tourist Information
AV. FONTES PEREIRA DE MELO
RODRIGO DA FONSECA
RUA CASTILHO
Estufe Fria
Parque
Picoas
ALM. BARROSO
PASCOAL DE MELO
Arroios
Parque Eduardo VII
AV. E. D. PACHECO
Marques Pombal
Monument
DUQUE DE LOULE
R. BONIFACIO
Rotunda
BRAAMCAMP
LUCIANO CORDEIRO
GOMES FREIRE
PENHA DE FRANCA
Anjos
R. A. HERCULANO
RUA DO SALITRE
Avenida
Jardim Botanico
AV. DE LIBERDADE
REIS
Intendente
MARIA DE FONTA
RUA DE S. BENTO
AV. ALMIRANTE
Museum of Religious Art
Tourist Information
Parliament
Estrela Basilica
Restauradores
Socorro
Graca Church
RUA DA GRACA
DA GLORIA
Rossio
Rossio
Camoes Memorial
Carmo Convent
St. George's Castle
Thieves Fair
Santa Engracia Church
Castle Belvedere
BONAVISTA
VASCO DA GAMA
ALECRIM
San Carlos Opera
RUA DO OURO
RUA AUGUSTA
RUA DA PRATA
ALFAMA
AV. 24 DE JULHO
City Hall
Cathedral
International RR Station
RUA ARSENAL
Black Horse Square
AV. INFANTE DE HENRIQUE
R. R. Station to Cascais
Placa do Comercio
AV. RIBEIRA DAS NAUS
Ferry Boat Station
Ferry Boat Station
METRO
Rio Tejo
Lisbon

The mystery of names is evident, too, in the Rossio, whose formal name is Praça Dom Pedro IV, after the king who stands atop a gigantic column in the center. Picadilly-like, with crowds passing by at all hours of the day and evening, the Rossio has been at the center of the action for centuries. Pigs were once slaughtered there, *festas* and *auto-da-fes* were held there. In one part of the square Jews were once massacred, in another João I was declared king. At the north end, where the neoclassical National Theatre of Queen Maria II now stands, was the palace of the Inquisition. Times change. Today the Rossio is a cacophony of honking auto horns, flower vendors with their dazzling displays, and spouting fountains.

While most of downtown Lisbon is 18th and 19th century, there are older monuments that survived the earthquake tucked here and there among the city's seven hills. One of the pleasures of sightseeing Lisbon is in discovering them. And the way best to do that is by walking.

You won't know Lisbon or catch its architectural surprises until you walk it, and you can't walk it in uncomfortable shoes. Two things conspire against the stroller: the undulating, tesselated sidewalks that are made, mosaic style, of white limestone and black basalt; and steep, sharply graded slopes that sometimes literally take your breath away.

IF YOU HAVE ONLY ONE DAY

Any Lisbon tour should begin at the top. A taxi, one of the city's prime bargains, will take you up to Castelo de São Jorge (St. George's castle) and from there it's all downhill—but only topographically. As you walk the ramparts that link the ten crenelated towers, you'll have the same knockout view of the Tagus and of Lisbon's six other hills as the Moors did and the Visigoths before them.

Look back, away from the water, down at the Largo da Graça. This was the site of Afonso Henriques's encampment that steamy summer of 1147 when the upstart Burgundian decided to challenge the Moorish rule of Lisbon. Even with the help of German, English and French crusaders it took him 3 months, well into October, before he drove the Moors out.

You'll understand why as you peer down into Alfama, at its labyrinthine streets that twist and coil around the hill. You can almost visualize the ambushes, sniping and other surprises the Moors had in store for anyone venturing up the hillside.

As you stroll, look for the door in the north wall where Martin Moniz, Afonso Henriques's friend, gave his life. He jammed his body into the door to keep it open, thus allowing the crusader forces to push their way into the castle grounds.

Castelo de São Jorge

There is nothing left of the elaborate palace that the Moors built here, but as you walk among the pines and cypress, in gardens redolent of orange trees and oleander, past ponds where black swans glide, you can understand why any conqueror would feel like King of the World in such a sweeping hilltop setting.

In the castle keep, rare birds play cock-of-the-walk—black-necked, red-beaked swans from Australia, polka-dotted guinea fowl and gold pheasants from China, flamingos from Florida. Behind a fence, where the Moorish kitchen once was, there are two coal-black, enormous ravens. The raven has been Lisbon's symbol and a special bird throughout Portugal since the time when, according to legend, two ravens guided the boat that brought the body of São Vicente safely ashore.

Don't be surprised if one of the birds greets you with a deep-throated "Olá!"

No one seems sure when the castle received its name, but it is often attributed to King João I, who carried St. George's picture on his banner when his forces fought the Spanish in 1385. Inasmuch as João I was married to John of Gaunt's daughter, and St. George was (and is) England's patron saint, there is some logic in this assumption.

Before beginning your circular descent into the maze of Alfama, via Rua Norberto Araújo, pause at the Largo Santa Luzia for one last wide-angle view of the Tagus and the red-tile roofed city below. You may also wish to visit the *Museum of Decorative Arts,* lodged in a salmon-pink 17th-century palace just around the corner. What you'll find is an extensive collection of luxurious 17th-, 18th- and 19th-century furniture handsomely displayed to show life as it was—for a few lucky souls anyhow.

* Museum of Decorative Arts. Facing is a marble version of São Vicente, Lisbon's patron saint

Attached to the museum is the *Fundação Ricardo Espírito Santo* (the Ricardo Espírito Santo Foundation), a professional workshop in which craftsmen learn to make and repair all the exquisite handmade *objets* of yesteryear: Arraiolos carpets, gold-leaf panels, hand-bound books, wood inlays, carved wooden cabinets.

Alfama

It is possible to stroll the steep streets of Alfama with map in hand, noting as you go the *judas* windows (peep holes) along rua da Regueira, the 16th-century mansion of the Counts dos Arcos (No. 22 Largo do Salvador) or the houses lined with the glazed, painted tiles called *azulejos* on pretty little Patio dos Flores.

Most of the churches and palaces in this former nobleman's district disappeared in the 1755 earthquake

Certain Alfama streets are so narrow—Beco do Carneiro (Sheep's Alley) for instance—the eaves meet overhead and you have to squeeze through single file. People were living in Alfama when the Visigoths arrived in the 5th century, and on Rua Norberto de Araújo you'll see the remains of a Visigothic wall. It was the Moors, though, who gave this section its permanent name, and you'll find part of *their* wall in a tower on Largo de São Rafael. Rua de São Pedro is Alfama's liveliest street, with tiny bars, fish and vegetable shops on either side and vendors hawking fish and fresh produce in between.

Alfama probably comes from the Arabic word alhama, referring to hot springs in the area

Sé

Below Alfama is Lisbon's cathedral, called *Sé* after the Latin word *sedes* for seat (episcopal seat or center). The origins are 12th-century Romanesque, though time and several earthquakes took their toll. Still, with considerable restoration it *looks* Romanesque once again, especially viewed from a distance, with its twin fortress-like towers intact.

National Museum of Ancient Art

It is a short cab ride from the Sé to the National Museum of Ancient Art, lodged in Pombal's old palace on Rua das Janelas Verdes. There's one main reason that this sleeper of a museum is an absolute must. It possesses Portugal's finest artistic treasure: a polyptych, *St. Vincent,* by Nuno Gonçalves. Painted as a church altar piece by a (now) little-known 15th-century Portuguese artist, the work is a visual poem, an epic of 15th-century Portuguese life. Surrounding the saint in the picture are faces from all levels of society —from Prince Henry the Navigator to simple fishermen—60 marvelous portraits in all.

Calouste Gulbenkian Foundation

Another cab ride will deposit you on the spacious grounds of the Calouste Gulbenkian Foundation. The *Gulbenkian Museum,* on the left as you enter the grounds, is stunning, both in the dramatic installations and in the breadth of the art collection. Here you'll find tomb figures from ancient Egypt, rare rugs from Turkey and Persia in an extensive Islamic grouping and delicate illuminated books from Armenia.

In the European wing of the elongated modern building you'll find old friends such as Gainsborough, Turner, Renoir, Rubens, Rodin, Rembrandt and Manet. There are also surprises: a room full of exquisite Art Nouveau jewelry designed by René Lalique; oriental tiles; 15th–18th-century furniture; three enormous 16th-century tapestries attributed to Guilio Romano of Ferrara; and a wall-length *La Pipee aux Oiseaux,* a marvelous 18th-century tapestry woven in Beauvais and designed by Francois Boucher.

IF YOU HAVE TWO DAYS

Belém, a suburb on the western edge of Lisbon, is so packed with riches it can keep you busy an entire second day. It is a short taxi ride from the city or can be reached by city bus No. 26 from the city center. Once in Belém, the various sights are all within a couple of walkable blocks.

Belém is almost a sacred site to Portuguese. On a humid July day in 1497 Vasco da Gama, in a tiny chapel where the *Mosteiro dos Jerónimos* (Jerónimos Monastery) now stands, prayed for a successful voyage. He then climbed aboard his caravel, *São Gabriel,* and sailed away to discover a sea route around Africa to India, thus opening up a whole new world of riches and power for Portugal.

In celebration of da Gama's triumphal voyage, and on the revenue from Indian pepper imports alone, King Manuel I built Jerónimos, a block-long monument that is a tribute in stone to Portugal's Age of Discovery.

As you face the monastery, on the right side of the complex is the church of Santa Maria de Belém. Linger long enough to savor the richness of the Gothic portal, dense with gables, pinnacles and niches filled with finely carved saints, kings and bishops.

Inside, the building seems to soar. The sense of spaciousness overwhelms. It seems impossible that such slender, elongated columns and vaulting could have withstood the 1755 earthquake, but they did. Consider the engineering skills involved. The 30-meter (100-foot) high vault above the transept has no visible means of support, no buttresses. The enormous structure depends on walls (outside) and piers (inside) less that 2 meters (6 feet) thick.

While the church's beauty dazzles, there is historical importance here as well. In the chancel are the tombs of 13 royal personages, including Manuel I. In the rear of the church are two side chapels, each with an over-decorated 19th-century version of a Manueline tomb. The one on the right, decorated with a caravel and Prince Henry the Navigator's cross, belongs to Vasco da Gama—who actually died in Cochin in 1524. Across from him is an equally lavish marble tomb, supported by crouching lions, with an effigy on the top wearing a laurel wreath. Ironies abound. The tomb is intended to honor Luis de Camöes, Portugal's most distinguished poet. Camöes died in 1580 of the plague and was buried in a pauper's grave.

Prepare yourself for the cloister, possibly the most beautiful in the Manueline style in all of Portugal. Two stories in height, its laciness is intensified by the double level. The embroidering of the stone arches looks like butterfly wings or plumed birds in flight. The effect is stunning. Gargoyles, including a most unusual grasshopper, compete with bas relief statues in niches for your attention. It's no wonder that Manuel I retreated to a private apartment here, the better to enjoy the quiet beauty of such surroundings.

At the far end of the monastery is the *Museu da Marinha,* the naval museum where Portugal's centuries of maritime brillance are delineated in ship models and replicas of famous ships such as João V's painted *galleotã grande.* Even landlubbers like us revel in the 1778 dragon-prowed royal brigantine with its gilded gondola and crew of 73 red-jacketed oarsmen, all in lifesize replica. A tiny *Sala do Oriente* reminds us—with its inlaid Chinese furniture and Japanese armor—of the long-armed reach of Portuguese ships.

"A gigantic marble bookend," is the way a Portuguese friend irreverently described the massive *Padrão dos Descobrimentos* (Monument of the Discoveries), which was erected near the Belém waterfront in 1960 to commemorate the 500th anniversary of the death of Prince Henry the Navigator. Behind Henry, who is at the prow of the stylized stone ship, are figures symbolizing the Age of Discovery—Vasco da Gama; King Manuel I carrying an armillary sphere; Camöes, who celebrated the era in his brilliant epic poem, *Os Lusiadas* (The Portuguese); the painter Nuno Gonçalves; as well as navigators, cartographers, cosmographers and monks. Even Philippa of Lancaster, Prince Henry's mother, is represented.

Nearby, at the water's edge, is the Torre de Belém, which was built as a defensive fortress right in the Tagus during Manuel I's era. The river changed course through time and the tower is now grounded. It remains as another Manueline tribute to that golden time. Architect Francisco de Arruba enriched the five-story building with Manueline, Gothic and even an occasional Arabic flourish. A graceful Renaissance loggia adds another dimension. When it was built the tower was just one of a series of forts set up as a defensive chain between Lisbon and Cascais.

As you amble along Rua de Belém toward the *Museu Nacional dos Coches* (Coach Museum), consider a stop for refreshment or light lunch at

O Rafael, 106 Rua de Belém, en route. On a lucky day you may pass the pink presidential palace (Belém Palace) when a new foreign ambassador is being received. If so, you'll enjoy watching the spectacle of dozens of spit-and-polish uniformed soldiers on horseback leading the dignitary's entourage.

Beyond the palace is the former Royal Riding School, a logical place, it would seem, to install the *Museu Nacional dos Coches.* The coach collection, which dates from the 16th to 19th century, is considered one of the largest in Europe. We counted 32 sculpted and gilded vehicles, but there are numerous smaller items on display as well—sedan chairs, minor carriages, litters and the like.

IF YOU HAVE MORE TIME

Lisbon is a great city for shopping, one of the last strongholds in Europe of hand-wrought craftsmanship. Even if shopping isn't high on your priority list, a stroll that combines a bit of shopping with sightseeing can lead to serendipitous discoveries—a *fin de siècle* fountain here, a tiny square or tile-faced church there.

Lisbon's two major shopping areas are the parallel streets of Pombal's "grid," Rua Augusta, Sapateiros and Aurea in the lower Baixa area and Chiado on a ledge above. Admiring the antique woodwork, gold lettering and vintage facades on many of the shops is a pleasurable part of any browsing–shopping stroll.

You might begin your walk in the Baixa where Lisboans shop for clothes, leather goods and jewelry. Rua Aurea, also known as do Ouro or the Street of Gold, has clusters of jewelry shops along it. For a coffee and pastry break, join the locals at Casa Macario, 272 Rua Augusta or Casa Brasileira, No. 267, across the street.

Turn from Rua Aurea at the corner of Rua de Santa Justa to ride the Santa Justa lift, Gustave Eiffel's Gothic grey steel elevator, up to the Largo do Carmo. As you get off the lift, A Quinta restaurant (good city views) is on the left. On the right is the *Igreja do Carmo,* facing the Largo. The 14th-century Carmelite church was destroyed by the 1755 earthquake and was left "as is," open to the sky. Inside is a minuscule Archaeological Museum with a few Roman and medieval antiquities and a rare coin collection.

From the Largo, where black and white pigeons roost eerily in feathery jacaranda trees, it is a short walk along Rua da Trindade to Rua Nova da Trindade, and finally, for the moment, the church of São Roque on Largo Trindade Coelho.

São Roque's grey stone Renaissance facade gives no clues to the ornate riches inside. The most famous chapel in this Jesuit church is that of São João Baptista, which looks like a display case of semiprecious stones. There are large columns made entirely of lapis lazuli (from Chile), agate and amethyst trim and wall mosaics, and cupids and angels carved in Carrara marble. The chapel was commissioned in Rome by King João V in the 18th century at a cost of $1 million. It had to be dismantled, shipped to Lisbon in three ships, and then reassembled. The ostentation staggers.

Near São Roque is the Solar do Vinho do Porto, 45 Rua de São Pedro de Alcantára, and it may be just the moment for time out from your walk to sit here, in the quiet of a handsome lounge, and sip a port. The Solar has the low-key ambience of a private club, but it is open to anyone who has the good sense to drop in. Basically, the Solar is a port wine bar with two sedate lounges for sitting, sipping, reading or just relaxing. The only libation available is port, but there are almost 300 different ones to choose among—supplied by 59 vintners—at about 35 escudos a glass. It could be a long day. (Solar is the Port Wine Institute's way of showing us all how many different varieties of port are produced. We'll drink to that!)

If you plan your meanderings right, you'll arrive at Tavares right about now. Tavares, 35-39 Rua da Misericórdia (phone 321112), is just down the street. One of Lisbon's most luxurious restaurants, it is small so reservations are almost a must here.

In the center of the small, bustling square, Largo do Chiado, is the seated bronze statue of Antonio Ribeiro Chiado, a 16th-century poet who has given his name to both the square and the entire district that runs from here, along Rua Garrett, to Rua do Carmo. Along Rua Garrett's five blocks you'll find the most fashionable shops in the city—for clothes, books, antiques, fancy foods, even musical instruments.

On the far side of the Largo do Chiado is the neoclassical church called *Italiana della Madonna di Loreto,* usually known as just Loreto, with pink marble interior walls an d *trompe-l'oeil* painted ceiling. There is usually a vendor or two below the church steps selling old books from a portable stall.

Another cab ride, another church. But the Madre de Deus is more of a museum than a house of worship. It is a *Museu do Azulejo* devoted to *azulejos,* those glazed earthenware tiles that the Portuguese have turned into a fine art form. By wandering through the church, the Manueline small cloister and the crypt, you will get a short course in the evolution of *azulejos* —Portuguese and foreign—from the 14th century onward.

Inside Information

Hotels

Three perks in all Portguese hotels: Continental breakfast and all taxes and all service charges are included in the quoted room price. The following are our personal preferences among a large number of hotels and restaurants.

It should be noted that all hotels in Portugal are government inspected and categorized from five (top) to one star (except the government-run *pousadas*). Our categories reflect our own preference for amenities, ambience and quality and are not necessarily the same as the offical ones. It should also be noted that a Portuguese penchant for cleanliness means even a one-star hotel is generally immaculate.

Keep in mind that *Expensive* in Portugal would be *Bargain* in some other countries. Our listing is relative, based on Portuguese price categories. For a double room: *Very Expensive,* 11,000–12,750 escudos; *Expensive,* 8,000–11,000 escudos; *Moderate,* 5,000–8,000 escudos; *Inexpensive,* 3,350–5,000 escudos; *Bargain,* 2,000–3,350 escudos.

★★★★★ 1. RITZ

**** Ritz Grill

88 Rua Rodrigo da Fonseca (phone 684131). Management by an international chain (Inter-Continental) hasn't diminished the special elegance of this spacious hotel. Convenient location, facing peaceful Edward VII park; 290 rooms and 20 suites with balconies; excellent restaurant (Ritz Grill); handy three-level snack bars; attractive shops; lounge and bar with live piano music each afternoon. *Very Expensive.*

★★★★★ 2. ALFA LISBOA

Avenida Columbano Pinheiro (phone 732121). A flagship and the only Portuguese property of the Spanish Husa chain, this new (1981) 21-story hotel is deluxe all the way: accoutrements, decor, size and furnishings of its 545 rooms. Its one drawback is its location, which is just beyond the edge of town (near the zoo). A planned-for swimming pool, sauna and other public rooms should help make it reasonably self-contained. Many rooms have a striking heads-on view of the 18th century aqueduct. Handsome "Pombalino" restaurant and folkloric "A Pousada" coffee shop. *Expensive.*

★★★★★ 3. LISBOA SHERATON

It's walking distance from the Gulbenkian Foundation

2 Rua Latino Coelho (phone 575757). The 388-room Sheraton is a focal point of Lisbon social life, a place to meet, lunch, socialize and people-watch. Swimming pool; rooftop restaurant (Panorama) on the 29th floor; many shops. *Very Expensive.*

★★★★★ 4. TIVOLI

185 Avenida de Liberdade (phone 530181). Comfortable, modern, with a handy location on the city's major promenade. This 350-room (including 20 suites), well-run hotel is a convenient springboard to sightseeing and shopping. Outdoor swimming pool. *Expensive.*

★★★★★ **5. AVENIDA PALACE**

123 Rua 1° de Dezembro (phone 360154). Lisbon's oldest deluxe hotel (built in 1894) has the air of faded grandeur. But its 95 rooms still have old-world elegance, impeccable maintenance and memories of glories past. Noisy street traffic makes an inner courtyard room almost essential. *Expensive.*

★★★★ **1. YORK HOUSE**

32 Rua das Janelas Verdes (phone 662544). Our favorite, this pousadalike treasure has been almost a private preserve of English and French visitors for decades, ever since Madame Andreé Goldstein turned the one-time 17th-century convent, then pension, into a small hotel. During World War II she sheltered escapees from Nazi Germany here. Each of the 46 superbly kept rooms is different, furnished with antiques and replicas. On warm days you can breakfast on the bougainvillea-draped patio under a plum tree. An unusually helpful English-speaking staff; good kitchen (a favorite with French embassy personnel). One drawback: no elevator and lots of stairs. Flash! New ownership and even better service. *Inexpensive.*

*** Restaurant here. You can stay also at their annex.

★★★★ **2. PRÍNCIPE REAL**

53 Rua da Alegria (phone 360116). A gem, resting on a quiet street just a marble chip's throw from bustling Avenida da Liberdade, this tiny 24-room hotel is a find; it's like staying in a private house, with each bedroom furnished differently. *Inexpensive.*

★★★★ **3. TIVOLI JARDIM**

7 Rua Júlio Machado (phone 539971). Located just behind its big sister, the Tivoli, this slick, 119-room edifice combines a handy location with colorfully decorated rooms and the amenity of a swimming pool (shared with Tivoli guests). *Inexpensive.*

★★★★ **4. LISBOA PENTA**

Avenida dos Combatantes (phone 740041). An outskirts location is compensated for by extras such as swimming pool, garden, shopping arcade, 592 rooms with balconies, roomy lounges and public areas. *Moderate.*

★★★★ **5. FLORIDA**

32 Rua do Duque de Palmela (phone 576145). Prime location off Avenida da Liberdade makes sightseeing, shopping, dining easy. Large rooms, simply decorated. Helpful concierge. *Inexpensive.*

★★★ **1. PLAZA**

Avenida da Liberdade at Parque Mayer (phone 370331). A Belle Epoque entrance telegraphs the theme throughout this attractive hotel, from Art Nouveau chandeliers in the lobby to logo, colors and bedroom furniture. Drawback: sometimes noisy adult amusement park next door. *Inexpensive.*

★★★ **2. DOM CARLOS**

121 Avenida Duque de Loulé (phone 539071). A comfortable 73-room (plus 17 suites) modern hotel, handy to the U.S. Embassy. Quiet rooms equipped with minibars. *Inexpensive.*

★★★ **3. DIPLOMÁTICO**
74 Rua Castelho (phone 562041). Popular with tour groups, this well-maintained 90-room hotel is handy to Praça Marquês de Pombal. Rooms with terrace views. *Moderate.*

★★★ **4. FENIX**
8 Praça Marquês de Pombal (phone 535121). Close to the busy Pombal square; roomy; with a respected Spanish restaurant (Bodegon). 114 rooms. *Inexpensive.*

★★★ **5. EMBAIXADOR**
73 Avenida Duque de Loulé (phone 530171). Central location; ample lounges; somewhat uninspiring rooms (100 in all). *Moderate.*

★★ **1. FLAMINGO**
41 Rua Castilho (phone 532191). Attractively decorated lounge, bar and public rooms make up for the 35 small bedrooms, which are nicely furnished, well kept and include minibar. *Inexpensive.*

★★ **2. JORGE V**
3 Rua Mouzinho da Silveira (phone 562525). The 49 double rooms are small for two (with much luggage), as are the baths; but they are neat and have balconies and views. *Inexpensive.*

★★ **3. HOTEL DA TORRE**
8 Rua dos Jerónimos, Belém (phone 636262). On a quiet, tree-lined street near São Jerónimos monastery. Some of the 49 rooms are small, but attractive and well kept, large lounges and friendly staff compensate. Trolley and bus stops nearby; 15 minutes from Lisbon center. *Inexpensive.*

★★ **4. PRESIDENTE**
13 Rua Alexandre Herculano (phone 539501). Good location, just off Avenida da Liberdade, near Praça Pombal. The 59 rooms are neatly furnished and serviceable, if nondescript. *Inexpensive.*

Restaurants

Our categories: *Very Expensive,* 1600–2600 escudos; *Expensive,* 1300–1600 escudos; *Moderate,* 800–1300 escudos; *Inexpensive,* 600–800 escudos; *Bargain,* 400–600 escudos. Prices per person for a three-course meal with wine. Most Lisbon restaurants are open for lunch from 12 A.M. or 12:30 P.M. to 3 P.M., for dinner from 7 or 7:30 to 11 P.M. daily. Reservations are advised, especially at all three- or four-star restaurants. Keep in mind that Lisbon's most expensive restaurants would be considered bargain-priced almost anywhere else.

Try the rabbit terrine with Cumberland sauce; sole in dry white Port wine with a spinach mousse

★★★★ **1. MICHEL**
5 Largo de Santa Cruz do Castelo (phone 864338). On a pint-size plaza near Castelo de São Jorge, this tiny (two-room) restaurant is Lisbon's French *nouvelle cuisine* oracle. The Portuguese–Moroccan owner Michel da Costa

demonstrates his skills on local TV as well. Open 12:30–3 P.M., 8–11 P.M.; closed Sundays and holidays. *Expensive.*

★★★★ 2. TAVARES

35 Rua da Misericordia (phone 321112). Mirrored elegance for some of Lisbon's finest dining. Continental and Portuguese specialties expertly prepared. *Very Expensive.*

★★★★ 3. TAGIDE

20 Largo da Biblioteca Publica (phone 320720). A hilltop view that sweeps from Castelo de São Jorge across the Tagus. One of the most elegant dining rooms in town. A pleasing mix of French (try the goose liver in Madeira wine sauce) and Portuguese *(arroz de pato a Minhota)* dishes. *Very Expensive.*

Ask for a table in room on the left, for a better view

★★★★ 4. AVIZ

12 B Rua Serpa Pinto (phone 328391). In an ambience that turns the clock firmly back to the 19th century, Aviz serves some of the best French and continental food in Lisbon—and has for 40 years. Seamless service reminds you how things *should* be done. One of the best wine cellars in town. *Very Expensive.*

★★★★ 5. BACHUS

8 Largo Trindade (321260). Super-stylish Art Deco accoutrements and exquisitely grilled fish have made Bachus the newest "in" place for locals to dine. *Expensive.*

★★★★ 6. O PAGEM

20 Largo Trindade (phone 373151). A new restaurant that features seafood and Continental dishes deftly prepared and presented. Grilled sole is superb. So are desserts. *Expensive.*

Dine outside on the terrace in warm weather

★★★★ 7. CLARA

49 Campo Martires da Patria (phone 570434). One of Lisbon's newer deluxe restaurants (but with a studied 1930s look). A Continental menu includes beef Wellington, veal Cordon Bleu. The wine list is extensive. *Expensive.*

★★★ 1. GAMBRINUS

23 Rua Portas das São Antao (phone 368974). In a cosy, *gemütlich* setting you'll dine on Portuguese specialties such as a wedge of *perdiz* (partridge) cut from a gigantic oven-hot-deep-dish pie. Here's the place to sample *vinho verde* (literally green wine); it complements the robust cuisine. *Expensive.*

You can lunch at the bar as well—on a starched white place mat

★★★ 2. ESCORIAL

47 Rua Portas das São Antão (phone 363758). Good Portuguese specialties. Similar in price and menu to neighboring Gambrinus. *Expensive.*

This street is restaurant row

★★★ 3. YORK HOUSE

32 Rua das Janelas Verdes (phone 662544). Real home cooking with a French accent is what you'll find in this 17th-century convent. Soup, fish, entree and dessert—for a remarkable 550$00. *Bargain.*

Popular with embassy crowds for lunch

★★★ 4. PAVILHÃO DE CAÇA

132 Rua do Século (phone 325740). Game is the specialty here—and it's well done. *Expensive.*

★★★ 5. GONDOLA

64 Avenida da Berna (phone 770426). Italian food in a pleasing setting—just opposite the Gulbenkian. If weather warrants it, opt for the grapevine-covered terrace. *Expensive.*

★★★ 6. BODEGON

8 Praça Marquês de Pombal (535121). Wide polished wood beams and copper pots on white stucco walls create a Spanish ambience, accented by well-cooked food. *Expensive.*

Note the number of Mercedes cars parked outside

★★ 1. 31 DE ARMADA

31 Praça de Armada (phone 676330). Don't be misled by the tacky exterior (the sign is the old-fashioned Coca-Cola type found in rural grocery stores). Three women cook and serve superb Portuguese dishes (try the seafood casserole, *A Corda de Mariscos,*) and the regional white wine *(Reguengos de Monsaraz)* in several tiny white-washed rooms. A "sleeper," very "in" with savvy locals, unknown to tourists. *Bargain.*

The name means "Love me, love me not"

★★ 2. MALMEQUER BEMMEQUER

25 Rua de São Miguel (phone 876535). Another tiny gem, in the heart of Alfama, a winner with its Portuguese and seafood dishes. Feast on gazpacho, grilled sole and *vinho verde. Inexpensive.*

★★ 3. BOTA ALTA

37 Travessa do Queimada (phone 327959). Located on a narrow, cobbled street (at the corner of Rua da Atalaia) in the *fado* district, Bairro Alto. A bistro-type restaurant, popular with Lisboans. *Inexpensive.*

★★ 4. FLORESTA DO GINJAL

7 Ginjal, Cacilhas (phone 2766013). Across the river, just a short ferry boat ride away, you'll dine on fresh fish and have a seagull's eye view of the river and Lisbon. *Moderate.*

★★ 5. QUEIJO E VINHO

4B Largo Contador-Mor (phone 867727). The emphasis here, as the name implies, is on wine and cheese—Lisbon's only such restaurant. Fondue is the specialty. Reservations are essential. Closed Sundays. *Inexpensive.*

★ 1. PORTO DE ABRIGO

16 Rua dos Remolares (phone 360873). Our favorite hangout in the low-rent category, this no-frills eatery is popular with knowledgeable Lisboans. Notice the well-dressed business types lunching in elbow-to-elbow quarters on paper-covered tables. A memorable must is *sole Porto Abrigo*—bathed in butter with a grated cheese edging. Try the Gaeiras white wine with it. *Bargain.*

★ **2. BONJARDIM**
10 Travessa de São Antão (phone 324389). Reliable, back-to-basics treatment of the house specialties: chicken roasted on a spit or barbequed suckling pig. Setting is folkloric, usually crowded. *Inexpensive.*

★ **3. CERVEJARIA DA TRINDADE**
20 Rua Nova da Trindade (phone 323506). Crowded, noisy, geared to a mob scene, the saving grace is good seafood (*bacalão* the specialty) at low prices. Handsome wall-to-wall blue and white tile scenes and barrel ceiling make the noise bearable, but the garden is quieter. *Expensive.*

Entertainment

Opera

The setting is sumptuous; the season extends from December through July and usually includes nine world-famous works. The 18th-century *Teatro Nacional de São Carlos* (modeled on Naples's San Carlos and Milan's La Scala) is among Europe's most beautiful opera houses. Address is Largo de São Carlos.

Theater

Theater is alive and active in Lisbon—and performed in Portuguese. There are the classics at the *Teatro Nacional Doña Maria II* (in the Rossio); more popular fare at the *Municipal Theater de São Luis,* and workers' theater at Teatro de Trindade (Rua da Trindade); experimental works at *Teatro Aberto,* near Gulbenkian.

Dance

Ballet is performed by the *Companhia Nacional de Bailado* and Ballet Gulbenkian in fall, winter and spring; sponsored by the Ministry of Culture. You can find out where, when and what is being performed at the National Tourist Office, Palacio Foz, Praça dos Restauradores, or by calling 706341.

Concerts

Concerts by Portuguese and international artists are performed at the *São Carlos Opera House, Teatro Municipal de São Luis* and the *Gulbenkian Foundation,* 45 Avenida de Berna. For information about the Gulbenkian's regular series, phone 762146.

Nightlife

Bars. Currently "in" include: *Procópio,* 21A Alto São Francisco (652851); *Foxtrox,* Travessa Santa Terezinha. *Mrs. Breton's Pub,* 6 r/c Rua Marechal de Saldanha (phone 365859).

"Fado" from Latin fatum, or "destiny". Fado clubs are mostly in Bairro Alto and Alfama. Reservations are recommended

Nightclubs. They include the rooftop *Panorama* at the Sheraton Hotel, 2 Rua Latino Coelha (phone 563911); and *Maxime,* 57 Praça da Alegria (phone 365366), with *fado* and folk dancing at 10 P.M., skin shows at 1 and 3 A.M. Minimums run 1,000$00 per person.

Fado Places. *Fado* is the music of Portugal's soul. Played on guitars and mandolins, these emotionally-charged songs are sung by men or women in intimate tavernlike settings. Most people go for dinner about 10 P.M. Performances usually begin around 11 P.M. Most fado places have a minimum (300–800 escudos average), but no cover, so dinner isn't obligatory. You'll find some of the best fado singing at *Senhor Vinho,* 18 Rua de Meio-á-Lapa (phone 672681), a favorite with Lisboans; *Lisboa a Noite,* 69 Rua das Gáveas (phone 368557), also popular and authentic; *Faia,* 48–56 Rua da Barroca (phone 369387), known for good food (especially Portuguese specialties).

Spectacles

Antigas are held only on fiestas and special occasions

The spectacle is the bullfight, especially the *antiga tourada* in which the *cavaleiros* wear 18th-century costumes, complete with periwigs and tricorn hats. The touradas take place from Easter until October at the *Campo Pequeno,* Lisbon's paprika-colored pseudo-Moorish bull ring (easily reached by metro). The tourada begins at 9:45 P.M. and features six or seven bulls.

The Portuguese bullfight is very different from the Spanish, and not just because the bull is not killed. Basically, it is the most stunning display of horsemanship and horseflesh this side of the Vienna Riding School. The thrills (and danger) escalate as the rider places "darts" in the bull's back and gallops away. Equally breathtaking is the display of gutsiness of the eight-man *forcado* who challenge the bull (after the darts have been placed) on foot, fling themselves over his horns when he charges and then subdue him. The bull is then herded out of the arena, alive. Bullfight tickets are from 180 to 500 escudos and can be bought through your hotel concierge or at the old-fashioned, green glass-covered *quiosque* (kiosk) in the Praça dos Restauradores. (Movie and theater tickets are available at the same kiosk.)

Weekday shopping hours: 9 a.m. to 7 p.m., but most shops close for lunch from 1 to 3 p.m. Saturdays most shops close for day at 1 p.m.

Shopping

You've probably at one time or another been part of a conversation decrying the breakdown of quality in modern life. The punch line is usually a plaintive "Why don't they make things like they used to"?

We've got news for you. In Portugal they still do. The joy of shopping in Lisbon is that superb custom-made, handmade objects are still relatively inexpensive. So if you've been thinking of replacing a carpet or covering a kitchen counter with tiles, bring your required measurements with you.

Carpets

Casa Quintão, 30–34 Rua Ivens—two floors of Portuguese Arraiolos carpets and throw rugs. *Jalco,* 44 Rua Ivens—antique carpets, as well as other antiques.

Tiles

Sant' Anna, 91–97 Rua do Alecrim—made-to-order tiles from 17th- and 18th-century designs. Also a large selection available on hand. *Ana,* Ritz Hotel, 88 Rua Rodrigo da Fonseca—fine selection of antique tiles, also modern reproductions. *Solar,* 68–70 Rua Dom Pedro—the definitive collection of authentic antique tiles, filed in stacks by century (from the 15th). Also other antiques—*santos* (wooden saint statues), gilded wooden baroque angels and other sculptures, pewter plates and candlesticks, furniture. *Fábrica Cerâmica Viúva Lamego,* 25 Largo do Intendente—for modern tiles and a wide selection of ceramics, plates, planters, pots.

Embroideries

Madeira Superbia, 75A Avenida Duque de Loulé—for exquisite Madeira-embroidered linens, pillow cases, tablecloths, place mats. There are other branches around town, but the widest selection is here. *Príncipe Real,* 12–14 Rua da Escola Politécnica—for luxurious sheets, tablecloths, lace and embroideries.

Porcelain

Vista Alegre, 18 Largo do Chiado—the showroom of Portugal's most famous porcelain producer—a fine selection of dinnerware available here.

Leather Goods

Galeão, 109 Rua Augusta—excellent selection of stylish handbags and luggage. *Casa Canada,* 232 Rua Augusta—also reliable, with good choices.

Jewelry

W.A. Sarmento, 251 Rua Áurea—best-known on a street of many jewelers, famous for filagreed silver and gold. *H. Stern,* Ritz Hotel, 88 Rua Rodrigo da Fonseca—a branch of the internationally famous company, known for its high quality precious stones, amethysts, emeralds and the like.

Antiques

Antiguidades, 34 Rua Dom Pedro V—antique ceramic plates, silver, pewter, *santos,* furniture. A choice collection on a street with numerous good antique shops. *Joachim Mitnitzky,* 1a Victor Cordon—many small bibelots, as well as museum quality furniture. *A.M. Salgueiro Baptista,* 85–89 Rua do Alecrim (next door to Sant' Anna)—excellent quality plates, etchings, small *objets.* Across the street, Nos. 48–50, is a shop specializing in old maps, rare books, interesting old engravings. *Dolls,* 26A Travessa da Queimada—an unusual tiny shop devoted to antique dolls and toys. On the same small street is *Lib-Lab,* No. 46—with oriental antiques and objects; and *1900–1930,* No. 33—offbeat art nouveau pieces (sculpture, lamps, glass).

Silver

Ourivesaria Aliança, 50 Rua Garrett—beautiful reproductions of antique silver and the real pieces as well, such as tea service sets, serving trays, candle sticks. While there, look up from the silver to the painted ceiling and bas relief decor—a delight. *Joalharia Mergulhão,* 162-B Rua de Sao Paulo, also has a superb collection of antique and reproduction silver.

Art

Galeria de São Francisco, 40 Rua Ivens—changing exhibits of contemporary Portuguese artists with works for sale. *R 75,* 75 Rua Castilho—a sleek gallery with avant garde art, changing exhibits (across from the Ritz Hotel complex). *Galerias Ritz,* Rua Rodrigo da Fonseca—on the corner, in the Ritz Hotel complex, with changing exhibits of contemporary paintings and sculpture. *GP Boutique,* 161 Rua Aurea—a small gallery featuring modern prints and ceramics.

Books

Libraria Bertrand, 73–75 Rua Garrett—a huge selection of art, travel and English-language books.

Food, Gourmet Specialties and Wines

Casa Pereira, 38 Rua Garrett—all kinds of chocolates (Portuguese and imports), teas and coffees. *Bolachas Nacionais Estrangeiras,* 23 Rua Garrett—a high-quality *supermercado* with wines, excellent cheese selection, (Alcobaça, serra, Évora Novo, among others), fruits and breads. Good place to stock up if you're planning picnic outings. *Martins & Costa,* 39–41 Rua do Carmo—famous for its fine selection of cheese, sausages, fruits and chocolates.

Open-Air Markets

The *Feira da Ladra* is Lisbon's version of a flea market. Held each Tuesday and Saturday, rain or shine, in the Campo de Santa Clara (just behind the Church of São Vicente, in the Alfama), this has become an old clothes market more than anything else. Visit it for local color if you like, but it's unlikely you'll find any hidden treasures.

Museums and Galleries (in addition to those mentioned in text)

★ **MUSEU NACIONAL DE ARQUEOLOGIA E ETNOGRAFIA (ARCHAEOLOGICAL MUSEUM)**

Mosteiro dos Jerónimos. Located in a 19th-century wing of the monastery, with Egyptian, Roman, Greek and prehistoric Iberian artifacts. Open 10 A.M. to 12:30 P.M., 2:30 to 5 P.M.; closed Mondays and holidays.

★ **COSTUME MUSEUM**
4 Largo São João Baptista, Lumiar. Interesting collection of period costumes displayed in a palatial setting—the 18th-century Palacio Palmela. Open 10 A.M. to 1 P.M., 2:30 to 5 P.M.; closed Mondays and holidays.

Lovely gardens and a good spot for lunch

Historic Buildings and Sites (in addition to those mentioned in text)

★ **AGUAS LIVRES AQUEDUCT**
More than 17 kilometers (11 miles) long, it took 20 years to build the 109 arches in the 18th century. The greatest height is 94 meters (213 feet). The aqueduct still brings fresh water from the Aguas Livres stream to the city.

The aqueduct survived the 1755 earth-quake

IGREJA SÃO VICENTE DE FORA (ST. VINCENT BEYOND THE WALL CHURCH)
Largo de São Vicente. A Renaissance church, damaged but rebuilt after the earthquake, it is notable for its thousands of *azulejos*, some depicting the Fables of Fontaine. It is also the pantheon for Portuguese monarchy, especially the Braganzas. Open 1 to 7 P.M., closed Sundays. Admission 10 escudos.

★ **PALACIO NACIONAL DA AJUDA (AJUDA PALACE)**
Cacada da Ajuda, Belém. A 19th-century palace whose ornate furnishings and tapestries often serve as backdrop for ceremonial occasions. Otherwise it's open to the public. Open 10 A.M. to 5 P.M.; closed Mondays. Admission 50$00.

Spectacles and Displays

Changing of the Guard. On the first and third Sunday of each month at 11 A.M. at the Praça Afonso de Albuquerque, Belém. Interesting if you're in the neighborhood.

Blessing the Fleet. This big event takes place in front of Mosteiro Jerónimos in Belém on the first or second Sunday in April. The bishop gives the blessing as the fishing fleet sets out on its annual cod-fishing expedition to the North Atlantic.

The Feast of São Antão. June 13, the birthday of Lisbon's native son, St. Anthony, is celebrated with gusto in the *bairro Alfama*. Costumed people, parades, decorations, bonfires through which daring men leap, song, dance and sardine gobbling are part of the dark-to-dawn fun.

St. Anthony only went to Padua; he was born in Lisbon near the Sé (cathedral)

Illuminations. Many historic buildings (such as Igreja do Carmo) are lighted at night from time to time. One of the most delightful illuminations is the *Fonte Luminosa* in the center of the Praça do Império, Belém. Jets of water (some 70 patterns) spurt and cascade through an hour-long performance.

Tours

Bus tours may not be your favorite way to see a city, but it may be helpful in Lisbon for several reasons: (1) in 3 hours you get a good sense of the city;

(2) Lisbon is extremely hilly, and its undulating sidewalks often require that you walk in the street—which means you may be spending more time watching out for traffic than enjoying the sights; (3) a professional guide conveys a tremendous amount of information that you can digest through individual headphones in the comfort of an air-conditioned bus.

Cityrama offers "Lisbon Citytours" year-round (except Christmas) in mornings and afternoons with pickups and returns at major hotels. Tariff: 1,300 escudos. Address 12 B Avenida Praia da Victoria (phone 575564).

Cityrama and other tour operators have an "Old Lisbon" tour that in half a day whisks you through Castelo de São Jorge, Madre de Deus, São Vicente de Fora and other churches. There's a stop to see the craftsmen at work at the Fundacão, Ricardo Espírito Santo.

"Tourist Lisbon" tour is a full day, with stops at the *Estufa Fria* in Parque Eduardo VII, Torre de Belém, Mosteiro do Jerónimos, the Coach Museum, and a tootle along the Tagus River.

There is also a "Lisbon by Night" tour that includes dinner, *fado* music and/or folk dancing and a drive around the city.

One interesting package includes dinner, a bullfight and transportation. A helpful feature is that the guide explains the bullfight action as it occurs. This tour can be booked with or without dinner—1,650–2,800 escudos—from tour operators such as Melia Tours or Cityrama.

Tagus River boat trips sail every Sunday, June through September, leaving from the Praça do Comerçio at 3 P.M., returning at 6 P.M. They offer splendid views of the city and river life. Tickets can be booked through any Lisbon travel agency.

Sports

Football. Soccer is the most popular spectator sport, and is played throughout Portugal from mid-August to the end of June, almost every Sunday, many times on Saturday and often on Wednesday evening. Lisbon has two First Division teams, Porto, has three, Braga and many other cities one. Ticket prices are from about $1.25 U.S. (for standing room) to $7.00 U.S. (the best seat in the stadium). Average price is $3.00 U.S.

Hunting and Fishing. You can arrange to go on expeditions (or assemble your own) through Retur, Ltd., 56 Rua Rodrigo da Fonseca. Retur puts it all together, giving you a choice of partridge, woodcock, quail or four-legged quarry such as fox or wolf.

Skin Diving. That super clear Atlantic water off the Lisbon coast beckons. Centro Portuguese de Actividades Subaquaticas, 37 Rua das Janelas Verdes, has expeditions going to prime diving spots many times a year. Some are nearby, others as far away as the Algarve. The Centro welcomes nonmembers on such trips.

GETTING AROUND

Lisbon on wheels is easier to manage and probably less expensive than any other capital city in Europe. A good thing, too, because the city is so hilly.

By Taxi

When we say wheels, though, we don't mean your own, but preferably a taxi. While rental cars are available from Avis, Hertz, Europcar (National), Inter-Rent (Dollar) and others, the city's narrow, twisting, sloping streets and unfamiliarity can be an exhausting challenge.

Our recommendation is to leave the driving to others. Taxi meters begin at 40 escudos and escalate slowly. For example, a 15-minute ride from the airport will cost you less than 300 escudos. There are some 3,500 taxis in Lisbon, and you should have no trouble hailing one. You can also telephone for a cab: phone (825061/2/3/4/5). You'll have to pay the meter amount plus the fare for the taxi's empty drive to pick you up. If your luggage exceeds 30 kilograms (66 pounds) or is so bulky it has to go in the trunk, there will probably be a 50% surcharge.

Hans Christian Andersen in 1866, complained that taxis were too expensive. They're one of Lisbon's best buys now

By Trolley

Trams range from yellow wooden Toonerville trolleys that look like they are from the 1890s to modern trolleys and cablecars that can climb some of the city's steepest hills. They are fun to ride and cost 32$50 escudos or less. (20-ride tickets are available for 11$25 each).

By Metro

The Metro is well-lighted, clean, quiet, practically graffiti-less. The trains run every five minutes or so from 6 A.M. to 1 P.M. Fares are 27$50, and you can buy reduced rate books of ten tickets for 18 escudos. One hitch: the routes are limited.

Buy a tourist ticket good for unlimited rides on any public transport in Lisbon for seven days, just 360 escudos

By Bus

Double-deck, tandem, conventional and big, new air-conditioned buses operate throughout Lisbon. Bus stops—called *paragems*—are posted with the numbers of the buses that stop there. With a route map, you can determine which bus will take you to your destination. Bus fares are 50 escudos or less; there's nearly a 30% discount if you buy a 20-ride ticket. Tickets can be purchased on the bus or trolley or at transit offices, such as the one at the base of the Santa Justa lift, Rua de Santa Justa, off Rua Aurea.

By Ferry

You can cross the Tagus from wharfs at Praça do Comerçio and Cais do Sodre. The cost is 30 escudos.

Directory

Embassies

U.S. Embassy, Avenida das Forças Armadas (ph. 725600). British Embassy,

37 Rua São Domingos a Lapa (phone 661191). Canadian Embassy, 2 Rua Rosa Araújo (phone 562547).

Tourist Information

The major Portuguese National Tourist Office is at Palacio Foz, Praça dos Restauradores (phone 363624); 86 Avenida Antonio de Aguiar (phone 575086): and the Miradouro de Santa Luzia, on the flank of Castelo de Sao Jorge (phone 870720). English language tourist information telephone numbers are 360450 and 575086.

Railway Stations

International and northern Portugal trains, Santa Apolonia (phone 864142); south and southeast, Sul e Sueste Station, Praça do Comerçio—east side (phone 367631); Estoril/Cascais line, Cais do Sodre Station (Phone 361121); Sintra and western routes, Rossio Station (phone 366226).

Telephone, Telegraph and Cable

Around the clock, 24 hours, at the post office, 58 Praça dos Restauradores and at the airport. International telegraph at "Radio Marconi," 20 Rua Dom Luis I, or 131 Rua de São Julião; or dial 10 and ask for "Telegrams Marconi" and have it billed on your telephone charges.

Places of Worship

Corpo Santo Church, Largo do Corpo Santo, and the English College, Rua dos Inglesinhos, both hold Roman Catholic services in English. St. Andrews Church, Rua da Arriaga holds a Church of Scotland service. The Baptist Evangelical Church, 36B Rua Filipe Folque, and Ugreha Evangelica Baptista da Parede, 19 Rua Machado dos Santos hold Baptist services. Shaare Tikva Synagogue, 59 Rua Alexandre Herculano holds Jewish services. Danish Seamen's Mission, 1 Patio do Pimenta holds Lutheran services the first Sunday of each month. Church of Jesus Christ of Latter Day Saints, 19 Rua Ten. Coronel Pessoa, in Cascais holds Mormon services.

Hairdressers

Most famous is probably Isabel Queiroz do Vale, Edificio Avis, Avenida Fontes Pereira de Melo. Also fashionable: Lucia Piloto, 12/18 Avenida da Liberdade (phone 320535); Brito & Brito, 236 Avenida da Liberdade (phone 572944); Adelina, 61-1 Rua Garrett (phone 321982).

Men's barber shops

Barbearia Brasilia, 1 Praça Marquês de Pombal (phone 535766); Barbearia Campos, 4 Largo do Chiado (phone 328476); Salão Brasileiro, 59 Rua de Santa Justa (phone 324430).

Lisbon's Environs—Day Trips

LISBON'S COAST

Day trips by car or bus are easy to the coast, or inland to Sintra, Mafra, Obidos or south of the Tagus River to Sesimbra, Setúbal or Palmela. Fast, frequent and inexpensive electric train service takes you from downtown Lisbon to the tawny sands of Estoril and Cascais in well under an hour.

Estoril

Estoril is the Grand Dame of the golden coast that stretches from Oeiras, west around the bend and then north as far as Ericeira. Our earliest awareness of Portugal's sun coast centered on newspaper stories of the deposed, exiled or retired kings and queens of Europe living in glorious tax-sheltered retirement in the palaces and villas that overlook Estoril's golden strips of sand.

The reality today is somewhat different. The palaces and villas are still there, respendent as ever. Some of the royals may even be luxuriating inside. The Palace Hotel and the nearby casino seem to prosper, but many other Estoril hotels are clogged with tour groups and at night the action seems to have moved west a few kilometers to Cascais. As a friend says, "Estoril is a great place to live, but no place for a visit."

Cascais

Cascais, whose humble fishing village origins go back to the 14th century, began drifting toward minor league resort status in the late 19th century. Nowadays, it has all the essentials for someone who wants sea, sun and sand, as well as good-looking boutiques, a wide choice of cosy pubs (the English influence), restaurants and a disco nightlife.

Beyond Cascais is the *Boca de Inferno* (Mouth of Hell), where the Atlantic waves have stabbed a hole through a cliffside cave. Remains of lookout fortresses—many from the 17th century—dot a morose and windswept seascape. Even Guincho with its powdery sand beach seems slightly sullen in the sun. Beyond it is *Cabo da Roca*—Europe's most western thrust into the Atlantic.

Estoril, pron. Shtoo-reel

John Bull is an "in" pub, 32 Praça Costa Pinto (283319). You can eat reasonably there, too. Also good: Duke of Wellington, on Rua Frederico Arouca

Try the lobster at Ericeira

By the time you reach Ericeira the mood changes again and becomes livelier, more gregarious. If you are driving, pause just before you reach Ericeira (heading north) for a head-on, long distance view of the monastery of Mafra, visible in sweeping perspective across the hills and valleys, like a mirage of architectural grandeur in the distance. Oddly, distance plays tricks. Mafra's towers seem taller and more stately than they do close up.

INLAND

Mafra

Mafra, built with some of the riches from the Portuguese colony of Brazil, was intended to be a celebration of the birth of a son and heir to King João VI and his wife, Carlota Joãquina. It was whispered that João saw it as his answer to Philip II's monumental El Escorial, but in truth João was more enamored of the French court of Louis XIV. Wags claimed that the 880-room palace-cum-monastery was built large enough so that João could take refuge from a nagging wife. In any case, the enormous, elongated edifice—the work of baroque architect João Ludovice—is a masterpiece. It looms so large that even standing as far away as possible across the square, you have trouble getting its profile in full perspective.

Mafra's last, but not finest, royal hour came in 1910. The palace sheltered 21-year-old King Manuel II and his mother the night before they sailed into exile from nearby Ericeira. The last Braganza, the last king of Portugal.

Sintra

Philip II of Spain retreated here. It was his kind of place, moody and majestic!

North of Estoril and Cascais, nestled into the Serra de Sintra hills, is Sintra and its triumvirate of palaces. "Sintra should only be seen on a clear day," say the Portuguese. But is Sintra ever completely free of the Valkyrian mists that have enchanted poets for generations? And would Sintra be Sintra without the romantic, mysterious mists that make such a natural backdrop for the theatrical palaces that perch on its hillsides?

Oldest is the *Royal Palace,* built on the site of a Moorish *alcázar.* With its ice cream cone chimneys and *boullabaise* of Gothic, Manueline and other architectural styles, the Royal Palace echoes to the sound of Portuguese history. For centuries it was the favorite royal summer escape hatch from Lisbon's heat. King Afonso V was born and died here. Young Sebastião planned his unfortunate expedition against the Moors here. And here you will see the bedroom where poor, befuddled Afonso VI lived for 9 years and died. (He was declared incompetent and his brother Pedro II seized both his kingdom and his wife.)

Don't miss the Magpie ceiling and the guide's story of the courtly gossip that led to its creation

Pena Palace, up a serpentine road, was built to the whim of Ferdinand of Saxe–Coburg–Gotha, husband of Queen D. Maria da Gloria and first cousin of Britain's Queen Victoria and Prince Albert. Smothered in its playful embrace is a 16th-century monastery, but most of the whimsical inventiveness is Ferdinand's and that of his architect–accomplice. The main tower was copied from the *Torre de Belém.* But take your pick, you'll find it all here: baroque portals, Renaissance cupolas, Manueline windows, Gothic vault-

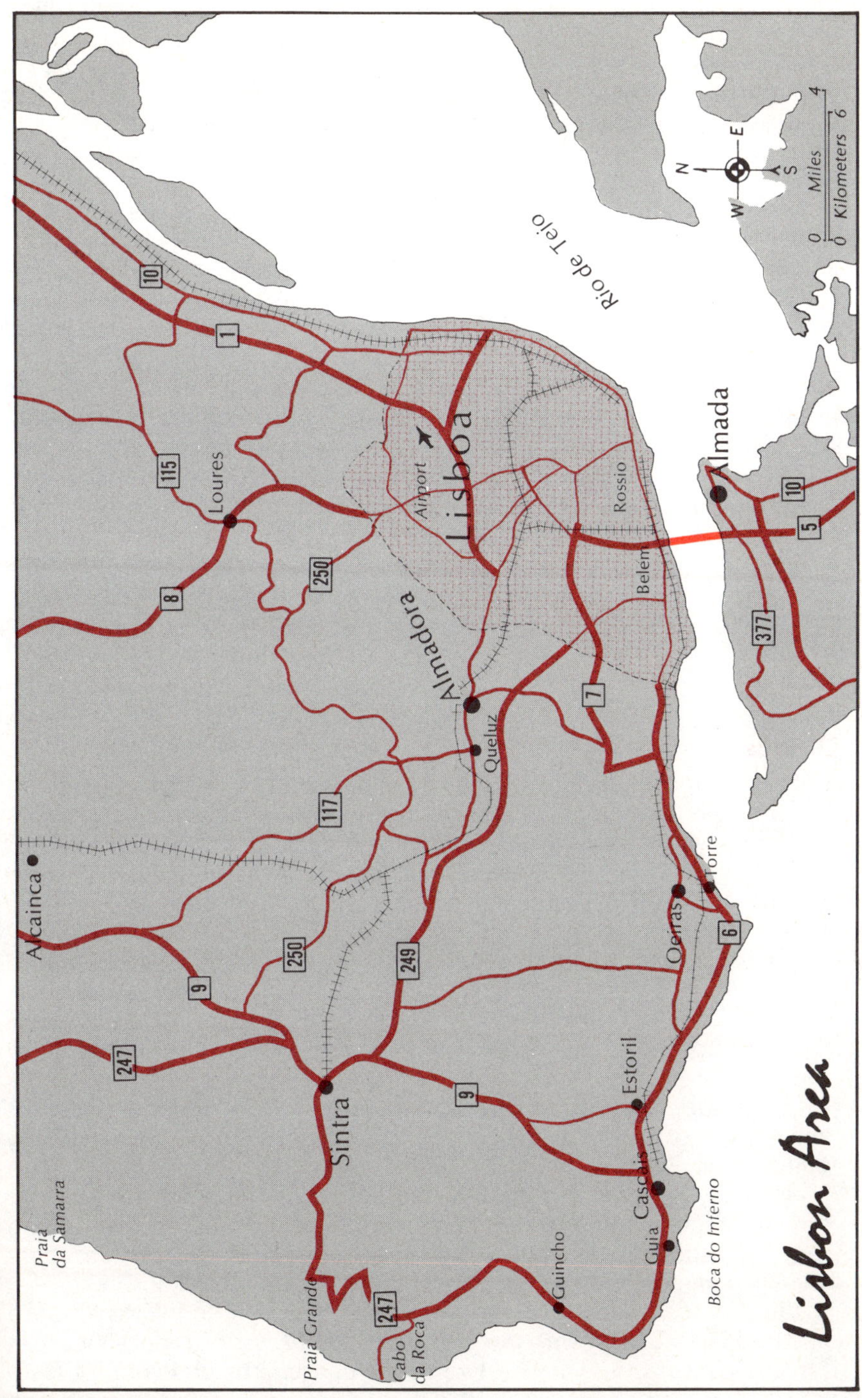
Lisbon Area
Lisboa
Airport
Rossio
Belem
Almadora
Queluz
Loures
Alcainca
Sintra
Estoril
Cascais
Guia
Guincho
Oeiras
Torre
Almada
Rio de Tejo
Praia da Samarra
Praia Grande
Cabo da Roca
Boca do Inferno
N
E
S
W
0 Miles 4
0 Kilometers 6
10
1
115
8
250
117
9
247
249
7
6
5
377

ing, Moorish minarets. Richard Strauss called it "the castle of the Holy Grail."

Local lore has Byron sleeping in as many houses as George Washington

The Hotel Lawrence where Byron, Bulwer-Lytton and other visiting English luminaries stayed, is no more. But there is a hotel in Sintra that had another life during the past century—*Seteais Palace.* It was built in the late 18th century by a Dutch consul named Gildermeester and is often called the Palace of Seven Sighs. The sighs have nothing to do with ghosts. No one ever accused old Gildermeester of haunting the place. Some say the sighs were his reaction when he got the builder's bill. Another version is that the palace was the scene of the signing of the Treaty of Sintra in 1807, in which the French agreed to leave Portugal but were permitted, by the British, to take much of their booty with them. The sighs came when the Portuguese heard the terms.

The pink palace of *Queluz,* just 13 kilometers (6 miles) or so from Lisbon, was built by King Pedro III, supposedly as a Portuguese Versailles. Versailles it's not, but it *is* an exquisite, beautifully integrated country palace (around which a small town has grown up) in the French style. Many of its 25 rooms come vividly to life. Note especially the *Salon de Toilette* (with the star designs in its parquet floor), the Don Quixote Room (with painted scenes from the novel framed in gilded medallions around the room), and the *Salon de Cha* (with delightful wall scenes of frolicking picnickers). Though now chiefly a museum, Queluz is sometimes used as a home away from home for foreign dignitaries on State visits. Queen Elizabeth II and the duke of Edinburgh stayed here in 1957.

Obidós

Further afield, but a possible day trip, is Obidós. It is much better, we must add, to spend the night, for the charming medieval town warrants two days for wandering. Its castle–*pousada* is a comfortable base for side trips elsewhere, such as the fishing village of Nazaré 25 kilometers (16 miles) or so up the coast, or inland to Santarém, which has a cluster of worthy sights waiting to be studied, photographed and enjoyed.

There are 7 churches in town to peek at

At first glance, Obidós is so much like a stage set village you are tempted to applaud. One narrow main street spins and twists and turns its way uphill to the castle. White-washed houses melt together all along the route. Many have been converted into shops with bright colored shirts and plates strung on the outside walls.

Take a tea break at the Alcaide, Rua Direita (95220), a "casa de cha" (house of tea) with nice views

The village goes back at least to Moorish times. In 1184 the Christians captured it and, under the guidance of a trio of kings—Dinis, Fernando and Manuel—enlarged and fortified it "just in case."

It is easy to be diverted by shopping in Obidós and rightly so, for some of the most interesting handcraft items in Portugal seem to find their way to the village's shops. Items made elsewhere are often available in greater abundance and variety here: pottery, fiber stools, woven tablecloths.

But Obidós is more than just another pretty space. In the Renaissance church of São Maria, down a few steps form the main street, Afonso V at age 10 married his cousin who was two years younger. The bride of King Dinis was so enamored of the village he did what kings could do then with elan —he made her a present of it. From then on, Obidós was part of the bridal package when a king married.

Palmela

The first stop from Lisbon might be Palmela. Here, on one of the highest hilltops within scanning distance, the Portuguese government had the good judgment to install a modern, deluxe *pousada* in the still-splendid ruins of an old castle of the Knights of St. James. You can "play castle," stroll the grounds, gaze out to sea from various lookouts and then lunch, dine or imbibe in the air-cooled wonder of the pousada's handsome rooms.

Down a few steps from the pousada is slightly more than a shell of a 15th-century Gothic church, *São Tiago* (Sant Iago in Spanish, St. James in English) with a Gothic portal. Inside is the sarcophagus of King João II's son, Jorge of Lancaster, as well as Gothic arches and remnants of blue-and-white tiling around the walls.

Setúbal

Setúbal—or St. Ubes as English sailors called it 100 years ago—is a mostly white town where some say the Algarve really begins. Romantics will tell you the town was founded by Noah's grandson. Be that as it may be, its salt was mined by the Romans, and its oranges are considered to be the best in Portugal.

In the big square called *Praça Miguel Bombarda* there is a tiny, understated masterpiece—the church of Jesus. The architecture is considered the earliest example of the unique Portuguese Manueline style. The building is the work—in 1491—of King Manuel's pet architect, Boytac, who later expanded and enlarged his twisted columns and stone "engravings" into a full-fledged Manueline style in Belém's São Jerónimo. "The stone looks like head cheese," a food-conscious friend observed, referring to the mottled reddish pink porphyry used throughout the church. Once through the flamboyant Gothic portals, you find yourself in a tiled wonderland of blue and white diamond shaped *azulejos* flanked by others in pale yellow and lavender.

Setúbal's main square, the palm-punctuated *Praça Bocage,* is watched over by a bronze statue of its native son, poet Manuel Bocage in knee breeches. Bocage is better known for his sonnets than for his Jacobin politics and his sympathy for Marie Antoinette.

You will want to drive past a terrain of cork and olives, wisteria and palms to the hilltop castle of *São Filipe,* which was built by Spain's Philip II during his short tenure as King of Portugal. Not only will you have the best view in town, but in the pousada tucked into the castle walls you can sip a *vinho verde* and watch the ships unload sardines and oysters way, way down below. In this idyllic setting King João II was married and, much later, stabbed his brother-in-law for plotting against the throne.

Inside Information

Hotels

For prices, see Lisbon, page 282.

*** Restaurant here

★★★★★ **1. PALACIO DOS SETEAIS**
8 Av. Barbosa do Bocage, Sintra (phone 2933200). An 18th-century delight, with two Italian Renaissance wings joined by a triumphal arch. Guest rooms furnished with museum-quality antiques and hand-painted walls, Flemish tapestries, aged rosewood and mahogany. Parklike, formal gardens, views of Pena Palace. 18 rooms. *Moderate.*

★★★★★ **2. ALBATROZ**
100 Rua Frederico Arouca, Cascais (phone 282821). Ensconced in a totally renovated 19th-century mansion, this is the Coast's most beautiful new small hotel (37 stylishly furnished rooms, three suites). Juts from rocks over water, with seawater swimming pool. Seamless service. Handsome dining room (★★★), *intime* lounges. *Moderate.*

**** Restaurant here

★★★★★ **3. HOTEL DO GUINCHO**
Praia do Guincho, 2750 Cascais (phone 2850491); 30 kilometers (20 miles) from Lisbon. This white stucco Moroccan mirage is built on a dramatic rock outcropping above the Atlantic in remnants of a 17th-century fortress. Thoroughly modern, decorated with *azulejos* and good taste; balconied rooms have limitless views of thundering waves, restless ocean. Member of Relais et Chateaux de Campagne association. 36 rooms, all different. *Moderate.*

★★★★★ **4. POUSADA DO CASTELO PALMELA**
Palmela, 8 kilometers (5 miles north of Setúbal) (phone 2351226). In the former 15th-century monastery of the Knights of St. James an ultramodern luxury inn has been installed, complete with elevator, marble-paved inner courtyard, king-sized guest rooms with leather chairs, handwoven rugs, spreads. One of the newest in the pousada chain and a real winner. Pool and parking. 28 rooms. *Moderate.*

★★★★★ **5. ESTORIL SOL**
Parque Palmela, Cascais (phone 282831). Though 20 years old, it's in mint condition. Rooms have balcony, clear views of beach and ocean, minibar, two bathrooms. Olympic pool, golf course, shops, sauna, gym, squash courts, organized functions. 310 rooms. *Expensive.*

★★★★ **1. POUSADA DO CASTELO**
Óbidos (phone 95105). Exquisite and exclusive are the words that classify this tiny castle, built as fortress by Moors in 12th century. Hand-carved furniture, suits of armor, walk-in, granite fireplaces, flowers; storybook village. Booked months ahead, understandably. Only six rooms. *Moderate.*

★★★★ 2. HOTEL DO MAR

10 Rua dos Combatentes do Ultramar, Sesimbra (phone 2233326). Built in tiers into the hillside 30 kilometers (20 miles) from Lisbon, its modern, functional rooms are balconied, have built-in furniture, views of pool and beach. Resort-type snack bars, saloon, restaurant with picture windows, views. 120 rooms. *Moderate.*

★★★★ 3. POUSADA SÃO FILIPE

Castelo de São Filipe, Setũbal (phone 23844). 50 kilometers (30 miles) south of Lisbon. Colorful *azulejos* brighten the walls of a former governor's house and is now the lounge and dining room high above the sea. Former gun rooms of this ancient fortress are now furnished with reproductions of antiques; fixtures are thoroughly modern, comfortable. 15 rooms. One drawback: many steps and no elevator. *Moderate.*

★★★★ 4. ESTORIL PALACIO

Parque do Estoril, Estoril (phone 268040). *The* place to stay for decades after it opened in 1942, this Grand Dame has been living in the past in recent years. Air-conditioned, with pool, sauna, three nicely furnished lounges. The hotel has new ownership and may soon again return to its five-star glory. But not now. Not yet. 200 rooms. *Expensive.*

Guest list reads like pages of Who's Who... includes Hirohito, Ibn Saud, Orson Welles

★★★★ 5. SINTRA ESTORIL

Estrada Nacional No. 9, Alcabideche, 2765 Estoril (phone 26907). Located 6 kilometers (3½ miles) north of Estoril on the national road, this resort hotel has much that a vacationer might want: air-conditioned rooms with terraces overlooking pool, gardens, tennis courts. Lounges and restaurant are modern; disco nightly; hairdresser. Drawbacks: Noisy on highway side; isolated location quite a way from beach and town. 192 rooms. *Inexpensive.*

★★★ 1. HOTEL DE TURISMO

Rua Porto de Rezés, Ericeira (phone 54545). In Europe's westernmost fishing village, this hotel is right on the water. For ocean view request first- or second-floor room with terrace and balcony. Pool, private beach, craft shops, parking, disco, garden for comfortable seaside holiday. 154 rooms. *Inexpensive.*

★★★ 2. ATLANTICO

7 Estrada Marginal, Monte Estoril (phone 2680270). On the shore between Estoril and Cascais this no-nonsense, modern hotel is a few steps from the Monte Estoril stop on the electric train from Lisbon. All rooms face water, are generous in size, unpretentious. Heated pool; restaurant on beach side. 183 rooms. *Inexpensive.*

★★★ 3. ESTALAGEM DO CONVENTO

Rua D. João de Ornelas, Óbidos (phone 95217). Just outside the walls of this museum town. Old monastery's rooms have blue and white tiles shoulder high on the walls, old-fashioned beds, modern bathrooms. From open terrace in rear to cozy, beamed ceiling restaurant with mosaic floor this one is a delight. 19 rooms. *Inexpensive.*

★★★ **4. CIDADELA**
Rua de 25 Abril, Cascais (phone 282921). It's a modern egg-crate-style building that has individual balconies for each room. Garden, hairdressers, supermarket, parking. 140 rooms. *Inexpensive.*

★★ **ALBERGARIA VALBOM**
14 Avenida Valbom, Cascais (phone 285801). This hotel *residencia* on a side street was built in 1977. It has garage parking and is a short walk from beaches and restaurants. 42 rooms. *Bargain.*

★ **1. BAIA**
Av. Marginal, Cascais (phone 281033). In the prime location on Cascais' beach, the Baia is a typical resort hotel—66 of its 88 rooms have balconies with beach views; lounge, restaurant, snack bar, sun terrace on top floor. Popular with tour groups. *Inexpensive.*

★ **2. INGLATERRA**
2 Avda. de Portugal, Estoril (phone 2684786). Old-fashioned family-style Victorian British establishment boasts pool and TV lounge, but guest rooms are prosaic. Some have balconies with views of park and sea. Limited parking. 49 rooms. *Bargain.*

Restaurants

For prices, see Lisbon, page 284.

★★★★★ **1. CASA DE CHA COZINHA VELHA**
Palacio Nacional, Queluz (phone 950740). This "tea house" was the kitchen for the national palace. Its dramatic interior has vast walk-in fireplace for roasting oxen, timbered ceiling, granite arches, coach lamp sconces, antique copper collection. Floral displays, regional and French specialties make dining memorable not only for the King of Spain, assorted presidents and Pope John Paul, but for the likes of us. Grilled sea bass with anchovy butter goes well with a Serradayres white wine. Hours 1–3, 7:30–10, seven days a week. *Expensive.*

The wine list is both good and lengthy

★★★★ **1. HOTEL DO GUINCHO**
Praia do Guincho, 2750 Cascais (phone 2850491). Diners are in a wide-angle seascape in suave, carpeted surroundings with burgundy upholstered chairs, table cloths. Menu is French–international–Portuguese, featuring tempters such as whiting with almonds, poached turbot *á la hollandaise,* Portuguese duckling with olives. Wine list is extensive. *Very Expensive.*

★★★ **1. PALACIO DOS SETEAIS**
8 Av. Barbosa do Bocage, Sintra (phone 2933200). The ground floor dining rooms of this historic Palacio face the formal gardens. Exquisitely decorated

with crystal sconces, matching soft green carpets and green and gold walls. Notable are *acepipas*—assortment of hors d'oeuvres. Peppery cream shrimp soup, whiting quenelles with periwinkles and curry sauce are among the delights. A fresh, aromatic Buçellas branco (white) wine from large wine list is a splendid choice. Hours 12:30–2:30 P.M., 7:30–9:30 P.M. *Expensive.*

★★★ 2. GALERIA REAL

Rua Tude de Sousa, S. Pedro de Sintra (phone 2931661). From its first-floor location above antique shops this rustic brick restaurant looks out on village road and gardens. A regional-cum-continental menu highlights sole, prepared meuniere or caprice style, and filet mignon. Good wine cellar. *Moderate.*

★★ 1. BEIRA MAR

6 Rua das Flores, Cascais (phone 380152). It should be called *Rua da Peixes* (fish) because this short street has seven seafood restaurants. *Beira Mar* (seashore) is closest to the bay and gets high marks for *lulas* (fried squid,) *cherne* (grilled needlefish) and other marine delights. Food arrives at table fresh, sizzling, without overkill. *Moderate.*

★★ 2. PO PIPAS

Rua das Flores, Cascais (phone 284501). A seaside bistro with sparkling crystal, starched linens in a room where barrel ends, garlic garlands, shallots and pineapples are decorative motifs. Excellent seafood. *Moderate.*

★★ 3. O BECO

24 Largo da Misericórdia, Setúbal (phone 24617). In a handy central location this restaurant has a rustic, charming interior and serves fresh seafood and regional dishes. *Moderate.*

★★ 4. O PESCADOR

Rua das Flores, Cascais (phone 282154). O Pescador (the fisherman), with a longer menu than its neighbors and more briny decorations (floats, nets), is well regarded by locals and visitors alike for both fish and meat dishes. *Moderate.*

★★ 5. O BATEL

4 Travessa das Flores, Cascais (phone 280215). Rustic, with beamed ceiling, whitewashed walls, flowers and fruit in profusion. Its menu has baked sole with cheese sauce, broiled squid with ham, prawns in garlic. *Moderate.*

★ RESTAURATE NAVAL SETUBALENSE

300 Av. Luisa Todi, Setúbal (phone 23674). Known as the Naval Club, this old-timer is a favorite for fresh red mullet and other sea treats. Prices are modest and match the setting. *Inexpensive.*

Entertainment

The *Casino in Estoril* (phone 2684521, 2684971, 2684995), reputedly Europe's largest, is more than a glorified gambling parlor. From 3 P.M. to 3 A.M. daily you can take a spin at the wheel, play baccarat or feed the one-arm bandits. (Remember to take your passport for admission to the casino.)

In addition to gambling, the establishment has a movie theater with current films, an art gallery with up-to-the-minute shows, a restaurant and a nightclub called The Wonderbar. There is a nightly floor show at 11:30 P.M. in the restaurant and at 1 A.M. in the Wonderbar.

Fado singing can be heard at half a dozen spots in the Estoril–Cascais area; two places that local residents consider best are: *Forte D. Rodrigo,* Estrada de Birre, Cascais (phone 2851373); and *Kopus Bar,* 3 Largo das Grutas, Cascais (phone 281901). Rodrigo opens at 10 P.M. and closes at 3 A.M. Kopus opens at 7 P.M. and closes at 4 A.M.

Fado singers don't warm up until midnight.

Shopping

International boutique–ish is a good description of much of the shopping on the Estoril–Cascais coast, but be prepared for surprises. In Cascais, for example, you can get exquisite, hand-embroidered (in the Azores) tablecloths and place mats at *Guida,* 7 Avenida 25 de Abril (phone 283708). Designer Marguerita Guida Arruda's specialty is matching tablecloth patterns to your porcelain dinnerware. Customers include various Rockefellers. Prices, as you might guess, are not budget but the quality is extraordinary.

Also in Cascais, *Isto e Aquilo,* Largo da Misericordia, features attractive pottery, weavings, gifts. Along Rua Frederico Arouca, a pedestrian mall, there are a number of off-beat shops.

During the summer months in Estoril a semipermanent market of handcrafts is set up near the railway station. It is known as *Feira do Artesanato* and features ceramics, wooden ware, woven and embroidered cloths. The arcade on the left side of the formal gardens facing the casino has a few shops sprinkled among the travel agencies and bank. A large shop, with a good variety of sweaters, caps, porcelain, pottery and unusual fishermen's stocking caps is *Regionalalia,* 27 Arcadas do Parque (phone 2681619). In the arcade on the opposite side is *Berenice* with a good assortment of English-language books and *Gal D'ouro* for imported foods and liquors.

As you emerge from the castle–*pousada* grounds in Óbidos, there are nice shops along the main street. And in Mafra, *Artesanato,* 20 Largo Conde de Ferreira (phone 52553), across from the monastery, has a big selection of fishermen's white knit sweaters, caps, gloves, and embroidered goods at very reasonable prices.

São *Pedro,* outside Sintra, has the liveliest market going. It is held twice a month on the second and fourth Sundays. Vendors from surrounding hills fill the streets and squares of the town with stalls, hawking everything from shoes and leather handbags to breads, cheeses, sausages, ham and wrought iron, straw goods and rugs. Even on non-market days, a number of intriguing antique shops are open along Largo 1st de Dezembro in *São* Pedro.

Museums and Galleries

Setúbal

MUSEU DE CIDADE

Municipal Museum, Pr. Miguel Bombarde. There are 15th- and 16th-century paintings of Portuguese primitives; especially the *Master of the Setúbal Altarpiece* pictures. Galleries are in a Gothic cloister. There is also collection of 15th–18th-century *azulejos,* which is great for tile fanciers. Open 10 A.M. –12:30 P.M., 2–6 P.M.; closes an hour earlier in winter. Closed Mondays and holidays.

Spectacles and Displays

Bullfights. From April to October at the Cascais Praça de Touros (Portugal's largest); usually on Sundays.

Tours

From Estoril, tours can be booked that include Queluz Royal Palace, Mafra and the three palaces in Sintra. They leave at 8:30 A.M., and return 10 hours later; they go twice a week, leaving from Estoril post office, Av. de Nice. Information from your concierge or Estoril Tourist Office, Arcadas do Parque.

Cruise from Cascais to Lisbon and back—A 4-hour trip leaving at 9 A.M., sailing up the Tagus River past forts, beaches and the monuments of Lisbon. Goes on Tuesdays, Thursdays and Saturdays from Cascais Marine Club—Pirata Tours.

Cruise on Cascais Bay for 2½ hours every afternoon at 3 P.M. to see beaches, landmarks and sealife. Departs from Cascais Marine Club—Pirata Tours.

Sintra and Cabo da Roca—A half-day tour to Europe's westernmost point and to either the Royal or Pena Palace in Sintra, winding through the mountains and along the shore. Mondays and Fridays at 9 A.M.; Wednesdays at 2:30 P.M. from Hotel Paris.

Mafra and Ericeira—A half-day tour to the monastery at Mafra, a stop at a ceramics workshop and another stop at the beach resort of Ericeira to see its colorful fishing fleet. Mondays at 2:30 P.M., depart from Hotel Paris.

Perks

The estate of a former viceroy of India, Don João da Castro, may be visited with permission. (He asked the king in 1542 for "a rock with six trees" and built this "paradise.") You'll have to write or request in advance from Exmº Senhor Ernesto Rau, Quinta da Penha Verde, Sintra. There are other *quintas* that may be visited with special permission. Inquire at Sintra or Estoril *turismo* offices.

The Naval Club of Cascais offers its facilities (restaurant, bar, terrace, rental of sail, motor and other craft) to interested visitors. International championships of star-class vessels held here.

Sports

You can hire steeds at Escola de Equitacão (Estribo Club) in Birre or at Hipodromo da Quinta da Marinha, Guincho.

Auto racing at the Autodromo just north of Estoril on the main highway. Check concierge or turismo office for schedule.

Golf is exceptionally challenging on the international championship course designed by MacKenzie Ross at Estoril Golf Club, one-half kilometer north of town on main highway. Contact hotel concierge or turismo office for details.

There are 71 fishing sites officially designated between Cascais and Guincho. Furthermore, fishing boats leave every Wednesday, Friday and Sunday at 9 A.M. on four-hour circuits from Cascais Marine Club. Bait and equipment are included in 1,500$00 fee.

Water skiing and underwater fishing equipment and training at the Cascais Marine Club. Estoril Coast's best beach is Carcavelos.

GETTING AROUND

From Cascais to Lisbon the electric train follows the shore and stops at key places. Fast, quiet, frequent and inexpensive (65$00 one way). Runs from 5:30 A.M. to 2:30 A.M. and takes 25 minutes, approximately, from Cais do Sodre station.

There is similar service from Lisbon to Sintra from Rossio Station, 25 minutes, about 100 trains per day at 65$00 one way.

Buses connect Cascais, Estoril, Sintra and other towns. They leave the Cascais and Estoril train stations hourly. To Cabo da Roca, for example, there are four departures daily. Inexpensive.

Taxis are inexpensive and can be found at train stations, taxi stands in front of Casino and Parque Estoril.

Chauffeur-driven cars may be hired with English-speaking drivers. Make arrangements through turismo office or concierge. Rates are according to type of car and may be by hour or kilometer.

Go in style. A horse-drawn landau can be hired at the stand by the Cascais garden on the main road. At Sintra's main square, the rate per hour is 1200$00 to Pena Palace (including waiting time) and return costs 1400$00.

Hire a fisherman's boat with crew and a *caldeirada* (fish stew) prepared for your family or group outing. You can take up to 12 persons. Arrange it at Estoril turismo office.

Directory

Airlines

Lisbon airport information; phone 802060.

Emergency Numbers

National emergency service; phone 115.

Cascais. Medical emergency; phone 2865454.

Estoril. Medical emergency; phone 2683387.
Ambulance; phone 2680189.
British Hospital, 49 R.S. de Carvalho (Lisbon phone 671007).
Police; phone 280061.

Railroad

Information; phone 326226

Telephone

European international service; phone 17. Intercontinental service; phone 329011. Telephoned cables international; phone 113.

Office of Tourism Information

Ericeira. 33A rua Eduardo Burnay; phone 63122.

Estoril. Arcadas do Parque; phone 2688013.

Palmela. Largo do Chafariz; phone 2350089.

Sesimbra. Largo do Municipio; phone 2233304.

Setúbal. Praç do Bocage; phone 24204; Largo do Corpo Santo; phone 22484.

Religious Services

Cascais. Roman Catholic mass in English, noon Sundays. Capela de São Sebastiao (Parque Castro Guimaraes) next to museum. Church of Jesus Christ of Latter-Day Saints, 19 Rua Ten. Coronel Jose Barros Pessoa.

Estoril. Anglican services, St. Paul's Anglican Church, Avda. Bombeiros Voluntarios.

The Algarve

Of all Portuguese regions, it is the south that gives you the most frequent reminders of the country's Moorish past. It took 100 years longer (until the 13th century) to force the Moors out of the cultivated terrain that they called Algarve. Still, with all the time that has elapsed since, there are at least 600 Arabic words that have remained entrenched in Portuguese. The name *Algarve—al-Gharb*—is among them.

You know there's change in the air almost the minute you cross the Tagus River from Lisbon and begin your southward journey. The sun bounces against the theatrically white houses with blinding intensity. North Africa seems a reality. The fretworked chimney pots, symbols of this part of Portugal, differ from house to house, but each reinforces the sense of Moorishness.

There is a belief that the mysterious word *al-Gharb* may have meant garden, and if you are here in winter when the almond covers the land like snow and the figs and orange and lemon trees are all abloom, you are willing to believe it.

We like the much-repeated story of the Nordic princess wasting away in her Algarve palace, homesick for the familiar sights of winter. Her Moorish prince lavished gift after gift upon her—to no avail. Then he planted an orchard of almonds, and when the trees bloomed, the princess smiled. She felt at home in the almond "snow."

The dedicated sightseer will head north and east in Portugal. It is the beachaholic who heads south. Oddly, with some 200 kilometers (120) miles of coves, cliffs and beaches available as a playground, the Algarve slept quietly for centuries. Only in the 1960s did it catch fire. Development since has been more tempered, and more controlled than, say, Spain's Costa del Sol. There are highrise hotel and condominium complexes, to be sure, but there are also fishing villages where people live much as they always have.

The Algarve, separated from the rest of Portugal by the Caldeirão and Monchique mountains and from Spain by the Guadiana River, is an entity to and of itself. New highways make road travel easier (though still not creamy smooth) from Lisbon and Évora. There is now an international airport at Faro, which represents the best solution for travelers with an absence of time on their hands.

If you fly to Faro, rental car offices make it easy to move along the coast at will (and at donkey's will, for sometimes traffic jams are beastmade as well as manmade here). A standard operating procedure is to base yourself somewhere on the coast and then beach, cove-and-village hop from east to west or vice versa.

In spite of what we have just said about sightseers traveling north, there *are* sights to be seen in the Algarve. They are just not as densely laden as elsewhere. The 1755 earthquake ruined most of the area's churches (its impact was felt even in Spain), so that most of the immaculate white-washed churches you see are not even 200 years old.

FARO AND POINTS EAST

Faro

Faro, a town of 22,000 or so, has been the Algarve's capital since the mid-18th century. Over a long, and now-and-then prosperous life, Faro has had its share of bad breaks. During the days of Philip II when Portugal was part of Spain, it inherited Spain's enemy, Britain, and in 1596 was burned to the ground by British raiders, Robert, Second Duke of Essex (Queen Elizabeth's pal) and Charles Howard. Before it could put itself right again, Faro was hit by not one but two earthquakes—in 1722 and 1755.

Essex "borrowed" Bishop of Faro's prize library, whose books became the nucleus of the Bodleian at Oxford

Still, for the dedicated, there are things to see. You may make the acquaintance of the *Sé* (cathedral), built on the base of a mosque first in the Gothic and then in the Renaissance style. You may be surprised to see the Chippendale chair on the altar and the red-and-gold pagoda-style baroque organ, a gift from the Portuguese colony of Macao.

After the Moors were driven from Faro across the ocean for the last time (by Afonso III in 1266), there existed for centuries an active Jewish colony. The Jews printed the first books in Portugal on their brand new 15th-century press. An 1820 synagogue and 1833 cemetery are considered the earliest *post*-Inquisition Jewish monuments to be found in Iberia.

Faro life revolves around its harbor, and as you admire the towering palms of the Manuel Bivar Gardens and the palm-bordered *Avenida de Republica,* you may doff your straw hat (or at least your sun glasses) to Dom Francisco Gomes's obelisk in Gomes Square. He's the Bishop and guiding light who helped the town put itself right after the earthquakes by building and planting as quickly and consistently as possible.

Sample the cataplana (ham, clams + pork in garlic-wine sauce) at * Roque in Faro

A short ferry ride or drive over a bridge takes you to *Praia de Faro* and a strip of sun-kissed beach. It's a place for swimming, water skiing, fishing or taking pictures of the Faro harbor across the water.

East of Faro

Ten kilometers (6 miles) east of Faro is *Olhão* with its sugar-cube white-washed houses stacked one above another on a cliffside. Oriental chimneys and fireplaces ornament what otherwise looks like a scene from North Africa. A short boat ride away is the *Ilha de Armona,* a harmonic beach considered prime by those who keep beach records.

For the best view of Olhão houses, climb the belfry of the Parish Church.

Nearby are *Estói,* and *Milreu,* where mosaics were discovered in 1876 that date from the Greek (5th century B.C.), Roman and early Christian period. You will see mosaics, ruins of a Roman bath, and fragmented columns, as well as the 18th-century *Palacio de Visconde de Estói.*

In *Tavira,* just 22 kilometers (13 miles) from the Spanish border, there is, in addition to a storybook all-white town, a seven-arched Roman bridge and the fine Renaissance church of Misericordia (1541). Facing Spain across the Guadiana is Vila Real de São Antonio, which could well have been named Pombaltown. It was a town built in 1774 in little more than 5 months at the order of Marquês de Pombal, who wanted to match the prosperous border town of Ayamonte across the river. Every door frame and paving stone was shipped to order from Lisbon, even the sunlike rays of the black and white stones of Praça do Marquês de Pombal, the main, orange tree-dotted square.

Glide across the river (by ferry) and into the trees of the very pleasant *Parador Nacional Costa de la Luz* (phone 320700) in Ayamonte, Spain, for lunch and scenic vistas of the area.

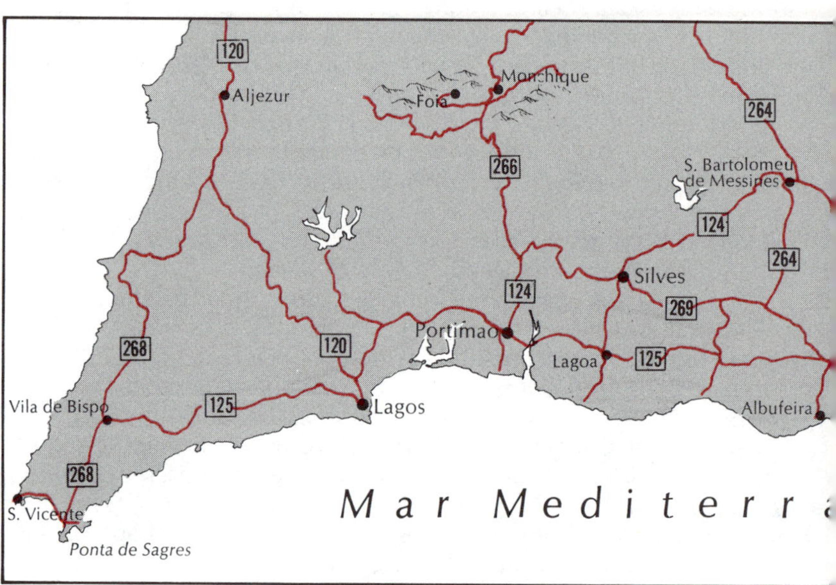

WEST OF FARO

Most of the action, admittedly, is west of Faro. What thrills us about the Algarve—even those of us who are not beach buffs—is the high drama of the Algarve coastline: beaches intercepted by massive craggy cliffs, surreptitious grottoes, and hovering hillsides. You can visualize the smugglers and pirates who might have holed up here in the past. It is a beautiful shoreline, artfully broken up by nature to prevent boredom. The coves and inlets are also natural buffers against sea winds.

All along this coast and undulating inland around pine and cork forests and orchards of figs and almonds are holiday villages, products of 1960–1980s planning. Among them are *Vale do Lobo* (Valley of the Wolf), an easy half-hour drive from the Faro airport, with a golf course designed by Henry Cotton, a Moorish look to the villas, and luscious plantings.

You could plan an entire holiday around the golf courses, most of them designed by specialists such as Cotton. Here now is *Vilamoura,* with golf, a

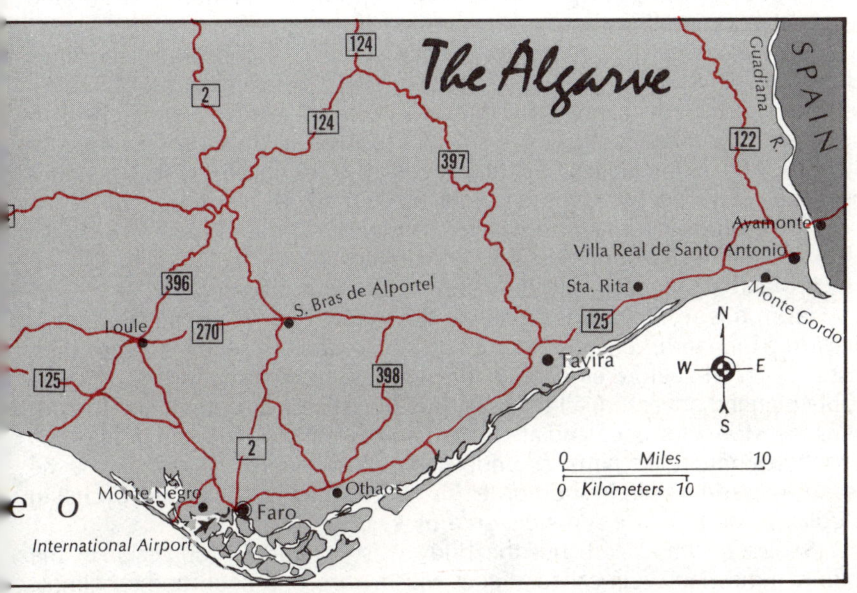

casino and a choice of hotels and rental villas. When building this enormous complex, remains of a Roman villa were discovered.

Salted and peppered among the holiday villages along the coast are bona fide fishing villages and sprinklings of deluxe and modest hotels. *Quarreira* used to bask in its artist colony image, but now serves as something of a refuge for golfing escapees from the more expensive resorts. *Albufeira* retains the look of the village it once was except during midsummer when it bursts its narrow seams with tourists. Locals like to call it "St. Tropez west." Try it in spring or fall when it's less crowded and you can really enjoy going through a tunnel to the beach, viewing the town hall that looks like a church (because of the belfry), and lolling about on the village's beaches, San Rafael to the west and Olhos d'Agua to the east. Albufeira was one of the Algarve's last Moorish holdouts, "liberated" in 1250.

West of Albufeira is *Carvoeiro,* tucked under steep rough-textured cliffs, surprisingly unspoiled considering that it hosts much of the coast's international nightlife. Nightclubs, English-style pubs, discos and bistros cluster in a passageway once used by fishermen to haul their boats by oxcart to the water. Some of Carvoeiro's beaches are so sequestered you can only reach them by boat. Next comes Portimão, a fishing center, with houses decorated with *azulejos,* pretty *praças* and charming streets.

Busy *Lagos* was a bustling town back in the 15th century when Prince Henry the Navigator used it as a "holding port" for as many as 147 ships. Its shipyards built the caravels that Henry's captains sailed to explore the then unknown universe. From Lagos, Gil Eanes took off to discover Cap Bojador in 1434. And in a small, well-made arcaded customs house, Henry's captains held their slave auctions, the first such slave markets in Europe.

The customs house is on *Praça da Republica,* a pretty square ringed with historic buildings. On one side is a 17th-century palace, identified by its coat of arms and a Manueline window, with a place in history.

From this window, it is believed, the young King Sebastião, Portugal's ill-starred monarch, romantic spinner of flawed dreams, gave his troops their last big pep talk before embarking for Morocco to fight the Moors. It was a badly planned adventure all the way, but Sebastião was determined to conquer the Moors for once and all. He led an assembly of youthful nobles and neophytes (much like himself), understaffed and underequipped, across the sea to Al-ksar el-Kebir. In short order his 15,000 men were savaged by Sultan Moulay Abd-al-Malik's superior force of 49,000.

Sebastião was killed, but the body wasn't returned for years. In the interim a messianic cult called "Sebastianism" arose. It flourished for almost 200 years. People refused to believe their young king had died. He was a prisoner; he was in hiding; he would return.

His death did more than skim off the cream of Portugal's noblest youth. It paved the way for Sebastião's Spanish uncle, Philip II, to take over the throne and led to 60 years of Spanish rule.

Sagres

If you skip all else on this breezy coast in a quest for a perfect tan free from sightseeing, save a few hours at least for a drive to *Sagres,* a desolate, forlorn point of land facing the ocean, which the Portuguese call their "Sacred Promontory." This is the site of Prince Henry's School of Navigation, long gone now. (A youth hostel stands on what is believed to have been the exact site.) The chapel where his sailors prayed before embarking in their caravels has been reconstructed, as has the villa where Henry himself lived. The fortress walls were rebuilt in the 17th century.

But more significant than manmade sights is the site itself. You can visualize Henry standing on this wind-lashed cliff, 75 meters (250 feet) above the Atlantic, watching as his ships took off, dreaming the impossible dream about what lay beyond "land's end," setting Portugal's future course for years to come. Henry gathered round him leading astronomers, astrologers, navigators, scientists. It was his perseverance—rewarded after his death—that brought riches, colonies and power to his small country, making it one of the two major sea powers of Europe for generations.

Just 5 kilometers (3 miles) from Sagres is *Cabo de São Vicente,* the most southwesterly point in Europe. The sunsets are spectacular here, a reminder that in ancient times people believed that the sun dropped off the edge of the world just beyond the cape's horizon.

If you have time you can continue north up the coast to *Sines,* where Vasco da Gama was born. The little chapel of Nossa Senhora das Salas on the cliff overlooking the harbor was rebuilt by this village's most famous native son.

When in Sagres, you may lunch or even spend the night at the Pousada do Infante, which is located on a second promontory overlooking a high cliff. The views are superb, and the restaurant is agreeable.

You can see a film at the Turismo Office here that relates the story of Henry & the Portuguese discoveries

INLAND

We have led you along the Algarve coast, but inland are a number of equally appealing villages, many with overhanging views of the sea. For example, weaving your way eastward from Sagres, you will first come to *Alvor* above Portimão. João II died here in 1495, but its history stretches back to Roman times when its *nom de ciudad* was Portus Hannibalis. Note the fine portal on its little Manueline church.

The countryside is wild and natural, with red poppies in bloom in springtime, buttercups, rock roses and other wild flowers decorating the earth much of the rest of the year. It is also a terrain of figs, cypress, eucalyptus and pine.

Caldas de Monchique, a spa town when the Romans were in these hills, is a spa town still. Its views are notable as are its many walks through surrounding hillsides. Try the bottled spa water and admire the many restored 17th-century buildings.

In *Silves* you might wonder about "what might have been." The capital of the Moorish Algarve, Silves was once bigger and more important than Lisbon. It now stands 11,000 strong. The 1755 earthquake dealt the town a blow from which it hasn't yet recovered, though its 13th-century cathedral of Santa Maria survives. Visit the restored red sandstone citadel, where the Moors held out for 6 weeks that fatal summer of 1189.

Loule, near Faro, fared better. Its reputation is as a market town, and if you want handcrafts this is where you will find coppersmiths, basket weavers and other artisans at work. Loule is also proud of its 12th-century Gothic parish church and its castle walls from the Middle Ages.

Hotels

For prices, see Lisbon, page 282.

★★★★★ **1. HOTEL DOÑA FILIPA**
Almansil, Vale do Lobo (phone 94141). In a beautiful wonderland of flowers and shrubs, this spacious resort hotel, like the many villas in the Vale do Lobo development, has a Moorish look. Just 18 kilometers (11 miles) from the Faro airport, this is a facility that has everything at its door: heated swimming pool, a children's pool, tennis (a new 12-court complex), minigolf, manicured grounds and public areas and at adjacent Quinta do Lago, a 27-hole golf course, considered one of the greats of Europe. Bedrooms with terraces, much use of tile and redwood throughout. 129 rooms. Now a Trust House Forte property. *Very Expensive.*

★★★★★ **2. LA RESERVE**
Santa Barbara de Nexe (phone 91474). Inland, secluded, this deluxe small (20 bedrooms) hotel has the style you expect of a member of Relais de Campagne. All rooms exquisitely decorated, with fireplaces, terraces overlooking two swimming pools. Tennis. Excellent restaurant. Six acres for wandering. Faro's beaches six miles away. Swiss-owned. *Very Expensive.*

★★★★★ **3. VILALARA**
Alporchinhos—Praia Redonda, Armacão de Pera (phone 32333). A luxury multilevel holiday village of individual rental villas on a spectacular strip of beach, the facilities here are great: two swimming pools, tennis, disco, indoor/outdoor restaurants, private access to beach, exquisite plantings, dramatic sea views. Villas in tiers along a cliff. 87 apts. *Very Expensive.*

★★★★★ **4. HOTEL DA BALAIA**
Praia Maria Luisa, Alto da Semina, Albufeira (phone 52681). In summer, Albufeira's the scene of the action, and this ultramodern, deluxe hotel is just 5 kilometers east of town, overlooking a love of a beach. Riding, tennis, minigolf, swimming pool are all there for a restful sportsy holiday. 150 rooms, each with a balcony tilted seaward. Manicured lawns. Public areas decorated with handsome modern art. *Very Expensive.*

★★★★★ **5. HOTEL PENINA GOLF**
Montes de Alvor, Albufeira (phone 22051). For the golfer who has everything, give him/her a week to master one of the great Henry Cotton courses, one 18-hole, two 9-hole, stretching across this 360-acre wooded and manicured property in the Monchique-backed hills. There's free golf and tennis, a larger than Olympic-size pool, sauna and all kinds of extras, including a private landing strip for planes and dancing every night to live music. 202 rooms. *Very Expensive.*

★★★★★ **6. HOTEL ALGARVE**
Avenida Tomas Cabreira, Praia da Rocha (phone 24000). The setting

couldn't be better for the committed beach lover. It faces the sea, with rock buffer between hotel and wide golden sand beach. All sports are here in a modern highrise setting: two saltwater swimming pools at cliff's edge above the beach, minigolf, sauna, fishing parties, water sports and a social director to make things happen. 164 rooms. Check the fantasy Oriental Suite. *Expensive.*

★★★★★ 7. HOTEL ALVOR PRAIA

Alcaria, Alvor, Praia dos Tres Irmãos (phone 24021). A never-leave-the-grounds vacation choice, with beach below (just a lift away), pool, sea and mountain views, two-level dining room with sea vistas, tennis, fishing boats, sauna, boutiques, riding and golf nearby. 201 rooms. *Expensive.*

★★★★ 1. TERRAÇOS DA RIA FORMOSA

Quinta do Lago (phone 94272). Strictly speaking, this consists of villas, studios and duplexes (some sleep four). It is not a single-unit hotel. We love the lawns with acacia and funny-mushroom-shaped pines, and the Moorish "feel." An ideal place to holiday for golfers; with golf packages and a super 27-hole golf course. It's a convenient centralized Algarve location to boot. *Expensive.*

★★★★ 2. SOL E MAR

Rua Jose Bernardino de Sousa, Albufeira (phone 52121/7). Built into the cliff overlooking Albufeira's golden beach, the hotel is a lively focal point for town life. 74 comfortable rooms with terraces overlooking the ocean. Large lobby is on top floor, with elevator going down five floors to the beach. Swimming pool, disco, restaurant and bar. *Moderate.*

★★★★ 3. HOTEL DE LAGOS

Rua Nova da Aldeia, Lagos (phone 62011). A dandy location on three hilltop acres overlooking Lagos. Free shuttle service to a private beach club, Duna. Heated pool at hotel; rooms with balconies and vistas. 273 rooms plus 12 deluxe suites. *Moderate.*

★★★★ 4. HOTEL ALCAZAR

Rua de Ceuta, Monte Gordo (phone 42184). An in-town location on the Algarve's east coast, this interestingly designed hotel is fun. It has pool, lounges, recreation rooms. 95 rooms. Well equipped. *Inexpensive.*

★★★★ 5. HOTEL DOM PEDRO

Vilamoura (phone 65412). If your taste is for large, this well-run hotel (part of the Dom Pedro Portuguese chain) has many amenities: tennis, 18-hole golf course (considered one of the Algarve's finest), three swimming pools, rooms with balcony facing marina. Not far from beach. 260 rooms. *Moderate.*

★★★ 1. BOA VISTA

6 Rua Samora Barros, Albufeira (phone 52175). Perched high on a cliff above the harbor, the hotel's compact, neat rooms (51, and three apts.) with balconies overlook the swimming pool, town and ocean. Pretty blue-white tiled lobby. A true "find." *Inexpensive*

★★★ 2. HOTEL DA ALDEIA

Areias de Sao Joao, Albufeira (phone 52031). Member of Glitter chain, this bright, well-run hotel is a short walk from Oura beach. 136 rooms, furnished in contemporary colors, with balconies overlooking lovely swimming pool. Caters to tours. Helpful concierge. *Inexpensive.*

★★★ 3. HOTEL ROCAMAR

7 Largo Jacinto d'Ayet, Albufeira (phone 56261). A cliffside view of the beach gives this sparkling "sugar cube" hotel its panache. 182 rooms with balconies. Good service. Convenient. Fine value. *Inexpensive.*

★★★ 4. POUSADA DO INFANTE

Sagres (phone 64222). The clifftop setting is a stunner, and the simple, classical interiors are in keeping with the rugged seascape unfurling before your eyes. 15 rooms. *Inexpensive.*

★★★ 5. HOTEL DA BALEEIRA

Sagres (phone 64212). The name of this cosy, all-white hotel means whaleboat, but the locale, high on a hill with an overview of the sea below, suggests "beauty." Dining room cantilevers over the sea; there's a saltwater pool, lounge and rooms with balcony views. 108 rooms. *Bargain.*

★★ POUSADA DE SÃO BRAS

São Bras de Alportel (phone 42305). Add a handy location—just 4 kilometers north of Faro—to the usual pousada tidiness, a certain rustic flair, and you've got a comfortable base for your holiday wanderings. 17 rooms. *Inexpensive.*

★ HOTEL ALCALÁ

Avenida Marginal, Praia da Rocha (phone 24062). Pleasant old house near beach, in town center. Modest lobby. Bar. 22 rooms. *Bargain.*

Restaurants

★★★★ LA RESERVE

Santa Barbara de Nexe (phone 91234). It's tucked away in the hills above Faro, but worth the hunt. Ensconced in a tropical garden with a tiny luxury hotel next door, this Swiss-managed restaurant features classic international fare with a French flourish. Try the sole mousseline or shish kebab caucasses style. Closed Tuesdays. Dinner only. *Very Expensive.*

★★★ 1. CASA VELHA

Quinto do Lago (phone 94272). Not only is this "Moorish" hideaway one of the prettiest restaurants around, it serves good food as well. Wander through the cavelike rooms, all whitewashed with low ceilings, decorated by one of Portugal's most prominent designers, Pedro Leitão, with banquettes, fireplace, a modern Algarve look. Try the Grand Marnier souffle. *Very Expensive.*

★★★ 2. O LEÃO DE PORCHES

Porches (phone 52384). We're partial to the country look of this 17th-century farmhouse in the little village of Porches. A cozy setting for regional and international (especially English) specialties. Closed Sundays. *Moderate.*

★★★ 3. OUTSIDE-IN

Faro-Loulé Road (phone 91443). French chef Yvan Cadiou demonstrates his *nouvelle cuisine* flair with pigeon, stuffed duckling, other delights. *Very Expensive.*

★★★ 4. ALPENDRE

Rua Barbosa Viana, Lagos (phone 62705). Dine fabulously in Lagos's center on such treats as filet of sole *flambé,* steak *flambé. Flambé* is the specialty here, even in desserts. Good wine cellar. *Expensive.*

★★★ 5. ROUXINOL

Monchique (phone 92205). On the highway between Portimão and Monchique, this attractive little place, with its terrace and fireplace, offers suckling pig as a specialty, also steaks and some international fare. *Moderate.*

★★ 1. SIR LANCELOT

10 Trav. da Mota, Faro (phone 29710). In a simple, folkloric setting, you'll dine on wild boar steak, rabbit or the Algarve specialty *cataplana* (steamed clams and pork). Try the almond tart for dessert. *Inexpensive.*

★★ 2. O AVENIDA

Avenida Jose da Costa Mealha Loulé (phone 62735). High ceilings, timbered walls, leather-backed chairs provide a rustic setting for *cataplana,* fresh fish and other specialties. A local favorite. *Moderate.*

★★ 3. A LANTERNA

Portimão (phone 23948). The emphasis of this little restaurant across the Portimão bridge is on seafood. A long-time establishment here, it knows what to do with fish. You'll find it fresh, grilled, delicious. Closed Sundays. *Moderate.*

★★ 4. DOM SEBASTIÃO

20 Rua 25 de Abril, Lagos (phone 62795). Popular locally for its fresh seafood, this is an attractive dining spot with its dark beamed ceilings and rustic ambience. *Moderate.*

★★ 5. A TRANCA

Almansil, near Vale do Lobo (phone 94237). In simple patio setting, prepare to tackle a wide array of charcoal grilled fish and meat prepared local style. Reservations are suggested, as A Tranca is both small and popular. *Moderate.*

★ 1. CASA ALGARVE

National Highway 125, Porches (phone 52682). Cosy one-room eatery with fireplace. Excellent *cataplana. Inexpensive.*

★ 2. O BICHO

12 Largo Gil Eones (phone 22977), Portimão. Heavenly fresh seafood, simply served in a bare-bones setting. No frills, but fun. *Inexpensive.*

★ 3. ANTONIO CATUNA

Albufeira (phone 55983). On the road from Albufeira to Guia. An Algarve landmark for years, noted for its grilled fish, chicken and meats. The food's the thing; there's no decor to speak of, but some nice valley and sea views. Closed Mondays. *Moderate.*

Entertainment

As you'd expect in a locale geared to international wayfarers, the Algarve is not bereft of giddy and gaudy things to do at night. There are three casinos: the *Alvor,* Montes de Alvor (phone 23141) (where we have found the meals generally very good); *Monte Gordo,* Praia do Monte Gordo (phone 42224) and *Vilamoura* (phone 65319).

There are numerous nightclubs, discos and even a few places where you can hear *fado.* In summer the larger hotels frequently have folk dance evenings. Luxury class hotels are often self-contained entertainment units themselves. A few have social directors to keep things lively. Most have bars, discos and live music.

The largest folk pilgrimage of the Algarve takes place in Loulé on Easter Sunday, when the heavy image of *Senhora da Piedade* is carried up a steep hill. There's also a lighter side with singing, dancing, fireworks. Faro's big annual fair is held July 15–31, with a similar hoopla of fireworks, procession, song and dance.

Shopping

Local crafts of special note are copperware, pottery, cork, knitted wool sweaters and caps. There is a duty-free shop at Faro's international airport. The buys to look for include perfumes, cigars, cigarettes and an assortment of Portuguese wines. The Algarve's own Medronho, a brandy made from small red berries, is a local specialty.

Specific shopping areas would have to be Faro's *Rua Santo Antonio* with pottery and art shops all along it. The town of Loulé is known as a craftsmen's center. Look especially at Rua 9 de Abril and the other streets leading off Praça Dom Afonso III for baskets, copper, esparto mats, braided ropes and reins, which make nice belts and bags. Loulé's Saturday market brings all the town crafts together in one place. Albufeira bursts with boutiques and small shops. Check out Charles Jourdan at St. James, Avenida Eduardo Rios (phone 55897) for name brand shoes at local prices. Casa Manesca, Travessa Candido dos Reis, off the main *praça,* has an unusually large selection of fishermen's sweaters, pottery, tea cosies, table runners, embroideries. At Infante D. Henrique House, 30 Rua Candido do Reis (phone 53267) there is a selection of high-caliber pottery in 17th-century designs.

Along the road between Albufeira and Portimão vendors sell a variety of Porches pottery. When you are in Portimão, look for branches of Solarte, 9 Rua São Gonçalo or 25 Rua 5 de Outubro; they stock a nice assortment of pottery and other regional handcrafts. Rua Santa Isabel is especially fertile shopping turf in Portimão. Note Galeria Portimão, at No. 5, for Portuguese art and some international prints by Picasso, Miro and others.

In Lagos you will find handcut and blown Portuguese crystal at Cristal Portugal, 21 Praça Luis Camöes; a good craft selection at Centro de Arte, Rua Barbosa Viana; and another Charles Jourdan at St. James outlet, 62 Rua 25 de Abril.

Perks

The entire coast is dotted with private cottages and white-washed villas, as well as condominiums, all available for holiday rental. Lists of rental agents can be obtained from the Portuguese National Tourist Office, 548 Fifth Avenue, New York, NY 10036.

Information on specific rental properties in the Algarve is available from Janina Bastos, 500 E. 83rd Street, New York, NY 10028; (phone 212-535–3262); and I.T.P. Worldwide Luxury Villa Holidays, 101 Bradley Place, Palm Beach, FL. 33480 (phone 800-327–4505).

Sports

The climate is so winning in the Algarve even in winter, when it averages 50 to 68°F., that sports of all kinds find this coast a safe harbor. Of the spectator sports, there are now bullrings at Albufeira, Lagos, Portimão, Quarteira and Vila Real de São Antonio with a season that runs from March to October. Handbills and posters at hotels keep you informed about the upcoming *corridas.*

Portimão has a first division soccer team, with a season that kicks off the middle of August and has a final whistle blown the end of June. Games are played each Sunday, and often Saturday and Wednesday evening as well.

There are tennis courts for day or night play and six superior golf courses with the climate to enjoy this sport to the fullest. You can ride Anglo–Arabian or Lusitano horses, by day or moonlight, on sandy beach or wooded piney paths. But not in summer. It's too hot and the horses are generally moved north to cool off. There is a Western Riding Center in Burgau near Sagres. The Centro Hipico on the edge of the Vilamoura complex is located in the stables of an 18th-century inn, with 50 mounts, a jumping ring, marked field trails, and individual lessons if desired. If you'd prefer trotting on your own two legs, there are jogging trails.

Wind surfing, water skiing, scuba diving and snorkeling are all tried and plied along the coast. You can big game fish—for swordfish, *mikos,* giant tuna and some 200 smaller species—from Portimão or Vilamoura Marina. You can rent charter fishing boats with or without crew. (It is also possible to join a fishing boat to watch a tuna hunt—but it means getting up early. The local turismo office at Lagos or Tavira will tell you where and how.)

Praia da Rocha and Tres Irmaos are 2 of the most famous of the Algarve's many marvelous beaches

GETTING AROUND

By Car

Avis, Hertz, Interent and other car rental agencies have offices at various towns along the coast. There's no question that driving is the most comfortable way to beach-and-village hop, stopping as you will to picnic or sightsee. But many of the roads beg for slow and patient going. Donkeys, motorcycles and devil-may-care fellow drivers are handicaps of the course, and gas is expensive.

By Bus and Train

There are local public bus and train services. You can get the schedules at the local tourist office. But be prepared for some irregularity and slow service.

North from Porto

PORTO AND ENVIRONS

Porto or Oporto, Portugal's second largest city—originally know as Portucale—has been called the Barcelona of Portugal. Lively, animated, businesslike, its commercial activities spill down one hillside (the right, looking downstream) of the River Douro and up the other (the left) to Vila Nova de Gaia and its profusion of wineries. Three bridges span the river, including one by Charles Eiffel (the all-metal railway bridge—Ponte de Doña Maria Pia) and a similar one by his disciple Don Luis. Anchored in the river, but with square sails billowing in the breeze, are the *rabelos* (flat-bottomed boats with long tillers) piled high with wine casks. They sit as daily reminders to anyone who might forget that wine is mother's milk in Porto. There are no wine tours *per se* up the Douro to the *quintas* where port wines are produced, but several of the vintners in Vila Nova de Gaia welcome visitors. The old city is much more than the sum of its ports. After good restaurants and better wines, you will welcome the exercise that sightseeing demands in this city of steep hills and sudden rapid descents.

By the end of a day spent viewing the splendid, mostly 12th-century Romanesque cathedral with twin towers flanked by buttresses, the monastery of the Serra do Pilar (see the round cloister with its 36 Ionic columns) and the church of San Francisco (still with its original rose window), you'll be happy to retire to *Solar do Vinho do Porto,* perhaps to sample a 1972 Diez Hermanos port (60 escudos a large glass) or a 20-year Niepoort port (130 escudos). This delightful wine bar, located in a hillside behind and below the Crystal Palace Garden, on the same grounds as the Romantic Museum, has a rose garden with an overview of the river. Like its Lisbon counterpart, but in a more open, expansive setting, this *Solar* has a lengthy (11 page) list of port wines that can be ordered very reasonably by the glass.

*** Pousada Barão de Forrester in Alijó is a new Douro wine country inn

Porto is the springboard to the Minho region, which extends north as far as the Spanish border. We recommend making a loop up the coast and coming back by an inland route. Radiating north of Porto are a number of fine sand Atlantic beaches. There's Póvoa de Varzim, still pretty much a fishing village. Beyond it is Ofir, with the best of two worlds—a sea and river location. It is popular for snorkeling, sailing and bass fishing.

Barcelos

Barcelos is a town with something to crow about, for this is the home of the shiny black ceramic rooster with the proud red comb—a symbol used in Portugal's official tourist literature. The Barcelos cock derives from a legend of medieval times. It is the Portuguese variation of the Spanish *Santo Domingo de la Calzada* pilgrimage story. In brief, a man is accused of stealing a bowl. To prove his innocence, he tells the judge a cooked chicken will stand up and crow. It does. Free at last. Another country, another cock-and-bowl story. You can see hundreds and hundreds of the jaunty Barcelos cocks in the Thursday market, which is held in the town's big open square, *Campo da Republica.* Vendors spread their pottery casseroles, pitchers, plates and other ceramics on the ground, and shoppers haggle and dicker from place to place. It's a colorful event. A few vendors repeat their act on Saturday, but the variety and volume make Thursday *the* day to be here.

Several appealing buildings 'feed into'' the square—a small octagon church, completely tiled inside in blue and white *azulejos* that relate the Way of the Cross; and an 18th-century church, *Igreja Nossa Senhora do Terco,* that was once part of a Benedictine convent. On a hill overlooking the 14th-century bridge (modified later) over the Cavado River are several other monuments. This area saw the birth of the ruling house of Bragança and you'll see the ruins of their 15th-16th-century palace. What remains has the look of a fortress but is now a small open-air archeological museum. From the various columns and chunks of marbled history, you can watch the women below at riverside doing their washing and stretching the clean clothes along the sand banks, just as they might have done in the days when the palace was mighty and intact.

Nearby on the same incline is a Gothic-style stone pillory; it's a medieval landmark, which can still be seen in most Portuguese towns. Here too is the collegiate church with a Romanesque portal. Leaving Barcelos, the road is lined with tiny, wild pink roses (in season); the terrain soon turns into a harvest of vineyards dotted with an occasional pine tree. You will see village and farm women walking alongside the road carrying huge loads on their heads. Ox carts are still part of the local lifestyle. The tempo is easy.

Viana do Castelo

The pace stays easy in Viana do Castelo, a town once described as *pulchra* by the Latin poet Rufus Festus Avienus. It is still beautiful—a lively settlement near the mouth of the Lima River. The Lima reminded Rufus's fellow Romans of the Lethe, the river in Dante's *Inferno* that caused forgetfulness (if you drank from it). Maybe there was a reason Roman soldiers never wanted to leave.

Remembering is more likely Viana do Castelo's stock in trade. Just stand in the main square, *Praça da Republica,* and relish the sights that crowd in on you. First, there's the graceful center fountain itself, the work (in 1554) of João Lopes Velho (the Elder). The square is almost a family affair, as its most prominent building, the Misericordia Hospital, was the work (in 1589) of João Lopes the Younger. It is a lovely sight to contemplate—an Ionic-columned arcade supports two levels of loggias, which in turn sit on stone caryatids.

Pause a minute over coffee and a sweet at the Pastelería Caravela opposite and enjoy the stone twirls and "pastry puff" embellishments in the facade that are counterpointed by red and purple flowers cascading from the window boxes on the loggias. It's a joyous place. The entire town gives us that feeling. Good restaurants (see Inside Information—Restaurants), streets geared for strolling and admiring the many manor houses and small palaces with their stone escutcheons in front, a municipal museum in an 18th-century palace with a collection of regional ceramics and an intangible cheerful quality to the ambience combine to make you want to linger.

We mustn't get so carried away that we forget one of Viana do Castelo's most important buildings, though you could hardly miss it on Rua Cabral near the main square. It is the 15th-century parish church, formally called *Igreja Matriz.* Though eclectic—a Gothic portal and majestic rose window with two square Romanesque towers as "sentries"—it works and sings. For an easy overview of Viana do Castelo drive to the top of *Monte de Santa Luzia* and, in the comfort of the newly refurbished Hotel de Santa Luzia, sip a little *vinho de regionales* and enjoy the views of the town, the not-so-lethal (Lethe) Lima and the sea beyond.

The coastal road is a beauty, evoking images of Old Portugal with ox carts, oxen with decorated wooden yokes and flowers growing with abandon everywhere. The distance of 53 kilometers (32 miles) from Viana to Valença speeds past.

Valença

Valença is a river town, guarding Portugal's Minho River frontier with Spain. Remains of Valença's 17th-century hilltop fortress call its neighbor's bluff (the town of Túy) across the river mist. Well, that was the intention. It never worked very well against the armies of León and Castile. Spanish armies still descend on little Valença. But nowadays they're welcome, for they are armies of shoppers, marching (or driving over the bridge) to comb Valença's cobbled, upwardly spiraling streets for glassware, pottery, clothes, almost any and every consumer item imaginable. The *peseta* seems to stretch further across the river, hence the manic shopping sprees.

For a non-Spanish visitor, Valença is a pleasing respite from the 20th century. Its hilltop *pousada,* with all-glass windows and wide-angle views of Túy, is tucked into the fortress grounds. A diversion on a sunny day is to ramparts-hop along any number of intriguing trails with different views. Valença has a quiet charm and is in a remarkable state of preservation. Houses have Manueline window frames and garlands of wrought iron balconies, and it is cheerful to contemplate them.

Braga

Braga has wonderful wide squares, like Largo Carlos Amarante, avenues and parks full of birds and flowers. These first impressions then give way to explorations. In Braga that means a peek at the Romanesque cathedral, which is in reality Romanesque-Gothic-Manueline-baroque. A generalization has it that in Portugal you find Gothic architecture in the south and Romanesque in the north. But in fact, so many generations have "improved" original buildings of whatever style that pure anything is hard to find anywhere.

The Braga cathedral is a case in point. The really ancient building on the site was destroyed by the Moors in 716. Ferdinand I of Castile recaptured Braga in 1040, and by the end of the century a brand new Romanesque cathedral was underway. But building tastes change. What you see now of the Romanesque original are a south door and arches over the main portal. Next came the Gothic portions: The main portico, the chapel of *Nossa Senhora da Gloria,* the Flamboyant Gothic altar-front, a few capitals in the cloister and the delicate and poignant *Our Lady Suckling the Holy Child* under a canopy.

The baroque interior then takes over with many marvelous additions of its own, such as the cherub-smothered gilded organ, gilded choir stalls (rather surreptitiously sexy in their carving), the Holy Sacrament chapel with its rich and lively three-dimensional altar panel called *The Church Triumphant.* Braga was at one time the seat of the Primate of All Spain and a major religious center. This translates into a treasury full of polychromed sculptures, ornately carved marble sarcophogi of archbishops and royalty, fresco-covered chapels, among other treasures.

Sacheverell Sitwell called Braga the "artistic capital of northern Portugal"

Braga also means a dozen or more churches, including *São João Marcos* (with a facade of *azulejos*), *São Victor* (16th-century facade) and, best of all, 3 kilometers from town on the Ponte de Lima road the church of *São Frutuoso,* a much-battered but still appealing 7th-century Romano-Byzantine church folded into a convent.

To the devout, Braga means climbing, on knees (yes, people still do), an ornate baroque double granite stairway 114 meters (381 feet) up a mountainside to *Bom Jesus do Monte,* a neoclassical church that is a major object of pilgrimage in Portugal. There's a funicular, if feet fail, and of course a road to drive on. This trip is worthwhile even for the non-religious because of the views of the city below. There's a *Casa de Cha* where you can sit on the terrace and drink a toast (beverage of your choice) to Braga's beauty, admire the spectacular vistas and perhaps even catch a touch of the sanctity in the air. Though truth to tell, a pilgrimage in Portugal has more the flavor of a family picnic—festive, relaxed, full of good cheer and minimal religiosity.

Try the Dão red wine from neighboring Viseu

Guimarães

Guimarães is considered the first capital of Portugal because Afonso Henriques was born here in 1111. But he is actually an Afonso-come-lately. Local lore says everything began much earlier with Wamba, king of the Visigoths. It seems that Wamba, then a chieftain, was asked to assume the mantle of Kingship. He said—in the best political tradition—"Never—unless leaves grow from my staff." You guessed it. The leaves sprouted and the Visigoths had themselves a king.

There are two focal points for your attention in town, first, the well-preserved castle (with splendid views) built just after the Norman invasion in 996; and second, *Largo da Oliveira,* a cobbled square with the Romanesque-arched collegiate church of Our Lady of the Olive Tree facing it on one side and the *Pousada Nossa Senhora da Oliveira* with its columned arcade on another.

In the castle's shadow is the palace of the dukes of Bragança, who cast their own shadow over Portuguese life for centuries. Much of the palace is restored, but even so, hall after hall is decorated with knock-out tapestries depicting historic events (Crusaders battling Moors; Hannibal; wild boar hunts medieval life). The tapestries were from the looms of Flanders, Aubusson and Gobelins workshops.

A few steps away is the tiny Romanesque chapel, *São Miguel do Castelo,* where Afonso Henriques was baptized. You will see the baptismal font.

The road from Guimarães to Viseu zigs curvaceously through Amarante, a river town edged in weeping willows where white geese dawdle, and then zags just as precipitously through Lamego, another pilgrimage city with a mountain-hugging baroque staircase of its own (the *Sanctuary of Our Lady the Redeemer,* a popular destination for a late August-early September pilgrimage).

Viseu

Raison d'étre for a visit to the bustling, wine-producing town of Viseu, with a population slightly under 20,000, is the *Grão Vasco Museum.* You will find all three treasured floors of it installed in the 16th-century *Três Escaloes* palace, located at a diagonal from the cathedral (which is worth a visit itself).

What makes the Grão Vasco special is its rare collection of primitive paintings and sculptures, mostly Portuguese, mostly the work of a school that flourished in Viseu during the 16th century. Luminaries of the school were two painters, Gaspar Vaz and Vasco Fernandes, better known as Grão Vasco. Both flirted with the style of Flemish artists such as Van Eyck and Quentin Metsys, but then developed their own individual signatures.

Chef d'oeuvres are three large paintings: a *Last Supper* by Gaspar Vaz and *Calvary* and *St. Peter* by Grão Vasco. Also of note are 14 paintings, once part of the cathedral altar piece, by other artists of the Viseu school. There are 17th-century Spanish paintings in the museum as well. The high ceilings, large halls and stone-arched doorways of the palace make a handsome backdrop for the art. Opposite the cathedral is a beautiful twin-towered Renaissance facade in white with deep grey granite borders, window and door frames. The flowing line of the roof and the flow of movement in the window frames provide a rhythm that borders on lyrical. The building is the *Misericordia* church. If it's Tuesday, you can walk to Viseu's weekly outdoor market to absorb the local color. There's not much for tourists to buy, just stall after stall of inexpensive clothing, home and farm products, a bit of utilitarian basketry and fresh produce. But it's a gypsy gathering place, and it *is* lively.

Viseu, for all its traffic jams and downtown noise, is an easy town for walking since many of the sights are compactly located. You may want to pay attention to several other churches—*São Bento,* with a fine painted ceiling and 17th-century *azulejos*; *São Francisco,* with an unusual hanging staircase and gilded baroque interior (also with choice antique *azulejos*); and *Carmo,* a full orchestra of baroque effects—gilded retable and pulpits, *azulejos* and no-holds-barred ornamentation. The last king of the Visigoths, Roderick, who fled Toledo in 711 or 712 is supposedly buried in *São Miguel do Fetal,* an 8th-century church. Save time to stroll along Rua Direita, Rua dos Andradas and Rua da Piedade, packed with 16th-18th-century houses adorned with wrought iron balconies, corbelling and unusual door knockers.

"Viseu were here" is not the town's motto, but it might well be.

Inside Information

Hotels

For prices, see Lisbon, page 282.

★★★★ 1. VERMAR DON PEDRO
4491 Póvoa de Varzim (phone 61041). This is perhaps the most elaborate and lavish resort hotel in northern Portugal. Shore location 26 kilometers (16 miles) from Porto makes it a magnet for beach people and a handy base for touring area. Has pool, tennis courts, disco; is on ocean; has a well-regarded restaurant. Rooms have balconies and ocean views and are tastefully modern; public areas eclectically overdecorated for our taste. 208 rooms. *Inexpensive.*

Has ** restaurant

★★★★ 2. POUSADA DE S. TEOTONIO
Valença do Minho (phone 22252). Modern building inside ancient fortress. Stunning views across river into Spain from rooms, patio, lounge, restaurant. Rooms furnished with antiques and handsome Portuguese handcrafted furniture, rugs, covers and drapes. 16 rooms. *Inexpensive.*

★★★★ 3. POUSADA DA OLIVEIRA
Apartado 101, Guimarães (phone 412157). Modern interior in 17th-century castle of Guimarães. Rooms and restaurant look out on Gothic gazebo and church; furnished with handmade beds, embroidered spreads, draperies and linen towels. A national landmark and no wonder. 16 rooms. *Moderate.*

★★★★ 4. INFANTE DE SAGRES
62 Praça D. Filipa de Lancastre, Porto (phone 28101). Lobby and lounge like an Edwardian mens' club, rooms with brass bedsteads, marble baths, handcrafted rugs; formal French restaurant decor. 84 rooms. *Moderate.*

★★★★ 5. DOM HENRĨQUE
179 Guedes de Azevedo, Porto (phone 25755). An international-style, high-rise hotel in center city. Public areas modern, white plastic, "with it" look; rooms comfortably modern, color coordinated with double lavatories, good reading lights plus TV and all usual amenities, including air conditioning. Vistas from rooms, bar and restaurant on top floors. 102 rooms. *Moderate.*

★★★ 1. HOTEL D. ELEVADOR
Parque do Bom Jesus do Monte, Braga (phone 25011). Antique-furnished rooms in a woodland retreat with superb views; steps from major pilgrimage shrine. It's quiet; remote from the city; old-fashioned. 25 rooms. *Inexpensive.*

★★★ 2. HOTEL DO PINHAL
Praia de Pinhal, Estrada do Mar, Ofir (phone 89473). In sand and pine resort area 45 kilometers (27 miles) north of Porto, completely modern hotel has huge rustic lounge, two pools, tennis courts, open-air restaurant. Rooms modestly furnished; some with showers, others with baths. 89 rooms. *Bargain.*

★★★ 3. TURISMO DON PEDRO
Av. João XXI, Braga (phone 27091). Modern, international-style hotel at edge of town. Rooms well equipped and comfortable; somewhat "loud" decorating. 132 rooms. *Inexpensive.*

★★ 1. GRÃO VASCO
Rua Gaspar Barreiros, Viseu (phone 23511). In the center of town on wooded grounds. Undistinguished building, with lovely gardens, pool, large marble halls, public areas. Ample guest rooms; conservative furnishings. Parking; terrace dining. 88 rooms. *Inexpensive.*

★★ 2. ESTALAGEM DO PARQUE DO RIO
Pinhal, Parque do Rio, Ofir (phone 89521). Rustic but modern solitude 45 kilometers (27 miles) north of Porto in wooded, camplike setting. Tennis; pool surrounded by guarded compound and hotel buildings. Compact, neat, quiet, relaxing. 30 rooms. *Bargain.*

★★ 3. HOTEL RESIDENCIA DE S. JOÃO
120–40 Rua do Bonjardim, Porto (phone 21662). Located on fourth floor of downtown office building. This small hotel has a tiny lounge with fine views of city; predominantly French clientele. 14 rooms. *Bargain.*

★★ 4. AFONSO III
494 Av. Don Afonso III, Viana do Castelo (phone 22699). Guest rooms are neat; balconies have river and town views; air-conditioned. Cavelike public areas; active disco. Free bus to beach. 89 rooms. *Bargain.*

Restaurants

For prices, see Lisbon, page 34. Pousadas offer five-course meals at all-in one price of 850$00 to 1,250$00, depending on the season.

★★ 1. POUSADA DE SÃO TEOTONIO
Valença do Minho (phone 22252). Fine regional cuisine: *Bacalhao dourado,* salmon with tomato, roast pork with clams. Generous samplings of desserts. Modern decor; fine vista across Minho to Spain. Dozens of wines listed. *Moderate.*

★★ 2. ESCONDIDINHO

143 Rua Passos Manuel, Porto (phone 21079). Folkloric tiled walls and beamed ceiling give cosy feeling. Menu has both regional and French dishes. *Sole meuniere* with fine herbs offers best of both worlds. Wine list has good choices. *Moderate.*

★★ 3. ALAMBIQUE

86 Rua Manuel Espregueira, Viana do Castelo (phone 23894). Hearty fare in agreeable setting. Slow service but fried Minho River trout, roast kid cutlets with vegetables in red wine sauce worth the wait. Kitchen open to view. Local *vinho verde* wine is inexpensive. *Inexpensive.*

★★ 4. ARCADA DO FERNANDO

Adjacent to Misericordia Hospital, Viana do Castelo. Atmospheric, with broad granite arches dominating spotless, tiny dining room. Kitchen open to view, equally immaculate. Short menu features local fish, with *bacalao* predominating. Local wines available at 80–480 escudos. *Inexpensive.*

★ 1. POUSADA SANTA MARIA DO OLIVEIRA

Rua da Oliveira, Apartado 101, Guimarães (phone 41893). The fresh, neat restaurant of the *pousada* looks out on the city square. The menu has pleasing familiars, no surprises: standard regional seafare (sole, hake, trout, bream, shrimp, clams) and land-based entrees (beef, pork, lamb, chops, filets). *Vinho verde* is pleasant choice. *Moderate.*

Vinho verde, lit. = "green," or fresh, wine"

O INACIO

Campo das Hortas, Braga (phone 22335). Rugged stone walls and fireplace, beamed ceiling and wood floors for mellow dining. A local favorite. Simple menu—broiled or roasted entrees, soups, omelets. Understandably inexpensive. Good wine list; pleasant *Dão tinto. Inexpensive.*

Entertainment

There are casinos in the resort towns of Póvoa de Varzim, 23 kilometers (14 miles) north of Porto, and Espinho, 18 kilometers (11 miles) south of the city. Both casinos feature dining, dancing and musical shows in addition to their basic stock in trade: roulette, baccarat, blackjack and slot machines. At Póvoa, *Casino Monumental* is in a seafront building that looks to be 1930s modern. *Grande Casino de Espinho* is three short blocks from the beach on Rua 19. Both are open from 3 P.M. to 3 A.M. daily. You'll need to show your passport.

Shopping

Northern Portugal is prime handcraft territory, with a variety of pottery, wooden objects (most popular are the adaptations of the traditional carved oxen yoke), baskets, embroidered tablecloths and place mats. In Barcelos there is the *Centro do Artesonato* in an old stone tower, Torre da Porta Nova. It has a wide selection of regional handcrafts (including Barcelos roosters) at modest prices. In Guimarães shops near and on the Largo da Oliveira sell the very delicate local embroideries in tablecloths and mats. Shopping in Porto focuses on five streets. For assorted gifts, look on Rua Santa Catarina leather goods (shoes and luggage), Rua 31 de Janeiro and Rua Sa da Bandeira; for jewelry Rua das Flores; for ceramics Rua Clerigos.

For specific shops in Porto that are extraordinary try: *Fabrica de Loica de Sacevem,* 40 Rua das Carmelitas (phone 22033) for ceramics of all kinds; *Casa dos Linhos*, 660 Rua Fernandes Tomas (phone 20044) for high-quality linens and embroideries; *Modeco*, 35 Rua de Ricardo Jorge (phone 27502), for charming, offbeat ceramics, clay figures, handicrafts; *Amazens do Porto* corner of do Conde Vizela and Clerigos, for terrific children's clothes. Look in at *Seculo Passado*, 665 Rua de Alegria for interesting antiques. Rua dea Junqueira (phone 64638) in Póvoa de Varzim probably handles more sales of gold and silverware than anywhere else in the country. You can see the silversmiths at work behind a glass partition. Valença is a Spanish shopper's dream for sizeable home furnishings and accessories. For items such as high-quality copper fondue sets, embroideried tablecloths and porcelain, drop by *Casa Victor*, corner of Rua do Conselheiro and Lopes da Silva.

Markets

In Barcelos the big market day is Thursday. Vendors come from all over the Minho area to sell ceramics, embroideries, baskets, wooden ware—all displayed in a 450 yard square Campo da Republica. Viana do Castelo's market day is Friday, and it too is a source of pottery and regional crafts such as embroideries, straw work, filagree jewelry. Quality varies at all the public markets. Braga's yoke fair is an artisans' market held each Tuesday on the fairgrounds. The "yokes" are the traditional yokes for oxen and are beautifully carved. They're more decorative than functional. Viseu's Tuesday market is somewhat mundane, as we said earlier.

Museums and Galleries (in addition to those mentioned in text)

Guimarães

★ ALBERTO SAMPAIO MUSEUM

Largo de Oliveira. In 13th-century Romanesque cloister, Gothic chapel, the museum includes paintings by Antonio Vaz, some fine early sculpture, much church silver and a triptych captured by João I from Spaniards at Battle of Aljubarrota. Open 10 A.M. to 12:30 P.M., 2–5 P.M.; closed Mondays and holidays.

Porto

★★ SOARES DOS REIS NATIONAL MUSEUM

Rua de Dom Manuel II. In an 18th-century palace. Painting collection has works by Flemish, Italian and French, as well as Portuguese primitives (including Grão Vasco), and 19th- and 20th-century Portuguese paintings. Has sculptures by Soares plus ceramics and furniture from earlier times. Open 10 A.M. 12 P.M., 2–5 P.M.; closed Mondays and holidays. Free admission on Sundays.

Viana do Castelo

MUNICIPAL MUSEUM

Rua Manuel Espregueira. Wall-blanketing *azulejos,* handpainted by Policarpo de Oliveira Bernardes in 1721, make the visit worthwhile. Also on view are ceramics from 16–19th centuries. Open 9:30 A.M. to 12:30 P.M., 2–5 P.M.; closed Mondays and holidays.

Historic Buildings and Sites

Braga

★★ SÉ (CATHEDRAL)

Terreiro de Sé. Largely baroque today, the 12th-century cathedral is augmented by cloister, courtyard, three chapels plus sacristies and treasury with sacred art museum (13th-18th century *santos,* 16th century *azulejos*).

★ BOM JESUS DO MONTE

5 kilometers east of city. Extraordinary shrine complex on hill overlooking Braga countryside. The church, built 1784–1811, has baroque chapels and staircase built zigzag fashion, boot-lacing their way up entire 116 meter (381 foot) hill that pilgrims scale on knees. Sanctuary in wooded park; water-powered funicular carries visitors to top.

Guimãraes

★ PAÇO DOS DUQUES

Palace of the Dukes of Bragança, Praça de Mumadona. Dating from 15th century, four restored buildings around a courtyard display armor, ceramics, antiques, paintings, carpets. Tapestries of Afonso V's campaigns, from Nuno Gonçalves's designs are standouts. Open 10 A.M.–5 P.M.; closed Tuesdays. Free on holidays.

Porto

PALÁCIO DE BOLSA

Pr. Infante D. Henrique. This stock exchange is truly palatial. See the Arabian Hall, derived from the Alhambra in Granada, and sculpture-decorated staircase. Open 9 A.M.-12 P.M. business days only. Ask porter to admit you.

Valença do Minho

★ **FORTRESS**

The 13th-century castle was enlarged and updated in 17th century; it now contains a town whose narrow, cobbled streets, tiled roofs, bustling shops and striking modern *pousada* attract droves of Spanish shoppers who flock to buy handcrafts and port wine. Mist-shrouded vistas are mysterious, ethereal.

Viseu

SÉ (CATHEDRAL)

Praça de Sé. Gothic with baroque overlay. Portuguese masons here made stone appear as flexible as rope or trees in their columns and network of ceiling ribbing. The 18th-century baroque altar piece is a gilded wonder. Visit choir loft and treasury.

Tours

Aveiro. Boat tours in summer leave from Canal de Cidade, Central Canal at 11:30 A.M. and return at 5 P.M. after circling through canals, islands, saltpans, fishing villages, viewing *moliceiros* (flat-bottomed boats) with intricate, swanlike prows working seaweed beds. Tour stops at *La Pousada da Ria* for lunch.

Douro River. Trips by train (by express, less than 2 hours) along the river through the gorgeous wine country. Lunch at Regua and return in afternoon. Arrange through concierge or travel agency.

Porto. Half-day tours of the city are offered by tour bus operators and travel agencies (see listing below).

Valença do Minho. Steam trains. Railway buffs will be interested in special tours on two 19th-century antique trains. One is kept at Valença the other in Porto. Request information from *turismo* offices in these towns.

Viana do Castelo. Festa tour, from May to October, goes by bus through Costa Verde. Includes local style dinner with wine, folk dancing and singing, fireworks and contemporary dancing. Arrange through travel agency, AVIC, in Viana.

Vila Nova de Gaia/Porto. Tour of port wine city and cellar. Tour bus with hostess. Daily, April-September. Visits wine cellar, includes tasting. Ask concierge or travel agency.

Vila Nova De Gaia. Three Bridges Cruise, May-September daily except Sundays and Saturday afternoons, on Douro River via launch from Porto Ferreira, 19 Rua da Carvalhosa, Vila Nova de Gaia.

Leading travel agencies in Porto are ABREU, 207 Avda. dos Aliados (phone 317921); Capristanos, 500 Rua de Sta. Catarine (phone 24571);

Melia, 269 Pr. Grl. Humberto Delgado (phone 310034); Star, 202 Av. dos Aliados (phone 23637); Wagons-lits et du Tourisme, 12 Rua Dr. M. Bastos (phone 25040).

Perks

Porto

Wine lovers will want to visit the port wine "lodges" across the river in Vila Nova da Gaia. There are 80 cellars, each a different vintner, easily reached by taxi across the Ponte de D. Luis I. The lodges are clustered within a few (large) blocks and welcome visitors. You will be ushered through the vat-, barrel- and cask-lined warehouses, shown the decanting and *solar* process and offered free samples of the products at a tasting bar. Among the most famous and best equipped to receive visitors are Sandeman, Croft, Taylor, Calem, Borges, Fonseca and Ferreira. The lodges are open daily during business hours, closed Saturdays and Sundays. Ask concierge or tourist office for map.

Solar de Vinhos de Porto is the name of the restful haven in an old quinta at Rua de Entre-Quintas where you can relax, sit on the enclosed veranda, sip a port selected from the 300 offered here. It's run by the Port Wine Institute and is open daily 10:30 A.M. to 11:30 P.M.

Sports

International Vintage Car Rallye. First week in July at Espinho.

Futbol. Played from mid-August through June almost every Sunday; also some Saturday and Wednesday nights. There are first division teams (the best) in Porto, Braga, Guimarães. Expect to pay 85$00 for standing and up to 700$00 for the best seat in the stadium.

GETTING AROUND

We favor going by car or van to the places in and around the countryside. For the convenience of leaving the driving to someone else, the tour bus, regular bus or train may be better. The rail and bus services are efficient and frequent and inexpensive. Check with concierge or turismo offices for schedules and departure points. In Porto, buses, trams and trolley buses cover the city; there are also inexpensive taxis.

Central Portugal – The Heartland

TOMAR, BATALHA, ALCOBAÇA AND NAZARÉ

Tomar

Begin in Tomar, which Somerset Maugham once called, with British reserve, "the most beautiful town in the world." Maugham was dazzled no doubt, as we all are, by Tomar's brilliant whiteness—its clean streets, white sugar-cube houses splashed with red geraniums and purple bougainvillaeas.

Tomar's first lure, though, is the monastery the Knights Templar built as their lookout fortress and headquarters high above the town. The knights had been leaders in the Crusades and had cleared this region of Moors in the Reconquest. King Afonso gave them another castle (Ceras) a few kilometers away. But the knights had something a bit more upscale in mind, and in 1118 they completed their masterpiece, a church–castle complex. Inside the church is an 8-sided temple, supposedly in the shape of the Temple of Solomon in Jerusalem. It was *the* popular architectural conceit at the time throughout Europe.

Standing inside the sanctuary of the dark temple itself, what surprises us is how small it is. Faded painted stone columns form a circle under a rotunda, reminding us of past glories. Around the outer edges are five of the original twelve 16th-century paintings that depict scenes from the life of Christ.

Pièce de résistance of the complex is the Manueline window in the facade of the Chapter House. Decay and a patina of golden lichen blur a part of the ornate designs, but it is still a window that commands respect—an incredible hammering of stone into the shapes of ropes, anchors, bows, sails and every other nautical symbol imaginable. And as if that weren't enough showing off, the masonic artistry extends to the towers on either side of the window. On the left is the Golden Fleece and on the right a stone belt and buckle, symbolizing the Order of the Garter. Above it are statues of Portuguese kings.

Tomar's lower town is a dazzler. As you wind your way down from the castle, stop at the chapel of *Nossa Senhora da Conceicão* to admire the carving on the capitals in this harmonious Renaissance building. Now may be the time for a sip of something cool at the *Estalagem Santa Iria* that overlooks the Nabão River and a creaking old Arab waterwheel.

Before leaving Tomar, stop at the *Synagoga Abraham Zacuto Luso,* a tiny 14th-century temple at 73 Rua Dr. Joaquim Jacinto, a geranium-intense street that is one of the prettiest in town. It is one street away from Tomar's loveliest square, *Praça do Republica.* Dominating the *Praça's* black-and-white checkerboard marble sidewalk is the bronze statue of Gualdim Pais with shield in hand. (His tomb, with that of other Templars, is in the Gothic church of *Santa Maria do Olival.*) Somehow the pigeons roosting cosily on his head seem to mitigate the militant stance of this once-powerful Templar. Across the square and well worth a look is the *Church of São João Baptista* with a flamboyant Gothic portal and several fine 16th-century Portuguese paintings.

Batalha

West of Tomar 30 kilometers (48 miles), following road 113 to No. 356, is Batalha, described irreverently by a friend as "the house that Jack built." To be more formal, it's the *Santa Maria da Vitoria* monastery that King João, or John, had erected in celebration (and thanks) for his army's victory against the Spanish at Aljubarrota 1 kilometer away. This was the time when João, illegitimate son of Pedro II, was anxious to consolidate his claim to Portugal's throne and struck an alliance with the English by marrying John of Gaunt's daughter, Philippa. The marriage lasted only until death, but the alliance has survived through centuries. So has the monastery. *Santa Maria da Vitoria* is one of Portugal's most beautiful monuments.

As you leave the highway and come suddenly upon this block-long masterpiece of Portuguese Gothic architecture, the sweep and power of it will leave you breathless, gasping. Even now, even after numerous visits, it has that effect on us.

Before entering, pause to admire the facade, reminiscent of York Minster with the rich panoply of kings, angels, saints and prophets—more than 100 of them—along the portal. And there in the vast monastery square is João's commander at Aljubarrota, Nuno Alvares Pereira, triumphant on horseback, fresh from battle, immortalized in bronze for all time, the sun striking him full in the face.

Inside the treasures reveal themselves slowly. Notice how the graceful vaulting gives the illusion of height. The tombs at the entrance to the Founder's Chapel are of Mateus Fernandes, the architect who built much of the chapel, and of Gonçalves Marcoda, who saved King João's life at Aljubarrota. In the Founder's Chapel, a silent, melancholic place, stands a huge sarcophogus—the tomb of João I and his English wife clasping hands through eternity. Tombs of all their children ring the alcoves in the sepulchral room. Camöes called the princelings *inclita geracão, altos Infantes* (the most illustrious generation of Princes). Only Henry the Navigator stands out now, with a Gothic stone crown above his head. Notice the delicacy of the star-shaped cupola above.

In the Royal Cloister, the question is where to look first. The interconnected arches are ripe with fantasies in stone. This is the Manueline style's finest hour. The embroidered thistle, lotus, globe and cross ornamentation enhance the simplicity of the slender Gothic arches—a stunning collaboration between architect and stone worker.

Gothic-style lights in the Chapter House commemorate two unknown soldiers of the Great War of 1914–1918. What is most remarkable about this room is the audacity of its concept: elongated vaulting unsupported by any columns—suspended by "magic." It is difficult, though, to concentrate on the ceiling and on the rare 16th-century windows illustrating scenes of the Passion of Christ, with two real live soldiers looking menacing in 1980s battle dress standing by, their hands on the triggers of real submachine guns. Is this war-like stance really necessary in such a sacred place? one might ask.

Alcobaça

Portugal's other great Gothic monument is at Alcobaça, 15 kilometers (9 miles) south on highway 1. It took 60 years to build. It is the Cistercian monastery of *Santa Maria,* which was founded in 1152 by the same Afonso Henriques who swept the Moors out of Lisbon. The facade on this largest, longest church in Portugal is as golden as Alcobaça peaches.

Renowned for its stark beauty, the monastery is even more famous to Portuguese lovers of romance. For this now silent place provides the setting for the denouement of Portugal's most tragic royal love story. As you face the altar, look at the sarcophagus to the left. It is a remarkable work of art; the marble has been carved with exquisite precision. The *Last Judgment* carved on one end has details such as the dead lifting the tops off their tombstones. Resting on the lid of the tomb is a woman, perfect except for her nose, which is chipped. Blame Napoleon's troops, some say, who thought the tombs contained treasure. This noble work is balanced on the backs of six crouching men with strange animal bodies.

And therein lies a tale. The tomb belongs to Inês de Castro, ill-fated Spanish lady-in-waiting to the wife of Pedro I, son of King Afonso II. Inês had the misfortune to catch Pedro's eye. When his wife died, Pedro supposedly married Inês in secret, but Afonso would have one of this liaison and Inês was mysteriously murdered. (Keep reading to find out where.)

Years later, when Pedro became king, he caught and executed two of the three murderers; he then exhumed his dead love, dressed her in royal robes and forced his courtiers to pay homage and kiss her mouldy, rotted hand. The six subhuman creatures supporting Inês's tomb were "portraits" of her betrayers at court. This episode may explain why Pedro was known as both Pedro the Just and Pedro the Cruel. History gives you a choice.

Across the aisle, to the right of the altar, is Pedro's tomb, equally ornate and Gothic, but supported as a king would have it by crouching lions. The two sarcophagi are so placed that on Judgment Day when the dead arise, the first thing Inês and Pedro will see will be one another.

There's more in Alcobaça. A guide will lead you (for a small tip) through a cloister heady with the scent of orange trees to the enormous kitchen where Rabelasian feasts were prepared for the 1,000 monks who once lived here. Here you'll see the canal of fresh water that flows into the room, the 6-ton marble slab table where meals were prepared and the gargantuan chimney suspended above a huge open hearth. Blue and white tiled scenes that relate the founding of the monastery by Afonso I cover the walls.

Nazaré

Nazaré is no longer the sleepy village it once was (so what else is new?). But the beachfront is still studded with fishing boats in basic blues, greens and reds. The women still wear layers of skirts and you'll occasionally spot the famous Nazaré plaids here and there. The craggy, textured cliffside rising from the water makes a memorable background.

Buçaco

Begin with Buçaco itself, a majestic 250-acre national park on the most northern end of the Serra do Buçaco Mountains. It *is* a forest primeval, with trees that *look* as though they date back to the 6th century when a group of Benedictine monks built a hermitage in this natural Gothic "cathedral" of towering pines, cedars of Lebanon and palms. In the 19th century new plantings were added from all over the world. There are more than 700 species (400 from Portugal alone) of flora, with eucalyptus, gingko, Himalayan pine, monkey puzzle, Japanese camphor and sequoia, among them. A great pleasure in walking the carefully delineated trails is that many of the trees are labeled, and you can identify even the most exotic.

Here's the Hotel Buçaco, begun as a hunting lodge for Ferdinand of Saxe-Coburg-Gotha, widowed consort of Queen Maria II. After he finished Pena Palace in Sintra (see section on Lisbon's Environs), Ferdinand wanted to do something else creative. With the help of an Italian architect, Luigi Manini, he built a Wagnerian fantasy of turrets, Manueline windows, double arches that echo *San Jerónimo* at Belém and walls faced with *azulejos* that tell the story of Camöes's epic *Lusiads.* It is an amazing bonbon of a place.

Just 3 kilometers (2 miles) outside the forest is the pastel spa town of Luso where the gouty and arthritic come to gulp the waters. (In fact, you'll find Luso bottled water on tables the length and breadth of Portugal.) Next door is Mealhada, the town that suckling pig and sparkling wine built—or at least made prosperous. This is a good place for lunch; stop at one of several restaurants on the main road that specialize in roast suckling pig to be washed down by the famous white champagne-like wine, Bomfinal.

Coimbra

Time now for Coimbra, Portugal's capital for 151 years. Ten kilometers (6 miles) south of Mealhada, a university town since the 14th century and an artistic center during Romanesque and Renaissance days, Coimbra is so rich in important sights you'll need a checklist.

The town of Coimbra exists on two levels: the bustling modern town below along the Mondego River and the old university town cerebrally above. If you are driving, we strongly recommend that you park your car on the lower level, perhaps along Avenida E. Navarro, a tree-shaded street near the *turismo* office. Then proceed on foot up the steep hill through the medieval Moorish Almedina gate up to the university with its splendid square, frescoed chapel, and extraordinary baroque library with each and every bookcase a painted and gilded work of art. Nearby is the notable *Machado de Castro Museum* in the Italianate Renaissance palace of a former bishop.

As you stroll, students will cross your path. You'll recognize them by their flowing black capes.

A major Coimbra jewel (among so many) is the Monastery of *Santa Cruz* on the town's lower level. It began life in 1131, courtesy of Afonso Henriques, but was rebuilt by Manuel I. He commissioned sculpture by noted Norman sculptors, Jean de Rouen and Nicolas Chanterene. Note especially the sarcophagi of the first two Portuguese kings, Afonso Henriques and his son, Sancho I, with the precise fine-tooled carving of Master Nicolas. The blue and white *azulejo* paneling in the church is wonderful. This is the place, they say, where Pedro forced his court to pay homage to his dead Inês.

Isabella (who was canonized in the 15th century) outlived her husband and retired to the *Santa Clara Velha Convent.* She was buried there, but frequent floods from the Mondego eroded the convent, and you'll now find Isabella's tomb up on a hillside in the new Santa Clara's. The old convent remains, now just a Gothic ruin. Down the road, Rua de Baixo, is *Quinta das Lagrimas* (Villa of Tears). This is the wooded park where Inês de Castro was supposedly waylaid and brutally killed. Her body was interred at the old Santa Clara's and later removed to Alcobaça.

Conimbriga

Ten kilometers (6 miles) south of Coimbra is Conimbriga. Here you can leap back to the times when Romans controlled the area and walk among ancient columns and admire mosaic pavements of the 1st century B.C. The town that was Conimbriga was a major link on the Roman road between Olissipo (Lisbon) and Braccaria (Braga) in the north.

IF YOU HAVE MORE TIME

Excursion possibilities multiply in this central band of Portugal. North of Buçaco, twisting through the Serra do Caramulo Mountains, is Caramulo, a surprisingly sophisticated little town perched pristinely on a hilltop peppered with pines, chestnuts and oak trees. A *pousada* juts from a ledge just below the town. Caramulo is a health resort at the invigorating altitude of 738 meters (2,460 feet). When you aren't hiking the hillside, you may want to visit the two fine museums that face each other in town: the *Auto Museum,* with 48 vintage cars in perfect running order and the *Museu do Caramulo,* with antiques, Old Master paintings, and, as titilating surprises, works by Raoul Dufy, Salvador Dalí, Fernand Leger, Chagall, Miró and Picasso.

Inside Information

Hotels

For prices, see Lisbon, page 282.

Has ★★★ restaurant. Peek at Presidential Suite, where Anthony Eden and bride honeymooned; has marble bath, own silver service & terrace.

★★★★★ 1. PALACE HOTEL

Buçaco National Park (near Luso) (phone 93101). *Fantasies:* You ascend a regal marble staircase at night and eyes in the suit of armor on the landing glow like hot coals; walk in the moonlight on the veranda lined with paintings-on-tiles of romantic derring-do; sip after-dinner liqueur in a baronial lounge in front of a walk-in stone fireplace with a uniformed butler at your sleeve. Those are for starters, and they're NOT fantasies. They're for real in this once-in-a-lifetime, fairy-tale palace in a 250-acre enchanted park. You'll be enchanted, too, with this dream castle, finished in 1909. It's an Edwardian adventure, Portuguese style. 64 rooms, 15 suites (all with forest views). *Moderate.*

★★★★ 1. ESTALAGEM DO MESTRE AFONSO DOMINGUES

Batalha (phone 96260). Each guest room in this well-appointed, immaculate inn is furnished differently—some modern, some in four-poster antiquity. Handy location across plaza from Batalha's major monument, Monastery of Santa Maria de Vitoria. 21 rooms. *Inexpensive.*

★★★★ 2. ESTALAGEM DE SANTA IRIA

Parque de Mouchao, Tomar (phone 32427). Located in the center of a serene, manicured park of palm trees, roses and pines, where a gigantic Moorish waterwheel reminds visitors of ancient days. This tiny, modern hotel is extremely attractive. All of its rooms have park or river views and the quiet is surprising since the city is just beyond the park's edge. Ten extremely simple rooms. *Bargain.*

★★★★ 3. HOTEL DOS TEMPLARIOS

Largo Candido dos Reis, Tomar (phone 33121). In one of Portugal's prettiest (and most historic) towns, this hotel overlooks a sleepy river. Rooms have large balconies; hotel boasts tennis courts, pool, parking, proximity to Parque do Mouchao. 84 rooms. *Inexpensive.*

★★★ 1. GRANDE HOTEL DAS TERMAS DO LUSO

Rua dos Banhos, Luso (phone 93150). A sleeper, so to speak. A modest facade screens comfortably large and cheerful rooms, each with a large balcony. Numerous lounges, card rooms; olympic-size pool; tennis court, minigolf. 157 rooms. *Bargain.*

★★★ 2. POUSADA DE SAN PEDRO

Castelo do Bode (phone 38159). A tranquil location overlooking a dam and, across the river, a pine-forested mountainside. Rustic flavor, individual attention in this small establishment near Tomar. 14 rooms (seven in annex). *Inexpensive.*

★★★ 3. POUSADA DE SAN JERONIMO

Caramulo (phone 86291). A whitewashed, tile-roofed "typical" Portuguese-style building perched on the hillside just below town. Idyllic for away-from-it-all-tranquility. Simple, strong, unsophisticated decor, comfortable lounge, handsome dining room. Easy-to-reach points of interest such as Viseu from here. Six rooms. *Inexpensive.*

★★★ 4. GRANDE HOTEL DA FIGUEIRA

Avenida 25 de Abril, Figueira da Foz (phone 22146). Beach views from large guest room balconies are standard in this resort hotel that faces the golden beach in Figueira da Foz. Popular with European tour groups; roomy enough for casual trippers, too. Live piano music in lounge most evenings. 111 rooms. *Inexpensive.*

★ 1. PENSÃO RIBAMAR

9 Rua Gomes Freire, Nazaré (phone 46158). This cosy pension with its beach location has a notable dining room. No wonder it's a beach lovers' favorite. (Only one-third of the rooms have baths—book accordingly.) 23 rooms. *Bargain.*

Restaurants

For prices, see Lisbon, page 284.

★★★ 1. PALACE HOTEL

Buçaco National Park (phone 93101). It's dining in style (and what style!) here: crystal chandeliers light a coffered *Mudejar* ceiling and polished parquet floors; chairs have needlepoint seats; carved Gothic sideboards counterpoint wrap-around pastel mural; waiters are positively Jeeves-ian. Fine food and wine add to a memorable dining experience. (The cellar is renowned; the wines from the region are notable, especially the Bairrada, Sangalhos and Dão.) The bargain price is memorable also: Four-course *prix fixe* menu only 1500$00. *Moderate.*

★★ 1. PEDRO DOS LEITOES

Highway 1, Mealhada. The name tells a lot: Pedro of the suckling pigs. This is the granddaddy of the roadside restaurants specializing in baby porkers in Mealhada. Be sure to have the local white wine with your meal—it's a crackling wine with champagne ambitions—and cracking good! *Bargain.*

★★ 2. BOA VIAGEM

Highway 1, Mealhada (phone 22191). One of the newest restaurants featuring the local specialty, suckling pig on a spit roasted over coals. Order *bairrada,* a regional sweet, for dessert; try the wine from the same area, too. *Bargain.*

★★ 3. BEIRA RIO

1–3 Rua Alexandre Herculano, Tomar. This low-key place is noted for good regional dishes competently prepared. Prices are modest. A Buçaco white wine would be a good choice to accompany your meal. *Bargain.*

★★ 4. TIPICO

Mealhada. While most of the suckling pig restaurants are *mais ou menos* the same, some local wisdom favors Tipico's treatment over rivals. Your palate, your move. It's competitive in price and quality, anyway. *Bargain.*

★★ 5. BELA VISTA

Rua Marquês de Pombal, Tomar. Whether you dine outside under the sky or inside in the simple dining room, you'll be surrounded by flowers and enjoying hearty, inexpensive fare. *Bargain.*

Entertainment

Figueira da Foz

The *Grande Casino Peninsular* offers the chance to win or lose at the slot machines and the wheel from 3 P.M. to 3 A.M. daily. In addition, its *Salão de Festas* has three movie theaters with films in three different languages. You can dine and dance in the Casino before the 11:30 P.M. and 1 A.M. shows, which feature international entertainers (and lots of skin). Tennis, swimming in pools or the Atlantic and the occasional horse race or bullfight offer diversion here.

Luso

This spa village has an elaborate schedule of entertainment during its May–October season. Most events are in the municipally owned former casino, a 19th-century confection of a building. They include folk dancing by regional groups, *fados,* concerts, bridge tournaments, handcraft exhibitions and gala balls. (The casino, incidentally, no longer deals, spins or rakes in the chips: The town now uses it for its tourist information center and for art exhibitions and public events.)

During the summer there are bullfights at rings in major towns of the area. Check with local *Turismo* offices as to specific dates.

Shopping

Most tourist-type shopping in Portugal is for handicrafts such as embroidered linens, handwoven rugs, copper, ceramics, basketry, silver. Best buys often come by "lucking into" a town or village on market day. In some towns the turismo offices have the crafts of the area displayed, often for sale.

In Coimbra, drop by the *Regional Handcraft Centre* run by the local *turismo* office. It is lodged in Anto's Tower, an old stone tower halfway down the hill between the old upper town and the modern city below. Two other shops of interest are *O Quebra Costas,* 45–51 Rua Quebra Costas, for original crafts, pewter and pottery especially; and *Bric A Brac,* 16 Rua Alexandre Herculano (phone 26483) for antiques.

Tomar is a good town for browsing. The street Rua de São João has several attractive boutiques and an antiques shop that invites poking around for treasures. It is *Velharias e Antiquidades de Americo Marques* at No. 121–123; there are especially nice vintage ceramic plates, carved wooden objects and silver.

Museums and Galleries (in addition to those mentioned in text)

Buçaco

MILITARY MUSEUM

Queen's Gate, Buçaco Park. This compact museum has everything military history buffs need to recreate or re-live Wellington's victory over Napoleon's troops here—uniforms, weapons, maps, prints, mannequins. Open 9 A.M.–6 P.M. Admission 10$00.

Historic Buildings and Sites (in addition to those mentioned in text)

PORTUGAL DOS PEQUENITOS

Avda. João das Regras. Not Disneyland, but a garden and miniature village built for kiddies. Wander through the miniature replicas of every type of house, building, chapel, church known to be in Portugal or in its one-time colonies. Open 9 A.M. to 7 P.M. Admission 20$00.

Fátima

20 kilometers (12 miles) southeast of Leiria. World famous since the day in 1917 when the Virgin Mary appeared to three children watching sheep. The spot has since become one of Christendom's great pilgrimage centers. Pilgrims pour in, especially the 13th of May, August and October.

Visited by Pope John Paul II in 1982

Parks and Gardens (in addition to those mentioned in text)

Tomar

PARQUE MOUCHAO

Avda. Marquêz de Tomar. A delightful riverside park in the city. Its walks are lined with asparagus fern, shaded by pines, palms and cypresses. An impressive Moorish waterwheel, 6 meters (20 feet) in diameter, turns unceasingly at park entrance.

Spectacles and Displays

Tomar's *Festa dos Tabuleiros* (festival of the trays) predates the Romans. A procession of virgins dressed in white who carry, on their heads, offerings of bread, wine and meat. Each display has 30 small breadloaves impaled on rods decorated with flowers and wheat. Oxen with gilt horns, garlanded, plus priests bearing silver crowns, and marching bands complete the procession. Not an annual event. Check with *turismo* office for date.

Sports

Fishing

You can arrange to go out with boats from Nazaré and Figueira da Foz after sea bass, bream, swordfish and mullet. For more information contact *Comissão Municipal de Turismo,* Esplinad Dr. A. Guimarães, Figueira da Foz; phone 22935, and *Comissão Municipal de Turismo,* Rua Mouzinho de Albuquerque, Nazaré; phone 46120.

Skiing

Skiers will find the runs almost as sensational as the scenery and views in the Serra da Estrela in the national park between Seia and Covilha. From December through May, winter sports rule in these mountains that reach more than 1,800 meters (6,000 feet) into the sparkling sunshine. The best runs are at Covoes da Torre, Loriga, Boi, Ferro, Piornos, Poios Brancos and Penhas da Saude. Information is available from *Commissão Regional de Turismo da Serra da Estrela,* Posto de Turismo, Largo do Mercado, Seia; phone 22272.

GETTING AROUND

Though local bus service and railway links connect most of the major cities and towns in this region, a car gives freedom, flexibility and access that public transportation can't match in the countryside. However, you could conceivably make one location, such as Coimbra or Tomar, your central headquarters and use bus or rail transport to go to beaches, resorts and other monuments or sights.

The Palace Hotel at Buçaco has worked out destinations closer than 60 kilometers (37½ miles) and will arrange for car with driver to reach them. Most car hire agencies operate from Lisbon, Porto or the Algarve. For the closest rental agency, check with *turismo* information office.

Évora and the Alentejo

ÉVORA

When Vasco da Gama, rich, famous, newly titled as Admiral of India and Count of Vidigueira, retired to a house in Évora, it seemed only natural. Everyone who was anyone—court painters, sculptors, scholars, statesmen—was here.

Da Gama's house, palace actually, has been much altered since his time. It is on the corner of Rua da Gama (of course!), a long white building with saffron trim and brick Arabic arches over the second-story windows. Later it became both the Court of Inquisition and palace of the Inquisitors. Today, a long journey over the centuries, finds it home to an Institute of Economy and Sociology.

Just up the hill and around the corner is Évora's most ancient site—a Roman temple dating back to the 2nd century A.D. Like much in Évora, its history is checkered. Its hilltop location made it ideal as a fortress during the Middle Ages when it was walled up and crenelated. Later, inexplicably, it was used as a slaughterhouse. Though it is called, romantically, Temple of Diana, scholars insist that's merely idle speculation. A current theory is that it was a temple to Jove.

Don't worry about the name. The 14 fluted and flowered Corinthian columns still intact are awesomely authentic. By scrambling up the foundation you can lean against one of them and contemplate the universe. Évora arouses such emotions. More pragmatically, you'll have a marvelous view of the countryside for miles.

Turn from the Temple of Diana to the lovely little *Igreja São João Evangelista* at the far corner of the Pousada dos Loios. Enjoy the ornamented Gothic portal as you wait for the custodian to let you inside and hope that he shows up (sometimes he does, sometimes he doesn't), for the interior is even more of a delight. Highlights are the floor-to-ceiling blue and white *azulejos* depicting the life of St. Laurence Justinian. They are the 18th-century work of Antonio de Oliveira Bernardes. The richness of the drawing, the vitality and sparkle, make it difficult to concentrate on anything else.

Churches, convents, monasteries, palaces—no wonder Évora is called a museum town. Even without a museum *per se* it would be. But it also has a museum, *Museu de Évora,* right behind the Temple of Diana, and it's a knock-out. Two floors of the former archbishop's palace are packed with surprises: a 16th-century Flemish *Virgin's Coronation* retable that leaps with lyricism, an intricate and charming 18th-century Indo-Portuguese oratorio—for starters.

The imposing building that was the palace of the dukes of Cadaval is now the Department of Roads. In 1390 the mayor of Évora gave it as a present to King João I. Its north tower was part of the medieval town walls. But still, all is not lost. Inside the palace a door on the left side opens to a tiny art gallery where there are several treasures—a 15th-century Gothic sculpture of a *Madonna and Child,* the smooth white stone evoking a remarkable sense of purity; and three 15th-century tombstones exquisitely, minutely engraved in brass.

The *Sé* or cathedral with its mismatched towers, added later to the finely vaulted Romanesque–Gothic building; the baroque church of *Espíritu Santo,* attached to the former Jesuit university (now a secondary school); the church of São Francisco, more satisfying for the spaciousness and grace of its high-ceilinged interior than for the somewhat prurient *Casa dos Ossos,* in which the bones of 5,000 monks have been formed into a Gothic-arched chapel—these will start you on your sightseeing days in Évora.

You may give up on Évora's dozens of churches. You may prefer just to savor the city's dazzling whiteness or to come upon a convent with a Moorish grill or a tiny park, such as the one overlooking Rua Mendo Estevens, a narrow cobbled street with a group of houses with unusual inlaid tiles in their facades. You may pause to look at Afonso Alvares's spherical marble fountain in *Praça do Geraldo.* At the top is a bronze crown. The baroque fountain, which dominates one end of the pleasing, open square, was commissioned by Cardinal Henrique, a power in Évora, in honor of Spain's Philip II. To make the fountain, the cardinal demolished a Roman arch. Ah well. It *is* a beautiful fountain.

IF YOU HAVE MORE TIME

Estremoz

A first stop is Estremoz, built in two layers like so many Portuguese towns, with its lookout castle–fortress on the hilltop and its business-as-usual town below. In Estremoz's lower level, especially its center, or *Rossio,* the lively Saturday market is held. Here's where you will find every kind of local pottery, sheepskin vests and caps, and gypsies, too.

In Estremoz's upper town a *pousada* has been built into an old palace within a 1258 castle. In the castle you'll see King Dinis's keep and the place where his wife, Queen Saint Isabella, died. We like to think of her sitting at the window weaving. The story goes that whenever she would drop her shuttle, birds would return it.

Borda and Vila Viçosa

From Estremoz it's just 15 kilometers (9 miles) to Vila Viçosa. In between is Borba, a town that "I dreamt I dwelt in marble halls" might have been written about. It is the marble center of the Alentejo. Even the most modest white-washed house in this all-white town is trimmed—doors, windows and stairs—with marble. Borba also has more than its per capita share of antique shops. Consider yourself forewarned.

Welcoming you to the huge stone square of Vila Viçosa is the bronze statue of João IV, eighth duke of Bragança and king of Portugal, sitting plume-hatted astride his spirited horse. The building to the left, as you face the palace, is the *Antigo Convento das Chagas* where all the Bragança duchesses are buried. Directly across from the palace is the twin-towered neoclassical *Convento dos Agostinhos,* pantheon of Bragança dukes where five generations of them have been entombed.

Inside, the palace is lavishly, if eclectically, furnished. Ghosts of Braganças linger in the high-ceilinged rooms. The ceiling paintings recall great mythological and biblical events—the exploits of Perseus, David and Goliath. You can visualize the Rabelaisian banquets, prudently planned marriages and theatrical performances held to quicken the attention of a bored court.

You will be shown the room where Jaime I strangled to death his adulterous wife, Leonor de Gusmão, in 1512. You will also see, midst the Aubusson and Brussels tapestries and Arraiolos carpets, the memorabilia of Carlos I, who left the palace for the last time February 2, 1908, just before the drive to Lisbon that ended in his assassination. It surprises everyone to see how talented are the paintings and watercolors of this second-to-last Bragança king.

Elvas

Elvas, one of Portugal's border towns, looms like a spotlight focused on Spain. A circumferential road leads you up and around the old castle walls, past the dried-out moat where wild poppies grow, up, up, up into the Praça da República at the old town center. Elvas's old walls are a remarkable example of 17th-century military architecture, perhaps the finest left in Portugal. Ramparts, parapets and fortified gates dot the horizon.

Marvão

Another Alentejo town that overlooks Spain is Marvão, which is north of Elvas. In the lounge of its hilltop pousada you can sip a Sagres beer or cup of tea and contemplate the centuries of "on guard" watchfulness that have plagued these border towns.

Castelo de Vide

If you drive to Marvão, a short 5-kilometer (3-mile) detour will take you to still another *blanc*-on-*blanc* town, Castelo de Vide, also ancient, also charming. A spa town, its rose-bedecked houses cling to a steep hillside topped by a 12th-century castle. Join the locals at a sidewalk café. Over your wine or Sagres you can enjoy the proportions of the Praça Dom Pedro V, with its 17th- and 18th-century buildings festooned with geraniums.

Inside Information

Hotels

For prices, see Lisbon, page 282.

A trip to the three E(s)—Évora, Estremoz, Elvas—can be planned around *pousadas,* for these government-run inns provide a comfortable, atmospheric way to enjoy the country life of the Alentejo.

★★★★ FOUR STARS

★★★★ 1. POUSADA DOS LÓIOS

Évora (phone 24051). The monks never had the comforts you'll enjoy in 28 rooms of their former home. Antique furnishings (but modern plumbing); a cloister dining room; helpful English-speaking staff; a 15th-century experience in 20th-century comfort. One drawback: no elevators. *Moderate.*

a deluxe pousada if ever there was one

★★★★ 2. POUSADA DA RAINHA SANTA ISABEL

Estremoz (phone 22618). A former royal palace inside a 13th-century castle keep overlooking the town and countryside. Superbly furnished with canopy beds, carved headboards, art treasures. 23 spacious rooms. No elevator. *Moderate.*

★★★ THREE STARS

★★★ 1. POUSADA DE SANTA LUZIA

Elvas (phone 22194). Located on the highway just below the old fortified town. More like a modern motel with 11 comfortable though undistinguished rooms. You may have to carry your own bags. The Pousada's true strength is its restaurant. Parking. Comfortable lounge and bar. *Inexpensive.*

Has ★★★ restaurant

★★★ 2. POUSADA DE SANTA MARIA

Marvão (phone 93201). From the highest point in a mountainous countryside, this nine-room inn is as quiet as an eagle soaring. Ideal as a getaway. Antiques and handicrafts furnish this isolated, other-worldly aerie. *Inexpensive.*

★★ TWO STARS

★★ PLANICIE HOTEL

40 Rua Miguel Bombarda, Évora (phone 24026). Facing a delightful little square, this 33-room hotel is simple, freshly decorated, attractive. Rooms open to deck with fine views of town and country beyond. *Bargain.*

There's a nice copper goods shop in the same square

★ ONE STAR

★ ESTALAGEM DON SANCHO II

20 Praça Don Sancho II, Elvas (phone 22686). An acceptable alternative to

Elvas's pousada. Located on the main square; decorated in tiles, handicrafts and rustic furniture; folkloric aspect to its cozy public areas. Most of the 24 rooms are spartan, but attractive. *Bargain.*

Restaurants

For prices, see Lisbon, page 284.

Don't be surprised if your waiter offers seconds & a sampling of the 17 desserts

★★★ THREE STARS

★★★ POUSADA DE SANTA LUZIA
Elvas (phone 22194). The line leading to the dining room here is standing room only from opening to closing time. Its secrets: the chef is an artist, the small menu changes daily, and the staff is friendly and professional. A fixed price menu features two hot, two cold appetizers; several kinds of homemade bread; soup; a fish choice; entree; choice of 17 desserts—all for 850$00. A bottle of wine—maybe the smooth Reguengas de Monsaras—and coffee can bring the total all the way up to 1,050$00. *Moderate.*

★★ TWO STARS

★★ AGUIAS D'OURO
25 Rossio do Marquês de Pombal, Estremoz (phone 22176). A second-floor location unfolds into an attractive modern-looking restaurant with white stucco walls, comfortable leather chairs. Specialties include pork *Alentejana* (with clams, garlic and coriander), veal in Madeira sauce, game in season such as partridge, quail, rabbit. *Moderate.*

★ ONE STAR

★ COZINHA DE SÃO HUMBERTO
39 Rua da Moeda, Évora (phone 24251). On a narrow street just off Praçado Geraldo, this 16th-century wine cellar-turned-cozy restaurant is popular with locals. Extremely inviting, with whitewashed walls decorated with tiles, plates, old utensils and teapots. Uncomplicated dishes are most successful, bread and cheese excellent. Wines 150–400 escudos by the bottle. *Inexpensive.*

★ FIALHO
14 Travessa do Mascarenhas, Évora (phone 23079). You may have trouble finding this tiny street. Once there, the plain but attractive restaurant is behind a walk-through bar. Regional dishes. *Inexpensive.*

★ O GIÃO
81 Rua da Republica, Évora (phone 23071). A well-kept, folkloric look makes this old standby sparkle. Robust regional dishes (pork *Alentejana*) are competently prepared. *Inexpensive.*

★ O TORREÃO
33 Rua da Cadeia, Elvas (phone 62983). Next door to the post office, this new restaurant is sleek and modern outside, vaguely old-fashioned inside, with high-backed chairs, rustic tables. Try the *baccalhau* or *pescada frita.* *Inexpensive.*

Cod or fried fish

Shopping

This is the region for handicraft lovers. In the Saturday market in Estremoz you'll find sheepskin rugs and vests, casseroles and other local pottery (low fired, so it's quite brittle). Évora is a particularly good shopping town. One street in particular—Rua Cinco de Outubro, leading down from the cathedral square—is lined with interesting shops where you can find the naive pottery plates of Redondo, brightly painted pottery figures (a regional specialty), fishermen's handwoven wool sweaters, copperware, fine knives, and embroideries. Note especially shops No. 31, 44, 48, 57A, 67A. In front of the public market, near the church of São Francisco, pottery vendors display their wares on the ground, and the selection of Redondo plates with charming folkloric scenes is usually a good one. Be prepared to negotiate prices, however.

Shops of special interest for handicrafts are as follows. *Marsanitas, Lda.,* 27–29 Rua da República, Évora; an all-encompassing selection of pottery, sweaters, sheepskin goods and other gifts. *Antonio Jose Morais Filhos,* 10 largo de Álvaro Velho, Évora; catty-corner from the Hotel Planicie, a modest-looking shop jammed with good buys in copper coffee pots, cups, cooking pots, decorative items. Good value in copper. *Artisanato Évora,* corner of Rua Cinco de Outubro and Alcarcova de Baixo, Évora; a nice assortment of crafts, especially pottery. *Sombrinha Boutique,* 5 Carreira de Baixo, Castel do Vide; porcelain, pottery, silver; in general a well-chosen gift selection in this corner shop.

Museums and Galleries (in addition to those mentioned in text)

Estremoz

RURAL MUSEUM

62B Rossio do Marquês de Pombal. In limited space, you get a vivid view of Alentejo life—local crafts artifacts and costumes. Open 2 to 6 P.M., closed Mondays and holidays. Admission 10 escudos.

Historic Buildings and Sites

Évora

The monuments are multifold. In addition to those already mentioned, the Antiga Universidade offers you the view of the Students Cloister, a lovely inner courtyard, classrooms faced with 18th-century *azulejos* and a richly ornamented portal. This Jesuit university, which attracted scholars from all over Europe in its heyday, was closed by Marquês de Pombal in 1759 when he drove the Jesuits out of Portugal. Open 10 A.M. to 1 P.M., 3 to 5 P.M., closed Saturday afternoons and Sundays.

Elvas

The four-tiered Armoreira aqueduct still brings fresh water to town from 8 kilometers (5 miles) away. It was begun in 1498 from plans drawn by Francisco de Arruda, but it took 124 years to finish.

Spectacles and Displays

This is the fair where the cavaleiros choose their mounts for bullfights

One of western Europe's last surviving horse fairs on a grand scale is held at Golega during the feast of St. Martin, early each November. Diplomats, aristocrats and royalty come to see the finest of horses paraded for sale by horse breeders of the Alentejo and Ribatejo regions. Wine flows freely from flower-bedecked loggias, while brightly garbed grooms and traditionally dressed breeders parade in style.

Evora's annual fair, June 23rd–July 2nd, is one of the biggest and best for those who like the vibes of market stalls heaped with fresh cheese, hearth-baked breads, sausages, intricately woven baskets, bonnets and blankets.

Music, dancing, fireworks, penitents' processions are part of the Romaria

September 20th–25th sees the big *Romaria do Jesus da Piedade* in Elvas. It's the season when country people flock into town for a massive cattle fair and a mix-match of religious and secular festivities.

Mid-August is the time of another colorful horse fair, this one at Vila Viçosa. But Vila Viçosa's main event is the Capuchin festival, a fair with bullfights held the second Sunday in September.

Perks

The tapestry workshop in Portalegre, a town between Elvas and Castel do Vide, can be visited on special tours from 10 A.M. to noon, and 3 to 7 P.M. weekdays, except in August. The workshop is located in a former Jesuit monastery. Just take the stairs on the first floor to the top, then ring the bell on the door on the left. The workshop is on Rua G. G. Fernandes.

GETTING AROUND

Your best bet for transportation in the Alentejo is a rented car or a car with driver. Though there are trains and buses serving the region frequently and inexpensively, a car gives you the flexibility to stop for photographs of a particularly scenic spot or to visit out-of-the-way villages.

Within each town, walking is easy. Most towns are too small for a bus or trolley network. Distances between sights—museums, churches, monasteries—are generally short, and you benefit from absorbing the "feel" of the place as you stroll its streets. Your pleasure is enhanced by small discoveries and the fact that the buildings are human scale. No highrise here!

Madeira

Madeira is 978 km southwest of Lisbon and 545 km off the African coast

A continually blooming garden, with green-clad volcanic peaks and rocky, dramatic coastline, Madeira is Portugal's year-round island in the sun. Closer to Casablanca than to Lisbon, it has nonstop, balmy, pollution-free weather, thanks to the Gulf Stream.

One of Henry the Navigator's captains, Joao Goncalves Zarco (the one-eyed), discovered Madeira in 1419 and was awarded the duchy of Funchal by the Prince. The primeval forests that once covered the island and gave it its name (*madeira* = wood) were timbered and cleared centuries ago but have been superseded by intensively cultivated hillside pastures, banana groves and vineyards tended by hardy islanders who live in thatch-roofed cottages.

Columbus married a woman from Porto Santo, lived there for some years and, say the locals, heard Madeiran sailor talk that inspired his Grand Design.

Centuries later, Madeira was an "R&R" stop for British colonials returning from duty in India and other outposts of The Empire. During the Napoleonic wars the British occupied the island and afterward many were reluctant to leave this halcyon hideaway.

Funchal, the capital, is a modern city studded with striking buildings that date back to its 15th-century origins. You'll find everything from luxury resort hotels to modest pensions, soignee night spots to seafront saloons, and everywhere you'll be welcomed by smiling, hospitable people and by the sight of flowers and trees in bloom.

Inside Information

Hotels

For prices, see Lisbon, page 32.

★★★★★ 1. REID'S

Estrada Monumental, 139, Funchal (phone 23001). Everything a world-class hotel should be in amenities, housekeeping and service, with superb views from this 1891 Victorian (but thoroughly modernized) cliff-hanging bastion of British tradition. Two heated seawater pools; facilities for water sports; tennis; ten acres of tropical gardens; health center with sauna and massage; cocktail bar with dancing. *Moderate.*

Afternoon tea as it should be... on the tea terrace, of course

★★★★★ 2. CASINO PARK HOTEL

Avenida do Infante, Funchal (phone 33111). Oscar Niemeyer's sleek ultramodern design provides guests with glamorous modern hotel luxury in a garden setting overlooking the harbor. Rooms with balconies and excellent views; tennis; heated pool; sauna; dancing nightly in panoramic Night Club. Part of the Casino and Conference Center complex. *Moderate.*

★★★★ 1. MADEIRA PALACIO

Largo Antonio Nobre, Funchal (phone 31031). With a hint of Miami, the Palacio has modern, open lounges, dining areas and rooms with balconies and sea views. Free transport to city. Features pool and terrace, tennis, shops. *Moderate.*

Restaurant rates ★★★

★★★★ **2. MADEIRA SHERATON**
Estrada Monumental, Funchal (phone 30001). From its craggy site the Sheraton offers fine sea views from comfortable, modern rooms decorated with local handicrafts. Tennis; heated pool; gym. *Moderate.*

★★★ **1. SAVOY**
Avenida do Infante, Funchal (phone 22031). This eclectic melange of buildings and styles provides modern rooms and amenities. Main feature: seaside terrace with heated pools and water sports; sauna; gymnasium. *Moderate.*

A local favorite for its cuisine

Restaurants

For prices, see Lisbon, page 34. Most restaurants serve lunch from noon to 3 P.M. and dinner from 7 to 11 P.M. daily. Reserve in advance.

Seafood is superb in Madeira. Don't miss espada, the deep-sea fish unique to the area. Warning: Shrimp and langostinos are as costly as lobster in the U.S.

★★★★ **1. GRILL ROOM, CASINO PARK HOTEL**
Avenida do Infante, Funchal (phone 33111). French and Continental cuisine deftly done, presented with flair. *Expensive.*

★★★ **1. JARDIM DO SOL**
Livramento (5 miles outside Funchal on the airport road) (phone 932123). This rustic inn specializes in robust local dishes. *Bargain.*

★★★ **2. CASA DE CHA DO FAIAL**
Sitio do Lombo, 1, near the north coast of the island (phone 57223). With a vista or verdant valleys and mountain peaks, this "tea house" has a no-nonsense menu, featuring grilled fresh local trout and the famous *espada* fish (try it with bananas and almonds). *Bargain.*

Shopping

Shops and business places are open 9 A.M.–1 P.M. and 3–7 P.M. daily and half-days on Saturdays. Banks: 8:30 A.M.–noon and 1–2:45 P.M., closed Saturdays.

The essential stop is Casa Do Turista, 2 Rua do Conselheiro, Funchal. This treasurehouse of crafts has outstanding selections of the famed Madeira embroidery, baskets, handbags, pewter, copper, faience, pottery, woodenware, leather goods, all at remarkably low prices. Gift wrapping free. Credit cards accepted.

Enjoy the help-yourself Madeira wine tasting bar. Go before 10 and take your camera — with flash

The Funchal market hops with activity from 6 or 7 A.M. until 2–8 P.M. except Sundays. Its fish market is a not-to-be-missed exposition of exotic sea creatures.

Entertainment

Concerts

The annual mid–June *Festival Bach* in Funchal features Brahms, Beethoven and other composers, and world-famous musicians and soloists. For tickets, write ahead to *Turismo* office.

Gambling

The Casino, on Avenida do Infante in Funchal, is open every night but Sunday for roulette, blackjack, French bank and slot machines. Its top-floor restaurant features dancing and a variety show at 11 P.M.; another show at 1 A.M. in the cabaret.

Folklore

Madeiran traditional dances are performed every day of the week at Funchal hotels. Check *Turismo* office or the *Madeira Island Bulletin* for schedules.

Unique to Madeira is its basket-sledge ride. From the village of Monte, 2,000 feet above sea level, to Funchal, you, seated in a huge, wicker basket with steel runners, slide down 2½ miles of steeply curving, cobbled streets. Two sure-footed, straw-hatted sledgemen guide your careening vehicle to prevent disaster.

Museums and Galleries

The *Sacred Art Museum,* Rua do Bispo, 21, Funchal—16th-century Flemish paintings the Dutch traded for Madeira's sugar. Open 10 A.M.–12:30 P.M., 2–5 P.M. weekdays; Sundays, 10–12:30; closed Mondays and holidays.

Historic Building and Sites

The 15th century *Se,* or *Cathedral* (★★★), Rua do Aljube, Funchal, has a spectacular three-dimensional wooden Mozarabic ceiling and remarkable choir stall carvings of the Apostles in Medieval dress.

Convent of Santa Clara (★★★), Calcada Santa Clara, completd in 1496, has Mozarabic wood ceiling, 17th-century *azulejo*-covered walls and Gothic tomb of Zarco's son-in-law.

Tours

You can visit a village in the crater of a sleeping volcano; enjoy the lush landscape as you travel to the north coast; scale Arieiro peak (1,810 meters); swim at Porto do Moniz; see the church where the last of the Habsburgs was buried and return to Funchal via basket-sledge. These day tours are offered for $12 U.S. per person, or less, by tour agencies: CAT, at Av. Arriaga 52; ATAM, Rua da Se; and Abreu, Rua Gorgulho, 1, all in Funchal.

Sports

Madeira is a game fishing center. World-record big-eye tuna, spearfish, blue marlin and blue sharks are taken locally. Day fishing can be arranged through the hotel porter, tour agencies and the Madeira Game Fishing Center, Avenida Arriaga, 73, Funchal (phone 31063).

GETTING AROUND

Taxis are plentiful and inexpensive—$2 U.S. will carry you from the city center to most hotels. The well-developed bus system is even more economical.

Events

Carnaval, the pre-Lenten festival, is a biggie, with parades and revelry in Funchal and the villages.

The flower festival during the first week in May in Funchal highlights flower exhibitions, parade, folkloric shows and music.

During Madeira's wine festival the third week of September, you'll enjoy folkloric dancing, music and wine tastings.

Food and Drink

Portugal's cuisine, like that of its big neighbor to the east, has evolved from its farm and seafaring traditions. But unlike its neighbor's, Portuguese seasonings are quieter, softer, less peppery. The cuisine, you might say, has the gentleness of the Portuguese themselves.

The Portuguese believe in cod (Sorry!). In fact, it's been called the most "faithful friend" of the Portuguese cook, and every bride is expected to have at least ten or 12 cod recipes in her dowry, an easy feat considering its prevalence. Try it with potatoes and olives *(Bacalhau a Gomes de Sa)* or in cakes with coriander, parsley and mint *(Bolinhos de Bacalhau).*

REGIONAL DISHES

Tripe <u>dobrada</u> is a Porto favorite, pork tripe stewed with chicken and pork knuckles

There are regional dishes and as you travel north and south you'll want to look for them. In Porto in the north, *the* dish, and every menu has one, is tripe. The story goes that in their enthusiasm to supply food for the fleet that was sailing to Ceuta to capture it from the Moors, the people of Porto slaughtered all their cattle and put the meat aboard the ships, leaving only the offal for themselves. That was in 1415 and they have been called *tripeiros* ever since. If you've never tried tripe, this may be the place to be adventurous; it's prepared in many different ways. A special way is *a moda do Porto,* a succulent stew with chicken, veal, ham, sausage and beans.

In the Minho area of the north, Spain's Galician and Portuguese cooking marry in their mutual affection for sea creatures, their dishes of Minho River lamprey (a special kind of eel) and even their soups. *Caldo verde* is the Minho's favorite; it's a mix of green cabbage, other vegetables, black pudding, olive oil and a base of mashed potatoes. It's much tastier than it sounds. This is also the region of *broa,* an unusual corn meal and rye bread that is unique and delicious. You will find it in Viana, Braga, Guimarães and most of the northern towns and villages.

A word, actually much more than a word, should be said about Portuguese bread baking. We defy you to have a poor piece of bread in the entire country. The baking skills are extraordinary. The breads vary from region to region—in shape, crusting and consistency. Each is wonderful—crunchy and crusty outside, light and flavorful within.

In the Alentejo, you will be in *porcine* heaven. Portuguese pork is among the finest in the world, and this is smack in the center of the producing area. We have already mentioned Mealhada near Coimbra in central Portugal as the home of contented pigs, but the Alentejo is wheat land, and after the wheat is harvested, black pigs are allowed in the fields to feast on acorns from the nearby oak trees.

Pork in this area around Évora and Estremoz takes the form of *carne de porco a alentejana* (marinated in wine, served with tiny stewed clams); a variety of pork sausages; *presunto,* a smoky ham; *paio,* spicy smoked tenderloin; bacon with a garlic–bay leaf pickling; and the more usual fresh pork.

Alentejo will introduce its other home-originated beauties. *Açorda* (bread soup) can be found all over Portugal. *Sopa a alentejana* is the local version; it's laced with coriander and garlic and embellished with a poached egg on top. Also try the ewes' milk cheese, *queijo do Alentejo,* and the sweet cheese tarts called *queijadas de Évora,* both of which are enhanced taken in tandem with the Bordeaux-like local red wine of Borba.

In the Algarve you'll learn to take your sardines neat, straight from the charcoal grill, as *sardinha grilhada*, often prepared right on the beach. The Algarve is a market basket full of choice seafood: *ameijoa* (the large clams with black shells), *conquilha* (a small flat clam), *buzio* (a spiky shelled crustacean), *mexilhao* (mussels), *ostra* (oysters), as well as the various fish that are netted each day. *Salmonete* (red mullet) is a favorite. Try the shellfish with Portugal's fine beer, Sagres or, if you want it in draft, Imperial.

Algarve sweets have an Arabic accent. You'll notice it in the *morgado de figos* (fig sweetmeat), *fios de ovos* (sweetened egg threads) and *Dom Rodrigos,* as well as in the many almond cakes and marzipan. Algarvian breads are different too. There's the crisp golden *papo seco,* a breakfast roll, or *pao integral,* a wholewheat bread. An insatiable sweet tooth will end a meal with a chaser of *medronho,* the ultrasweet Algarve brandy.

DRINKS

You may have more kinds of thirst quenchers to choose from in Portugal than you were aware of. There are excellent bottled waters, generally in half- and full-liter bottles. Available everywhere in the country is *Luso water,* bottled at the famous health spa, or *Vidago* or *Castelo water.* They can be had with or without carbonation or *aeration* and are served ice cold.

The beer in Portugal is also very good. One of the best is *Sagres,* available in regular, light or dark *(preta).* Beer is almost invariably served chilled.

Portugal has ideal soil and climate conditions for wine grapes. In a country the size of Ohio, it produces four times as much table wine as California! Portuguese like wine—they drink 95 liters (25 gallons) per person per year. Fortunately, there's a bit left over for others to enjoy.

Port wine is produced from grapes grown in the upper Douro River Valley. Brought down river to Vila Nova de Gaia's "port lodges" by truck, the liquid is kept in barrels from 2 to 50 years. The resulting wine may be red or white, dry, medium or heavily sweet, depending on the grapes and processing. White port generally is a dry or semi-dry aperitif. The reds are likely to be medium, heavy and even full and fat for afterdinner or dessert.

Madeira wine is produced in the islands and is similar in range to port.

Of Portugals's table wines, its *rosés* are undoubtedly best known abroad. These are available in Portugal, but don't limit yourself to them. The major wine types available are as follows:

Vinho Verde. "Green wine" is actually either red or white! These are young wines, light in alcohol (usually 8% to 11%) and *petillant* or crackling. The white is nearly as clear as water and extremely refreshing. The red is deep in color and pleasant, not heavy. Vinho verde comes from the region north of the Douro and Tamega rivers, with Braga at its center.

Dão. Dão is another type of wine from a region of granite hills and sandy soil along the Dão, Alva and Mondego rivers in the north. White Dão wines are pleasing, if a bit astringent. The reds, with a little age, can be large, fruity, clean and smooth. Those that have aged a decade or more can be remarkably good, vying with similar Riojas in quality. You'll find Dão reds throughout the country. Viseu is the largest city in this wine-producing region.

Colares. From near Lisbon, on the Atlantic coast, these full, smooth red wines have been famous for centuries.

Buçelas. It's produced north of Lisbon and is a dry, fresh white wine, clean tasting and flaxen colored.

Bairrada. These white wines from Coimbra to Aveiro have champagne characteristics at table wine prices. Very festive.

Setúbal. This city produces a superb muscatel dessert wine; it improves with age.

Rosé Wines. They are produced in various areas of the country. Those bottled by Mateus are processed at Vila Real.

Look also for the reds of *Torres Vedras, Ribatejo, Alcobaça* and *Agueda.* Dry wines are now coming from the Algarve around *Lagoa.*

Label language

Vinha—vineyard
Quinta—farm, estate
Colheita—vintage
Reserva—better-quality, aged wine
Garrafeira—private cellar or best quality
Vinho verde—green or young wine
Vinho de mesa—table wine
Vinho de consumo—ordinary wine, not bottled
Maduro—old or mature
Engarrafado na origem—estate bottled

Branco—white
Tinto—red
Rosado—rosé
Clarete—light red or dark rosé
Séco—dry
Doce, Adamado—sweet
Espumante—sparkling
Adega—cellar (like Spanish *bodega*) or cave

The Cultural Scene

Some 3500 years ago, give or take a century or two, the Celts and Iberians subdued the aboriginal people of what the Romans later called their province of Lusitania—present day Portugal. Until 1263 when Afonso III finally pushed the Moors out of the Algarve, a series of conquerors occupied and left their marks on what is now Portugal. Then, as an independent kingdom, the Portuguese did plenty of exploring and conquering of their own.

For 125 years this tiny country on the far edge of the European continent was a major world power that wrote history in remote places, changing the lives of millions. The achievements were extraordinary for a country measuring at most 560 kilometers (350 miles) long and 218 kilometers (137 miles) wide—an area slightly larger than the state of Maine. And at the time it had a population of less than 2 million.

Portuguese poet laureate Camöes celebrated his beloved country as well as her intrepid explorers in his epic, *The Lusiads:*

> High, as the brow of Europe
> Is Lusitania set;
> Here is the world's end
> And here in the ocean waves
> The sun sinks to rest each night.

Observing the Portuguese today—the assorted blonds, redheads and brunettes—one wonders which spring from the 300 years of Roman rule, which from Visigothic, which from Moorish antecedents (not to mention Greek, Carthaginian, Phoenician, Vandal, Suevian and assorted other settlers or occupiers). And which of these ancestors is responsible for the long-suffering forbearance of the Portuguese, seen in the patience of the people—pilgrims, fruit pickers, fishmongers and farmers? Who can identify the forebears whose hot blood is evident in the manic auto driving of present day Portuguese?

Does the stoicism, if not fatalism, come from their Arab lineage? Or is that the strain that makes them so devoted to the land? Is it the eight centuries of existence as a nation and 300 years of independence that have given

Portuguese their deep but not overweening pride in nationality? Is it their Greek heritage that makes them so hospitable to foreigners? Which node in the double helix has given them their extraordinary craftmanship? One looks, fascinated, and wonders. Will these characteristics change?

For change is sweeping Portugal in many ways. You'll notice evidence of it first in graffiti—in the political murals and posters on nearly every available wall. Obviously there are passionately held political views here. These are the undercurrents and outpourings of the bloodless revolution of 1974 that made possible open political opposition and free discussion for the first time in almost half a century.

For most of those previous 50 years there had been a political deep freeze, enforced by the country's long-time ruler and dictator Antonio de Oliveira Salazar, who died in 1970. But now Portugal is awake—like Sleeping Beauty. The impact of this new awakening is uneven, however.

For instance, in the golden fields of Alentejo women wearing men's felt hats with their faces covered with scarves, still till the fields with their skirts tucked around their legs like knickers. Yet in the shops and stores of Porto or Portalegre other women are in jeans or casual skirts and tee shirts, familiar uniforms around the world. The colorful, traditional costumes that once distinguished one Portuguese town from another (that we as tourists so appreciate) are now relegated to *feiras* and festive occasions.

You still hear *fados* and folk music, but more likely it will be some variation of soft rock, that pours out of a cassette or radio or speaker in hotel lobbies and restaurants. Radios are universal and televison has become so widespread that in most scenic areas you'll find it difficult to photograph rooftops that have no TV antennas fingering the sky.

Some changes have been fundamental. Portugal is, after all, a country where one out of every three citizens is tied to the land, deriving his livelihood from agriculture or forestry. Farms, fields and vineyards cover 30% of the land and forests cover another 35%. (Another third of the population lives in the two cities of Porto and Lisbon.)

Today, in the large fields south of the Tagus, plowing, planting and cultivation are done by tractor and machines. In small hillside plots in the north farmers use portable gasoline-engine cultivators to work the ground. Road-building programs have changed rural transportation. You may see an occasional flock of sheep or herd of cattle meandering down the road these days. But far more often you'll meet a tractor rather than a donkey cart. Even the farmer who still uses a horse-drawn cart is sure to have one with tires instead of wooden wheels.

Travel on foot has been superseded by inexpensive local bus, bicycle or motorbike. Towns, therefore, have become much more accessible and have made available new items—those power Rototillers and blue jeans—that change traditional ways of life.

Such changes mean that modernization is coming as inexorably as tomorrow's dawn, unless Portugal slips into the grip of some austerity-minded regime. Is that likely? Hardly. Portugal's major sources of foreign exchange are not her cotton textiles nor wines (her two largest exports), but the money Portuguese emigrants send home and money people like you and us—the 7 million tourists who visit each year—spend in the country. It would be an unusually xenophobic regime that would jeopardize those golden geese.

What can you expect to find in today's Portugal? Certainly not a Walt Disney production, where kindly, eccentric character actors in quaint costumes perform Broadway-choreographed folk dances in quaint town squares. As kindly and colorful as the Portuguese may be, they are too pragmatic to wear rare and expensive costumes when less costly garments are readily available and accepted by their peers. Yet they are romantics, too, and sensitive. Portuguese have an expansive, time-honored sense of hospitality that changes of the past decade have not dimmed. This unostentatious graciousness invites you to share with them their most precious possessions: green and golden landscapes, shimmering seas, silken beaches, food, wine, a wonderful way of life and the monuments of their glorious past.

LITERATURE

If great themes beget great writers, it is no wonder that Luis Camöes became the Dante of Portugal. He lived (1525–1580) and fought for his king in Africa and India. Though he wrote plays, it was his epic poem *The Lusiads* (1572), a paean to the heroes of the Portuguese discoveries, that won him immortality. Gil Vicente, who was active before this, was the court playwright and is considered the father of Portuguese theater. Vicente stopped writing in mid century as the Inquisition increased its power.

In Portugal's towns and cities you will find streets named after Bocage, (Portugal's leading poet of the 18th century), Garrett (a 19th-century romantic poet), historian Alexandre Herculano and novelists Eça de Queiros and Castelo Branco.

The major writers in this century have been poets Joao Gaspar Simoes, José Regio and Fernando Pessoa and novelists Ferreira de Castro and Fernando Namora, Miguel Torga and Aquilino Rebeiro.

ARCHITECTURE

Though the Visigoths were in Portugal for centuries, there is little architectural trace of their presence. The Roman residue is only slightly better: the so-called "Temple of Diana" in Évora, the ruins of Cetóbriga near Setúbal and the excavated town of Conimbriga (present-day Coimbra). Of course, Roman, Visigothic and Moorish buildings generally disappeared because they were recycled into churches and monuments.

Examples of Moorish buildings are few, yet the African impact on Portuguese architiecture was strong, as seen in the Moorish castle sites in details such as window screens and interior decorations as well as house and roof construction. The Moors' most unique legacy was undoubtedly *azulejos*. Among the many reworked Moorish castles are those at Santarém, Setúbal and São Jorge's in Lisbon.

Romanesque architecture arrived in Portugal with Henri of Burgundy, along with his new title—count of Portugal—and new bride, Teresa, daughter of Alfonso IV of Castile and León, who had bestowed both title and wife upon Henri. It was a package deal in gratitude for help in the reconquest.

Romanesque was the fortress architecture of the 11th century in Portugal, for battles with the Moors were still raging. The cathedral at Coimbra is an example. Its massive granite construction was as much for defense as for worship. There were also strong architectural influences from Galicia at this time, especially from Santiago de Compostela, the great medieval pilgrimage goal.

One of the most remarkable Romanesque buildings surviving is the octagonal 12th-century rotunda of the Knights Templar at Tomar. Supposedly inspired by the Temple in Jerusalem, it is unique. Most examples of Romanesque are found in northern Portugal—the south was in Moorish hands during this period.

Gothic building took inspiration from French models such as the Abbey at Clairvaux. Among its Portuguese descendents are the Alcobaça Abbey, the Lisbon and Évora cathedrals and the Cistercian cloisters at Coimbra—all built in the 14th century. The apogee of Portuguese Gothic was reached in the monastery at Batalha.

Manueline was the exuberant style that drove masons to be pastry chefs in stone. It takes its name from Manuel I, 1490–1520. It was a unique Portuguese variation of Gothic that combined flamboyant with Spanish Plateresque, with additional Indian and Oriental flourishes derived from Portugal's voyages of discovery. Themes from the sea are woven into the stone fabric of churches, cloisters, libraries, towers and tombs. Hallmarks of the Manueline style are twisted columns, rich embellishment around windows, arches and doorways, nautical motifs such as ropes, hawsers, knots and the sea-going armillary sphere—all in stone. Outstanding examples are the Belém Tower of the Arruda brothers, Diogo and Francisco, and São Jerónimo Monastery in Lisbon by Diogo Boytac (who originated the style in the church of Jesus at Setúbal), João and Diogo de Castilho. Manueline elements of the Batalha monastery were the work of Mateus Fernandes.

The Renaissance had its own Portuguese flavor in the work of Miguel de Arruda at Batalha and Diogo de Torralva in Tomar's convent of Christ. The patronage of Cardinal Georges d'Amboise brought to Coimbra a remarkably talented group of French artists—Nicolas Chanterene, Jacques Buxe, Jean de Rouen and Philippe Houdart—as well as the Portuguese Castilho brothers, João and Diogo. You'll see their works in the Machado de Castro Museum in Coimbra. They used the soft-as-plaster Ança stone to carve low reliefs and highly decorated doorways, pulpits and tombs. This influenced development of a richly ornamented architectural style that was widely adopted.

Jesuit patronage led Italian architect Filippo Terzi and Baltasar Álvares to introduce baroque to Portugal. Their designs resulted in severely plain ground plans—rectangular churches with simple interiors without apses or ambulatories (São Roque church in Lisbon)—early in the 17th century. Later, after Portugal's independence from Spain, incredibly rich and ostentatious ornamentation—gilded cherubs, angels and swags of foliage—became the vogue (as in Braga's cathedral). Among the architects of this period were João Turiano, João Nunes Tinoco and João Antunes.

Though Manuel I commissioned almost 100 architectural projects, he may have been eclipsed in expenditures by João V. In the 18th century João brought Friedrich Ludwig from Germany and Mardel from Hungary to build the monastery, basilica and palace at Mafra—which some call a Portuguese Escorial. Mateus Vicente designed Queluz Palace, often referred to as Portugal's Versailles.

SCULPTURE AND PAINTING

Roman sarcophagi, mosaics and sculptures may be seen in museums in Évora, Coimbra and Lisbon, which also have Romanesque and Gothic sculpture. Portugal's 14th-century Gothic sculpture hit a high note in the tombs of star-crossed lovers Inês de Castro and Dom Pedro I in Alcobaça Abbey.

During the Manueline period sculptors came into their own, embellishing every square inch of stone with flowers, leaves, scales, rope and the ubiquitous cross of the Order of Christ. Two Flemish sculptors, Jean d'Ypres and Olivier de Gand, came to Portugal and worked on the altar piece of Coimbra cathedral and strongly influenced other sculptors. Two important Flemish painters, Francisco Henriques and Frei Carolos, worked in the country at this same time. The most outstanding Portuguese painter of his age was Nuno Gonçalves, who is justly famous for a single work, his six-panel St. Vincent polyptych.

An entire school of painting developed around Vasco Fernandez, known as "Grão Vasco", in the town of Viseu. Gaspar Vaz also did notable work at this time.

Machado de Castro, perhaps the leading sculptor of his era (1731–1822), worked in Braga, Porto and Coimbra. His equestrian statue of João I is seen by most visitors to Portugal: It's in Praça do Comercio in Lisbon, which is also known as Black Horse Square. Also active was the portrait painter Domingos Antonio de Sequeira (1768–1837).

In the 20th century, two Portuguese painters have become widely known. Both worked in Paris: Amadeo de Souza Cardoso (1887–1918), who was associated with Modigliani; and Maria Helena Vieira da Silva.

AZULEJOS

Though the Moors introduced the art of colored tiles into both Spain and Portugal, these glazed earthenware ceramics became such a rage in Portugal and were developed to such a degree that it is fair to call them an indigenous art form. Nowhere else will you find the variety of subject matter or uses (portals, walls, fountains, ovens, seats, and so on) that are to be seen in Portugal. They are used as paintings to tell stories, to relate history—in short, as visual record.

The first homemade tiles were manufactured in Portugal in 1565—before that they were imported from Spain or Morocco. But it was after 1650 that they were used on a grand scale in public buildings—biblical and mythological scenes, floral and fanciful decoration and architectural trimmings—and the demand was so great that Dutch tiles almost ran the domestic product out of the market. However, Antonio and Policarpo de Oliveira Bernardes in the 18th century established a tile-making school. By 1740, the *azulejos* were being turned out *en masse* and after the 1755 earthquake the Rato Royal

Pottery Factory produced a type suited to rococo styles and uses of the period.

FOLKLORE

If you are interested in folklore—crafts, music, dance and events—you will find in Portugal an *embarras de richesses*. The crafts are alive in every corner of the country. If you have an eye and appetite for fine crafts you will find something to please you among the carved *cangas* (ox yokes of Barcelos), the lace of the shore villages, baskets from the northeast, *Arraiolos* carpets or Portalegre silk tapestries, the gold and silver filigree work of Gondomar and the variety of ceramics from towns from the Algarve to Coimbra.

Folk dances and songs are best seen at the fairs and festivals of the patron saints in each town. Be sure to check our listing of these; for definitive information, check with the Portuguese tourist information offices in the towns.

The religious festivals called *romarias* in which people gather for religious ceremonies honoring a patron saint are impressive. These usually include religious ceremonies and processions followed by a huge picnic, folk dancing, music by bagpipers and tambourine players, fireworks and a craft fair.

BULLFIGHTS

For spectacle, horsemanship of surpassing beauty, low comedy and displays of sheer insanity (as when the *forcada* of men on foot challenge and subdue the bull) there is nothing to match the Portuguese *tourada*. By all means try to see this when the 17th-century-style *antiga Portuguesa Corrida de Gala* is on. In it you'll see a horse-drawn coach and periwigged *cavaleiros.* The bull is not killed in Portuguese bullfights.

MUSIC

The live music scene centers about Lisbon opera, ballet and concert series (see Lisbon listings) and discotheques and places for dancing. Each town has its share, and the tourist information office can advise.

The *fado* tradition is continued in the late night *fado* places in Lisbon and Estoril (see text).

Index

Portugal index starts on page 371.

SPAIN

PORTUGAL